AF531190

PURDUE AT 150

A Visual History of Student Life

{The Founders Series}

PURDUE AT 150

A Visual History of Student Life

David M. Hovde, Adriana Harmeyer, Neal Harmeyer, and Sammie L. Morris

PURDUE UNIVERSITY PRESS | West Lafayette, Indiana

Printed in the United States of America.

Cataloging-in-Publication data is on file at the Library of Congress.
ISBN: 978-1-55753-834-5

Unless otherwise noted, all photographs are from the Archives and Special Collections, 1869–2018, at the Purdue University Libraries, West Lafayette, Indiana. Specific collection and creator are specified in image captions.

Information about individuals, organizations, places, and events in photographs has been provided to the extent that it is known.

The text of this book is set in the Centaur typeface, designed by Bruce Rogers, Purdue Class of 1890.

[Table of]

CONTENTS

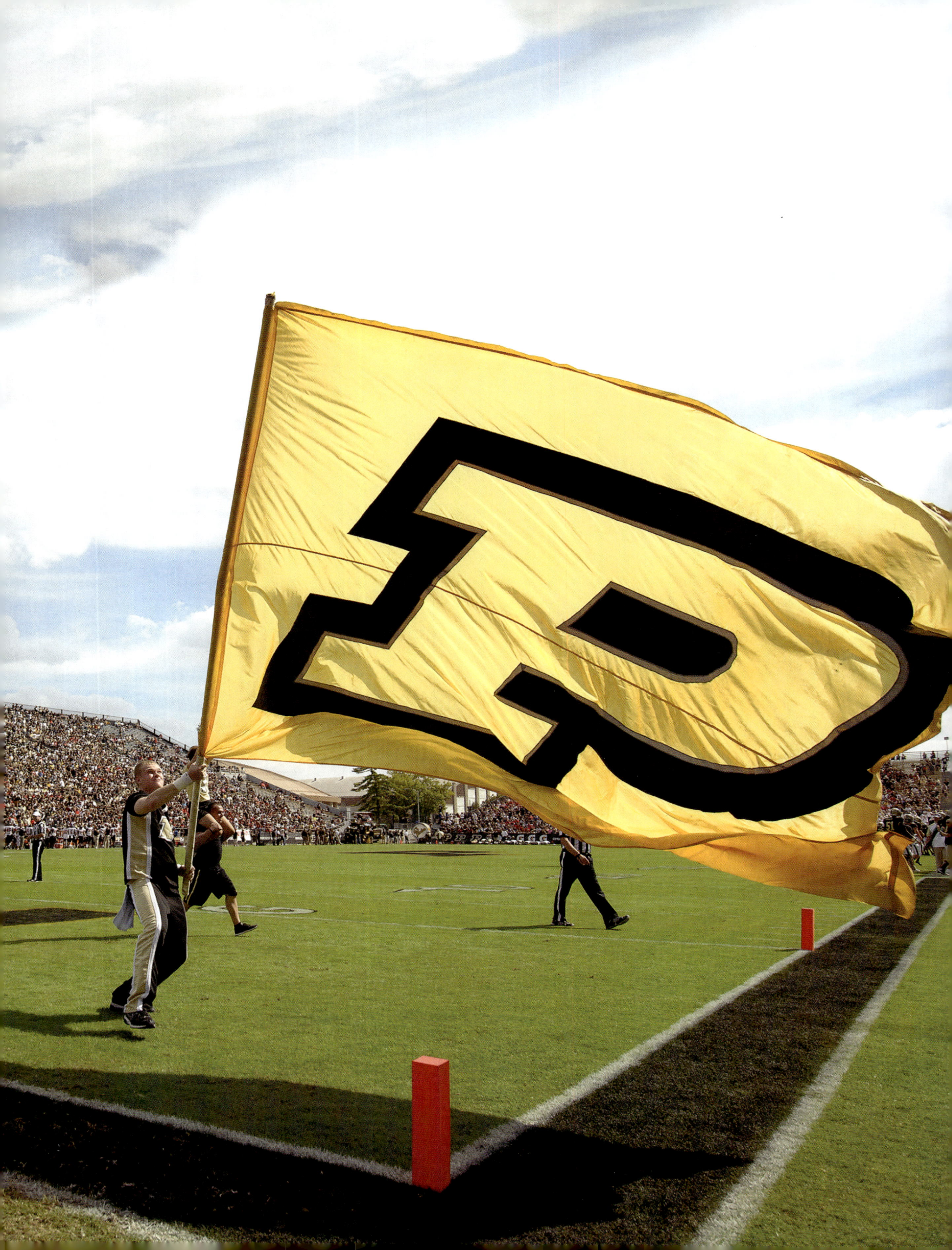

[Foreword]

With the extraordinary number of Purdue University alumni who have made their mark around the world, we are honored and humbled to share our story for *Purdue at 150*.

I'll be honest. I did not know much about Purdue when a representative came down in December of 1996 to watch one of my high school football practices. I remember my coach leaning over and whispering that the man in the black and gold jacket on the sideline was there to see me. We were preparing to play in the 5A state championship game at Texas Stadium, and despite a remarkable season, I had resigned myself to the fact that I probably would not be recruited to play college football. But Purdue saw something in me, and for that I am forever grateful.

Purdue took a chance on me, coming out of Westlake High School in Austin, Texas. Joe Tiller had been hired as the head football coach in November of 1996 and was scrambling to put together a recruiting class to sign the following February. I had suffered a torn ACL in my knee as a high school junior but came back to lead my team to an undefeated 5A state championship season as a senior. Still, the combination of my knee injury and being only six feet tall scared off many college recruiters. But not coach Tiller. He believed I could run the one-back spread offense he was about to introduce to the Big Ten Conference.

Our recruiting class was ranked dead last in the Big Ten in 1997, but we made the commitment to one another that we would turn around a program that had not seen a winning season or bowl appearance in over a decade and leave as champions. Over the next four seasons, Purdue was the talk of college football. We had so many remarkable victories, culminating in a win over rival Indiana on a bitter cold night in November 2000 to secure a Big Ten Championship and Rose Bowl berth. As the Purdue faithful rushed the field that night, as they had for wins over Michigan and Ohio State in earlier weeks at Ross Ade, the feeling of pride and gratitude set in that we had made true on our commitment to leave as champions.

Waving the Purdue flag during the 2013 Homecoming game. Photo by Charles Jischke. *(Purdue University Marketing and Media collection)*

Certainly, football was a huge part of our Purdue experience, but not the only part. We both received world-class educations—Drew in industrial management and Brittany in organizational leadership and supervision—and often refer to Purdue as the "Ivy League school of the Midwest." That is why we were compelled to support the development of the Brees Academic Performance Center for Purdue Athletics in 2007.

During our time at Purdue, the composite grade point average of all the student-athletes surpassed the general student body for the first time and has continued to do so on a regular basis. That impressive distinction reinforces our belief that all Boilermakers can be successful in competition and in the classroom—win championships and earn meaningful diplomas.

Purdue also taught us the importance of giving back and using our platform as athletes to influence young people in a positive way. In addition to raising our four young children (Baylen, Bowen, Callen, and Rylen), Brittany runs the Brees Dream Foundation full-time in its mission to provide care, education, and opportunities for children and families in need, especially those suffering from the debilitating effects of cancer. The Brees Dream Foundation has contributed over $35 million since its inception in 2003.

Leadership and personal growth development are additional qualities we learned at Purdue. We continue to be inspired by the pioneers and innovators who walked the campus before us . . . John Wooden, Neil Armstrong, and Amelia Earhart to name just a few. Their courage and commitment to excellence have set the standard and created a road map for all of us to carry forward as we make our mark on this world. From business to technology, agriculture to medicine, sports to philanthropy, Purdue continues to make Giant Leaps that move society forward with a great respect for the past.

We are so grateful for our time at Purdue. We have developed lifelong friendships and are part of a university family that extends globally. Everywhere we travel, we meet Purdue alumni, and the feeling of pride and excitement is always present. As good as the past has been, we feel like our best is yet to come.

Purdue at 150 is the definitive visual history of student life at our beloved alma mater, recalling stories through rare images and artifacts as well as words. Whether you are a long-time alum or a recent graduate, we know you will enjoy the trip down memory lane. We thank all Boilermaker fans for your ongoing support.

Boiler Up!

Drew and Brittany Brees
New Orleans, Louisiana

Drew and Brittany Brees Student-Athlete Academic Center. Photo by Rebecca Wilcox. *(Purdue University Marketing and Media collection)*

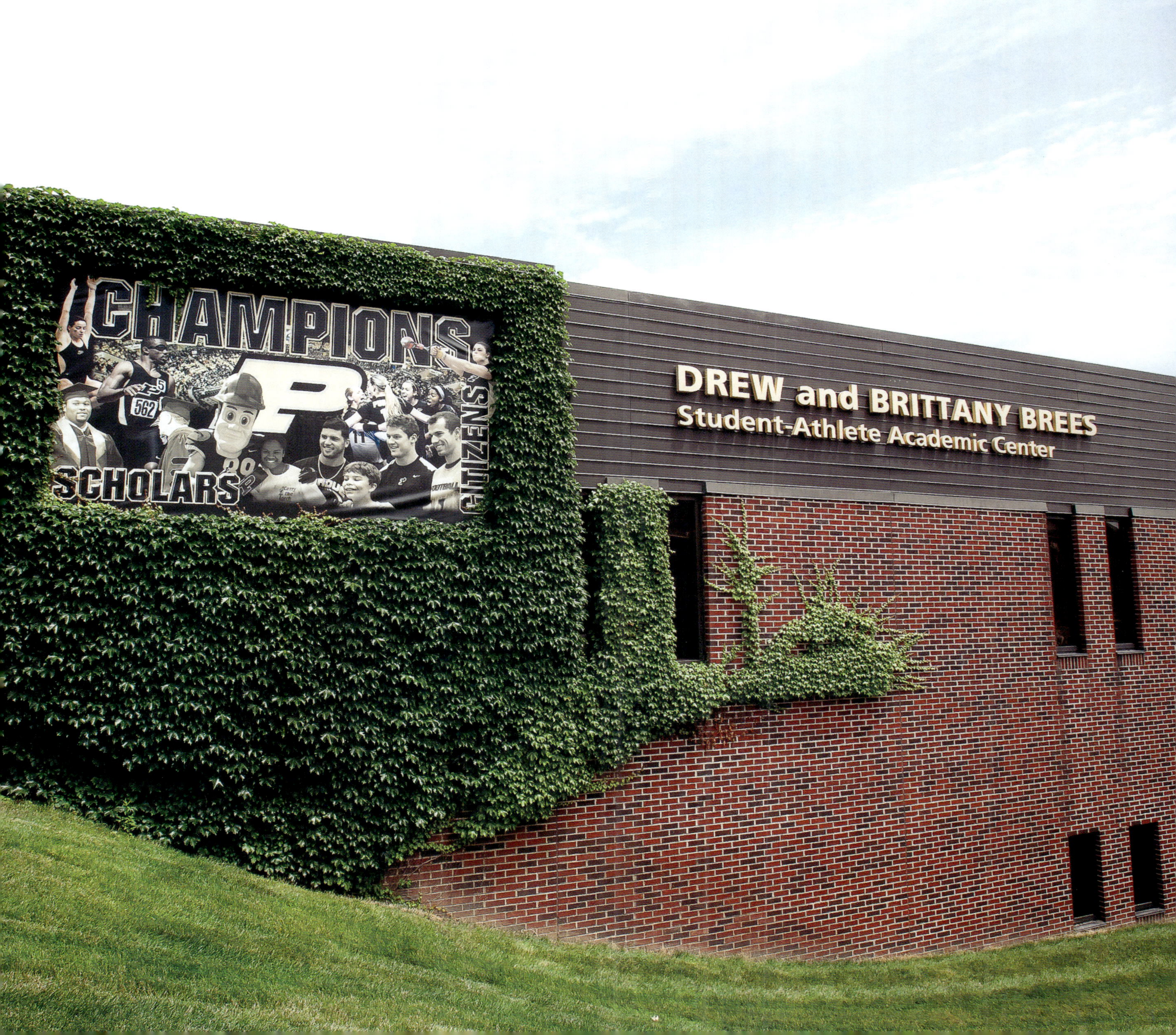
CHAMPIONS
SCHOLARS
CITIZENS
DREW and BRITTANY BREES
Student-Athlete Academic Center

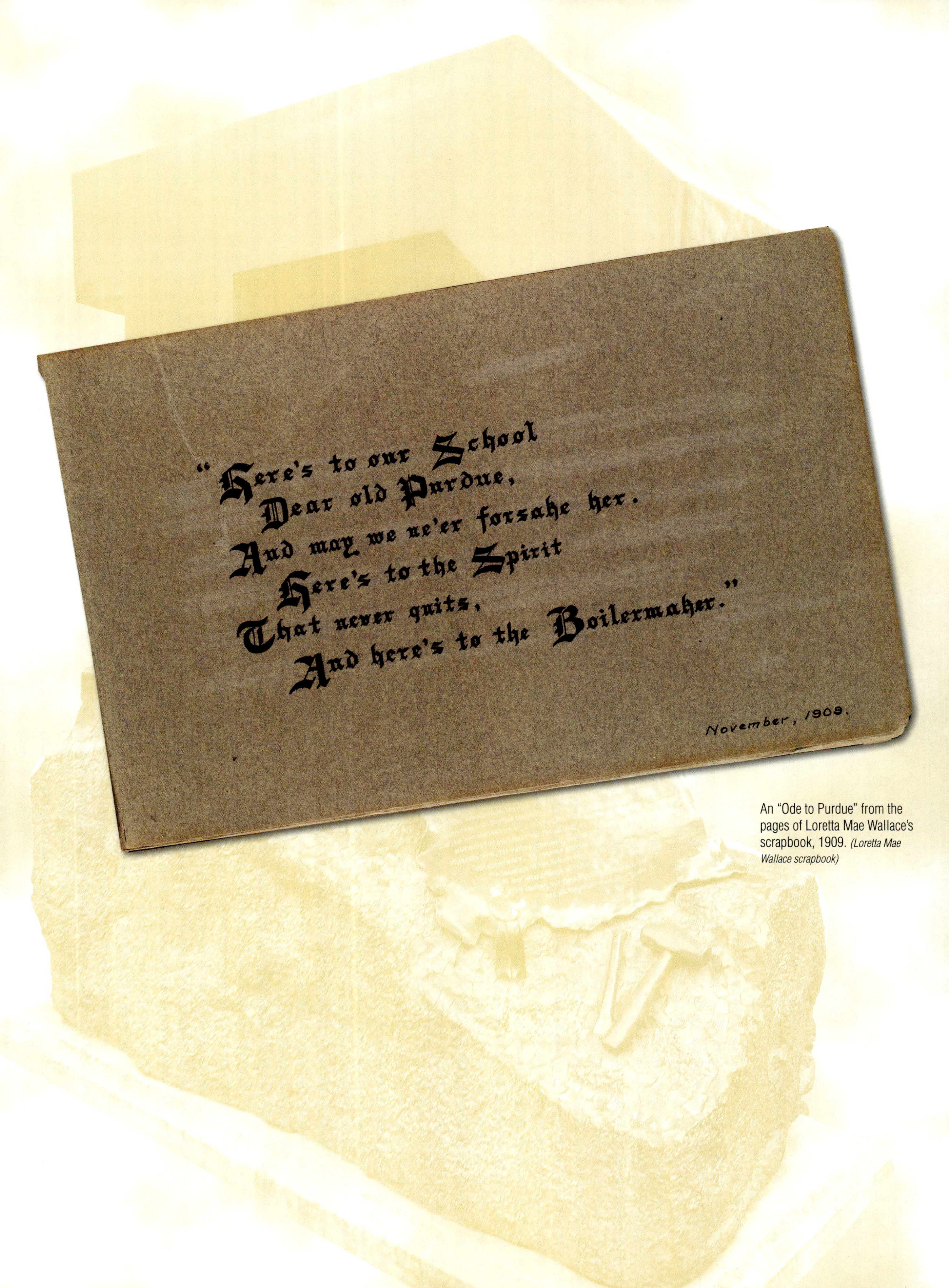

An "Ode to Purdue" from the pages of Loretta Mae Wallace's scrapbook, 1909. *(Loretta Mae Wallace scrapbook)*

[Preface]

STUDENT LIFE

Each semester, Purdue students arrive in West Lafayette shortly before classes begin. They find their rooms, introduce themselves to their roommates, and learn where on campus their classes will meet. Students purchase textbooks, notebooks, and supplies and determine which places have the best food. In the subsequent evenings, they join organizations and explore the areas around campus.

Some students carried slide rules while others carried laptops. Some worked on the campus farm for agriculture credits while others developed code for computer science classes. Aspects of student life have changed over time, yet much of the student experience has remained the same for 150 years.

In this book, we hope to show you how student life has changed over time yet remained undeniably true to Purdue. Through photographs, documents, and artifacts, you will experience the lives of students throughout Purdue's history. Note the similarities that tie together all Purdue alumni while recognizing the people, places, and events that have made each era of Purdue's history unique.

The full story of Purdue would fill countless volumes. This book is limited in scope to focus on the student experience through the lens of materials in the Purdue University Archives and Special Collections. Like a student filling the pages of a scrapbook, we have surrounded ourselves with the artifacts of Purdue history and selected a small sampling of representative images to affix to these pages.

"In presenting thus in formal phrase a record . . . so unavoidably condensed, the editors are sufficiently aware that the shell is here but not the life. The victories, nay even the defeats, of bygone years still live in memories of onlookers and participants."

—*William Hepburn and Louis Martin Sears*[1]

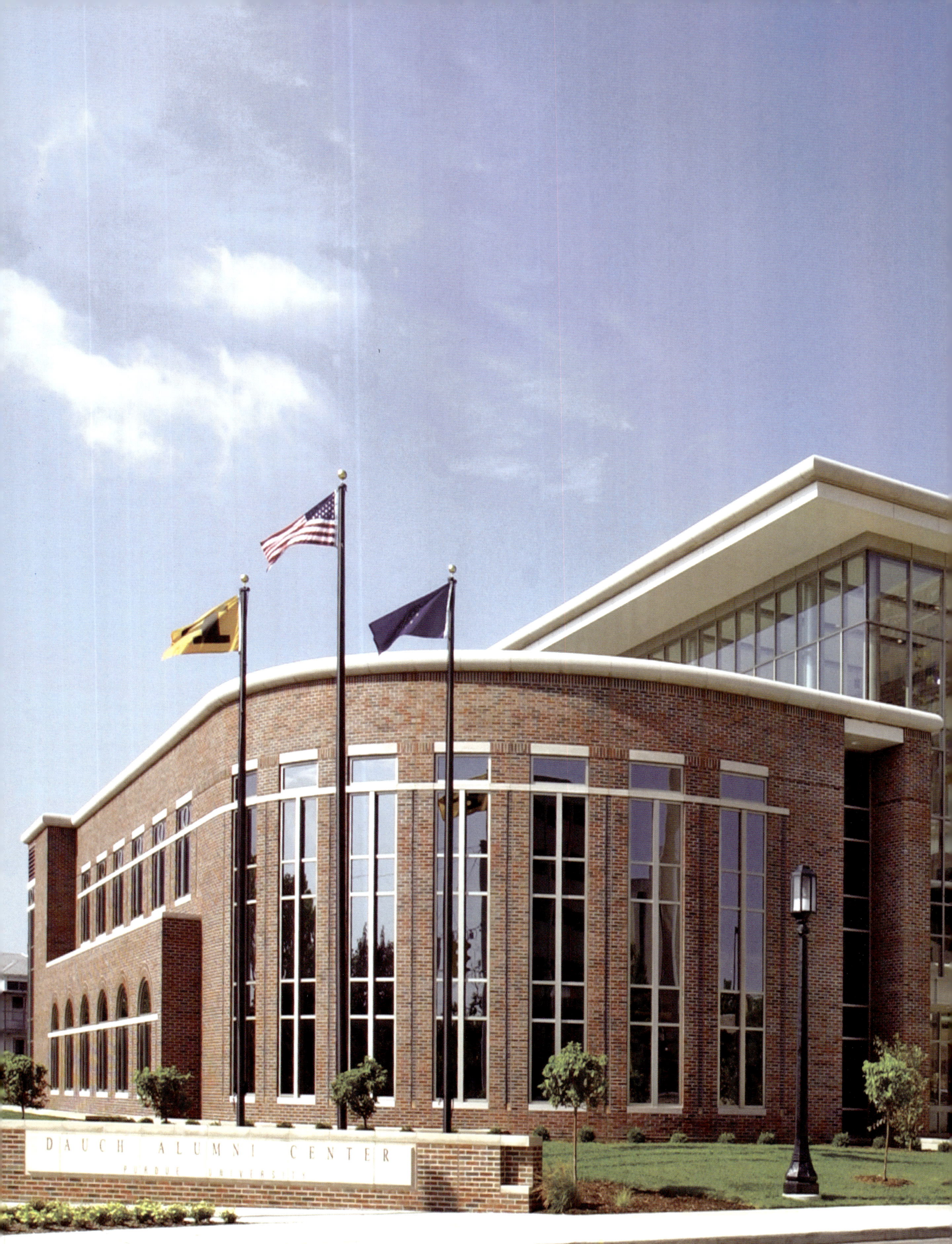
DAUCH ALUMNI CENTER
PURDUE UNIVERSITY

[Acknowledgments]

This book would not have been possible without the tireless efforts of several individuals who contributed their time and expertise. First, the authors wish to thank Bryan Shaffer, Katherine Purple, and their colleagues within the Purdue University Press for their support for this project; their professionalism and commitment to their craft cannot be overstated. Our thanks to Cliff Harrison and Allen Bol, who spent hours carefully digitizing many of the photographs, postcards, documents, and artifacts found in these pages. Many staff members within Purdue University Archives and Special Collections (ASC) contributed short essays and feedback. Heartfelt thanks to our ASC colleagues Carly Dearborn, Gene Ann Fausett, Tracy Grimm, Stephanie Schmitz, Mary Sego, and graduate assistants Virginia Pleasant and Jennifer Sdunzik. In addition, a contingent of ASC student employees aided in our quest. Many thanks to Amanda Burdick, Meghan Diamond, Jon Hathaway, Sarah Kenny, Elizabeth Kriebel, Bhavika Lakhani, Molly Lynch, Heidi Shaw, Evalyn Stow, Tatum Theaman, Claire Werner, Tabitha Wyant, and Michelle Zhang. We have been thrilled to have so many current Purdue students be able to contribute their time, work, and enthusiasm toward this publication.

We must also thank William Hepburn, Louis Martin Sears, George Munro, John Norberg, Robert Topping, and all who have devoted their energies to researching and documenting the history of Purdue University. Our work would not have been possible without theirs.

Finally, thank you to every individual who has contributed to Purdue University Archives and Special Collections. Without your donations of collections and financial support we would not have been able to tell the story of Purdue through the perspectives of students past and present. The documents, photographs, and related memorabilia you have donated to the Archives have allowed us to preserve and share Purdue's history with current and future generations.

Sincerely,

David M. Hovde, Adriana Harmeyer,
Neal Harmeyer, and Sammie L. Morris

The Dauch Alumni Center, July 2004. *(Purdue University photographs)*

WARRANTY DEED.

By this Deed, John Purdue

of Tippecanoe County in the State of Indiana **Convey and Warrant**
to the State of Indiana for the use of Purdue University of Indiana
of Tippecanoe County, in the State of Indiana for the sum of
One Dollars, the following described **Real Estate,** in
Tippecanoe County, in the State of Indiana, to-wit: the North East quarter of the South West quarter of Section nineteen, in township twenty three North, of Range four West. Containing forty acres, also Eleven & one quarter acres off the West side, of the North West quarter; of the South East quarter of Section nineteen, in township twenty three, North of Range four West, said Eleven and one quarter acres being a Strip of equal width across the entire west Side of the North West quarter of the South East quarter of said Section Nineteen, also the North West quarter of the South West quarter of said Section nineteen, Town 23 Range 4. Containing thirty Eight Acres and three fourths, acres also ten acres off of the East Side of the North East quarter, of the South East quarter of Section twenty four, in said township twenty three, North of Range five West, said ten acres being a Strip of equal width across the entire East Side of said North East quarter of the South East quarter of said Section twenty four, in Consideration of the Sum of one dollar to him in hand paid the receipt whereof is hereby acknowledged, and also in Consideration of the location of the Purdue University in said County according to the provisions of an act of the General Assembly of said State Entitled "An act accepting Certain donations from John Purdue and others, and locating "and naming the College contemplated by the Act of Congress, approved July 2. 1862, providing "for its organization and management, adding a member to the Trustees of the Indiana agricultural College and changing the Corporate name of said Trustees, and declaring an "Emergency" Approved May 6.th 1869.

In Witness Whereof, The said John Purdue
has hereunto set his hand and seal ~~and affixed the Government Stamp~~, on this twenty Second day of August A. D., 1876

Revenue Stamp

John Purdue (SEAL.)

SEAL.

SEAL.

SEAL.

The State of Indiana,
Tippecanoe County. } SCT.

Before me Frank W. Spencer a Notary Public within and for the County and State aforesaid, personally came John Purdue the grantor in the foregoing deed and acknowledged the execution of the above conveyance to be his act and deed for the purposes therein mentioned.

IN TESTIMONY WHEREOF, I have hereunto set my hand and Notarial Seal, this 22nd day of August A. D., 1876.

Frank W. Spencer.
Notary Public

Warranty deed signed by John Purdue for land given to Purdue University. *(Warranty deed signed by John Purdue)*

[Introduction]

A LAND-GRANT UNIVERSITY

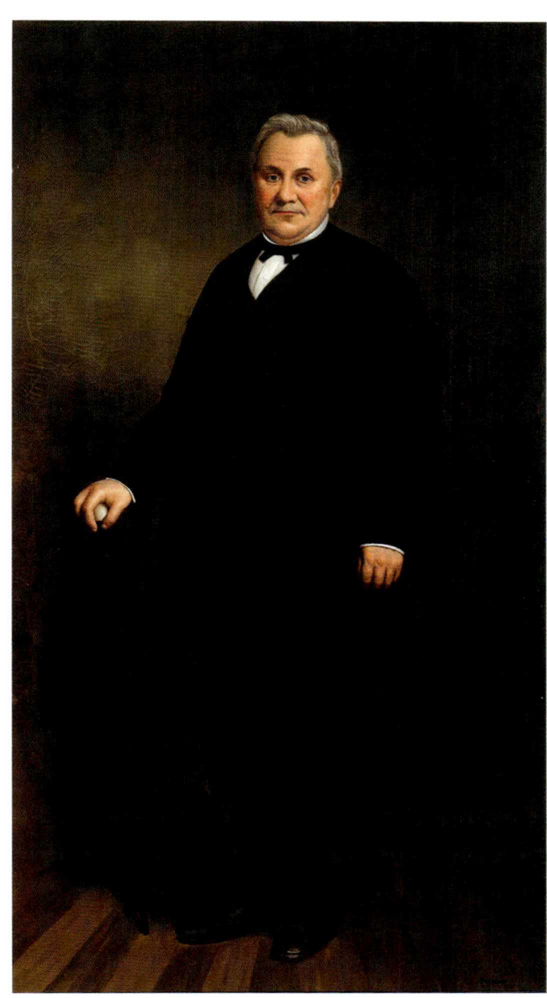

Portrait of John Purdue, circa 1870s, which hung in the Library in University Hall and for many years in the Office of the President before being transferred to the Purdue University Archives and Special Collections for display. *(Purdue University Archives and Special Collections)*

On July 2, 1862, President Abraham Lincoln changed the face of higher education in America by signing the Morrill Act into law. This act, introduced by Senator Justin Morrill of Vermont, spurred the development of a new form of publicly funded educational institution, one in each state, known as land-grant colleges. These were colleges for the children of the working classes, meant to improve the lives of each state's citizens, bring modern methods of industry and agriculture to the states, and improve the social and economic fabric of the nation.

The legislation required each state to sell thirty thousand acres of public lands and invest the proceeds in government or other safe stocks to create a perpetual fund for "the endowment, support, and maintenance of at least one college where the leading object shall be, without excluding other scientific and classical studies, and including military tactics, to teach such branches of learning as are related to agriculture and the mechanical arts, in such manner as the legislatures of the States may respectively prescribe, in order to promote the liberal and practical education of the industrial classes in the several pursuits and professions of life."[1]

On March 6, 1865, Indiana formally accepted the federal grant, and later that year the trustees of the newly established Indiana Agricultural College met for the first time. Counties, towns, and existing colleges from across the state submitted proposals to host the new institution. In May of 1869, the Indiana House and Senate accepted an offer from Tippecanoe County, largely due to an additional $100,000 pledged by local businessman John Purdue.[2] The next five years were spent constructing a university by establishing policies, hiring staff, and building a campus on Indiana farmland. Classes commenced in 1874. Purdue University became the fifteenth higher education institution in the state of Indiana.[3]

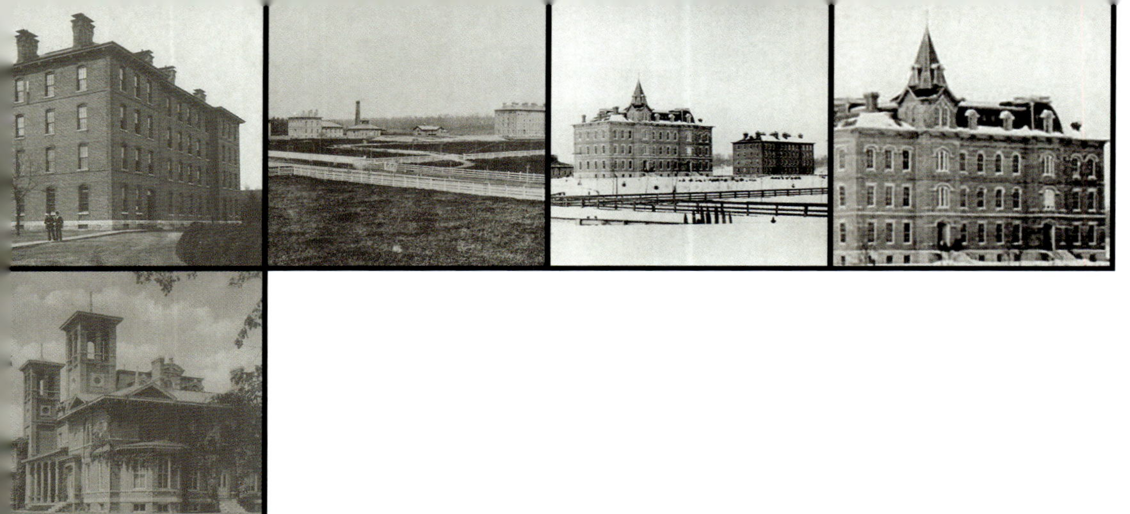

Campus plat, 1874–1894, projecting Purdue's growth in its earliest decades. Reality did not match the plans, as other structures came into existence during this period. *(Campus Maps collection)*

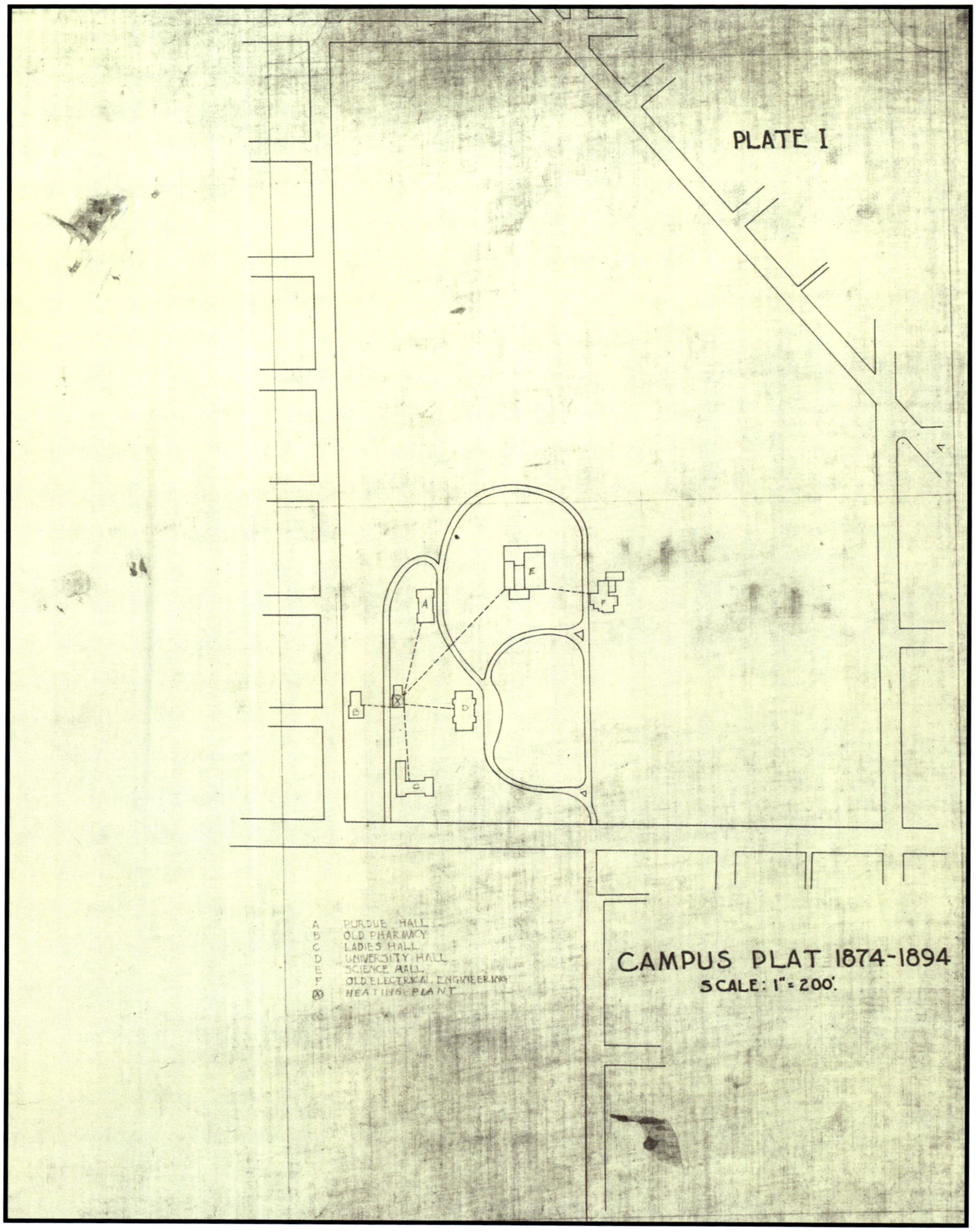

PLATE I

A PURDUE HALL
B OLD PHARMACY
C LADIES HALL
D UNIVERSITY HALL
E SCIENCE HALL
F OLD ELECTRICAL ENGINEERING
(X) HEATING PLANT

CAMPUS PLAT 1874-1894
SCALE: 1" = 200'

{ Enrollment in 1870: 0 students }

[The 1870s]

PURDUE AT 10

"There was no organization of classes or duties. Everyone was a sort of bloc and attended all the recitations if he wished. And the faculty was as inchoate, for they taught whatever was assigned them whether in their line or not. It was a willing, facile, mobile gathering that made the beginning of Purdue and did their work perhaps better than they knew. It was the true Hoosier spirit which was to do as well as possible whatever the hand found to do."

—*Chase S. Osborne, preparatory class of 1874–1875 through freshman class of 1876–1877*[1]

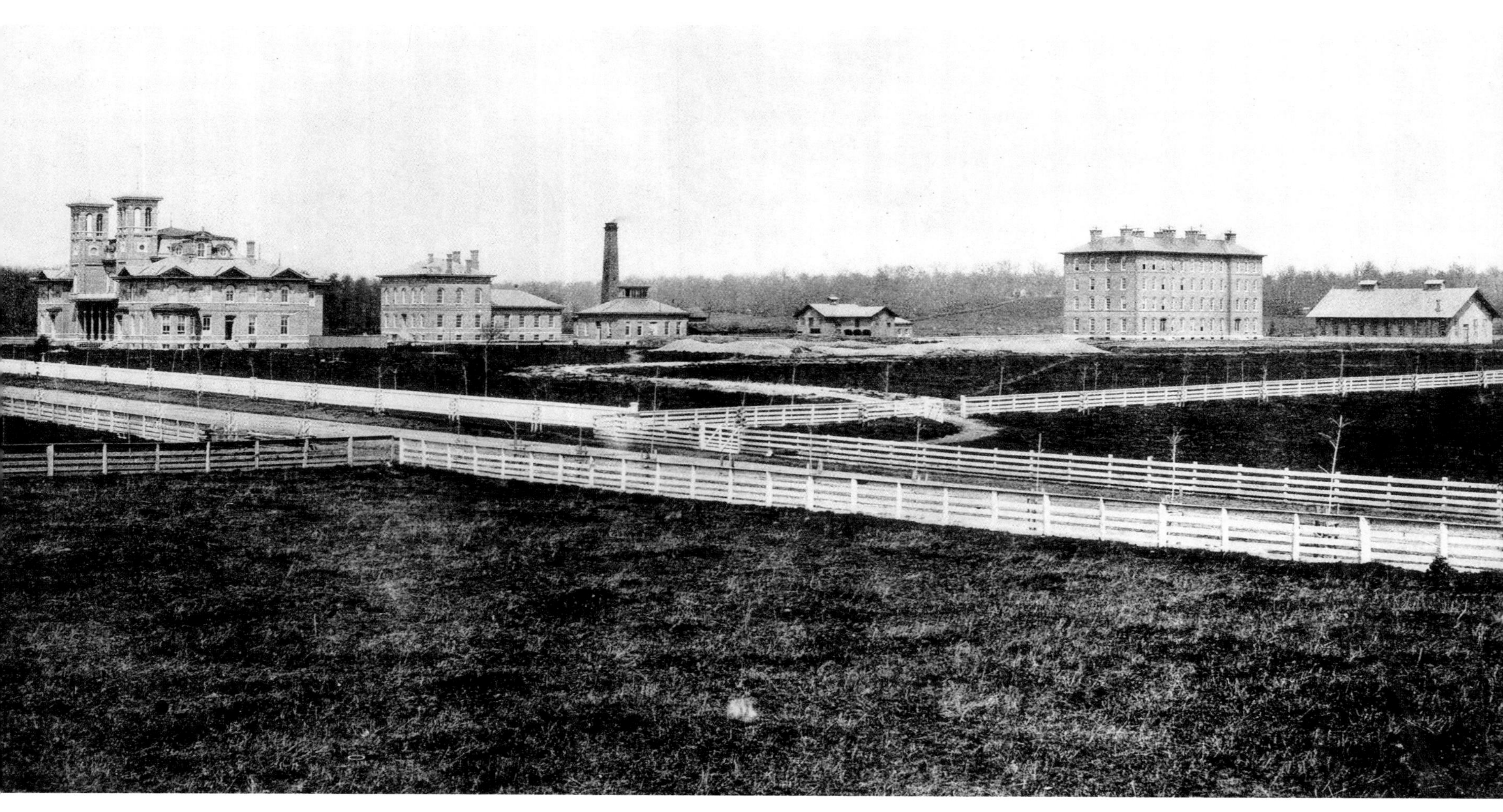

The oldest known photograph of Purdue's campus, circa 1876, showing the Boarding House (later known as Ladies Hall), Laboratory (later known as Building Number 2), Boiler and Gas House, water closet, Men's Dormitory, and Military Hall and Gymnasium. *(Purdue University photographs)*

For the 1874–1875 academic year, tuition at Purdue was free for in-state students and $20 for all others.

On September 16, 1874, thirty-nine students, John Purdue, the Board of Trustees, University president Abraham C. Shortridge, five faculty members and their families, and the staff awoke to begin a new adventure. The students began to arrive cn campus that day, greeted by a mix of newly constructed buildings and old farm structures standing behind whitewashed wooden fences along dirt roads and pathways. Purdue's most iconic building, University Hall, was not yet built.

Students could work for two to three hours per day on the farm, the college grounds, or the vegetable garden to help pay their expenses.

The students who traveled westward to campus on foot or omnibus passed through Lafayette, across bridges over the Wabash River, and finally up a hill to Chauncey, as West Lafayette was known at the time. The town consisted of two or three stores, some houses, and a blacksmith shop.[2]

Trees and hedgerows were a prominent feature of the early campus, helping to distinguish the University from the fields it replaced. The one-hundred-acre university farm south of State Street was beginning to take shape; its red brick farmhouse and barn were the first buildings on campus. Eighty-six acres of campus north of State Street housed the University's main buildings. The stately Boarding House served as a residence hall for faculty and their families and a dining hall for students. The Laboratory housed shops for engineering courses and labs for scientific research. The Men's Dormitory provided accommodations for up to 120 male students. A horse barn and water closet were nearby. The Boiler and Gas House provided hot water, steam heat, and gas to the Boarding House, Laboratory, and Men's Dormitory. The Military Hall and Gymnasium, a simple wooden structure, was the most northerly building on campus.

By the time the academic year began in September, five faculty members had been hired:

Eli F. Brown, English Literature and Drawing
John S. Hougham, Physics
John Hussey, Botany and Horticulture
William B. Morgan, Mathematics
Harvey Wiley, Chemistry

Though Purdue University was originally known as the Indiana Agricultural College, none of these first professors specialized in agriculture or animal husbandry. Purdue's first president, Richard Owen, left before the University opened. Abraham C. Shortridge, the second president, joined the University in June of 1874 and was president when classes commenced.

In 1874, Purdue offered courses in agriculture, chemistry, civil engineering, physics, and mechanical engineering. Postgraduate and special courses were available in engineering, natural history, chemistry, metallurgy, and physics and were intended for transfer students from "literary college[s]" who wished to "fit themselves for professional efficiency" in those disciplines.[3] By 1876, those special courses were also open to students who completed general science requirements in their first two or three years at Purdue.

In these early days, the University had two academic units. In addition to college-level coursework, Purdue also offered a Preparatory Academy for students who were not academically prepared for college-level studies. Indiana was only one generation beyond the end of its pioneer period, and Indiana's common schools—today's public schools—had not been fully developed. The Academy helped students from rural areas prepare for the university coursework that would train them for professional careers.

After an initial examination in September, one senior, two sophomores, and thirteen freshmen were deemed ready for college coursework. Twenty-six students were assigned to the Preparatory Academy, where they took courses in spelling, arithmetic, geography, and grammar. A second examination added a sophomore and a freshman to the roster. By the end of the first semester, forty-five students were enrolled at Purdue.

PURDUE UNIVERSITY,

LAFAYETTE, INDIANA.

A Rare Opportunity to Obtain a Scientific or Practical Education.

PURDUE UNIVERSITY is well organized, with an efficient Faculty and excellent facilities for scientific instruction.

The University Academy, in charge of Prof. E. E. SMITH, affords young people a fine opportunity to review the common branches and take an elementary course in Physiology, United States History, Physical Geography, Algebra, Zoology, Botany, Physics, Industrial Drawing, and Book-Keeping. Applicants for the first year's course are admitted without examination, if they have devoted sufficient attention to the common branches to indicate a fair knowledge of them. Applicants for the second year's course are examined in Reading, Writing, Spelling, Arithmetic, Geography, English Grammar, and Physiology. United States History will be accepted as a substitute for Physiology.

The regular course in the College of General Science covers a period of four years. The physical sciences, (Botany, Zoology, Chemistry, Physics, Astronomy, and Geology) constitute the leading element of the course. Applicants for admission to the Freshman class are examined in the common branches, and also in Elementary Algebra (including quadratic equations), United States History, Physical Geography, and Physiology. Their knowledge of these preparatory studies must be sufficient to entitle them to a teacher's certificate of good grade. Applicants for an elective course are also required to pass an examination in the above branches of study.

The examinations for admission to the College classes and also to the second year's course in the Academy will be held Sept. 10, beginning at 9 a. m. The Fall Term opens Wednesday, September 11, at 9 a. m.

The expenses incurred in attending Purdue University are very low. The entrance and incidental fee is only $5 per term. The cost of board is $3.00 per week, and of room, heat, and light, 50 cents per week. Boarding can also be obtained in private families, in Chauncey, on very favorable terms. Accommodations for self-boarding and club-boarding can be secured in Chauncey, and the expenses may thus be reduced to about $2 per week.

Students appointed by County Commissioners are entitled to tuition, room, heat, and light without charge. Each county can thus send two students.

For further information send for a catalogue. Address,

Purdue University, Lafayette, Indiana.

1878 advertisement for Purdue University. *(Collection of early Purdue University publicity materials)*

FIRST

Annual Commencement,

—OF—

PURDUE UNIVERSITY,

LAFAYETTE, IND.

Thursday Morning, June 17th, 1875.

PROGRAMME.

MUSIC.

March, ... V. E. Becker

Arion Glee Club.

PRAYER.

MUSIC

Wanderer's Return, . . . Franz Abt

Arion Glee Club.

ORATION

The Search for Truth, . . . John B. Harper

MUSIC.

Must I, then, Part from Thee, . . . F. Otto

Arion Glee Club.

Presentation of Diploma. . By Gov. Hendricks

MUSIC.

Waltz, ... F. A. Vogel

Arion Glee Club.

BENEDICTION.

Program from the First Annual Commencement of Purdue University, June 17, 1875. *(Board of Trustees meeting minutes)*

During the third faculty meeting on September 8, 1874, rules were set to establish the culture of the university: "In the estimate of the faculty the use of profane language and intoxicating liquors is immoral, and the use of tobacco in any form is considered highly injurious. And that in making up the monthly standing of students in deportment and morals, the habitual use of these articles be considered against them."[4] Students who lived on campus could not visit Lafayette in the evening without permission and were expressly forbidden to visit establishments that sold alcohol, such as a popular but off-limits cider mill on the levee along the Wabash River. On one occasion, Guilford Lawson Spencer successfully snuck to Ladies Hall in the middle of the night to deliver a pitcher of cider to Jennie Spencer and her friends.[5]

Purdue used a three-term system for many years. The first term ran from September to Christmas, followed by a two-week break. The second term ran from early January through late March, followed immediately by a third term that ended in mid-June. These terms were punctuated with field trips, including visits to local iron furnaces and a natural history trip to Mammoth Cave, Kentucky.[6]

The graduation of John Bradford Harper, the first Purdue graduate and only member of his class, took place on a rainy June 17, 1875. Various dignitaries including Indiana governor Thomas Hendricks, John Purdue, trustees, faculty, students, and local citizens assembled in the Military Hall and Gymnasium. Harper gave an address entitled "A Search for Truth," which expounded on limitless human intellect, and received his diploma from Governor Hendricks.

Purdue's Early Graduates

John Bradford Harper, the University's first graduate, earned a chemistry degree and later became a railroad and civil engineer. (Perhaps Purdue's first true boilermaker!) He is remembered for building canals and dams in the southwest.

Charles J. Bohrer, who graduated with a bachelor of science degree in 1876, wrote Purdue's first thesis, "Beer and Its Physiological Effects." He applied his findings to the family business, the Newman & Bohrer Brewery of Lafayette.

Franklin Pierce Clark graduated in 1877 with a bachelor of science degree. He also received a postgraduate degree in chemistry. A year later he became a faculty member at Purdue in chemistry. Clark operated a drugstore in North Baltimore, Ohio, for thirty-three years.

William King Eldridge graduated with a bachelor of science degree in 1877 and then completed an advanced degree in civil engineering at the University. He was Purdue's first engineering graduate and subsequently worked as a Lafayette city civil engineer, architect, and engineer for various firms.[7]

With the opening of the fall term in 1875, eight female students were admitted to the Preparatory Academy. Sarah Oren was hired that year as the first female faculty member, and her daughter, Cata Oren, was among the Preparatory Academy students. One year later, in the fall of 1876, six women were admitted into the University. Worth Reed, in his reminiscences of early Purdue life, recalled, "Young women came the second year and then things moved much better. The young men began wearing collars, blackening their boots—we all wore boots then—and fixing up generally."[8]

The first Purdue University thesis, "Beer and Its Physiological Effects," submitted by Charles J. Bohrer in 1876.
(Charles J. Bohrer thesis)

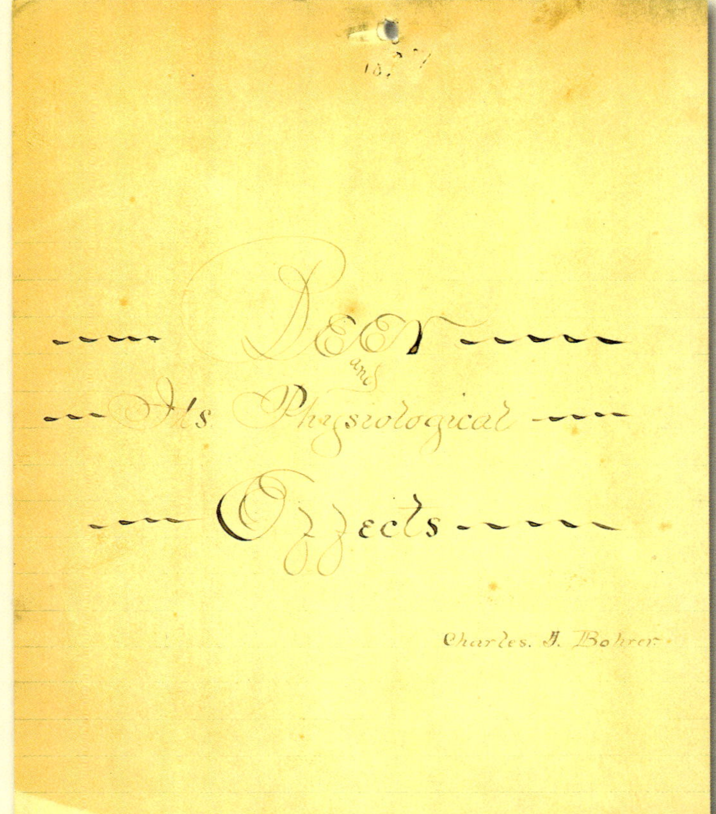

Beer
and
Its Physiological
Effects

Charles J. Bohrer

The Boarding House, renamed Ladies Hall when it began housing female students.
(Purdue University photographs)

Irving 1876.

– Exhibition –

Purdue University

Thursday evening, Dec. 21, 1876.

Invocation – – Music

Salutatory F. P. Clark, Pres.

Essay – A Noble Purpose – Lewis Owens.

Oration – A Thirst for Knowledge – F. Goodwin

Paper – Part First Geo. Jamison

– Music –

Declamation – Egyptian Ruins – W. E. Beach

Discussion – Resolved, That Co-education should exist in our colleges & universities.

Aff: J. C. Van Natta.

Neg. J. H. Blair.

Declamation – Our system of Public Instruction should distinctively inculcate a love of country. D. W. Noble

Paper Part Second – Geo. Jamison

Music.

Programme

Prayer.

Opening By the President.

Addie Borum.

Music – Quartette – Drifting with the tide

Essay – Modern manias – Fannie Taylor

Declamation – "Bernardo del Carpio" Nannie Baldridge

Music – Guite de Couer – Alice McClure

Essay – Names – – – Hattie Taylor

Oration – Civil service reform – Lora Miller

Music Fantaise Brilliante – Florence Taylor, Alice McClure

Paper – – –

Declamation, "Virginia", Hattie M. Brown

Duett "La chasse Infernale" Hattie Taylor, Lora Miller

Quartette – "Good Night."

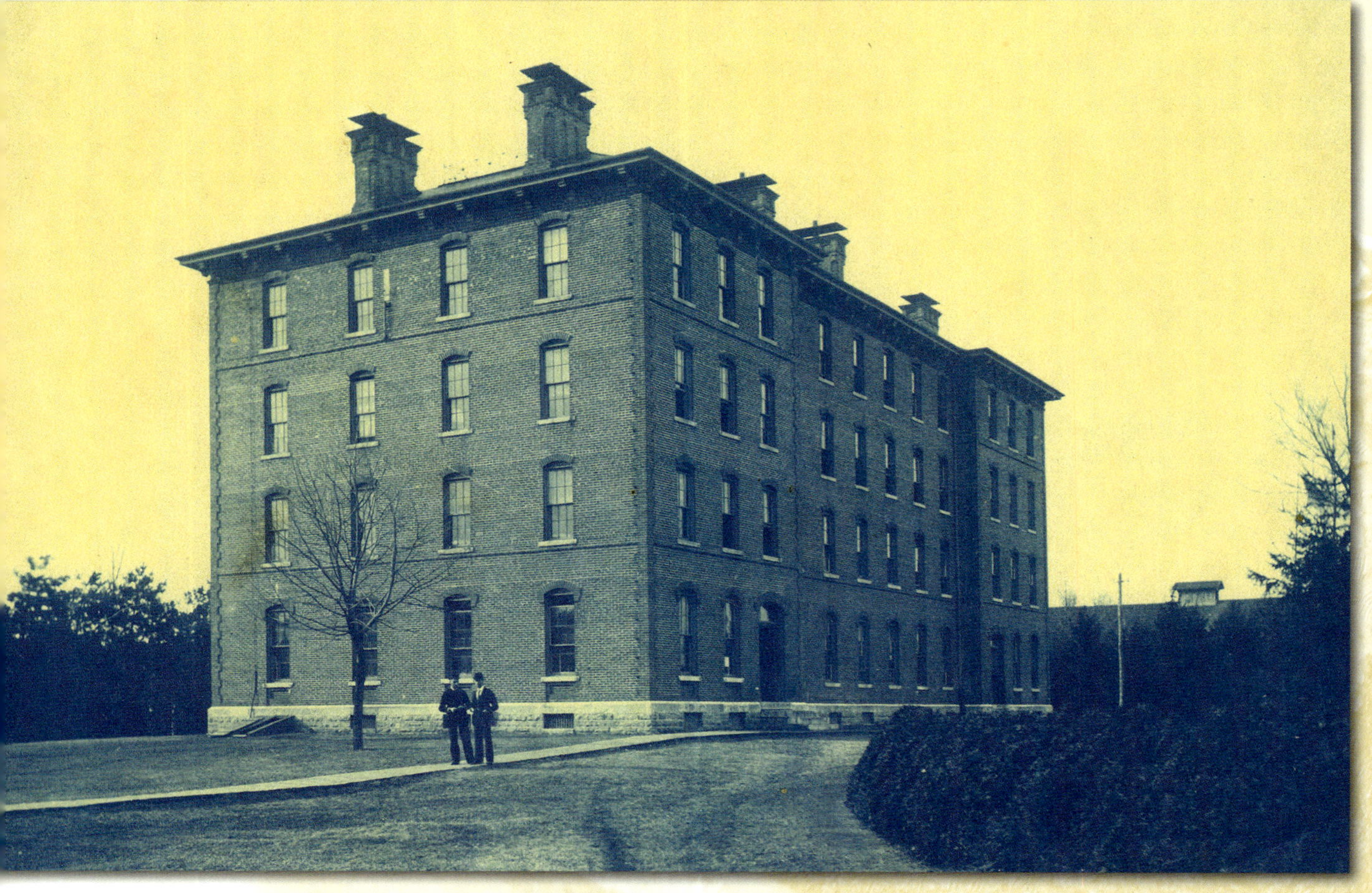

Above, left: Handwritten program for an exhibition of the Irving Literary Society, December 21, 1876. The exclusive, and exclusively male, society formed in January 1875 to focus on the growth and development of the mind, public speaking, research skills, and open discussion of a wide variety of topics that included religion, politics, and education. *(Irving Literary Society records)*

Above, right: Handwritten program for the Second Annual Exhibition of the Cereal Society of Purdue University, June 12, 1877, a group formed by female students in the Academy in the spring of 1876. In the fall of 1877, after the Cereal Society disbanded, the Philalethean society formed with a focus on dramatics and writing.[9] *(Philalethean Literary Society records)*

Left: Men's Dormitory, circa 1890s. *(William Chester Halstead photographs)*

The Delta Delta Chapter of the Sigma Chi fraternity, an unofficial student organization, formed on campus in 1875 with seven members. Fraternities were strongly discouraged by Purdue and other universities at the time, as evidenced by the *Annual Circular of 1876–77*: "A regulation of the University forbids the organization of any society by the students, except by the consent of the Faculty."[10]

In April of 1875 the first campus newspaper appeared on the scene, *The Purdue*. John Bradford Harper and Professor Wiley led the enterprise. Articles covered such topics as note-taking, chemistry, medicine, and chess. *The Purdue* was short-lived, publishing just a few issues in the subsequent months.

Students found many ways to entertain themselves. The Military Hall and Gymnasium was furnished with a bowling alley, a trapeze, parallel bars, a punching bag, a mattress (likely for tumbling), and other exercise equipment.[11] In Purdue's first year of existence, students and faculty joined together to form a baseball team, which won all four of its games that year against Lafayette area teams.[12] On one occasion, Professor Wiley pitched a ball that struck catcher John Bradford Harper in the mouth, forcing his cigar down his throat.

Military exercises were also a large part of student life. During the first years, Professor Wiley led military instruction as captain of the volunteer "Purdue Army," as it was unofficially known. In the spring of 1876, Wiley and the cadets had their first long-range march and encampment, traveling eight miles north along the Wabash River before pitching camp. The trip included the theft of chickens from a nearby farm and a river rescue to save a nearly drowned Wiley.[13] The students were required to wear the regulation United States Army cap and blouse, and the unit was sworn in as part of the Indiana state militia in 1877.

In December of 1876, a nearly blind and ill President Shortridge resigned. He was replaced by Emerson White, a well-known educator who joined the University with a plan to completely reorganize the institution. The Preparatory Academy was separated from the University and the faculty consolidated. White embraced the primary mission of the institution: mechanical arts and agriculture. In his first address as president he stated, "It is better to teach a few applied sciences well than to teach many in a superficial manner."[14]

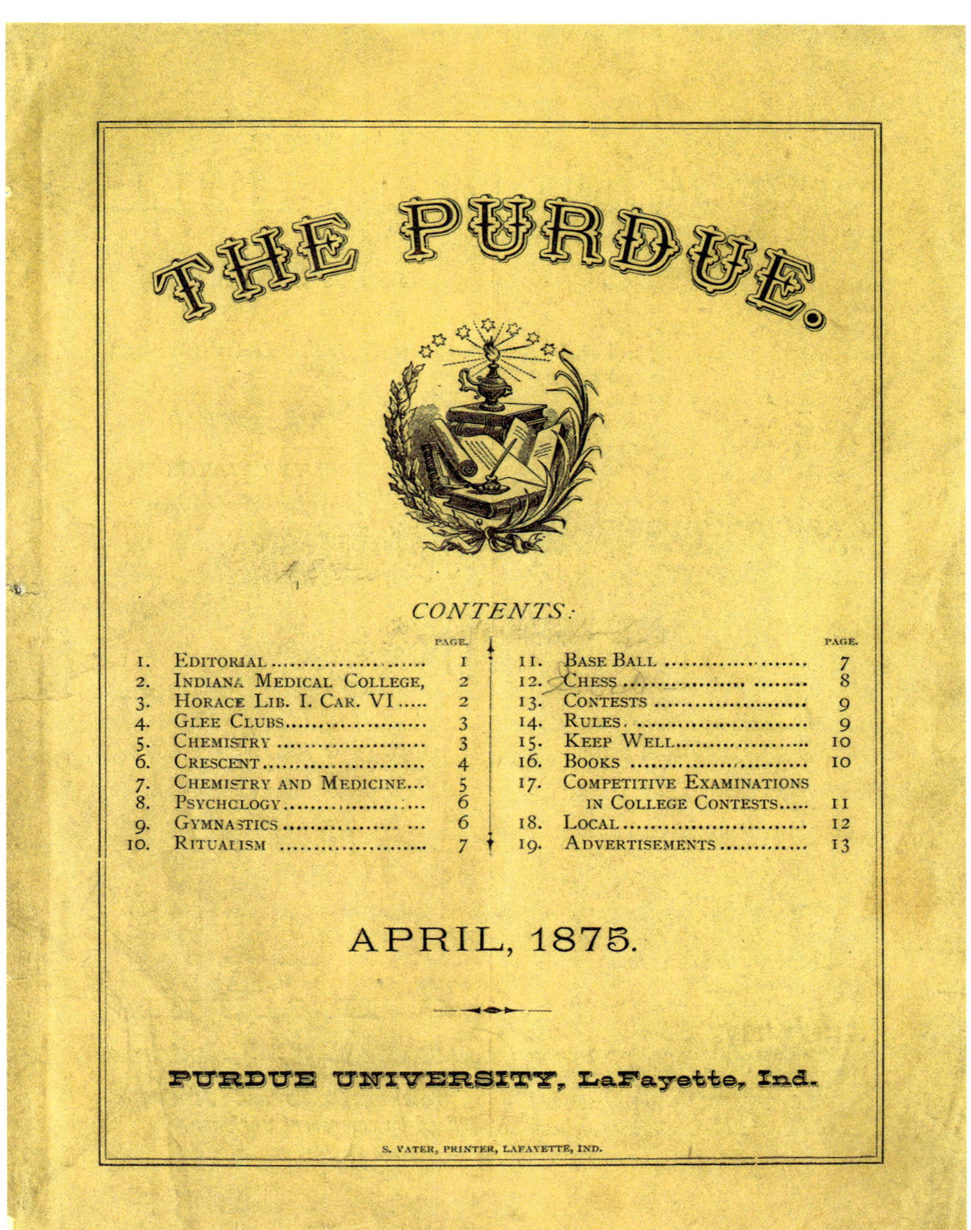

THE PURDUE.

CONTENTS:

APRIL, 1875.

PURDUE UNIVERSITY, LaFayette, Ind.

S. VATER, PRINTER, LAFAYETTE, IND.

Cover of *The Purdue*, April 1875.
(The Purdue)

On the night before the opening day of classes for the fall of 1876, John Purdue died. Due to his importance to the community and the University, his body lay in state with a student honor guard. Purdue was buried the next day in front of what was to become University Hall.

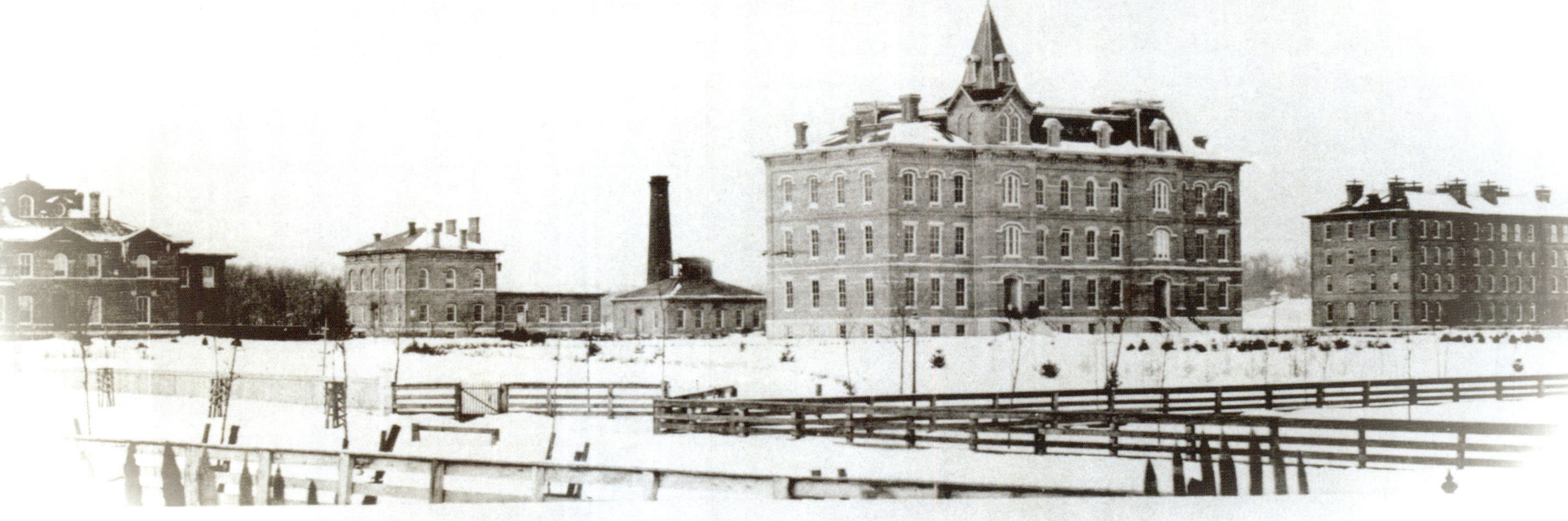

That same year, the University purchased a direct current Gramme magneto-electric machine, the first machine to produce electrical energy at a commercial scale. Professor Wiley installed it in the Laboratory Building, powered by a steam engine, then placed an arc lamp and reflector on the roof of the Laboratory and lit up the night sky. This moment marked the first electric light produced by a dynamo west of the Allegheny Mountains. Hundreds walked from Lafayette to the levee to look at this marvel. One man held his pocket watch over the dynamo to test its effects and was forced to send his watch to Boston for repairs.[15] Purdue was beginning to make a name for itself in the fields of science and engineering.

Purdue University, Nov. 1, 1877.
The dedication of the new College Building of Purdue University, will occur on
WEDNESDAY, NOV. 21st,
at 2 P. M. and it is hoped that the occasion may be one of special interest.
The laboratories, cabinet museum, library, recitation rooms, etc., will be open from 9 A. M., to 2 P. M., affording visitors an opportunity to see the University in session. The steam and gas works, farm, etc. may be visited at any hour of the day.
You are cordially invited.
E. E. WHITE, President.

Top: Snowy campus scene in 1877, the year University Hall was completed. *(Purdue University Marketing and Media collection)*

Right, top: Postcard invitation to the University Hall Dedication Ceremony on November 21, 1877. *(University Hall records)*

Right, bottom: Commemorative plaque placed outside the Laboratory in 1932 when it was renamed Building Number Two to honor its history as the second building on campus. *(Purdue University Archives and Special Collections artifacts collection)*

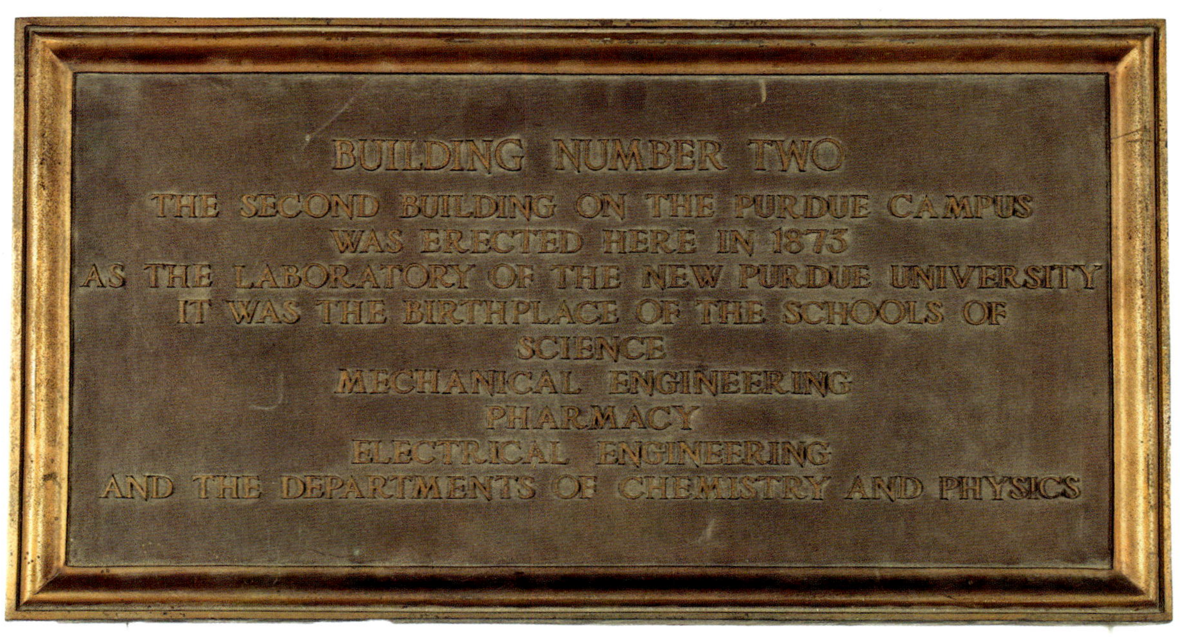

Eulora Miller, First Female Graduate

Eulora Miller of Lafayette enrolled at Purdue in 1876, part of the first class of women to enroll in the University. Her younger twin sisters, Maude and Mabel, enrolled that same year in the Preparatory Academy. Years later, she recalled that her arrival was looked upon as an invasion by the men in her class.

Miller especially enjoyed surveying courses, which allowed her and her fellow students to spend time outdoors. She graduated with a bachelor of science degree in 1878, one year ahead of schedule, becoming Purdue's first female graduate. After graduation, Miller became Purdue's second librarian. In 1887 she achieved yet another first as one of twenty students to enroll in the initial year of Melvil Dewey's library instruction program at Columbia College (now University) in New York, the first of its kind in the world.[16]

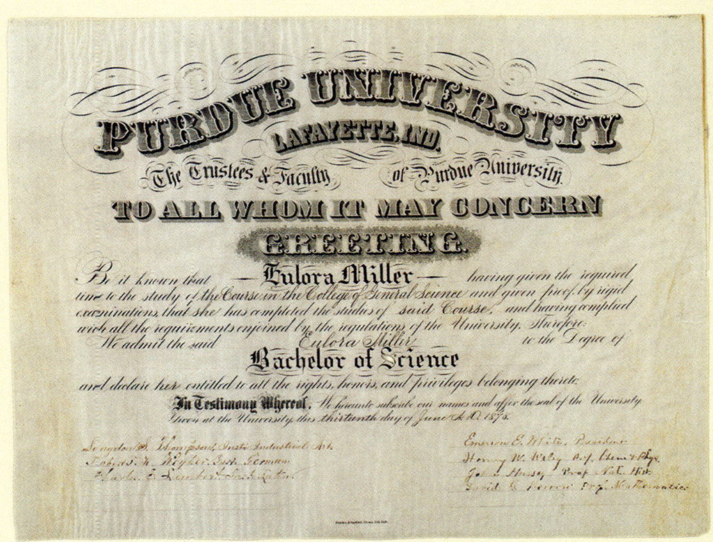

PURDUE UNIVERSITY
LAFAYETTE, IND.
The Trustees & Faculty of Purdue University
TO ALL WHOM IT MAY CONCERN
GREETING.

Be it known that — Eulora Miller — having given the required time to the study of the Course in the College of General Science and given proof by rigid examinations, that she has completed the studies of said Course, and having complied with all the requirements enjoined by the regulations of the University, Therefore
We admit the said Eulora Miller to the Degree of

Bachelor of Science

and declare her entitled to all the rights, honors, and privileges belonging thereto.

In Testimony Whereof, We hereunto subscribe our names and affix the seal of the University
Given at the University, this thirteenth day of June A. D. 1878.

Emerson E. White, President

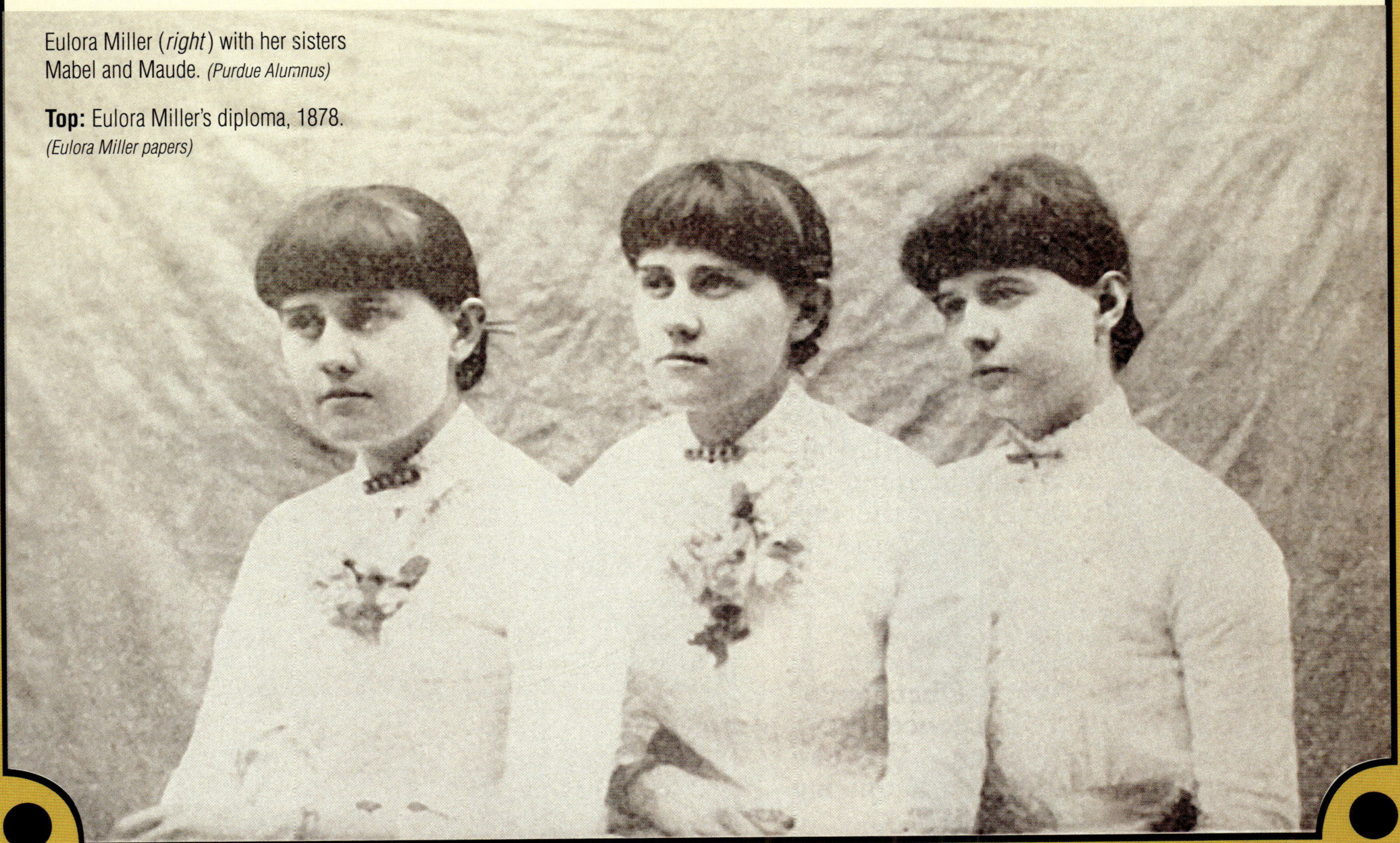

Eulora Miller (*right*) with her sisters Mabel and Maude. *(Purdue Alumnus)*

Top: Eulora Miller's diploma, 1878. *(Eulora Miller papers)*

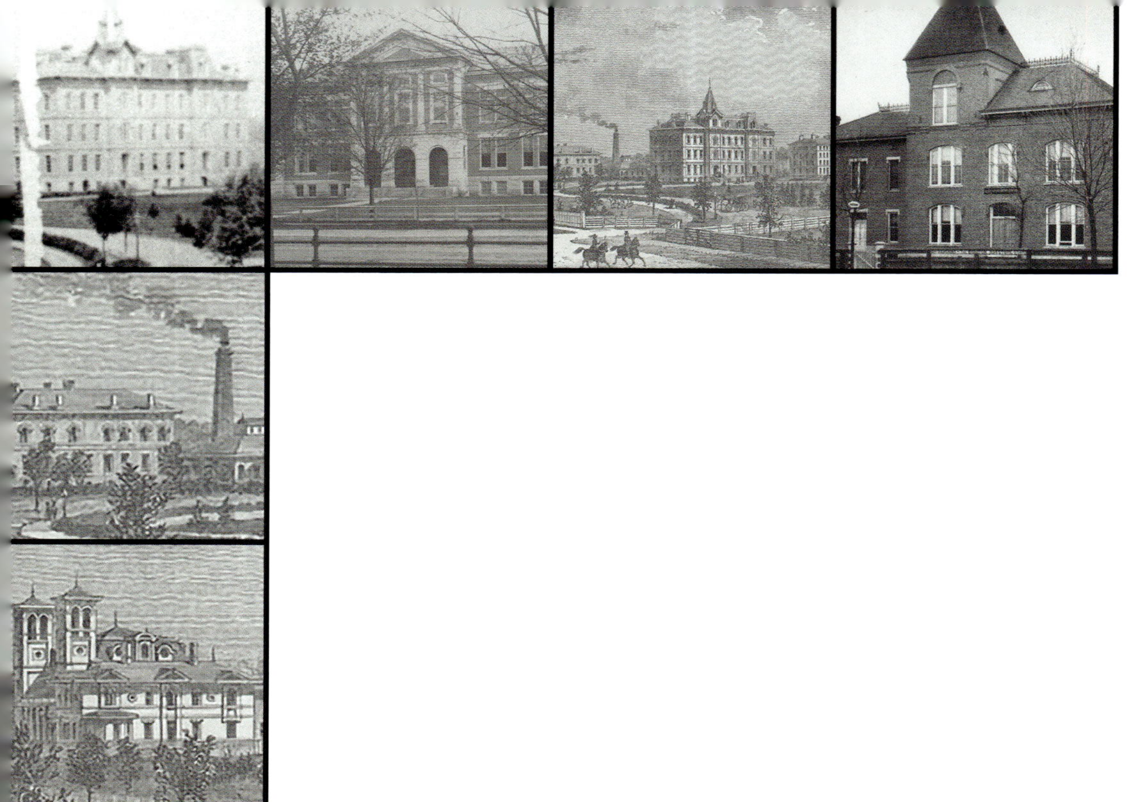

Campus view, circa 1881. New campus maps were not produced during the 1880s; in their stead, this artistic rendering of the "Old Main" portion of campus was used in publications such as course catalogs to visualize the academic buildings. *(Annual Register of Purdue University)*

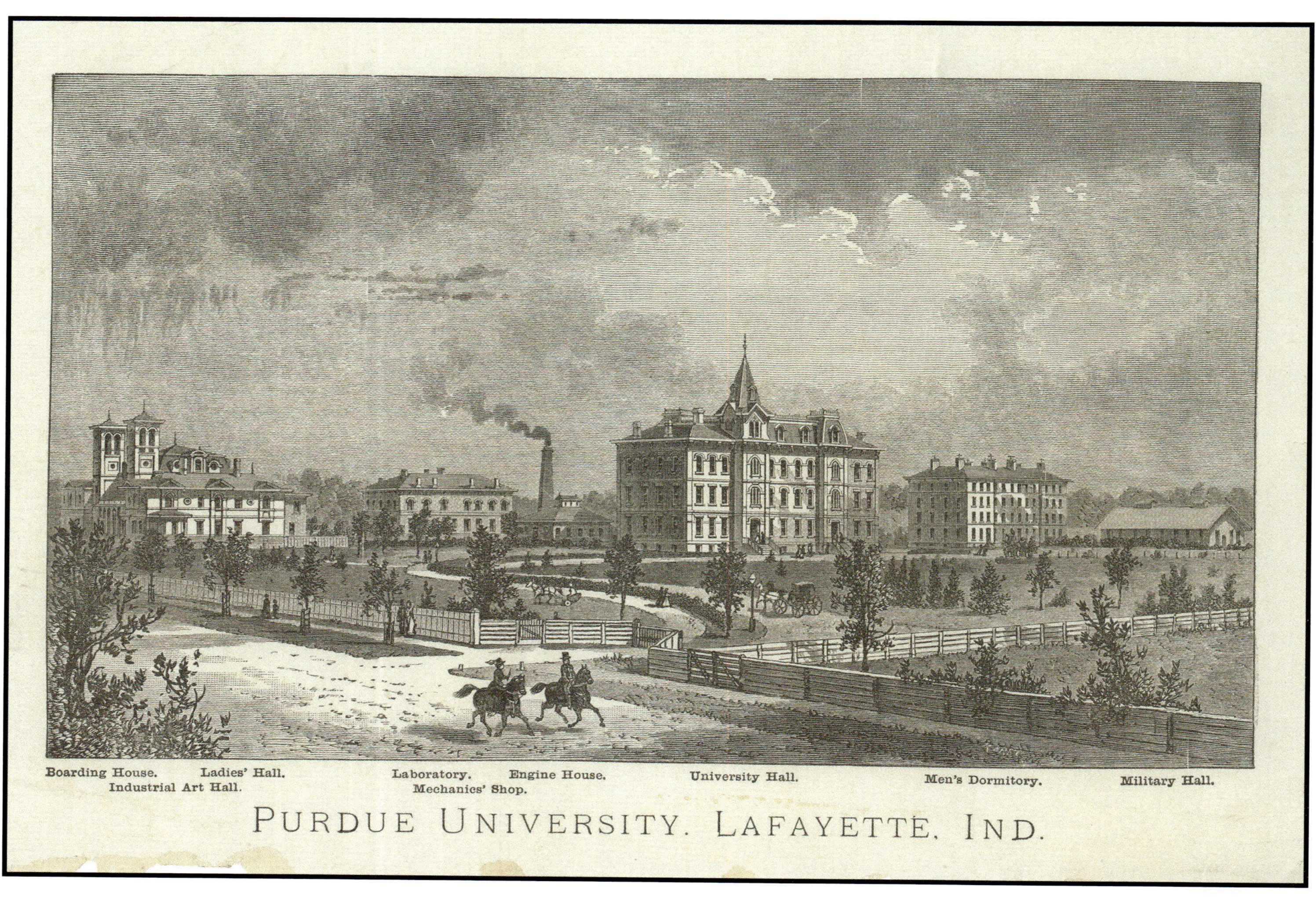

{ *Enrollment in 1880: 254 students*[1] }

[The 1880s]

PURDUE AT 20

"Wednesday Mar. 2nd 1881

A.M. I arose at 6-Oclock. Attended classes as follows: Drawing from 9 to 10 o'clock—Geometry from 10 to 11—Trigonometry from 11 to 12. Had good lessons.

P.M. Taught Book Keeping class from 1½ to 2½. recited Latin from 2½ to 3½. Under Prof. Maxwell. I do not think he has as much vim as a teacher ought to have."

—*From the journal of E. C. White,*
Purdue student and instructor at the Academy[2]

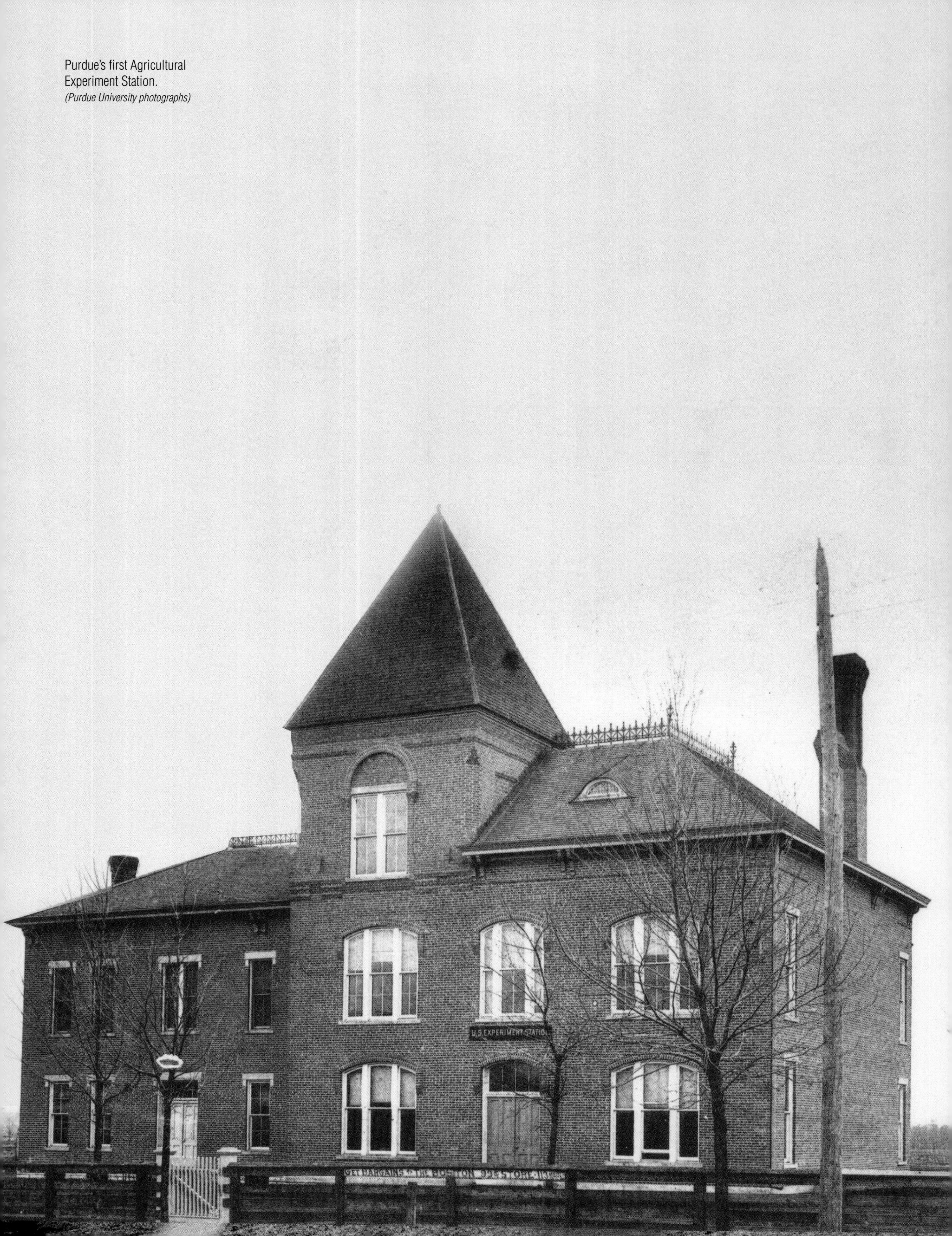

Purdue's first Agricultural Experiment Station.
(Purdue University photographs)

In 1880, nearly every student enrolled at Purdue was from Indiana. Only five did not call Indiana home, and among those, the furthest traveler was Charles C. Georgeson from College Station, Texas. Fortunately for these students, tuition was free, but the university did charge fees for room and board, heating, light, and laundry. Those students who wished to live off campus did so in boarding houses within walking distance of class.[3]

Purdue's School of Agriculture introduced winter short courses in 1886, which meant that Purdue students became not just young men and women who lived on campus but farmers from across the state of Indiana who looked for educational opportunities outside the growing seasons. In 1888, Purdue created its own experiment station and expanded the experimental crop-testing fields on campus, again expanding its role in agricultural education across the state.

President White and Sigma Chi

President Emerson White was strongly opposed to fraternities. Beginning in 1877, students were required to sign a written pledge to not join a Greek or secret society. All violations were severely punished and could lead to dismissal from the university. Rather than disband, members of the nascent Sigma Chi fraternity went underground. When found out, many of its members were expelled in the ensuing years.

Thomas Hawley, a Purdue student who had withdrawn from classes, joined Sigma Chi and had his application for readmission rejected when he refused to sign the pledge against Greek societies. Hawley's case went to the Tippecanoe County Circuit Court and lost, but an appeal to the Indiana Supreme Court ruled in part in favor of the students.

President Emerson E. White.
(Purdue University photographs)

White continued his opposition following the Supreme Court verdict. The students and their supporters moved their fight to the state legislature, where in 1883 amendments were brought forward to require Purdue to remove its rules against fraternities. The new legislation tied state funding to the university's acceptance of student organizations. The legislature adjourned before passing a funding bill and Purdue received no money from the state that year.

In September of 1885, after the resolution of the court cases and White's resignation from office, six students received permission from the faculty to join Sigma Chi. Kappa Sigma fraternity was established on campus that same year and fraternities became a permanent part of student life at Purdue.

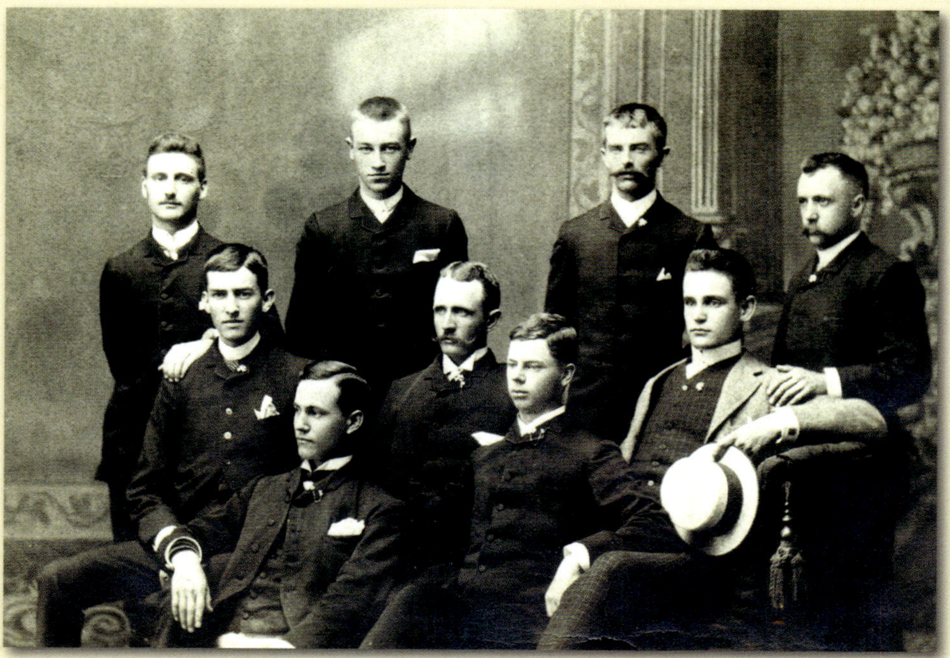

Members of the Delta Delta Chapter of Sigma Chi, May 1886. Standing (*left to right*): Bennett Taylor, James F. Bruff, Shrewsbury B. Milles, Worth Reed. Seated: George Ade, Charles A. Marsteller, Colfax E. Earl, Ernest V. Claypool, Henry H. Vinton. *(George Ade papers)*

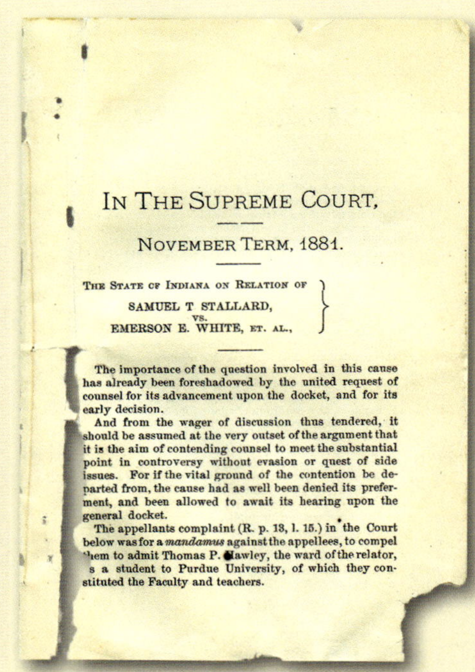

IN THE SUPREME COURT,

NOVEMBER TERM, 1881.

THE STATE OF INDIANA ON RELATION OF SAMUEL T STALLARD, vs. EMERSON E. WHITE, ET. AL.,

The importance of the question involved in this cause has already been foreshadowed by the united request of counsel for its advancement upon the docket, and for its early decision.

And from the wager of discussion thus tendered, it should be assumed at the very outset of the argument that it is the aim of contending counsel to meet the substantial point in controversy without evasion or quest of side issues. For if the vital ground of the contention be departed from, the cause had as well been denied its preferment, and been allowed to await its hearing upon the general docket.

The appellants complaint (R. p. 13, l. 15.) in the Court below was for a *mandamus* against the appellees, to compel them to admit Thomas P. Hawley, the ward of the relator, as a student to Purdue University, of which they constituted the Faculty and teachers.

Record of the Indiana Supreme Court, November Term 1881, regarding the Sigma Chi case. The Supreme Court ruled in favor of the students.
(Collection of Sigma Chi Fraternity Court Case materials)

Left: President Smart in his University Hall office. *(William Chester Halstead photos)*

Below: Military cadets marching through Purdue's main gates. *(Josiah H. Andrews scrapbook)*

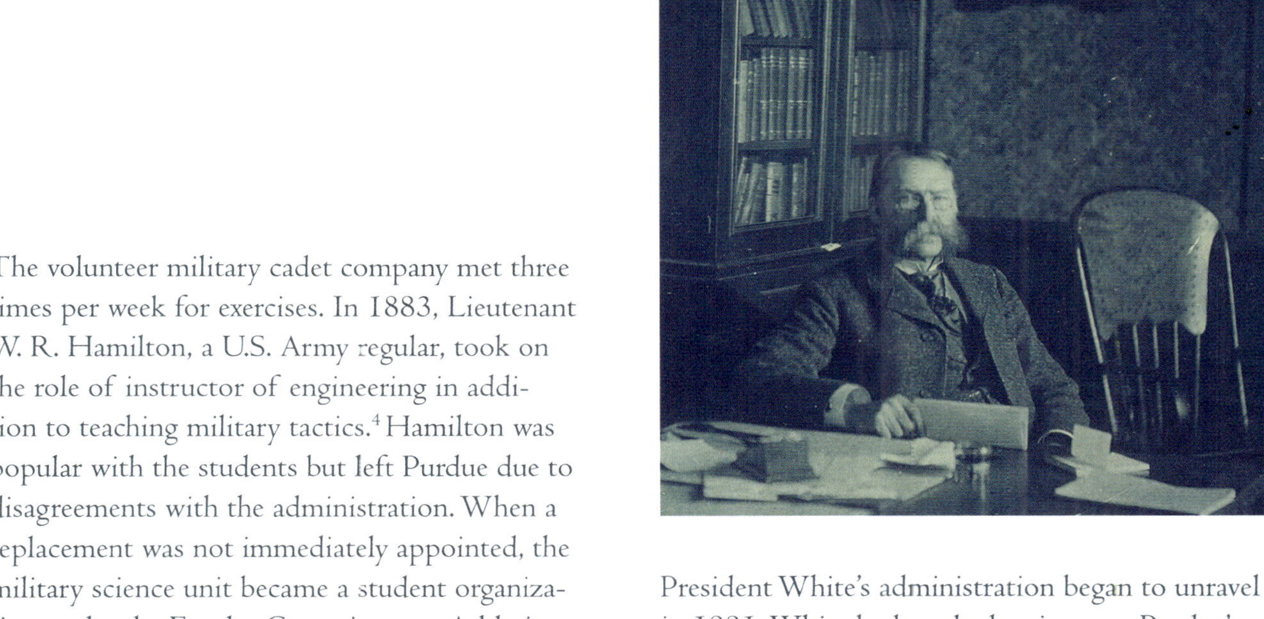

The volunteer military cadet company met three times per week for exercises. In 1883, Lieutenant W. R. Hamilton, a U.S. Army regular, took on the role of instructor of engineering in addition to teaching military tactics.[4] Hamilton was popular with the students but left Purdue due to disagreements with the administration. When a replacement was not immediately appointed, the military science unit became a student organization under the Faculty Committee on Athletics. Drill was suspended from the spring of 1887 until West Point graduate Lieutenant Abner Pickering was hired in 1888. Beginning in the 1889–1890 academic year, all freshman male students at Purdue were required to join the military science program for a minimum of two years. Pickering organized the students into a battalion of infantry, a battalion of artillery, a drum corps, and a signal corps. The drum corps would become known as the Military Band, a precursor to the Purdue Marching Band.

President White's administration began to unravel in 1881. White had worked to increase Purdue's entrance requirement standards and as a result, enrollment declined. The drop in numbers led to criticism from a state legislature focused on growth. Furthermore, most of the students were from Tippecanoe County, and the state demanded a state institution, not a county institute.[5] President White resigned in March 1883 due to these pressures and the circumstances surrounding the Sigma Chi court cases. The Board of Trustees subsequently hired James H. Smart as the fourth president of Purdue.

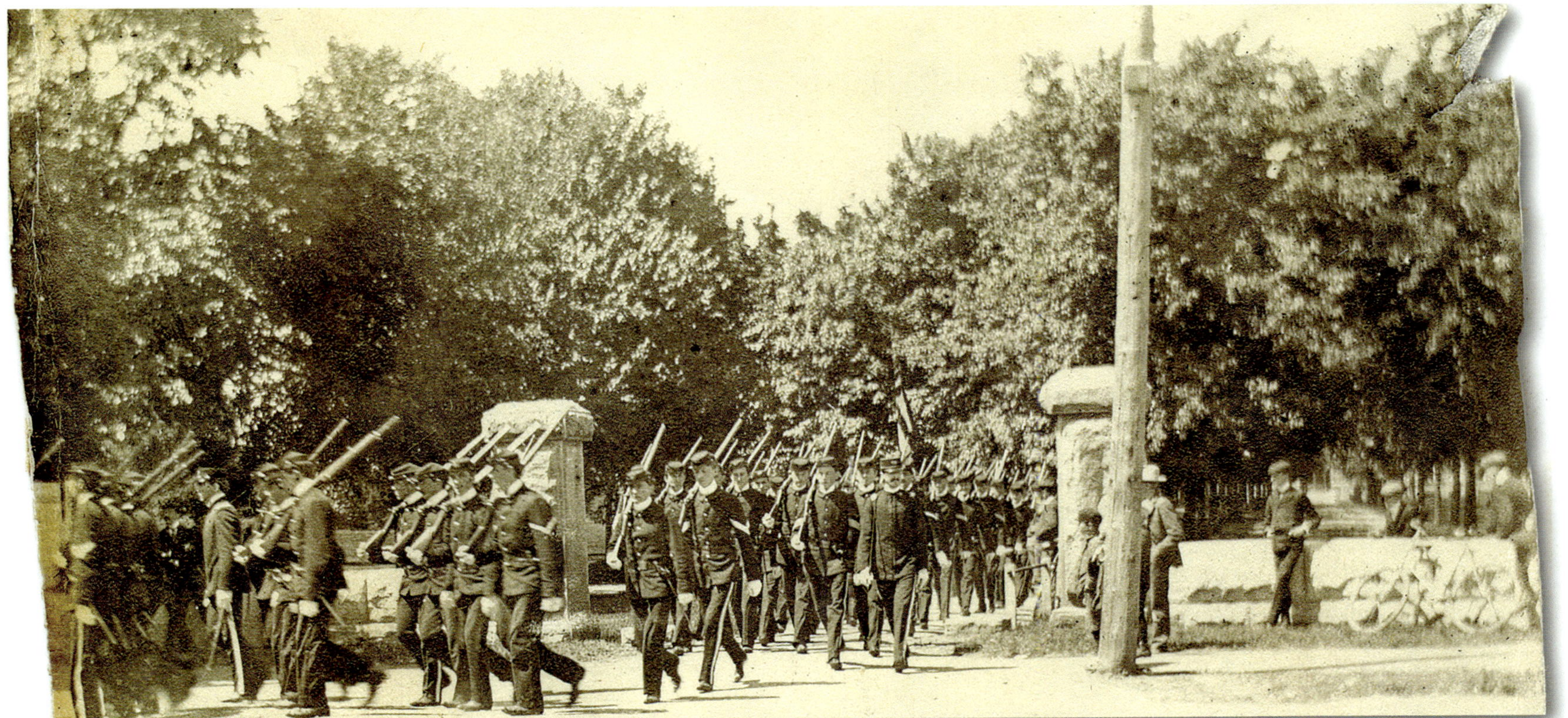

Many of Purdue's oldest and most enduring traditions began in the 1880s, including the selection of old gold and black as the official Purdue colors, the band, the *Debris* yearbook, and the *Purdue Exponent* student newspaper.

In 1887 the student athletic association voted to have a football team. Only two members of the team had ever seen a game. The team paid for its own uniforms, the coach's salary, and transportation. An athletic field did not exist on campus, and the team chose to practice in front of the Men's Dormitory. They had one week of practice before the first and only game of the season against the more experienced team from Butler University. The day before the big event, a self-appointed committee of faculty and students met in University Hall after the team members realized that Purdue did not have distinctive team colors. Football captain John Breckenridge Burris suggested using orange and black, the colors worn by Princeton's successful teams, but in the interest of being distinctive, old gold was substituted for orange. The university had chosen its iconic colors. The game against Butler ended in an unceremonious 48–6 defeat; the results telegrammed to President Smart simply stated, "It's a Waterloo."[6] No team formed for the 1888 season.

On June 8, 1887, Purdue held its first interclass athletic Field Day on the Parade Ground, or Oval, an area that later became known as Memorial Mall. For many years, the four undergraduate classes formed their own teams in baseball, football, and other sports. With limited opportunities to play intercollegiate sports, these rivalries were often just as important as contests against other schools.

The 1887 football team, the originators of old gold and black. *(Purdue University photographs)*

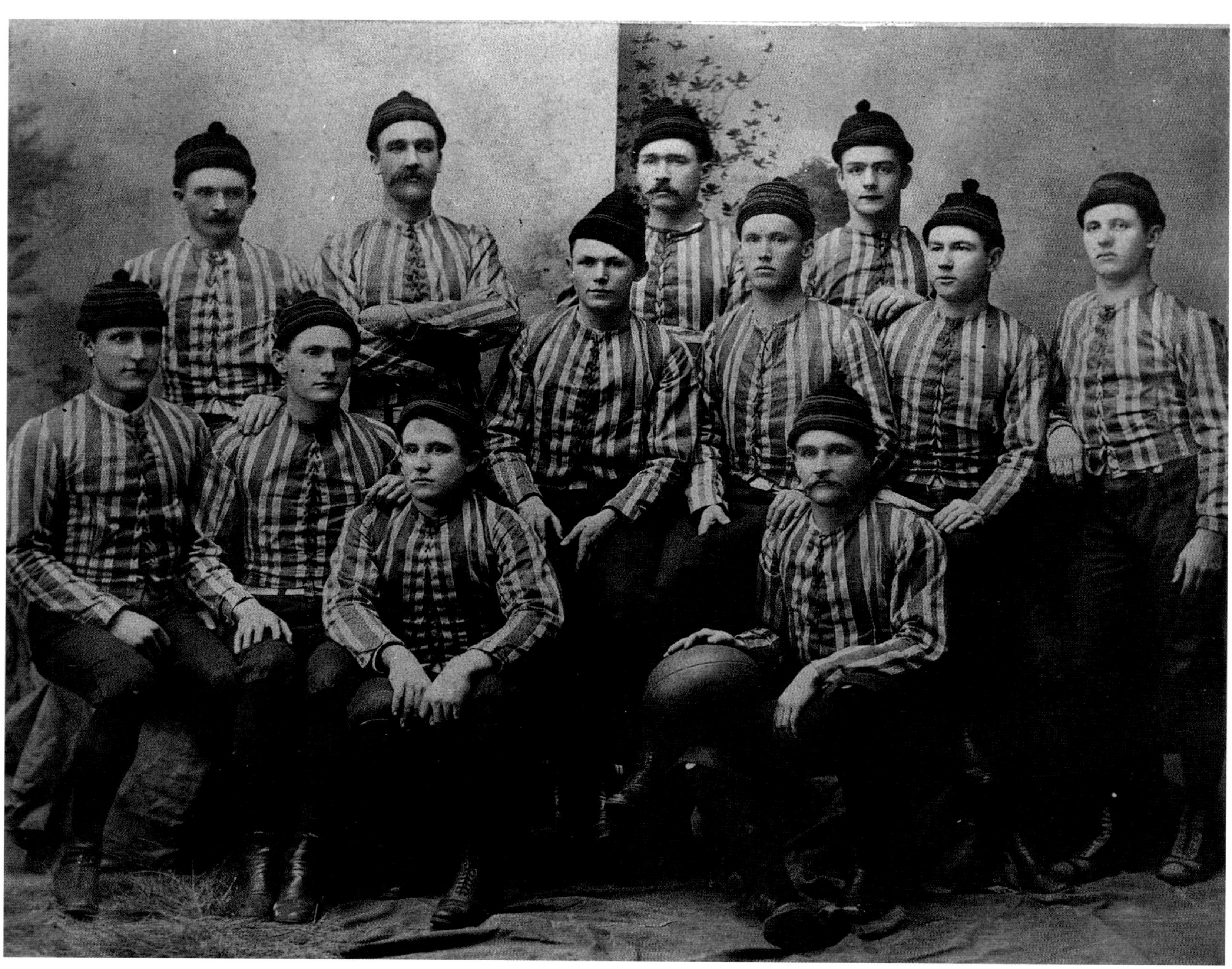

Left: Program for the Annual Address before the United Literary Societies, June 31, 1889. *(Philalethean Literary Society records)*

Right: Cover of John S. Wright's history notebook, 1889. *(John S. Wright papers)*

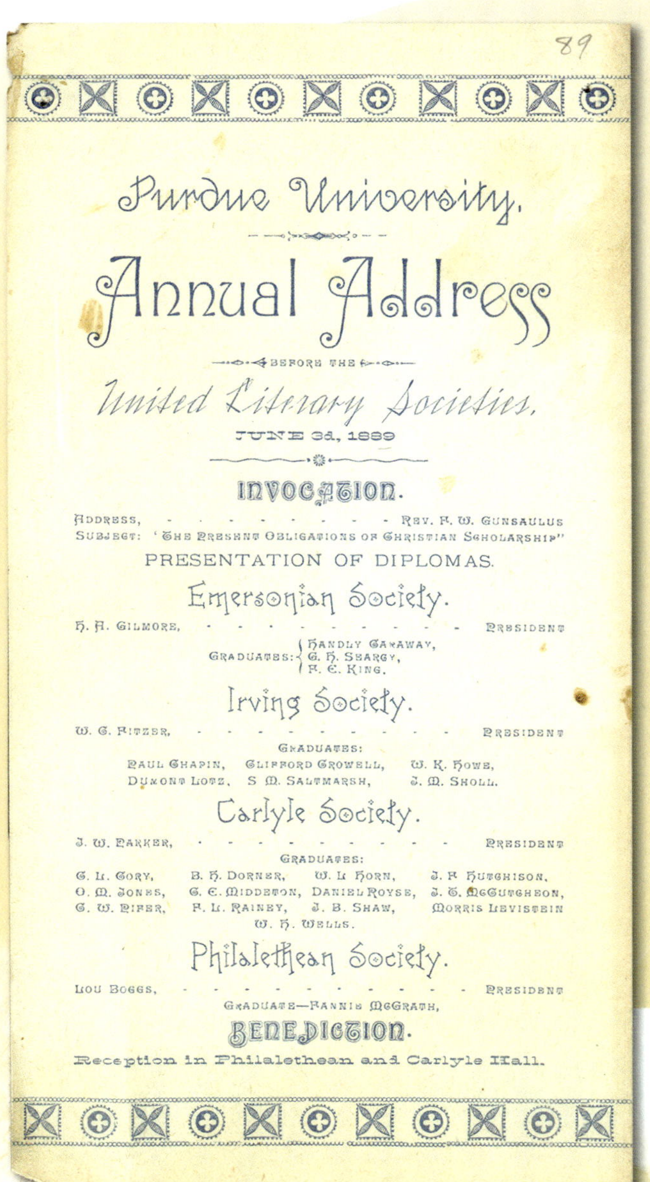

89

Purdue University.

Annual Address

before the

United Literary Societies,

June 31, 1889

INVOCATION.

Address, - - - - - - - - - - Rev. F. W. Gunsaulus
Subject: "The Present Obligations of Christian Scholarship"

PRESENTATION OF DIPLOMAS.

Emersonian Society.

H. A. Gilmore, - - - - - - - - - - President

Graduates: Handly Caraway, G. H. Seargy, F. C. King.

Irving Society.

W. G. Fitzer, - - - - - - - - - - President

Graduates:
Paul Chapin, Clifford Crowell, W. K. Howe,
Dumont Lotz, S M. Saltmarsh, J. M. Sholl.

Carlyle Society.

J. W. Parker, - - - - - - - - - - President

Graduates:
C. L. Cory, B. H. Dorner, W. L Horn, J. F Hutchison,
O. M. Jones, G. E. Middeton, Daniel Royse, J. T. McCutcheon,
C. W. Pifer, F. L. Rainey, J. B. Shaw, Morris Levistein
W. H. Wells.

Philalethean Society.

Lou Boggs, - - - - - - - - - - President

Graduate—Fannie McGrath,

BENEDICTION.

Reception in Philalethean and Carlyle Hall.

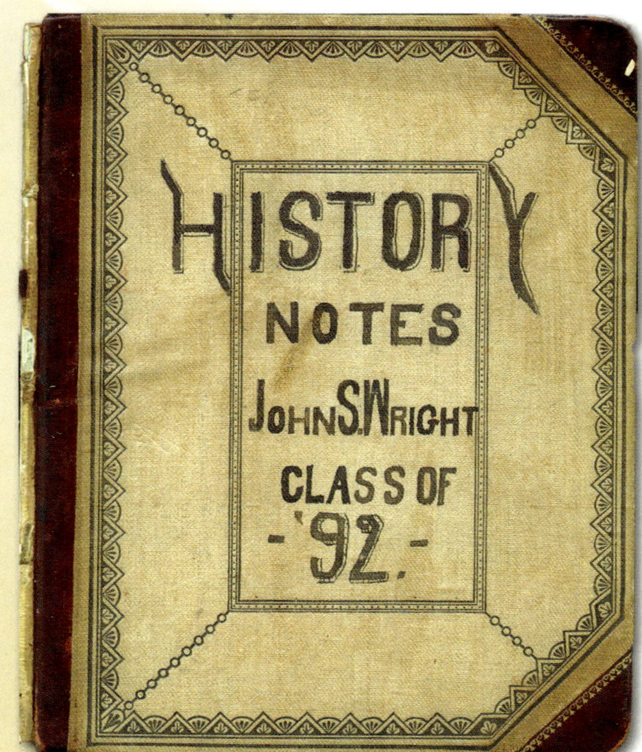

5

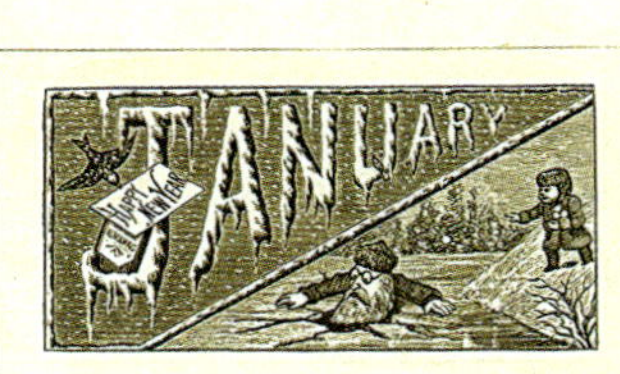

1st. 1882. Sunday.
I arose at. 8:00 o'clock. Cold & snowed.
I am now 23 years old. A Junior in
Purdue University, taking Scientific course.
I also am instructor in Book Keeping in
Academy; belong to Bond Presbyterian
Church; Am corrospondent for La Fayette
Sunday Journal and Litery Editor of
Christian Worker; also Critic in the
Irving Literary Society and I am
in good health and weigh about 145
lbs. I am in a poor condition financially
but will be in a better one before 3 yrs
rolls by. if God permits. I am in
Handcock Co. Ohio on a visit to H. Loup.
Read some in "Figs and Thistles"

E. C. White, class of 1883, documented his Purdue experience in a daily journal. His entry on January 1, 1882, provides an overview of his situation, stating, "I am now 23 years old. A Junior in Purdue University. Taking Scientific course. I also am instructor in Book Keeping in Academy; belong to Bond Presbyterian Church; Am correspondent for La Fayette Sunday Journal and Literary Editor of Christian Worker; also Critic in Irving Literary Society and I am in good health and weight about 145 lbs. I am in a poor condition financially but will be in a better one before 3 yrs rolls by, if God permits." *(E. C. White papers)*

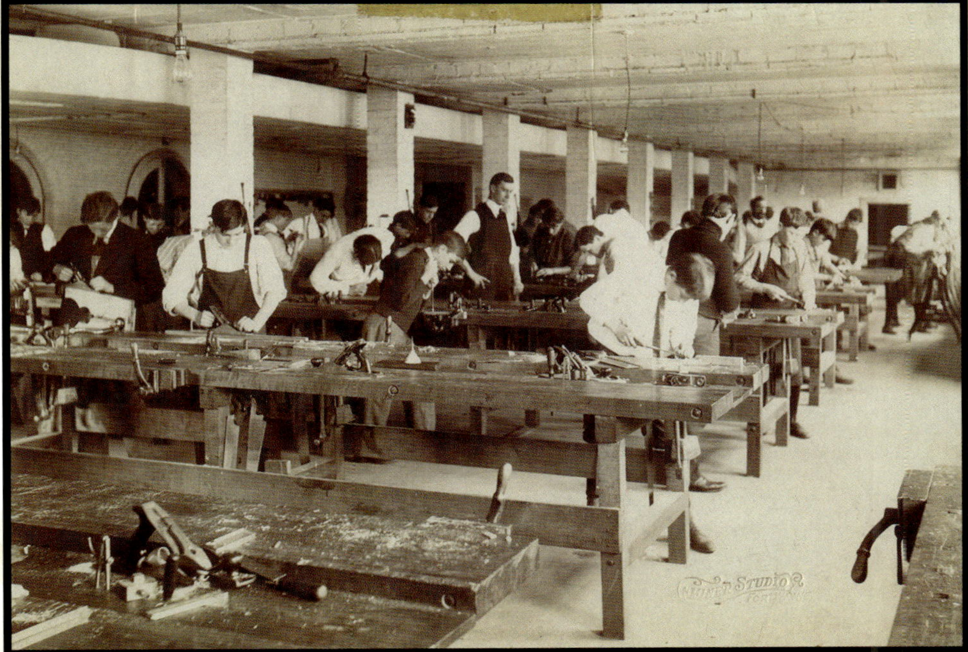

Woodworking class in a room with electric lights. *(Purdue University photographs)*

The original student newspaper of the 1870s, *The Purdue,* had a short life but was revived in the fall of 1882 as a monthly publication. *The New Purdue* was a combined effort of the Irving, Philalethean, and Carlyle literary societies. The content involved short literary, scientific, and engineering pieces; poems; and campus news from departments, clubs, and literary societies. The publication continued until the spring of 1888, when tensions between the faculty and student staff led to its demise.[7]

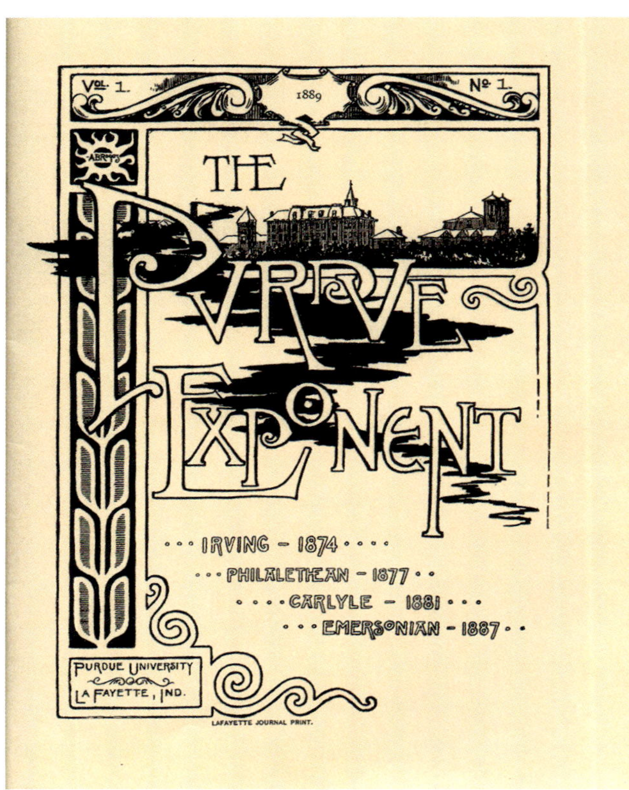

First edition of the *Purdue Exponent,* December 15, 1889. *(*Purdue Exponent*)*

The *Purdue Exponent* followed in December 1889 as a monthly publication. Much like the earlier student news publications, the first issue contained features concerning news, sports, the literary societies, and departmental activities, as well as essays.[8]

Another enduring publication that began in 1889 was the *Debris* yearbook, produced annually by the senior class until 2008. Funding for the yearbook came from subscriptions, student organizations, and advertising. Throughout its existence, the *Debris* shared class histories, personal stories, cartoons, school rivalries, and social activities. Pulitzer Prize winners Booth Tarkington and John T. McCutcheon contributed regularly during its formative years. The yearbooks document otherwise unrecorded histories of the university from the student perspective.

The Ancient Order of Dormitory Devils formed as a secret society on campus and soon became legendary for its members' pranks, which ranged from placing animals and wagons on the roof of the Men's Dormitory to pouring buckets of water on unsuspecting pedestrians walking beneath open windows. On one occasion, the Devils captured a victim to douse in the water pump only to be met with cries of "I'm President Smart, I'm President Smart!" None of the Devils were punished for the indiscretion. In perhaps their biggest stunt, the Devils climbed the tower of the Boiler and Gas House on a very cold night, intent on silencing the bell that woke them in the morning and signaled class times. They turned the bell upside down, filled it with water, and waited for it to freeze solid. When the morning arrived, no bell rang to wake them.[9]

Below: Views of student life illustrated by John T. McCutcheon in the *Debris* yearbook, 1889. Activities include late-night card games, sneaking cider from the cider mill, Dormitory Devils escapades, and painting the class year at the top of the Agricultural Experiment Station, a precursor to the Tank Scrap. *(*Debris *yearbook)*

Bottom: Daniel Royse, Samuel Saltmarsh, Dumont Lotz, Clifford Crowell, Oliver Jones, Handly Caraway, and John McCutcheon, editors of the first *Debris* yearbook. *(*Debris *yearbook)*

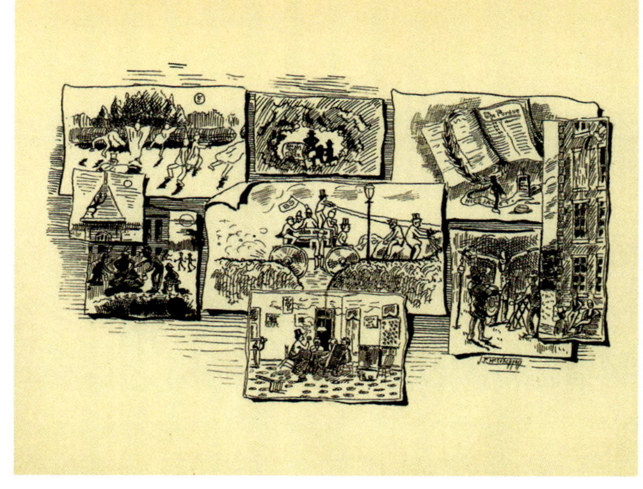

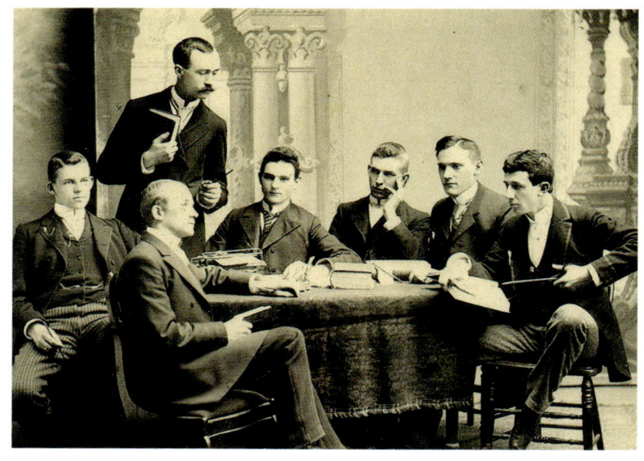

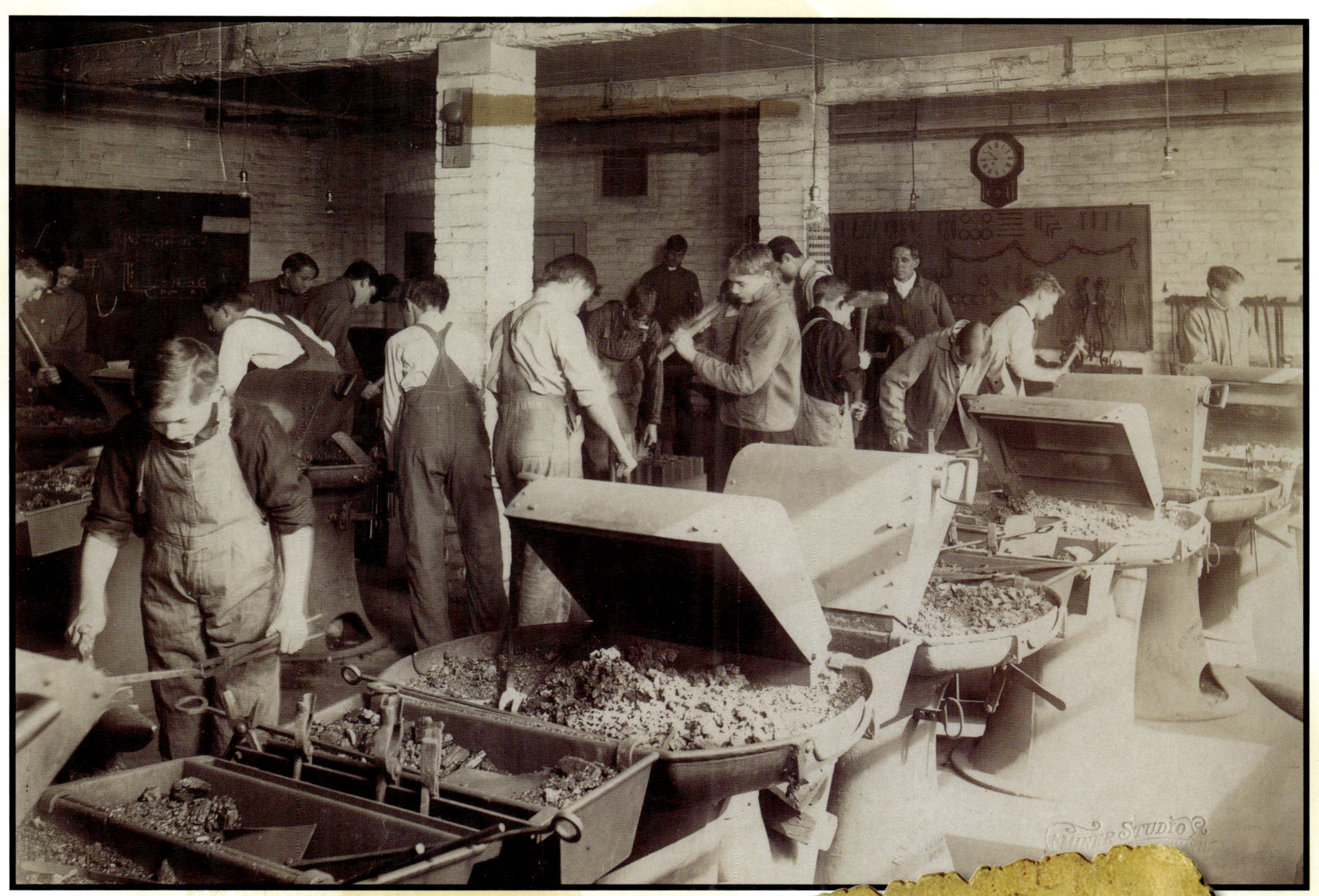

Class of '88
will Picnic at Jewettsport,
May 22d, 1886.

Boat leaves at 8 a.m. sharp. See list for company.

Invitation Committee:
Jas. S. Shortle. Miss Jessie Born. J. C. Ross.

Above: Blacksmithing class.
(Purdue University photographs)

Right: A Class of 1888 picnic invitation includes a penciled note at the top: "Get a Girl and let's go!"
(Paul Million papers)

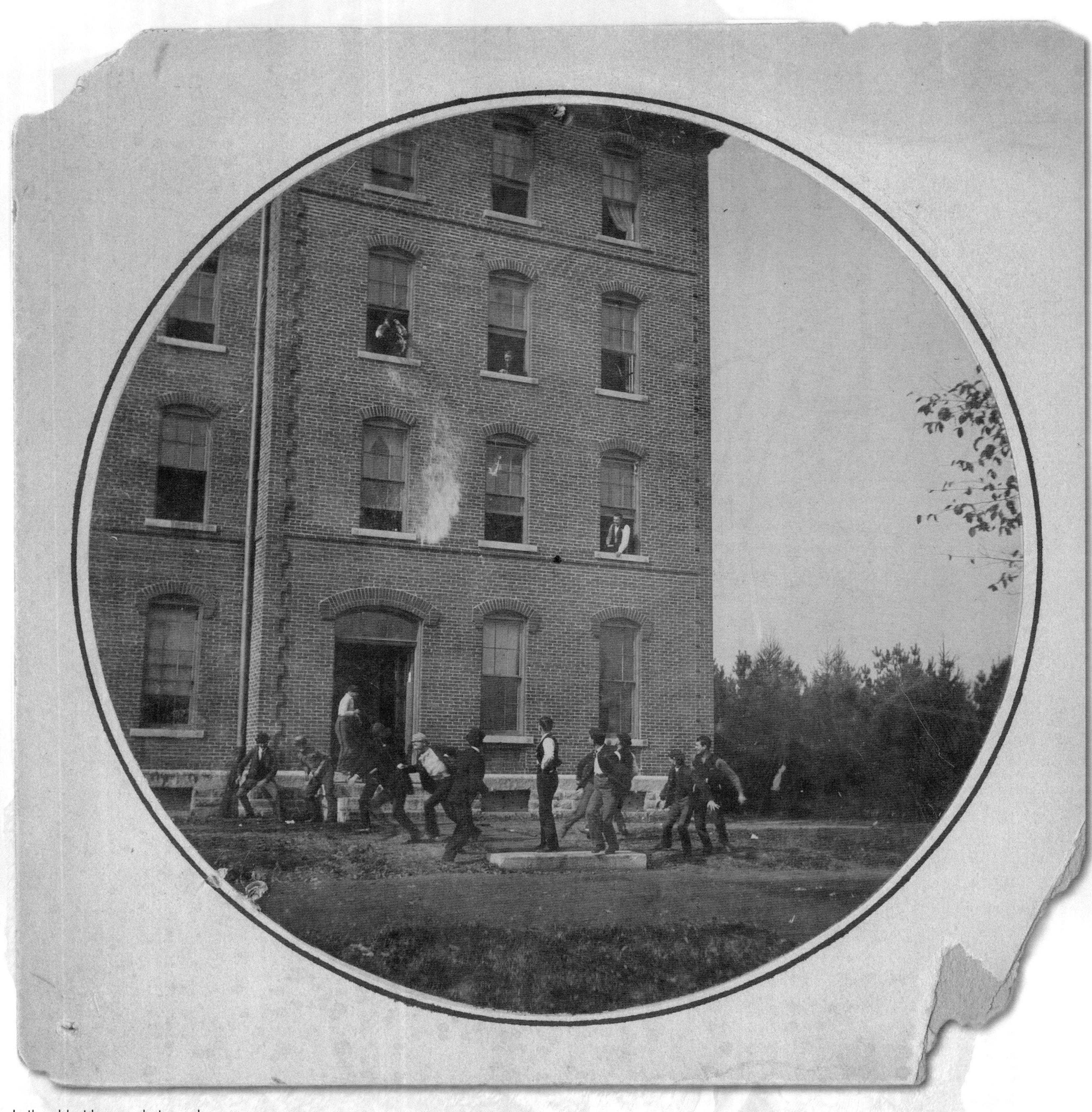

In the oldest known photograph of students on campus, a man pours water from a third-floor window of the Men's Dormitory onto a group of students below.
(Purdue University photographs)

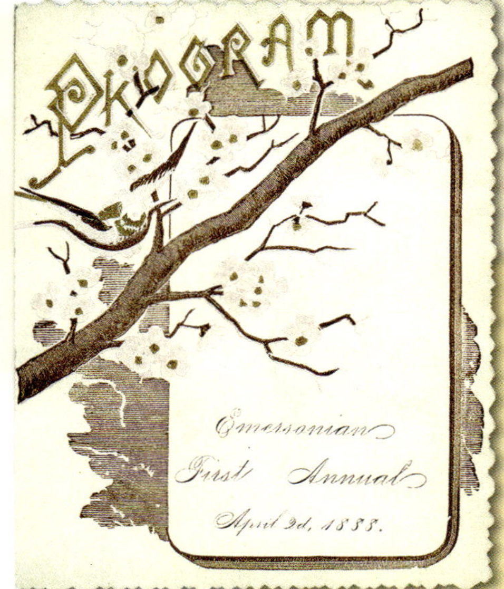

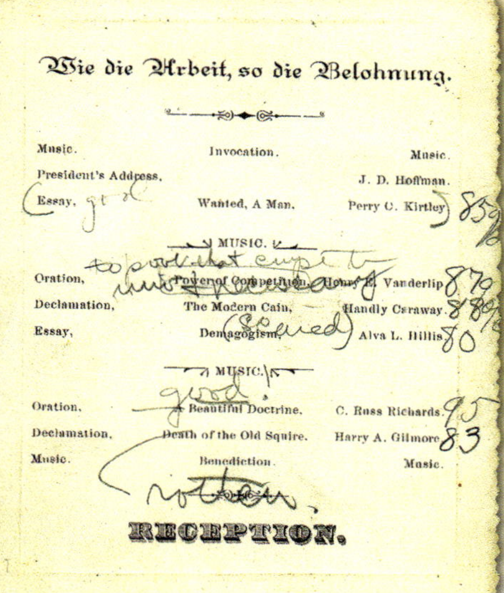

Wie die Arbeit, so die Belohnung.

Music.	Invocation.	Music.
President's Address,		J. D. Hoffman.
Essay,	Wanted, A Man.	Perry C. Kirtley.
	MUSIC.	
Oration,	Power of Competition,	Henry E. Vanderlip.
Declamation,	The Modern Cain,	Handly Caraway.
Essay,	Demagogism,	Alva L. Hillis.
	MUSIC.	
Oration,	A Beautiful Doctrine,	C. Russ Richards.
Declamation,	Death of the Old Squire.	Harry A. Gilmore.
Music.	Benediction.	Music.

RECEPTION.

PREPARATORY CLASS

OF

Purdue · University

LaFayette, Ind. Dec 20 1888

Report of Charles Thompson

for the Term ending Dec 19 1888

BRANCHES OF STUDY.	Recitations.	EXAMINATION.	AVERAGE $\frac{2R+E}{3}$
Algebra,	76	71	71
Arithmetic,	83	54	74
Agriculture,			
Shop Work,	75		
Mechanical Drawing,	65	82	71
English,	87		
History, U. S.	88		
Industrial Drawing,			
Physiology,			
Physical Geography,			
Elocution,	98		
Natural Philosophy,			

Excused Absences .... Unexcused Absences ....

Tardiness Unexcused, ...

Remarks: ....

☞ 100 is the standard of perfection; and 70 is the standard of lowest approved attainment. Parents will please compare the pupils' mark with the standard.

Erastus Test, Principal.

Far left: Program for the Emersonian Society First Annual event, April 2, 1888. Student George Ade made notes about the speakers, ranging from "good" to "rotten," and assigned them grades. *(George Ade papers)*

Left: December 1888 report card for Charles E. Thompson, student of the Preparatory Academy. *(Charles E. Thompson collection)*

Below: Female students working in the greenhouse with Professor James Troop. *(Purdue University photographs)*

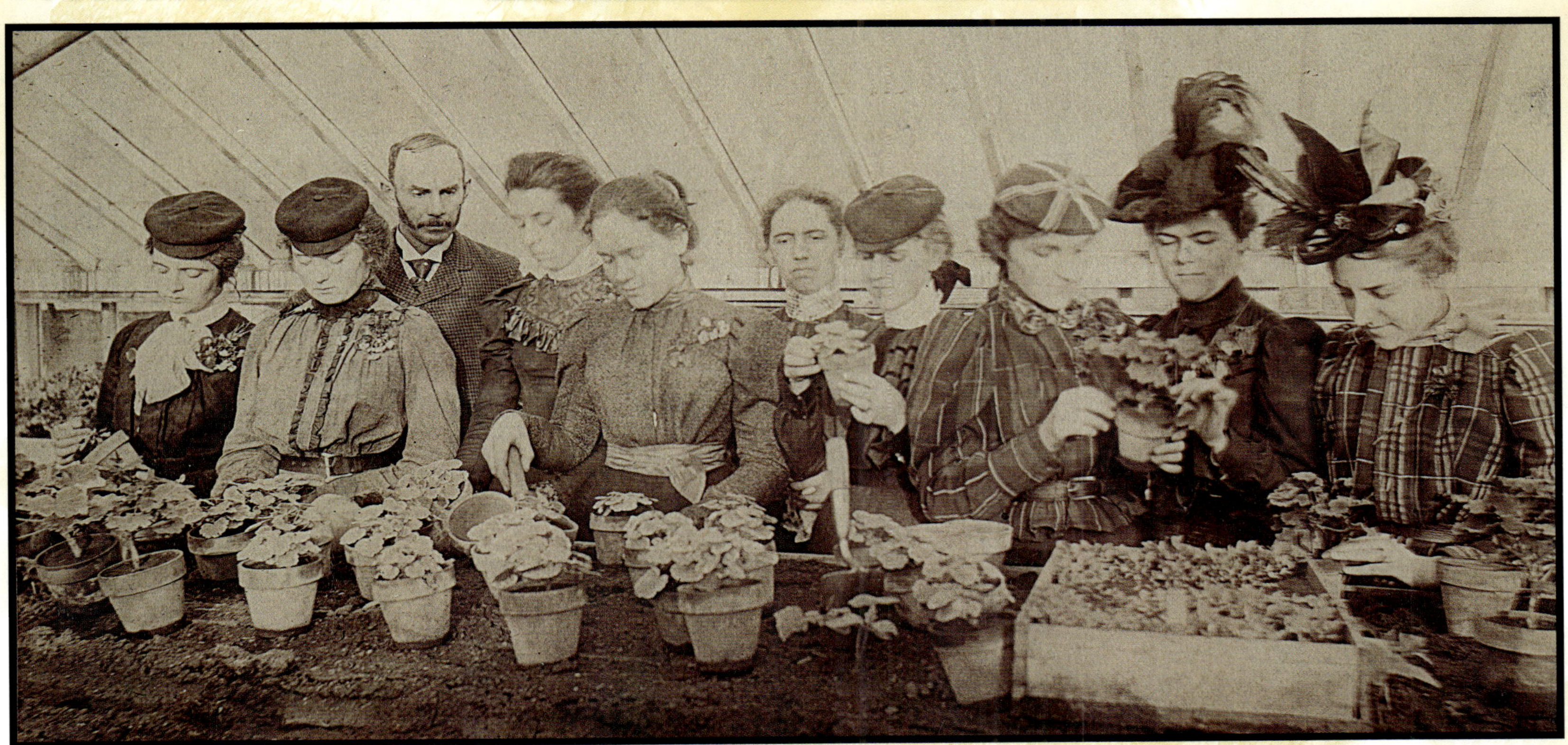

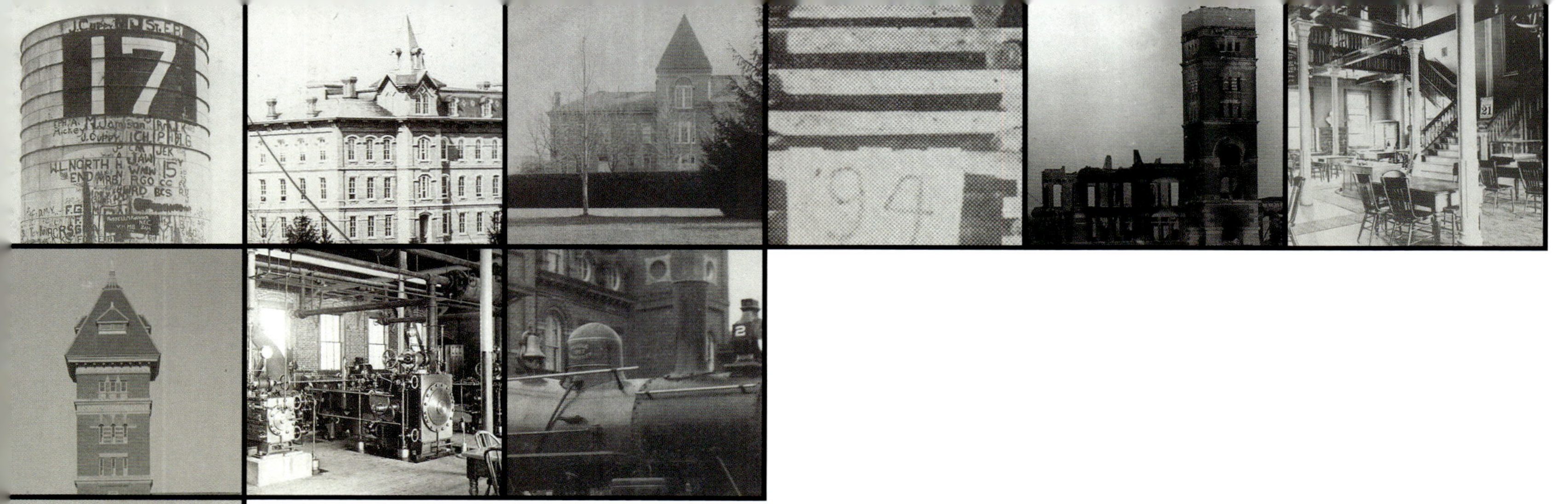

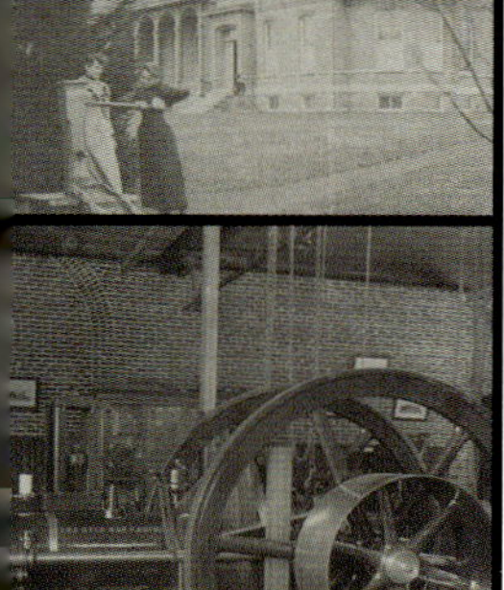

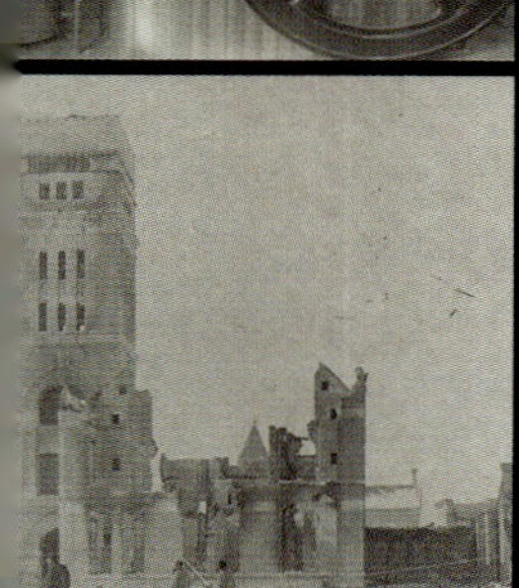

1898 West Lafayette campus map. *(Campus Maps collection)*

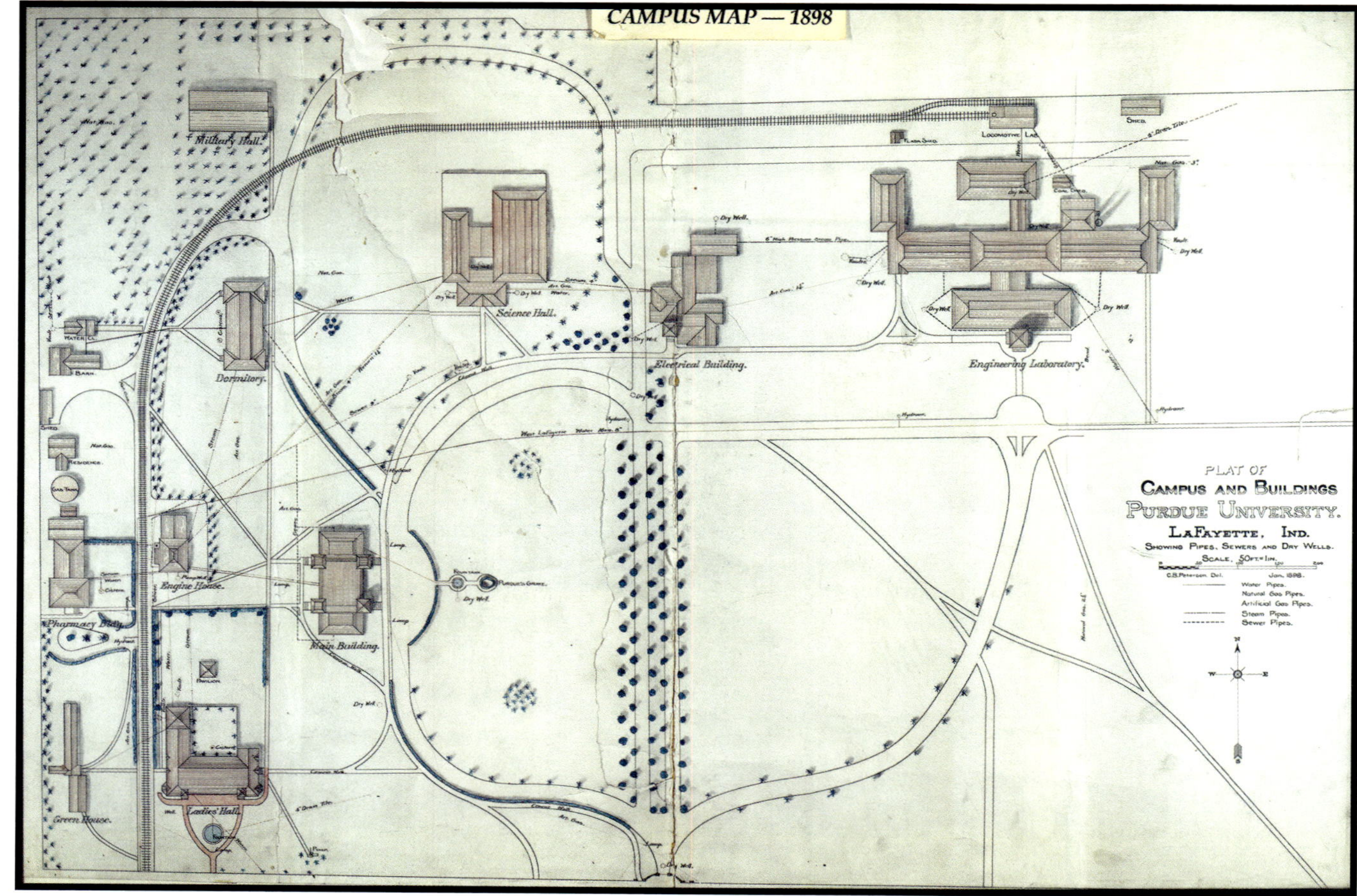

{ Enrollment in 1890: 530 students[1] }

[The 1890s]

PURDUE AT 30

"I went directly to Professor Stone and told him that I found it was pretty easy for me and that I would like to try and make the course (graduate) in three years. He said, 'No, don't be in a hurry; just take your time. Go on up in town to the skating rink and enjoy yourself.' But that didn't satisfy me, and I kept talking until finally he permitted me to try and make the course in three years instead of four. So, I had plenty to do from that time on."

—*DeWitt "Buck" Buchanan, class of 1898*[2]

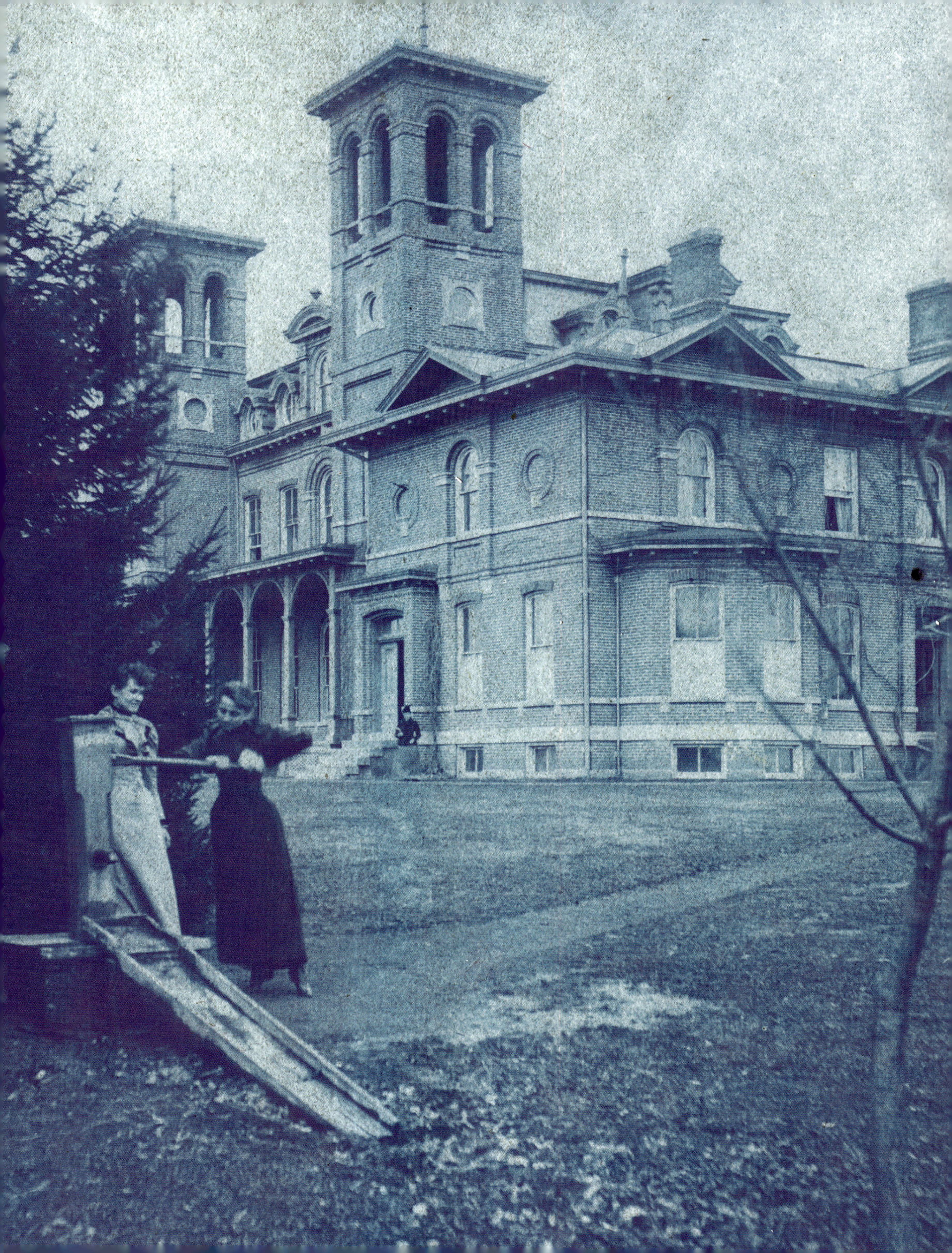

In 1890, tuition remained free for in-state students and $25.00 for students outside of Indiana.

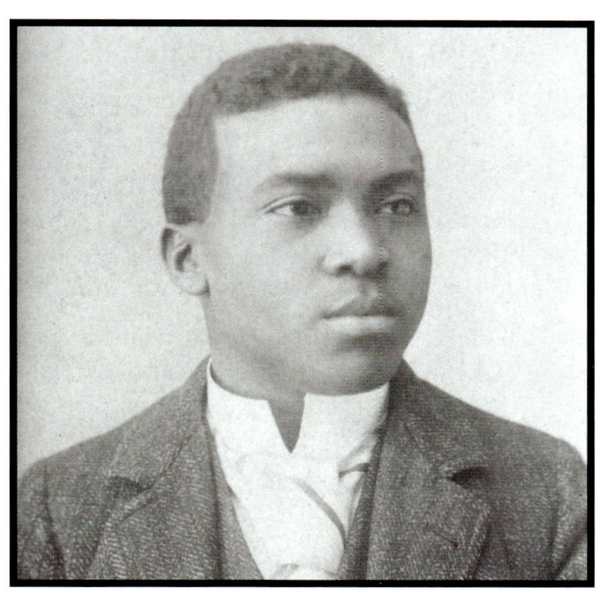

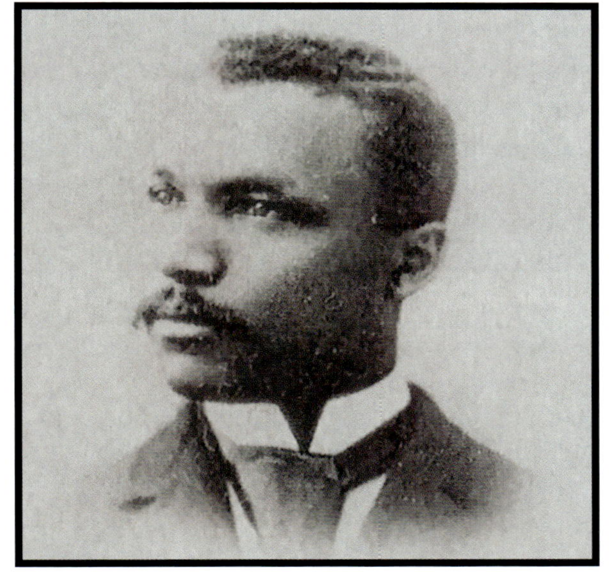

Top: George W. Lacy, 1890.
(School of Pharmacy and Pharmacal Sciences records)

Bottom: David Robert Lewis, 1894.
(Debris yearbook)

Opposite page: Students at the water pump outside Ladies Hall, a popular meeting spot for male and female students.
(William Chester Halstead photos)

The students of the 1890s came from eighty-two Indiana counties, eighteen states and the District of Columbia, and three countries—Canada, Japan, and Spain. Enrollment grew so much that campus facilities were inadequate for hosting major events; lectures and ceremonies were held in tents or event halls in Lafayette.

In 1890 George W. Lacy, or Lacey, completed a degree in pharmacy, becoming the first African American graduate of Purdue. At the time, Pharmacy was an academic organization separate from the university, and as a result, Lacy's success is sometimes overlooked. In 1894 David Robert Lewis of Greensburg, Indiana, completed his bachelor's degree in civil engineering, becoming the first African American graduate of a traditional four-year program at Purdue.

The Heavilon Hall Fire

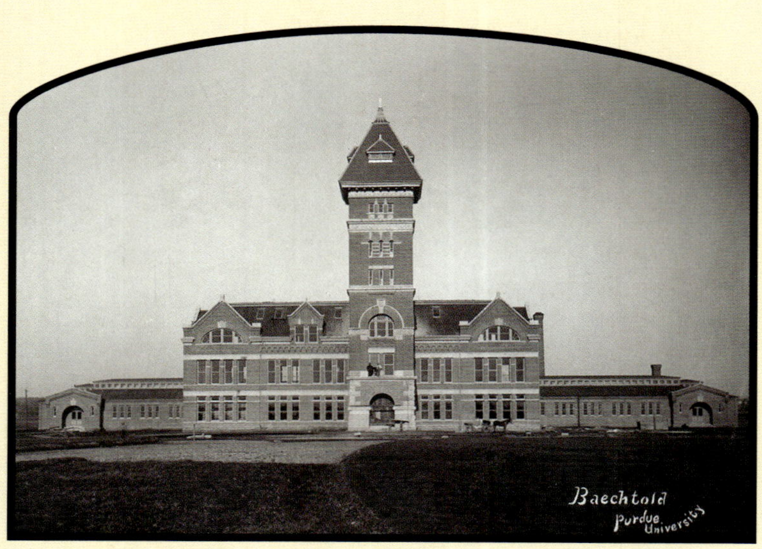

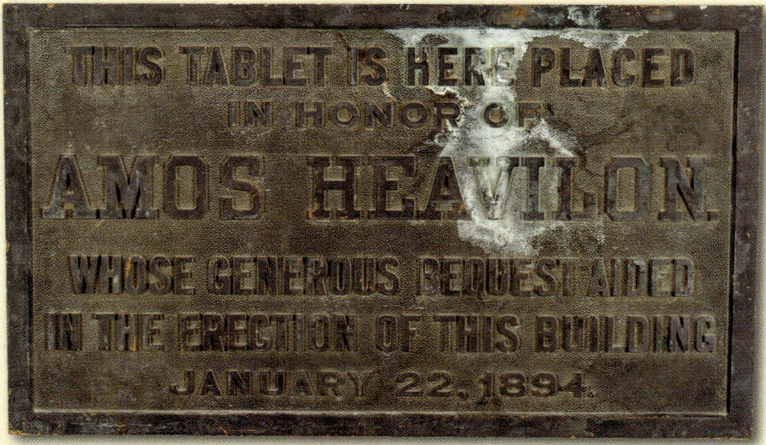

On January 19, 1894, Purdue dedicated its new mechanical engineering building, commonly known as Heavilon Hall, in honor of benefactor Amos Heavilon. The governor and several faculty members gave speeches to the assembled throng, and during the dance held that evening the building was illuminated so brightly it was visible from Lafayette. Purdue University was justifiably proud. The new state-of-the-art building had been constructed around the existing Mechanical Laboratory and contained a foundry, a woodshop, an engineering laboratory, a machine room, a forge room, offices, classrooms, a museum, and a boiler room. It would house the Schools of Mechanical Engineering and Civil Engineering and the Department of Practical Mechanics.

Four days after its dedication, on the evening of January 23 at about 8:30 p.m., a fire broke out in the boiler room. A strong northwest wind fanned the flames through the laboratories. Students, staff, faculty, and neighbors ran into the building and removed whatever machinery and furniture they could. The entire engineering laboratory, machine room, and forge room were engulfed in flames; the famed Schenectady locomotive was trapped amid the destruction. By the time fire brigades arrived, much of the three-story building was beyond saving. Only a portion of the building containing the foundry and woodshop remained standing. Almost everything was lost, including faculty book collections, years of research data, engines, drill presses, lathes, and other valuable machinery. President Smart stood by in tears.[3]

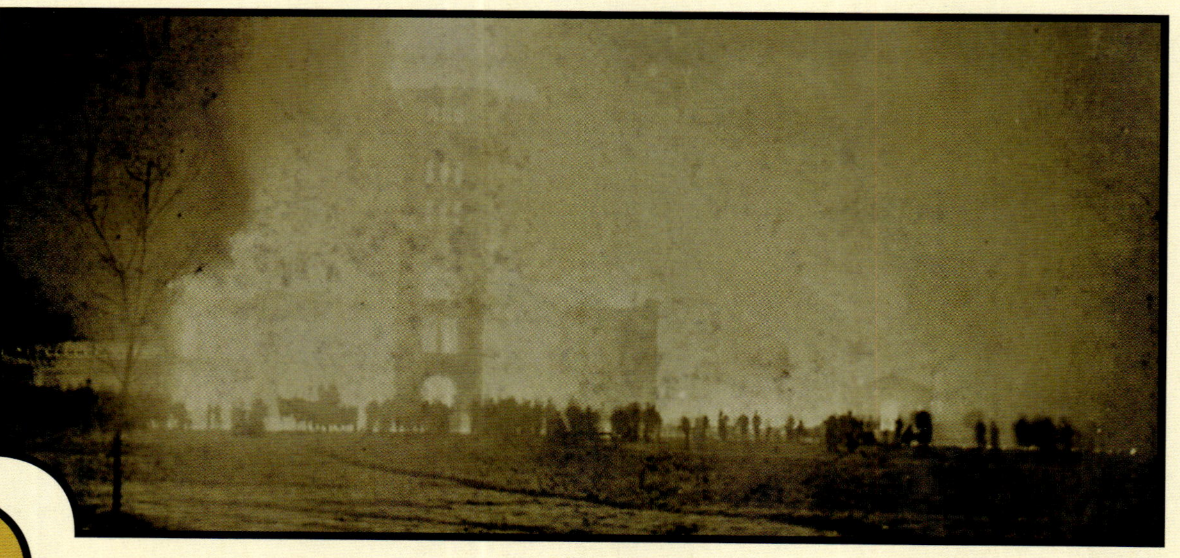

Top: Heavilon Hall before the fire, 1894. *(Purdue University photographs)*

Middle: Sign that stood outside the first Heavilon Hall, 1894. *(Heavilon Hall records)*

Bottom: The Heavilon Hall fire occurred four days after the building opened in January 1894. *(Purdue University photographs)*

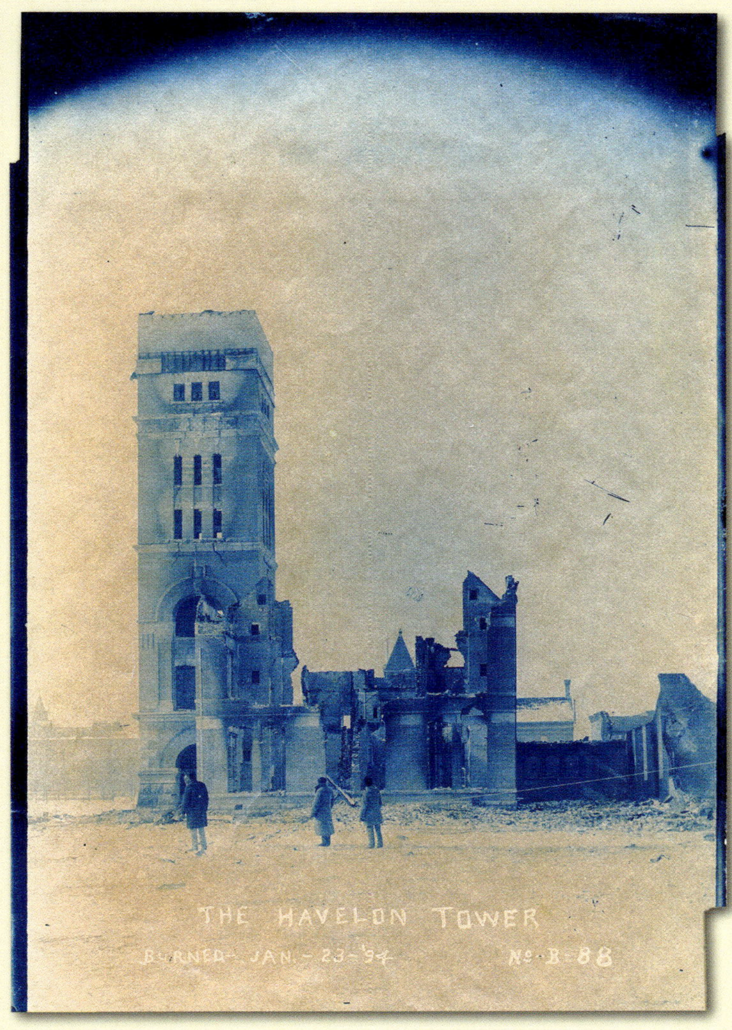

We the undersigned do pledge ourselves to pay on or before Aug 1st 1894, the sums set opposite our names, the same to be forwarded to President Smart of Purdue University & by him applied toward the rebuilding and equipping of the Heavilon shops.

(Heavilon Shops)

George W. Ross '86	$25.00
George Ade '87	25.00
C. V. Kimball "89"	10.00
R. B. Strong "89"	10.00
Jno. O'Gara '88	25.00
R. D. [illegible] '92	
A. N. McCoy '92	25.00
W. J. [illegible] '92	10.00
Jno. T. McCutcheon '89	20.00
Pd. Y. E. King "89"	10.00
Albert Scheible	15.00
Philip Potter	10.00
[illegible]	10.00
C. C. [illegible]	10.00
James F. Hutcheson	$5.00 Pd.
[illegible]	5.00

The next morning, the newest jewel of Purdue's crown was a blackened shell. Chapel services that morning were attended by visibly tired and grief-stricken students, faculty, and staff. In this moment, President Smart stood before those gathered and shared a vision that has guided the university. Smart stated: "We are looking this morning to the future, not to the past. I am thankful that no one was injured. . . . But I tell you young men that tower shall go up one brick higher."[4]

Work began immediately on restoring the building as local organizations and alumni groups contributed to the fundraising effort. Dealers and manufacturers replaced equipment for free or at reduced cost. The Schenectady was returned to the manufacturer and restored. Temporary classrooms were built in six days with repaired and replaced machinery in use two weeks later. By June, the laboratories had been rebuilt and were ready for the fall term.

The rebuilt Heavilon Hall tower was built nine bricks higher (rather than one) and included a clock purchased from funds donated by the Class of 1895, the Ladies' Matinee Musicale of Lafayette, and the student Mandolin Club. The clock tower would stand as an icon of the university for decades.

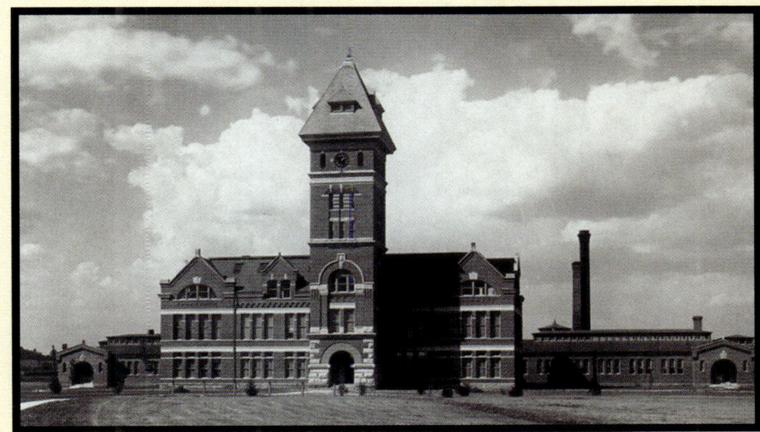

Top left: The morning after the Heavilon Hall fire. *(Purdue University Marketing and Media collection)*

Top right: Contributions by members of the Chicago Alumni Association to the Heavilon fund-raising campaign, 1894. Contributors include George Ade and John McCutcheon. *(Purdue Club of Chicago scrapbook)*

Bottom right: The second Heavilon Hall. *(Purdue University photographs)*

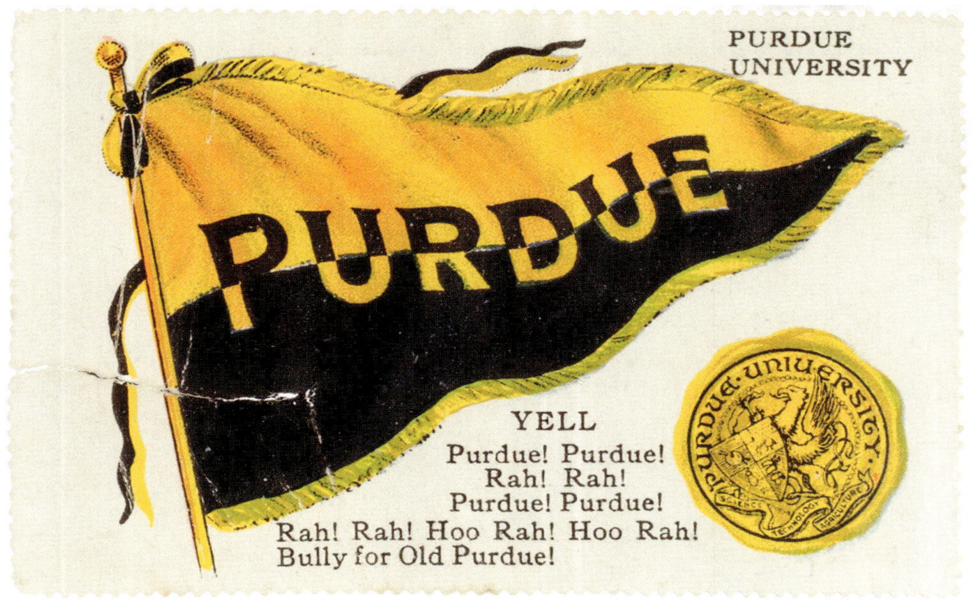

Bruce Rogers, noted typographer and creator of the Centaur font, graduated from Purdue in 1890.

In addition to building school spirit, student handbooks also helped students identify extracurricular activities on campus. The number of options grew steadily throughout the decade. Three new fraternities appeared on campus alongside Sigma Chi and Kappa Sigma: Sigma Nu in 1891, Phi Delta Theta in 1893, and Sigma Alpha Epsilon in 1893. Career-oriented clubs formed for students interested in science, civil engineering, electrical engineering, agriculture, and pharmacy.

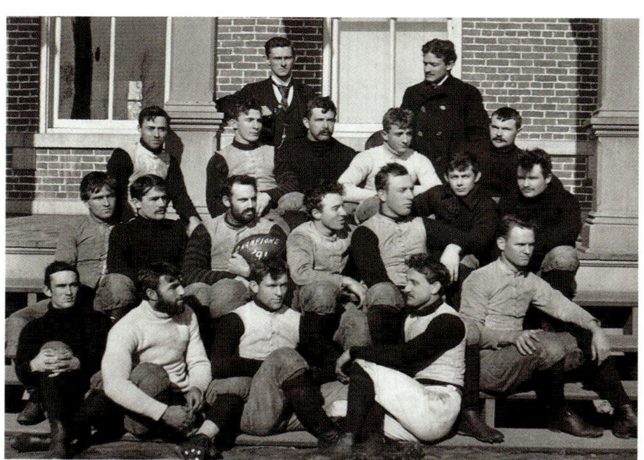

Top: Cigarette advertisement card with Purdue pennant, seal, and yell. *(Purdue University Archives and Special Collections Artifacts collection)*

Bottom: The football team after the 1891 season. *(George Ade papers)*

On October 24, 1891, the still relatively new Purdue football team played its season opener against Wabash College. Over the course of the game, Purdue was accused of multiple underhanded tactics, including the selection of recently graduated Purdue team captain Robert Allen Lackey as referee and the use of iron cleats on their shoes. Ultimately eight Wabash players left the field due to injuries, some caused by Purdue's cleats, and Purdue won the 40-minute-long game 44 to 0. Afterward, the Crawfordsville newspaper reported that the game had been a "slaughter of the innocents" and Wabash had been "snowed completely under by the burly boiler makers from Purdue." Though intended as an insult, Purdue embraced the nickname and the team has ever since been known as Boilermakers.[5]

Until 1892, the few outdoor athletic activities and military exercises at Purdue took place on Memorial Mall. That year saw the creation of Stuart Field, an integrated track, football, and baseball field located just east of the Armory. Stuart Field later became the site of military programs and exercises, memorial services, band practice, and student rallies.

Due to increasing concern about professional sports interfering with university athletics, President Smart teamed with other Midwestern university administrators to form an athletic conference that would regulate intercollegiate sports. In 1896, the Intercollegiate Conference of Faculty Representatives was born, later known as the Western Conference. During the twentieth century, the conference became better known as the Big Ten.

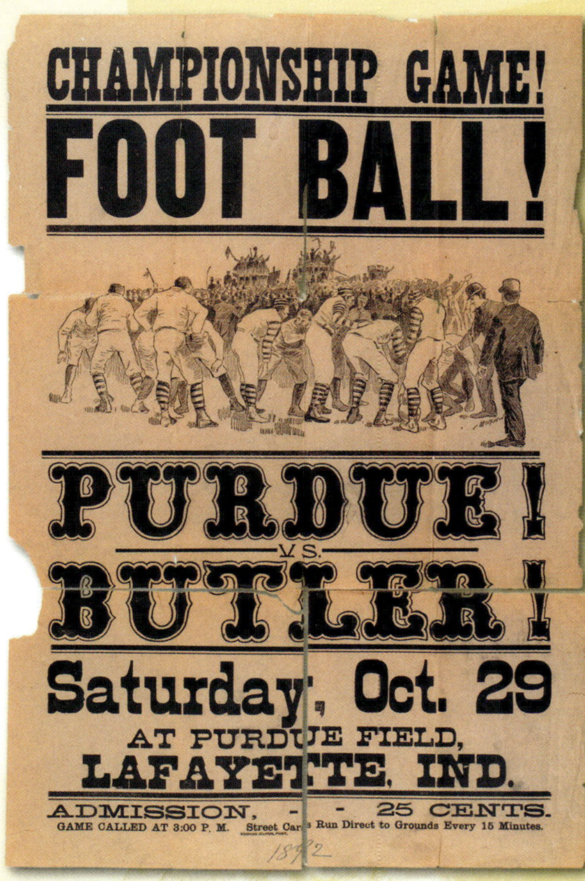

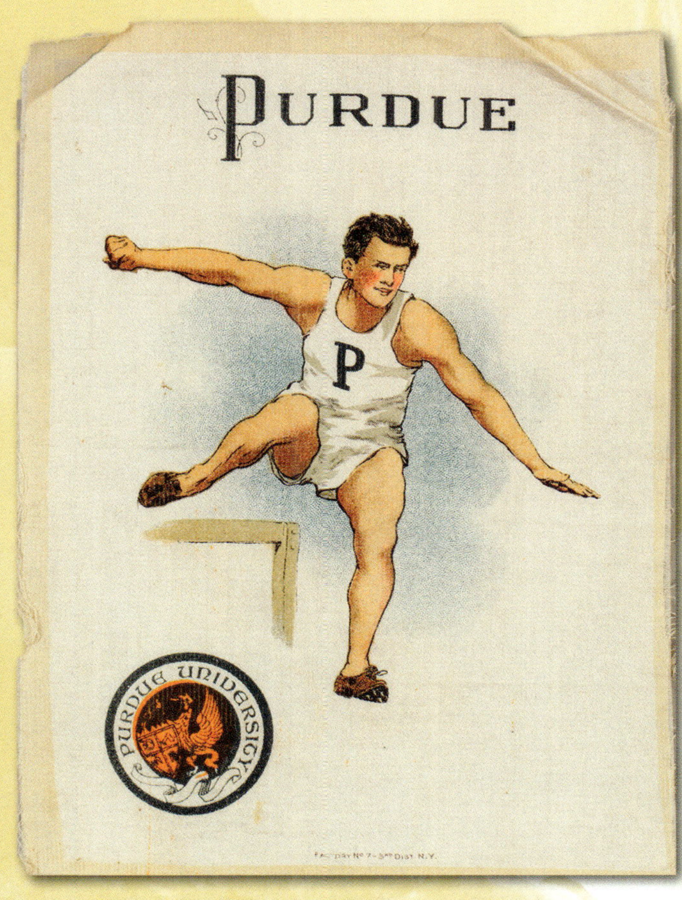

Far left: Poster for the Purdue vs. Butler football game, October 29, 1892. *(Purdue Broadsides collection)*

Left: Silk square with the Purdue seal and a track and field athlete. *(Purdue University Archives and Special Collections Artifacts collection)*

Below: Boxing match in front of the Dormitory, circa 1894. *(William Chester Halstead photos)*

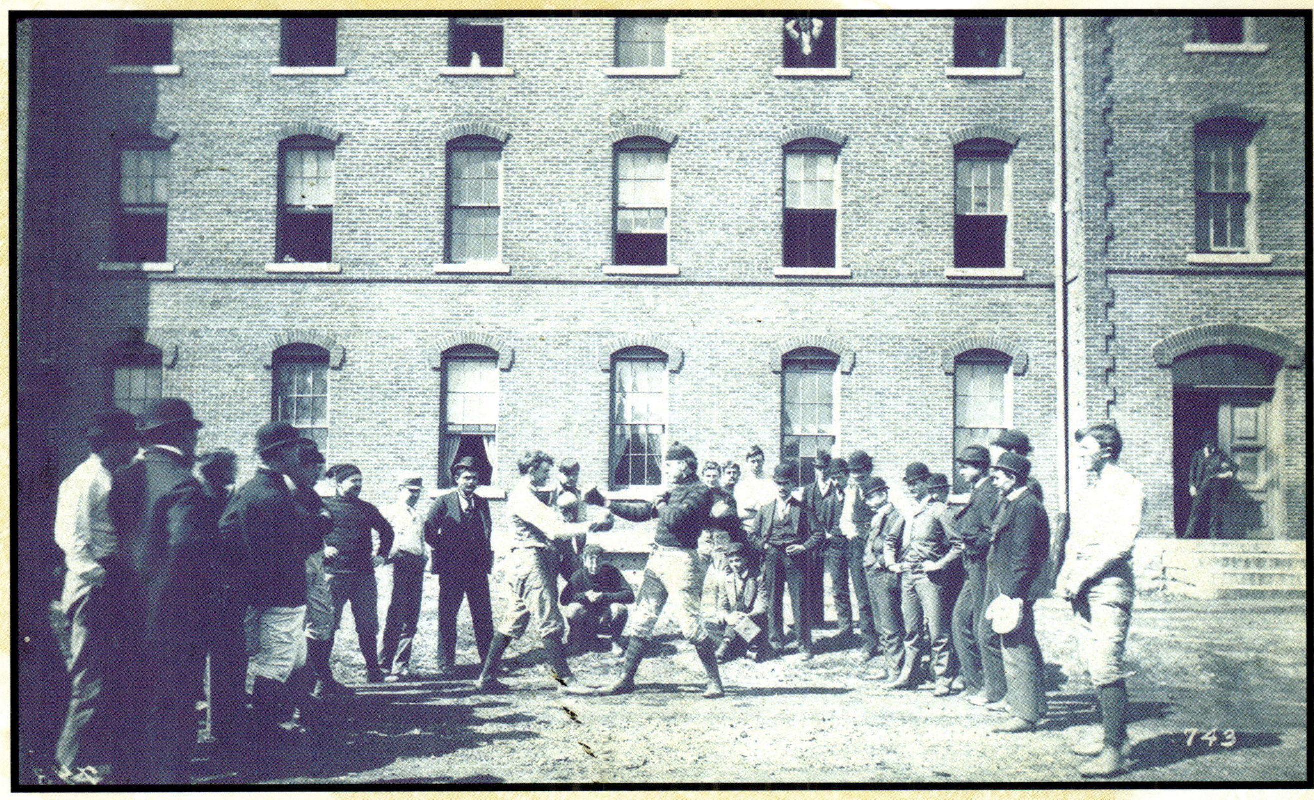

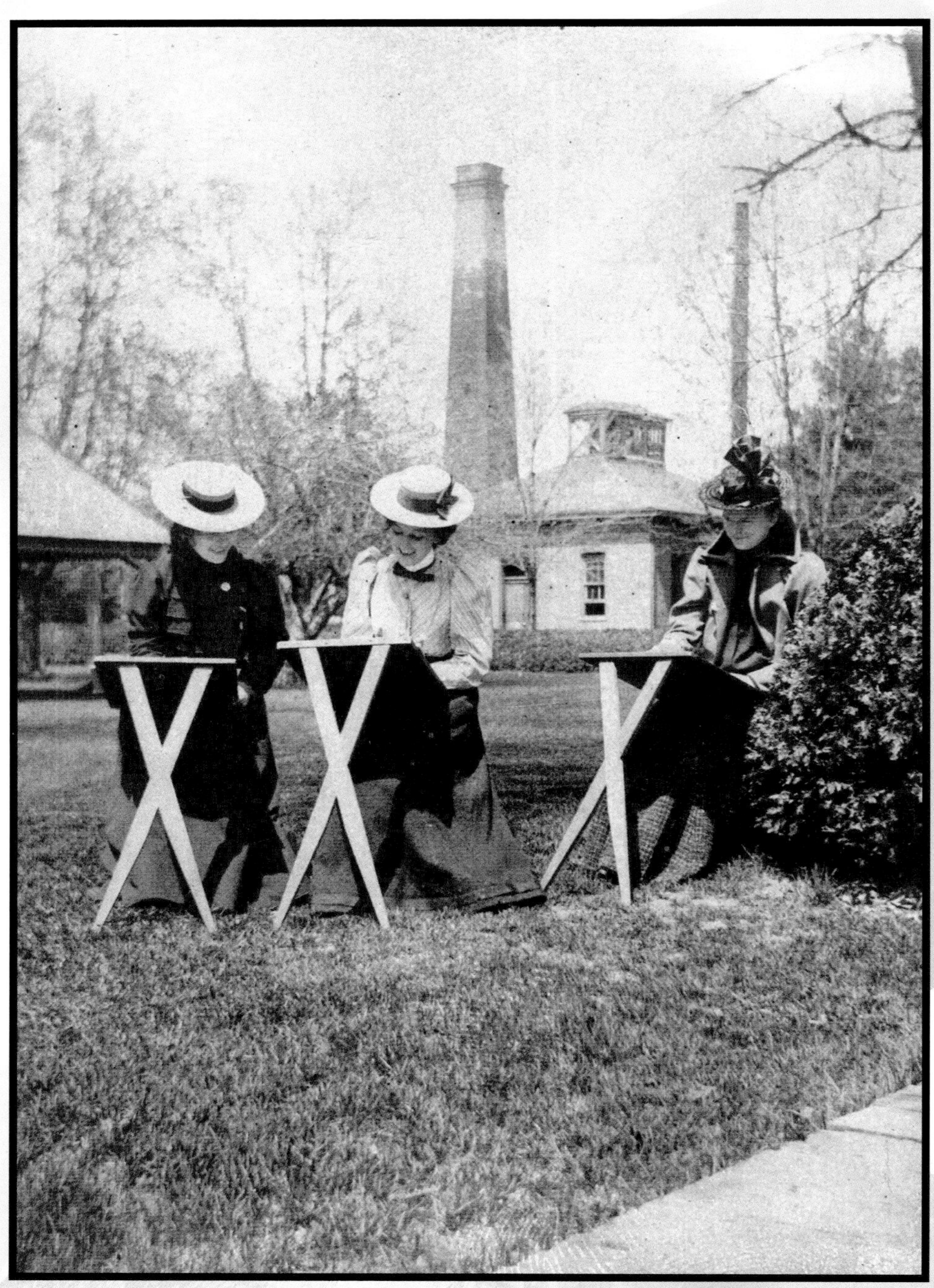

Left: Female students completing art projects outside Ladies Hall. *(Josiah H. Andrews scrapbook)*

Below right: Woodworking class, 1891. *(Purdue University photographs)*

Middle right: Crops laboratory class studying the germinating power of differently aged seeds. *(Purdue University photographs)*

Bottom: Richard A. Smart, class of 1891 and son of President Smart, working with the No. 7 Otto gas engine in Heavilon Hall before the fire. *(Purdue University photographs)*

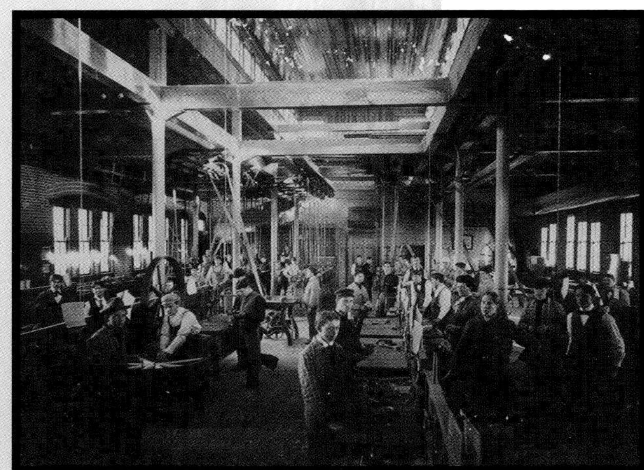

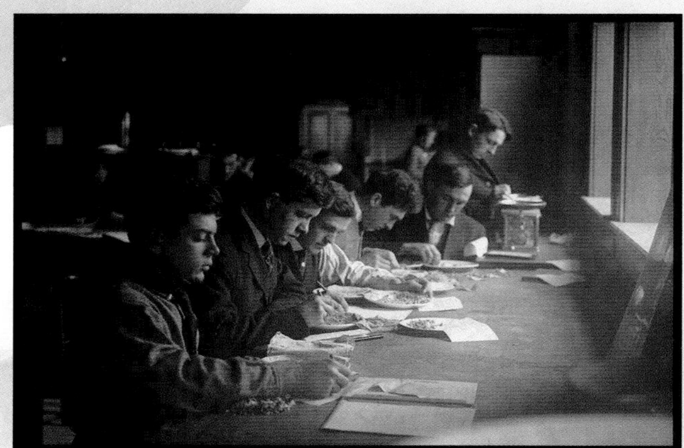

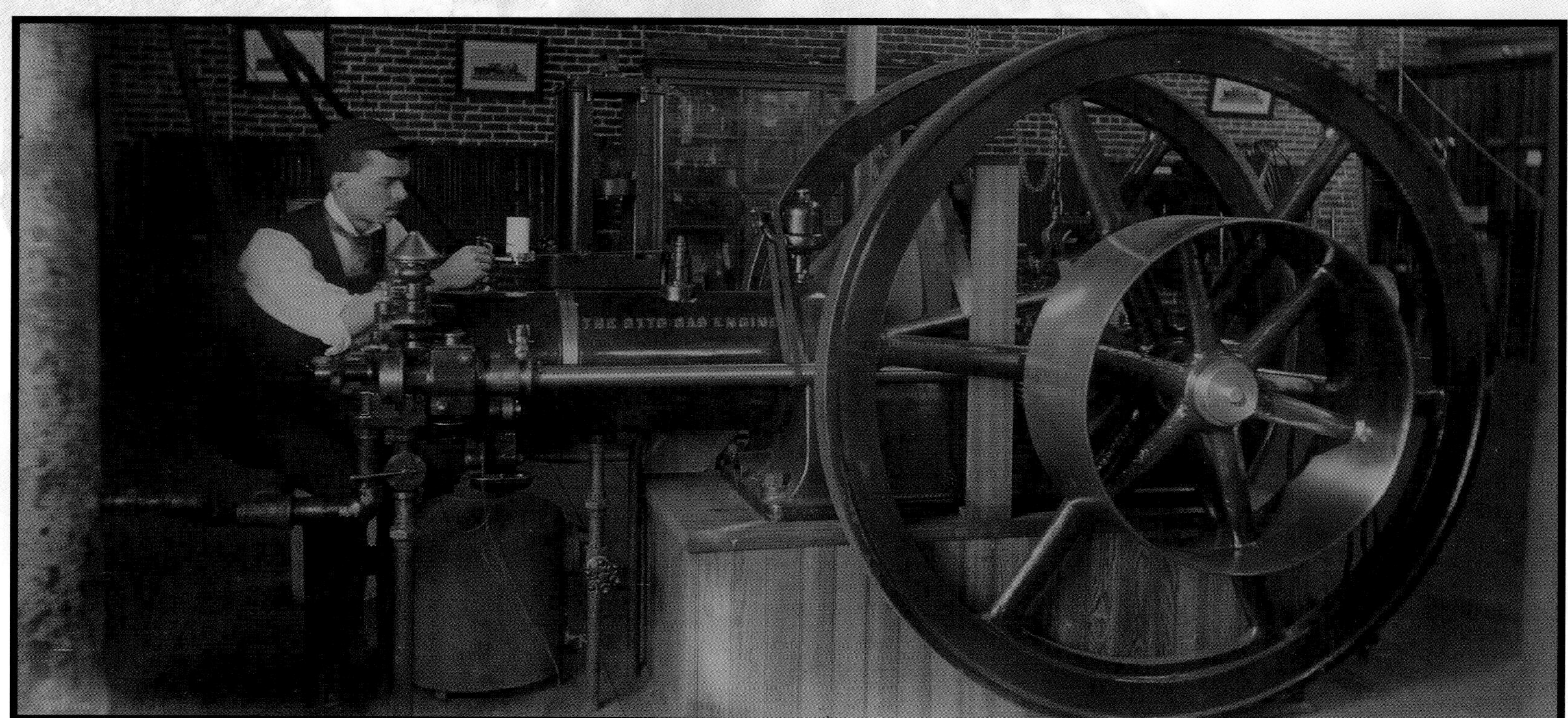

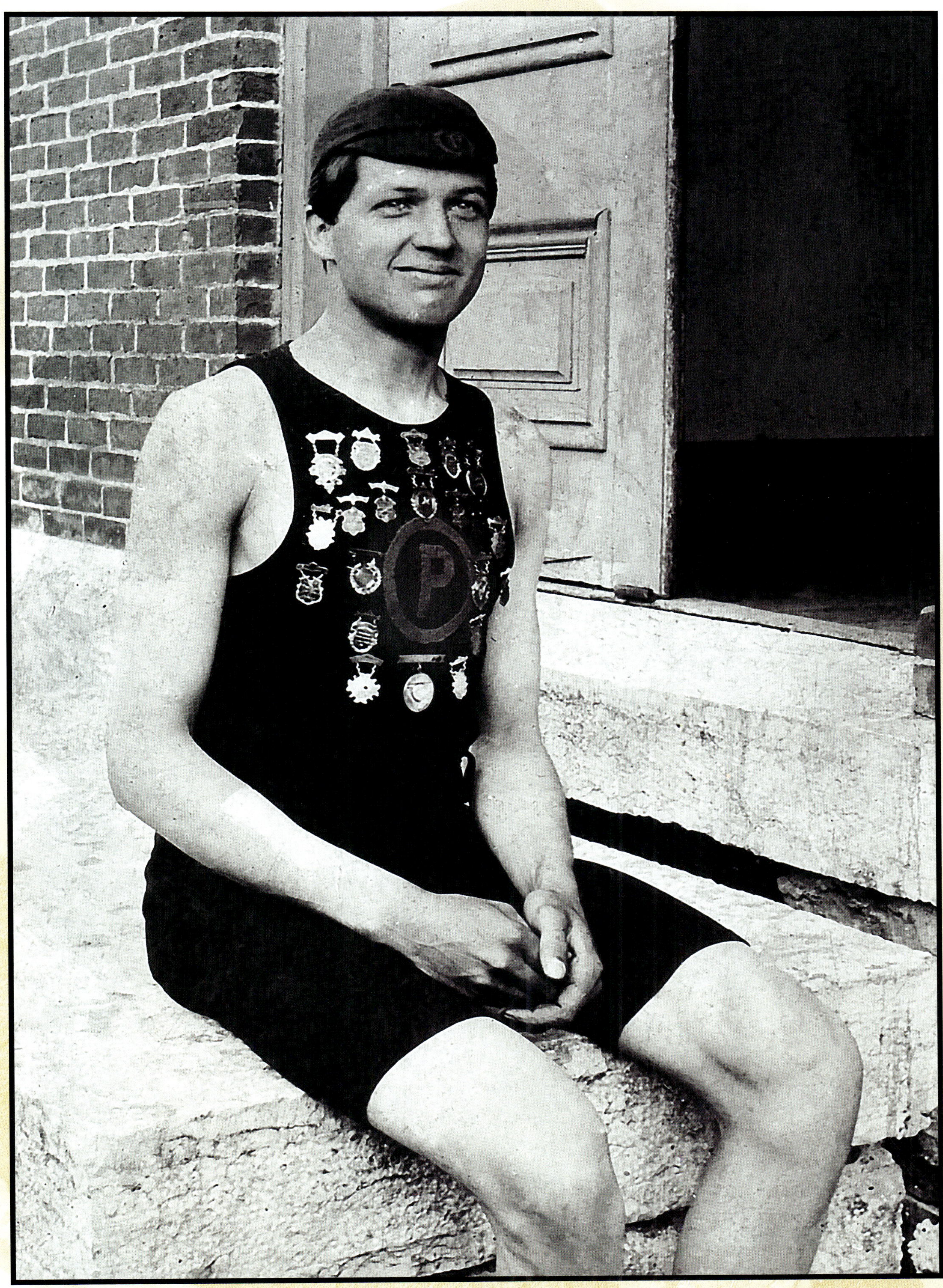

Raymond "Deac" Ewry was an eight-time Olympic gold medalist and the first Purdue graduate to participate in the Olympics. He completed the 1900, 1904, and 1908 Olympic Games. Ewry also held world records in the standing high jump and standing broad jump. *(J. C. Allen and Son Inc. photographs and negatives)*

Left: The Library in University Hall, October 21, 1899. *(Purdue University photographs)*

Below: Norris Hebbard Harding, class of 1894, and H. R. Wait, class of 1897, in their Purdue Hall dorm room, December 14, 1893. The students are violating both the no smoking and no firearms regulations. *(Purdue University photographs)*

Bottom: Panoramic view of campus, 1898. State Street is visible to the left and Grant Street appears in the lower right. *(Purdue University photographs)*

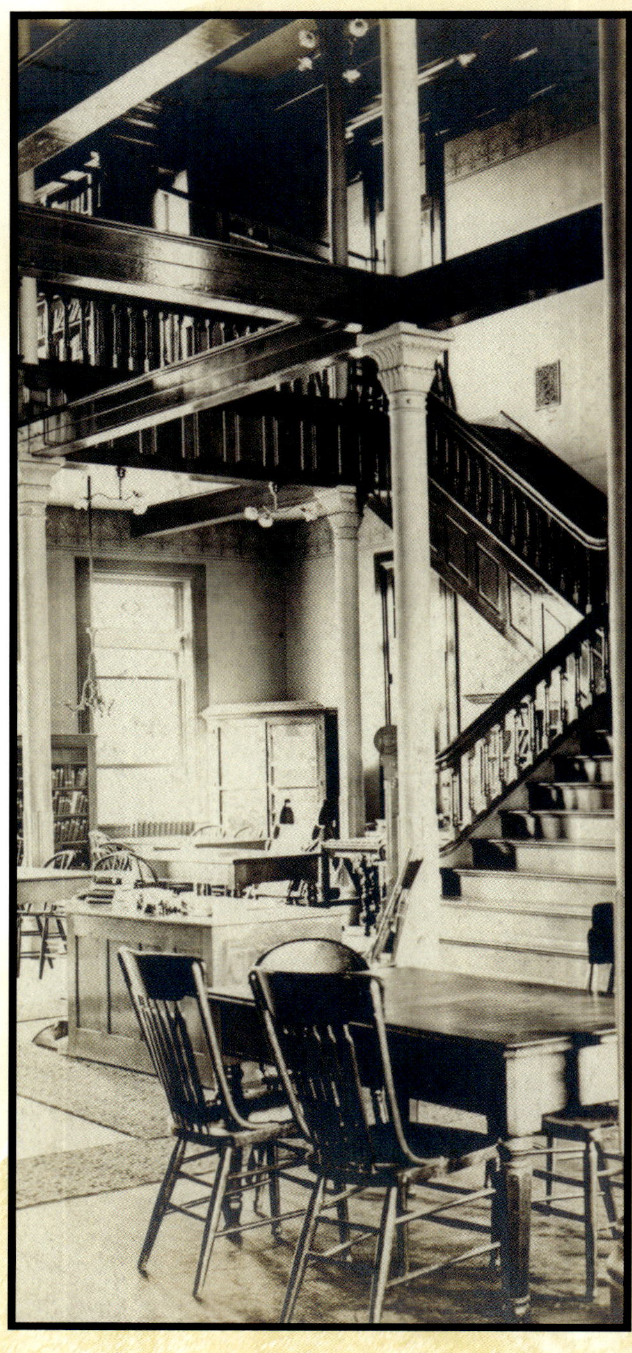

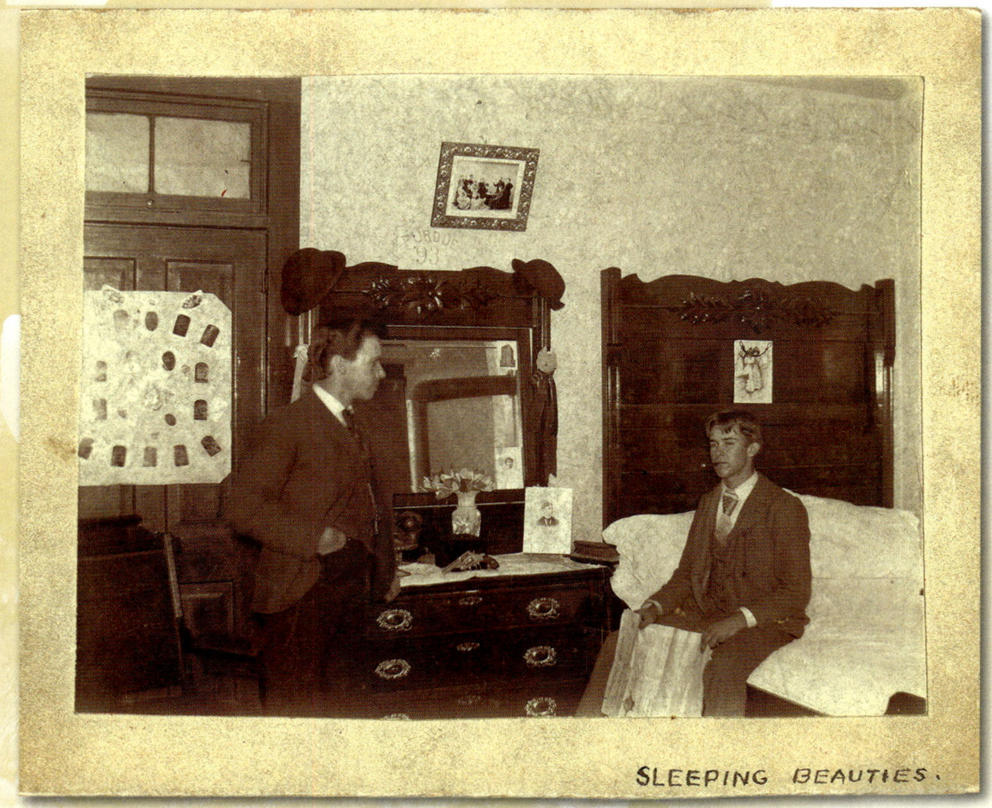

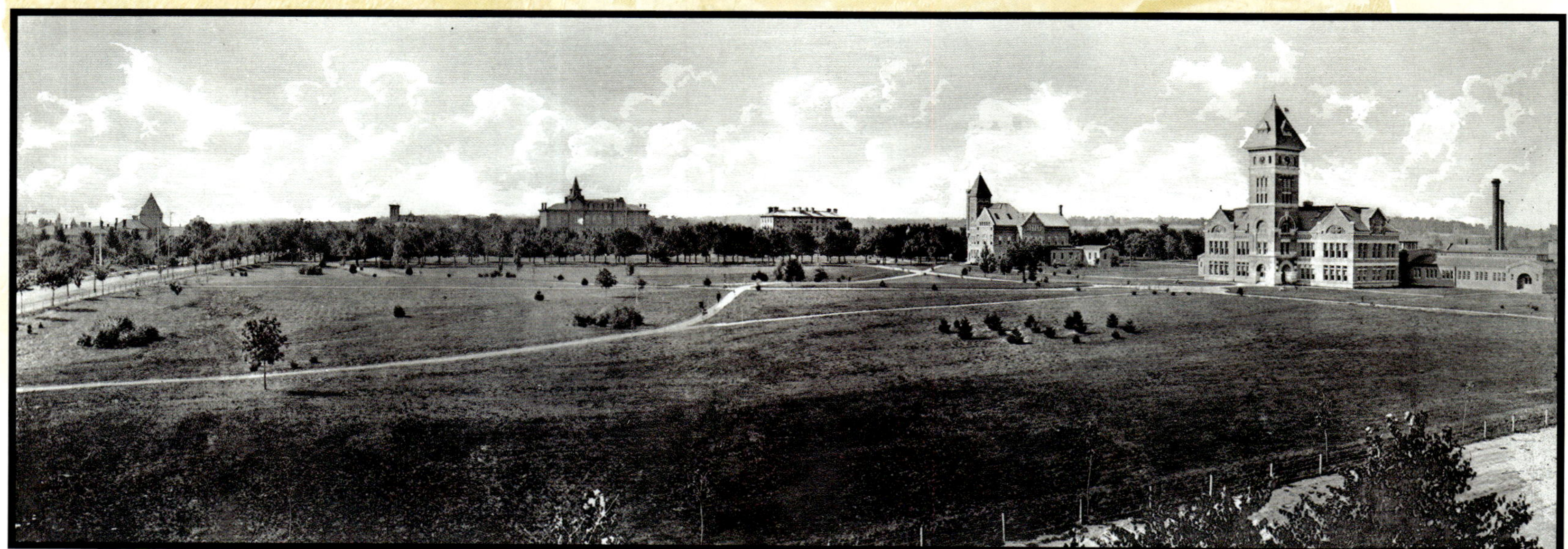

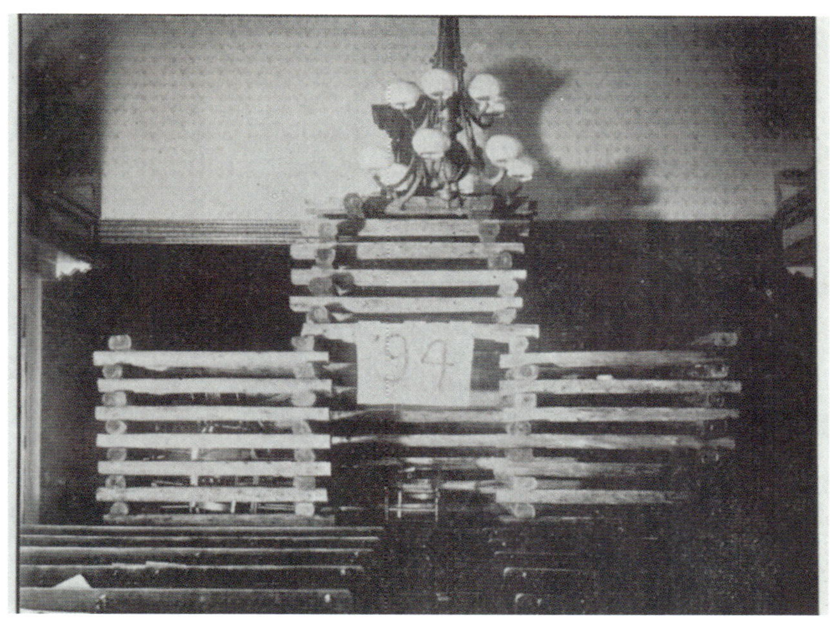

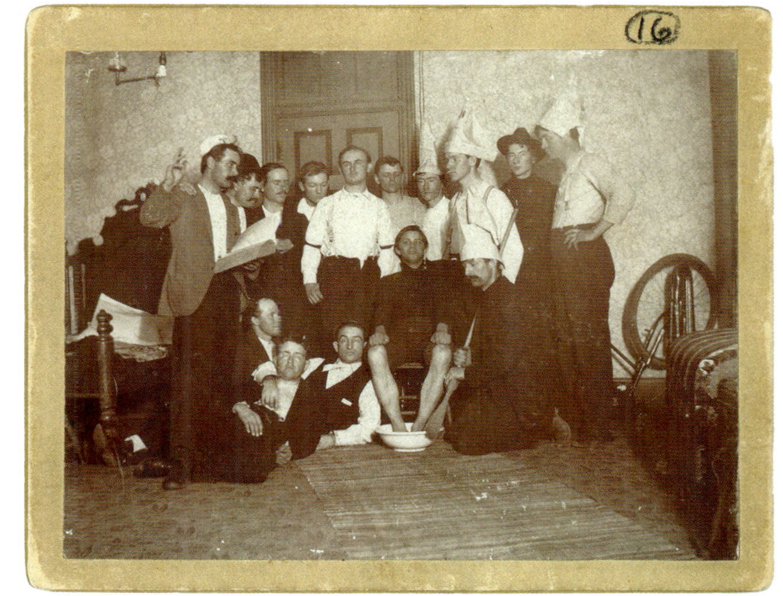

Students were required to attend morning chapel service every weekday before classes, and these meetings were a frequent target of the Dormitory Devils. On one occasion, they placed roosters in the organ, which caused great disruption when the organist began playing the next day. The Devils of the Class of 1894 planned a more elaborate prank involving railroad ties being used to lay the track for the Purdue Railroad. (The track was initially built to move the rebuilt Schenectady steam engine to the Testing Laboratory.) They piled the railroad ties in the front of the chapel, placing the pulpit and the Bible at the top. As chapel services were about to start the following morning, the faculty noticed the room unusually crowded with students. When President Smart arrived he was not at all pleased. Years later, 1905 alumna Bernice Nelson Grant retold the story shared with her:

> Dr. [Erasmus Test] went down stairs two steps at a time after a bible. The Pres. complimented the students upon the beauty of their work and spoke of the great future before them on a mechanical line, he then opened the singing book at random and said "We will sing 256." The pianist played and the student body sang: "Blest be the tie that binds."[6]

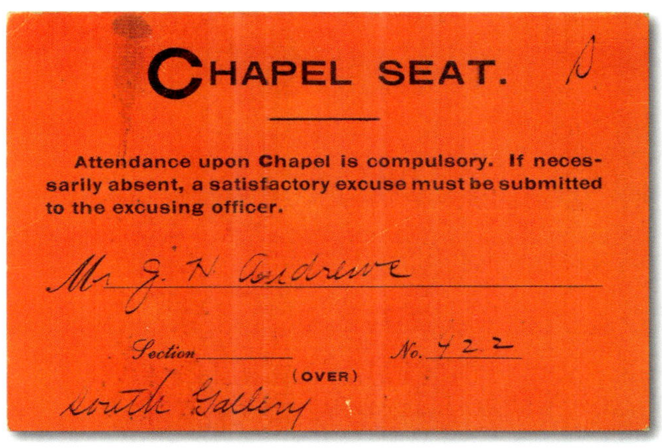

CHAPEL SEAT.

Attendance upon Chapel is compulsory. If necessarily absent, a satisfactory excuse must be submitted to the excusing officer.

Mr J. H. Andrews

Section ______ No. 722

(OVER)

South Gallery

Top left: Railroad ties stacked at the front of the chapel with the podium on top. *(Debris yearbook)*

Top right: The initiation of a new member of the Dormitory Devils, 1900. *(Purdue University photographs)*

Bottom: Assigned seat card for chapel services. *(Josiah H. Andrews scrapbook)*

The Tank Scrap

In a description of an early tank fight,

William T. Berkshire, class of 1902, recalled:

So we went out one night, possibly 15 or 20 of us. . . . We hadn't been out there very long when a great crowd of the Class of 1901 came out, and they overpowered all of the boys practically. They had twine with them. They tied hands behind backs of the fellows, and they tied their feet together. And they rolled them down in a little ravine that was back of the tank.

But another man by the name of Branigan, who was in my class, and I saw that we were so outnumbered that we weren't getting anywhere, so we hightailed it across the road into an apple orchard. We climbed up into some trees. And we waited, and we waited, and we waited. Finally, the '01 people had done what they intended to do, and they left. So, we climbed down out of the trees, and by yelling, we had no lights, we located our men and untied them. Inadvertently the '01 boys had not disturbed our paint or the rope tackle we were to use to scale the side of the tank. Then, we started to paint the tank. Just as the sun was up, we had the job finished. There was a football game that afternoon, and the '02 stood out plain on the tank.[7]

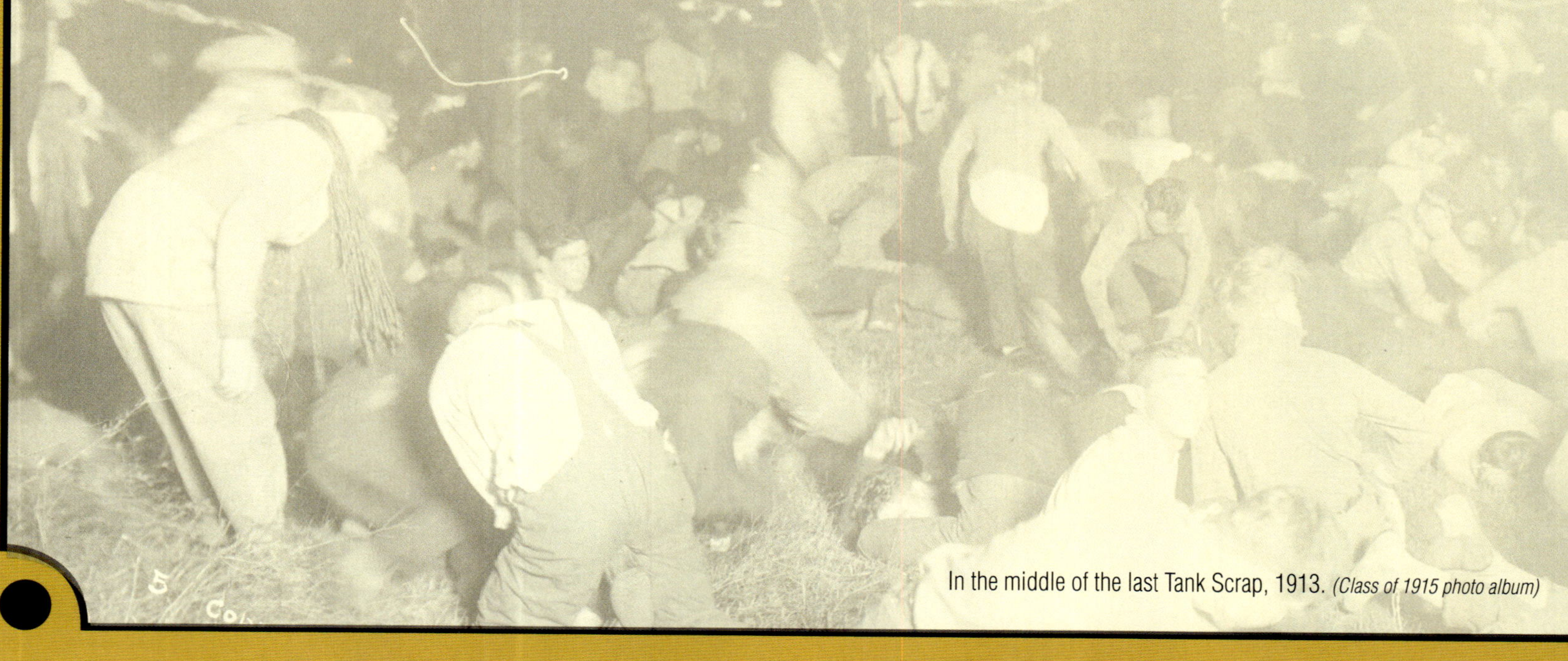

In the middle of the last Tank Scrap, 1913. *(Class of 1915 photo album)*

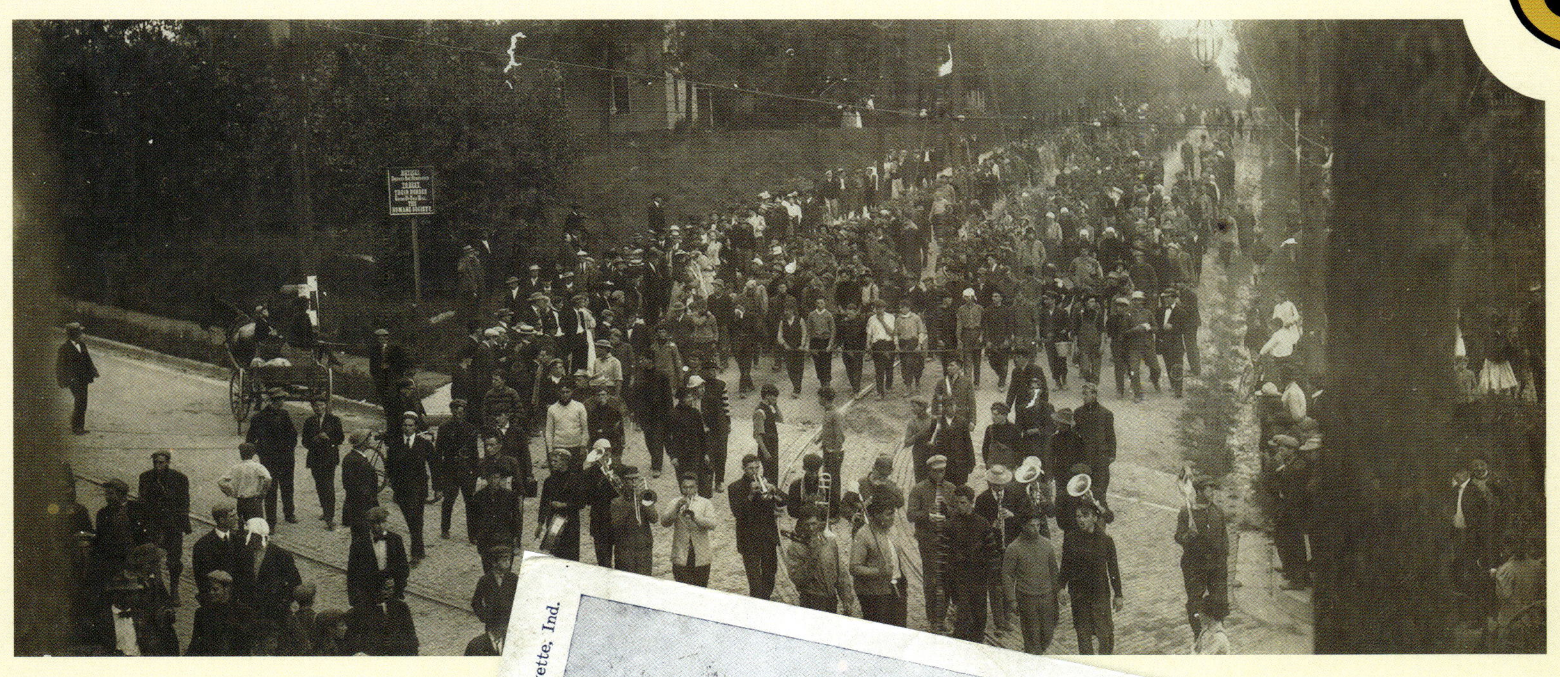

Above: The victorious Class of 1910 marches its opponents into town after a Tank Scrap. *(Purdue University photographs)*

Right: Postcard featuring the Purdue Tank Scrappers with the tank indicated in the background, 1907. *(Purdue University Postcard collection)*

Published by O. L. Foster, Commercial Photographer, LaFayette, Ind.

Purdue
"Tank Scrappers"

Show this to Leo and tell him he ought to have been here then.
Where the mark is is the tank
answer soon as possible
M. S.

In late 1894, a fifty-foot-high water tank was installed near the land that became Grand View Cemetery on North Salisbury Street in West Lafayette. The tank could be clearly seen from campus and quickly became a target of graffiti artists, including students, who painted their class graduation year on the tank. Soon, painting the tank became a subject of interclass fighting; these combative physical battles led to the establishment of an annual "scrap" between male freshmen and sophomores to determine which graduation class year would appear on the tank. In the formative years of the event, classes scrapped multiple times over the course of a few weeks, never accepting defeat. However, the impracticality of constant fighting soon became apparent and the scrap became a once-a-year event with a recognized routine.

In the weeks leading up to the annual Tank Scrap, juniors advised freshmen and seniors advised sophomores in strategy. Participating students formally requested the university president's permission to hold the event and raised money for expected medical expenses. The students then coordinated with local police for traffic and crowd control. At its height, up to ten thousand people would gather on a nearby hillside to watch the spectacle.

By 1907 the standard practice for the freshmen was to start assembling by the call **"Freshmen *Out!*"** They gathered behind the Civil Engineering Building early in the evening. Sophomores assembled an hour later at the Stuart Athletic Field. The freshmen filed through West Lafayette behind a marching band to the tank, where they took up positions downhill from their target. Around 2:00 a.m. the sophomores arrived and the battle was opened at the firing of a signal rocket. The sophomores then charged down the hill into the freshmen. Generally, both sides held men in reserve in case the battle turned against them. In some years, the brawl lasted a couple of hours and in others as little as twenty-five minutes. Once the upperclassmen declared the winning class, the victors were clear to emblazon the tank with their graduation year. However, the scene was far from over. The winning class also painted the losing side and marched the tied and chained defeated into downtown Lafayette, where the losers were required to perform their opponent's class chants and other embarrassing stunts.

As the event evolved, rules were established, expanded, and modified. By 1901 it was established that no fisticuffs or weapons of any sort were to be used. To prevent injury, padlocks and chains were introduced in 1902 to replace the ropes.

Finally, in 1905 official rules were published:

1. *None save Freshmen and Sophomores shall engage in the contest.*
2. *It shall occur in the night and end before daylight on the morning of the first football game on Stuart field.*
3. *No contestant shall use any weapons, nor be permitted to strike with his fist.*
4. *The class having the fight won on the morning above mentioned shall be declared the victors and their numerals remain on the tank at least through the football season.*
5. *In case the fight is declared a draw, the numerals actually on the tank shall declare the victors.*[8]

The Tank Scrap came to a sudden and grim end in the fall of 1913. On the night of the Scrap, Purdue's freshmen and sophomores marched to the tank as in years past and prepared to brawl. Amid the scuffle, student Francis Obenchain was fatally injured. It was initially reported by the Tippecanoe County medical examiner that he had suffered a heart attack in the excitement, but after his body was sent home to Whitley County it was found that his neck had been broken. Students gathered the day after the Scrap and unanimously voted to cease the dangerous tradition.

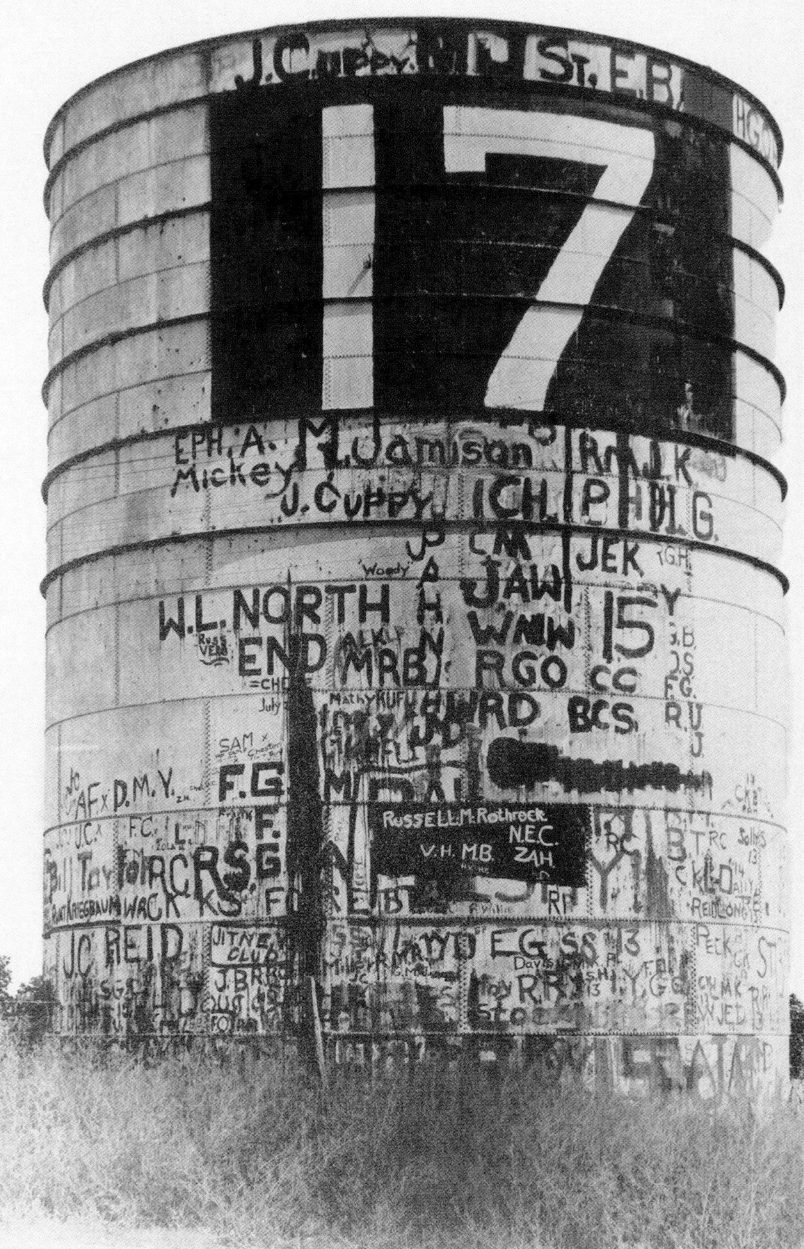

The Tank after the last Scrap, 1913.
(Purdue University photographs)

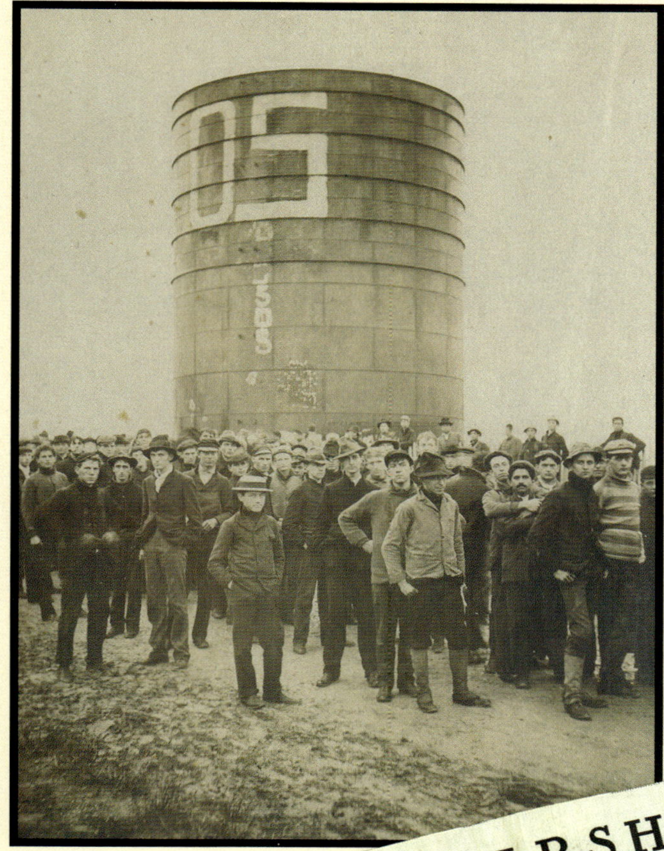

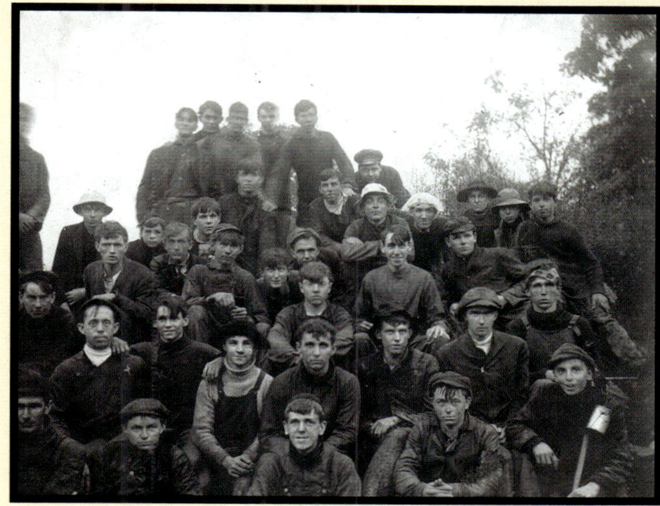

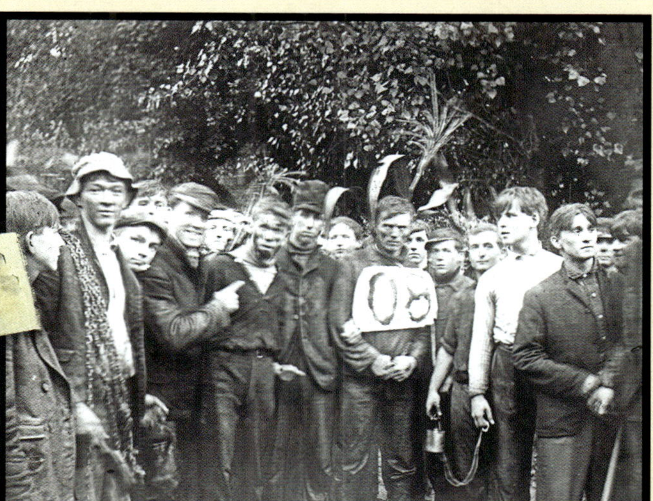

Top left: After the Tank Scrap, circa 1901–1902.
(Purdue University photographs)

Above left: Tank Scrap marshal ribbon, circa 1900.
(Otis E. Griner papers)

Top right: A group of victorious students after the Tank Scrap.
(Henry C. Balcom collection)

Above right: The "chain gang" comprising members of the (losing) Class of 1908 after the Scrap.
(Henry C. Balcom collection)

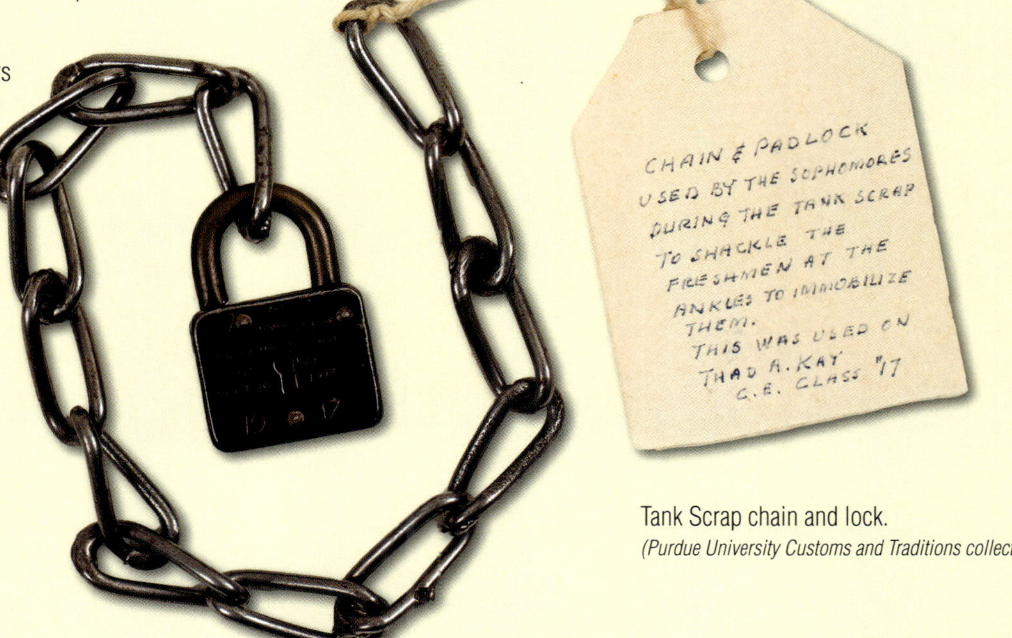

Tank Scrap chain and lock.
(Purdue University Customs and Traditions collection)

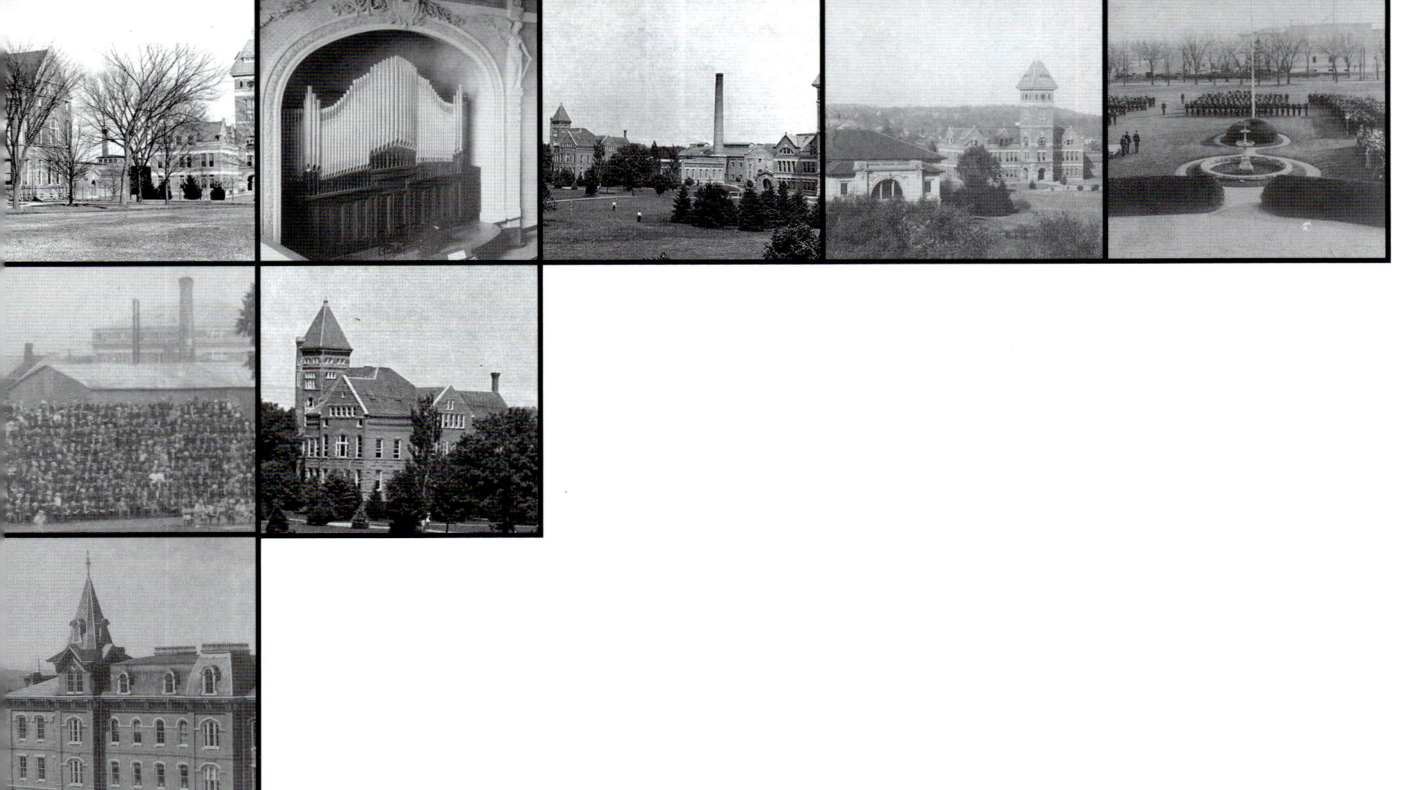

Campus map by J. B. Truman, circa 1902. *(Campus Maps collection)*

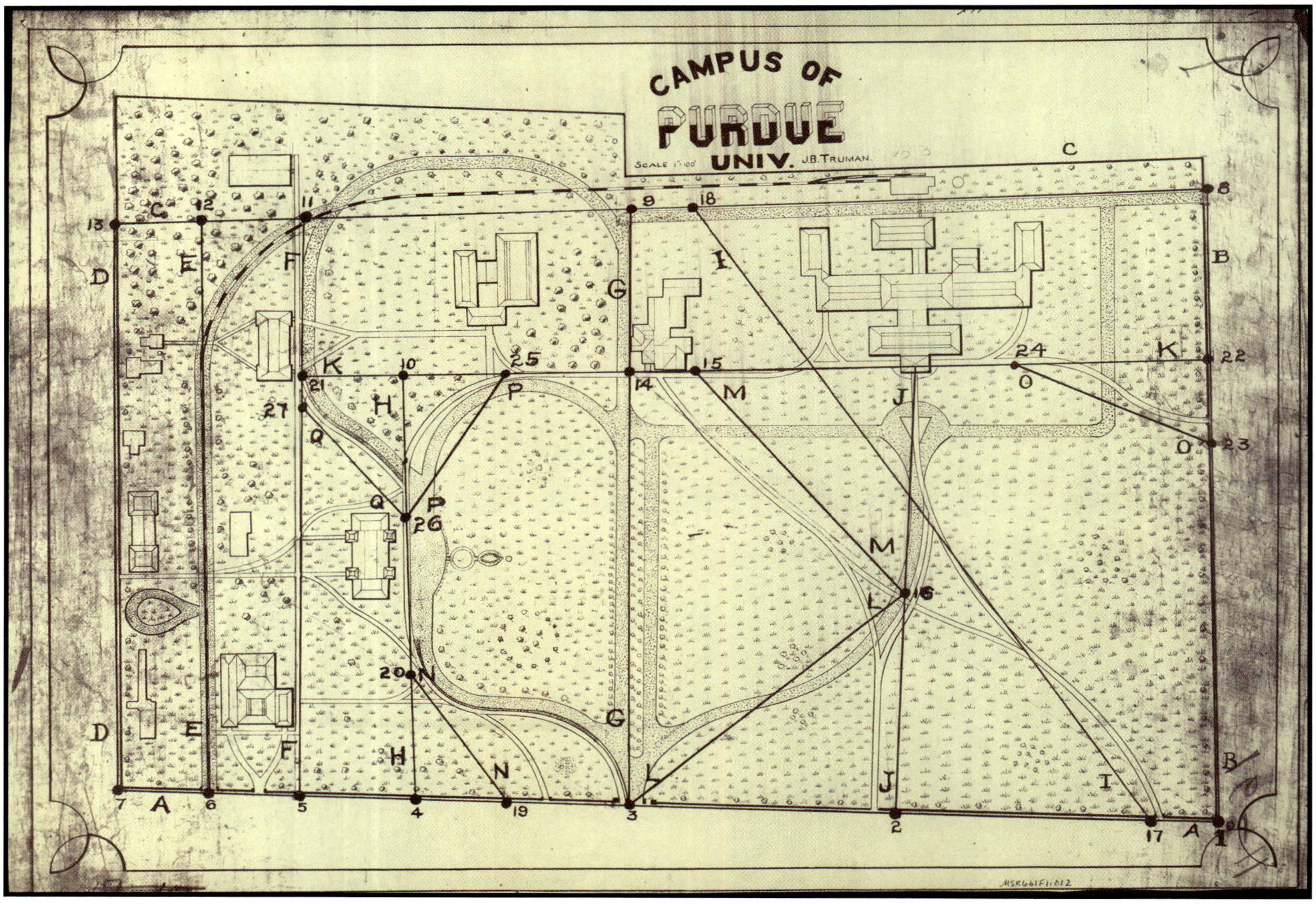

{ *Enrollment in 1900: 1,043 students*[1] }

[The 1900s]

PURDUE AT 40

"We had a full morning from about eight o'clock, except we had to go to chapel in what is now the University Hall. In our freshman and sophomore years, we had to work in the shops—either the carpenter shop, the machine shop, the foundry, or the forge. We learned how to do things with our hands."

—*William T. Berkshire, class of 1902*[2]

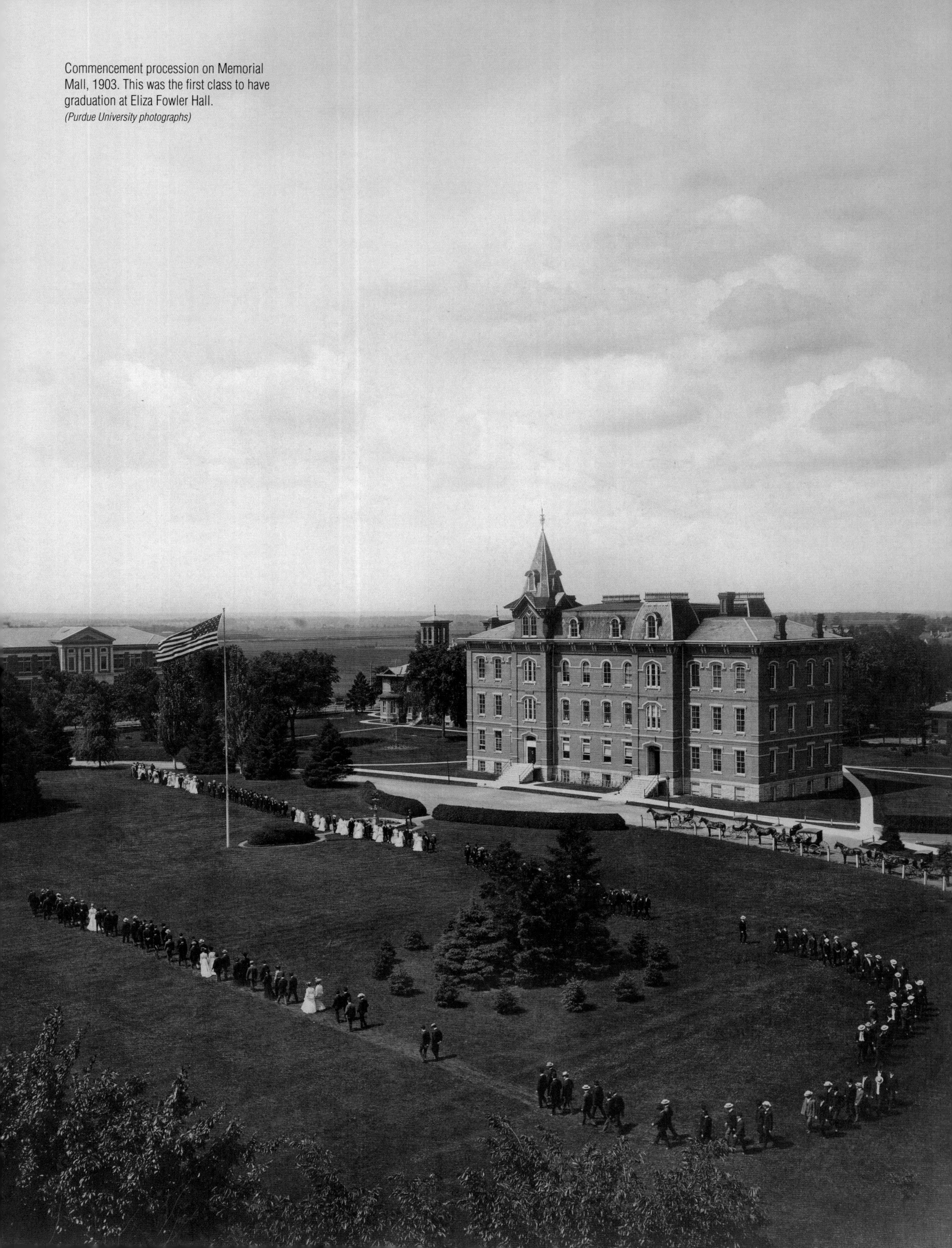

Commencement procession on Memorial Mall, 1903. This was the first class to have graduation at Eliza Fowler Hall.
(Purdue University photographs)

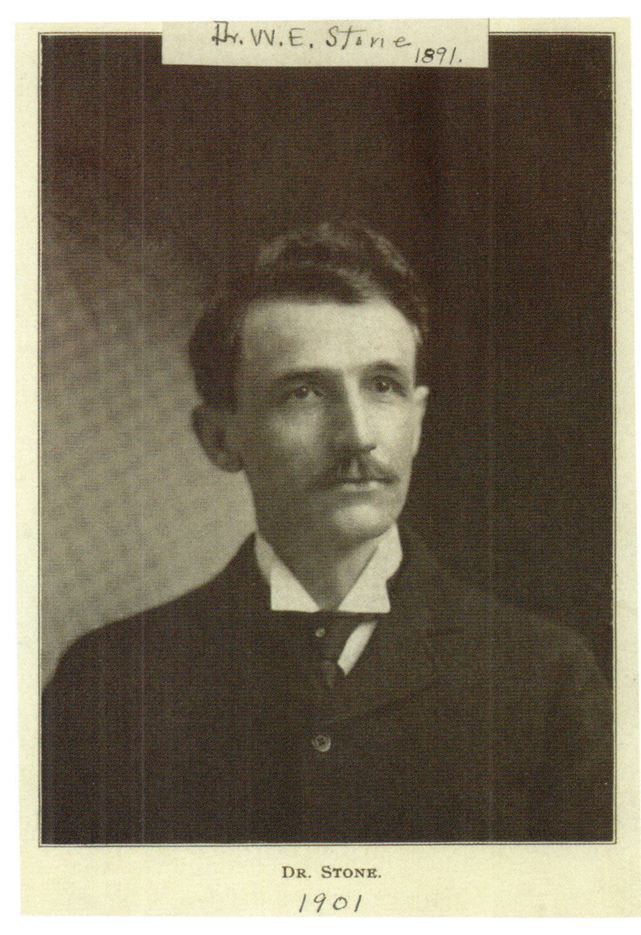

Winthrop Stone, 1901.
(Winthrop E. Stone papers)

During the first decade of the twentieth century, many fledgling campus activities cemented themselves as Purdue traditions. As the university continued to grow, a burgeoning alumni base provided the word-of-mouth and written stories to encourage students to carry the traditions from one generation to the next.

President Smart faced serious health issues at the turn of the century, and much of the management of the university fell to Winthrop Stone, professor of chemistry, who took on the role of vice president. When Smart died on February 21, 1900, Stone became the first Purdue president hired from within the institution and the first who had not specialized in education. Stone, only thirty-eight years old at the time, was a popular choice among the students.

Lauson Stone, class of 1904, was the younger brother of President Winthrop Stone.

The Train Wreck

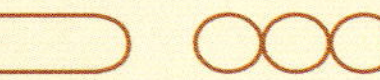

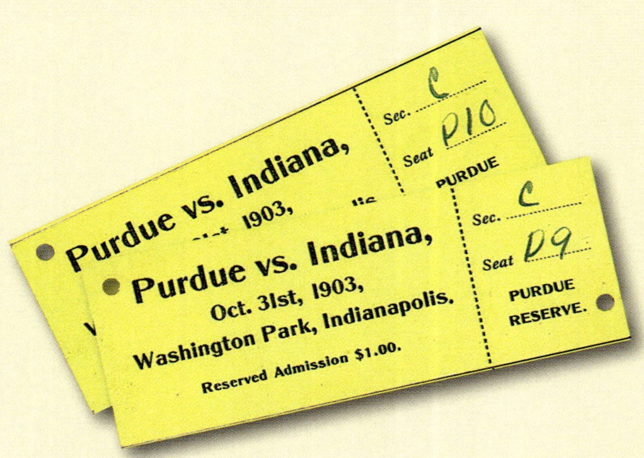

On the morning of October 31, 1903, 950 people joined the Purdue football team on a train bound for Indianapolis and a game against Indiana University. President Winthrop Stone and his family, along with students, faculty, staff, and townspeople, were among those on the Purdue Special. As the fourteen-car train rounded a curve in northwest Indianapolis, it plunged into a coal train backing up on the same tracks. The front car, carrying the football team, was destroyed, landing on top of a coal car. The second car, carrying the band, derailed and slid down a fifteen-foot embankment. The third car was seriously damaged when it struck the other cars. Sixteen people were killed immediately and another died later from his injuries. Hundreds more were injured, some seriously.

Homer Thomas was thrown from the wreck and was the only player to avoid injury. Fred Kassebaum was thrown from the car and landed, badly injured, in one of the coal cars. Irwin Osborne, team captain, and Ferdinand M. Hawthorne both recalled being thrown through glass windows and flying through the air for what "seemed like minutes." Conrad W. Zimmerman remembered dodging endless splinters and other debris, only to discover he had landed on the tracks.[3] William Moore was found—his right leg broken and severe cuts to his head—being bandaged by two elegantly dressed young women in blood-covered dresses.[4] Similar scenes occurred all day near the wreckage.

The crash was heard from blocks away. Dazed passengers, nearby workmen, and neighbors rushed to the demolished cars. Blanche Miller, a Purdue librarian and favorite of the student body, was one of those who immediately began treating the injured and giving comfort.[5] President Stone, who had been traveling in the fifth car, kept handwritten notes tracking the dead and injured. Dozens were taken to area hospitals. At Purdue, Professor William Goss and others answered telegrams from worried parents as President Stone relayed information back to campus.

Top: Tickets to the Purdue vs. Indiana football game on October 31, 1903. *(1903 Train Wreck materials)*

Below: Aftermath of the train wreck. *(Purdue University photographs)*

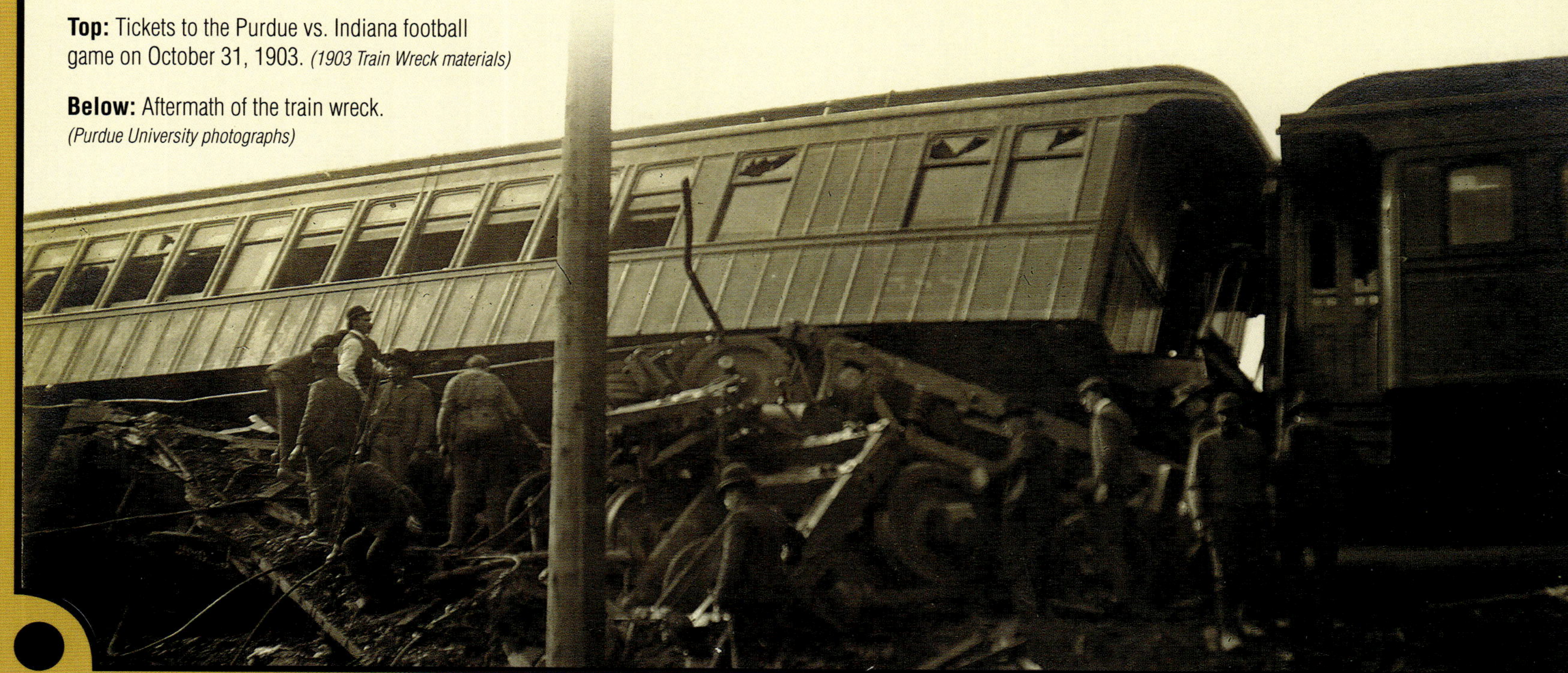

Faculty members crossed the country to attend many funerals in the subsequent days. On November 11, 1903, a memorial service was held on campus to honor the sixteen dead. They were Lafayette businessman Newton Howard, assistant coach Edward Coll Robertson ('01), team trainer Patrick McClair, and thirteen students: Thomas Albert Bailey ('07), Joseph Collins Coates ('06), Gabriel S. Drollinger ('05), Charles Elwood Furr ('05), Charles G. Grube ('05), Jay Quincy Hamilton ('06), Walter Daniel Hamilton ('06), Roswell Johnston Powell ('05), Wilbert Price ('04), Walter Lucas Roush ('04), George Leslie Shaw ('07), Samuel Plummer Squibb ('07), and Samuel Campbell Truitt ('07). On November 30, 1903, Harry O. Wright ('07) succumbed to his injuries, becoming the seventeenth and final victim of the tragedy.

Among the survivors, some faced slow and painful recoveries, some sustained injuries that plagued them for life, and some never returned to complete their studies. Others returned to Purdue to mourn their friends and try to resume their lives.

In the weeks following the funerals, the community called for a memorial gymnasium to honor the victims. In late November, President Stone published a formal call for contributions.[6] Donations arrived from hundreds of Purdue alumni, faculty, staff, and students and the surrounding community. The Memorial Gymnasium was dedicated during Memorial Day weekend on May 29, 1909, with state-of-the-art facilities, a swimming pool, and reportedly some of the first glass backboards of any university basketball facility. (The structure was renamed Felix Haas Hall in 2006.) In memory of those lost, seventeen steps lead up to the main entrance.

Below: List of the dead maintained by President Stone. The use of various pens and pencils in the list illustrates the fluid nature of the tragedy. *(Winthrop E. Stone papers)*

Bottom left: Cover of the memorial edition of the *Purdue Exponent* after the train wreck, November 11, 1903. *(Purdue Exponent)*

Bottom right: The 1903 Purdue University football team. *(Purdue University photographs)*

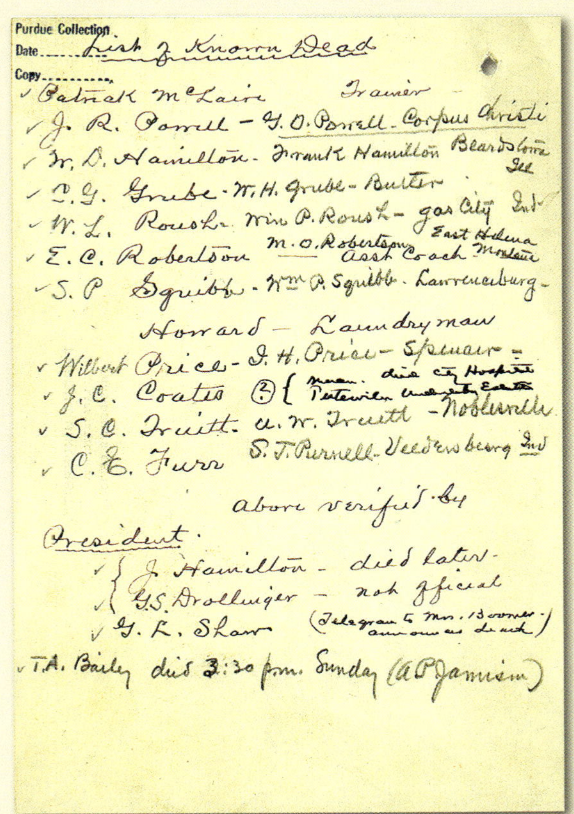

Purdue Collection
Date List of Known Dead
Copy
✓ Patrick McLaire   Trainer
✓ J. R. Powell – G. O. Powell – Corpus Christi
✓ W. D. Hamilton – Frank Hamilton Beardstown Ill.
✓ C. G. Grube – W. H. Grube – Butler
✓ W. L. Roush – Wm P. Roush – Gas City Ind
✓ E. C. Robertson   M. O. Robertson – Asst Coach – East Helena Montana
✓ S. P. Squibb – Wm P. Squibb – Lawrenceburg –
Howard – Laundryman
✓ Wilbert Price – J. H. Price – Spencer –
✓ J. C. Coates (?) { died city Hospital
✓ S. C. Truitt – A. W. Truitt – Noblesville
✓ C. E. Furr   S. T. Purnell – Veedersburg Ind
above verified by
President.
✓ { J. Hamilton – died later –
✓ { G. S. Drollinger – not official
✓ G. L. Shaw (Telegram to Mrs. Boomer – announces death)
✓ T. A. Bailey died 3:30 p.m. Sunday (A. P. Jamison)

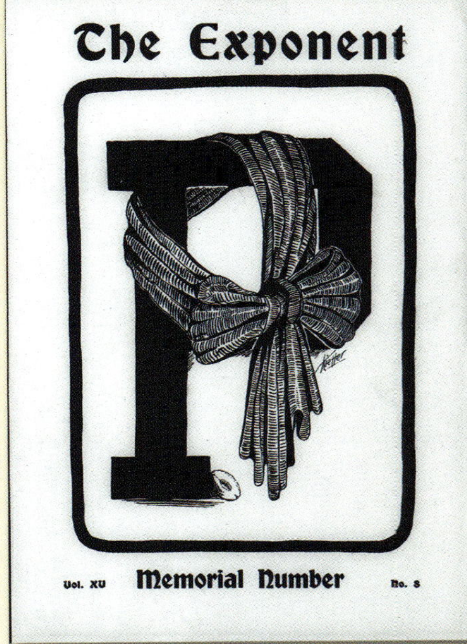

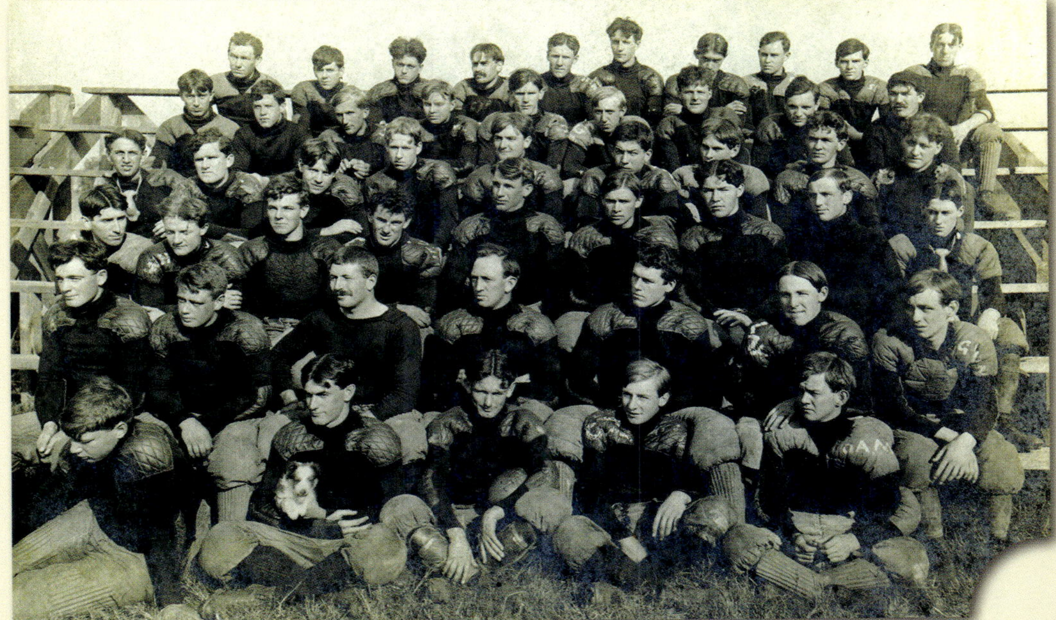

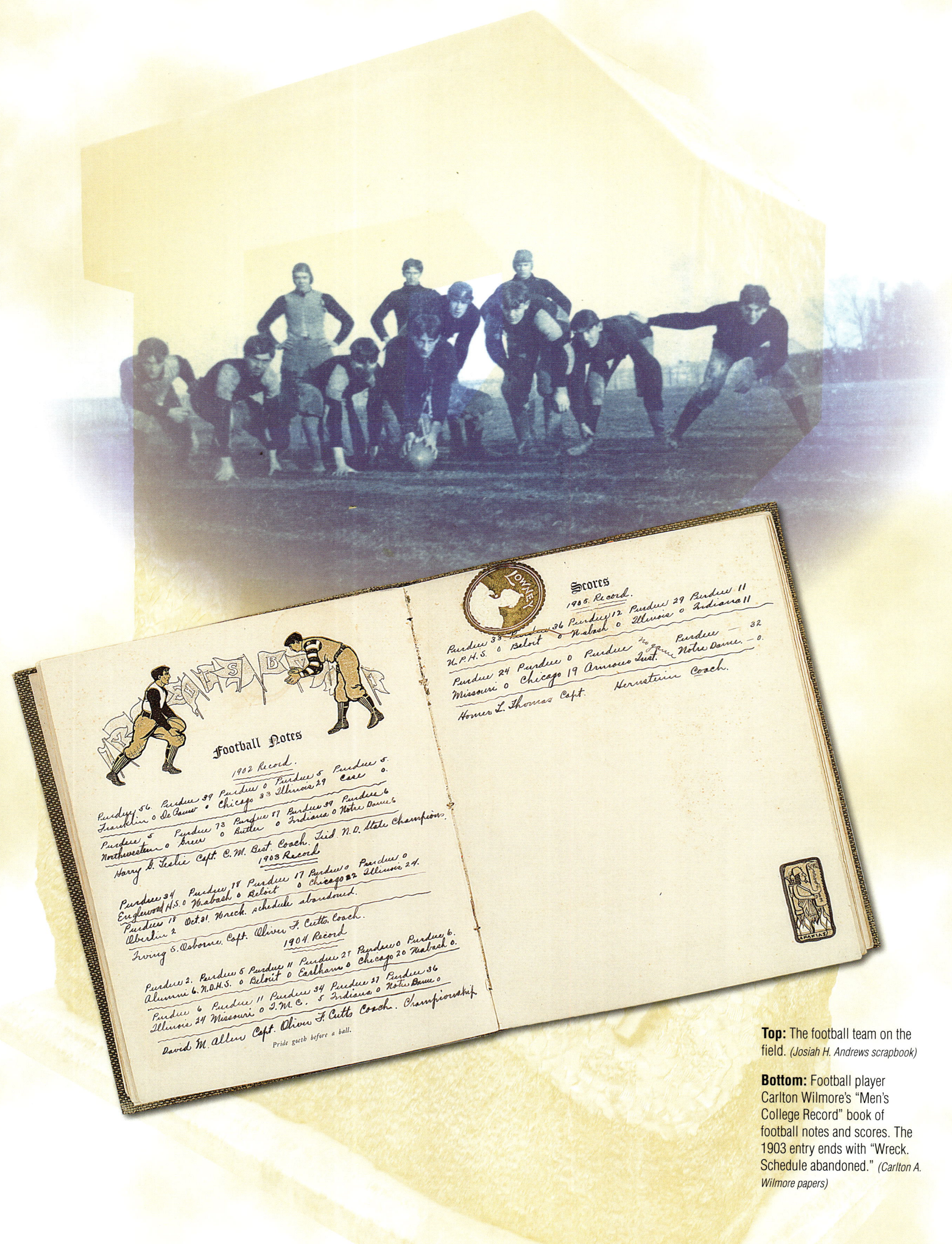

Top: The football team on the field. *(Josiah H. Andrews scrapbook)*

Bottom: Football player Carlton Wilmore's "Men's College Record" book of football notes and scores. The 1903 entry ends with "Wreck. Schedule abandoned." *(Carlton A. Wilmore papers)*

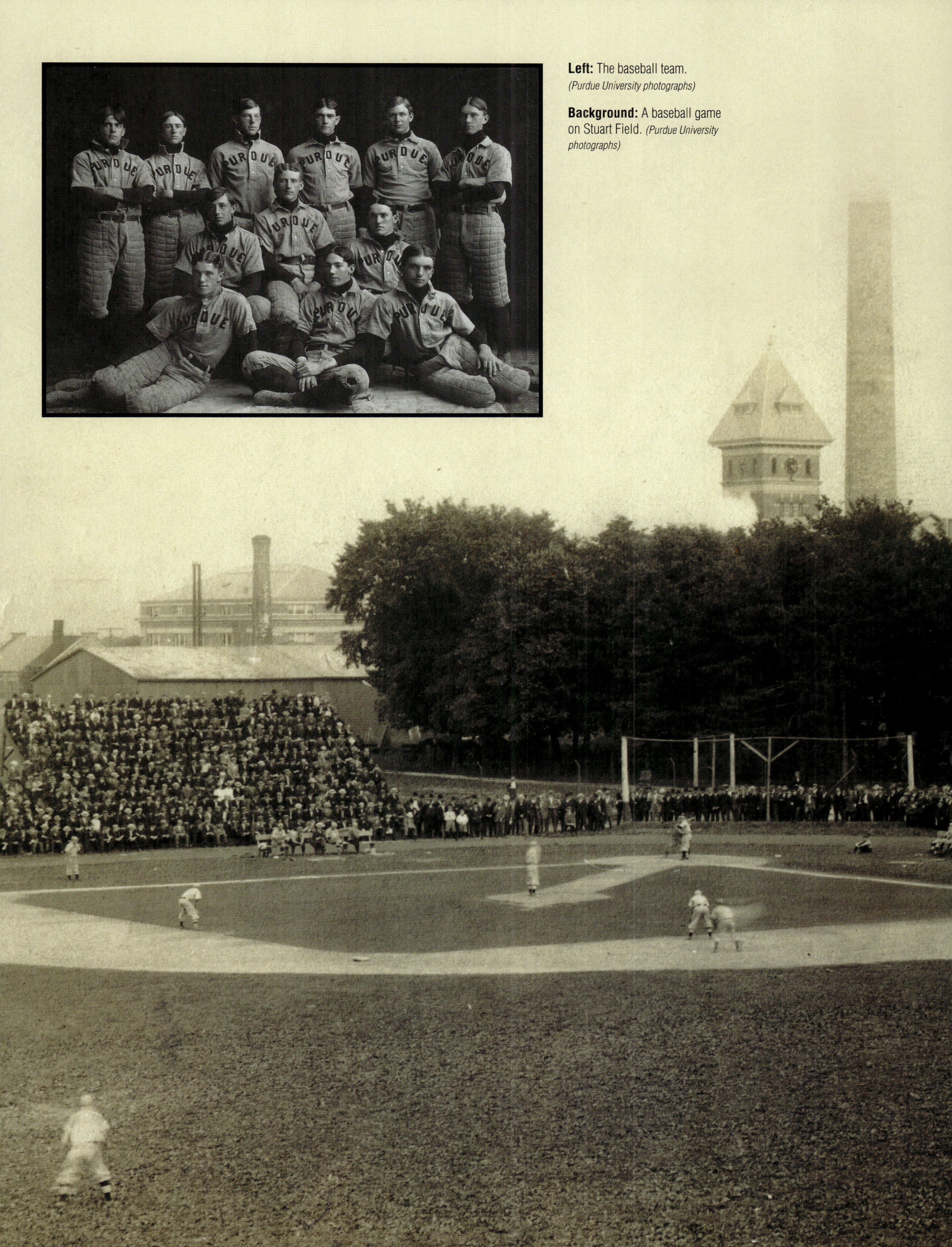

Left: The baseball team. *(Purdue University photographs)*

Background: A baseball game on Stuart Field. *(Purdue University photographs)*

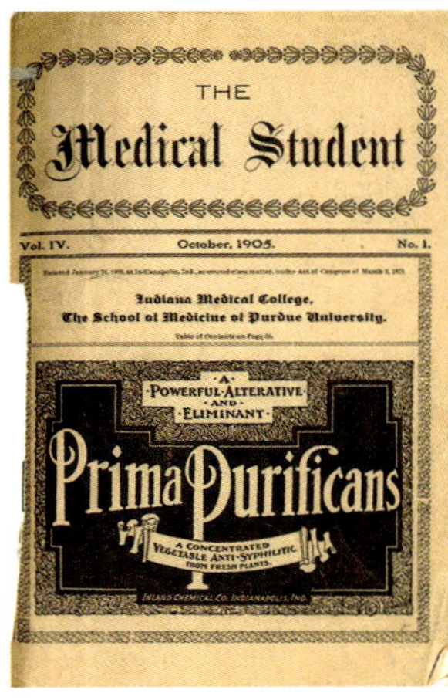
THE

Medical Student

Vol. IV. October, 1905. No. 1.

Indiana Medical College,
The School of Medicine of Purdue University.

A Powerful Alterative and Eliminant

Prima Purificans

In 1905, Purdue opened the School of Medicine in Indianapolis, a consolidation of three existing medical schools in the state. Immediately, Indiana University opposed the new program and created its own school. Contrasting bills were presented in the state legislature, but ultimately Purdue conceded, and Indiana University took control of the medical school in 1909.

A lesser-known student tradition was the Night Shirt Parade, rumored to have taken place since the earliest days of Purdue athletics. Generally, when a Purdue team returned from a victory, the male students would assemble on campus dressed in their nightshirts, parade to downtown Lafayette, and disrupt the town with songs and cheers as they greeted the victorious team at the train station. On May 17, 1904, celebrating a baseball victory, the students first brought a bell along for the celebration.[7]

Following a football victory against Indiana University on November 12, 1904, the Night Shirts raided the Locomotive Museum in the shops on campus and took a large bell. They carried this bell on a wagon and repeatedly hit the bell with a hammer during the parade toward the train station. This bell was left behind at the Tippecanoe County Courthouse after the revelry and had to be retrieved by the university. Afterward, the bell and its abandonment became part of the Night Shirt routine. President Stone tired of using university resources to resecure the bell and ordered it to be hidden from the students. Consequently, the bell was buried twenty-five feet deep in a gravel pit on campus, but later, after a three-week search, students removed the bell from its grave.[8]

After the bell's recovery, a committee formed to properly manage the bell and its use. Bernard R. McBride, William D. Dudding, and John S. Gettrust from the Class of 1907 and Charles W. Leber and Henry E. Ballard from the Class of 1908 formed the plan to build a carriage for the bell. That carriage, built by the Peter Anderson Carriage Works and Purdue instructor John Francis Keller, carried the bell through much of Purdue's history. The bell was known as the Purdue Bell until the 1920s, when it was re-ordained as the Victory Bell.

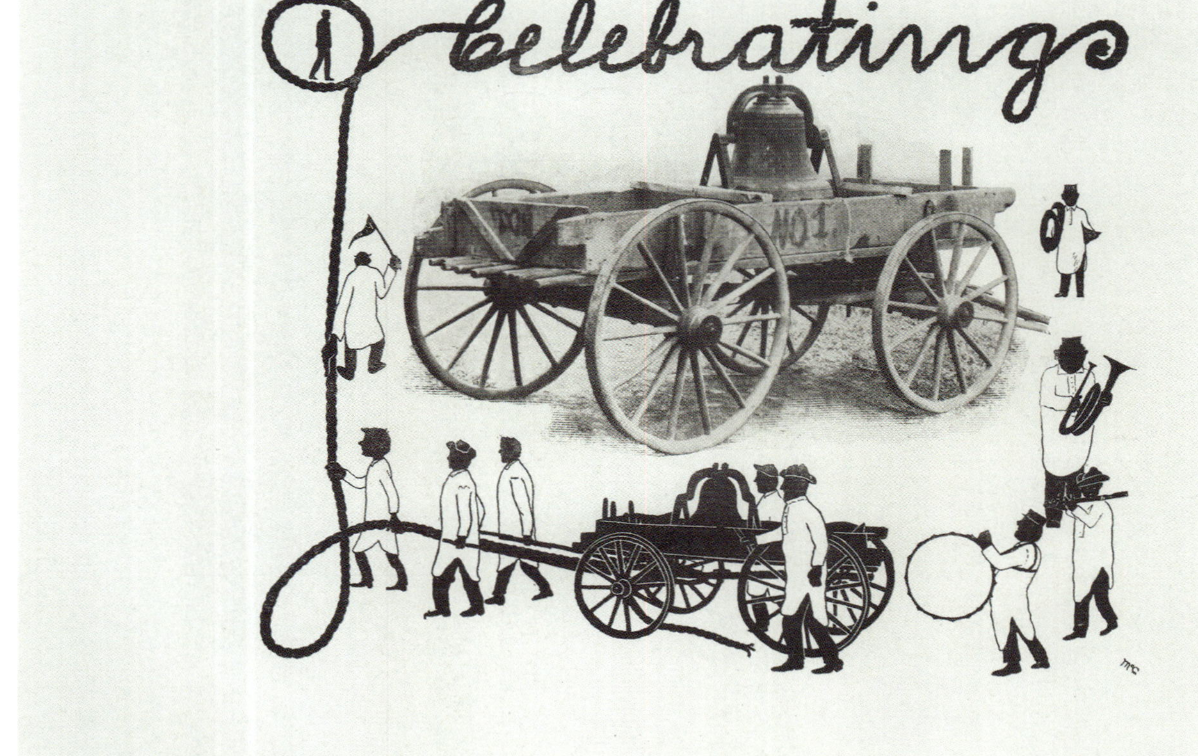

Top: October 1905 edition of "The Medical Student," a monthly publication of the Purdue University School of Medicine in Indianapolis. *(Purdue University School of Medicine collection)*

Right: An illustration of the Night Shirt Parade, complete with Victory Bell, from the 1905 *Debris* yearbook. *(*Debris *yearbook)*

The Cosmopolitan Club

Purdue's branch of the Cosmopolitan Club, the university's first international student organization, was founded in the fall semester of 1907. Its purpose was to bring international and domestic students together, and the group motto was "Above All Nations is Humanity." In its first year, the club counted forty-nine members from ten different countries. Interestingly, the 1908 *Debris* yearbook lists eleven countries including Puerto Rico, though it had been a part of the United States since 1898. The two Puerto Rican students, F. S. Virella and Jose Mateo Garcia y Abreu, are likely the first Latino Purdue students.[9]

Club membership continued to grow in the ensuing years, yet the onset of World War I decreased its numbers. The club reformed again following end of the war until World War II. Again, the outbreak of war caused a decline in membership; this time, the club did not continue.[10] In 1945, students formed the International Association of Purdue, which took over many of the purposes of the Cosmopolitan Club. Like its predecessor, the IAP brought international students together and sought to address important socio-political questions of the day via guest speakers and round tables.[11]

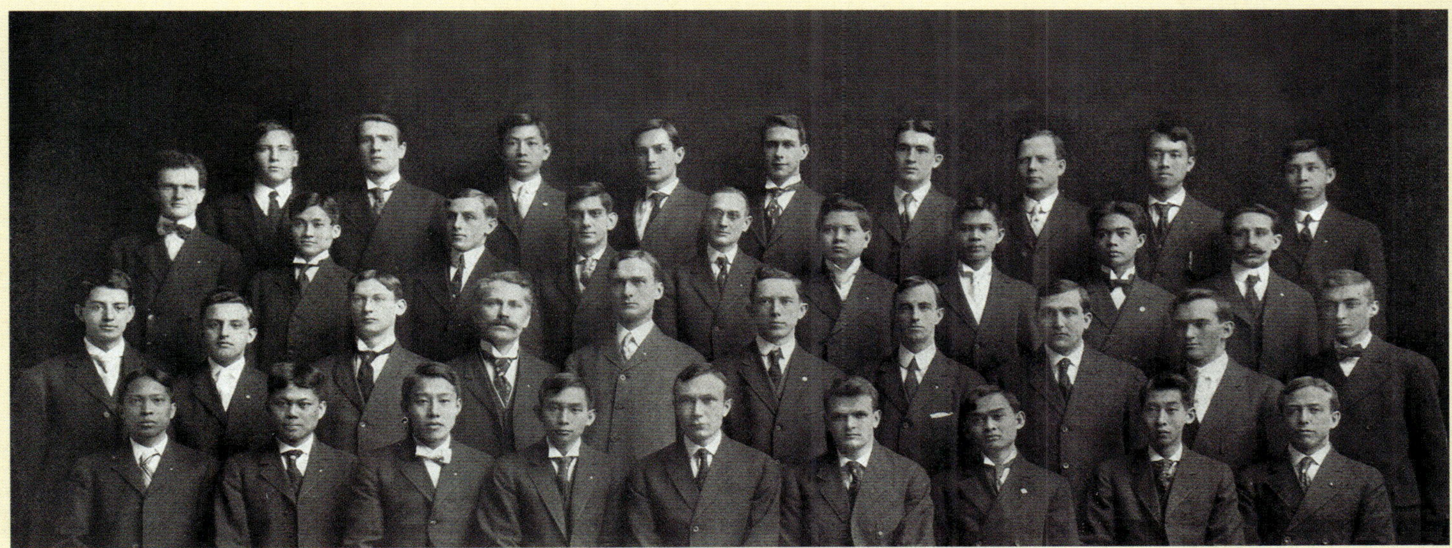

The first Cosmopolitan Club, 1908.
(Debris *yearbook*)

Clothing Traditions

Throughout much of the twentieth century, Purdue students wore distinct clothing and accessories that identified their class years, extracurricular activities, and clubs. The clothing was often emblazoned with personal touches.

In the fall of 1904, seniors Edward Wyllys Hyde Jr. and Daniel Bernard O'Brien were looking in the window of the Taylor Steffen Company tailoring shop at 306 Main Street in Lafayette and saw a bolt of yellow corduroy fabric that they thought would make good trousers.[12] They shared the idea with their classmates and a tradition was born. The cords immediately became the fashion statement for the senior class. The 1905 senior class formally adopted them, and the cords became, by custom, a garment specifically reserved for seniors alone. Men wore their cords as trousers and women wore corduroy skirts. By the 1940s, seniors personalized their cords with designs including their majors, clubs, cartoons, and jokes, with designs becoming more elaborate each year. As time went on, seniors added derby hats, coats, and canes to their upperclassmen uniforms. By the late 1960s, the senior traditions faded away. Though many students since that time have worn cords around campus, never again has it been a class-wide tradition.

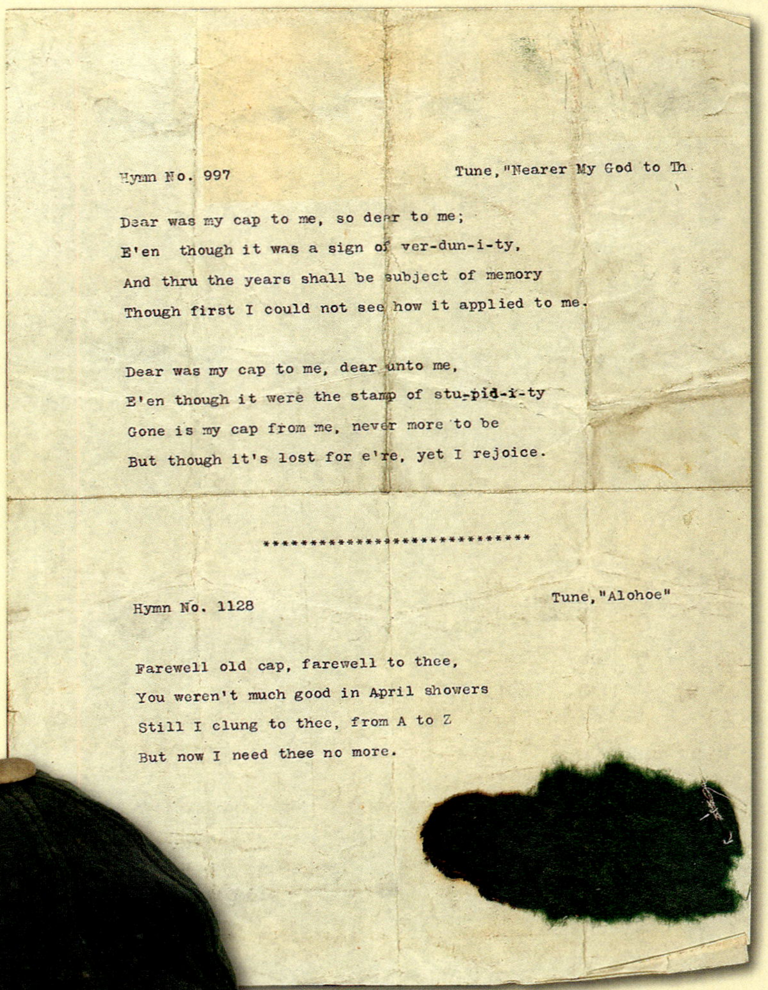

Beginning in 1904, the men of the junior class developed their own clothing-based tradition by adopting junior hats. The style of hat changed from year to year, chosen by the members of the class based on the class colors. Junior hats continued until the early 1930s.

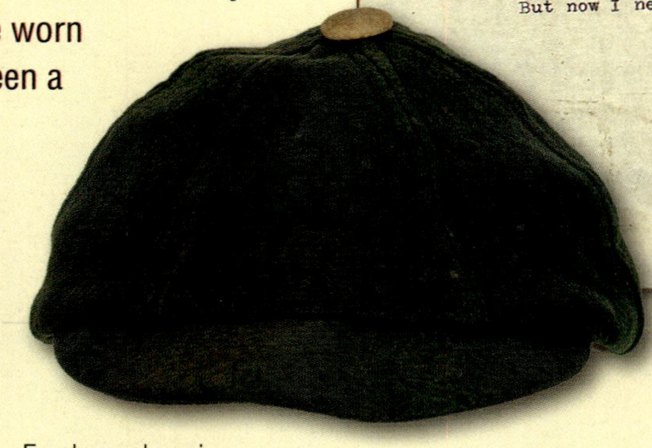

Hymn No. 997 Tune, "Nearer My God to Th

Dear was my cap to me, so dear to me;
E'en though it was a sign of ver-dun-i-ty,
And thru the years shall be subject of memory
Though first I could not see how it applied to me.

Dear was my cap to me, dear unto me,
E'en though it were the stamp of stu-pid-i-ty
Gone is my cap from me, never more to be
But though it's lost for e're, yet I rejoice.

****

Hymn No. 1128 Tune, "Alohoe"

Farewell old cap, farewell to thee,
You weren't much good in April showers
Still I clung to thee, from A to Z
But now I need thee no more.

Scrap of fabric saved from a burnt freshman cap affixed to a page of cap-themed hymns, 1920. *(Robert T. Hatt scrapbook)*

Freshman beanie. *(Leslie and Ruth Vaught papers)*

Like many colleges in the United States in the early part of the twentieth century, Purdue's upperclassmen enforced a tradition of freshman caps, or beanies. These small green felt caps were selected to make the freshmen stand out as the newcomers to campus; for many years the color of the button on the top of the hat indicated the wearer's major. On St. Patrick's Day, the caps were thrown into a bonfire to symbolize the freshmen were no longer green.

Many of Purdue's student organizations had distinctive hats, known as pots, typically made of felt or cloth. Each club's pot had a distinct style and color, sometimes featuring the insignia of the club. Wearers sometimes customized their pots with buttons and pins from other organizations. Although the exact date of adopting pots is unknown, they first appear in the *Debris* in 1937. Like cords, pots had disappeared from widespread popularity at Purdue by the early 1970s, but the Reamer Club has continued the tradition.

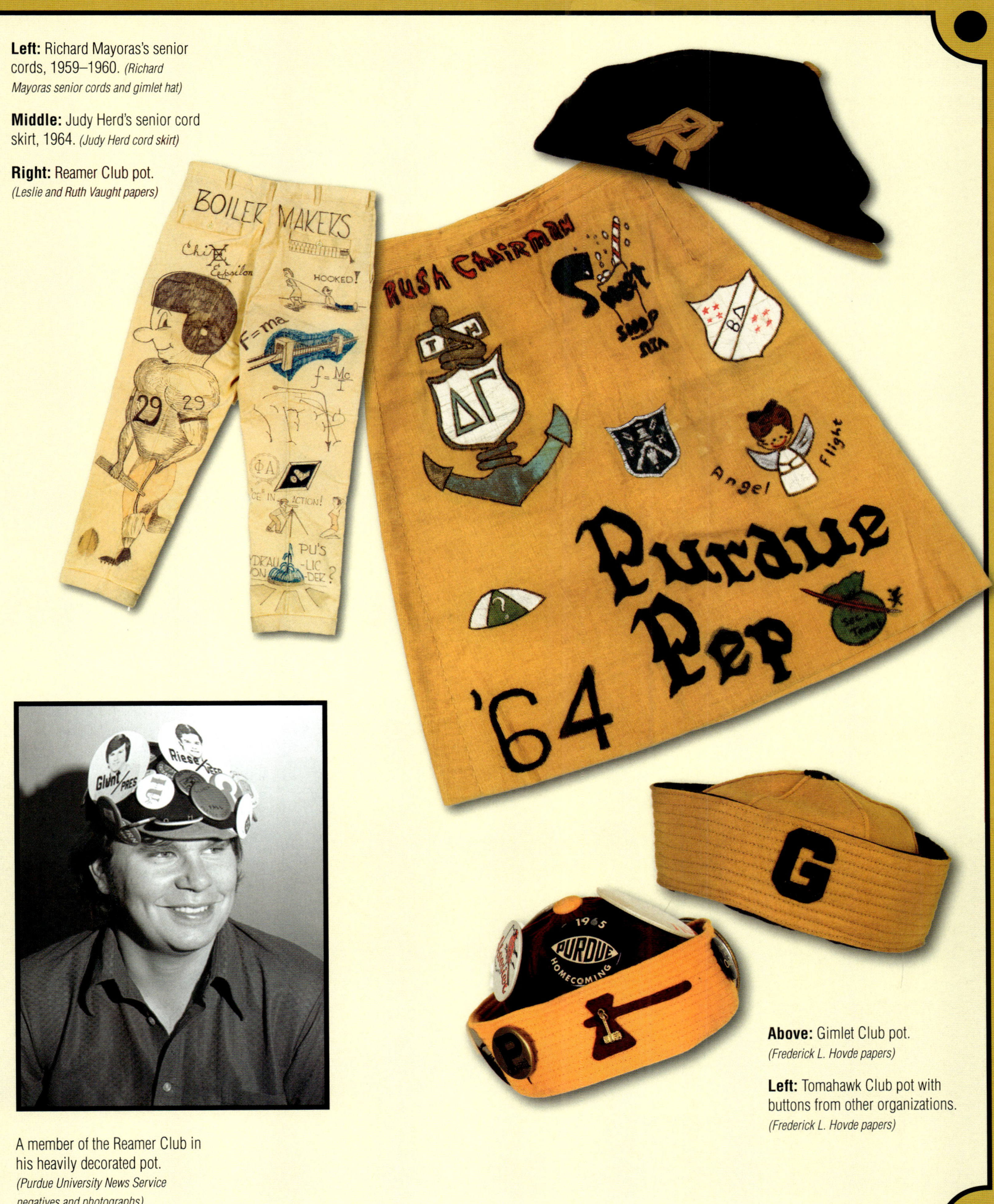

Left: Richard Mayoras's senior cords, 1959–1960. *(Richard Mayoras senior cords and gimlet hat)*

Middle: Judy Herd's senior cord skirt, 1964. *(Judy Herd cord skirt)*

Right: Reamer Club pot. *(Leslie and Ruth Vaught papers)*

A member of the Reamer Club in his heavily decorated pot. *(Purdue University News Service negatives and photographs)*

Above: Gimlet Club pot. *(Frederick L. Hovde papers)*

Left: Tomahawk Club pot with buttons from other organizations. *(Frederick L. Hovde papers)*

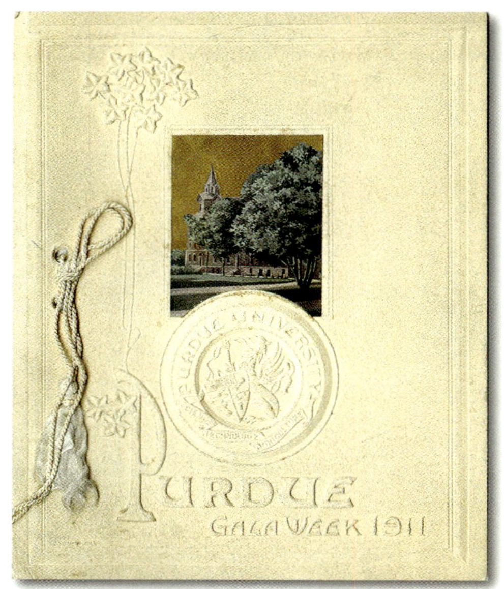

Right: Program for Gala Week, 1911. *(Charles M. Romanowitz papers)*

Bottom: The Marching Band leads alumni past Heavilon Hall on a parade through campus during Gala Week. *(Purdue University photographs)*

Commencement activities typically consisted of not only a graduation ceremony but also three to four days of events, including art exhibits, luncheons, and recitals. In 1904, the event was expanded to a full five days of activities known as Gala Week. The week of class reunions included campus tours, parades, bonfires, dances, and alumni class athletic competitions. Activities changed from year to year, yet a wreath laying at the grave of John Purdue held as a long-standing tradition.

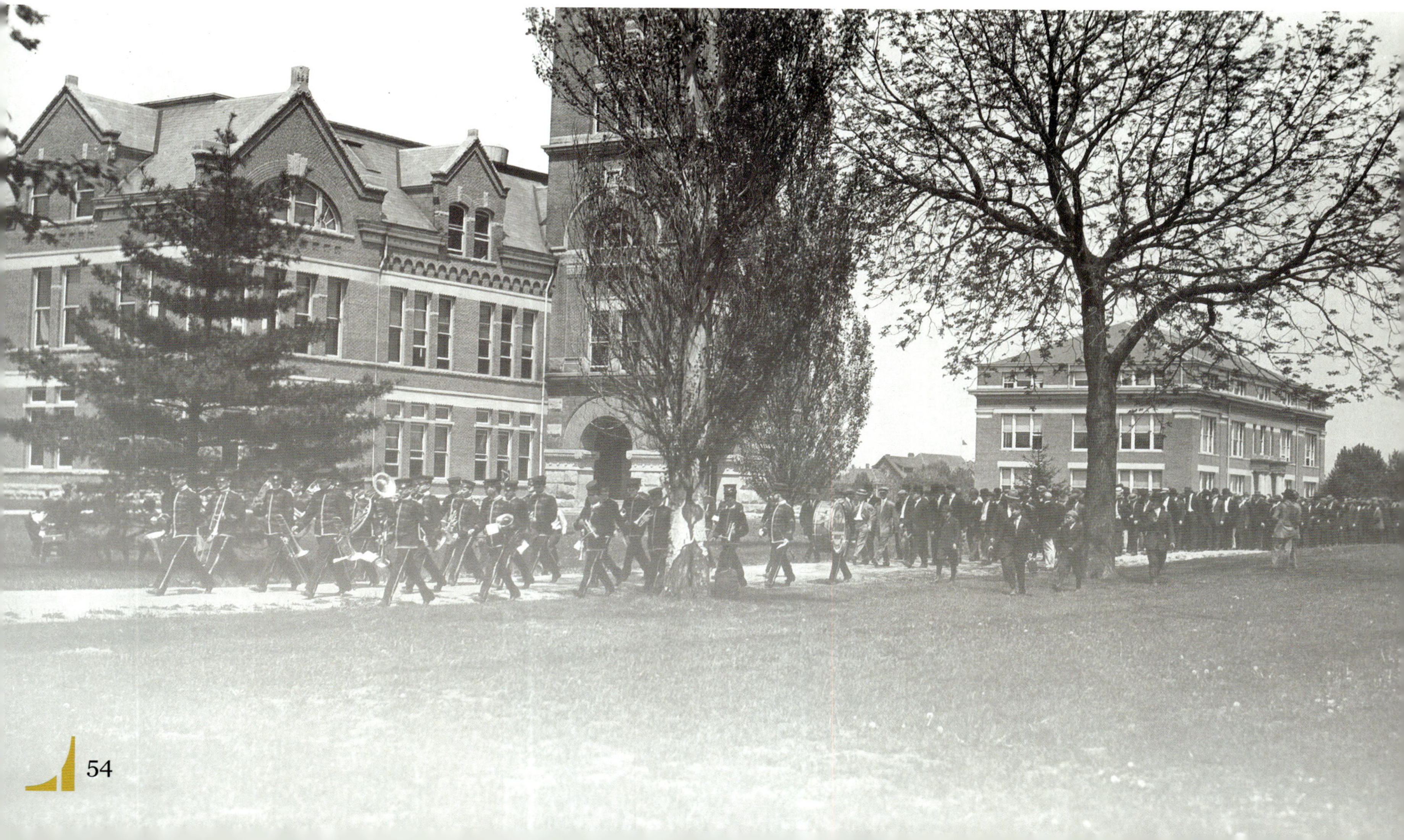

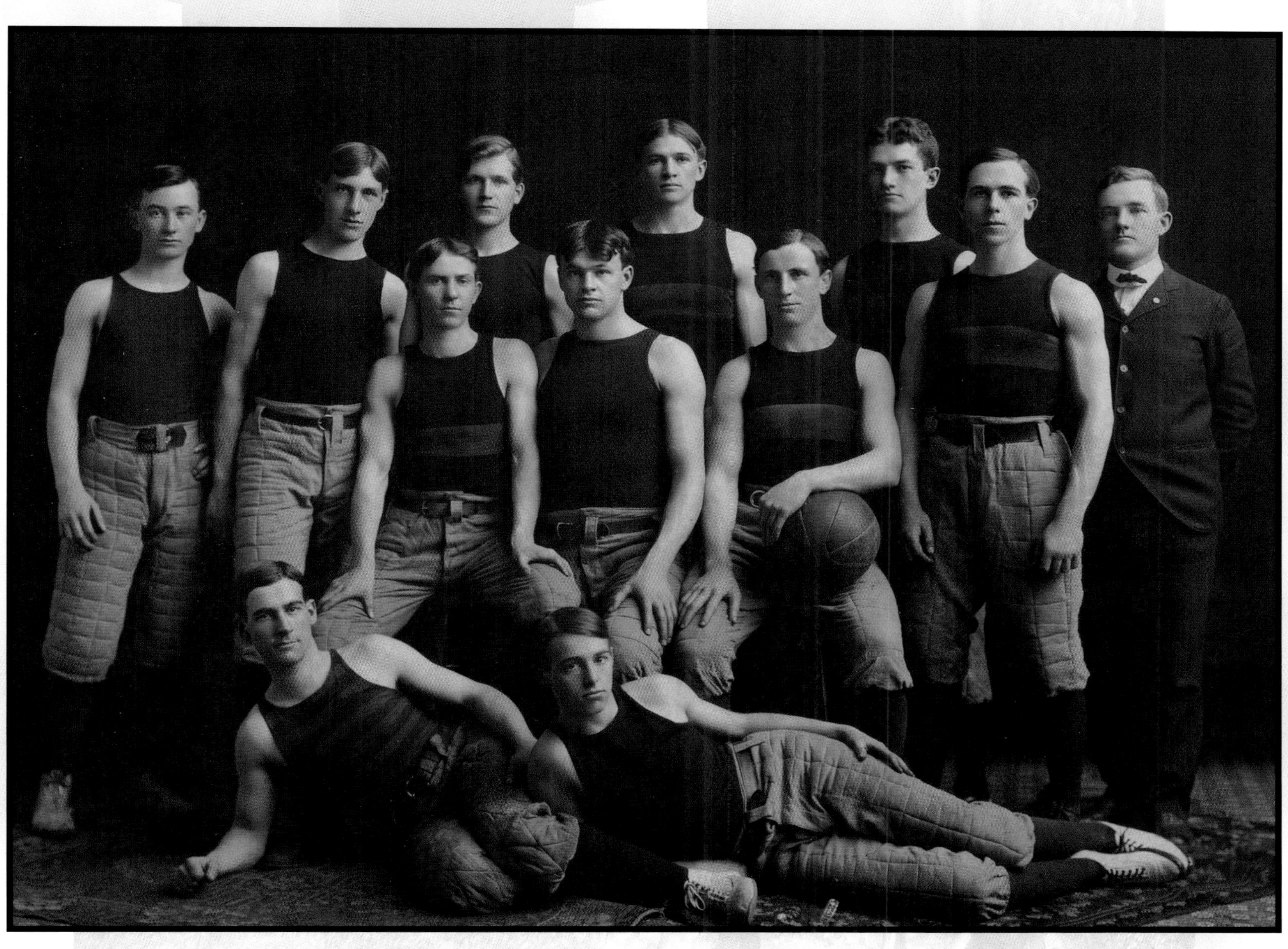

The undefeated 1903 basketball team.
(Purdue University photographs)

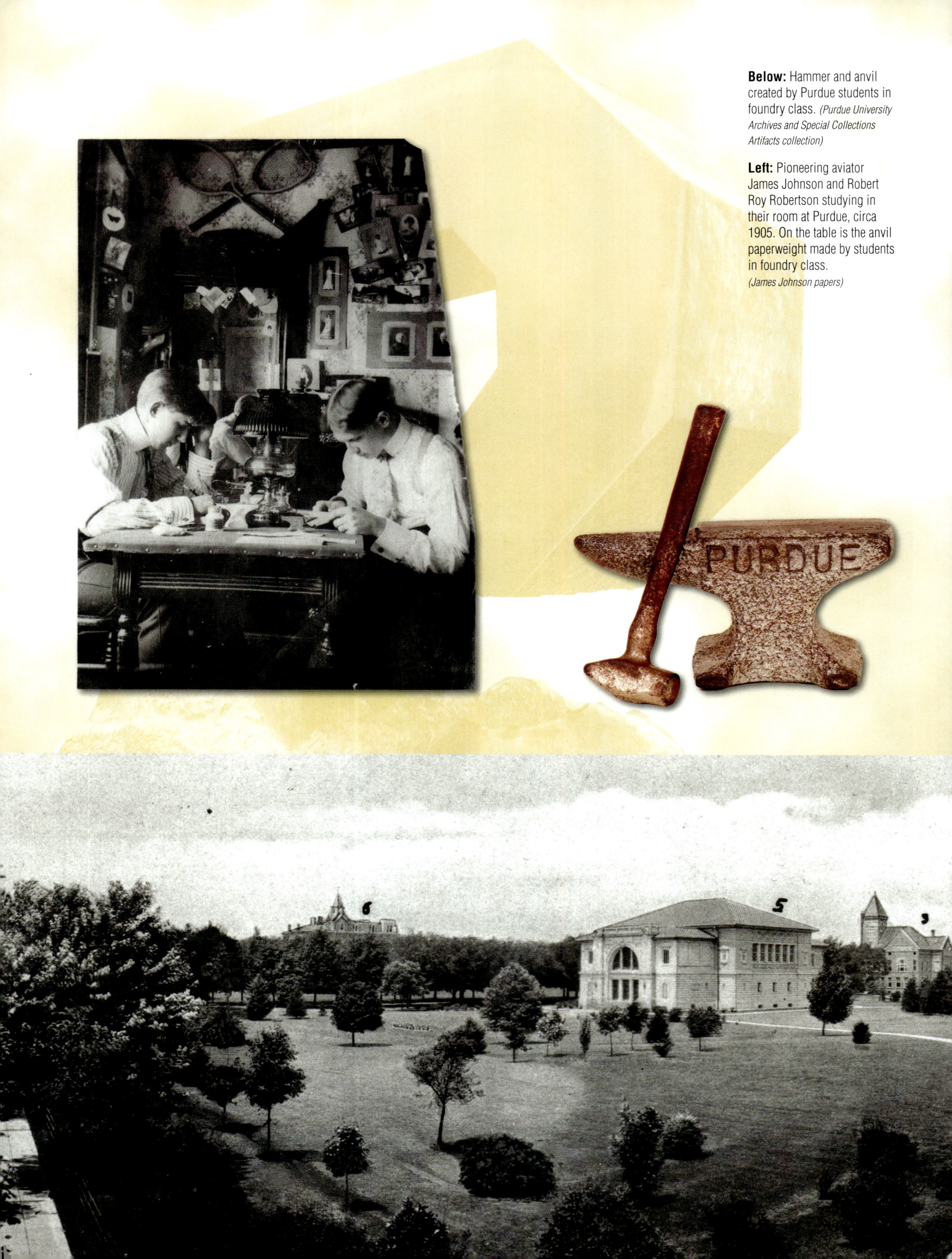

Below: Hammer and anvil created by Purdue students in foundry class. *(Purdue University Archives and Special Collections Artifacts collection)*

Left: Pioneering aviator James Johnson and Robert Roy Robertson studying in their room at Purdue, circa 1905. On the table is the anvil paperweight made by students in foundry class. *(James Johnson papers)*

The Dubois Club.

The ten negro students attending Purdue this year met last Friday night and organized under the above name. The scope of the club is broad. Its object is to develop among its votaries a higher moral, intellectual and social life. The business transacted was the choice of a name and the election of officers. At the next meeting on Friday, November 5, Mr. J. W. Gentry will read a biological sketch of Professor Dubois, from whom he received instruction while attending Wilberforce university a few years ago. Since organizing word comes that the colored students of Indiana university, Bloomington, have also organized under the same name, a happy coincident which may result in affiliation and an intercollegiate organization. The officers are: Edward R. Richardson, president; Clarence Marshall, secretary; Miss R. G. Webb, treasurer.

Left: The Dubois Club formed by the ten black students attending Purdue in 1909 to follow the "higher moral, intellectual and social" example of W. E. B. Dubois.[13] Among its members was Treasurer Rhoygnette Webb, the earliest known black woman to attend Purdue, who studied pharmacy with the Class of 1911 and later became a well-known nurse in Chicago.[14] *(Purdue Exponent)*

Below: Panoramic postcard of campus with buildings numbered and identified on the back alongside a message from student Charles Romanowitz to Miss Ruth Ritchie of Ludlow, Kentucky, 1906. "This is only six of the buildings. The other are near the Library but do not show here. I have recitations in three of these. Under the two you can see the tank where many battles were fought, but looks very small as is more than a mile away." Romanowitz identified University Hall as "Library and English Building." *(Charles M. Romanowitz papers)*

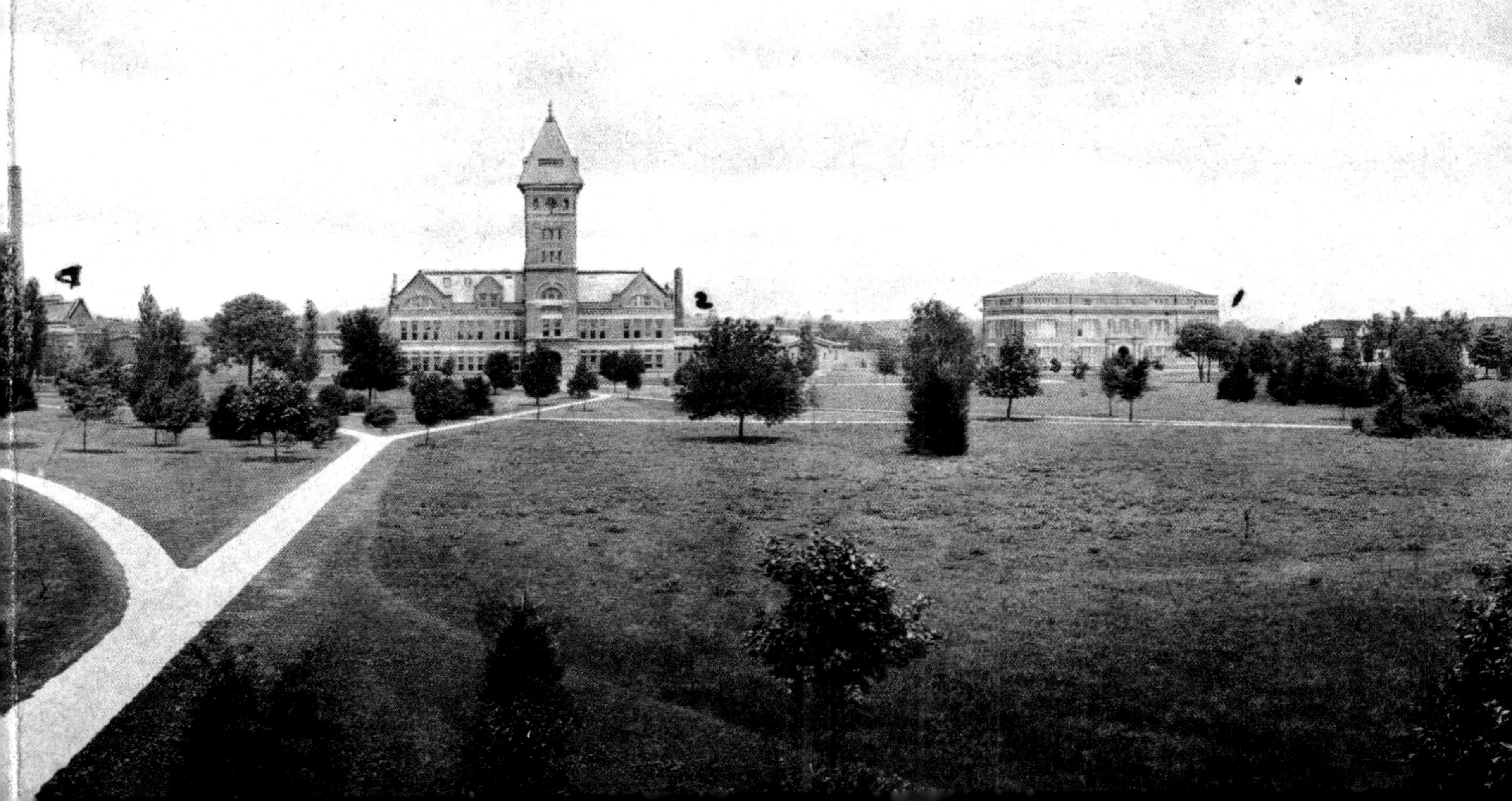

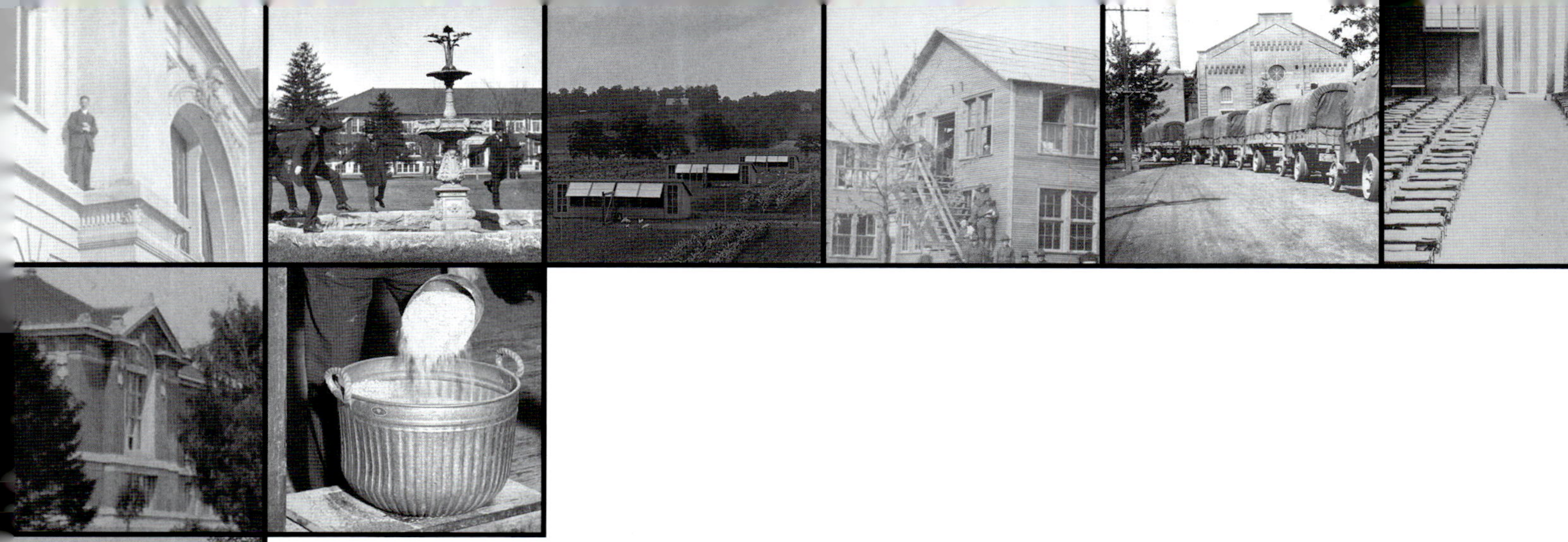

Campus map, 1910. *(Campus Maps collection)*

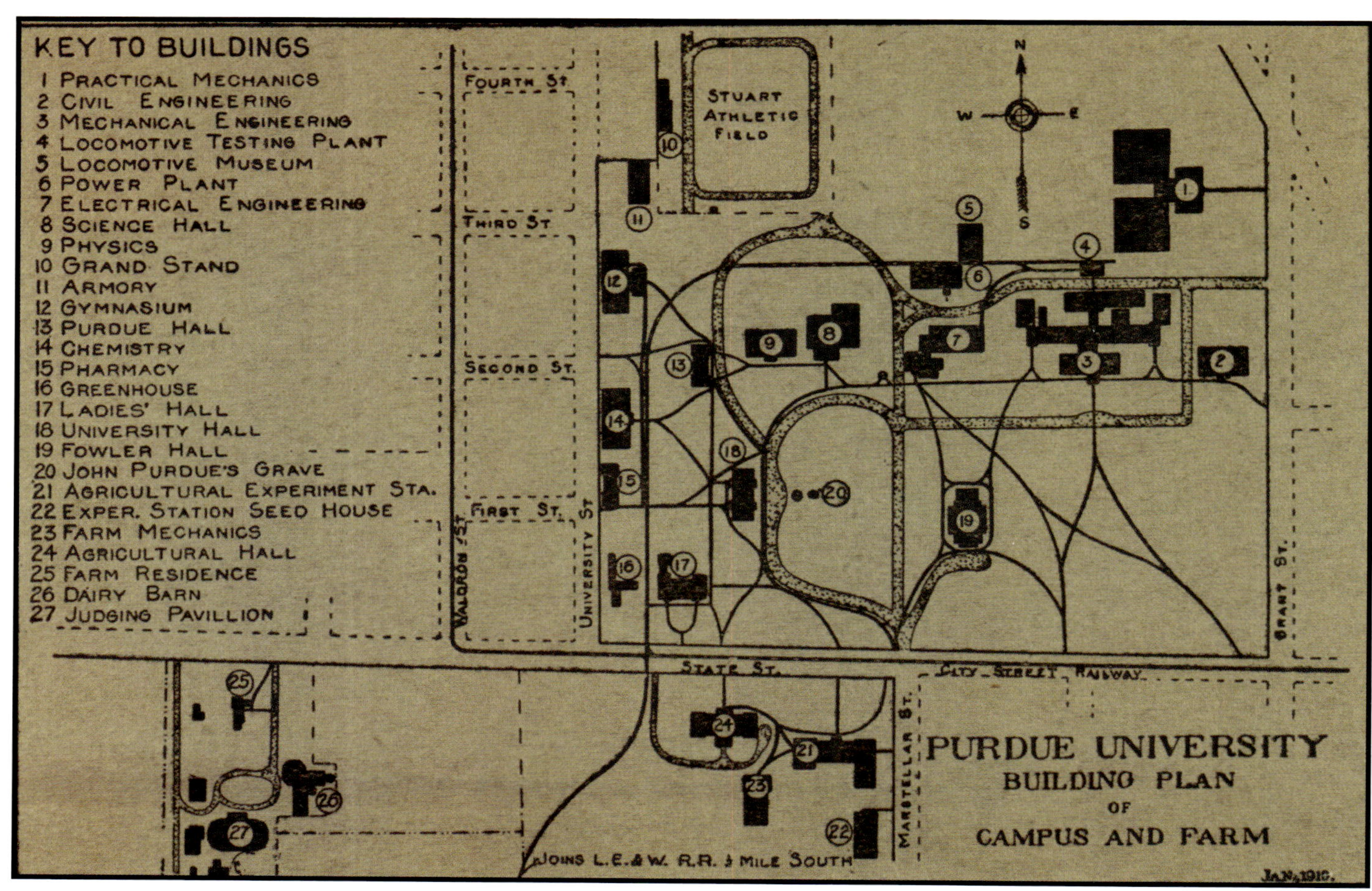

{ *Enrollment in 1910: 1,855 students*[1] }

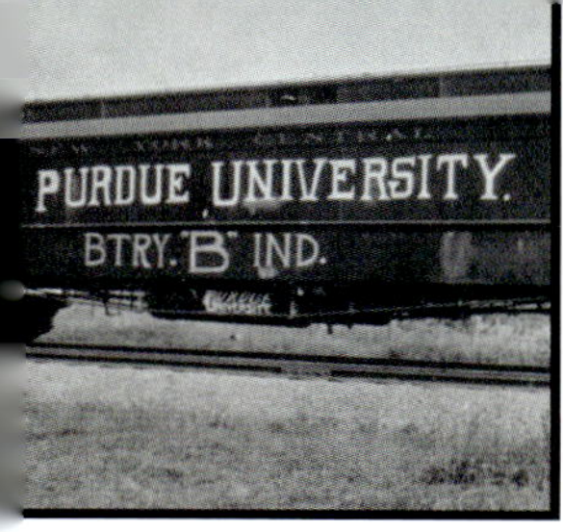

[The 1910s]

PURDUE AT 50

"Climaxing our campus days was a glorious Senior year. We appeared in our corduroys, derby hats and canes on October 3, at the opening of the football game, with Wabash. Purdue won, 27 to 3."

—*Purdue class of 1915*[2]

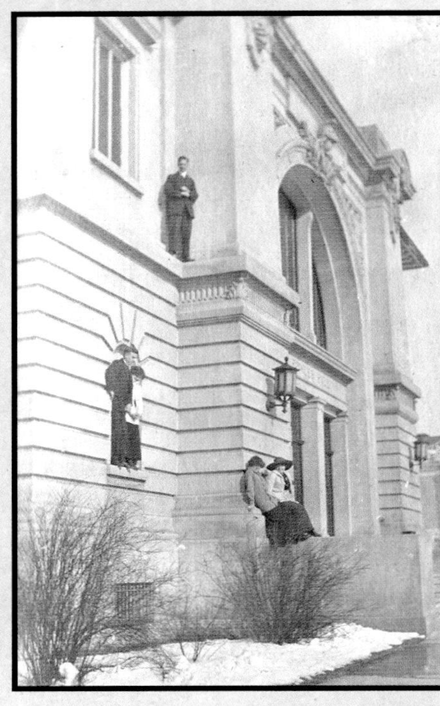

Left: "Statuary" of students on the side of Eliza Fowler Hall, circa 1913. *(Class of 1915 photo album)*

Background: Students posing around the fountain on Memorial Mall, Stanley Coulter Hall (then known as the Biology Building) in the background. *(Glennard Miller photo album)*

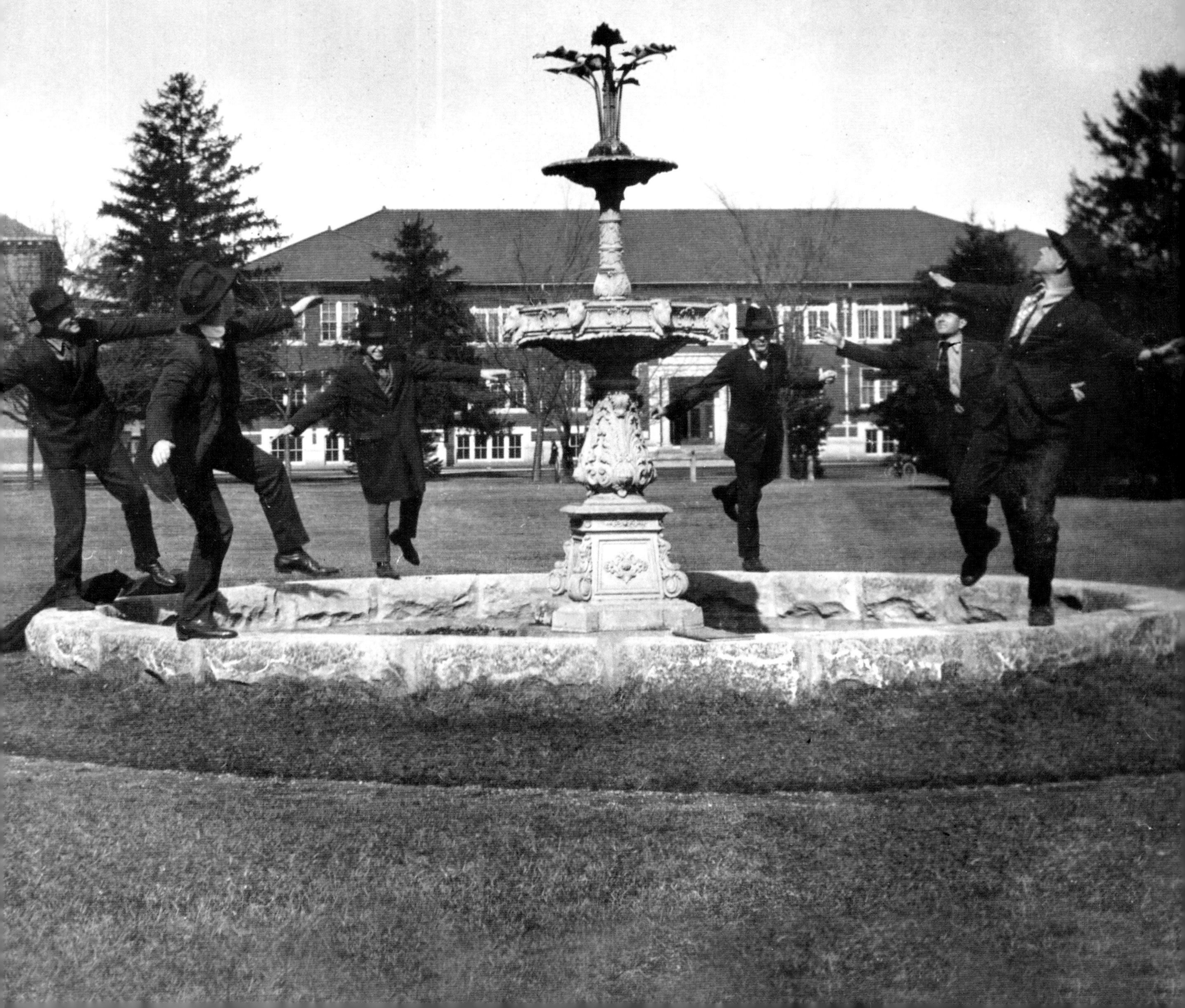

In 1919, Lillian Louise Lamb became the first woman to graduate from Purdue's College of Agriculture.

After decades of formalizing the operations of Purdue and increasing enrollment, the 1910s were one of the most radically transformative decades of Purdue's short existence. Established traditions such as the Tank Scrap ended, new traditions began, and repercussions of world war reached the Purdue University campus. Ultimately, the Purdue of 1919 looked very different from the early days of the decade.

Below left: Score for "A College Town for Me" from the Harlequin Club production *One Moment Please!* *(Purdue University Harlequin Club collection)*

Below right: Students with their house dog. *(Otis E. Griner papers)*

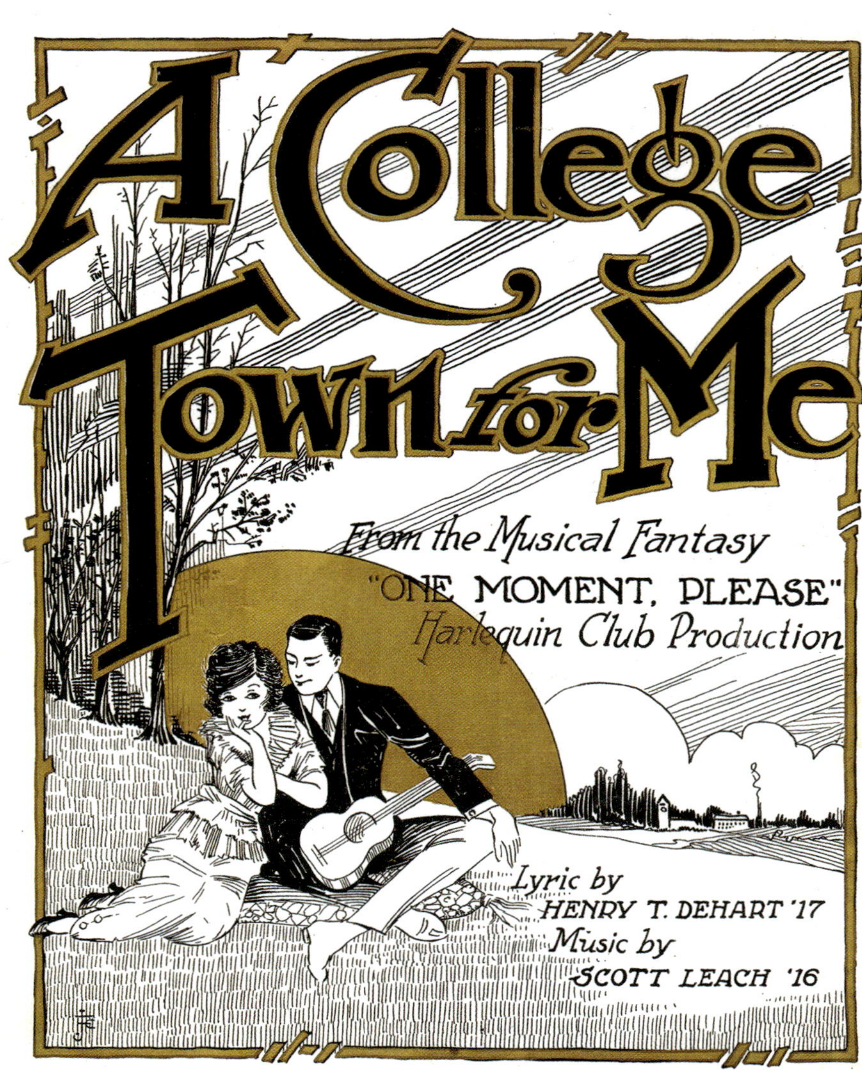

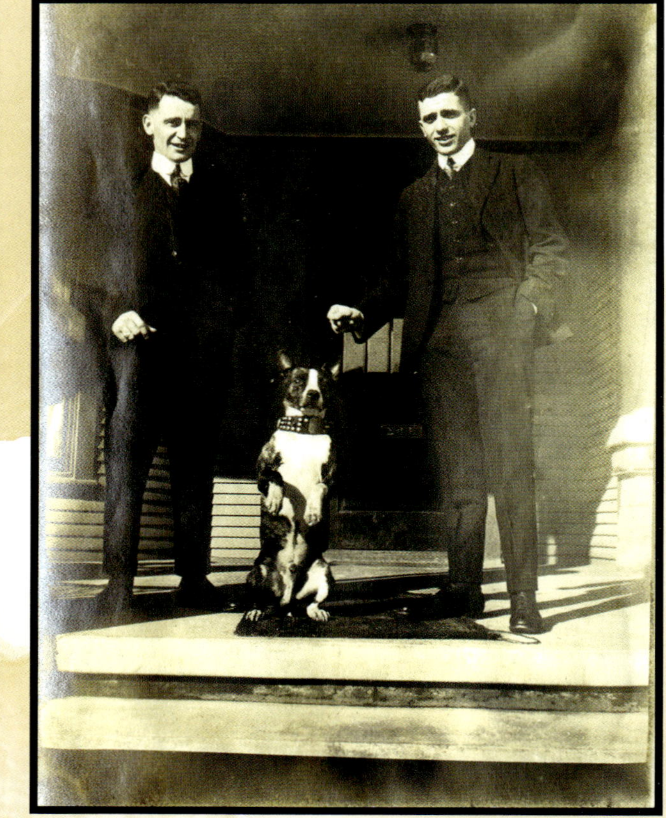

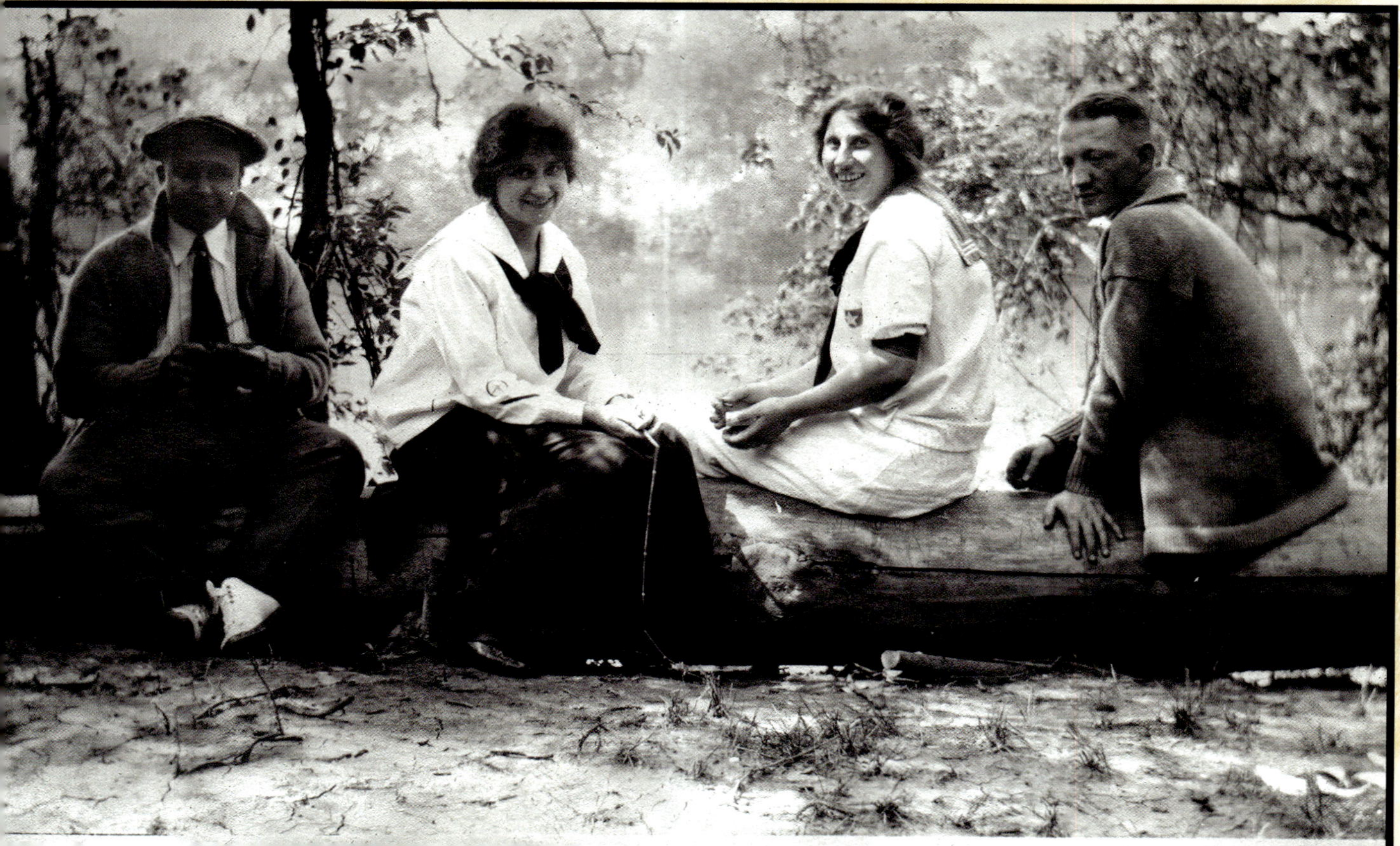

Students at Happy Hollow Park. *(Otis E. Griner papers)*

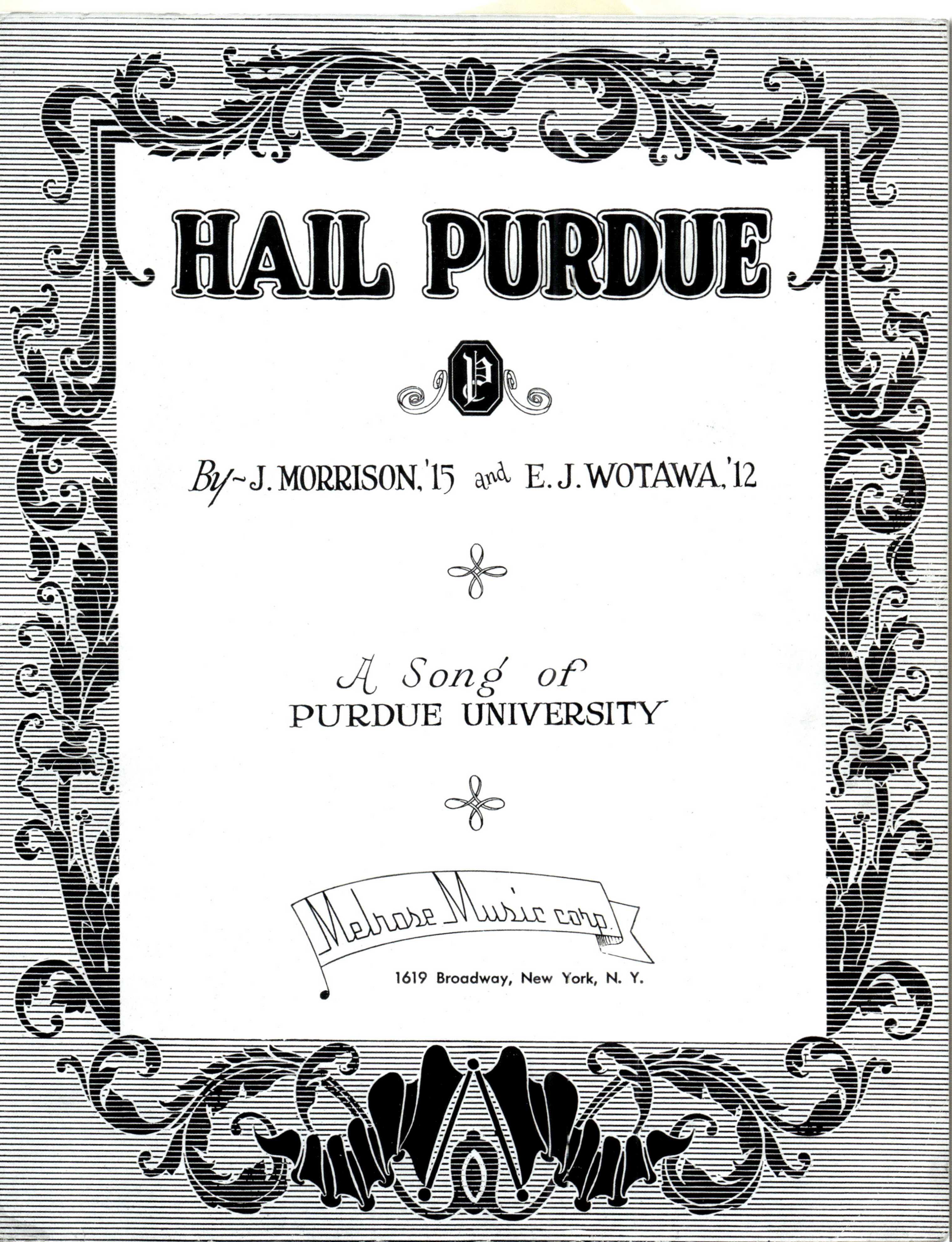

Sheet music for "Hail Purdue."
(Purdue University Musical Organizations records)

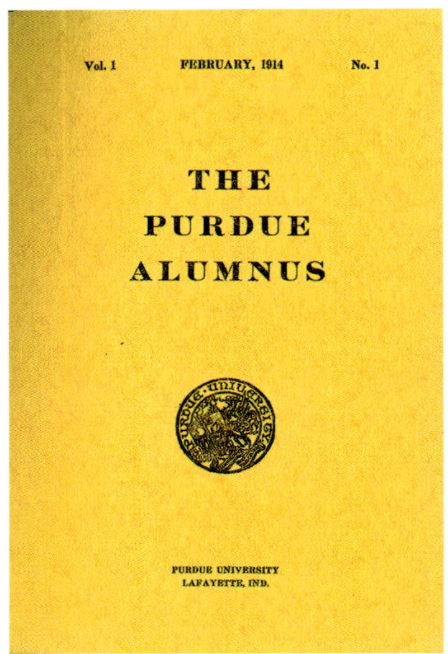

The first *Purdue Alumnus* magazine, 1914. *(Purdue Alumnus magazine)*

The Purdue Alumni Association, which Purdue's first graduate brought together in 1878, took its recognizable modern form in 1914 when the long-running *Purdue Bulletin* newsletter became the *Purdue Alumnus* magazine. This publication allowed Purdue alumni around the world to stay informed about activities on campus as well as the accomplishments of their fellow Boilermakers.

Purdue's School of Agriculture educated not only traditional four-year students, but also attendees of eight-week short course programs held January through March each year. These short course students were known as "Shorthorns" and participated in student activities during their two-month stint on campus. They fielded a team in interclass athletic events and joined in some campus traditions. In early 1910 and again in January 1912, the Shorthorn students opted to get involved in the Tank Scrap. Their approach, however, avoided the "scrap" part of the activity entirely and instead involved sneaking to the water tank in January and painting the letters "S.H." over the class year of the previous fall's victors. The Class of 1912 and the Class of 1915 were not pleased when they saw the unscheduled paint job on the tank that obscured their victories.[3]

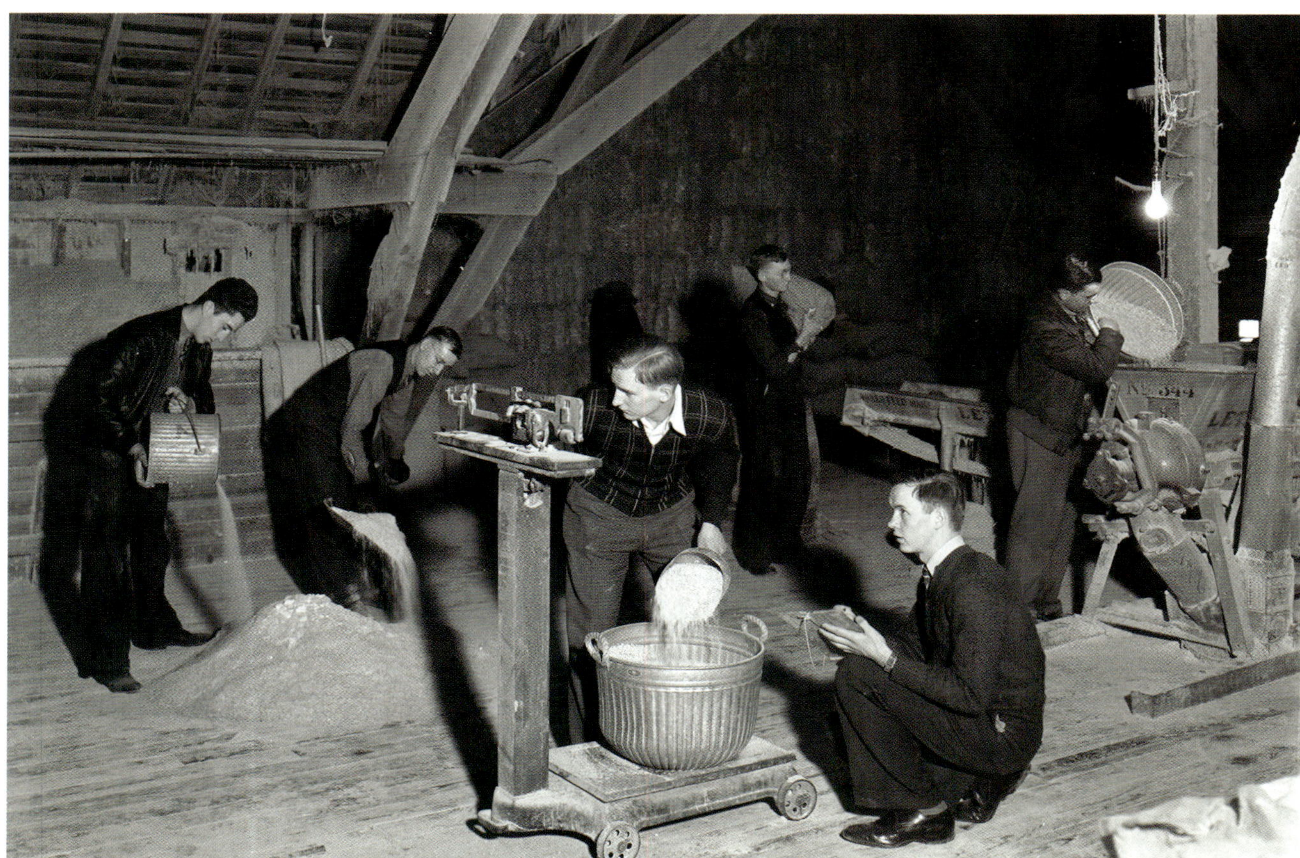

Short course students grinding, weighing, and mixing feed, 1937. *(J. C. Allen and Son Inc. photographs and negatives)*

Action during the Purdue vs. Wisconsin football game, October 18, 1913.
(Purdue University photographs)

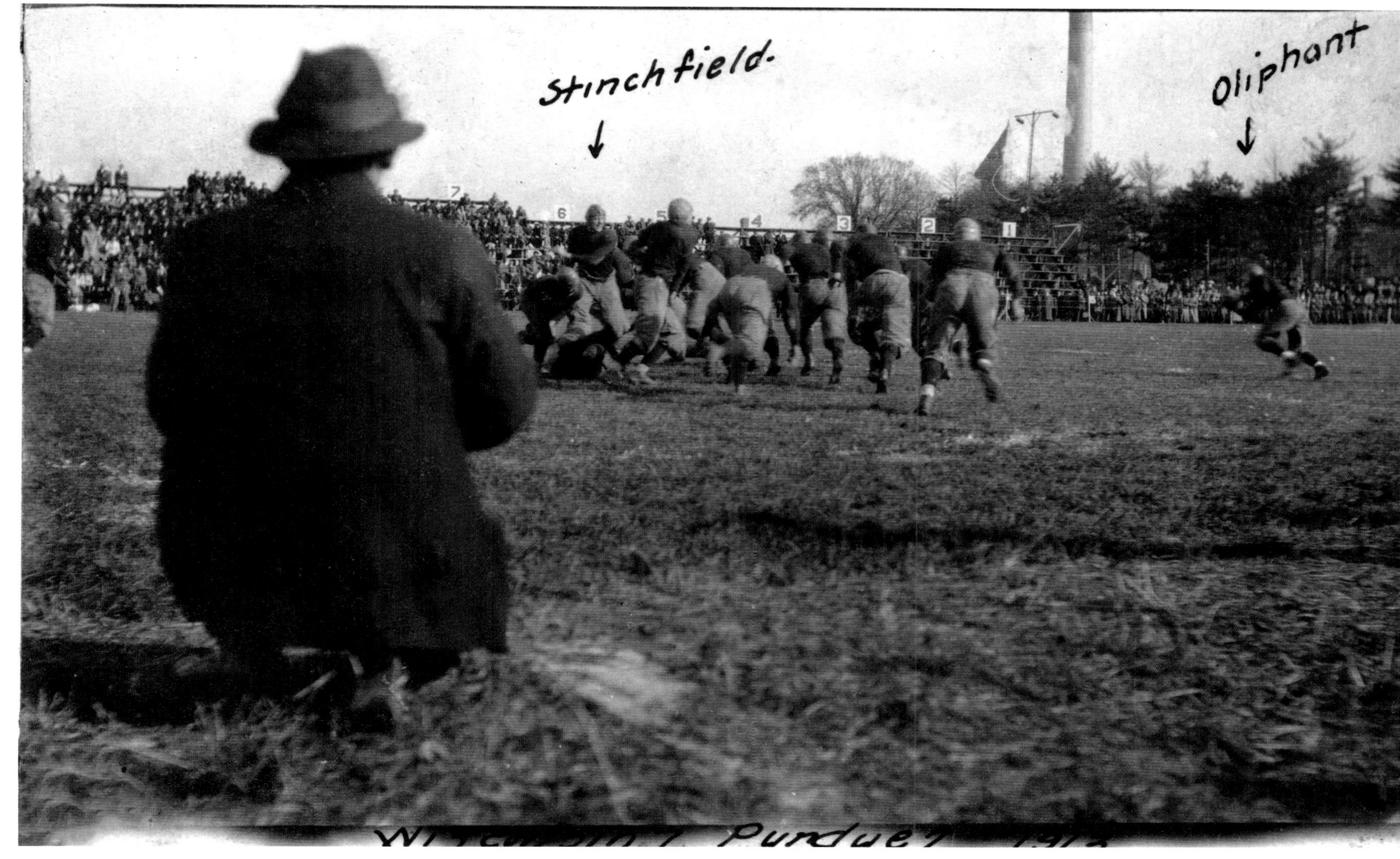

The biggest name in Purdue football of the 1910s was Elmer Q. Oliphant. He was the first Purdue athlete to letter in four sports (football, baseball, basketball, and track), was the first football All-American, and, according to legend, once kicked a game-winning field goal with a broken ankle, then fainted from the pain. The Purdue vs. Wisconsin football game held on October 18, 1913, was called "the grandest exhibition of football ever staged" at Purdue due to a seventy-yard touchdown run by Oliphant and ended in a 7–7 tie between two strong teams.

Mechanics Burning

The McAnnix, Mack Kannix, or Mechanics Burning was a significant student event on campus from 1903 to 1912. Mechanics Burning was an elaborate mock funeral ceremony held by the seniors who had just finished their year-and-a-half-long mechanical engineering program. The 1903 *Purdue Exponent* detailed the first such event as students "desiring to express their joy at deliverance from the all-absorbing subject."[4] At the height of the ceremony, the seniors threw their accumulated textbooks into a large bonfire.

SACRED

TO THE

MEMORY

OF

I. P. C. McANNIX

McMX

LAST SAD RITES AND CEREMONIES

Program cover for the 1910 Mechanics Burning. The I. P. C. in the victim's name stood for Irving Porter Church, author of the textbook. *(John Heiss collection)*

On the day of the funeral, the seniors formed a procession and a parade soon after chapel exercises. In the tradition's formative years, a large mockup of the textbook was displayed at the head of the parade and carried on a stretcher to the site of the ceremony. Eulogies and sermons, all with titles similar to 1904's "A Body at Rest Must Remain at Rest Forever," were laced with mathematical formulas and engineering references. These were followed by hymns, the reading of the will, and finally the application of "midnight oil" before the textbook was set on fire. The ashes were later carefully gathered and presented to the president of the junior class. In later years a fabricated "body" replaced the textbook.[5]

In 1911 the funeral service was replaced by a trial. The 1911 ceremonial booklet contains a lengthy play with a judge, attorneys, a jury, and a long list of witnesses for both sides. The outcome was guaranteed to be a guilty verdict, as proven by the oath administered to the witnesses: "Do you solemnly swear that the testimony which you are about to give will in no way favor the prisoners and will not give them a chance to escape the punishment which is due them, so help you Consul?"[6]

The activity in 1912 was similarly grand in scale. However, the increasing protests of faculty and complaints about insulting, profane, and sacrilegious aspects of the event ultimately led to its demise, and the Class of 1913 opted not to attempt another Burning. The tradition quickly faded from memory.

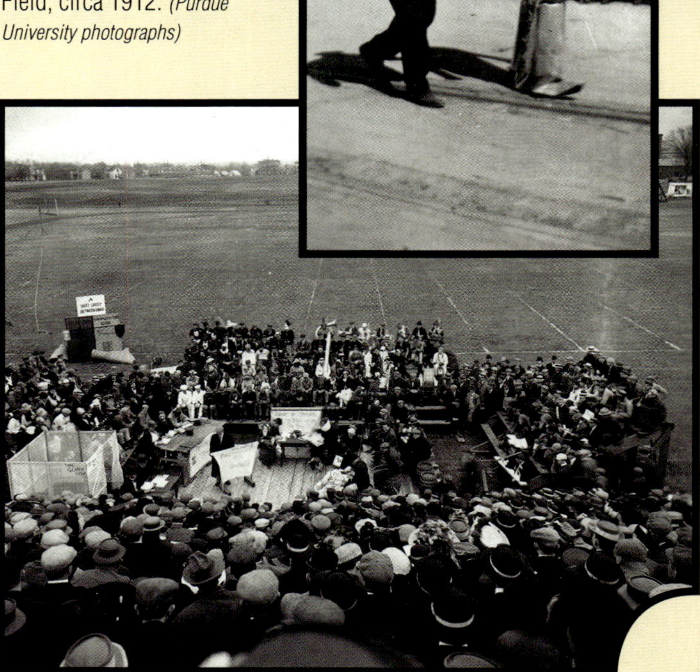

Right: A mechanical man in the Mechanics Burning parade. *(Otis E. Griner papers)*

Below: The trial on Stuart Field, circa 1912. *(Purdue University photographs)*

The Purdue Circus

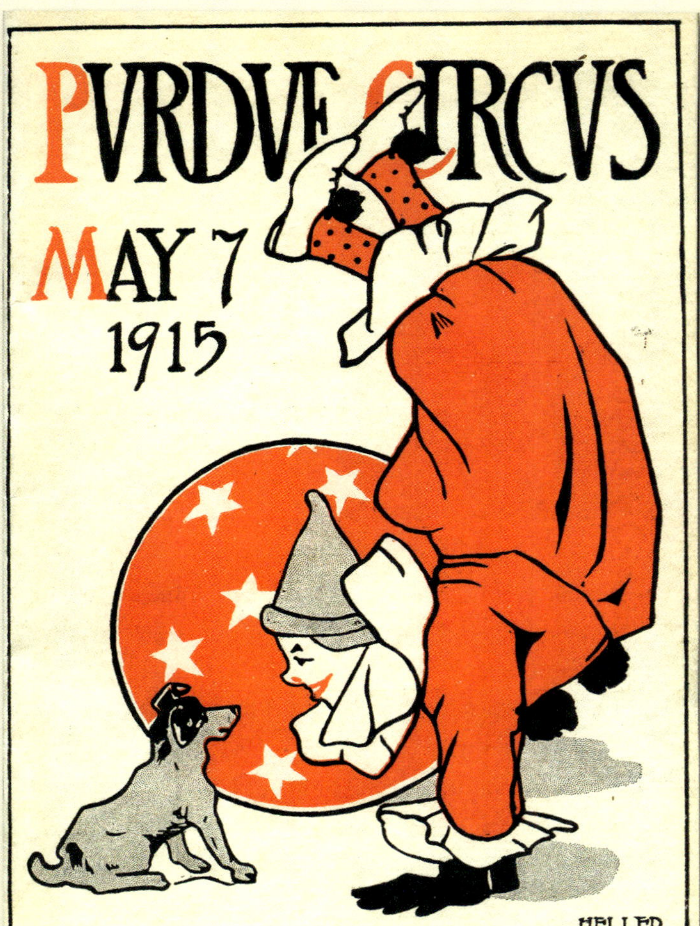

Program from the 1915 Purdue Circus.
(Purdue University Customs and Traditions collection)

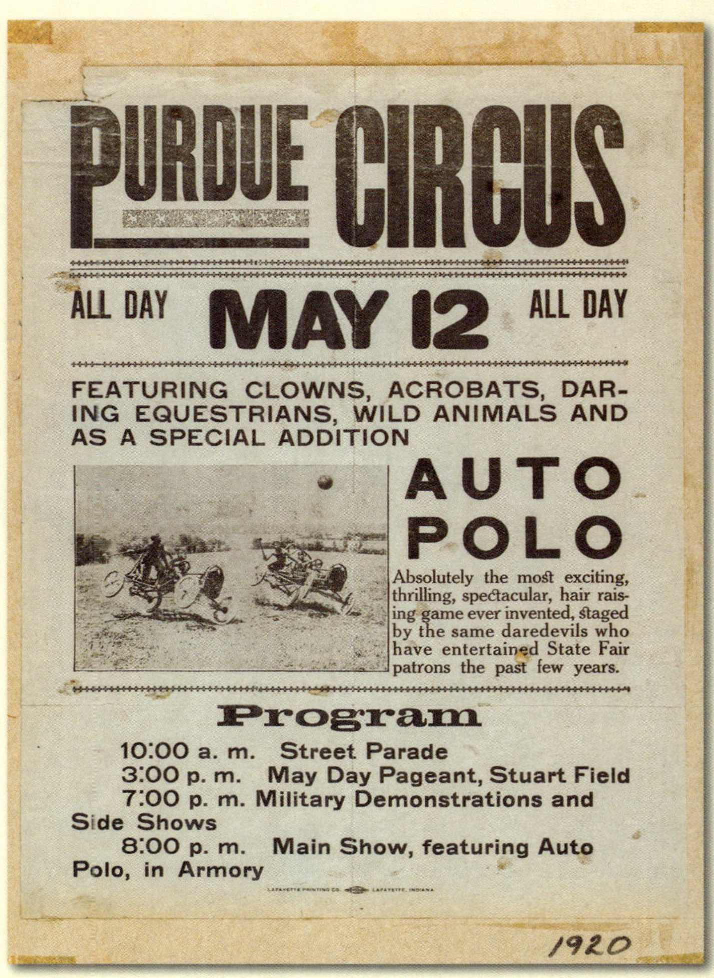

Poster for the Purdue Circus featuring Auto Polo as the spotlight event, May 12, 1920. *(Purdue Broadsides collection)*

The first Purdue Circus was held on May 1, 1913, organized by the senior class. The events commenced with a morning parade through campus, West Lafayette, and Lafayette with floats, bands, animals, and performers.[7]

The afternoon included sideshows on Stuart Field with such highlights as the Palace of Mysteries, the Electric Show, and "Some Chicken Show featuring Fatima the fat hen, and her five hundred flippant, frolicsome, singing, bouncing, bounding, boxom, chick, charming, chattering, chirping chickens" arranged by the Poultry Club.[8]

The Circus itself began around 8:30 in the evening, featuring stunts, tumblers, acrobats, animals, a chariot race, clowns, and many activities invented by student groups. In 1920 the lineup included Auto Polo, a polo game with cars swapped in for horses.

The Circus grew each year until 1917, when it was canceled due to the United States entering the war in Europe. The event was revived after the war, but it quickly lost popularity and disappeared from Purdue after 1922.

May Day and End of the Year Celebrations

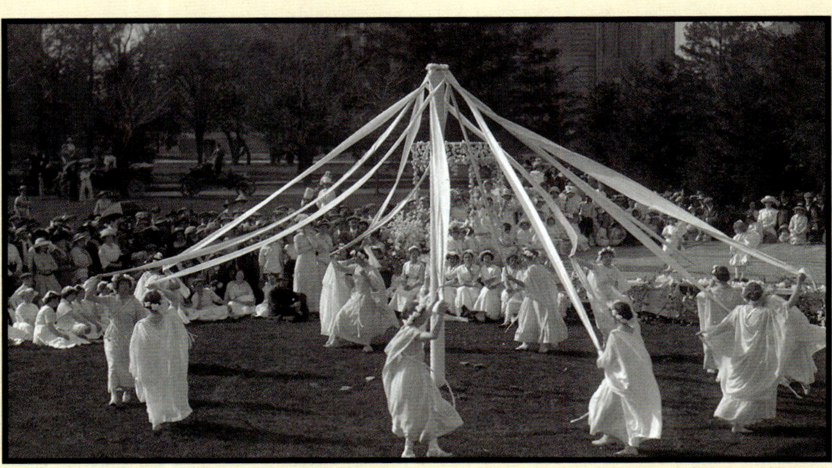

Along with the Purdue Circus, the May Day Pageant of 1913 was considered a more wholesome and inclusive replacement for the Tank Scrap and Mechanics Burning. May Day, a common celebration of spring at academic institutions across America, featured plays, poetry readings, and dances, culminating in the traditional maypole dance. Purdue's May Day activities were held on Memorial Mall on May 1 and featured musical accompaniment provided by the symphony section of the Purdue Band. The festivities were presided over by the May Queen and her court, elected by the student body in the weeks preceding May Day. Purdue's female students, led by the women of the senior class, organized the entire event.

In the 1920s, several springtime activities, including May Day, Mother's Day, and community sings, merged into a single weekend event.[9] This was apparent in 1946, when the May Day Queen was "crowned during the University Sing on Mother's Day Week-End."[10] University Sing, or U-Sing, was a singing competition between housing units organized by the Student Union. It grew out of earlier community sings and continued as a regular part of campus life for decades after formal May Day activities ceased. The May Queen, the last remaining piece of May Day, was crowned annually at U-Sing until 1969.[11]

Above: The Maypole Dance at Purdue's first May Day, 1913. *(Purdue University photographs)*

Below: The crowd at Purdue's first May Day, 1913. *(Purdue University photographs)*

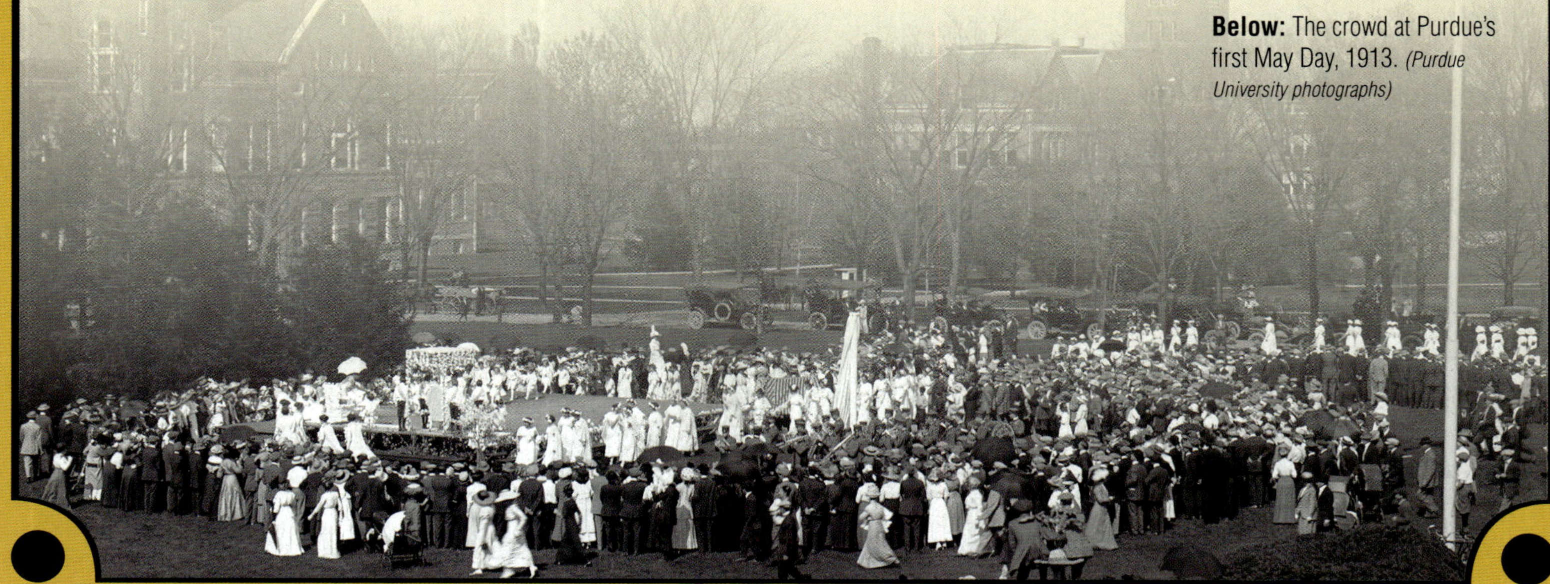

Below: Trainees outside the SATC barracks. *(Robert T. Hatt scrapbook)*

Bottom: "Purdue University Training Detachment. May, 1918. This picture does not give a very good idea of the size of the Armory. The flag, about half of which is here shown, is about 30 ft long and hangs 12 ft above the floor. There are 509 bunks." *(Purdue University photographs)*

The second half of the 1910s at Purdue, like in the rest of the world, was defined by World War I. Though the United States joined the war effort late and its involvement lasted barely more than a year, every activity, every person, and the entire campus was reshaped to serve the needs of the country during wartime.

Thanks to Purdue's military training requirement for male students, the University had hundreds of ROTC-trained men ready to serve their country when the call came. Some even enlisted with foreign armies before the United States formally entered the war in 1917. However, Purdue's largest contribution to the war effort was the establishment and implementation of the Student Army Training Corps (SATC), a military training program adopted at universities across the country to allow students to receive military training along with their academic coursework. Due to the opportunity presented by the SATC as well as the presence of a training unit of the United States Naval Reserve, Purdue's population dramatically increased in 1918. To accommodate the influx of men, Purdue built temporary barracks on the north side of campus at a location that later became the Mechanical Engineering Building along the Engineering Mall.

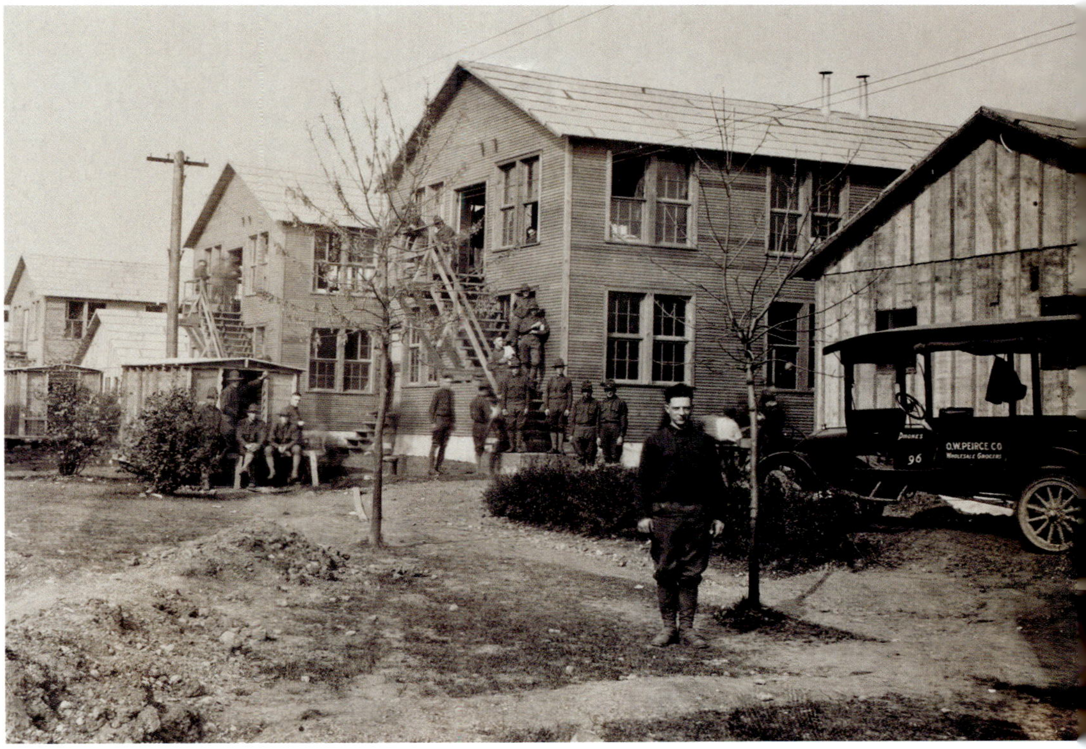

Lieutenant Julius Born, class of 1913, put his mechanical engineering education to good use during the war. In a letter to his parents, Born describes the many skills required of an artillery officer:

> [He m]ust of course know every nut and bolt in all of the different guns and some of the larger ones are very complicated. In addition he must be a bit of a chemist and thoroughly understand all of the different kinds of powders and their actions, and projectiles of which there are many kinds. He must also be a mechanic and a mathematician, understand the care and feeding of horses, be a wireless operator and a telephone central, and know how to build field fortifications. At the same time he has to be a topographical expert and be able accurately to map any kind of country, and above all be a good horseman.[12]

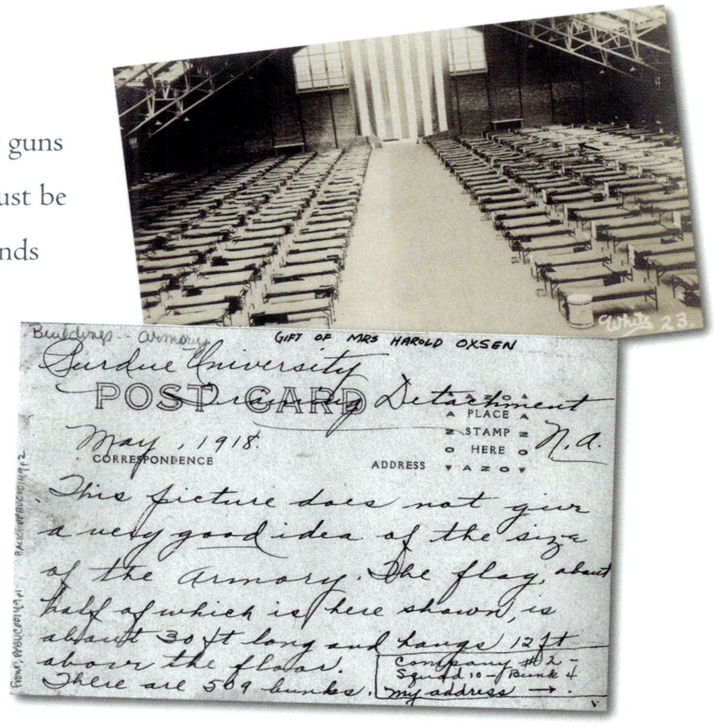

OFFICIAL BULLETIN
PURDUE UNIVERSITY

no. 12

October 1, 1918 TUESDAY

IMPORTANT NOTICE

ALL MEN STUDENTS are directed to assemble on Stuart Field PROMPTLY at 11:00 a. m. today to take part in the nation wide ceremony of inaugurating the STUDENTS' ARMY TRAINING CORPS. It is important that everyone be prompt, as this ceremony is to be simultaneous in all S. A. T. C. colleges of the country.

W. E. Stone, President

By the fall of 1918, the war's impact on campus became tangible. The *Purdue Exponent* ceased publication for the semester as "all the members of the staff have been either in the SATC here or in training camps elsewhere," but the Lafayette *Journal* as well as the *Courier* increased coverage of Purdue topics to fill the gap and ensure that the Purdue community remained informed about both local and international events.[14]

Many athletic events were canceled, as there were not enough young men on campus to fill the teams at Purdue or other colleges. Many clubs and literary societies were put on hold for the duration of the war, and even after, many struggled to regain their momentum and folded within the following few years. For the first time, French surpassed German as the most popular foreign language on campus.

Above: Official Bulletin Number 12 announcing the inauguration ceremony for the Student Army Training Corps, or SATC, October 1, 1918. *(Purdue World War I Announcements and Publications)*

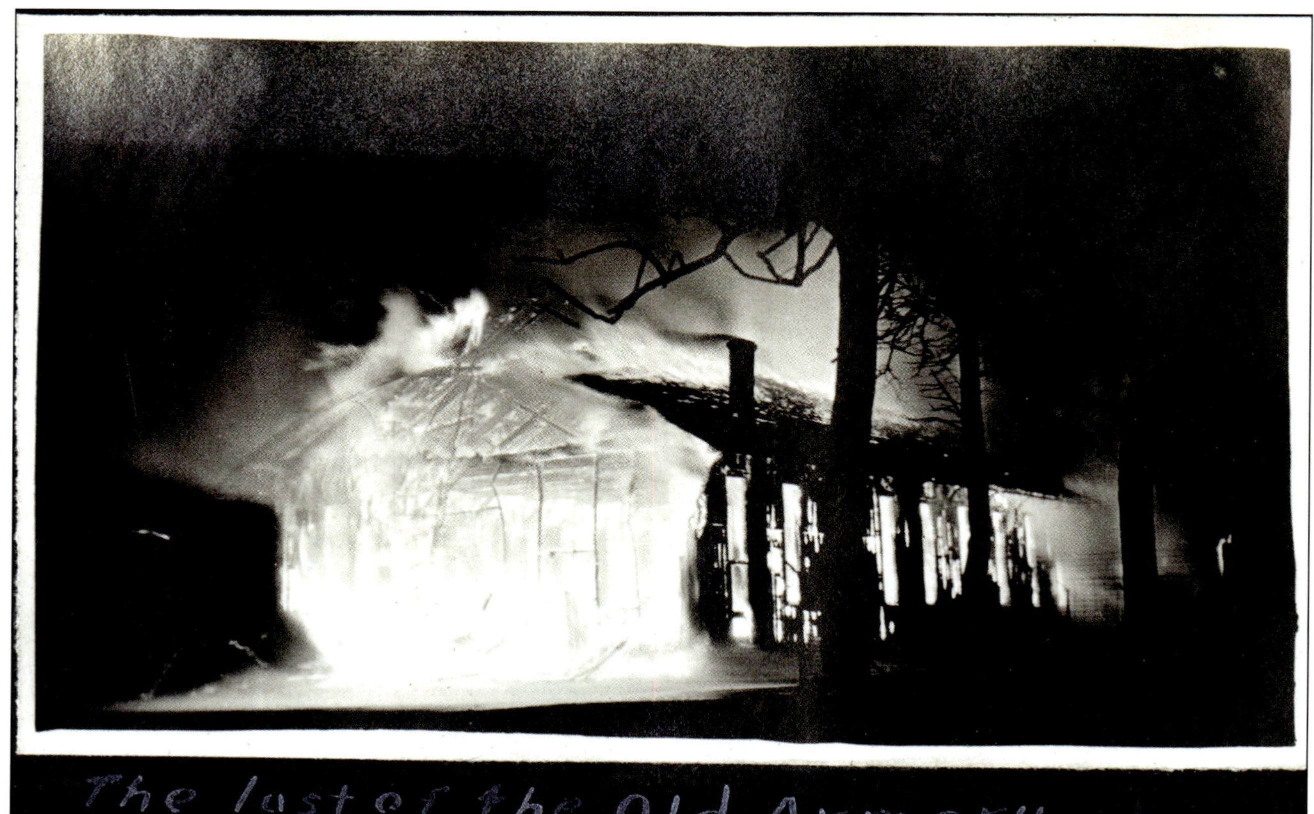

Right: Purdue's Armory, an original campus building from 1874 that had previously been called Military Hall and Gymnasium, was completely destroyed on February 24, 1916. A fire broke out in the middle of the night, likely due to a failure to fully extinguish the fire in a coal-burning stove, and it spread too quickly to be contained.[13] A completely new Armory was constructed at the same location in 1917. *(Arthur H. Fisher papers)*

Battery B

In the summer of 1916, Purdue's Battery B became the only military unit of Purdue students to be called into federal service and stationed in a combat zone. The unit formed in 1914, when a group of students interested in forming an artillery (rather than infantry) unit organized. They were known as Battery B of the Indiana National Guard. In 1916, National Guard units from across the country were called up to serve in the Border War, protecting the border with Mexico against raids by Mexican revolutionaries.

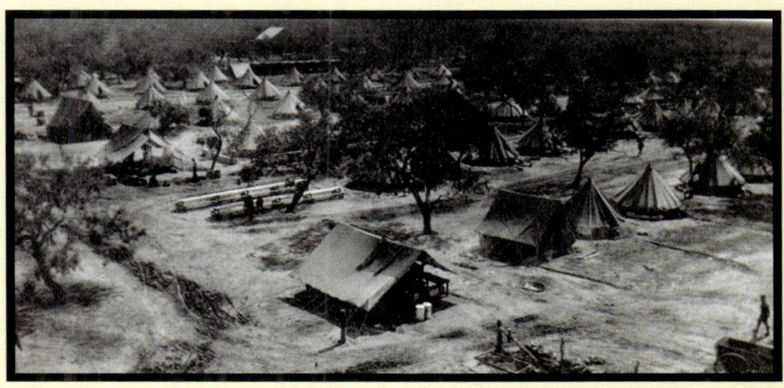

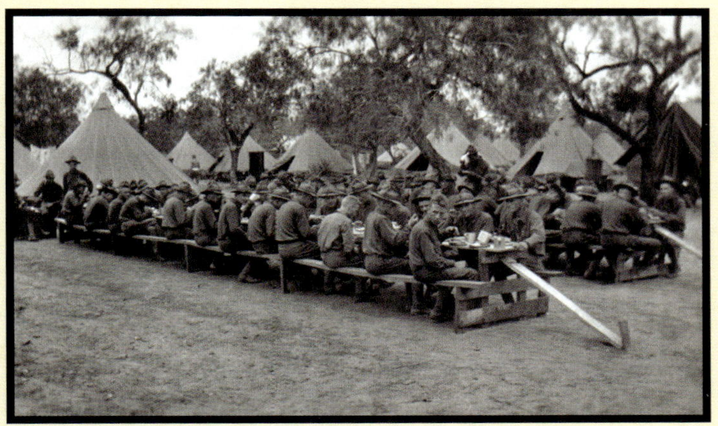

Battery B left West Lafayette on June 23 amid great fanfare. Along with Indiana National Guard Batteries A and C, they trained at Fort Benjamin Harrison in Indianapolis for two weeks before shipping out as the First Battalion Indiana Field Artillery. They reached their camp near the border in mid-July and remained until the men were granted leave to return to Purdue for the beginning of classes in the fall. Battery B was mustered out of service on September 27. They saw little action during their weeks of service, but the Border War proved an important experience for 100 of the 150 Battery B men, who later served in World War I.

Top right: Battery B's camp. *(J. Holmes Martin Battery B papers)*

Above left: Soldiers at mess in camp. *(J. Holmes Martin Battery B papers)*

Right: The Battery B train in Missouri on its way to the Mexican border. *(J. Holmes Martin Battery B papers)*

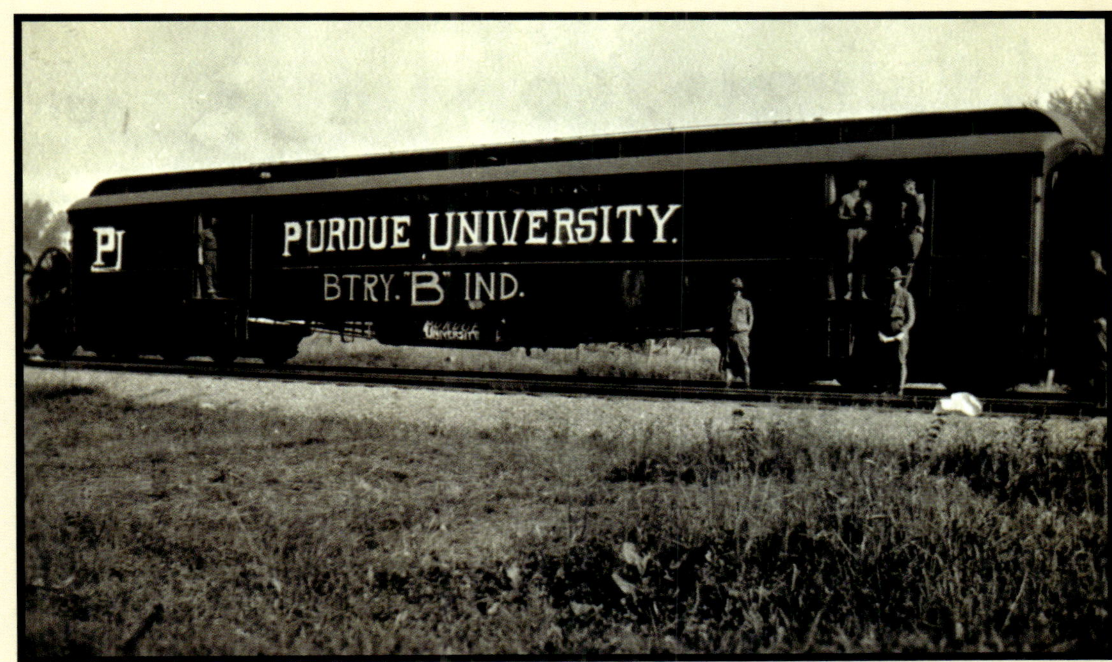

Purdue University Glee Club

ENTERTAINMENT DE LUXE

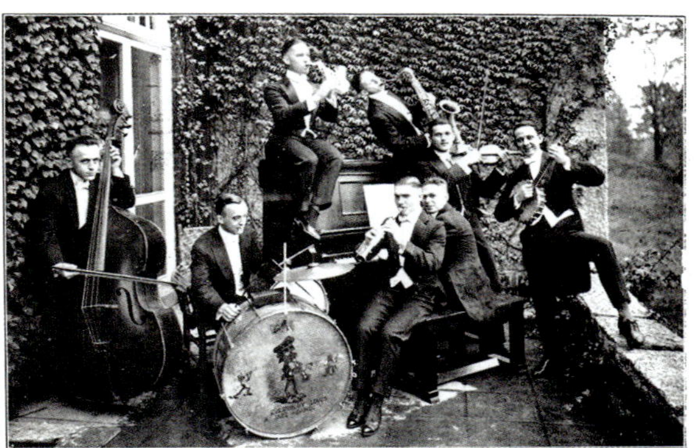

Glee Club Jazz Band

Latest musical hits rendered in an original way makes this number our biggest feature. Such a combination of instruments has never before been used, and the result is far beyond expectation.

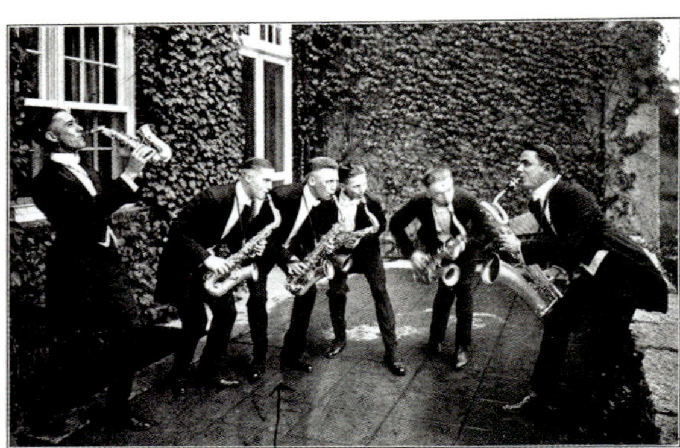

Glee Club Saxaphone Sextette

"THE BROWNLETS." Playing music as furnished by the famous Brown Brothers Sextette, in a manner which causes jealousy from the members of that organization.

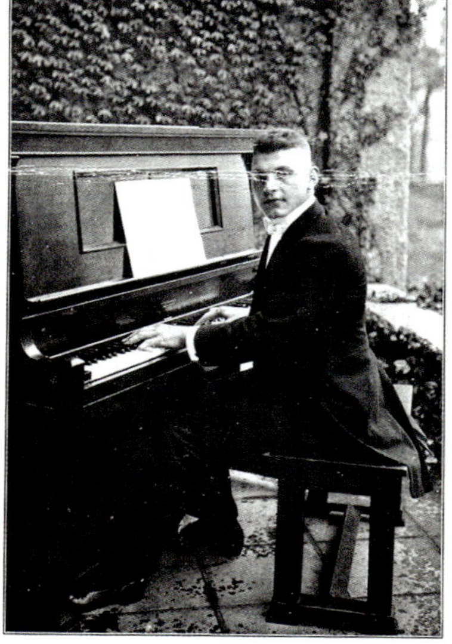

K. W. HUFFINE, Piano Soloist

Assists in Jazz Band

HUFFINE, Captain of the Varsity Foot Ball Team, and the best "Line Plunger" in Western Schools, is just as successful at the Piano as upon the Gridiron, rendering classical jazz music in a manner which makes a Piano sound like a sixty piece band.

Other Features:

Male Quartette

Violin Solo

Whistling Solo

Piano Duet

Comedy Pianologue

Classical Numbers by 5-piece Orchestra

Interesting Sketch Showing Life at Purdue

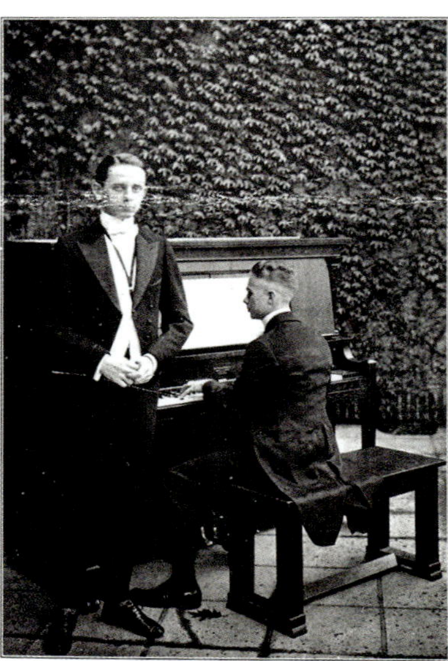

EDWARD NELL Jr.,

Baritone Soloist, accompanied by W. E. McDougle. An artist rendering both classical and popular solos with unusual musical ability.

Purdue University Glee Club poster. *(Robert T. Hatt scrapbook)*

PURDUE UNIVERSITY

ANNOUNCES

A Course for Women

IN

Dairying

April 8 to May 4, 1918

under the direction of

School of Agriculture

"I urge upon women everywhere to encourage the training of healthy young women for their country's service. They are the Nation's army of women defenders."

Faithfully,

(Signed) ANNA H. SHAW,
Chairman Woman's Committee, Council of National Defense.

A "Win the War" Course

Left: Purdue's short courses were modified during World War I to suit the needs of the war effort. "A Course for Women in Dairying," taught April 8–May 4, 1918, taught women practical skills such as milk testing, dairy bacteriology, and ice cream making. *(College of Agriculture, Administration of the College of Agriculture, records)*

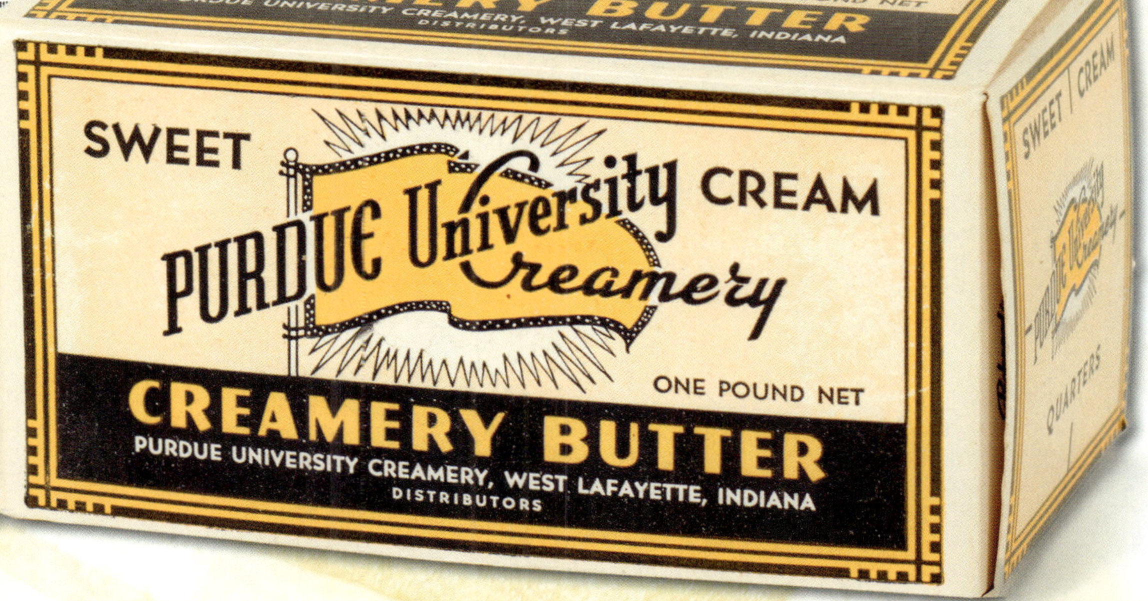

Below: Sweet Cream butter packaging produced by the Purdue University Creamery. *(College of Agriculture, Administration of the College of Agriculture, records)*

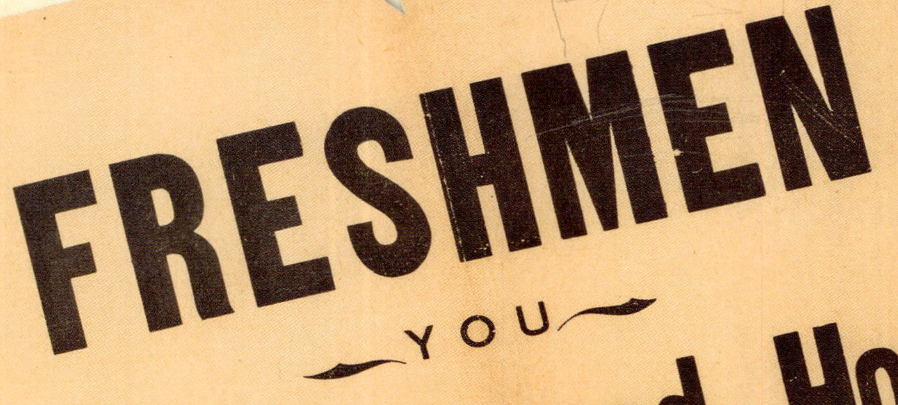

FRESHMEN

YOU

White Livered Hogs

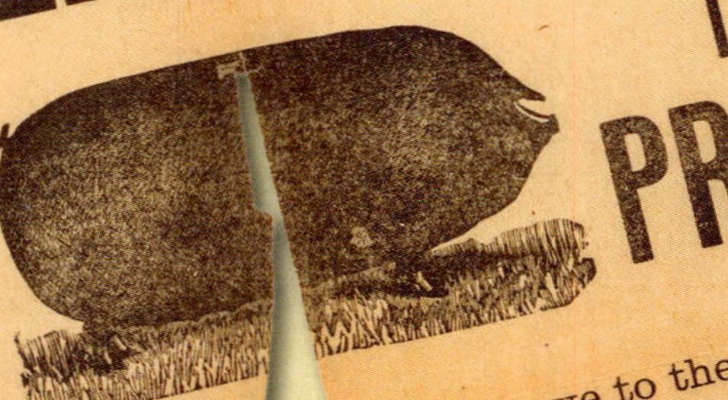

STOP LOOK

BEWARE PREPARE

FRESHMEN, ye slimy sluts of section, harken ye to the indisputable edict of your Hermeneneutical Superiors, the FEROCIOUS CLASS OF 1915.

REMEMBER, ye rabid runty reprobates, ever to bow thy hairacious heads in reverance before the Omnipotant CLASS OF 1915.

EVER cover thy Sanguiferous Sarconic Scrofulous Scurvied skulls with a slimy smear of Green.

SLOBBER, Slivered Saponaceous Skunks, Ye Evil Smelling Sausage Suckers, consign ye your Class Pins and Kindergarten Garb to the blistering heat of Perdition.

HEED ye and harken to our counsel ye Miserable Dogs or thou shalt be forever under the curse of your masters, the mighty CLASS OF 1915.

MUSTY Muck-rakers, hang your Hebdomadary Hides in the haunts of your Harlots. Forget ye thy Lady Nicotine when thou enterest the Portals of the Campus. Touch not the sacred fire water of the East Side, least Ye have visions of Hell.

EFFECTUALLY we will Edulcorate your Exzematous Effeminacy by an Efflux of Effulgent Effrontery. Ye Endospermic Ebullience of Euchyma.

NEVER Forget, Ye Vilest of Vipers, Ye Putrid Presuming, Boil-suckers, Ye Slimy Scum of the Earth,

WE HATE YOU ALL!

CLASS OF 1915

Poster addressed to "Freshmen, You White Livered Hogs" from the Class of 1915.
(Purdue Broadsides collection)

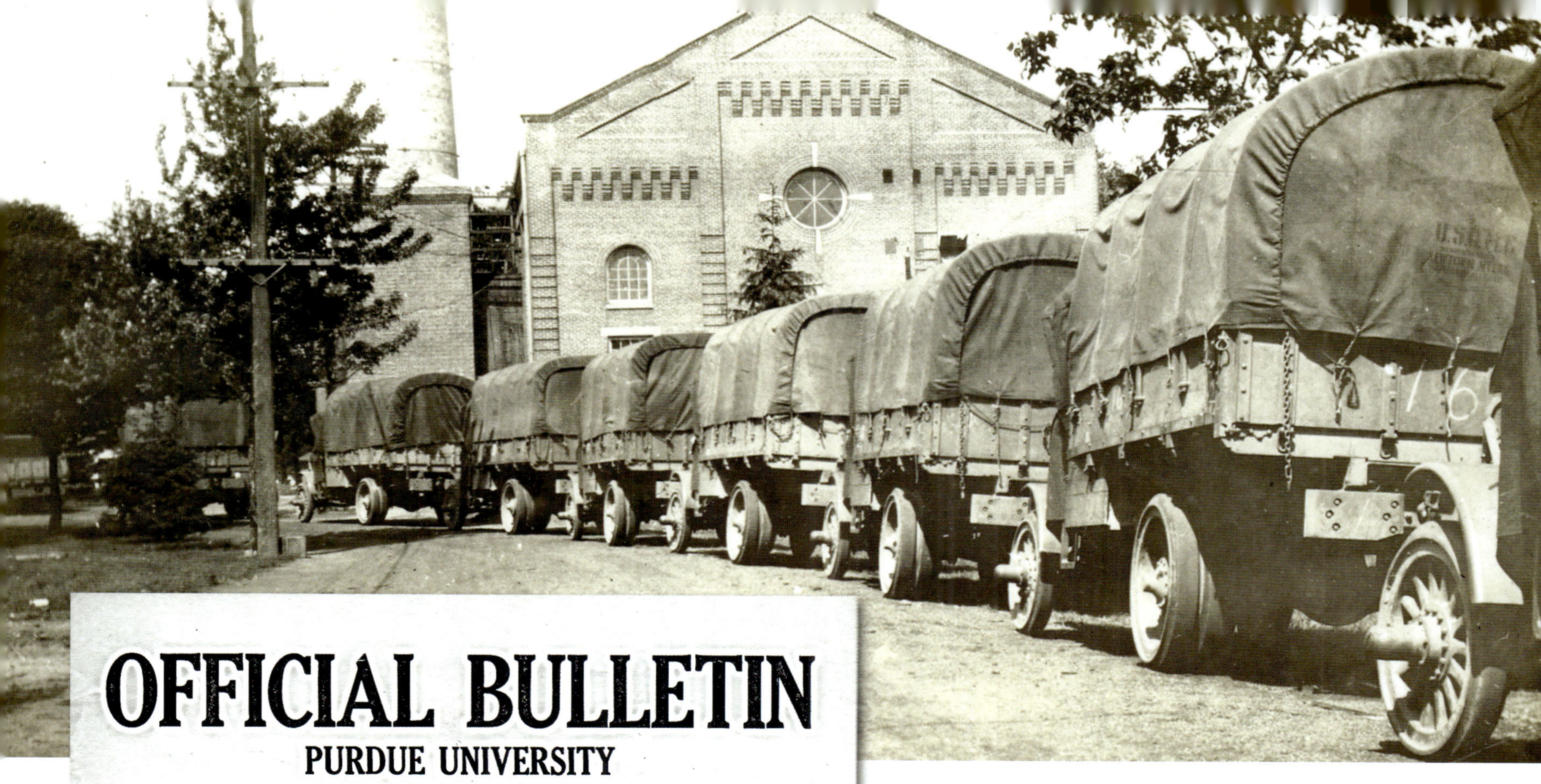

OFFICIAL BULLETIN
PURDUE UNIVERSITY

Number 17

October 11, 1918 Friday

NOTICE

BY ORDER OF THE STATE BOARD OF HEALTH, UNIVERSITY CLASSES ARE SUSPENDED UNTIL OCTOBER 20TH. THIS DOES NOT APPLY TO MEN UNDER MILITARY CONTROL. UNLESS ORDERS ARE PUBLISHED TO THE CONTRARY, ALL CLASSES WILL BE RESUMED MONDAY MORNING, OCTOBER 21ST.

W. E. STONE, PRESIDENT

GAME IS CANCELLED

BY ORDER OF THE STATE BOARD OF HEALTH, THE FOOTBALL GAME FOR SATURDAY, OCTOBER 12TH, IS CANCELLED.

ATHLETIC COMMITTEE.

PARADE NOT AFFECTED

THE ORDER FROM THE STATE BOARD OF HEALTH DOES NOT AFFECT THE PARADE OF VOCATIONAL AND S. A. T. C. TROOPS SCHEDULED FOR 9 A. M. SATURDAY, OCTOBER 12TH.

ED JACKSON, Major U.S.A., C. O.

Top: Military trucks outside the campus power plant. *(Glennard Miller photo album)*

Bottom: Official Bulletin Number 17 stating that classes were to be canceled October 11–20 due to the influenza outbreak. The cancellation was extended and the university did not resume regular operations until October 30. *(Purdue World War I Announcements and Publications)*

Near the end of the war, an outbreak of influenza that caused tens of millions of deaths across the world reached Purdue. To combat the quick spread of the deadly illness, the university suspended "all civil activities" and canceled classes from October 11 through October 30, 1918, though military activities had to continue despite the risk. Ultimately eleven people died at Purdue during the flu outbreak.[15]

By the end of the war, more than four thousand people associated with the university had served in some capacity and sixty-seven Purdue men had died in the service from injury or disease.

Though service members began returning home from Europe after the armistice declaration on November 11, 1918, the specter of war was still a presence at Purdue for several more months. To help returning students catch up, the university extended the 1918 fall semester through March 1, 1919. This had the effect of shortening the spring term by one month, though the amount of work expected from each student was not reduced. In the January 6, 1919, *Exponent,* the first issue since June of the previous year, Professor Thomas Moran wrote a column encouraging students to embrace "a new start" with their college careers, noting that the "old-time activities will soon be with us again."[16] For the first time since before the war, the academic year ended with May Day celebrations and the Circus.

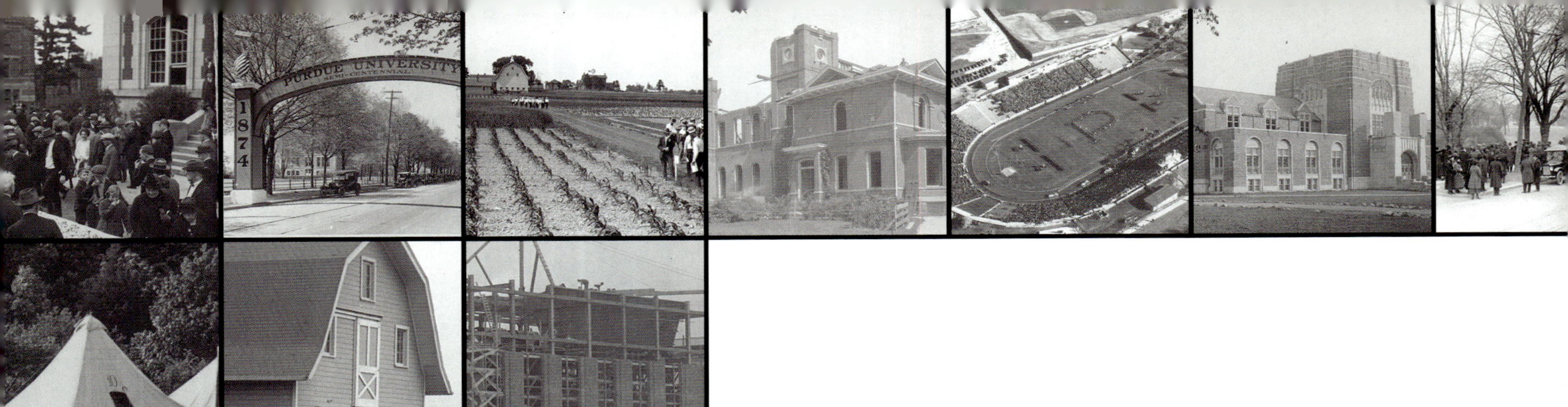

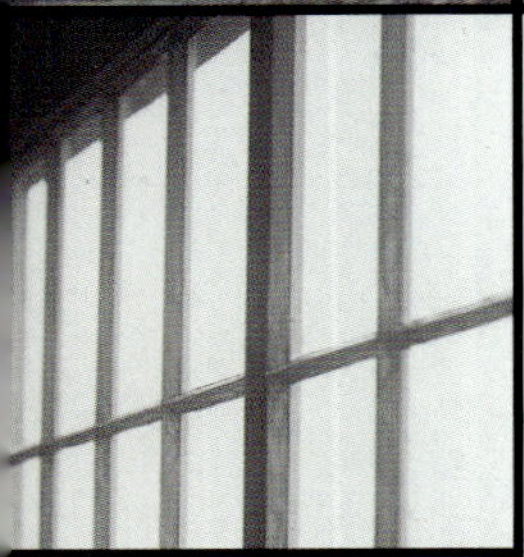

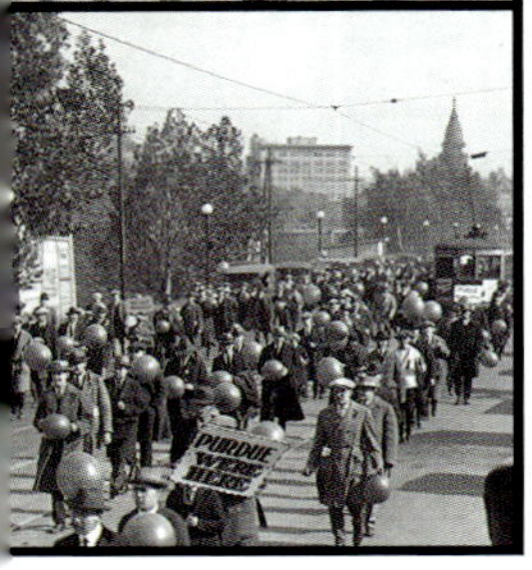

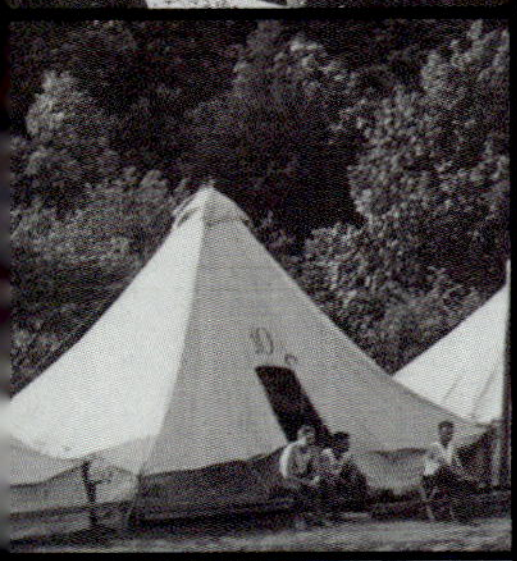

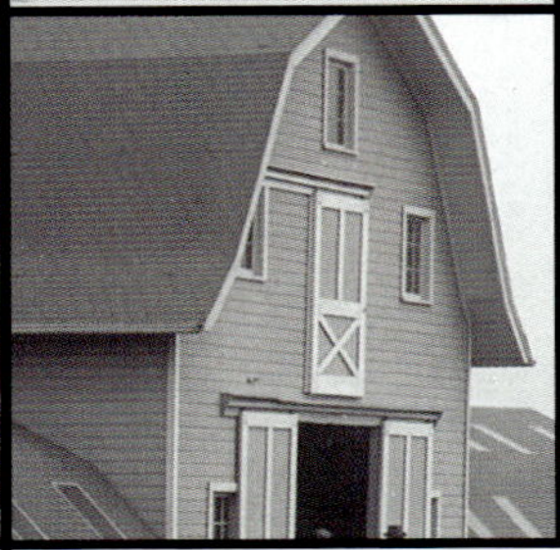

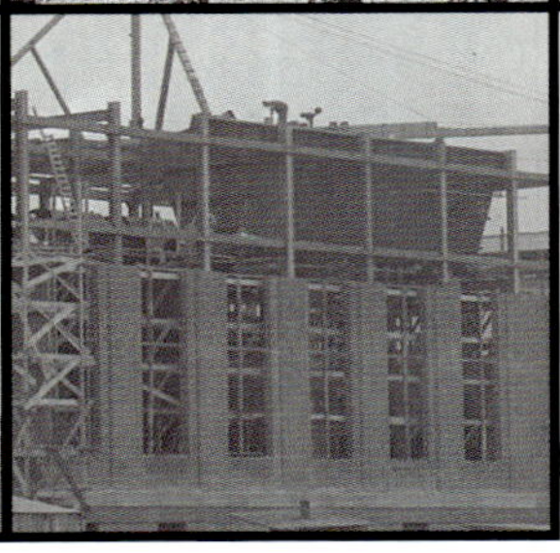

Campus map, 1924. This is the first map to include Ross-Ade Stadium. *(Campus Maps collection)*

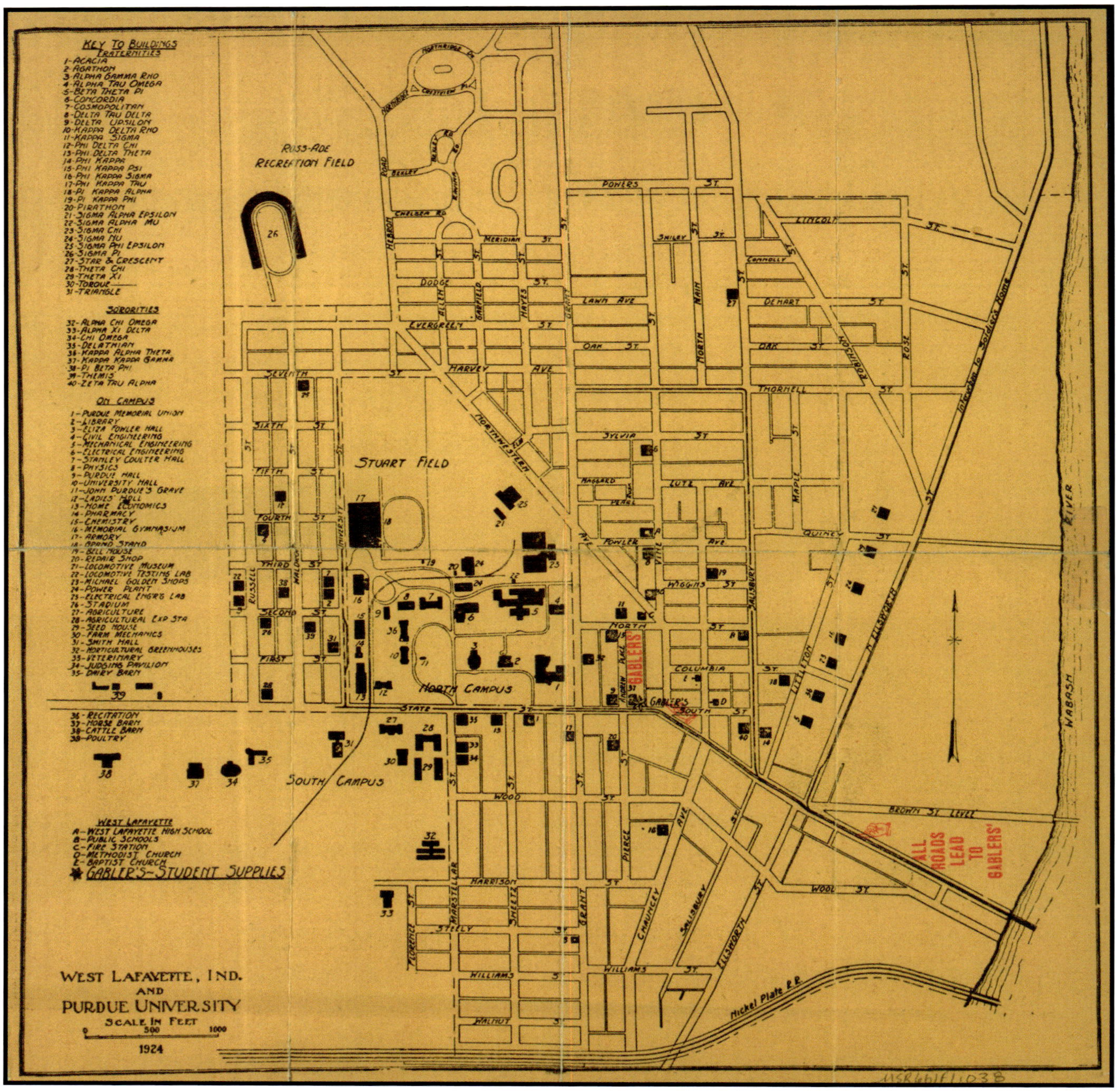

{ *Enrollment in 1920: 3,110 students*[1] }

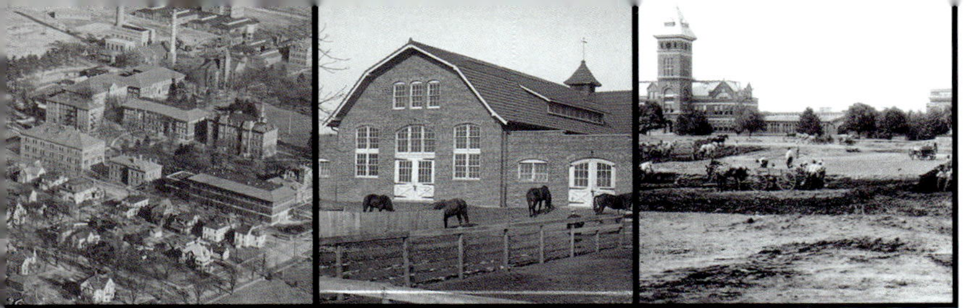

[The 1920s]

PURDUE AT 60

"Our class has been able to watch the progress of the Purdue Memorial Union and has seen the construction of the building from the beginning. . . . We feel that this will be a wonderful home for the various student activities of our beloved institution and we hope the other classes, which are yet to come, will support this worthy undertaking as our own class has done."

—*J. Meyer Holland, president, and Anna B. Cochran, secretary, class of 1925*[2]

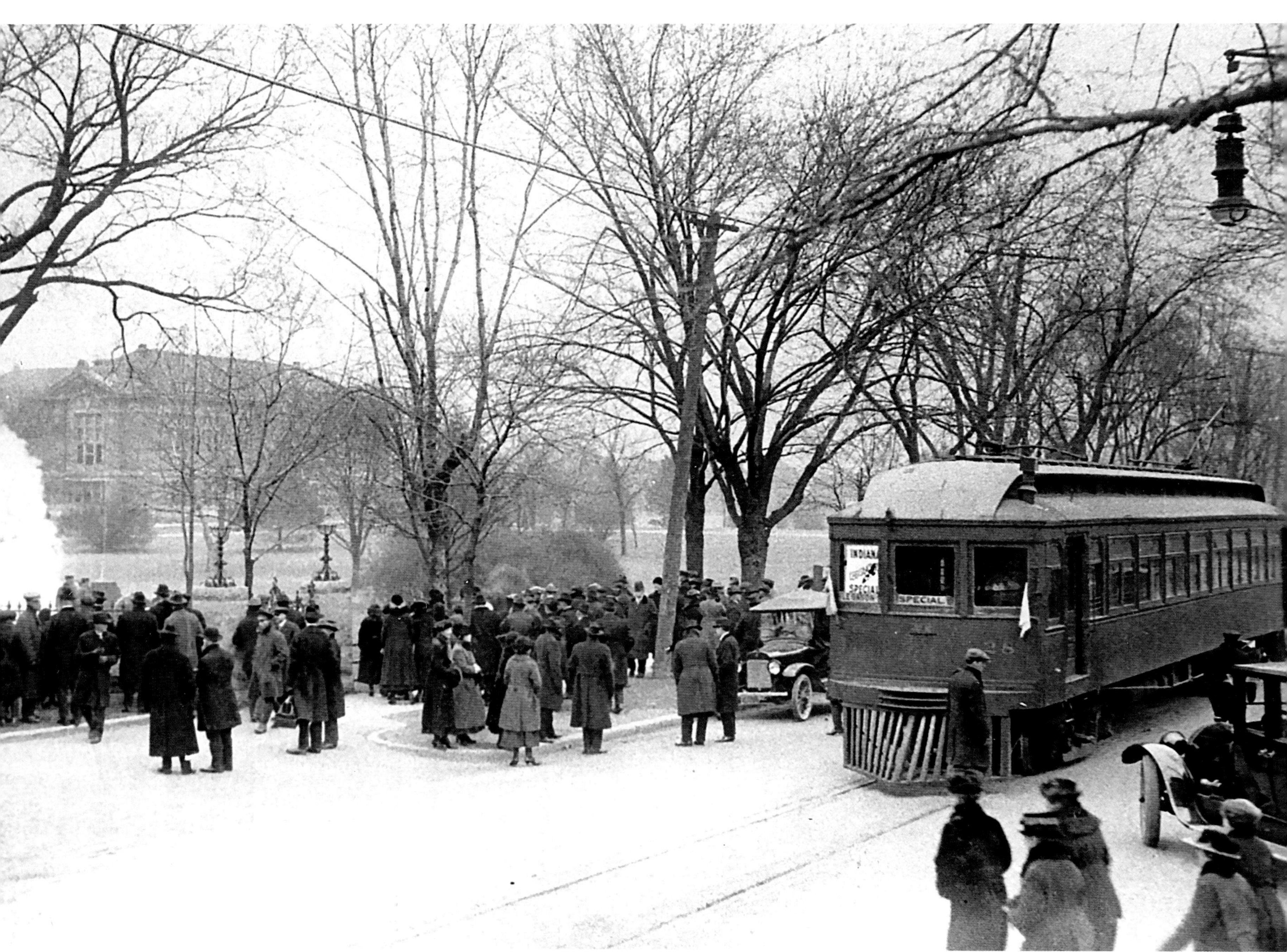

The Indiana Special trolley moves along State Street at the gates to campus. *(Purdue University Marketing and Media collection)*

Students in the 1922 graduating class were the first to wear caps and gowns, adopting a common tradition that Purdue had resisted for many years.

After World War I and the 1918 influenza outbreak, the 1920s arrived at Purdue with the promise of change and a return to stability. Students could fill their days with clubs and activities, returning to the typical lives of college students placed on hold in 1917. The university itself saw increased enrollment, growth of both old and new academic programs, new buildings, and new student activities during the decade.

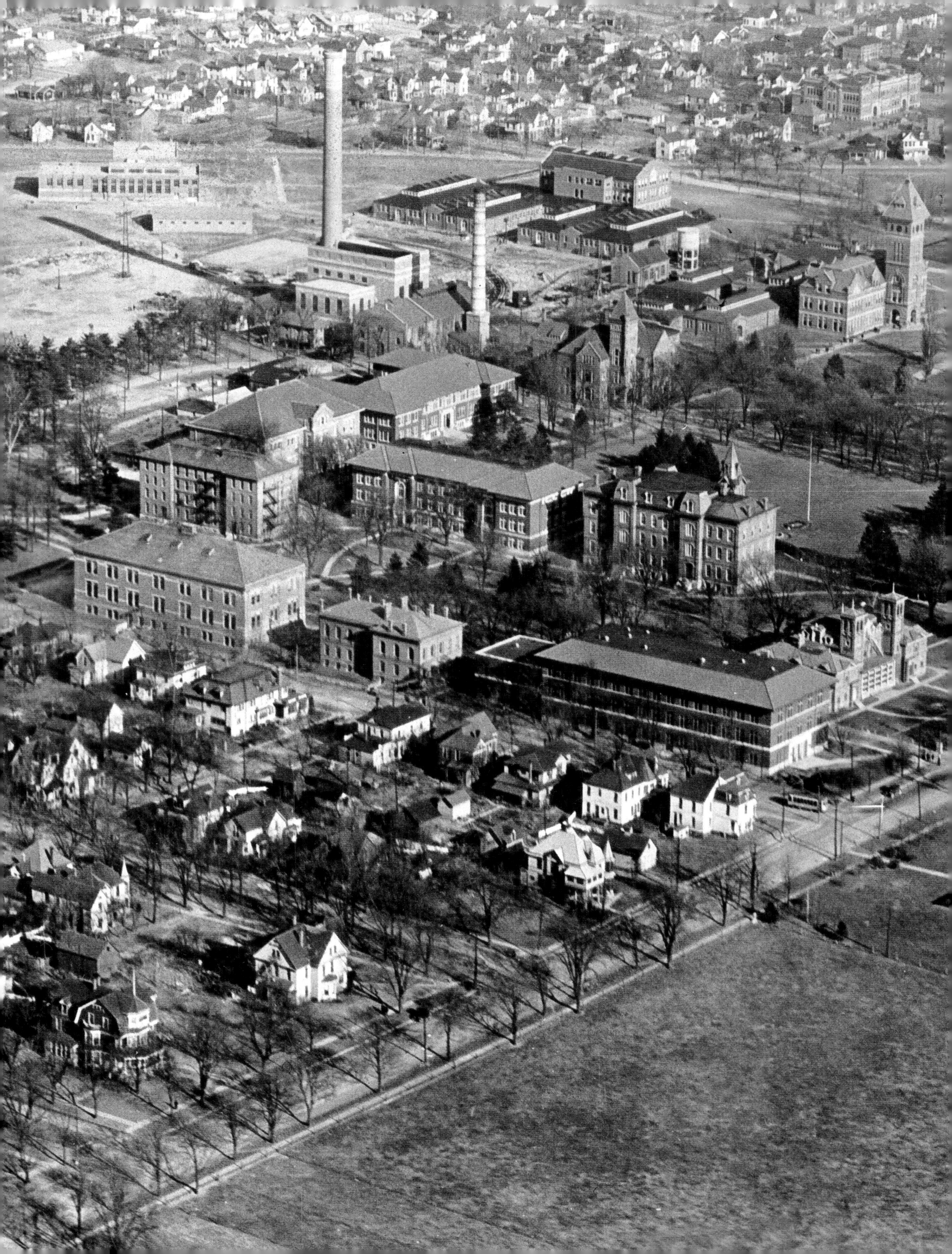

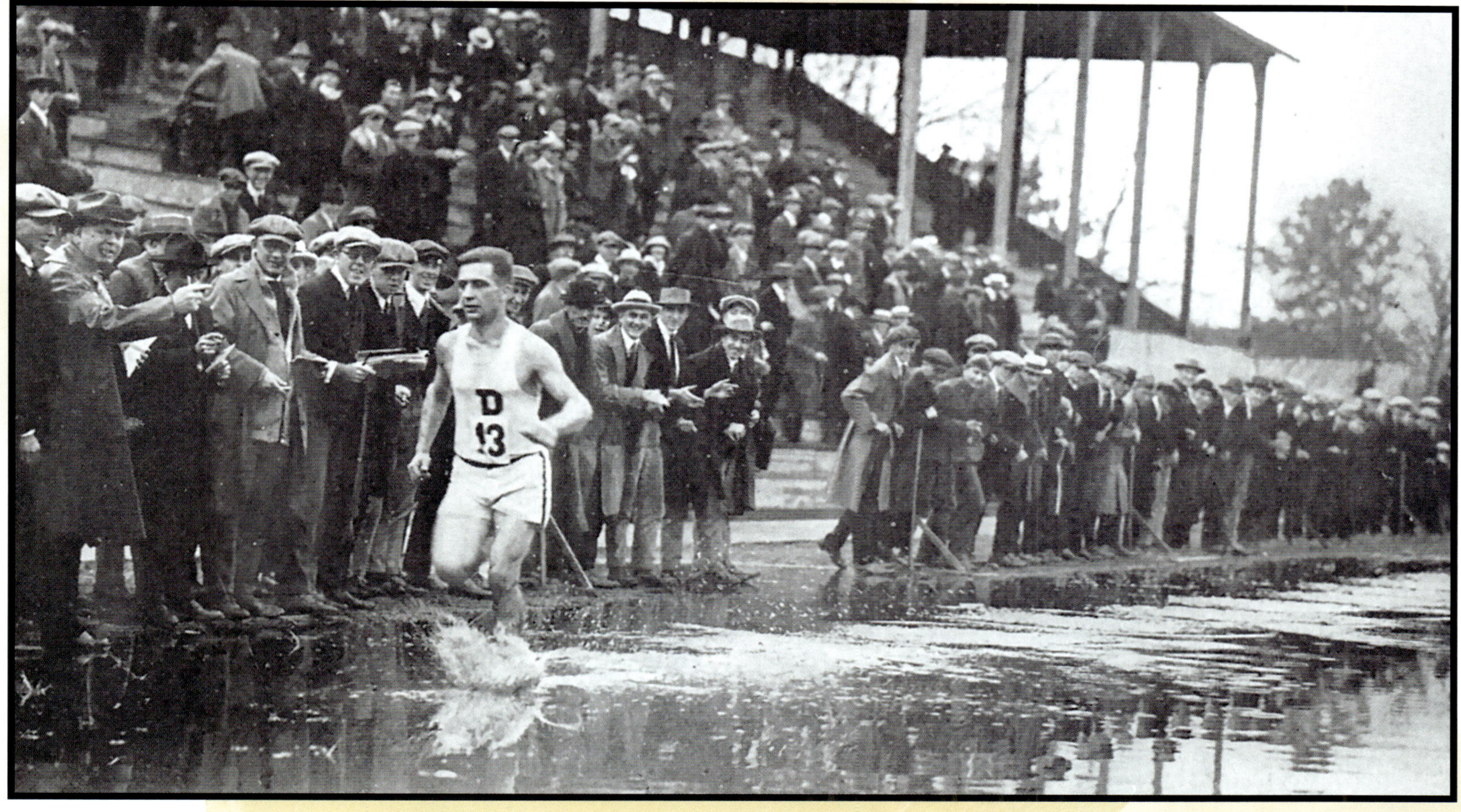

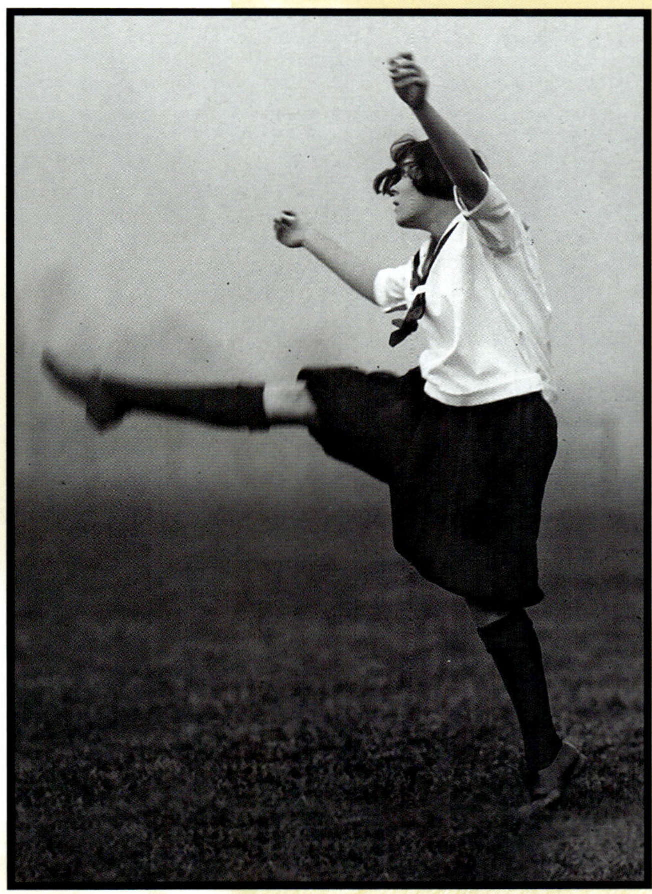

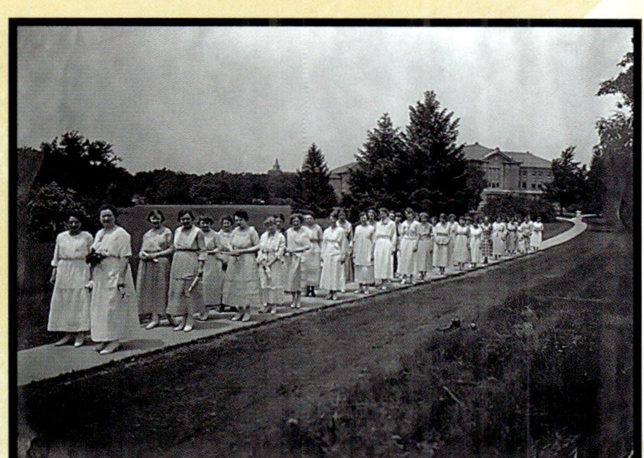

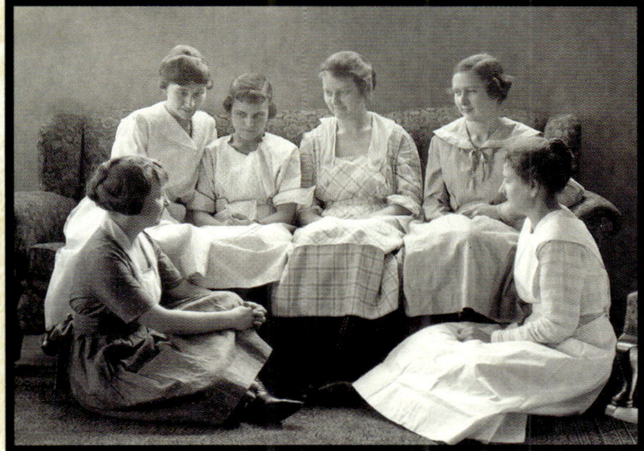

Clockwise from top:

Clifford C. Furnas, class of 1922, runs through ankle-deep water at a state track meet. In 1920, Furnas represented the United States at the Olympic Games held in Antwerp, Belgium. *(Debris yearbook)*

The School of Home Economics 1920 graduating class. *(Purdue University photographs)*

The first occupants of the Home Economics Practice House, 1920. As part of their senior coursework, the women took full responsibility for managing the house, establishing and following a budget, and entertaining guests in open house events. Responsibilities rotated every five days so that each woman had a chance to serve in each of six roles in the house: hostess, housekeeper, assistant housekeeper, cook, assistant cook, and waitress.[4] *(Purdue University photographs)*

Women's soccer team player, December 3, 1925. *(Purdue University photographs)*

Opposite Page: Aerial view of Purdue University campus, circa 1924–1927. *(Purdue University photographs)*

Top: Fictionalized "Extracts from the Diary of a Chinese Student at Purdue" from the Chinese Students' Year Book, 1927. *(Purdue University Chinese Students collection)*

Bottom: The Chinese student basketball team, 1925. *(J. C. Allen and Son Inc. photographs and negatives)*

DIARY

Extracts from the Diary of a Chinese Student in Purdue.

SEPT. 3rd. Arrived today by the Big Four from Chicago. A taxi carried me across the Wabash bridge to the West Side. What a nice little town it is! Wide streets relieve traffic congestion, and beautiful trees give quite a comfortable shade. Had a hard time in getting a room. Most landladies, some with a suspicious air, would say, "Sorry, the room's just taken." Put up at Wang's place for the night.

Sept. 4th. Got my room at last. Landlady was especially kind; she had had Chinese students with her and said, "I prefer to have Chinese students." Maybe prompt payment of rent was one of her chief preferences. Went to Purdue State Bank. Not anything like guarantee required in cashing and depositing checks. Thanks to those who established good credit.

Sept. 5th. Took lunch at the Memorial Union. Nice and cheap. That's some place they have; a barber shop, a pool and billiard room, a soda fountain, lounge rooms, card, chess and checker tables and an assembly room for dances and banquets.

Oct. 1st. Had my lunch in the College Inn. Ran to library for some reference books. Gee! the reading room was full—lots of co-eds. Some buried their heads in their books, evidently digging hard. Others whispered (loudly enough to be overheard) with each other and could not refrain from smiling all the time. Was particularly embarrassed when the fair eyes stared at me through curiosity.

Oct. 3rd. Sent Dad an account of monthly expense, thus:—Rent, $12.00; Meals, $25.00; and Miscellaneous, $10.00. A little allowance was made in the last two items for going to Mars and Luna Theatres.

Oct. 11th. To save the five-cent fare downtown I bought a second-hand Ford. Plenty of trouble with the machine but as much fun. Took quite a talk to convince Dean Fisher that the car was for convenience before he gave me the permit to drive.

Oct. 26th. Watched the ball game with Wisconsin. The town was decorated with the colors of both Universities. A big affair! Got quite excited during the game and felt tired afterwards.

Nov. 6th. Went to the Men's Gymnasium and played basketball for awhile. A shower bath followed by a dip in the swimming pool made me feel exceedingly fine.

April 27th. Drove to Black Rock with the bunch. It was about 15 miles away from the town. Facing the Wabash river and with several nice cottages on the rock, it was an ideal place for picnic. Many other spots such as Soldiers' Home, Battleground, Columbia Park, etc., are attractive; but this place furnishes the best natural scenery.

May 9th. Had some boating in the Wabash river. The paddles went down harmoniously and the boat glided gracefully through the glassy water. Those having boating experience only in the pools could never imagine what a great time I had to-day!

15

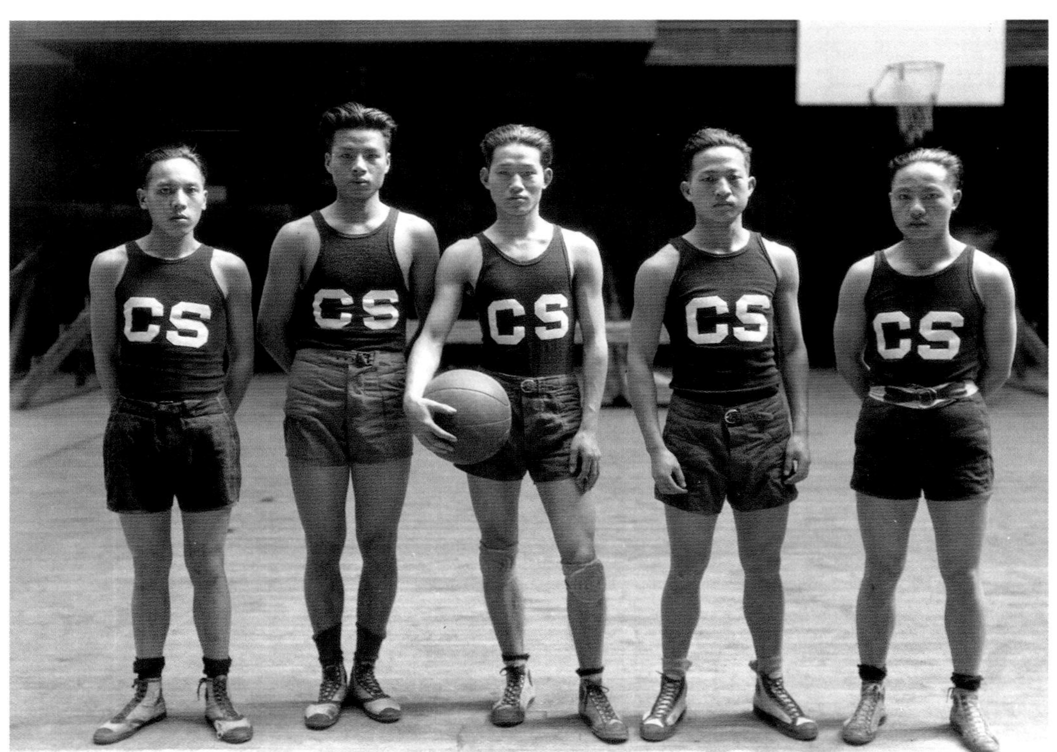

The international student population continued to grow throughout the 1920s, as did Purdue's international reputation. In 1925 an estimated fifty-two foreign students were enrolled at Purdue, with the majority (thirty-one) from China, followed by the Philippines, India, and Japan. International students were still not completely integrated into Purdue student life. Chinese students formed their own recreational athletics teams and competed in the interchurch basketball league on campus; the largely nonreligious students took pleasure in competing as "the Chinese" against such teams as the Methodists and the Presbyterians.[3]

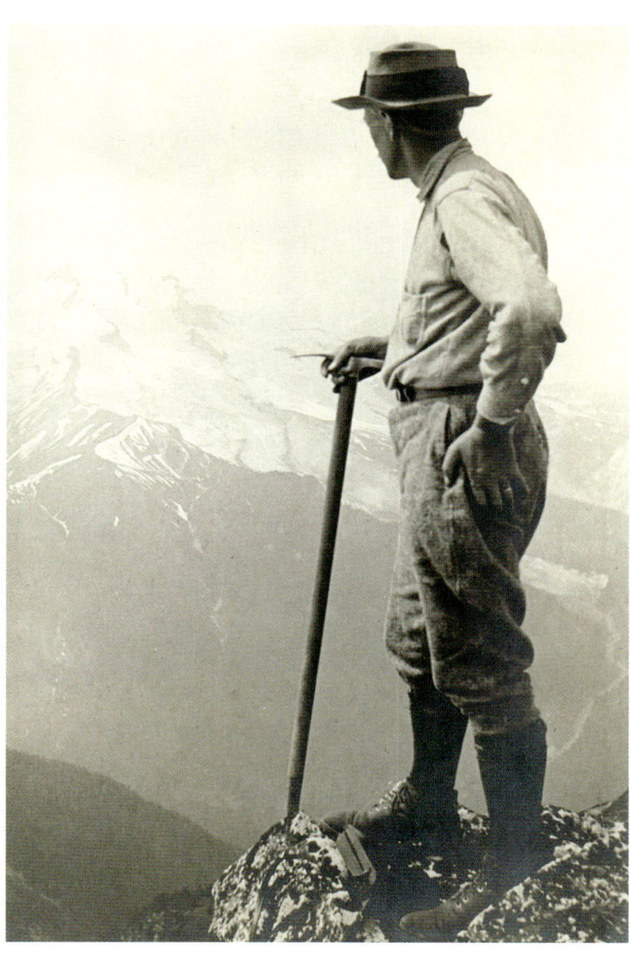

Tragedy struck Purdue in July 1921 when President Winthrop Stone died in a mountain climbing accident. The Purdue community was shocked by his unexpected death and hosted a funeral for Stone soon after his death, followed by a full memorial service on October 12. Henry Marshall, chairman of the Executive Committee of the Board of Trustees, served as interim president with the title of vice president until Edward C. Elliott was hired in the summer of 1922.

RESOLUTIONS

On the Death of Dr. Winthrop E. Stone

President, Purdue University.

WHEREAS, Death has entered our midst and has removed from our ranks our honored President, Winthrop E. Stone; and

WHEREAS, For these many years he labored for the welfare of Purdue University, which by his unfaltering devotion to duty he lifted the plane of the great educational institution of the country; and

WHEREAS, Through the years he never faltered in serving the best interests of alumni and students, many of whom were advanced by his wise guidance to positions of honor and trust; and

WHEREAS, Through the years he bound himself by strong ties of affection to those of our number who were so fortunate as to come in contact with him in a personal way; therefore be it

RESOLVED: That we, as members of the Purdue Alumni Association do deplore the loss of a leader whose wisdom and foresight have made the University what it is; and furthur be it

RESOLVED: That we, as individuals, do deplore the loss of a friend who gave in the full measure of loyal devotion, and furthur be it

RESOLVED: That we convey to the wife and other relatives of Dr. Winthrop E. Stone our profound sympathy in their bereavement; and to his official family in the University our feeling of loss in the death of a leader to whom they had consistently and constantly proved their loyalty.

Purdue Alumni Association.

By its officers:
E C DeWolfe, '96, president.
A E Kemmer, '02, vice president.
Ella Shearer, '04, secretary.
S S Cromer, '14, treasurer.

And the Advisory Council:
W G Kaylor, '05.
E C DeWolfe, '96.
O C Ross, '95.
L Murray Grant, '04.
S S Cromer, '14.
E D Jackson, '96.

8/23/21

August 15, 1921.

Left: Winthrop Stone on a mountain climbing expedition. *(Purdue University photographs)*

Right: Resolution by Purdue Alumni Association upon the death of President Stone, 1921. *(Winthrop Stone papers)*

Purdue Memorial Union

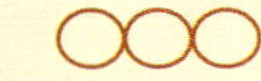

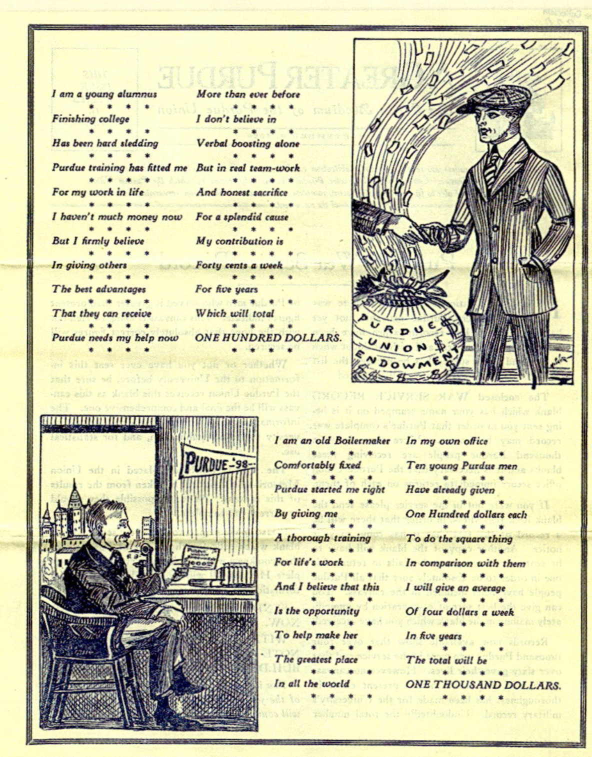

I am a young alumnus
Finishing college
Has been hard sledding
Purdue training has fitted me
For my work in life
I haven't much money now
But I firmly believe
In giving others
The best advantages
That they can receive
Purdue needs my help now
More than ever before
I don't believe in
Verbal boosting alone
But in real team-work
And honest sacrifice
For a splendid cause
My contribution is
Forty cents a week
For five years
Which will total
ONE HUNDRED DOLLARS.

I am an old Boilermaker
Comfortably fixed
Purdue started me right
By giving me
A thorough training
For life's work
And I believe that this
Is the opportunity
To help make her
The greatest place
In all the world
In my own office
Ten young Purdue men
Have already given
One Hundred dollars each
To do the square thing
In comparison with them
I will give an average
Of four dollars a week
In five years
The total will be
ONE THOUSAND DOLLARS.

Perhaps the biggest and most lasting change to appear on campus during the 1920s was the construction of the Purdue Memorial Union. The Union was first proposed during the early 1910s, but efforts were postponed due to World War I. After the war, the students sought a new building to serve not only as a center of campus activity but also a tribute to all those who had served during the war. Students and alumni spent months raising funds and implored their classmates to contribute to the Union fund with large signs on campus. Enough funds were gathered to begin construction in 1922, and a groundbreaking ceremony took place during Gala Week in June. Alumnus David Ross, at that time a university trustee, laid the cornerstone for the building on November 25, 1922, in a ceremony attended by Indiana's governor, Warren T. McCray. Fundraising continued throughout the building's construction, which was occasionally delayed due to funding issues.

The building officially opened on September 9, 1924, quickly becoming the center of student activity on campus. It has been expanded and renovated multiple times.

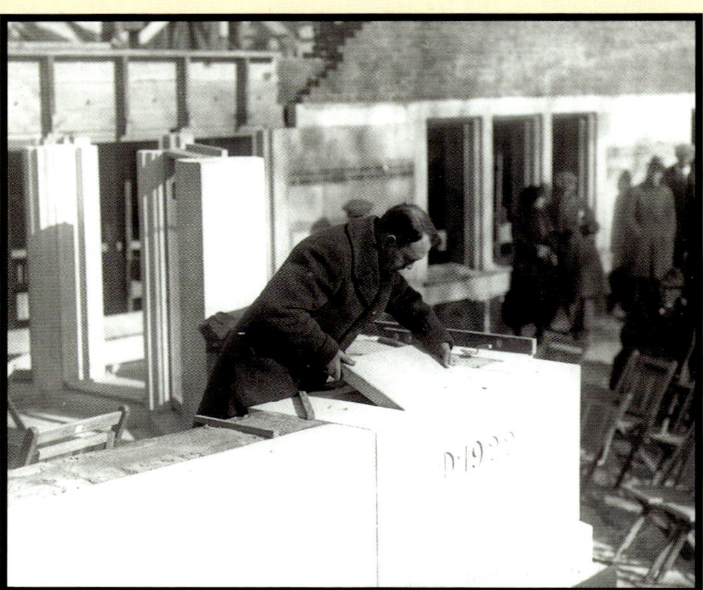

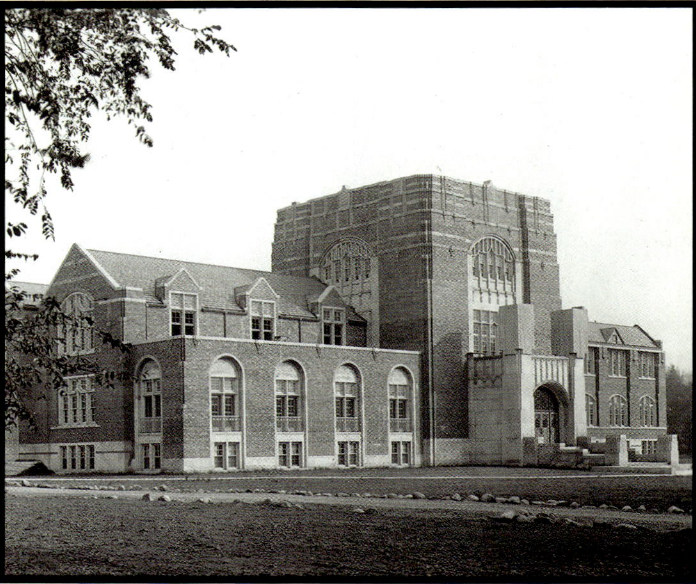

Top: Poems and cartoons encouraging donations to the Purdue Memorial Union Fund from students and alumni. *(Purdue Memorial Union records)*

Above: David Ross lays the cornerstone for the Purdue Memorial Union, November 1922. *(Purdue University photographs)*

Purdue Memorial Union near the end of its initial construction. *(Purdue University photographs)*

Pappy's

The Sweet Shop has been a favorite meeting spot for more than ninety years. If the walls could talk, they might tell tales of romance, struggles, friendships made, and futures forged. The first true Sweet Shop appeared in its own separate space in the Purdue Memorial Union in 1927 and expanded in 1957. When it first opened, Purdue students often referred to it as the "Sweet Shop Lab" and scheduled time in the "lab" for the social side of their education.

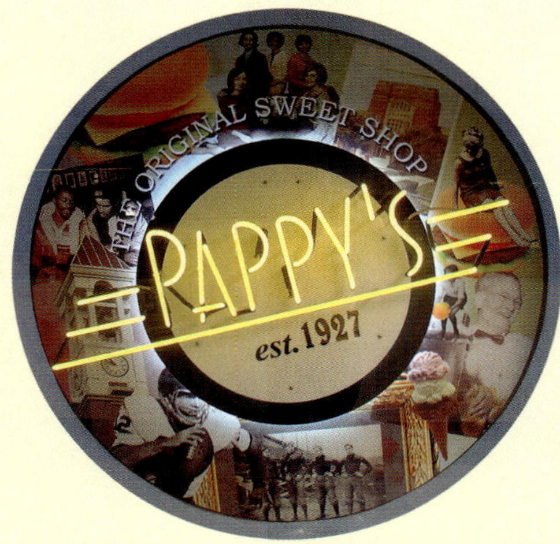

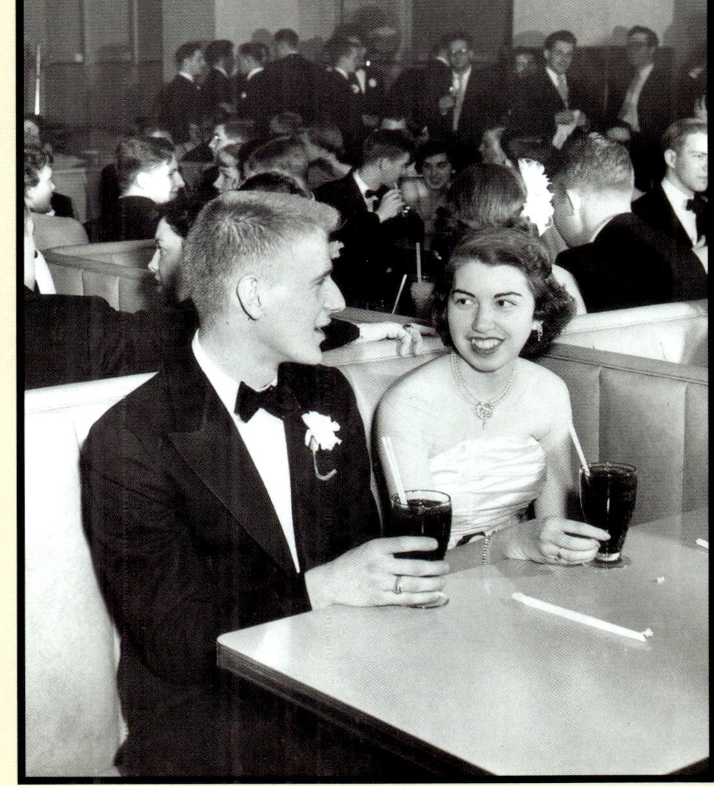

Frank "Pappy" Fox started working in the Sweet Shop in the 1920s and was a beloved fixture there for over thirty years. Per a Memorial Union brochure, "Frank served up sound advice and sympathy for student problems with his coffee, sandwiches, ice cream, and sodas. In return, the students showed great pride and respect for the Sweet Shop and quickly added a 'Sweet Shop Lab' to their schedules."[5]

The early Sweet Shop's favorite and standard snack was a ham salad sandwich. Fox planned the original menu for the Sweet Shop and developed his own chocolate sauce and blend of coffee.

After renovations, the Sweet Shop became known as Pappy's Sweet Shop to honor Fox. Pappy's celebrated its ninetieth anniversary in 2017.

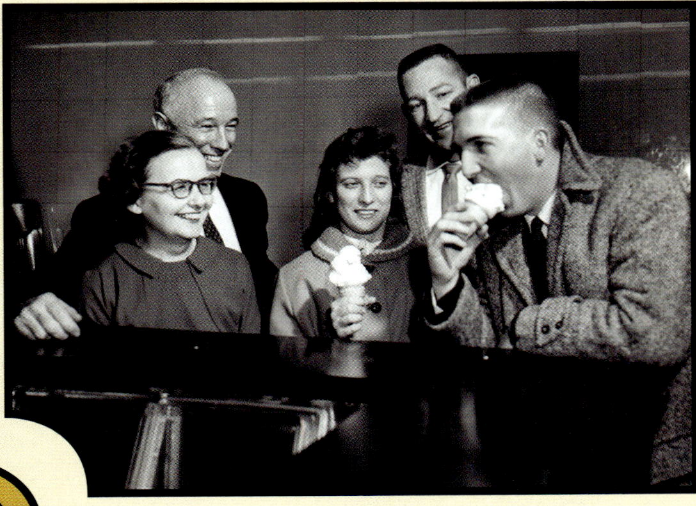

Top left: A colorful neon sign welcomes visitors to Pappy's. Photo by Teresa M. Brown. *(Purdue University Libraries records)*

Top right: Students in the Sweet Shop during a dance, 1950s. *(Purdue University photographs)*

Left: Students enjoying ice cream at the Sweet Shop, circa 1960. *(Purdue University photographs)*

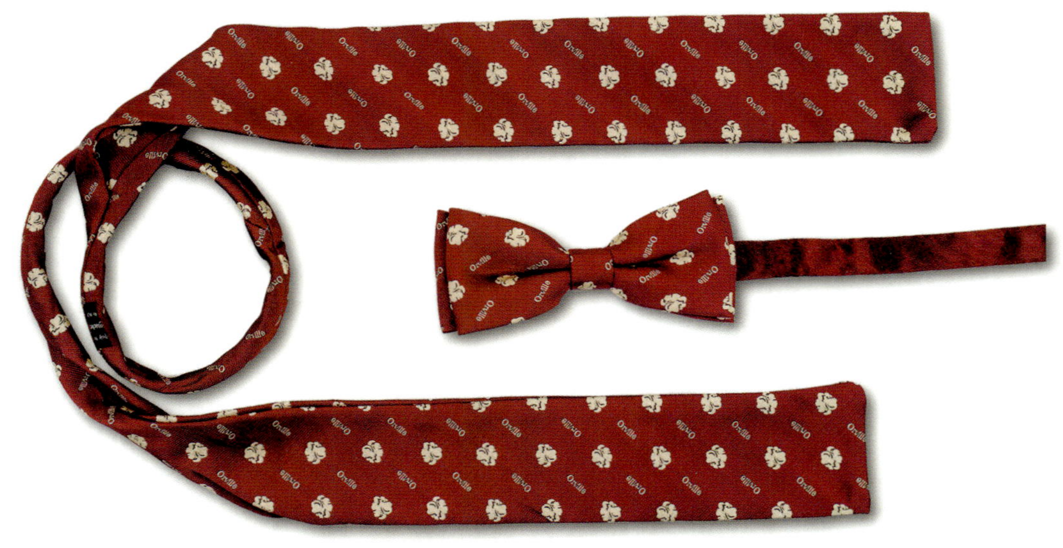

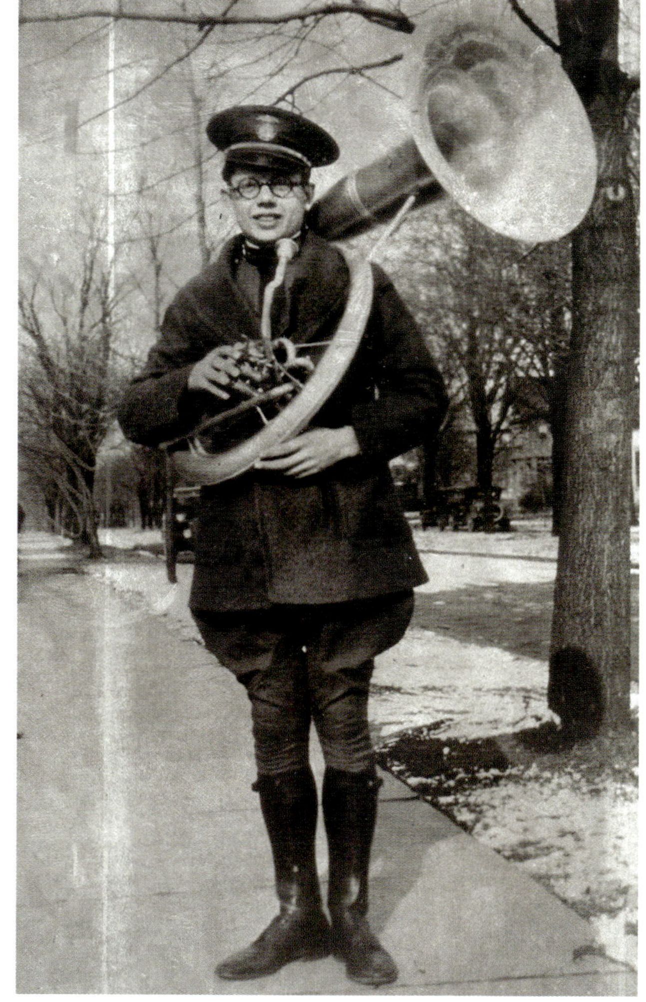

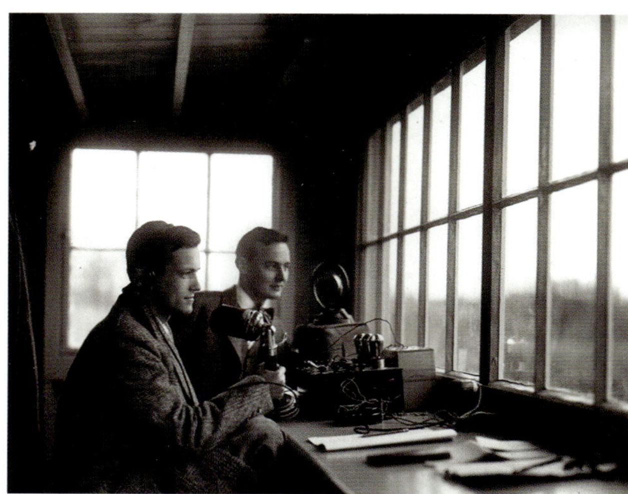

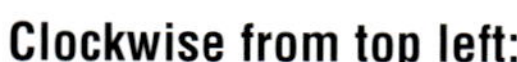

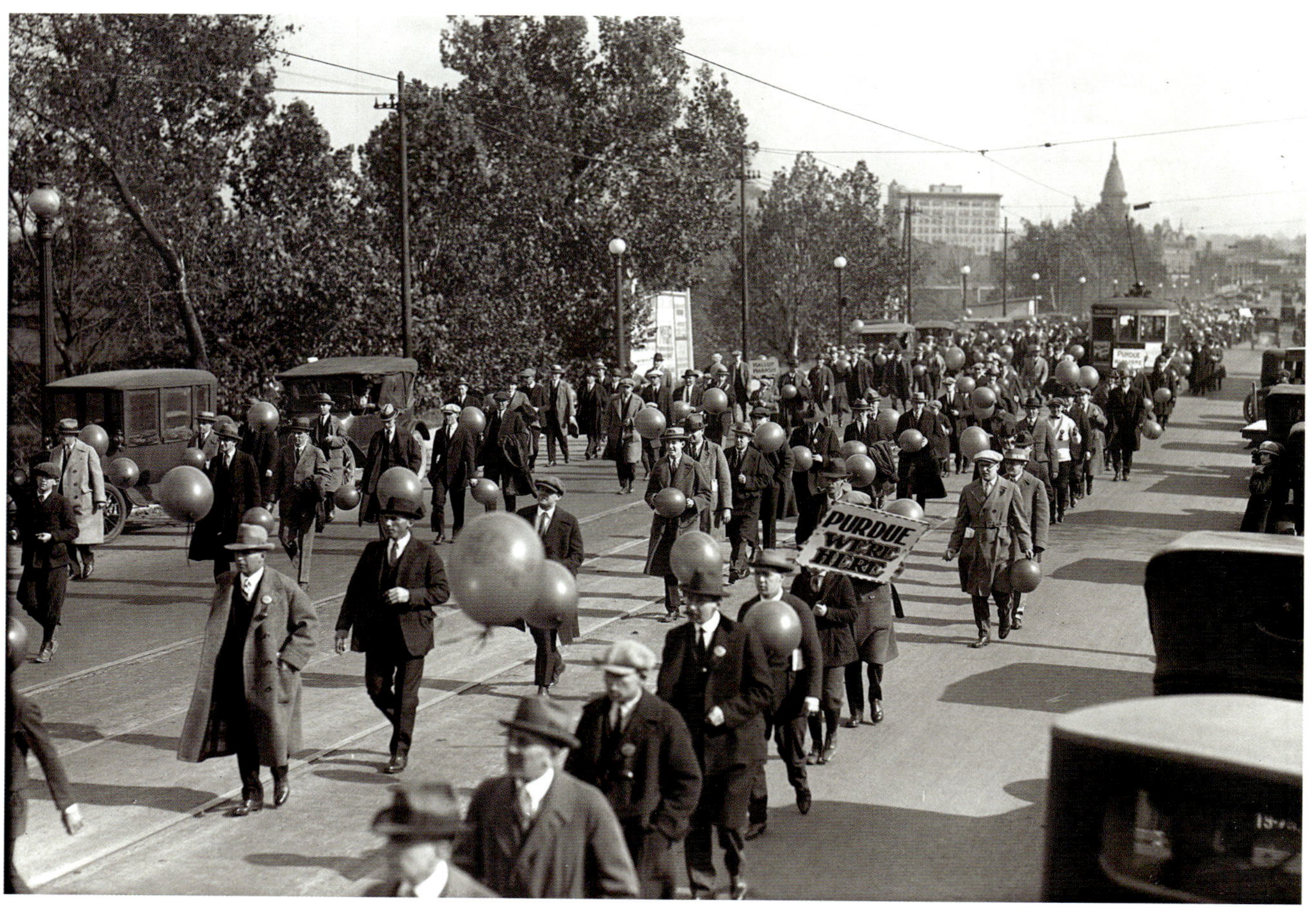

Clockwise from top left:

Orville Redenbacher's bow tie with popcorn embroidery. *(Orville Redenbacher papers)*

Orville Redenbacher, 1928. *(Purdue University photographs)*

Lafayette Day crowds marching across the river from Lafayette carrying gold-colored balloons emblazoned with the words "Let's Go, Purdue!" in 1923. *(J. C. Allen and Son Inc. photographs and negatives)*

The press box at Ross-Ade Stadium, 1927. *(Purdue University photographs)*

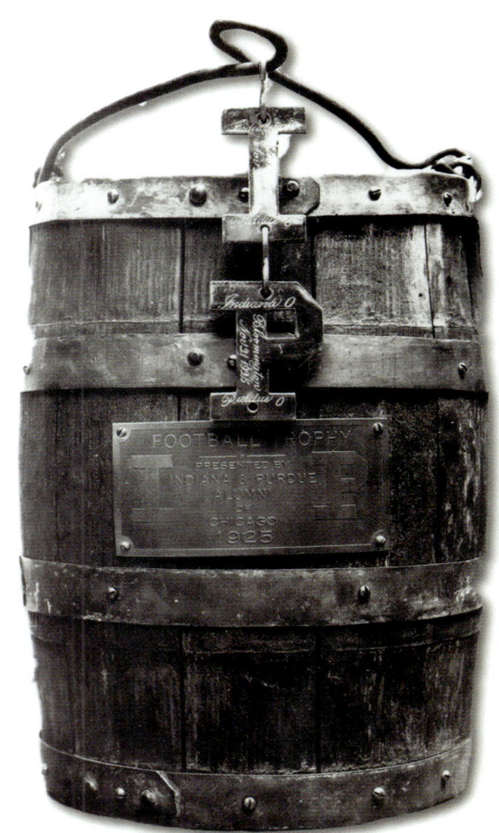

The 1920s was a revolutionary decade for Purdue athletics. On November 22, 1924, Purdue's Homecoming game against Indiana was the first to be held in the new Ross-Ade Stadium. The 1925 football game between rivals Purdue and Indiana introduced what became one of the oldest continued prizes in college football, the Old Oaken Bucket. The teams had played an annual rivalry game since 1891, but the introduction of the Bucket, a trophy that represented the shared agricultural heritage of both Indiana schools, sparked even greater interest in the annual game. The Old Oaken Bucket became an emblem for the Purdue football team even outside the annual game against Indiana. Its image appeared on promotional materials for Purdue Athletics and on tickets to football games.

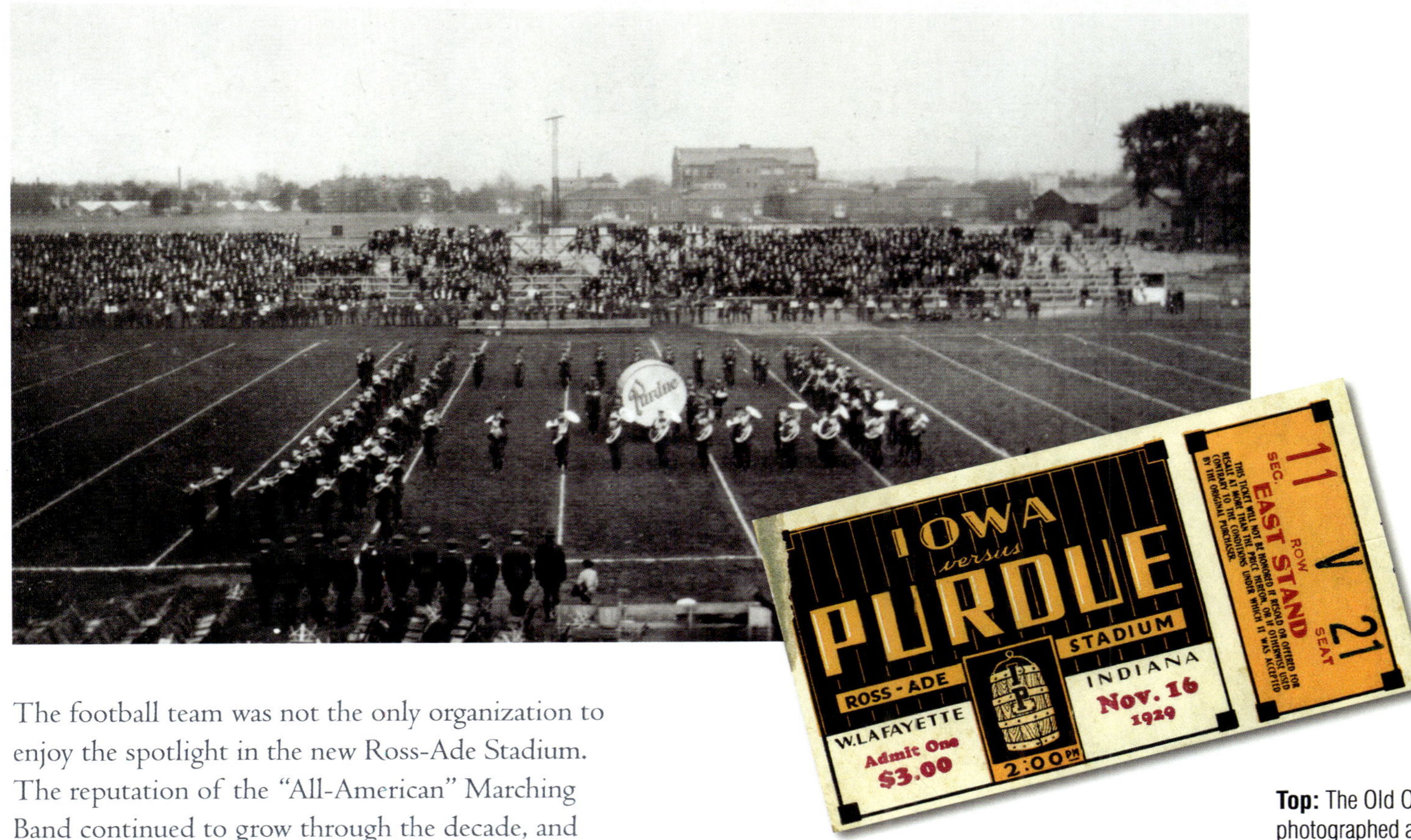

The football team was not the only organization to enjoy the spotlight in the new Ross-Ade Stadium. The reputation of the "All-American" Marching Band continued to grow through the decade, and the Class of 1928 included one of its most famous alumni: Orville Redenbacher.

Not to be outshone by its gridiron counterpart, Purdue basketball also excelled. Led by coach Ward "Piggy" Lambert, Purdue won more games than any other team in the Big Ten Conference in the 1920s. The Boilermakers ended the season on top of the conference in 1921, 1922, 1926, and 1928.

Top: The Old Oaken Bucket photographed at the time of its introduction in 1925. *(Purdue University photographs)*

Above right: Iowa vs. Purdue football ticket featuring the Old Oaken Bucket. *(Purdue University Athletic Collection)*

Above left: The "All-American" Marching Band in Block P formation on Stuart Field. *(James R. Eaton photo album)*

Celebrating Purdue's Semicentennial

The university chose to celebrate its fiftieth anniversary in 1924 since the first classes at Purdue were taught in 1874. Purdue spent months planning every aspect of the semicentennial celebration, as ten different committees of administrators and faculty members planned everything from invitations to music. Approximately 750 alumni returned to campus for three full days of events, including class reunions, picnics, banquets, and a football game against Indiana. Decorations covered campus, West Lafayette, and even downtown Lafayette, where banners hung across streets, and storefronts featured decorations celebrating the milestone.[6]

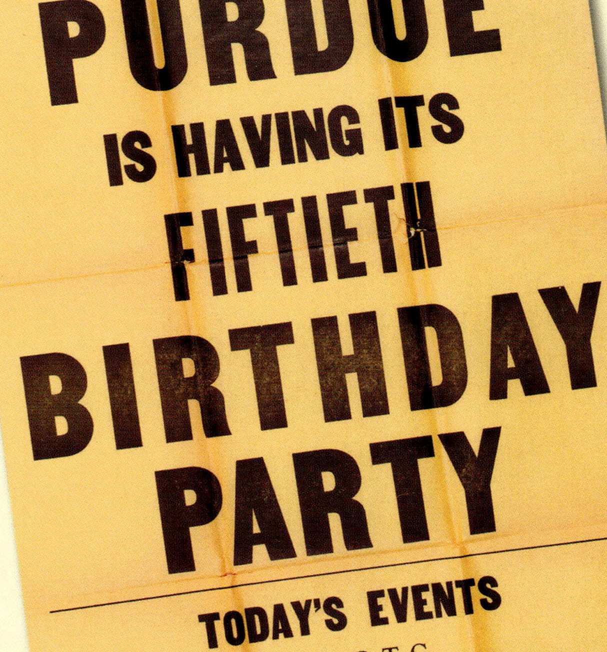

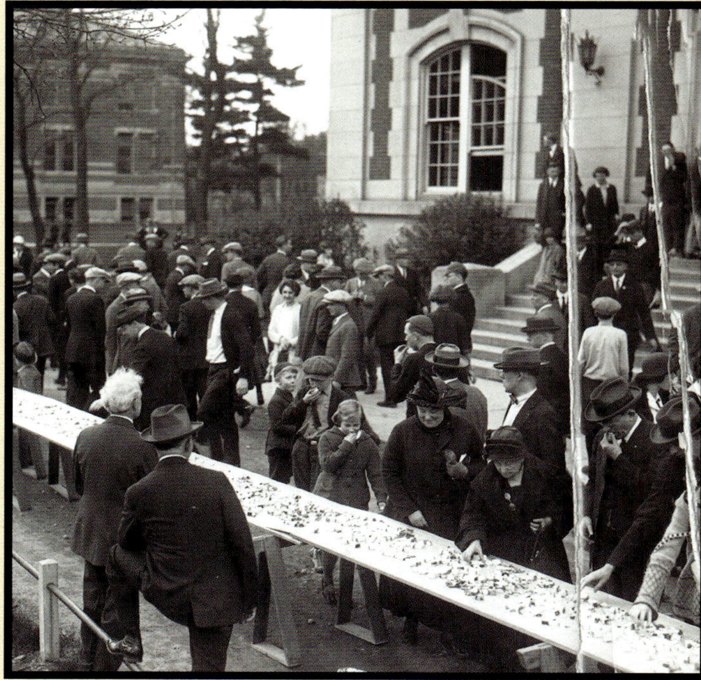

Above: Semicentennial event poster: "Purdue is Having Its Fiftieth Birthday Party." *(Purdue University Semi-Centennial collection)*

Left: Crowds enjoy the semicentennial birthday cake outside Memorial Gymnasium. *(Purdue University photographs)*

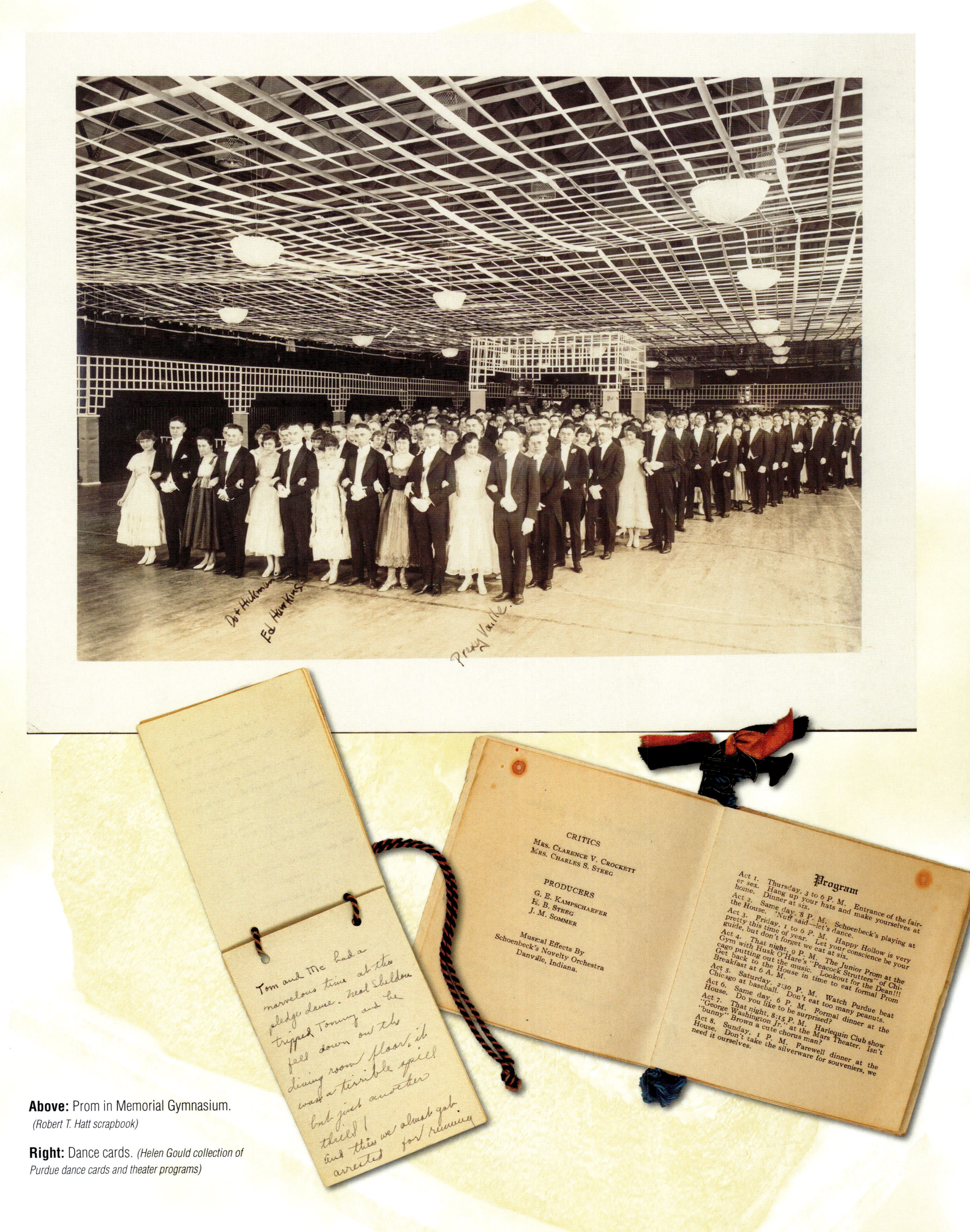

Above: Prom in Memorial Gymnasium. *(Robert T. Hatt scrapbook)*

Right: Dance cards. *(Helen Gould collection of Purdue dance cards and theater programs)*

Right: The Electrical Engineering Building with WBAA broadcast towers on the roof. *(Purdue University photographs)*

Bottom: Architectural rendering of Cary Quadrangle by architect Walter Scholer. *(Purdue University Architect records)*

Franklin Levering Cary Memorial Hall, the first building of a planned residential complex to house male students, opened in 1928. Frank and Jessie Levering Cary of Lafayette donated $50,000 to build the dormitory in memory of their son, Franklin Levering Cary, who died suddenly of appendicitis shortly before his anticipated college enrollment date in 1912. Cary, later known as Cary Quadrangle, became the first men's residence building on campus since the Men's Dormitory was renovated into classroom space in 1902. Purdue paid tribute to dormitories past by inviting former members of Purdue Hall's "Order of Dorm Devils" to the cornerstone-laying ceremony on November 5, 1927.[7]

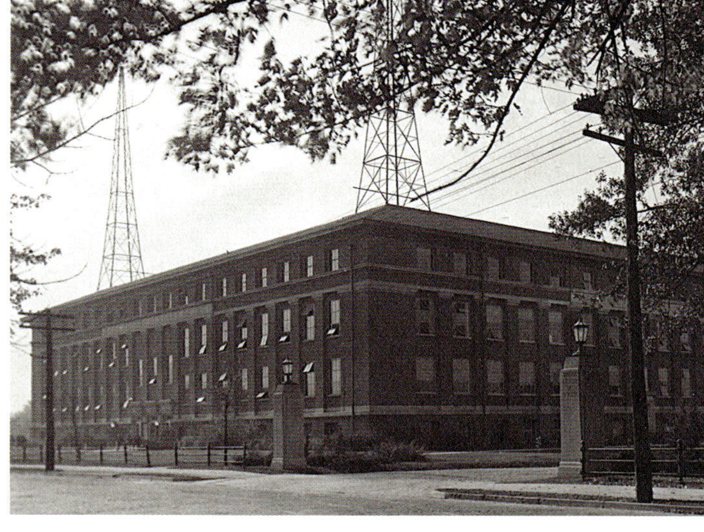

Purdue gained its voice on April 4, 1922, when radio station WBAA received its broadcast license. WBAA, which replaced the amateur station 9YB, was the first radio station licensed in the state of Indiana.[8] The student-run station was based in the School of Electrical Engineering. Its first broadcast was an Arbor Day message from the secretary of agriculture simultaneously broadcast by radio stations across the country. Regular programming included lectures, news, and music. In 1929 WBAA ceased operations for a time after a March 14 fire destroyed the entire studio and its equipment in the Electrical Engineering Building. But the station was rebuilt with "modern equipment in a new and improved broadcasting unit" and was back on the air within a year.[9]

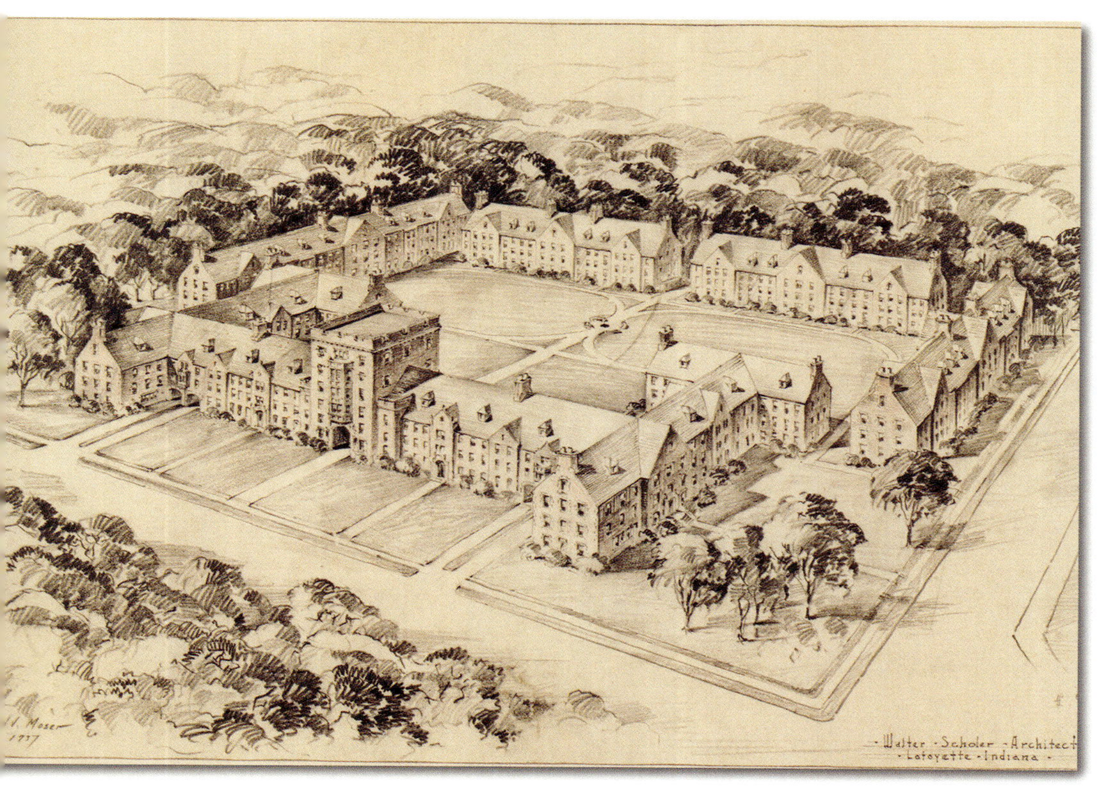

From 1914 to 1960 Purdue held an annual summer surveying camp to allow civil engineering students a chance to gain hands-on experience without impacting their course load during the traditional academic year. In its early years, the camp was held in multiple locations across Indiana and Michigan, including a stint from 1924 to 1928 at McCormick's Creek State Park. In 1926, David Ross purchased a plot of land southwest of West Lafayette along the Wabash River and donated it to the university to establish a permanent home for the camp. Students first used the land during the 1928 camp session, when their primary activities included construction of buildings, roads, and a septic system to form the permanent infrastructure.

Left: Students complete surveying assignments during civil engineering camp at McCormick's Creek State Park, 1925. *(Purdue University photographs)*

Right: Girls Rifle Team practices in University Armory, 1925. *(Purdue University photographs)*

Bottom: Ross Civil Engineering Camp participants, 1941. The student in the back row, far left, is wearing one of the earliest shirts featuring Purdue Pete. *(Purdue University photographs)*

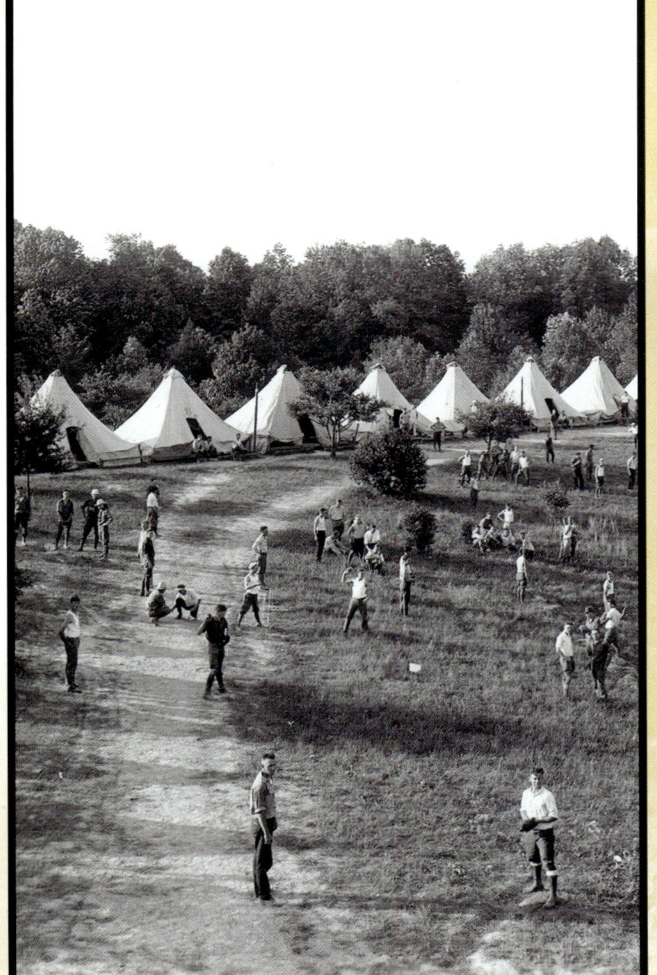

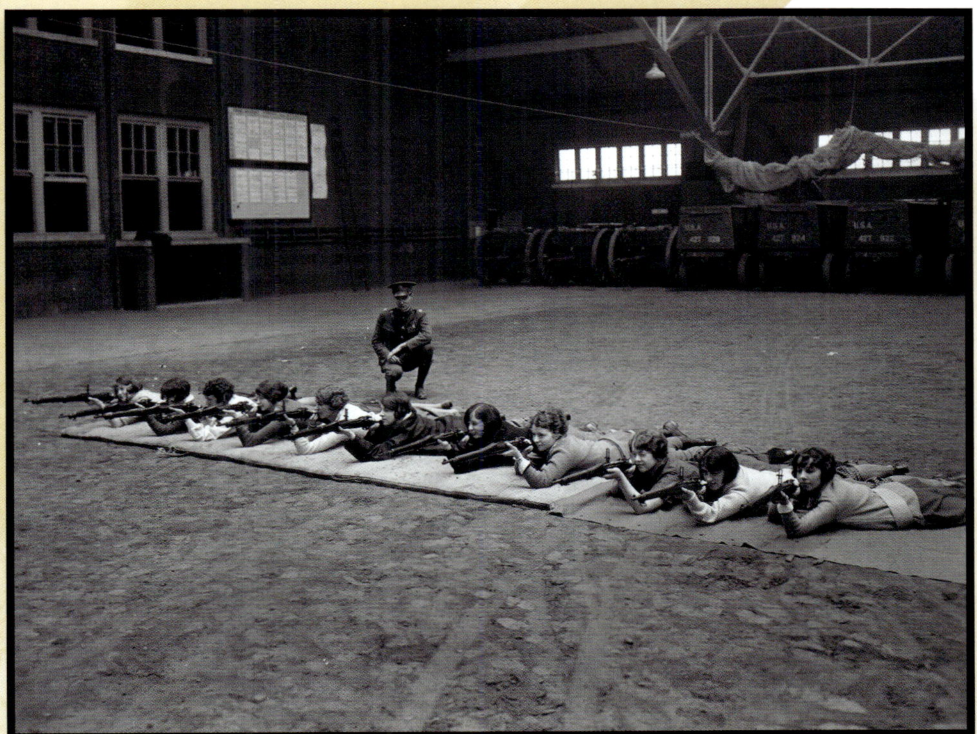

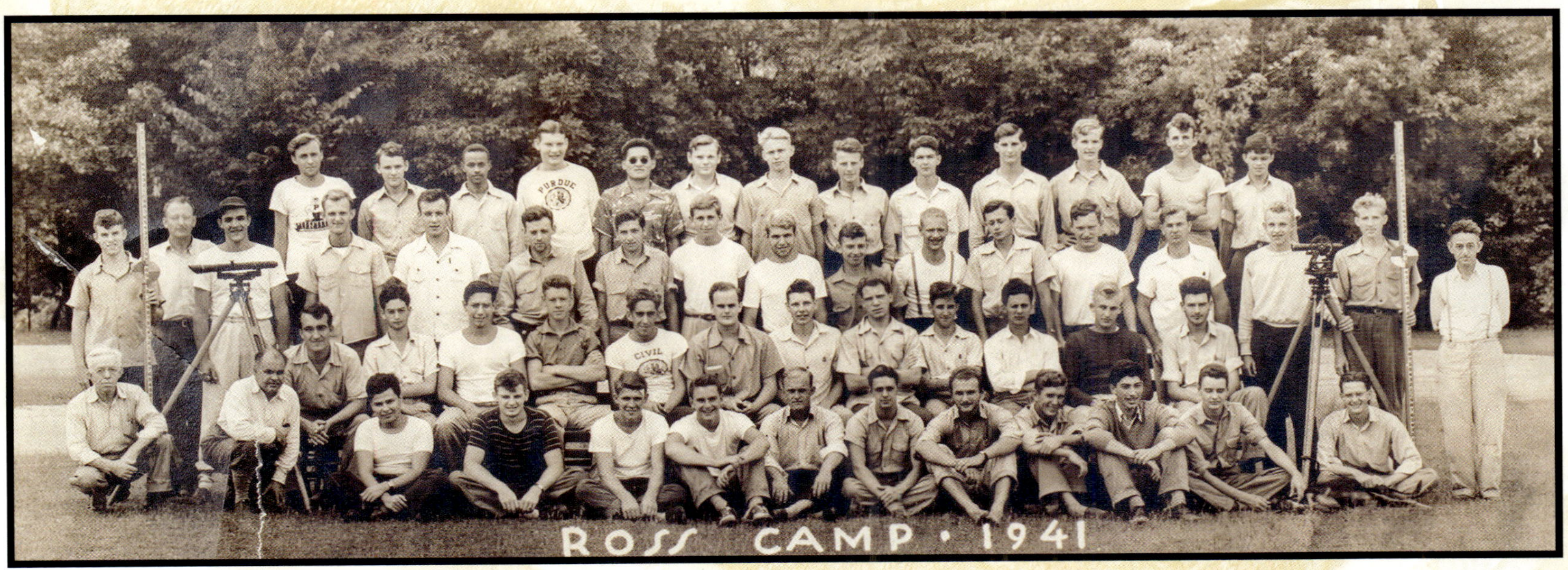

Do's and Don'ts for Freshmen

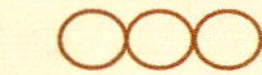

1. All Freshmen when on the Campus shall wear their regulation green caps or toques as the weather permits. This type of head gear was adopted by the Freshman Class nine years ago, and has been followed by each Freshman Class since.
2. Freshmen shall occupy the balcony in Fowler Hall during all general student assemblies.
3. During Class football games and 'Varsity practice, Freshmen shall occupy the east bleachers.
4. Freshmen shall upon meeting them, salute the President of the University and the Commandant.
5. Freshmen shall not wear mustaches.
6. Smoking is prohibited on the Campus.
7. Follow the walks on the Campus.
8. Do not ride motorcycles on the Campus walks.
9. Do not wear high school insignia.
10. Learn the 'Varsity yells and University songs.
11. Try out for the teams.
12. When in Purdue do as the Boilermakers do.
13. Failure of any student to show proper respect for the good order, morality, integrity, and the rights of others, will be regarded as reason for exclusion from the University.[10]

22 PURDUE UNIVERSITY

TO THE 1924 CLASS

On enrolling in Purdue you become members of the '24 Class and your first duty is to maintain that membership in good standing by making a passing grade in each subject for four years. Try out for the Freshman 'Varsity Teams and if you fail to make them do not stop but come out and work all the harder for a position on your Class Team. Purchase a Coupon Book which admits you to all the home games and be at every game backing the Team till the final whistle.

When the time comes to select your Class Officers, do so with care and before casting your final ballot be sure that you know something about the man for whom you are voting. Too often has it been true that a man renown for his prowess as an athlete has been elected president of his class only to fail in keeping up his work in the University. After electing your officers back them up and when your President calls a class meeting, do not think that it will get along all right without you, but be there. It is your class and it is up to you individually to make it the best class that has ever gone through Purdue.

DO'S AND DON'TS FOR FRESHMEN

1. All Freshmen when on the Campus shall wear their regulation green caps or toques as the weather permits. This type of head gear was adopted by the Freshman Class nine years ago and has been followed by each Freshman Class since.

2. Freshmen shall occupy the balcony in Fowler Hall during all general student assemblies.

3. During Class football games and 'Varsity practice, Freshmen shall occupy the east bleachers.

HANDBOOK 23

4. Freshmen shall upon meeting them, salute the President of the University and the Commandant.

5. Freshmen shall not wear mustaches.

6. Smoking is prohibited on the Campus.

7. Follow the walks on the Campus.

8. Do not ride motorcycles on the Campus walks.

9. Do not wear high school insignia.

10. Learn the 'Varsity yells and University songs.

11. Try out for the teams.

12. When in Purdue do as the Boilermakers do.

13. Failure of any student to show proper respect for good order, morality, integrity, and the rights of others, will be regarded as reason for exclusion from the University.

CLASS DISTINCTION

All except the Sophomore class have a distinguishing custom of dress. The Freshmen, nine years ago, adopted the green skull cap as their emblem, with the green toque for winter. Colored buttons indicate the school of the wearer as follows: Agriculture—orange, Civil—red, Mechanical—blue, Electrical—white, Science—black, Chemistry—purple, Pharmacy—brown. The Juniors adopt a class hat bearing their colors, and wear it during the last two years of their course, and the Seniors wear corduroys.

Each class organizes itself into a unit body and elects a President, Vice-President, Secretary, Treasurer, Historian, Sergeant-at-Arms, Yell Leader, and representatives to the Student Council and the Athletic Association

Excerpt from *Purdue University Hand-Book, 1920–1921.* *(Purdue University Hand-Book)*

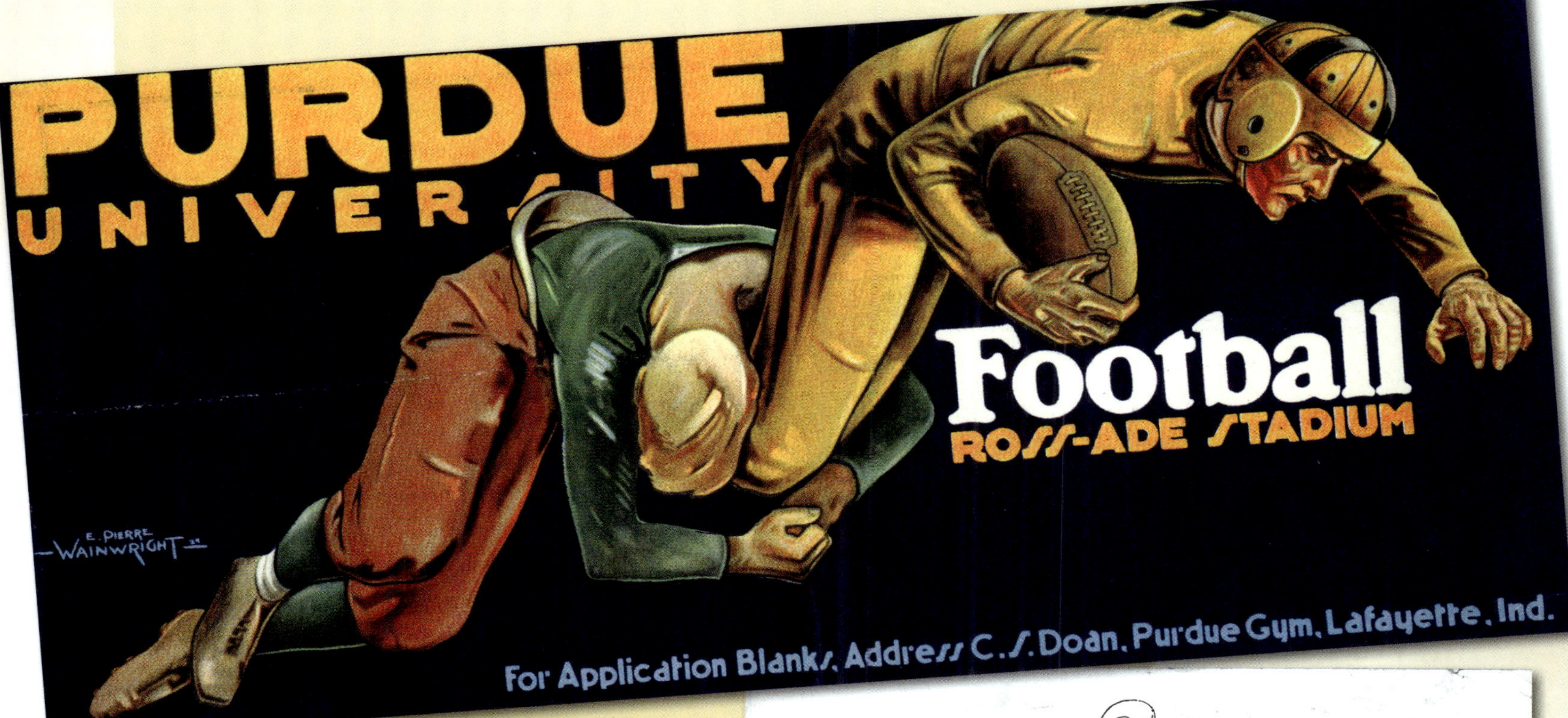

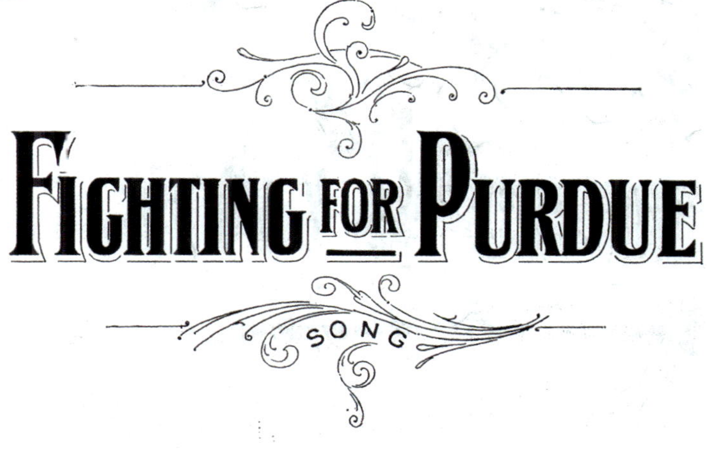

Above: 1929 Purdue University football booklet. Illustration by E. Pierre Wainwright. *(H. C. Dimmich papers)*

Right: Sheet music for George Ade's "Fighting for Purdue," meant to become a fight song for Purdue Athletics but never widely adopted. *(Purdue University Musical Organizations records)*

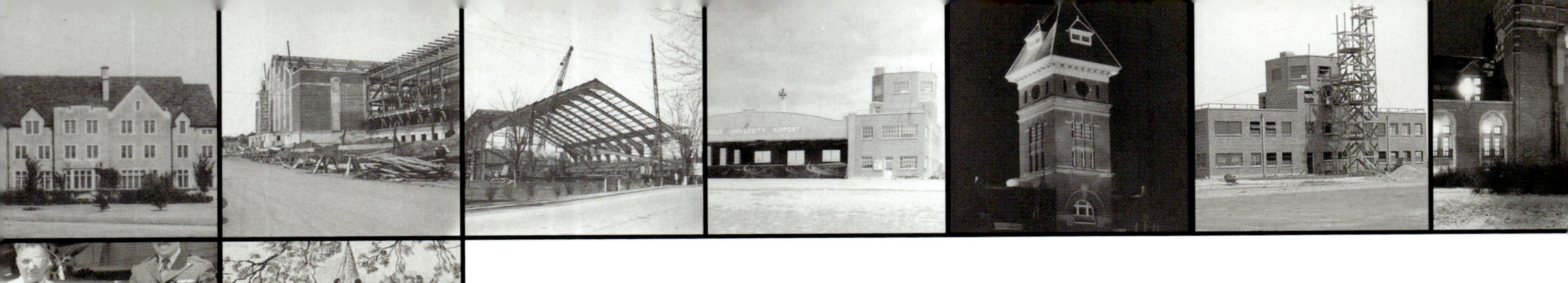

Campus map, January 1930. *(Campus Maps collection)*

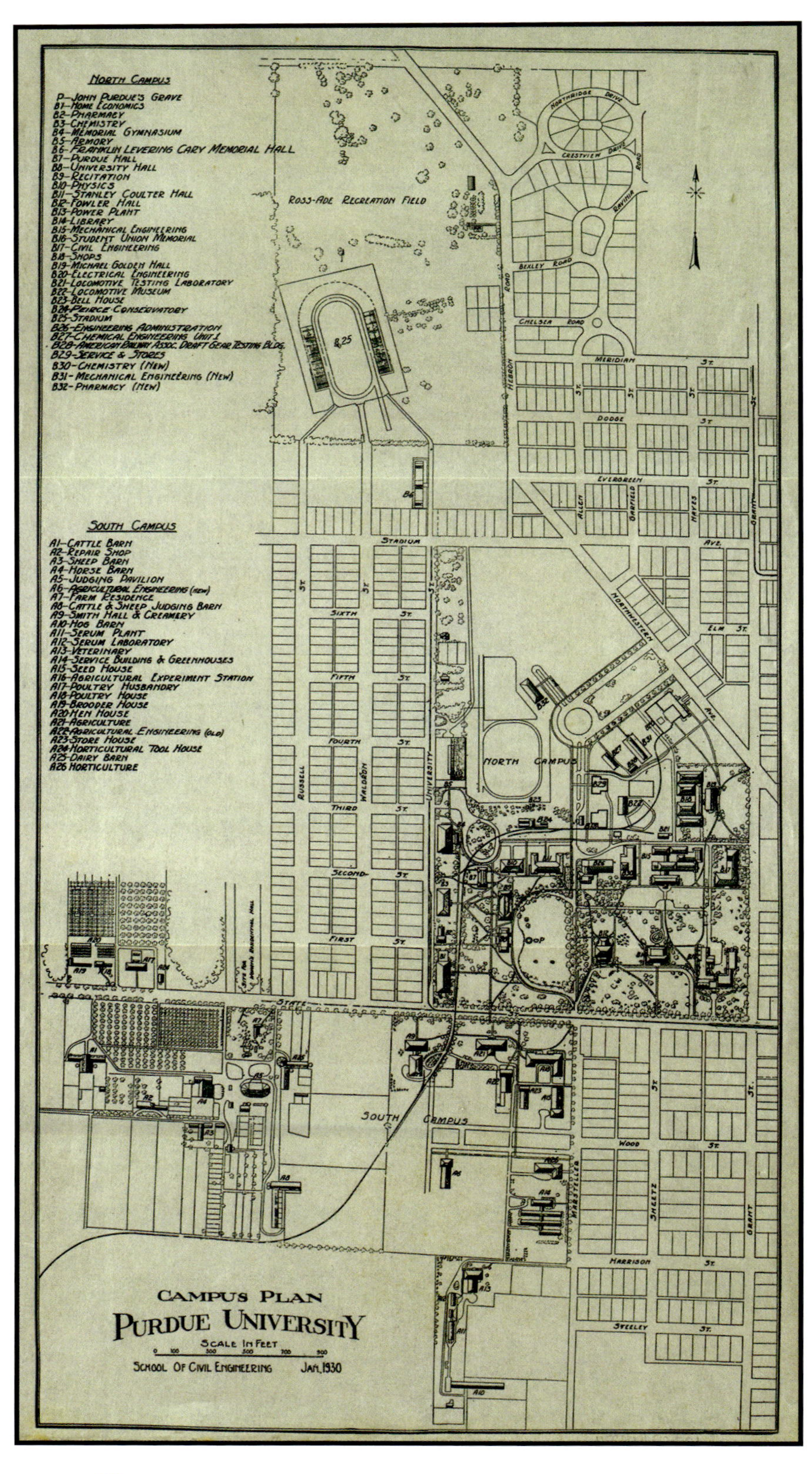

{Enrollment in 1930: 5,745 students[1]}

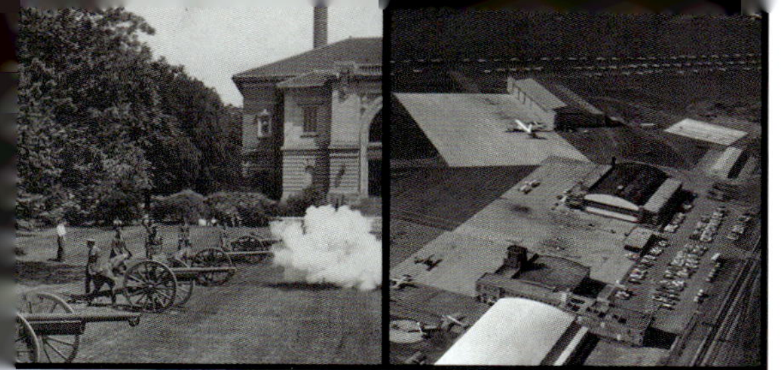

[The 1930s]

PURDUE AT 70

"I had a lot of fun in engineering. We thought we were pretty hot stuff, carrying around our slide rules. . . . There are two important things that opened up for me at Purdue, things I look back to with gratitude. . . . [T]here was the English department. . . . We wrote a lot of junk which I thought was great then, but which would make me shudder now to have to read a paragraph of it. But the whole enterprise was for me such a liberating and liberalizing experience—plus some actual practice in writing. . . . I can still almost smell the inside of that old University Hall."

—*Edward Mills Purcell, class of 1933*[2]

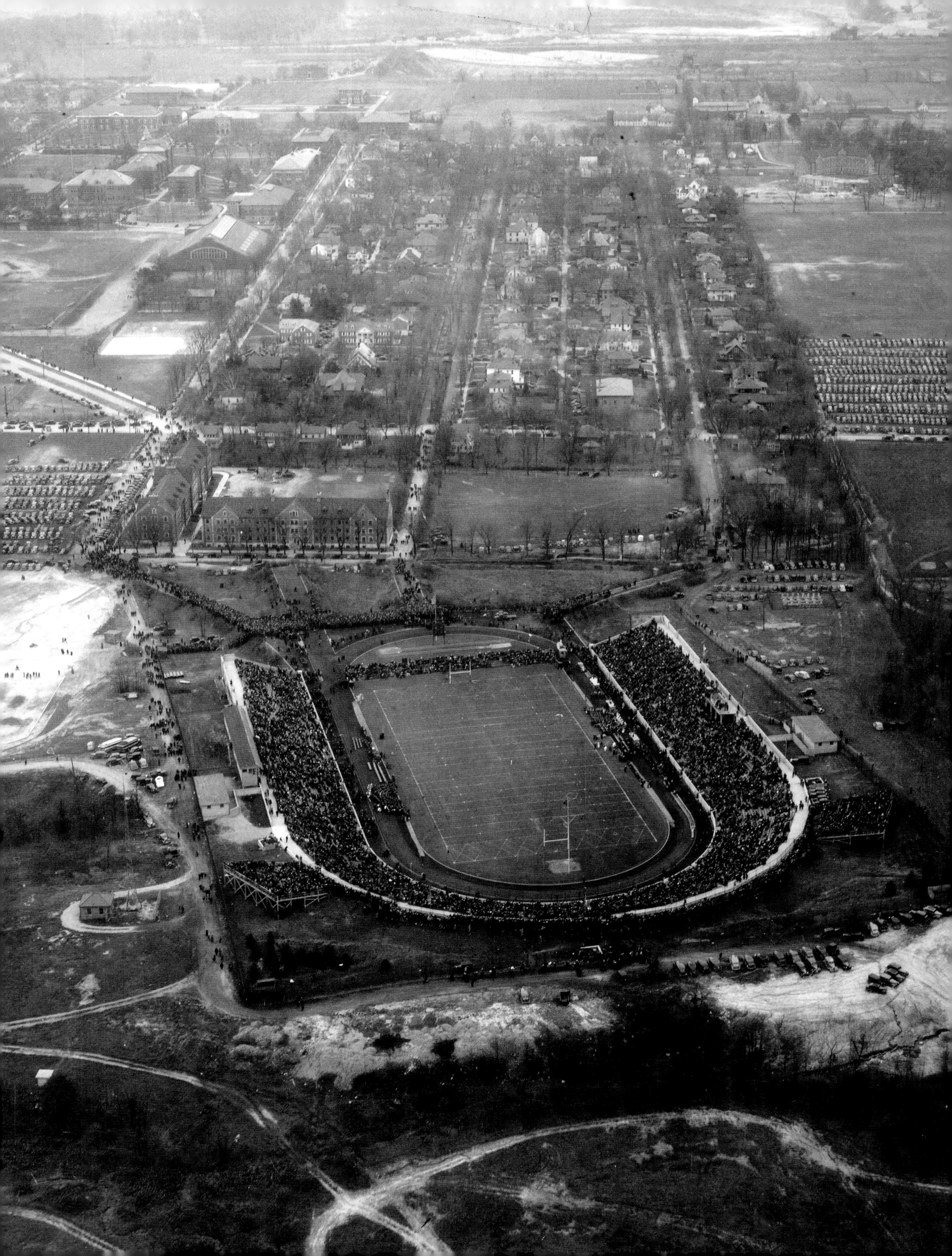

Opposite page: Aerial view from the north of Ross-Ade Stadium and Purdue campus, circa 1937. *(Purdue University photographs)*

Below: Amelia Earhart sitting on top of her Lockheed Electra plane with students Virginia Gardner, Rufina Sexton, Barbara Sweeney, Betty Spilman, Barbara Cook, Louise Schickler, Mary Johnston, Mary Louise Hinchman, Dorothy Hewitt, and Gaby D. Roe, September 20, 1936. *(Amelia Earhart at Purdue)*

The 1930s brought great progress, athletic victories, and famous faculty members to Purdue. As the demographics of the university's faculty and students saw increasing diversity, Purdue saw increasing success in a variety of areas.

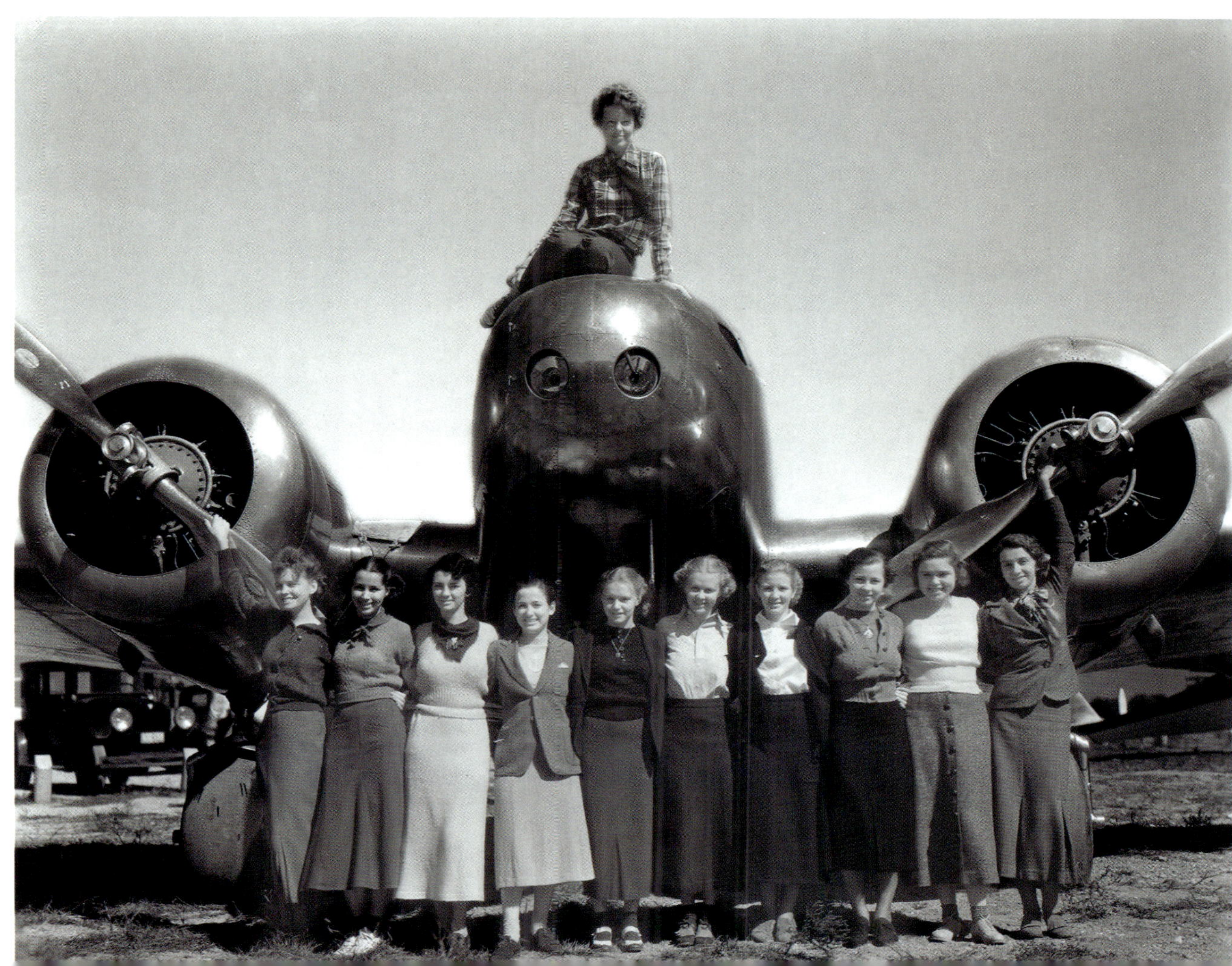

Purdue's international student population grew throughout the 1930s and the University created promotional materials tailored to young people around the globe. In a 1934 booklet, "Personal Letters from Purdue University to Students of the World," President Elliott, current international students, and alumni appealed to prospective students in other countries to enroll at Purdue. As Elliott wrote in his introductory message: "From the beginning there has been a steady stream of students from beyond the borders of the United States. It is a matter of great pride that this stream continues to flow in spite of great difficulties arising from the disturbed states of world affairs."[3] The booklet demonstrated the breadth of Purdue's global reach via its international alumni, and the editors encouraged alumni around the world to distribute copies in their home countries. The publication featured personalized letters from members of Purdue's international student clubs written in a variety of languages.

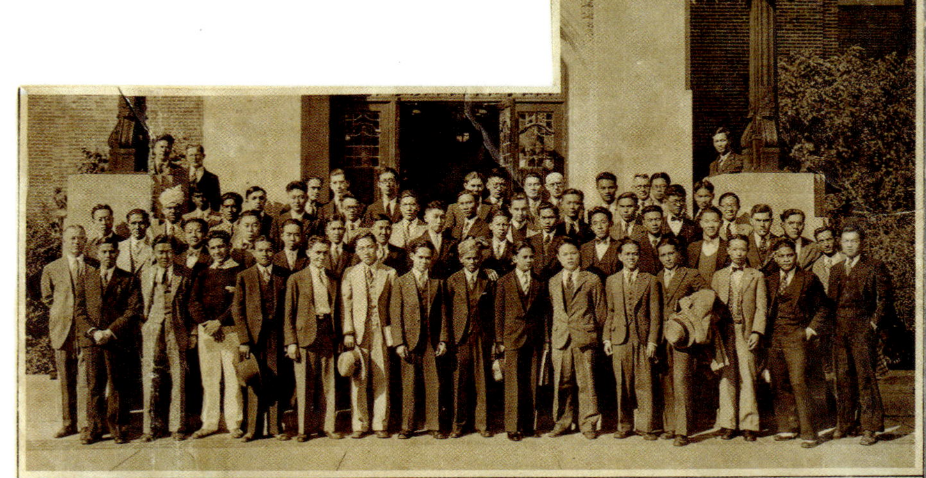

FOREIGN STUDENTS ENROLLED AT PURDUE UNIVERSITY—Twenty-two different countries are represented by this group. First row, left to right: Y. C. Hou and George T. Y. Woo, China; Zareh K. K. Saradjian, Persia; Teofilo A. Alemania, Philippines; Nuk Mars, Greece; J. V. Ogai, Korea; F. F. Gorospe, Philippines; Konigapogn Joseph Devadanam, India; Rosendo M. Palafox, Philippines; M. H. Wu, China; Lionel T. Bation and Potenciano Lesaca Jr., Philippines; C. L. Wang, China; F. L. Dongallo; C. Y. Kang, China. Second row: H. M. Baldwin, faculty adviser; S. J. Kansi, Hawaii; T. T. Mou Chi C. Wang, K. C. Meng and H. L. Shen, China; C. H. Kim, Korea; A. E. Park, Siberia; L. W. Thong, China; T. E. Estonilo, Philippines; A. R. Chen, S. T. Wang and T. E. Shaw, China; M. Soifer, Poland; C. D. Tchalovsky, Jugoslavia, and J. H. Coyaji, India. Third row: H. J. King, China; C. S. Speake and K. K. Puri, India; T. H. Wang, H. T. Jiu and S. C. Liu, China; A. E. Tonsay, Philippines; L. W. Brohman, Germany; C. C. Sun, C. T. Liu, K. K. Yang and S. J. Yang, China. Fourth row: Y. C. Woo, China; Bruno Beckmann, Germany; S. K. Sur, India; J. G. Adashko, Poland; Guillermo L. Franco, Mexico; V. P. Ormachea, Bolivia, S. A.; P. L. Li, China; W. S. Solomekin, Russia; M. C. Li, Y. C. Li, C. C. Hsu, J. Cheng, C. T. Hsin and J. C. Lee, China. *(Allen.)*

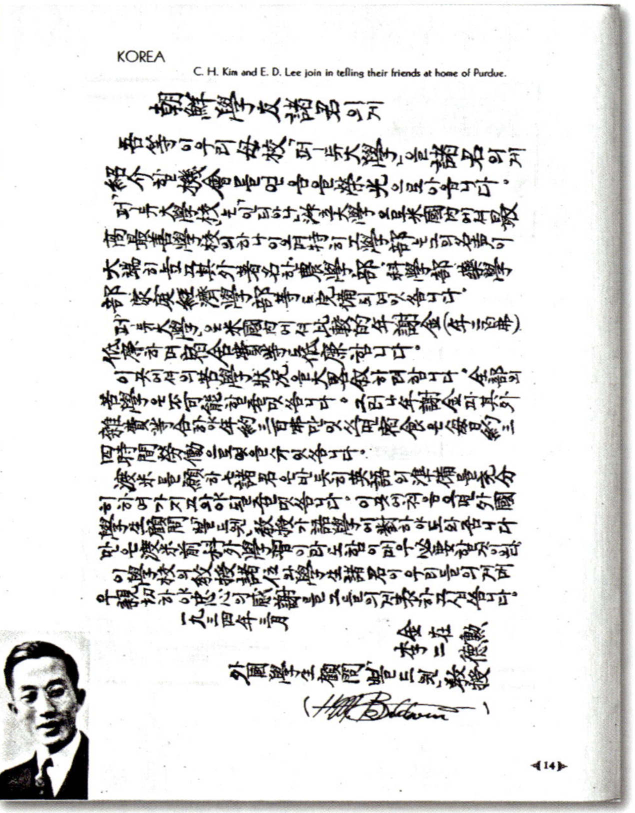

KOREA

C. H. Kim and E. D. Lee join in telling their friends at home of Purdue.

朝鮮學友諸君의게

[illegible]

◄14►

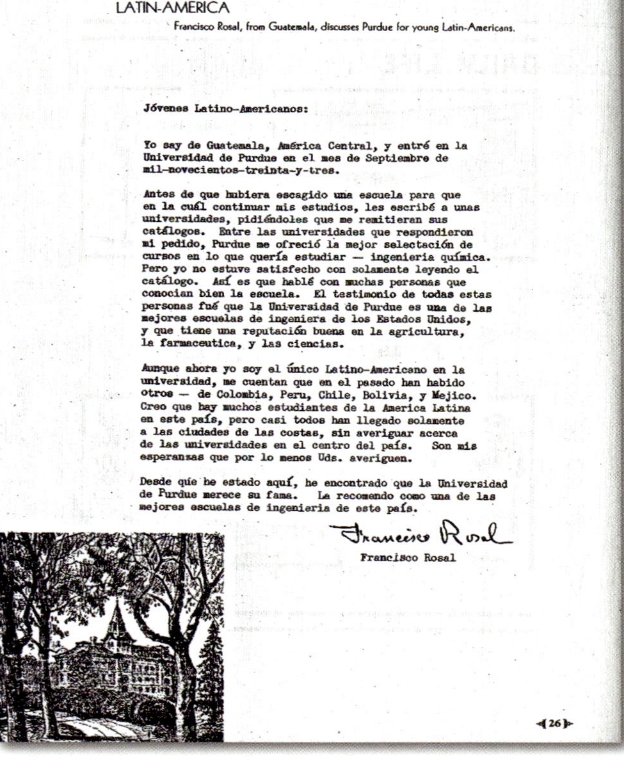

LATIN-AMERICA

Francisco Rosal, from Guatemala, discusses Purdue for young Latin-Americans.

Jóvenes Latino-Americanos:

Yo say de Guatemala, América Central, y entré en la Universidad de Purdue en el mes de Septiembre de mil-novecientos-treinta-y-tres.

Antes de que hubiera escagido una escuela para que en la cuál continuar mis estudios, les escribé a unas universidades, pidiéndoles que me remitieran sus catálogos. Entre las universidades que respondieron mi pedido, Purdue me ofreció la mejor selectación de cursos en lo que quería estudiar — ingenieria química. Pero yo no estuve satisfecho con solamente leyendo el catálogo. Así es que hablé con muchas personas que conocian bien la escuela. El testimonio de todas estas personas fué que la Universidad de Purdue es una de las mejores escuelas de ingeniera de los Estados Unidos, y que tiene una reputación buena en la agricultura, la farmaceutica, y las ciencias.

Aunque ahora yo soy el único Latino-Americano en la universidad, me cuentan que en el pasado han habido otros — de Colombia, Peru, Chile, Bolivia, y Mejico. Creo que hay muchos estudiantes de la America Latina en este país, pero casi todos han llegado solamente a las ciudades de las costas, sin averiguar acerca de las universidades en el centro del país. Son mis esperanzas que por lo menos Uds. averiguen.

Desde qúe he estado aquí, he encontrado que la Universidad de Purdue merece su fama. La recomendo como una de las mejores escuelas de ingenieria de este país.

Francisco Rosal

Francisco Rosal

◄26►

Top: International students at Purdue, 1930. *(Purdue University International Students collection)*

Right: Letter from Korean students C. H. Kim and E. D. Lee to the Students of the World, 1934. *(Purdue University Archives and Special Collections Vertical Files)*

Far right: Letter from Guatemalan student Francisco Rosal to the Students of the World, 1934. *(Purdue University Archives and Special Collections Vertical Files)*

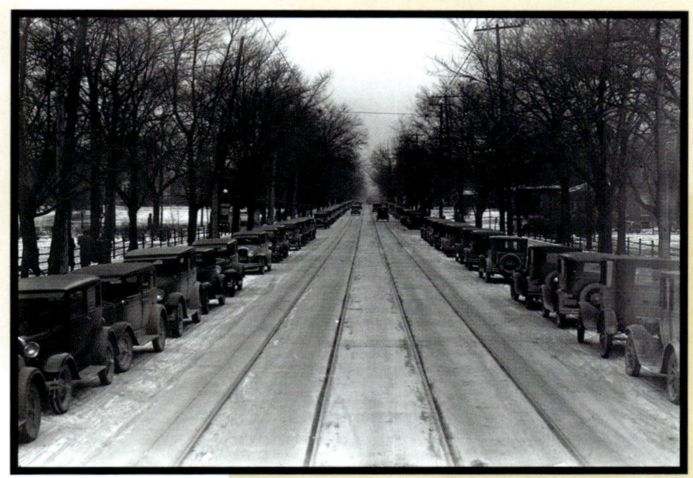

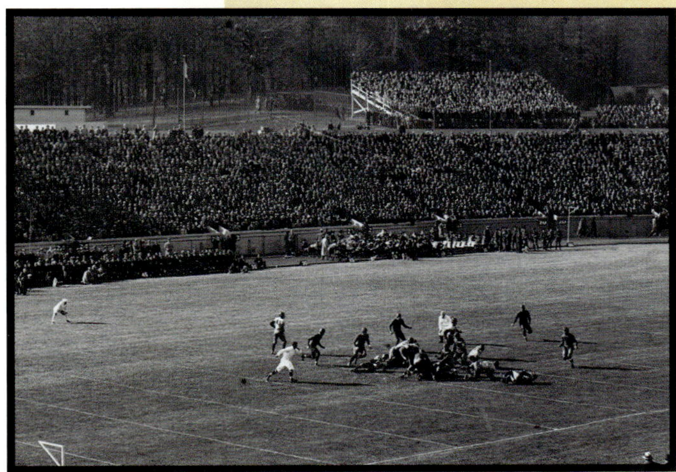

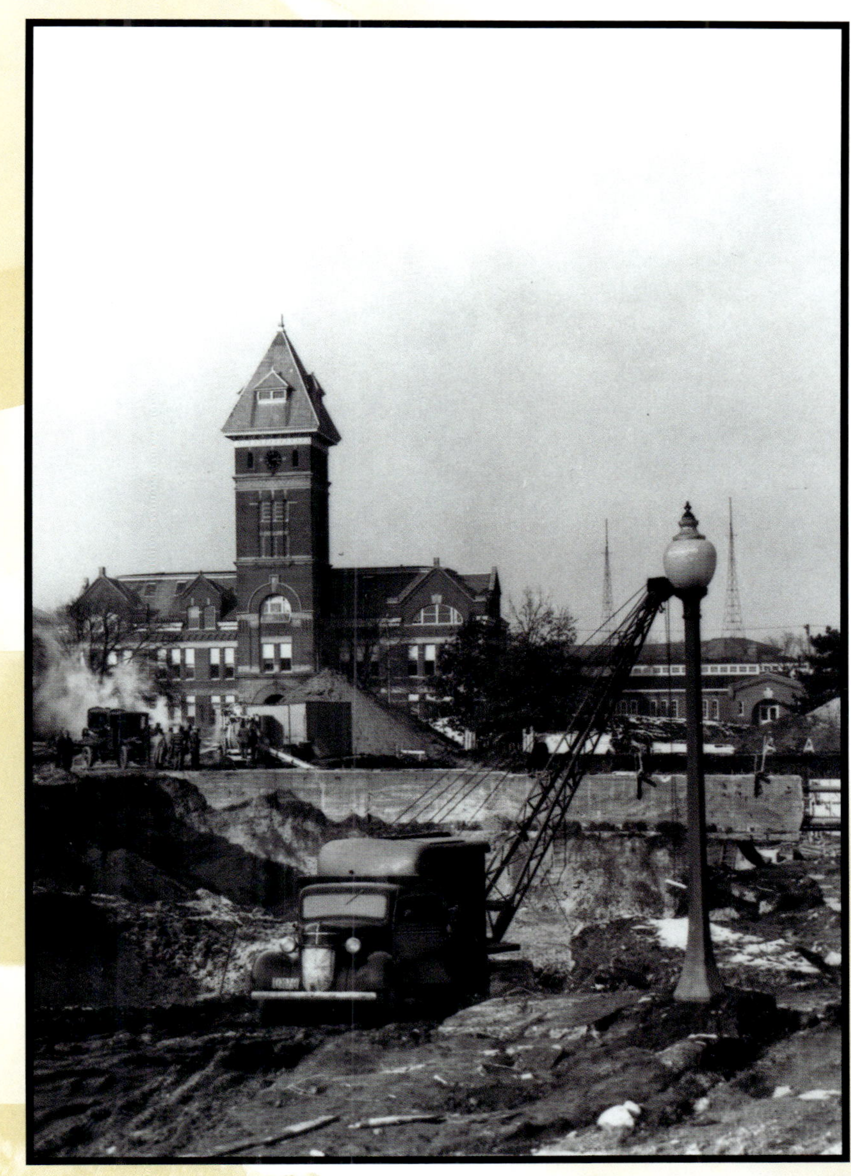

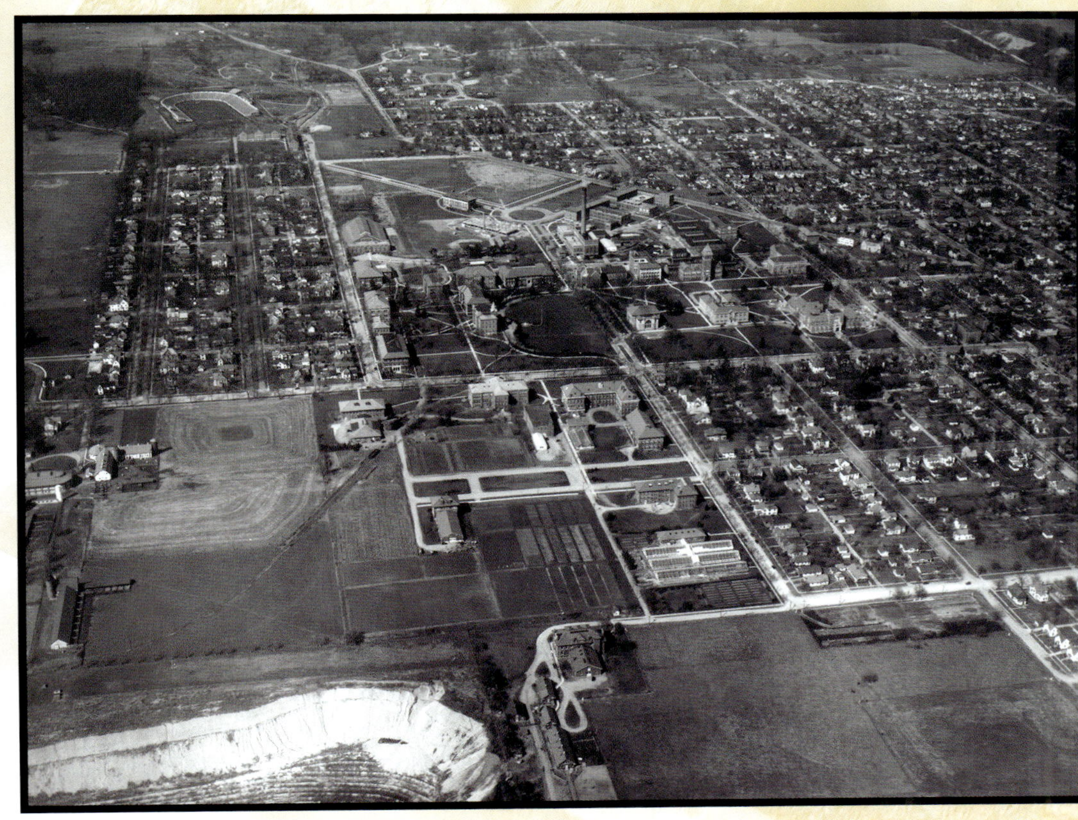

Clockwise from top left:

Automobiles lined up along State Street during the January 1930 Agricultural Conference. Streetcar lines are visible in the center of the street. *(J. C. Allen and Son Inc. photographs and negatives)*

Renovation to Purdue Memorial Union, 1939. *(Purdue University Marketing and Media collection)*

Aerial view of Purdue University campus, circa 1936. *(Purdue University photographs)*

Football game, Purdue vs. Wisconsin, October 1930. *(Purdue University photographs)*

Below from top:

Freshman belt buckle, 1939. *(Horace W. Payne collection)*

A record number of freshmen participate in student registration in the Armory, Sept. 9–11, 1931. *(Purdue University photographs)*

Students at work in the *Purdue Exponent* office, March 1933. *(Purdue University photographs)*

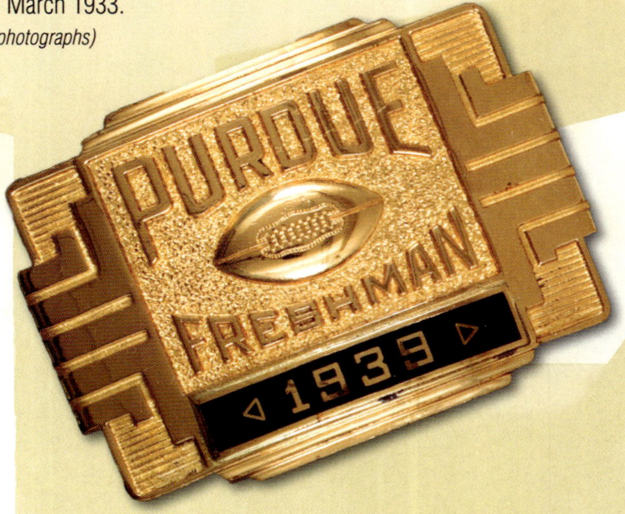

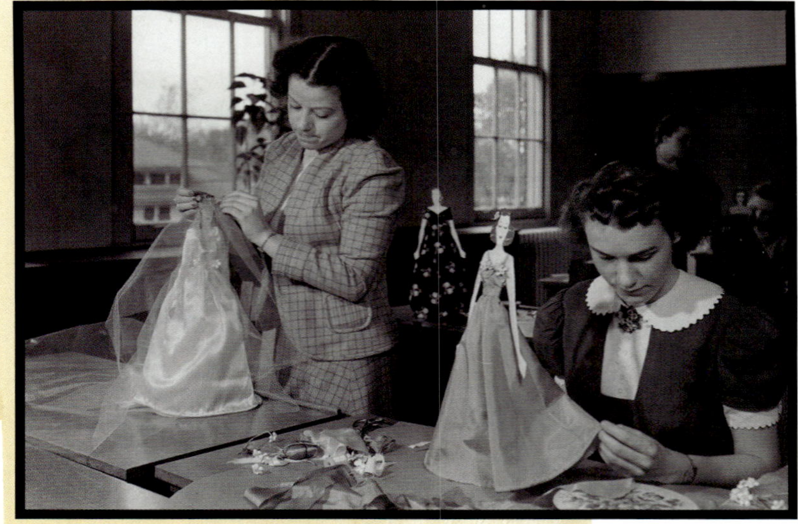

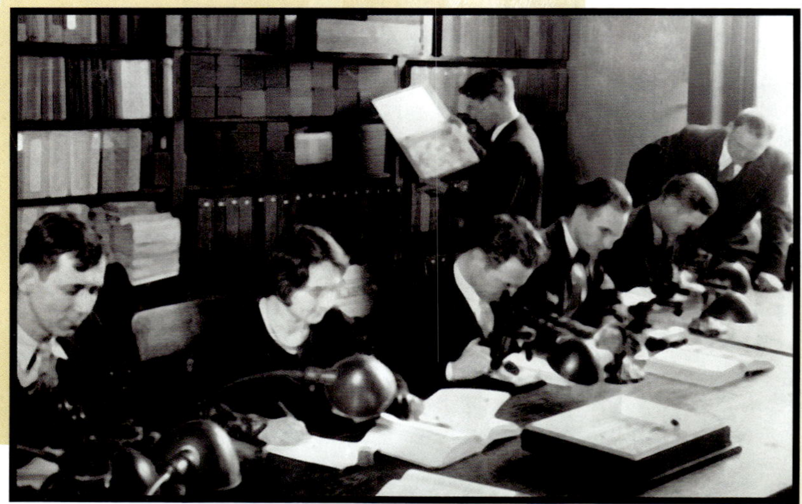

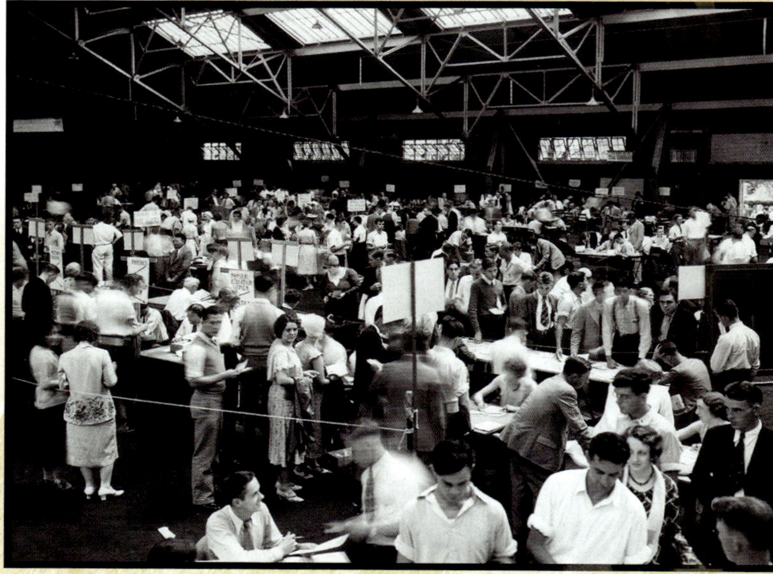

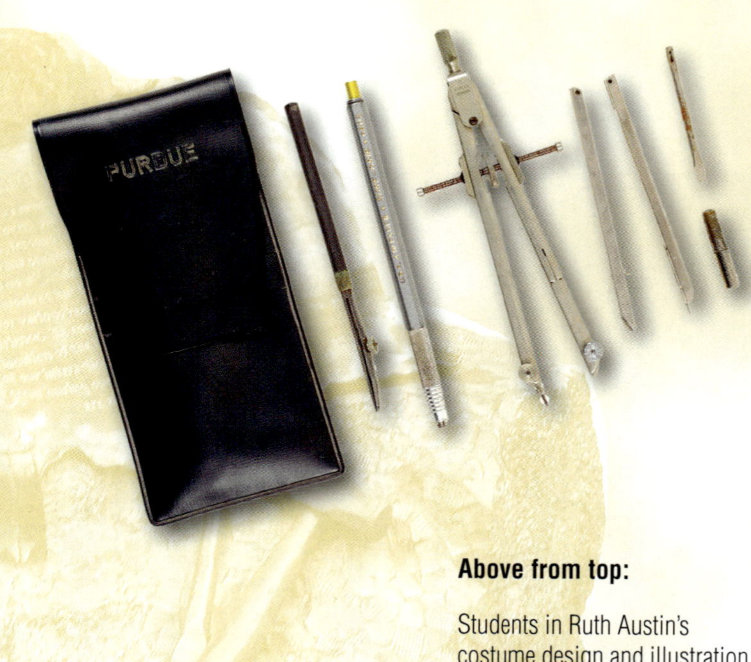

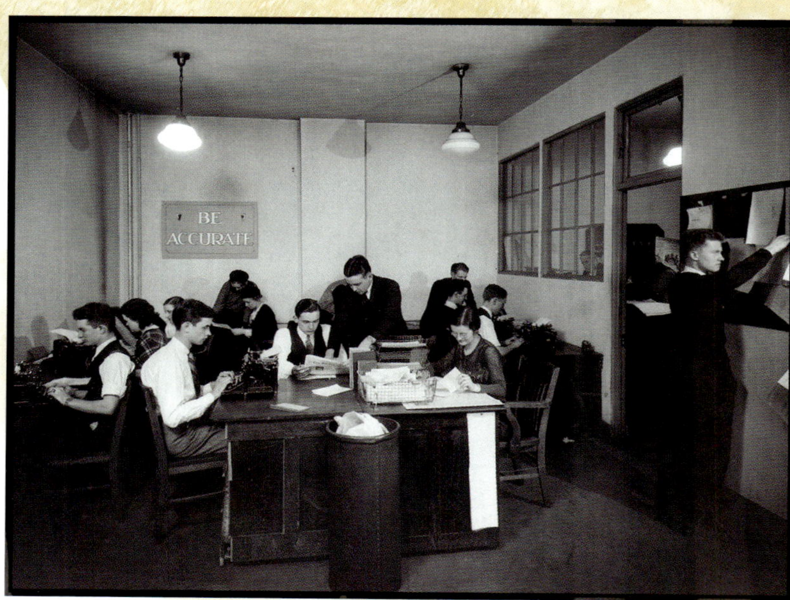

Above from top:

Students in Ruth Austin's costume design and illustration class in the Department of Applied Design, 1938. *(Purdue University photographs)*

Students in entomology class. *(Purdue University photographs)*

Purdue student engineering tools, including a compass and rulers. *(Robert Gagen engineering tools)*

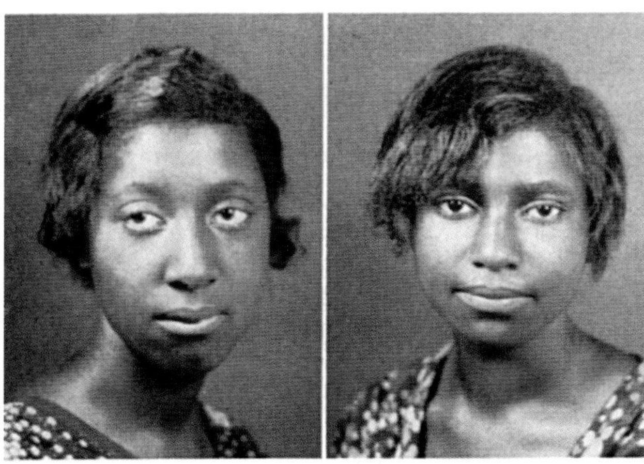

Left: Yearbook photos of sisters Delia (*left*) and Ella Belle Silance, class of 1932. *(Debris yearbook)*

Bottom: Amelia Earhart and Captain G. W. Haskins teaching a class in aerial navigation to aerodynamics students at Purdue University Airport. *(Amelia Earhart at Purdue)*

Just as Purdue's international student population grew rapidly in the years following World War I, so too did the number of female students. Three of Purdue's early African American women graduates earned their degrees in the 1930s. Thelma F. McDonald received her bachelor of science in 1931.[4] Delia Silance, who earned a scholarship, and her younger sister Ella Belle each earned a bachelor of science in 1932.

To help address the needs of the female student population, President Elliott hired two women with international reputations to join the University in 1935: pilot Amelia Earhart and motion study pioneer Lillian Gilbreth. Elliott believed that Earhart and Gilbreth, with their professional achievements, would serve as role models for women seeking careers after graduation and their affiliation with the university would provide valuable publicity. Although at first glance the two women seemed very different, both were committed to education and equal opportunities for women. Each championed women in the workforce while serving as real-world examples of women who achieved success in male-dominated professions.

During the 1930s Purdue's engineering and science coursework remained on the cutting edge, allowing students opportunities to conduct research and prepare for future careers. Nobel Prize-winning physicist Edward Purcell, who graduated from Purdue in 1933, recalled that "quantum mechanics had been discovered in '26–'28 and here, by golly, I was an undergraduate at Purdue in 1932, just four or five years later, doing experiments with electron diffraction."[5]

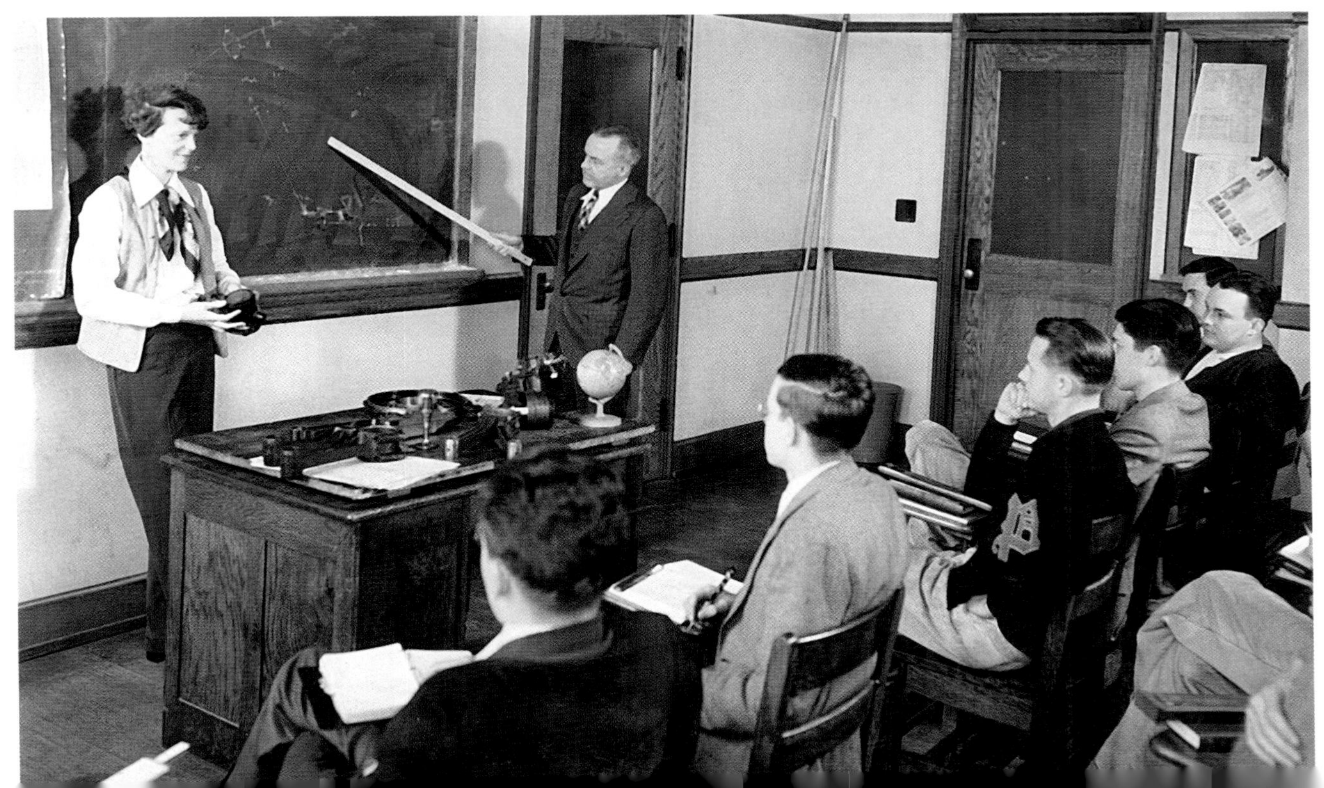

Purdue Airport

Since its inception, the Purdue Airport has been more than a landing strip and decidedly more than an airport: it has been a classroom of hangars, machine shops, research laboratories, a control tower, tarmac, and sky. The Purdue Airport officially opened on September 4, 1934, following a few years' hiatus through difficult economic times, then eight months of development and renovation as a federal works project of the Civil Works Administration.

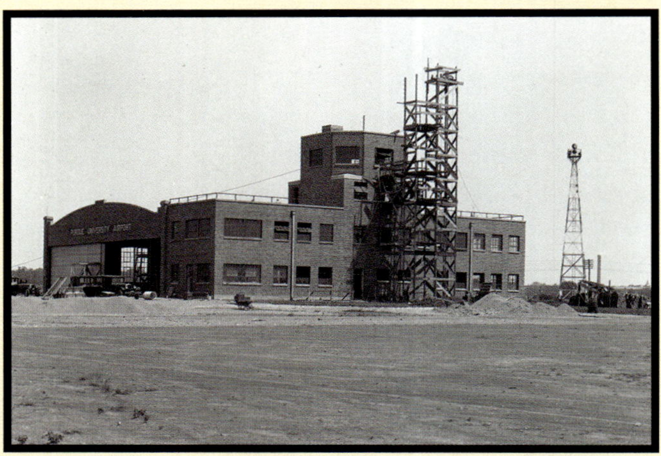

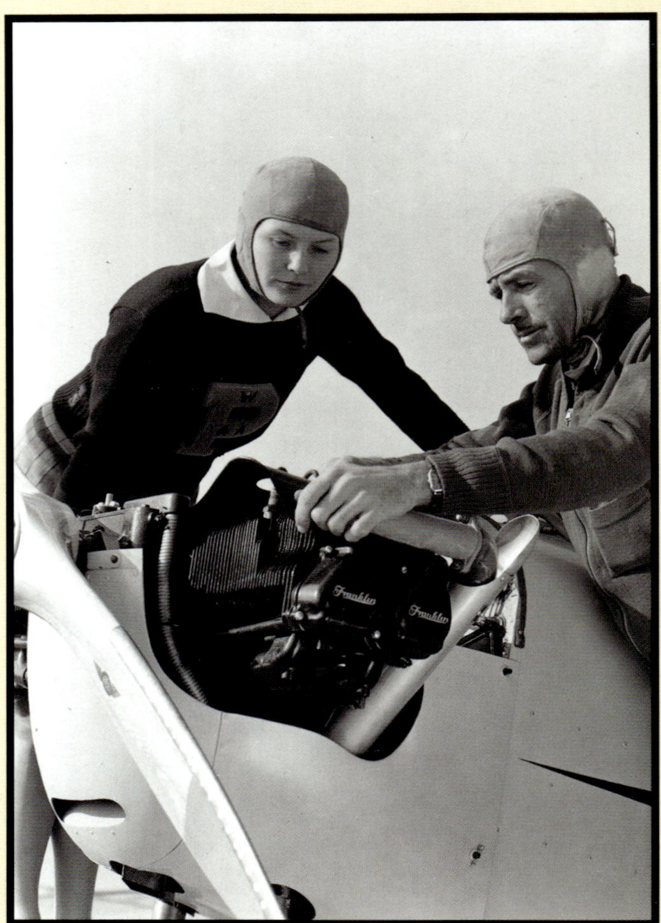

The first Purdue student flight training took place in the summer of 1930. The students received technical instruction from faculty and flying lessons from a representative of the Curtiss-Wright Flying Service. Though enrollment that summer was low, the class included two Chinese students.[6] The Purdue Glider Club formed in 1932 and would be just one of the numerous student clubs the Airport would host over the decades. The Purdue Aeromodelers, Aero Club, Flying Club, Purdue Pilots Inc., Women in Aviation, Drone Club, Purdue Flight Team, and others have followed.

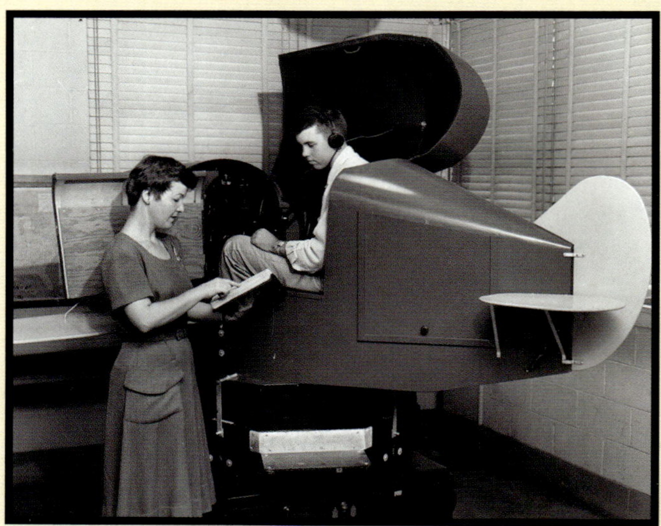

Above: Airport under construction, 1934. *(J. C. Allen and Son Inc. photographs and negatives)*

Right top: Aviation instructor Captain Lawrence I. Aretz examining an airplane engine at the airport with a female student. *(Purdue University photographs)*

Right bottom: Aviation technology student receives link trainer instructions from Jill McCormick to prepare for copiloting DC-3 airplanes. *(Purdue University photographs)*

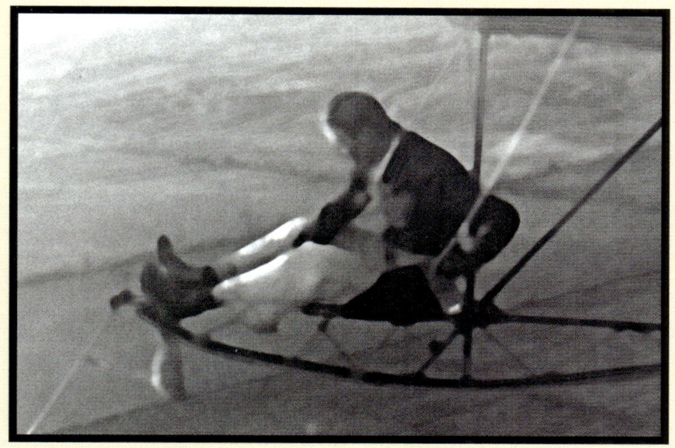

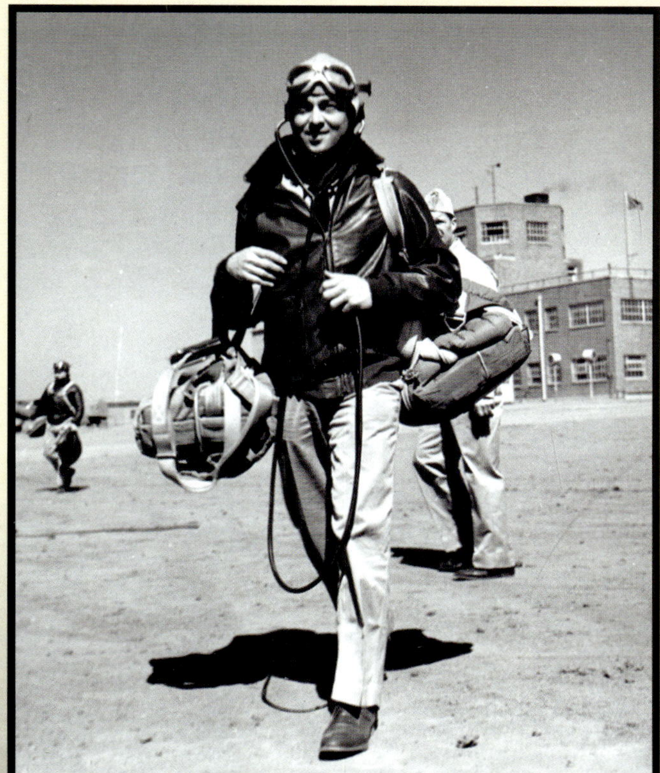

In the 1930s, the Purdue Airport played host to aviation rock stars such as Wiley Post, Jimmy Mattern, and Amelia Earhart. In 1939, Purdue became the first university to implement the U.S. Civilian Pilot Training Program, preparing five hundred special pilots to serve in World War II; during the 1940s, Purdue Airport served to support the war effort as did much of the rest of campus. Beginning in 1943, Purdue collaborated with the U.S. War Training Service program, and the airport became a training facility for the Navy Flight Instructors School and later hosted basic flight training for aviation cadets.

The 1940s saw air transportation develop as a curriculum in the School of Aeronautics, and in the 1950s, the airport took off as a laboratory for aviation. The first engines class, taught by James Maris, began in the fall of 1955, firmly establishing the airport hangars as laboratories. The 1950s also saw the establishment of Purdue Aeronautics Corporation. PAC would allow students to get practical laboratory experience and training with aircraft on the ground and in flight. Since the 1960s and 1970s, aviation technology students have hosted intercollegiate flying meets and sent teams to compete in the Air Race Classic. Nearly a century after its inception Purdue University Airport continues to expand opportunities for students in its classrooms, laboratories, and hands-on aviation programs.

Top: A student soars four hundred feet in the air on a glider plane, circa 1950s. *(Purdue University Marketing and Media collection)*

Bottom: Student of the Navy Flight School at Purdue Airport, circa 1943. *(John C. Franks papers)*

Background: Aerial view of Purdue Airport, circa 1960. *(Purdue University photographs)*

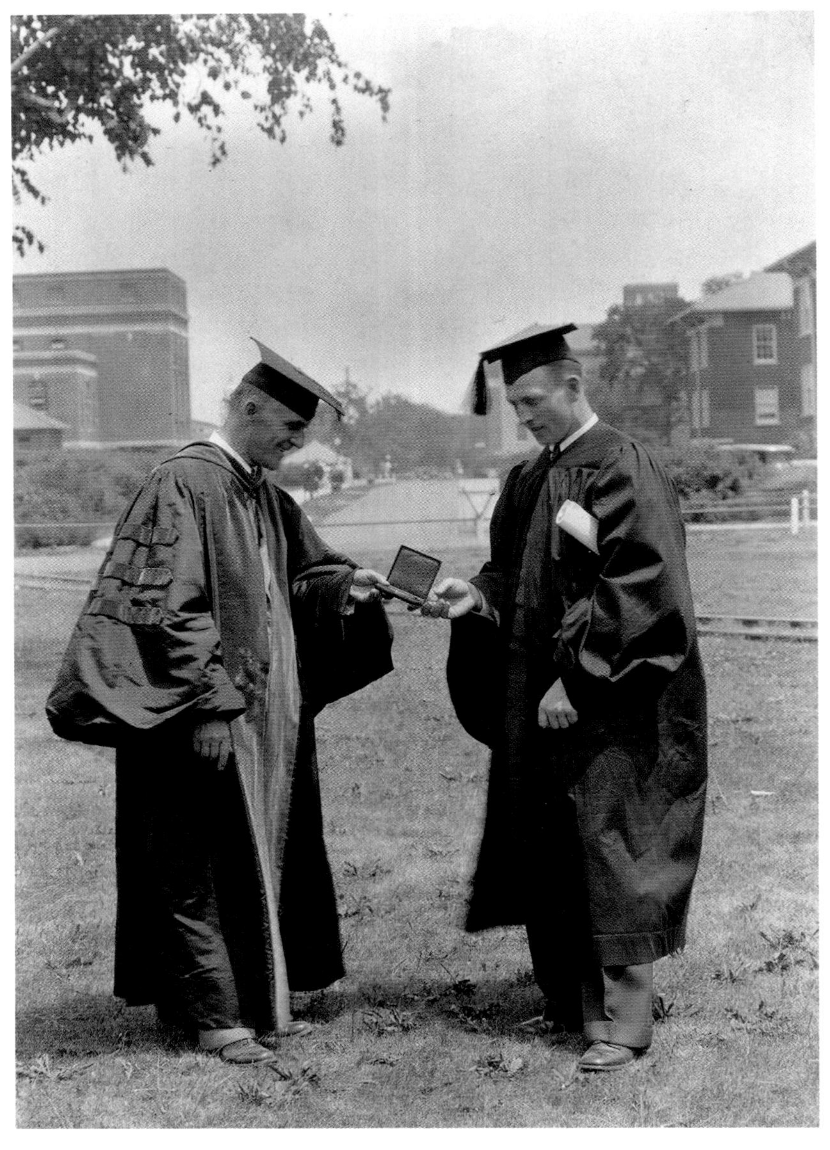

The success of athletics during the 1930s also helped boost school spirit. Under the leadership of coach Piggy Lambert and star player John Wooden, the Purdue basketball team was a powerhouse. Wooden was an All-American in basketball in 1930, 1931, and 1932.[7] After outgrowing its space in the Memorial Gymnasium, the basketball team played all of its home games for the 1933–1934 season at Jefferson High School.[8] The team won the Big Ten Championship in 1930, 1932, 1934, 1935, 1936, and 1938 and claimed the national basketball championship of 1932.[9] Purdue ended the 1939–1940 basketball season with a 34–31 win over Illinois, winning the last of its eleven Big Ten titles under Lambert. When invited to play in the two-year-old NCAA tournament, Lambert, who did not like postseason play, declined. Instead, Purdue recommended Indiana for the spot, and Indiana defeated Kansas for the national title that year.[10]

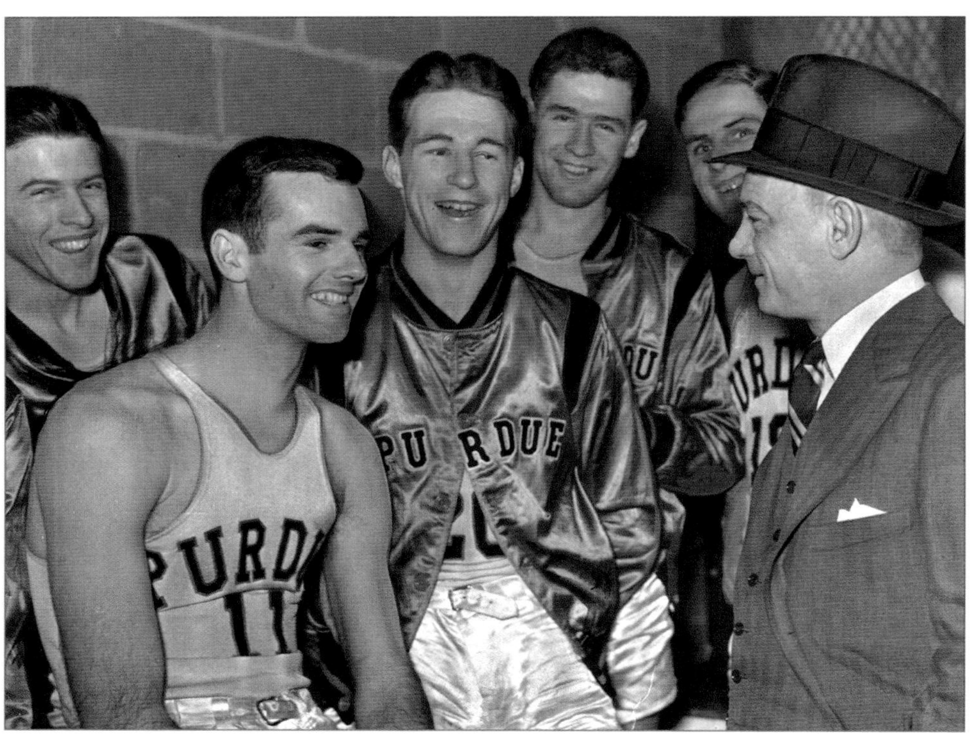

Top: Student and basketball star John Wooden receiving the Big Ten medal for combined proficiency in athletics and scholarship from President Edward C. Elliott at commencement in 1932.
(Edward C. Elliott papers)

Left: Basketball players Fred Beretta, Gene Anderson, Tom Dickinson, Dan Fisher, Elwood Yeager, and Coach Lambert after defeating rivals Indiana, February 27, 1939.
(Purdue University photographs)

The Purdue Majorettes first performed with the "All-American" Marching Band in 1939.

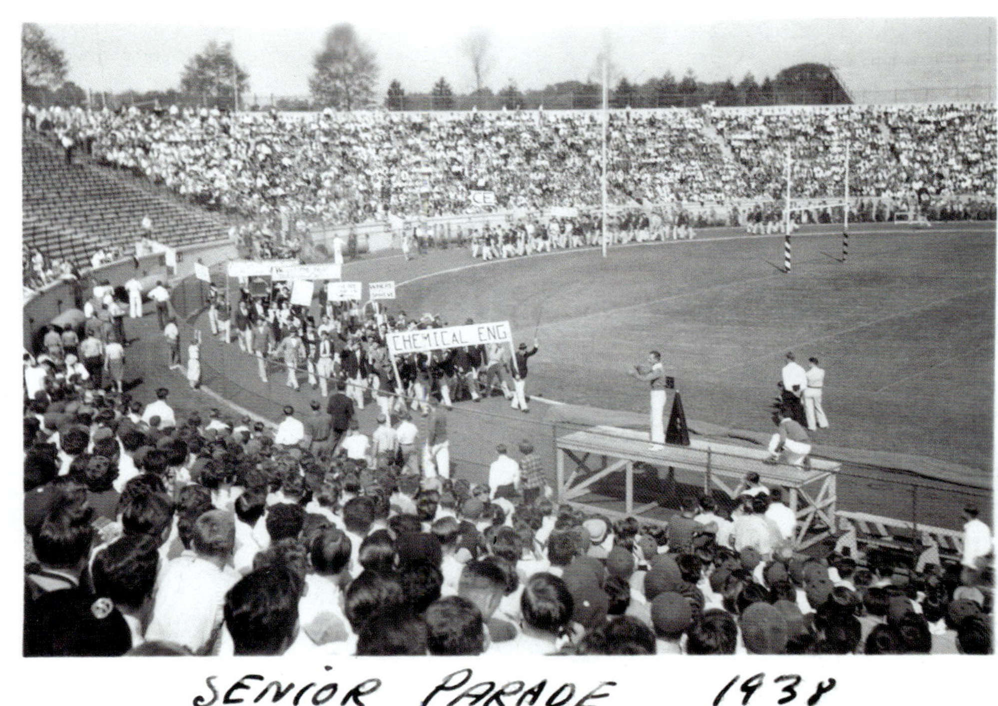

Football also flourished in the first part of the decade under coach Noble Kizer. His first four seasons at Purdue were incredible, resulting in twenty-nine wins, four losses, and two ties.[11] Purdue's football team co-won the Big Ten Championship in 1931 and 1932.[12]

In 1938 the intense competition between Purdue and Indiana University over who would win the Old Oaken Bucket led to a new custom—the burning of Miss Indiana. Members of student clubs (Reamers, Gimlets, and Skull and Crescent), the "All-American" Marching Band, and four thousand fans carried out last rites for Miss Indiana. The ceremony included singing "For the Honor of Old Purdue" and a bonfire where an image of Miss Indiana was burned at the stake alongside a Bloomington city limits sign. Football coach Mal Elward gave the keynote, stating that Purdue's "great football team doesn't have to be afraid of a d— thing Indiana has."[13] Purdue went on to win the Bucket, 13–6.

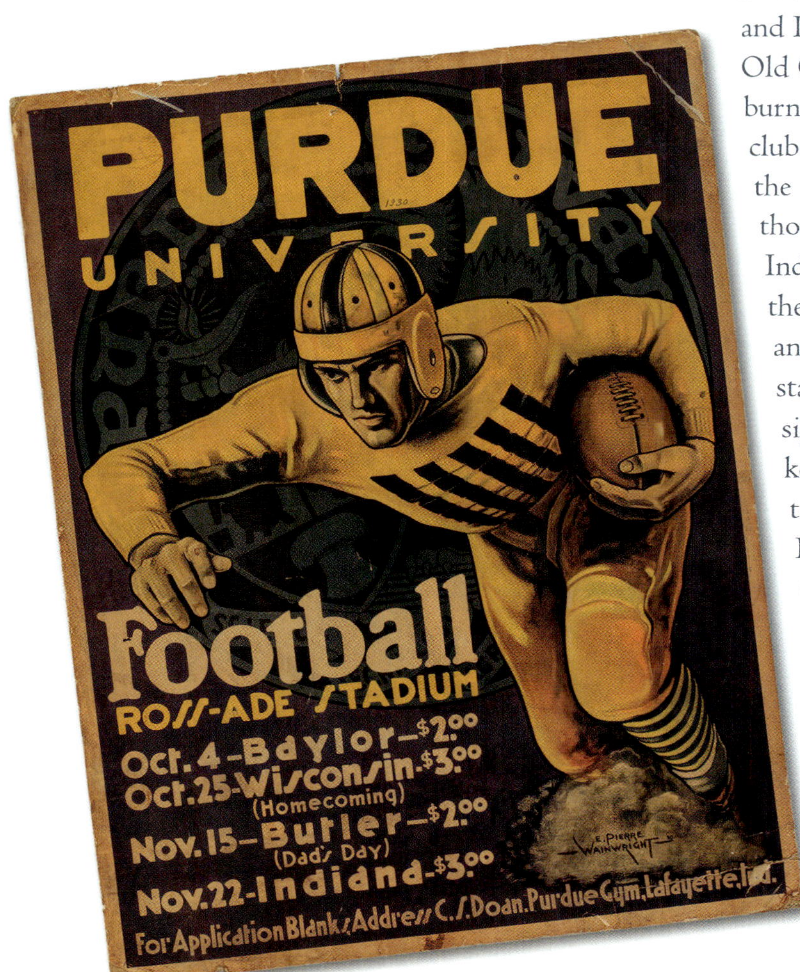

Top: Senior parade at a 1938 football game. *(Arthur and Roberta Bitzer papers)*

Left: Purdue University football poster for the 1930 season, illustrated by E. Pierre Wainwright. *(Purdue Broadsides collection)*

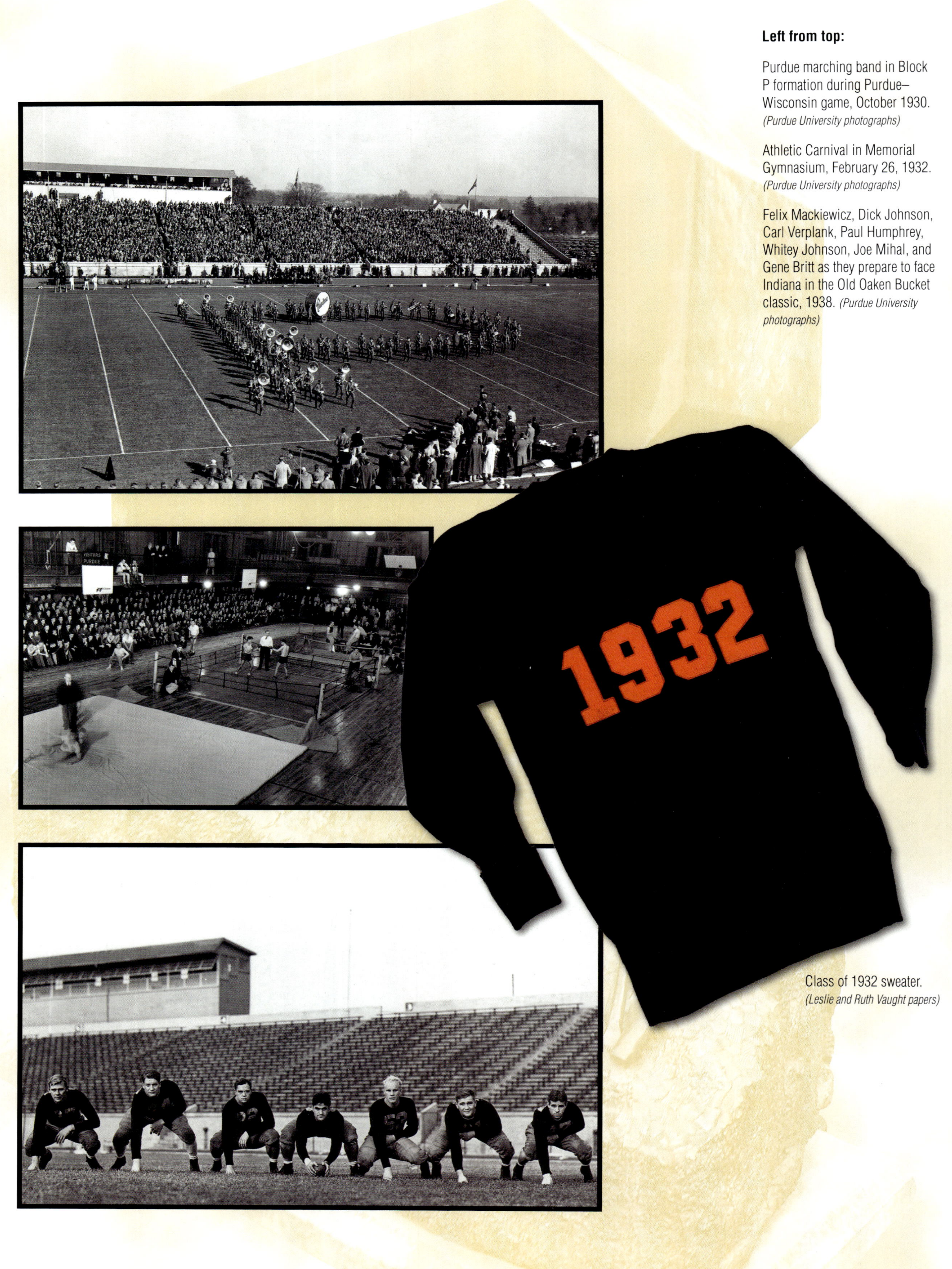

Left from top:

Purdue marching band in Block P formation during Purdue–Wisconsin game, October 1930. *(Purdue University photographs)*

Athletic Carnival in Memorial Gymnasium, February 26, 1932. *(Purdue University photographs)*

Felix Mackiewicz, Dick Johnson, Carl Verplank, Paul Humphrey, Whitey Johnson, Joe Mihal, and Gene Britt as they prepare to face Indiana in the Old Oaken Bucket classic, 1938. *(Purdue University photographs)*

Class of 1932 sweater. *(Leslie and Ruth Vaught papers)*

The "All-American" Marching Band saw success and innovation throughout the decade. In 1930 the Band set a new record by including fanfare trumpets on the football field during a performance.[14] In 1933 it performed two days of concerts at the Chicago World's Fair. Under director Spotts Emrick, the Band wowed crowds by adding lights to its performances in 1935, becoming the first band to perform a halftime show with lights on its instruments and uniforms.[15] The Band brought its light display to a night performance at the Kentucky Derby Festival Parade in April 1935, where it won the contest for best college band in the parade.

Al Stewart became director of the Women's Glee Club in 1930 and of the Men's Glee Club in 1932. The following year, President Elliott approved the formation of a Purdue Choir, though he initially refused to "spend one dime on music" at Purdue.[16] With the Men's and Women's Glee Clubs and the Purdue Choir, Stewart began to build a positive reputation for what became known in 1933 as the "Purdue Musical Organizations." Their most famous performance, the annual Christmas Show, was first held in 1933 and soon outgrew its home in Fowler Hall.[17]

The rapid growth in the campus landscape of the 1920s slowed somewhat in the early 1930s, a result of the economic toll of the Great Depression. Enrollment declined as well, and President Elliott called for increased efficiency and reductions to student expenses.[18] By mid-decade, the buildings program picked up pace again, giving rise to numerous new facilities or expansions to existing structures. With a growing international student body, successful athletic teams, a nationally recognized band, and major developments in flight training and housing research, Purdue's national reputation made significant strides in the 1930s.

Glee Club performance broadcasting from the Purdue Memorial Union. *(Purdue University photographs)*

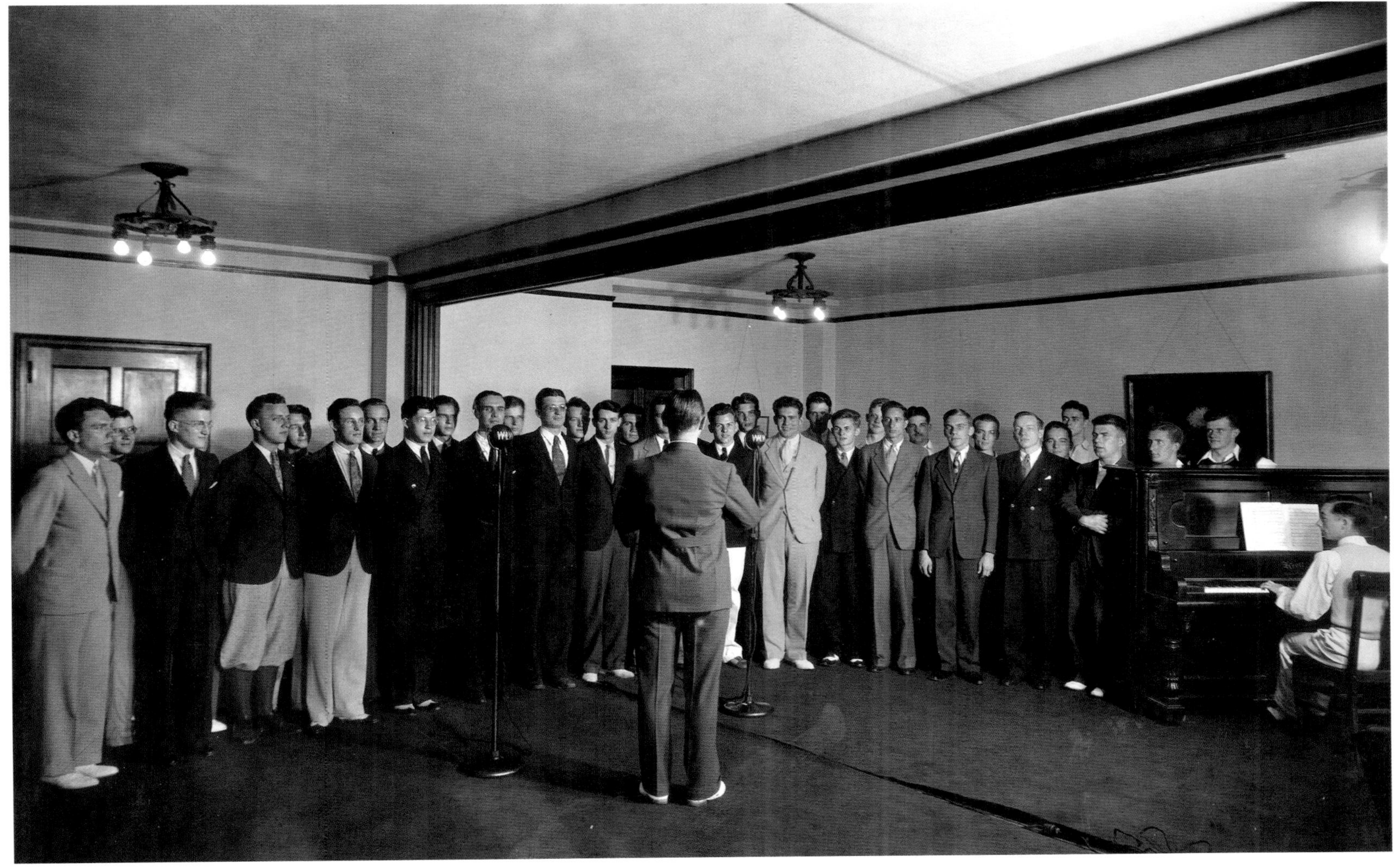

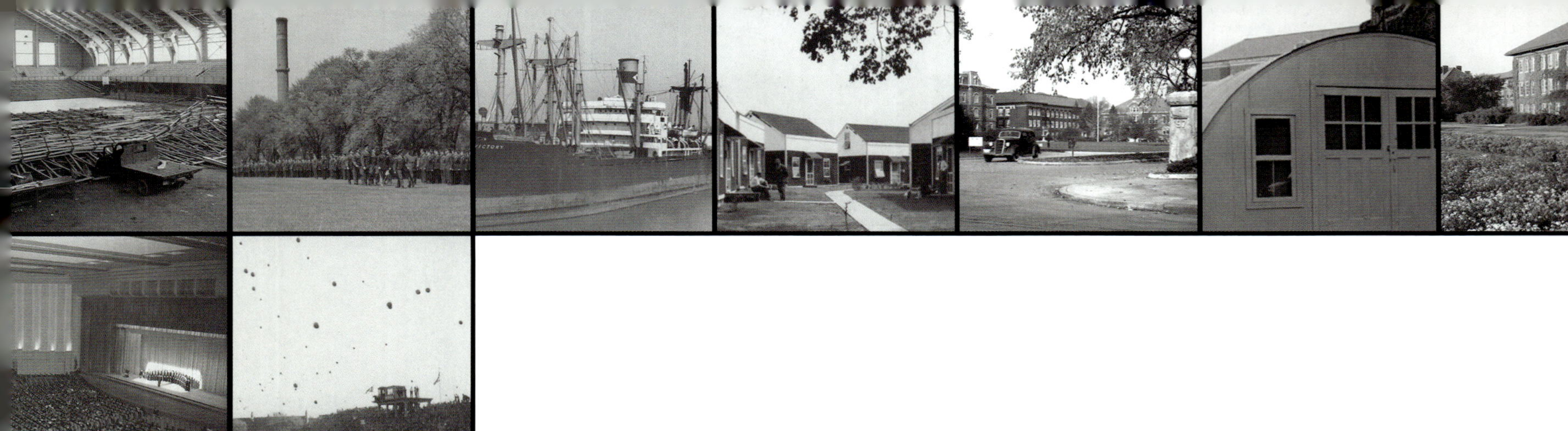

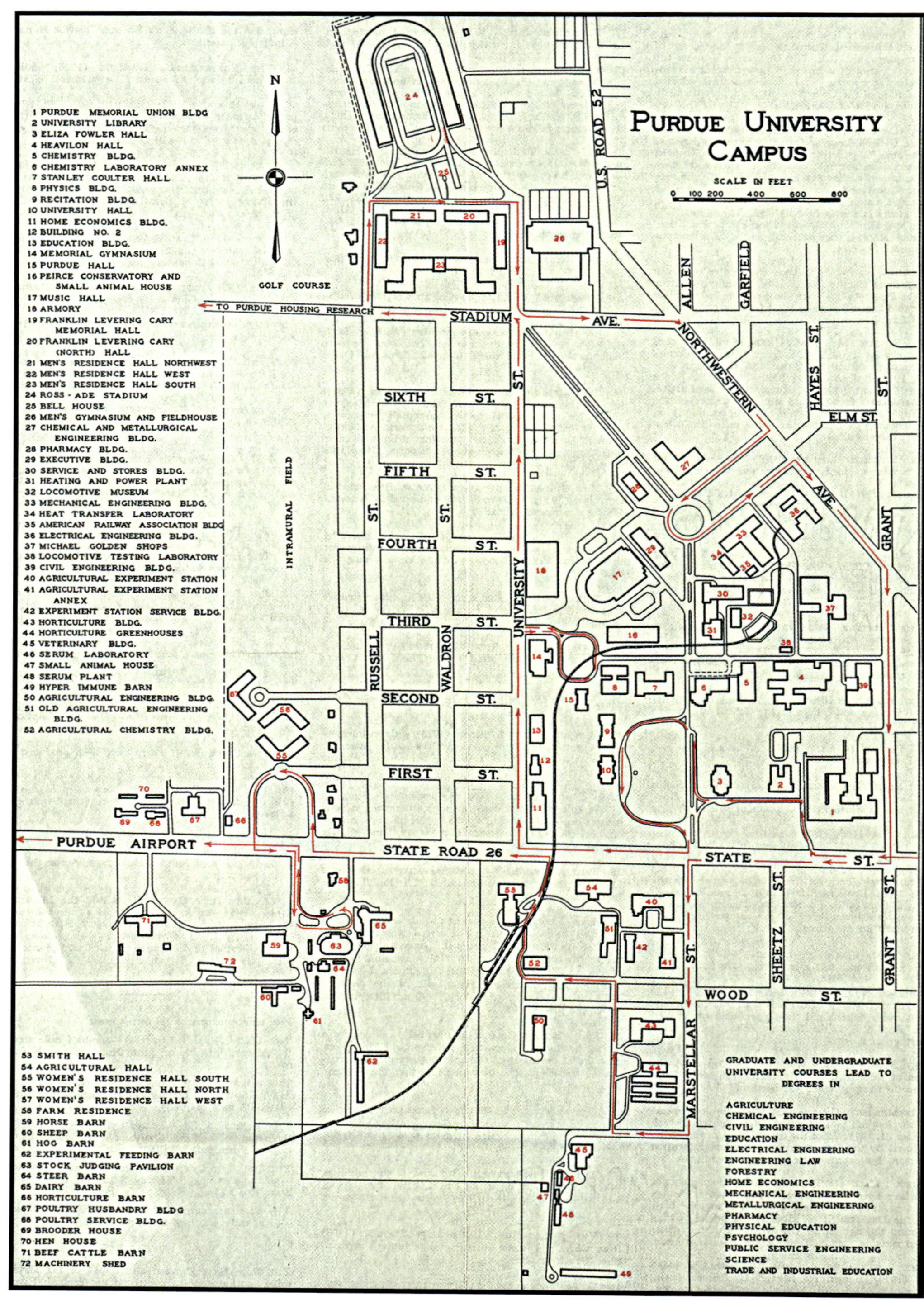

Campus map, circa 1941. *(Campus Maps collection)*

{Enrollment in 1940: 8,279 students[1]}

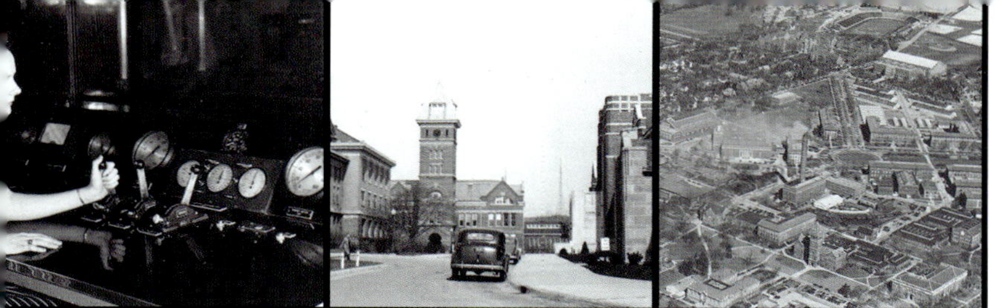

[The 1940s]

PURDUE AT 80

"From the corners of the campus, through the paths of shady trees, around impressive stone buildings, changes have crept over Purdue University. The white bell trousers of the sailors, the khaki neatness of the soldiers, the gold braid and insignia of their superior officers have invaded the homeland of the original sloppy joes. Coeds, in this day of 1943, attend classes twelve months of the year and practice correspondence at night to the armed forces here or overseas. . . . At Purdue University, serious patriotism has scattered the pre-war, carefree college ways to the four corners of the war-torn world."

—*Editorial Staff of the* Debris *Yearbook*[2]

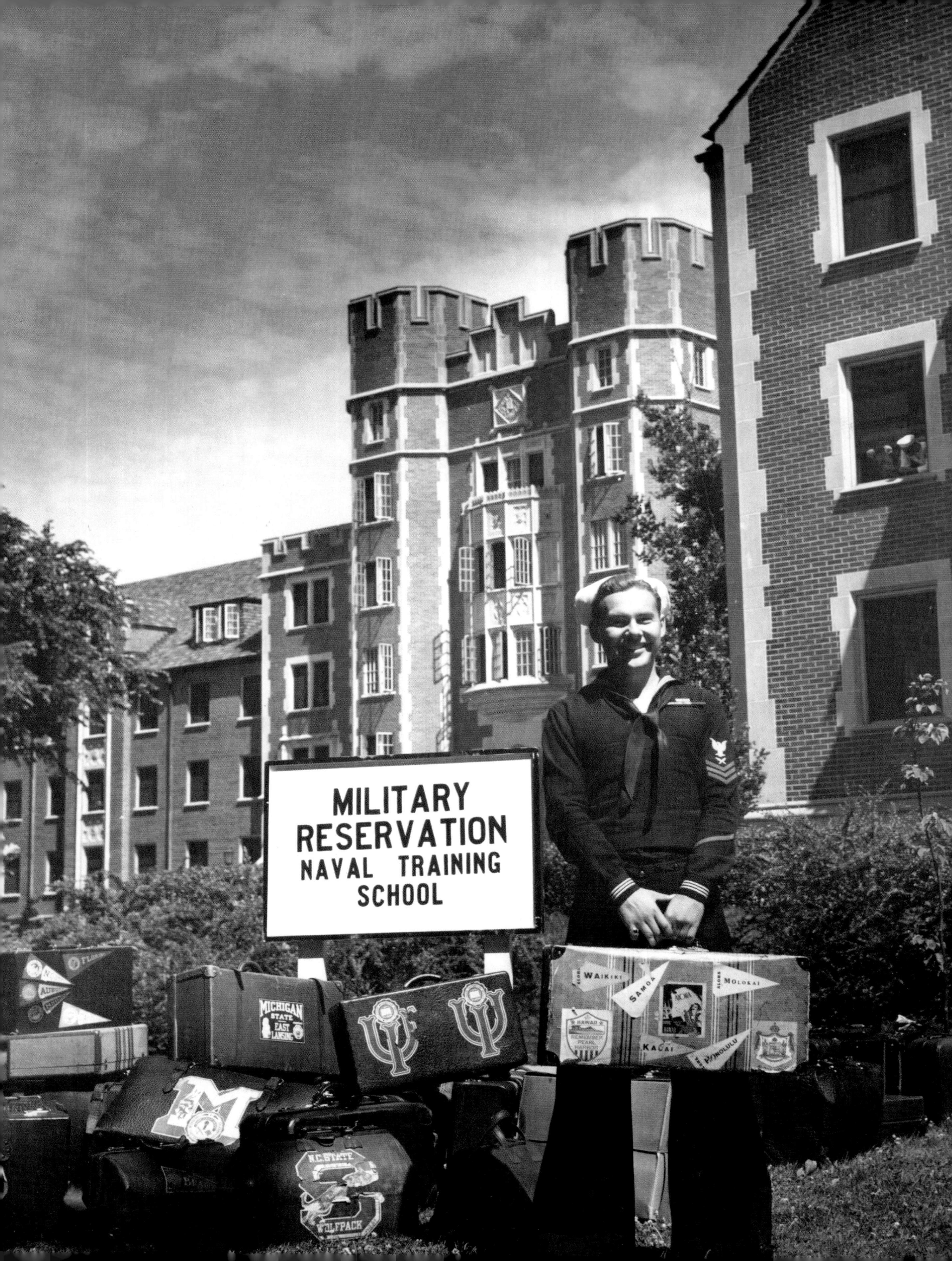
MILITARY
RESERVATION
NAVAL TRAINING
SCHOOL
MICHIGAN STATE EAST LANSING
WAIKIKI
SAMOA
MOLOKAI
REMEMBER PEARL HARBOR
N.C. STATE
WOLFPACK

Opposite page: Student Warren Harding entering the V-12 program at Purdue, 1943. *(Purdue University photographs)*

Below: Purdue War Training Courses brochure, listing available programs and courses. *(Purdue World War II Announcements and Publications)*

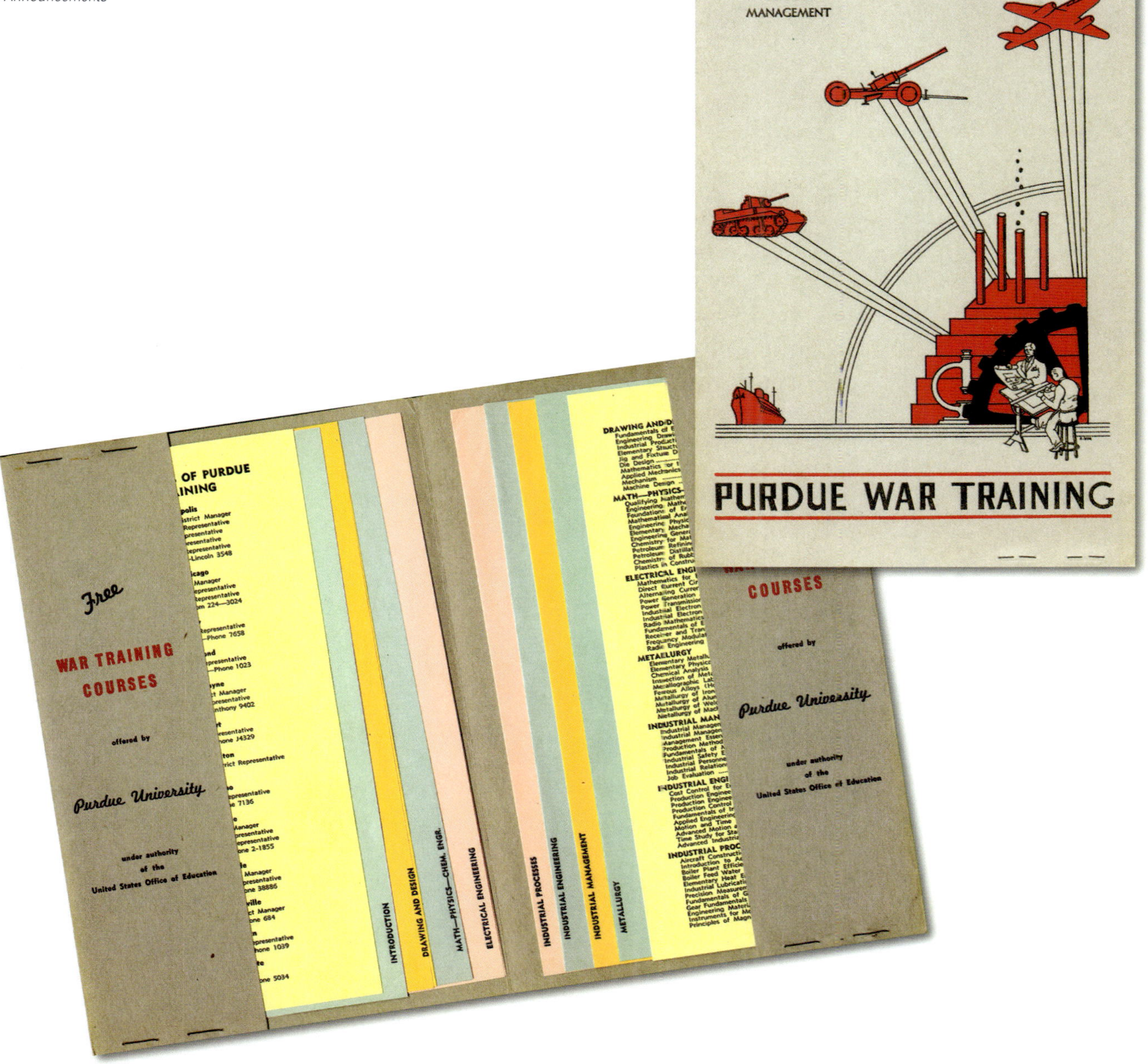

For the first half of the 1940s, Purdue focused on helping the nation and contributing to World War II. Purdue established the Defense Training Office, later known as the War Training Office, to administer training programs for workers in the defense industry.[3] Through this office, the University's Engineering-Science-Management War Training program helped train approximately sixty thousand workers.[4]

Cadette Johnny Hemphill working on a disassembly project, October 1943. *(Totsye Harper Winslow papers on the Curtiss Wright Cadettes)*

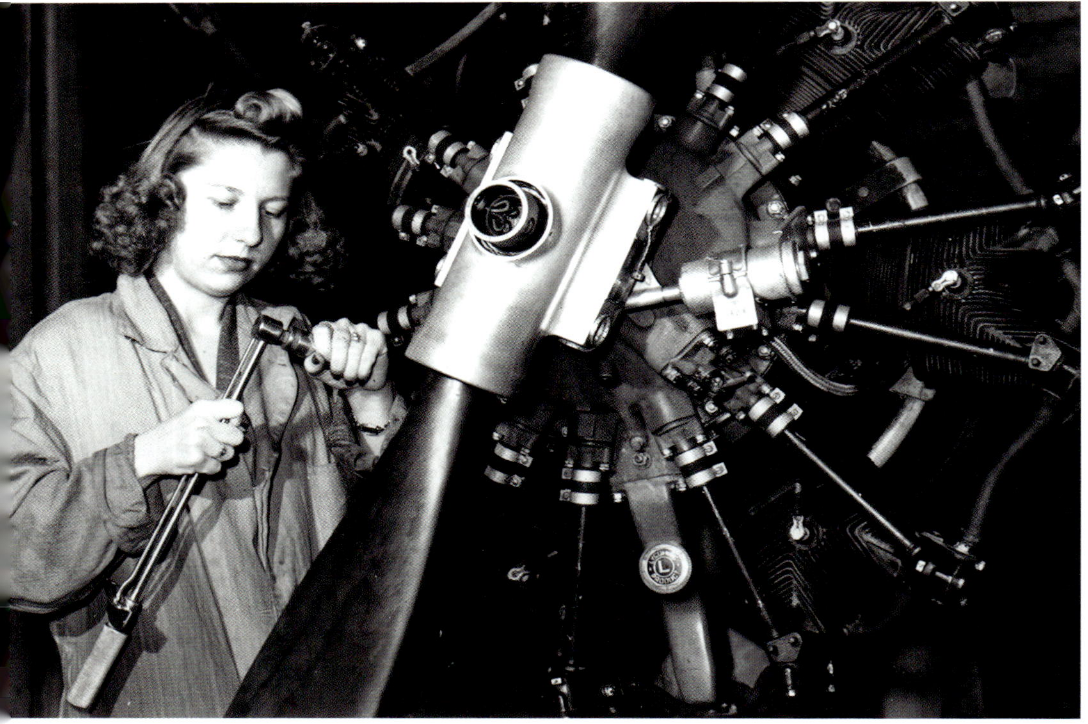

In 1941, the U.S. Navy began selecting men for the first squadron of the Flying Boilermakers, a group of naval aviation cadets who would go through training as a group.[5] The following summer, trainees in a course on explosives set off test explosions behind the Chemical and Metallurgical Engineering Building. Student registration dropped in September 1941, after the activation of the Selective Service, and students struggled to choose whether to enlist, seek employment, or continue their education.

Byron Anderson, class of 1948, recalled:

> There were a number of Navy people here, they called them V-12s, and the Army had some people here at the time, too, and they had a flight school out here . . . it was a much smaller university. . . . Of course, the war is on and everything's different, and you're on rationing, and so forth, and can't get gasoline, it's hard to go anyplace, and nobody had any money anyway. . . . [I]f you didn't have a uniform on, you were really sort of out of place, because nobody had any money to buy clothes, so we just wore our uniforms.[6]

Three wartime programs to prepare women for filling engineering jobs were hosted at Purdue from 1943 to 1945: the Curtiss-Wright Cadettes, the RCA Cadettes, and the Wright Field Cadettes.[7]

Both the Army and the Navy opened training programs at the University in 1943.[8] The Navy V-12 Program, inaugurated at Purdue in July 1943, offered college-level instruction to selected high school graduates, college-level students, and others to provide an ongoing supply of officer candidates in special fields required by the U.S. Navy, Marine Corps, and Coast Guard.[9]

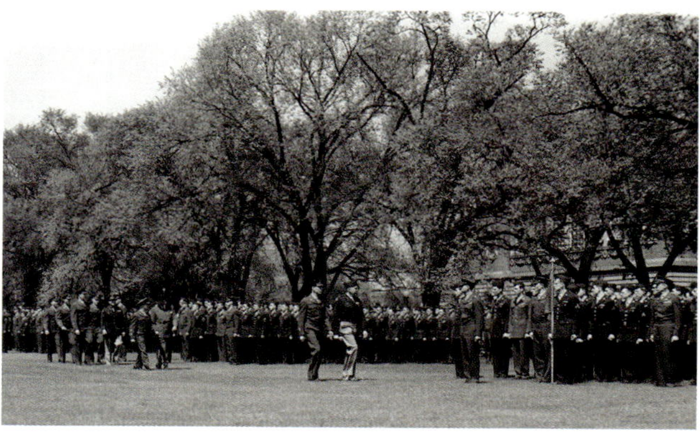

Inspection of Purdue University ROTC by War Department representatives, 1947. *(Purdue University photographs)*

The first woman officer who was a full-fledged member of the Civil Engineering Corps of the Navy, Kathleen F. Lux, graduated with a civil engineering degree from Purdue University in 1942.[10]

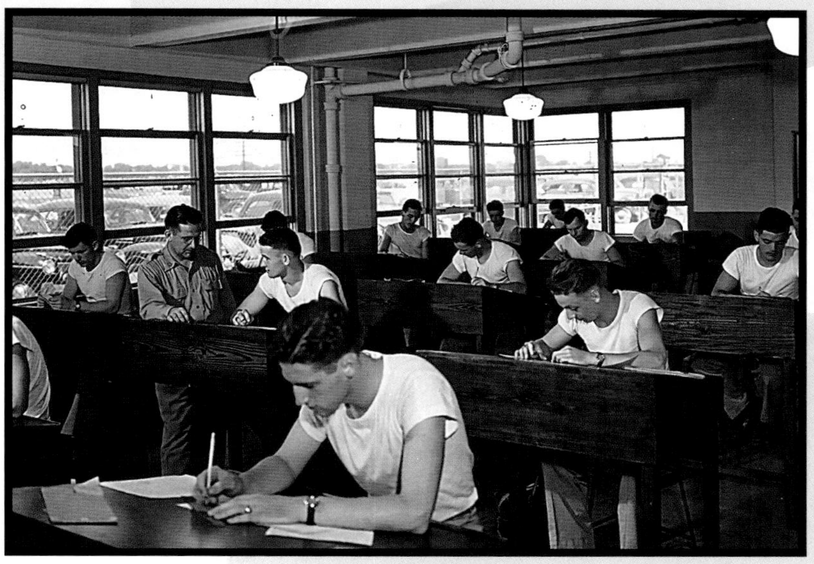

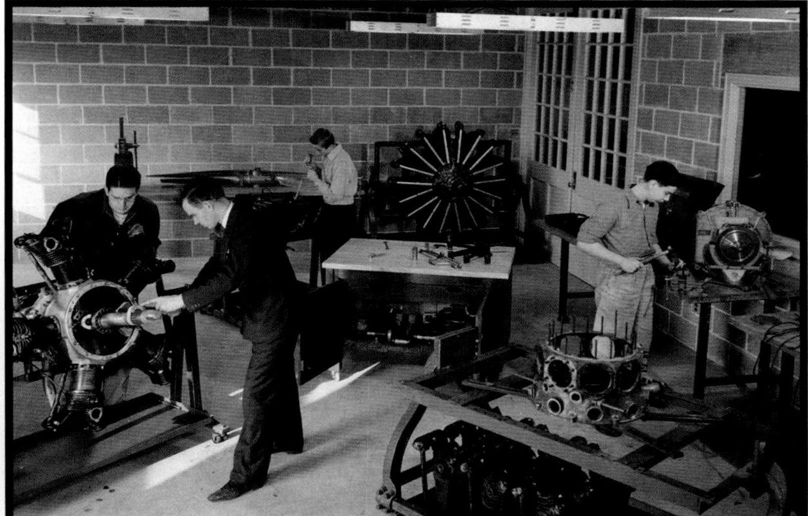

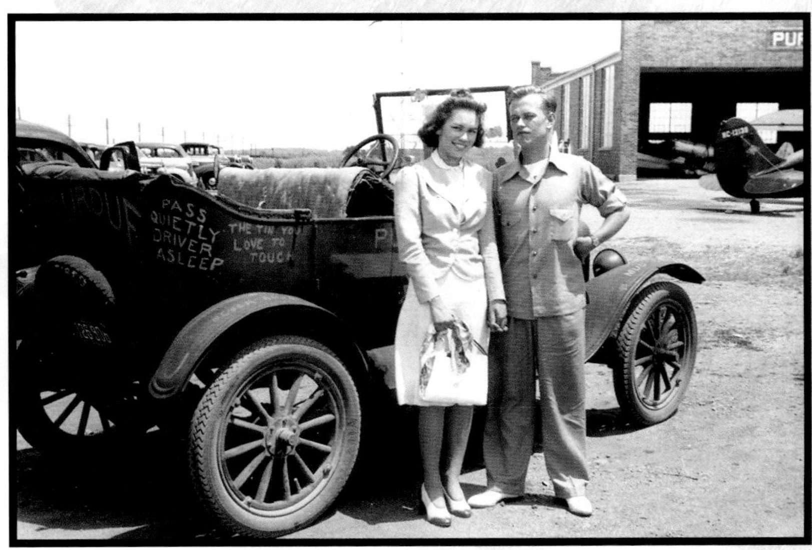

Top: V-5 trainees in the classroom, School of Aviation Technology, 1944.
(Purdue University photographs)

Middle: V-5 trainees working on engines, 1944.
(Purdue University photographs)

Bottom: Miller J. Tonkel and his girlfriend pose in front of a decorated Purdue-themed car at the Purdue Airport, 1940.
(Miller J. Tonkel papers)

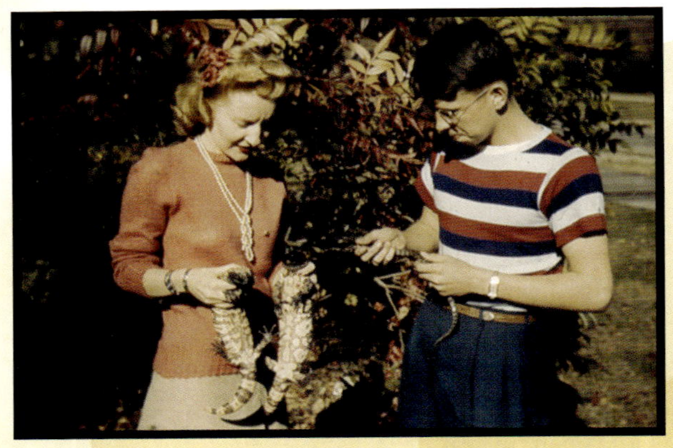

Top: Science students with reptiles, circa 1946. *(Purdue University photographs)*

Middle left: George Yock, Lyle Crist, Dick Frazer, and Don Cripe broadcast for WBAA from a basketball game, 1945. *(WBAA records)*

Middle right: Students participating in Purdue's physical preparedness program, 1942. *(Purdue University photographs)*

Bottom: Elliott Hall of Music during its dedication, May 3, 1940. At the time of its construction, the Hall of Music's seating capacity of six thousand was among the largest in the world. *(Purdue University photographs)*

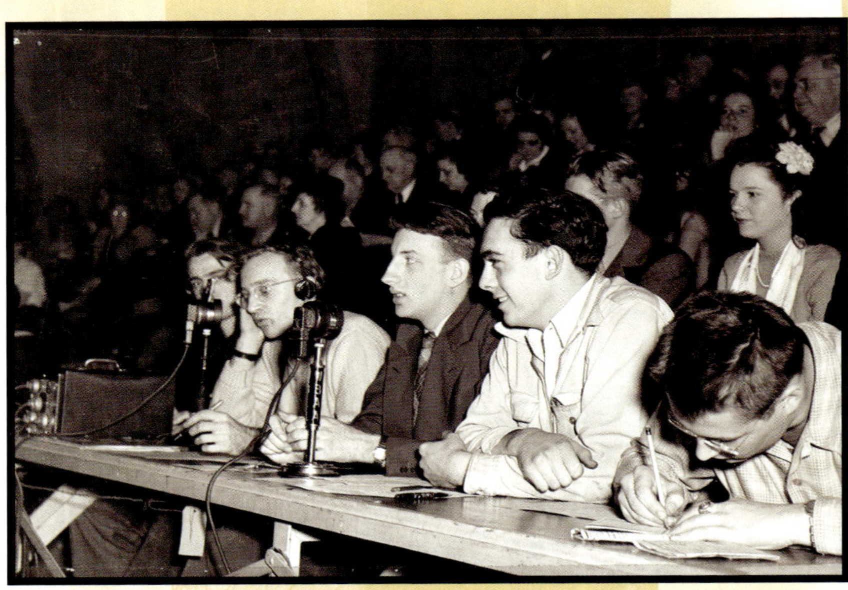

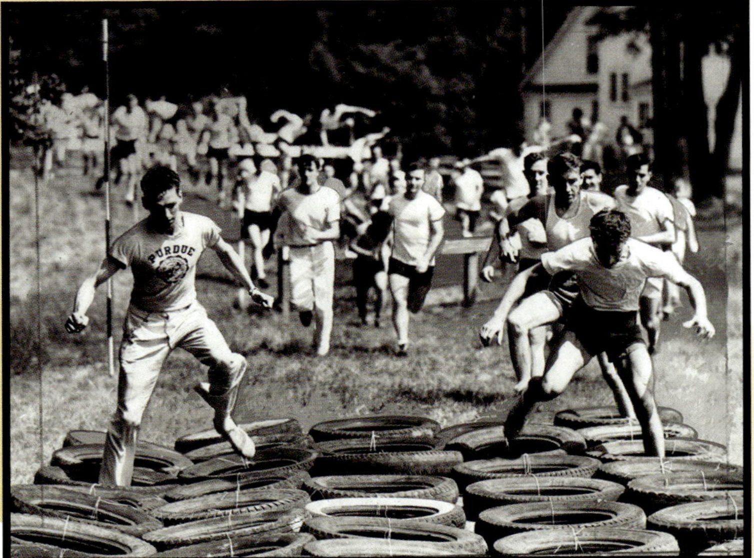

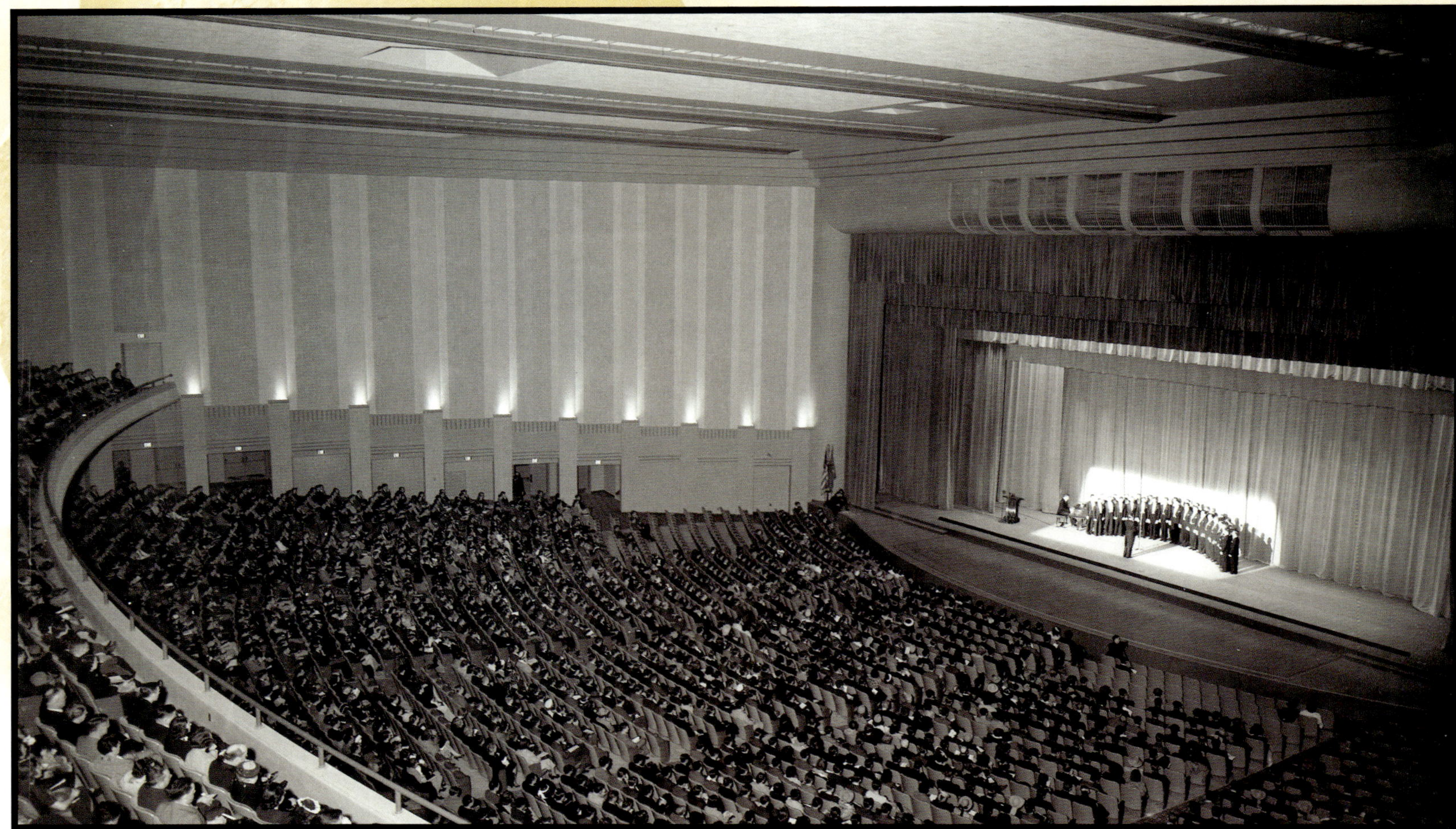

A wartime Christmas letter from Purdue University to the Purdue community, 1944. *(Purdue World War II Announcements and Publications)*

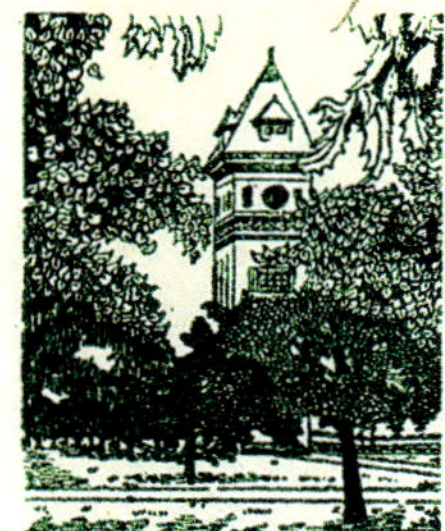

Christmas Thought Of You
From Your Old Purdue

December, 1944

Dear Boilermaker:

May this Purdue signal pass the barriers of time and space and battle fronts. May it reach you packed with the meaning of our hopes for you, hopes understood by all those who mark the Christmas season.

May this be the last of the years of war, and the beginning of a year when a new peace is created for all nations and new hopes are born in the hearts of all men.

Thus, our gift of sentiment. We await your answering signal.

Space pioneer Iven C. Kincheloe Jr. graduated from Purdue in 1949.

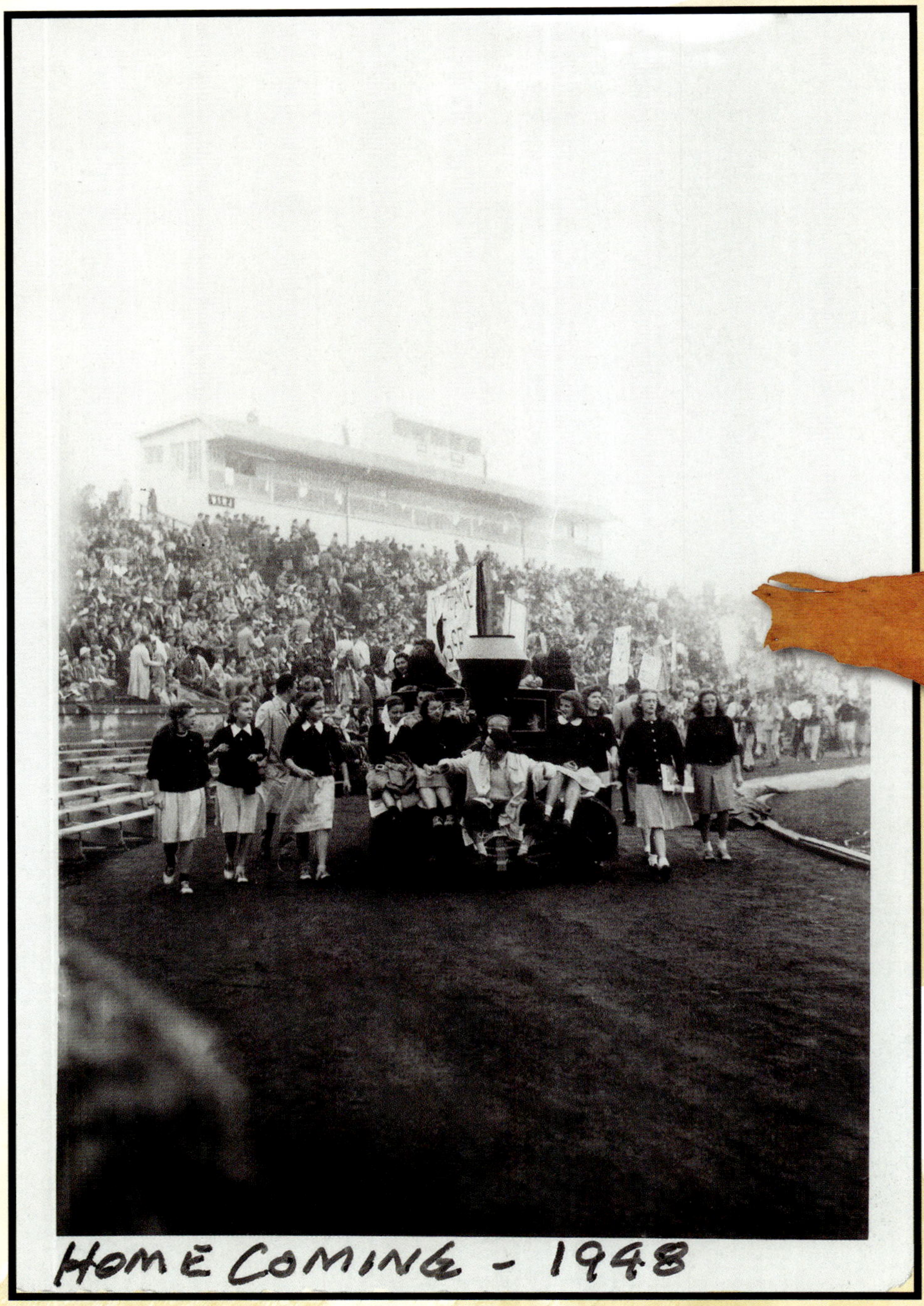

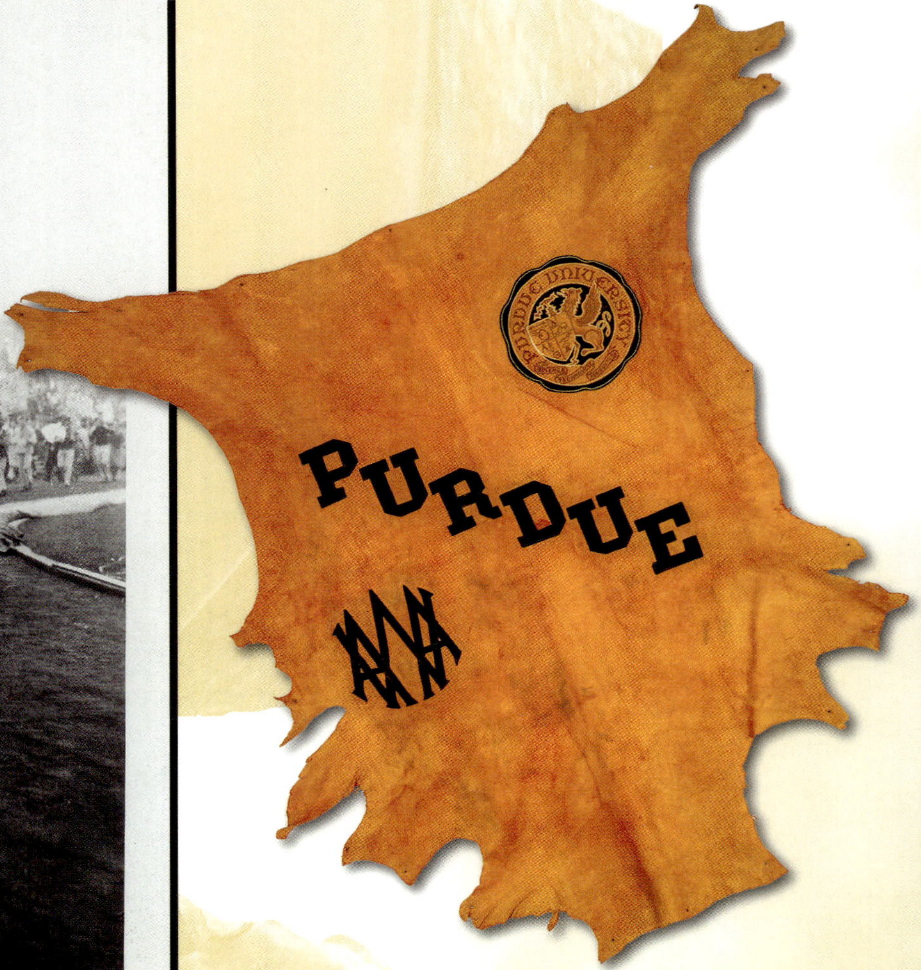

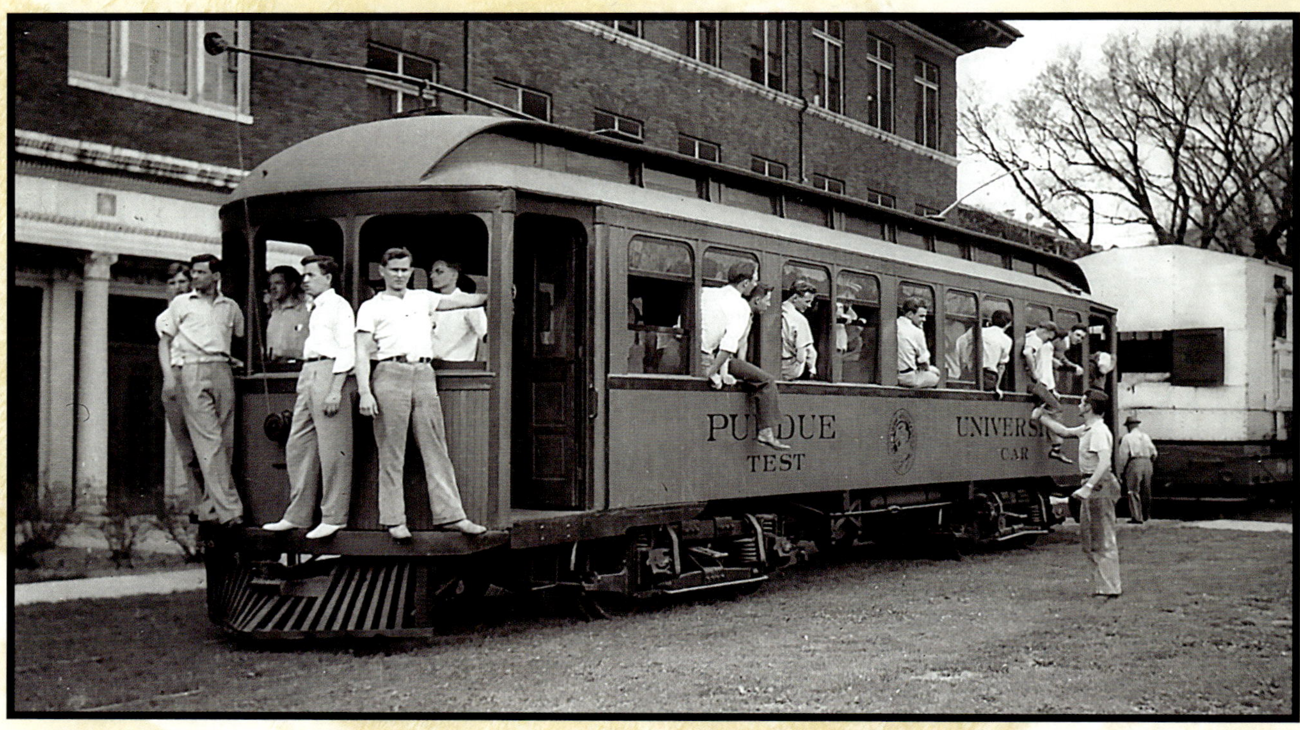

Top left: Students riding the Boilermaker Special, Homecoming 1948. *(Purdue University photographs)*

Top right: Leather skin awarded to Eleanor Harrison by the Women's Athletic Association in 1942. Each year, the WAA awarded a skin to one outstanding senior in the group. *(Eleanor Harrison collection)*

Right: Men on Purdue test car, May 1940. *(Purdue University photographs)*

The Way It Was at Purdue, 1941–1945

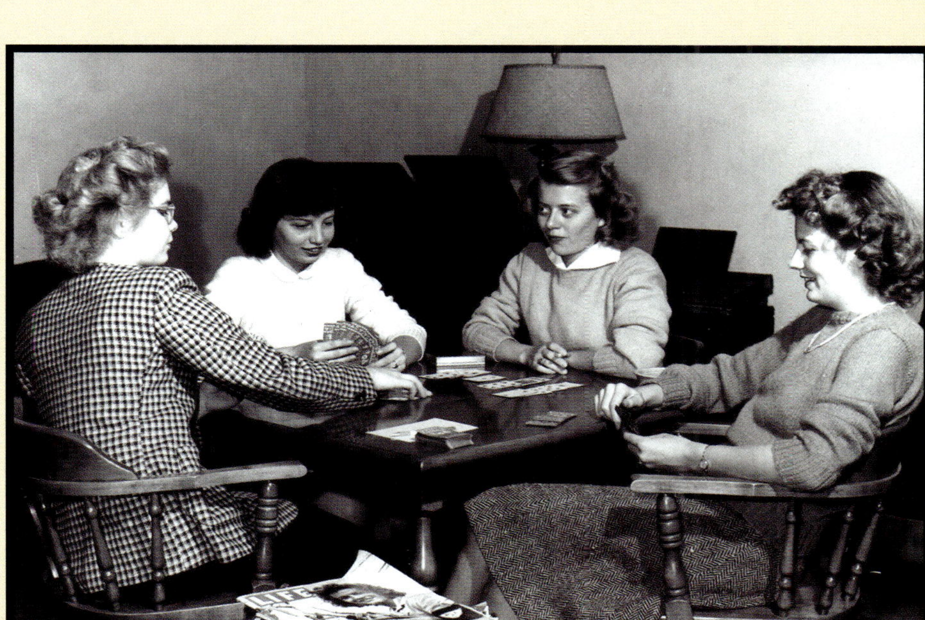

I came to Purdue as a freshman in September 1941. There were four male students for every female student. . . . We were welcomed by the University President, Edward C. Elliott, after which another man spoke and among other things told us to look first to our right, then left, and by the end of the year one of the three would still be a Purdue student.

Everyone registered for class assignments in the armory at the beginning of each semester. The "Green Guard" was an honorary group of upper level women students which helped new women with registration. . . . Each student received a "Passport" on which were our photographs and which allowed us to attend . . . games, convocations, some dances and other activities. All freshmen, both men and women, were expected to wear freshman beanies, small green felt caps.

Slacks for women were not permitted on campus and none of my friends even owned slacks or jeans. Saddle shoes and ankle sox were common footwear for coeds and skirts and sweaters or sweater sets were normal attire for attending class. However, in the dorms, women were required to wear heels and hose at dinner time. Six girls were seated at each table and one of them served as a hostess for the table—this assignment changed every evening. Only the hostess was permitted to speak to the waiter on behalf of her table mates when asking for any additional needs, such as coffee, water, milk, etc. . . .

Each dormitory had a house mother, and each floor had a "smoker" (room). . . . Washers and dryers were in the basement; but many students had heavy card board boxes about 24 × 15 × 4 inches in which laundry was mailed home to be washed, ironed, and returned, perhaps with some treats tucked inside the clothing.

—Esther Conelley Boonstra, class of 1945[11]

Above: Students relax with a game of cards. *(Totsye Harper Winslow papers on the Curtiss Wright Cadettes)*

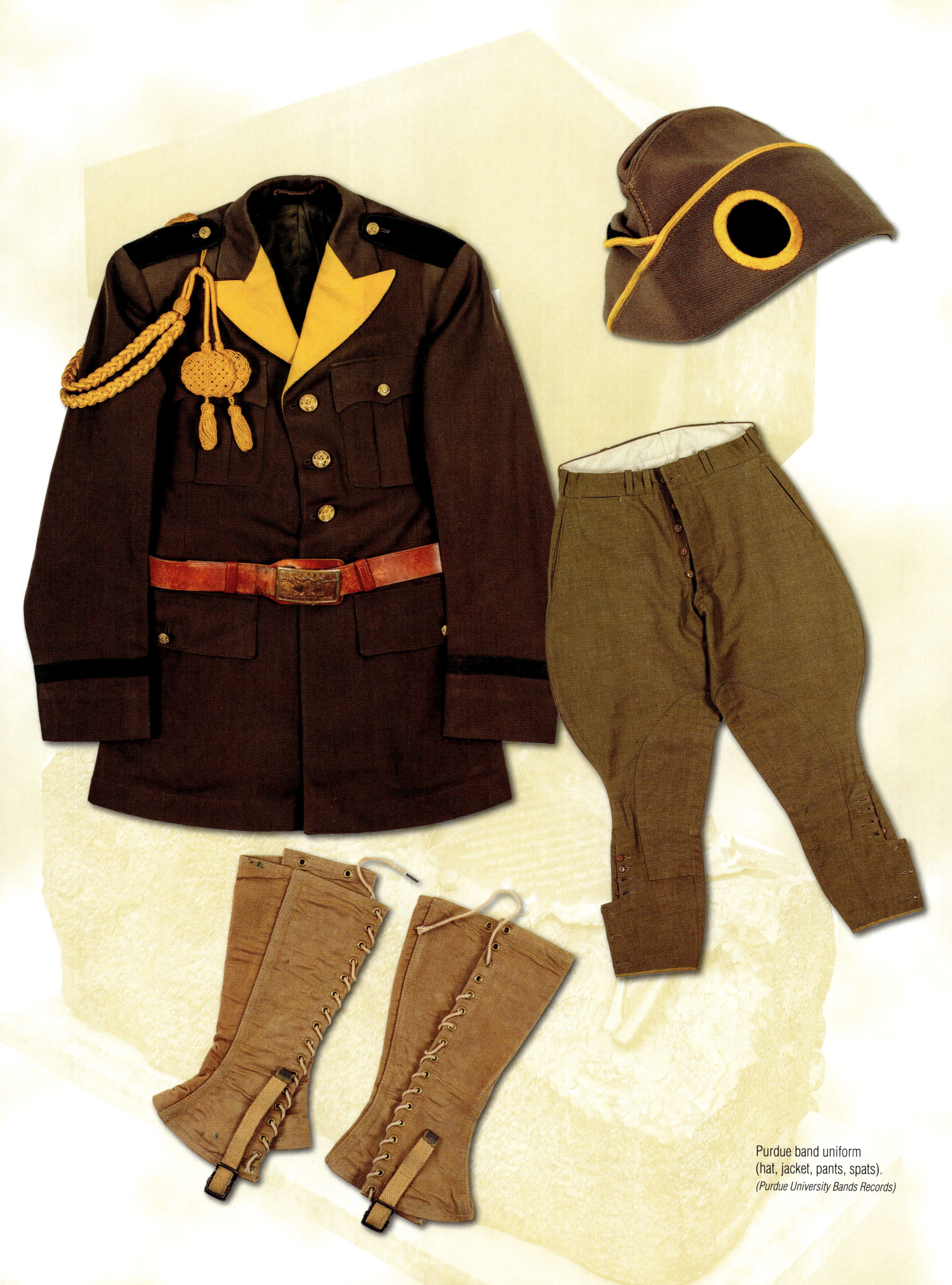

Purdue band uniform
(hat, jacket, pants, spats).
(Purdue University Bands Records)

Perhaps because of the influx of men in military training programs, Purdue had an outstanding football team for the 1943–1944 year. The Navy V-12 program brought athletes to Purdue from other schools, including Anthony J. Butkowitz of the University of Illinois, who became an All-American.[12] The Boilermakers were undefeated in the 1943 football season, the only such major team in the country.[13] Perhaps just as importantly, Purdue defeated its rival, Indiana University, for the Old Oaken Bucket in a 7–0 game that year. As the student editors of the yearbook proclaimed, "This was the first time Indiana had been scoreless since the old days when 'Boilermakers' were literally Boilermakers."[14]

After the War Department changed a policy about the organization of Army Field Artillery units, Purdue began admitting African American students to the ROTC in 1942.[15] Frederick C. Branch, the first African American commissioned officer in the United States Marine Corps, was among those who received Navy V-12 training at Purdue.[16]

During these tumultuous war years new student traditions were born—most notably two of Purdue's most iconic symbols for school spirit: Purdue Pete and the Boilermaker Special. Students, faculty, and staff with war on their minds needed time for fun activities such as attending dances, pep rallies, and sports competitions. The Boilermaker Special and Purdue Pete helped bring the Purdue community together and display its pride.

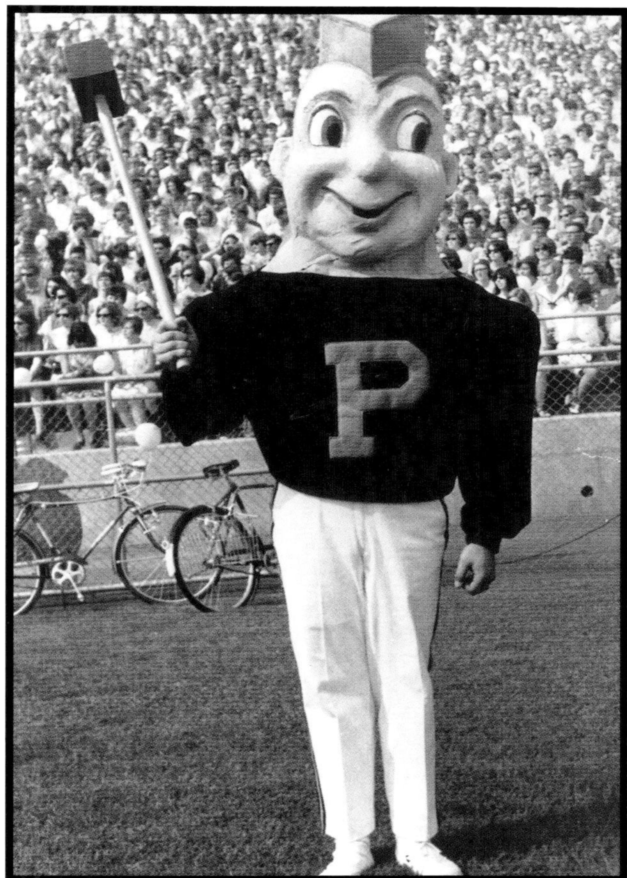

Purdue Pete, or Boilermaker Pete as he was first known.
(Purdue University photographs)

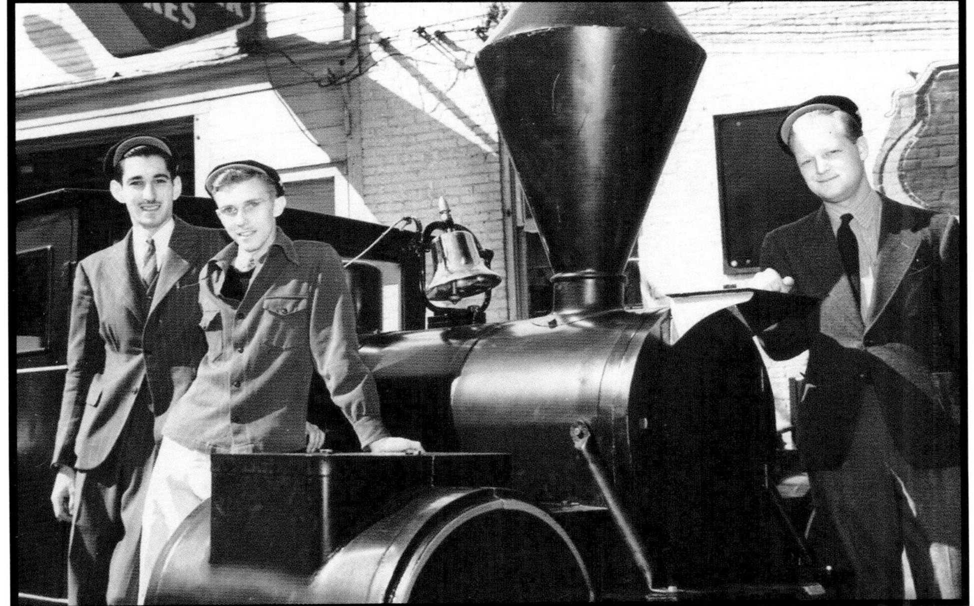

Reamer Club members Israel Selkowitz, Warren Archibald, and Elbert S. Bohlin, who were instrumental in the creation of the Boilermaker Special.
(Purdue University photographs)

Right: Pete in the *Debris* yearbook. *(Debris yearbook)*

Below: A Quonset hut at the north end of the Armory served as an ROTC classroom. *(Purdue University photographs)*

The cover of the *Debris* yearbook for 1944 displayed a character that would become forever after interwoven in Purdue's history. This barrel-chested figure, often shown carrying a hammer, was first introduced as Boilermaker Pete. The editors of the yearbook described Pete as "a familiar campus personage" who was stepping "into the spotlight with his busy role of wartime duties and service" by symbolizing the spirit of Purdue.[17] According to some sources, prior to his appearance in the yearbook, Purdue Pete was created as an advertisement logo by University Bookstore founders M. C. "Red" Sammons and Bob "Doc" Epple.[18]

The Varsity Glee Club, composed of men from the University Choir, performed at Carnegie Hall in 1942 as finalists in the National Glee Club Competition sponsored by popular radio host Fred Waring. The group was named runner-up but gained national attention for the strength of its performance.[19] That same year the Purdue Musical Organizations director, Al Stewart, formed a new musical group, the Purduettes. This singing group of thirteen women students was created in response to the temporary disbanding of the Concert Choir during the war.[20]

Campus overcrowding became a serious problem as veterans returned to campus after the war, many taking advantage of the G.I. Bill. Enrollment nearly tripled, and facilities, many of which had been minimally repaired and maintained during war years, were unprepared for this dramatic growth.[21] Temporary housing erected on campus helped alleviate some housing problems. In 1946, due to shortages in classroom and housing facilities, Purdue was forced to turn down five thousand registrants for the fall semester. Students lived in attics and basements of some buildings, faculty stayed in rooms in the Union, and some fraternities "acquired Quonset huts to take care of their returned G.I.'s."[22]

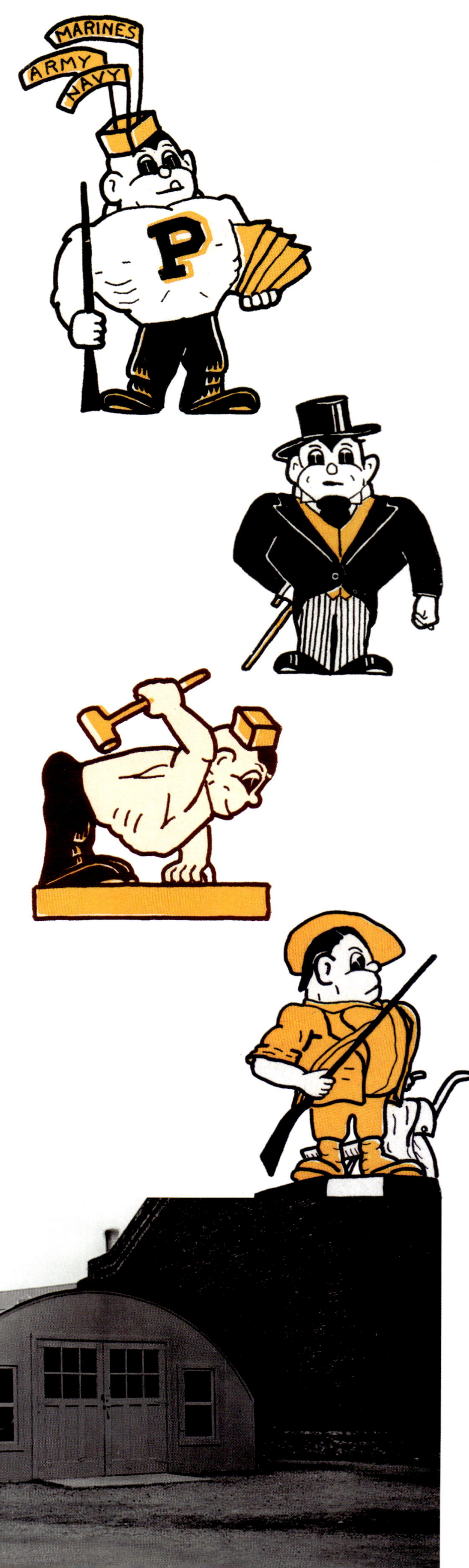

The beginnings of what would become known as Purdue's branch campuses in Fort Wayne, Indianapolis, North Central, and Calumet all began in the 1940s. Fort Wayne, Indianapolis, and North Central first held classes in 1941–1942; the first regular university classes at Calumet were held in 1946–1947.[26]

Long-time president Edward C. Elliott retired in 1945. In recognition of his leadership and service, the Board of Trustees designated him as the first president emeritus of Purdue University.[23] Dean of Engineering A. A. Potter served temporarily as acting president until Frederick Hovde began his term as president in January 1946.[24]

For African American students on campus, the 1940s were a time of growing dissent and hard-won gains in status. Young men who had fought for the rights of others during the war came back to face limited rights imposed by segregation. The April 17, 1946, Board of Trustees minutes note an African American student's request to be admitted to the Men's Residence Halls. No action was taken at that time. Following pressure from Indiana governor Ralph Gates, Purdue desegregated student housing in 1947, allowing African American students to be housed in campus dormitories. An African American attorney and alumnus, Willard Ransom, challenged the segregation of sports at Purdue. Following a student protest, the University allowed a black student, Herman Murray, to play football.

In 1948 the trustees discussed the refusal of barbers in the Purdue Memorial Union to cut the hair of black students. This issue was brought to their attention by a letter-writing campaign from a non-campus organization, the Social Action Committee. In this meeting, President Hovde described his work trying to convince the barbers to cease discrimination against African American students. In response, the Board of Trustees unanimously reaffirmed its nondiscrimination policy "in all University activities."[25]

Purdue's first female swimmer, Jeanne Wilson Vaughan, competed in the 1948 Olympic Games.

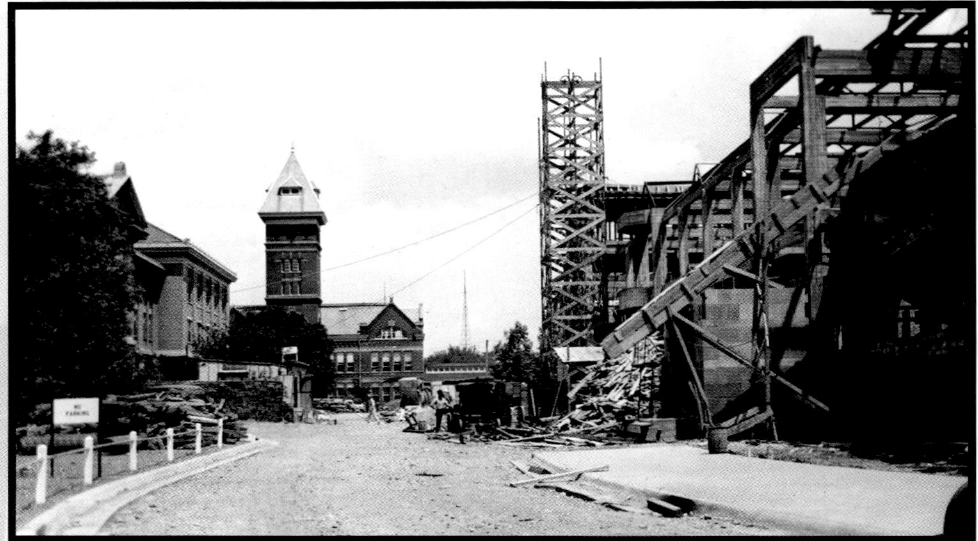

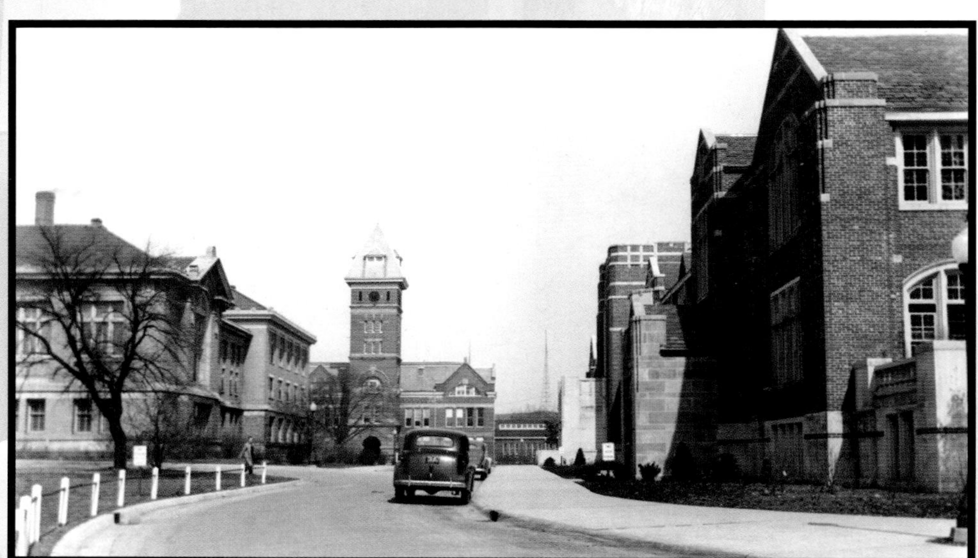

Top: During construction on an addition to the Purdue Memorial Union with the Library and Heavilon Hall visible on the left. *(Miller J. Tonkel papers)*

Middle: After Union construction, Library and Heavilon Hall visible on left side of image. *(Miller J. Tonkel papers)*

Bottom: The entrance to Purdue's campus looking over Memorial Mall, 1940. *(Miller J. Tonkel papers)*

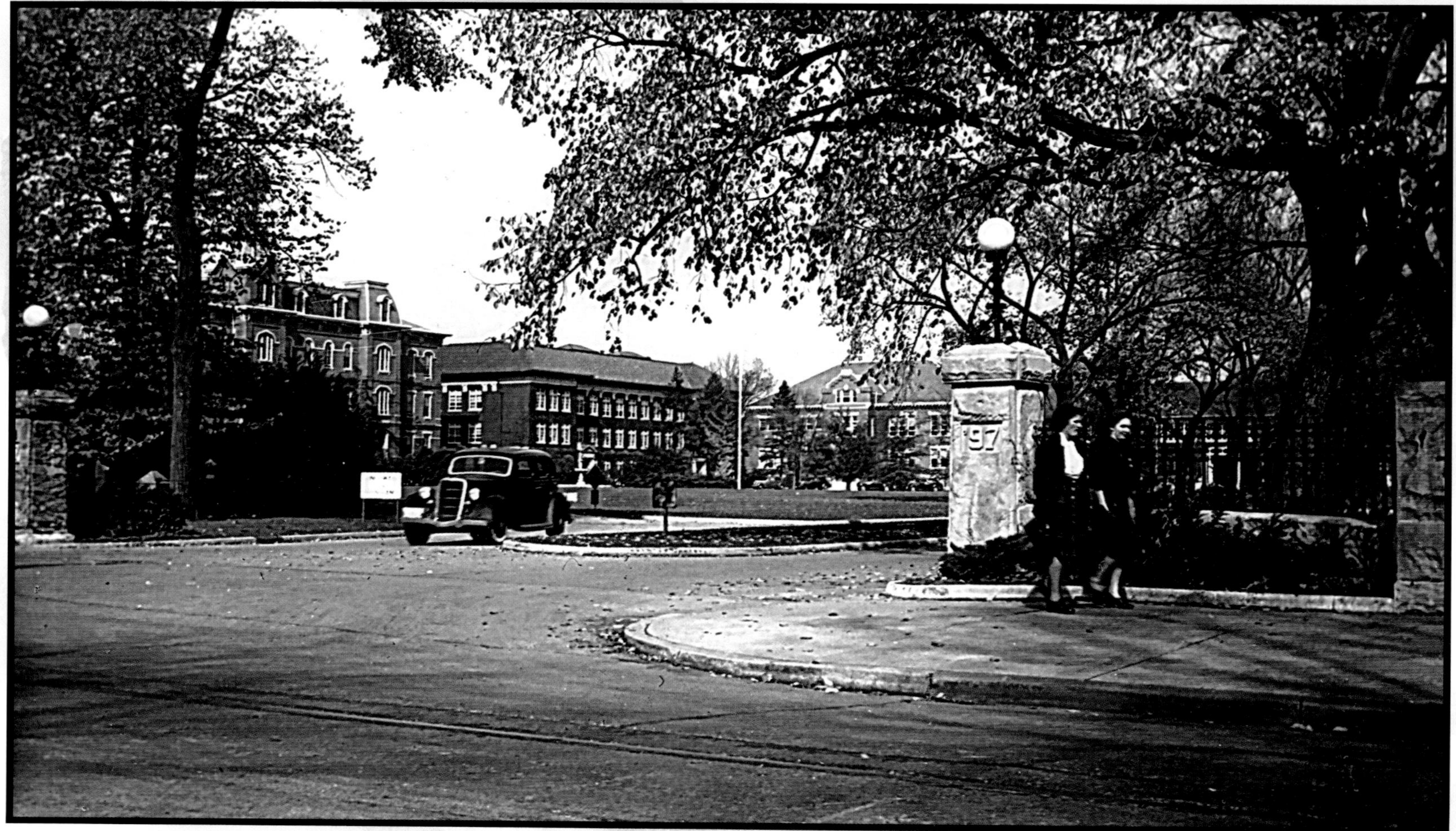

World record balloonist Malcolm D. Ross graduated from Purdue in 1941.

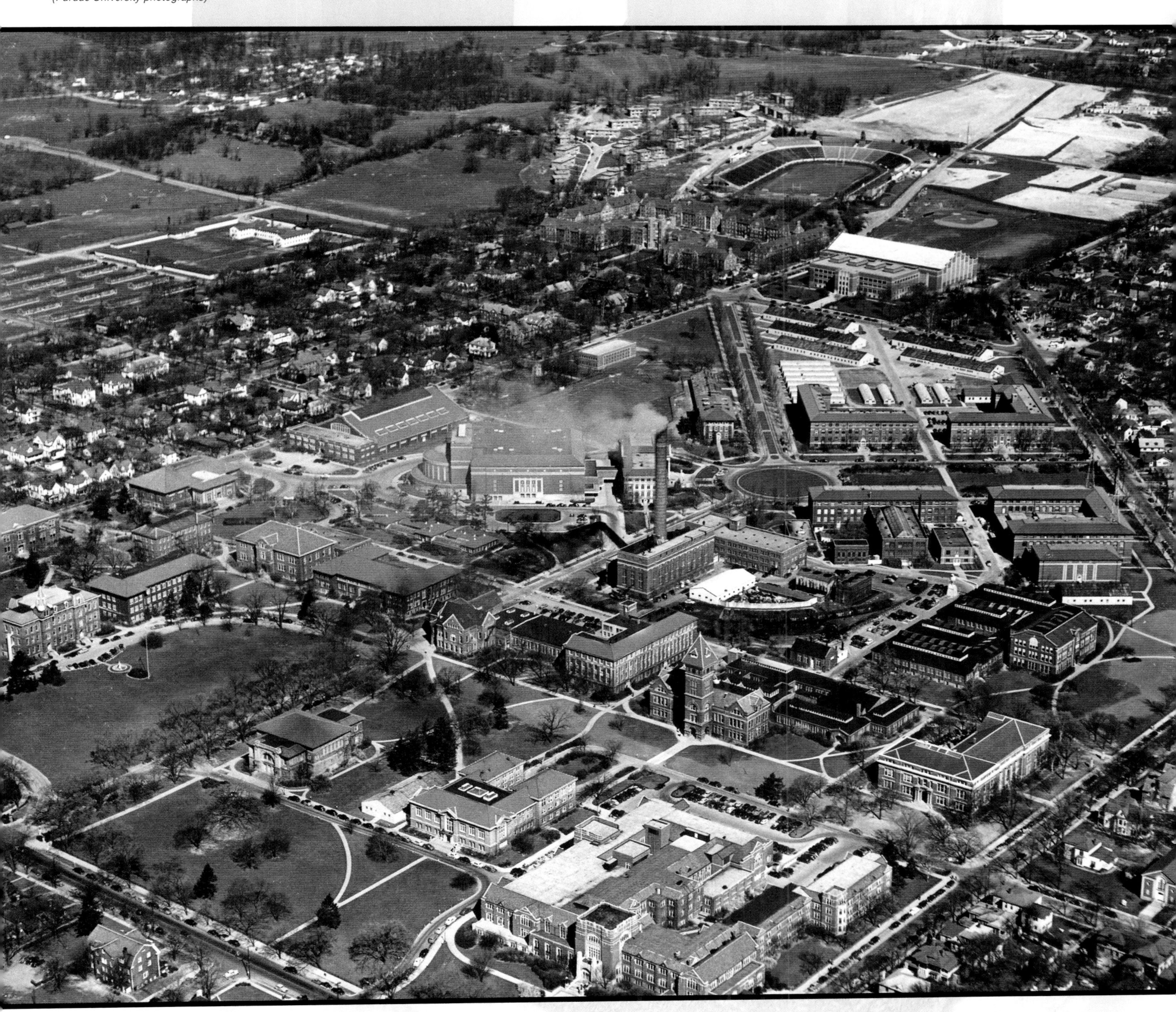

Aerial view of Purdue University campus, 1940s.
(Purdue University photographs)

Below: In a 1947 letter to Margaret Kennedy, student Thomas Hendrix alludes to an injury he sustained in an accident on campus, likely the bleacher collapse of February 1947. *(Thomas Hendrix letters to Margaret Kennedy)*

Purdue experienced one of its greatest campus tragedies in 1947. During the Purdue–Wisconsin basketball game on February 24, shortly following the players' departure from the court at halftime, the temporary bleachers holding approximately thirty-six hundred fans collapsed. The crowd did not panic, and spectators at the game immediately began offering help to individuals who were trapped under fallen beams. Members of the local community provided vehicles for transporting the injured to area hospitals. Three Purdue students—Roger Gelhausen, William Feldman, and Ted Nordquist—died and over five hundred people were treated for injuries by the Student Health Service and local hospitals.[27]

Graduate student Robert C. Forney described his experience from the bleachers:

> I heard a shout and some noise to my right which would be down towards the center of the grandstand. I turned around and faced in that direction but there were a lot of people standing up and I couldn't see anything. . . . Just about that time somebody in the balcony said "there she goes," and I . . . thought actually the balcony was moving. There was no sensation of motion of the grandstand at all but very shortly the balcony began to move upward and I came to the conclusion that we were falling.[28]

16 April 47

Dear Margaret,

Oh! Buddy what wonderful weather we have. at the present time it is snowing and it is really cold out. I went to class today and yesterday for the first time in seven weeks.

I had to stay here during Easter but it wasn't to bad. about three more of the kids are here with me from the accident.

In June I expect to graduate as I had planned but I will be short a couple of hours. The university is going to help me graduate. They should do something.

This summer I don't guess I can work as I had planned. I may go to school. I can take a few hours and get paid on the G.I. Bill. I may go to Emory.

I may get to take my cast off next week and get a brace. That will make life a little easier.

Well be good. at the present about all I can do is be good.

Love
Tom

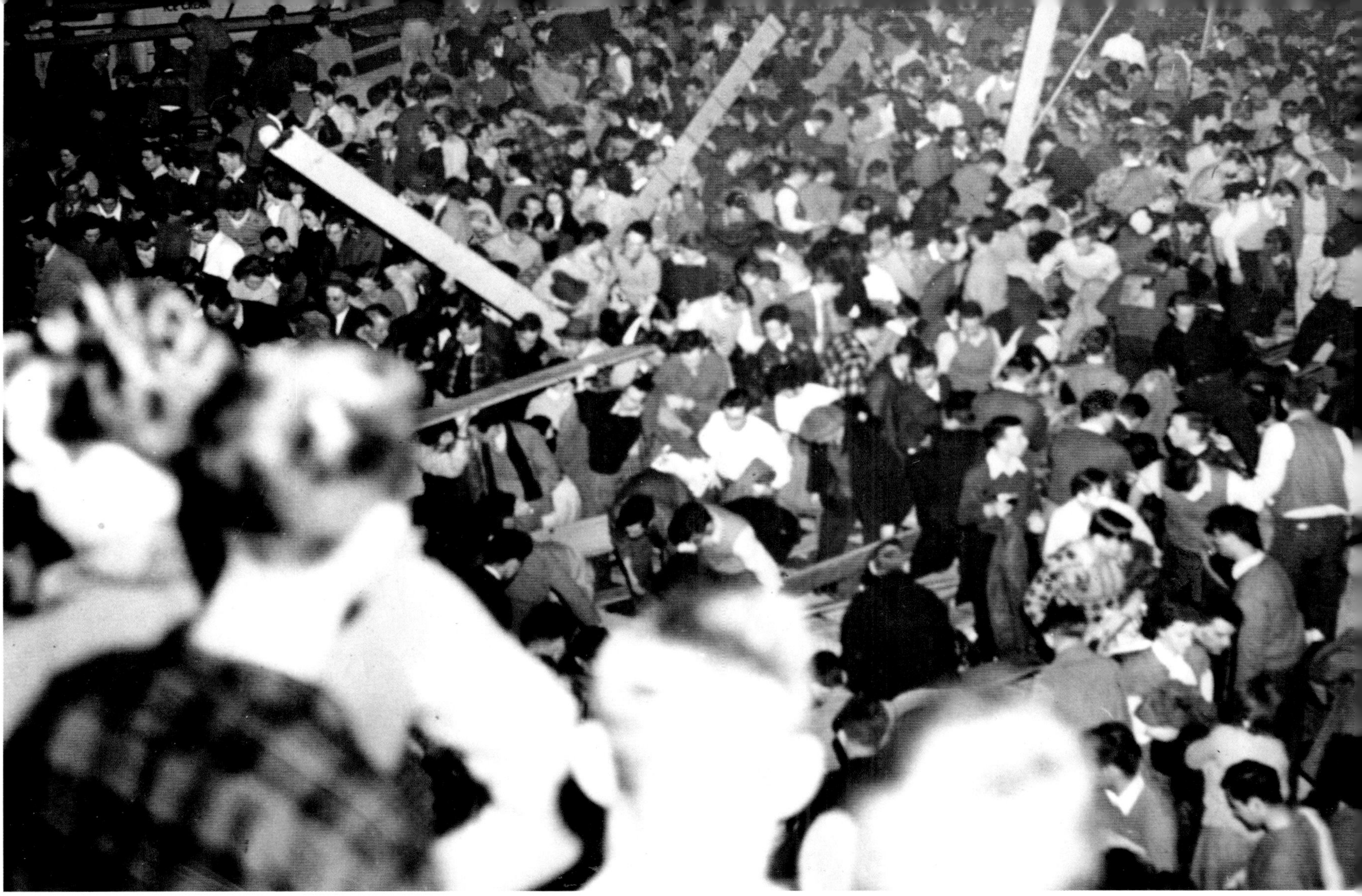

President and Mrs. Hovde visited injured students in the local hospitals and asked members of the faculty to pay them visits and provide them with reading material. The investigative committee concluded that the manufacturer's metal connections were insufficient for the load, resulting in structural failure. As noted in the student yearbook, the bleacher collapse was a tragedy that marked a "never to be forgotten game" in Purdue history.[29]

In 1949 the campus came together to form a more positive memory when the Disney movie *So Dear to My Heart* held its premiere at the Purdue Hall of Music. Partly filmed in Brown County, Indiana, and featuring 4-H Club work, the film was enthusiastically welcomed by the Purdue community. Walt Disney and the cast attended, and Purdue hosted a "Walt Disney Night." That same year, the Glee Club was chosen to represent the country's land-grant institutions by performing at the presidential inauguration ceremonies of Harry Truman.[30]

The 1940s was a decade of ups and downs—war, new student traditions, overcrowded conditions, and changes in gender and racial dynamics on campus. After the end of World War II, the University identified 14,000 names of alumni and former students who had served with the armed forces during the war. Thousands of alumni and former students were unreachable during the turbulent war years, and the records were incomplete. The University estimated that 17,500 men and women from Purdue contributed to the war effort by the time it ended.[31] More than 500 of them gave their lives to the war, and their names were listed in the Purdue Memorial Union on the Roll of Honor.[32]

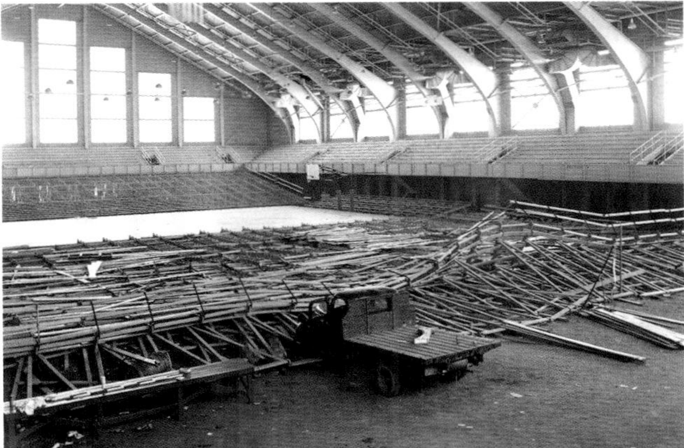

Above: The scene of the bleachers collapse at Lambert Fieldhouse, February 24, 1947. *(Purdue University photographs)*

Below: The aftermath of the bleachers collapse. *(Board of Trustees records)*

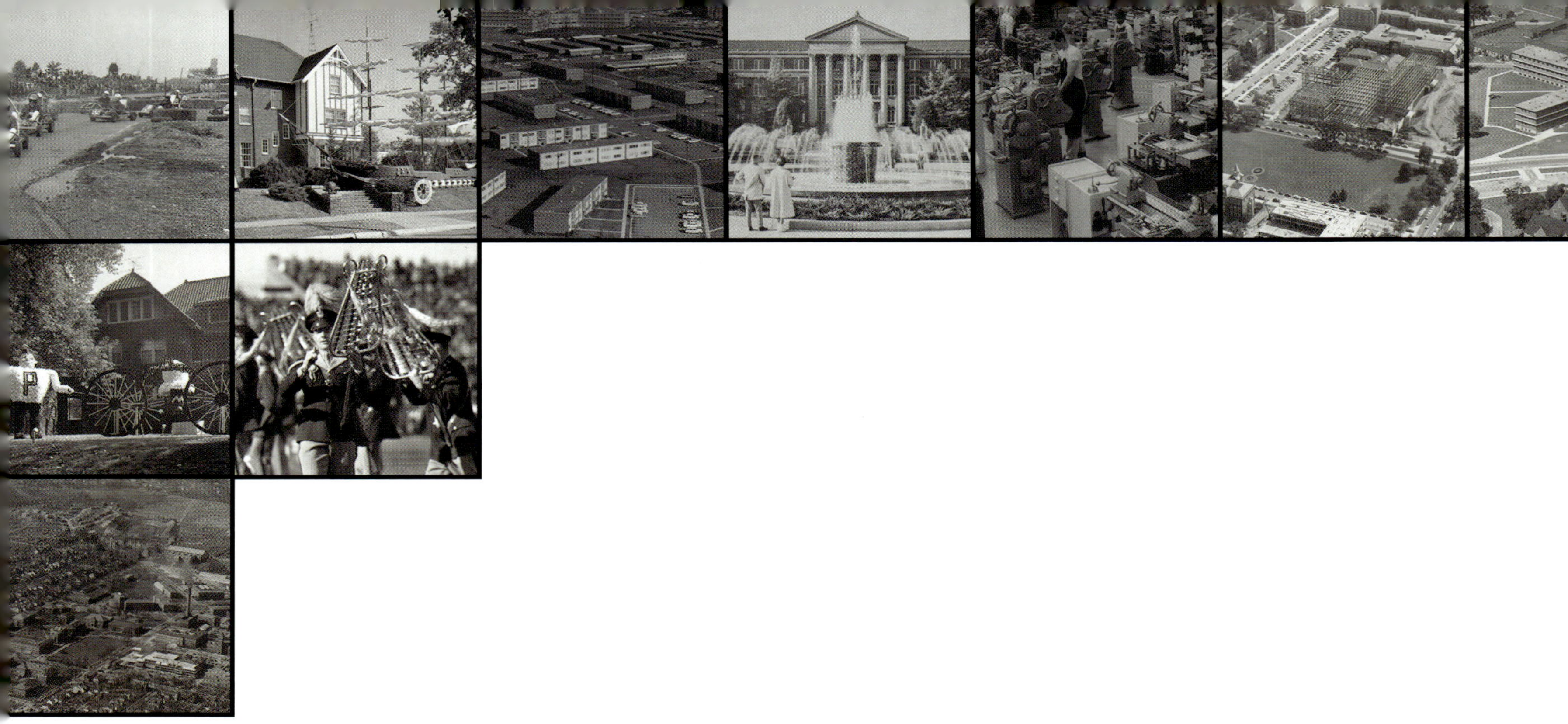

Bird's eye map of campus, 1951. *(Campus Maps collection)*

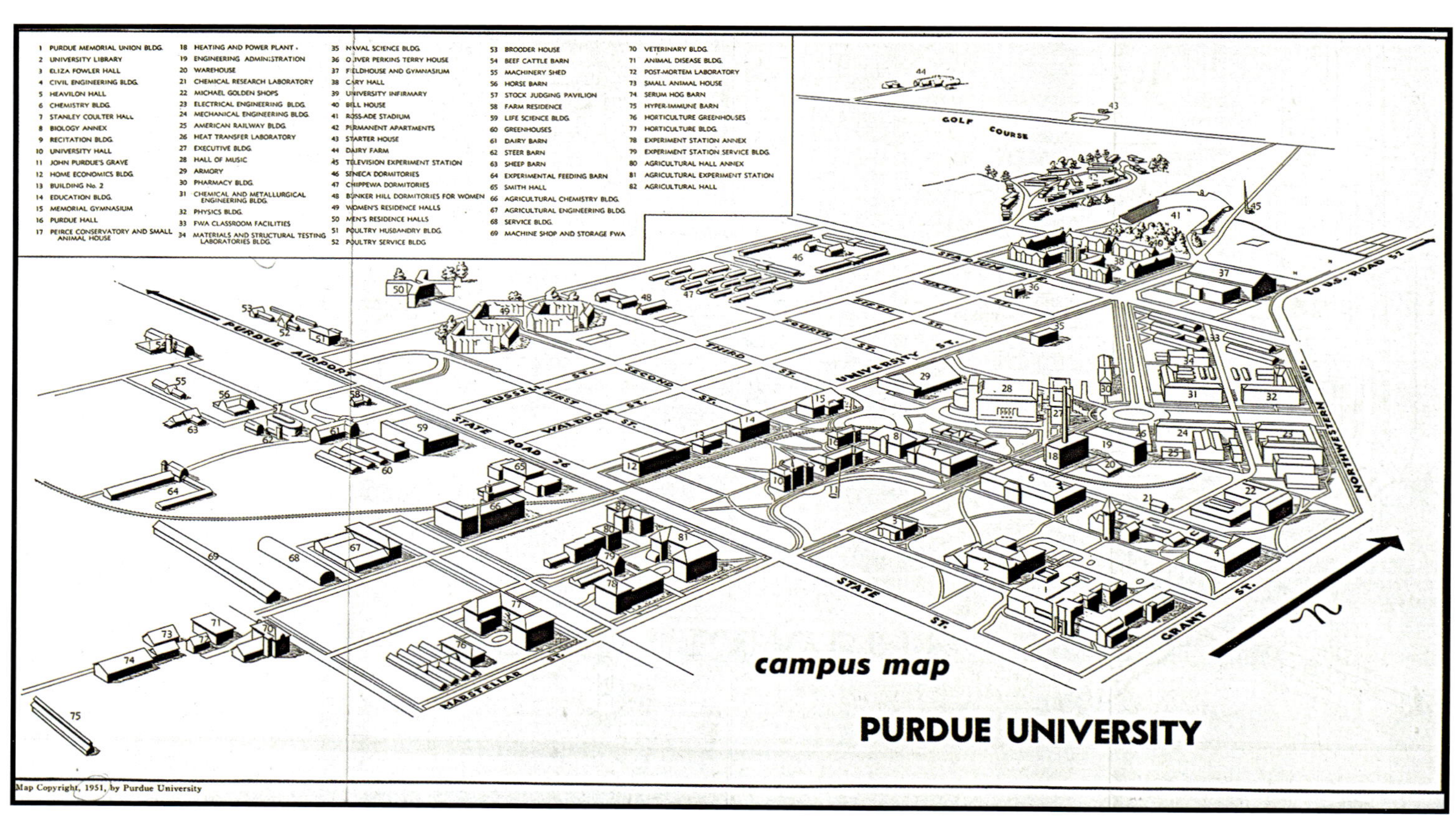

{ *Enrollment in 1950: 13,010 students*[1] }

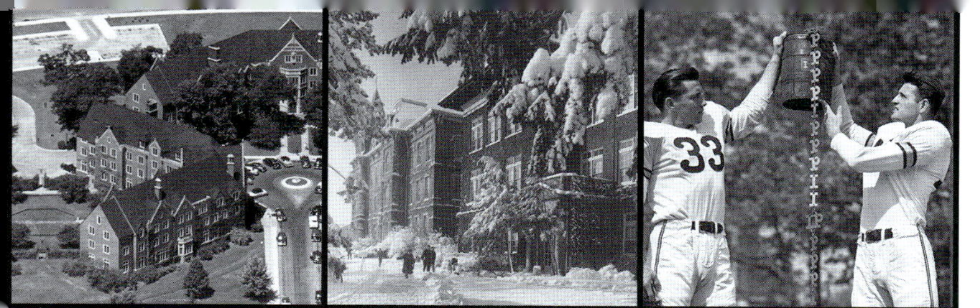

[The 1950s]

PURDUE AT 90

"Purdue was at its peak enrollment for a decade there with the G.I. Bill. I was thrust into classes as a seventeen-year-old with captains and colonels from the army who were 25 and 28 years old. I was amazed at the competition. They weren't just kids like me. These were G.I.s, and they were determined to get an education. It was an awakening."

—*Richard E. Grace, class of 1951*[2]

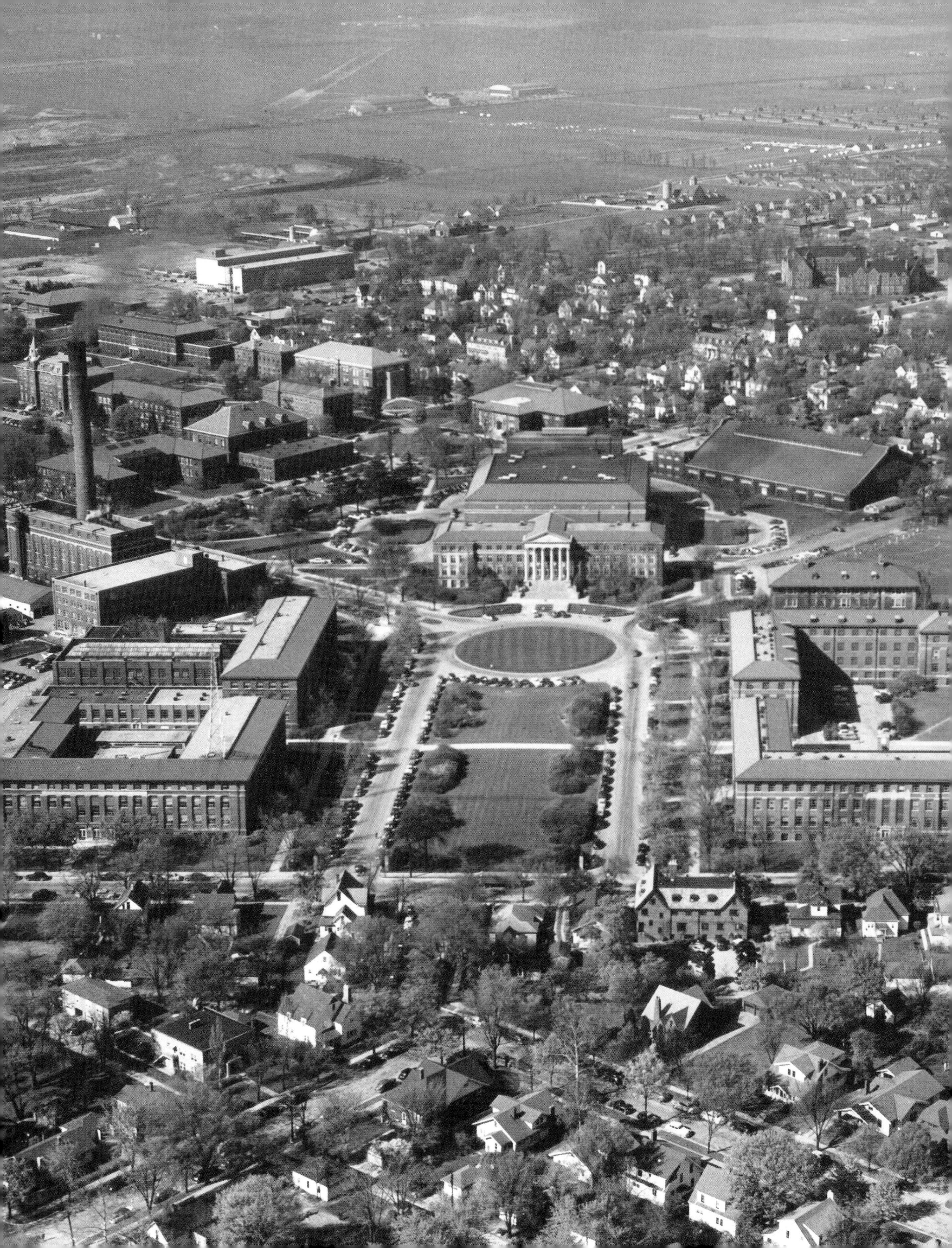

Commander Richard L. Duncan, U.S. Navy, was awarded the first PhD in the School of Aeronautical Engineering in 1950. Maurice Zucrow, who in 1928 had become the first person to receive a PhD in any field at Purdue, was his advisor.[3]

Aerial view looking to the southwest of the Purdue University campus, circa 1952. *(Purdue University photographs)*

The excitement of starting a new academic year in September of 1950 was tempered by the fact that the Korean War had started on June 25. ROTC cadets knew what they would be doing upon graduation, and many others wondered if the next few years would be as trying as those during the last war. Purdue's enrollment dropped by nearly 15 percent from 1949 to 1950, easing some of the overcrowding on campus that had resulted from the large influx of veterans attending school on the G.I. Bill after World War II. However, by 1954 the war was over and the Purdue population was back on the rise.

Mock P

Every four years from 1952 to 1968, the Mock Political Convention, or Mock P, gave Purdue students a hands-on opportunity to understand the mechanics of modern politics. Mirroring the national political process during the year before a presidential election, Purdue students were assigned to represent states based on their housing units, researched major political issues and public opinion on those issues in the states they represented, campaigned for their platforms and preferred presidential candidates in other dorms and residences, and finally, fought to have their voice heard on the floor of the political convention.

The three-day convention of the Purduvian Party, much like the national Democratic and Republican conventions, included a keynote address from a noted national political figure, the establishment of a party platform, and finally the selection of a presidential candidate. Delegates had to understand the political process thoroughly in order to conduct roll-call votes, propose amendments, and motion for recesses and adjournments. Since the voting age at the time was twenty-one, this was the only chance most students had to participate in a major national election.

Alumna Mary Lou Siefker remembered: "I was a freshman when they had Mock P, and we had meetings, we talked about possible political candidates, and then we would go out and campaign across campus. We would go to the other dorms and carry our signs and pass out brochures. Then we met in the fieldhouse, I believe it was, for the convention. It was row upon row upon row of delegates to the convention. Each housing unit had their own area, just as states in a political convention would have. And we would, at certain times and when certain things happened, get up and march around the stadium, chanting for our favorite possible candidate; that was a really exciting time and very enlightening time."[4]

In its first year, the Purduvians nominated Ohio senator Robert A. Taft, who lost the Republican primary to eventual president Dwight Eisenhower. In all four subsequent conventions, however, the candidate favored by the Purduvians won the presidency: Eisenhower, Kennedy, Johnson, and Nixon. In 1960, nominee John F. Kennedy adjusted his campaign schedule to accept his nomination in person, stating that "as Purdue goes, so goes the nation."[5]

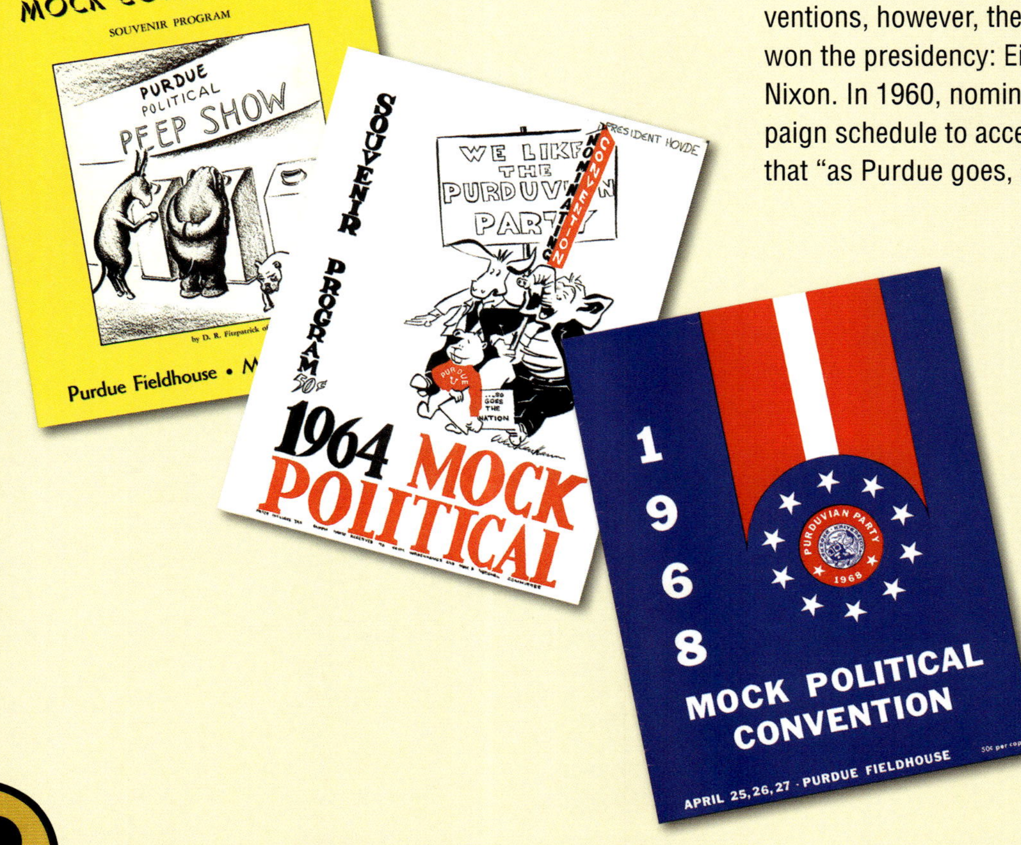

The 1952, 1964, and 1968 Mock P Convention programs. *(Frederick L. Hovde papers)*

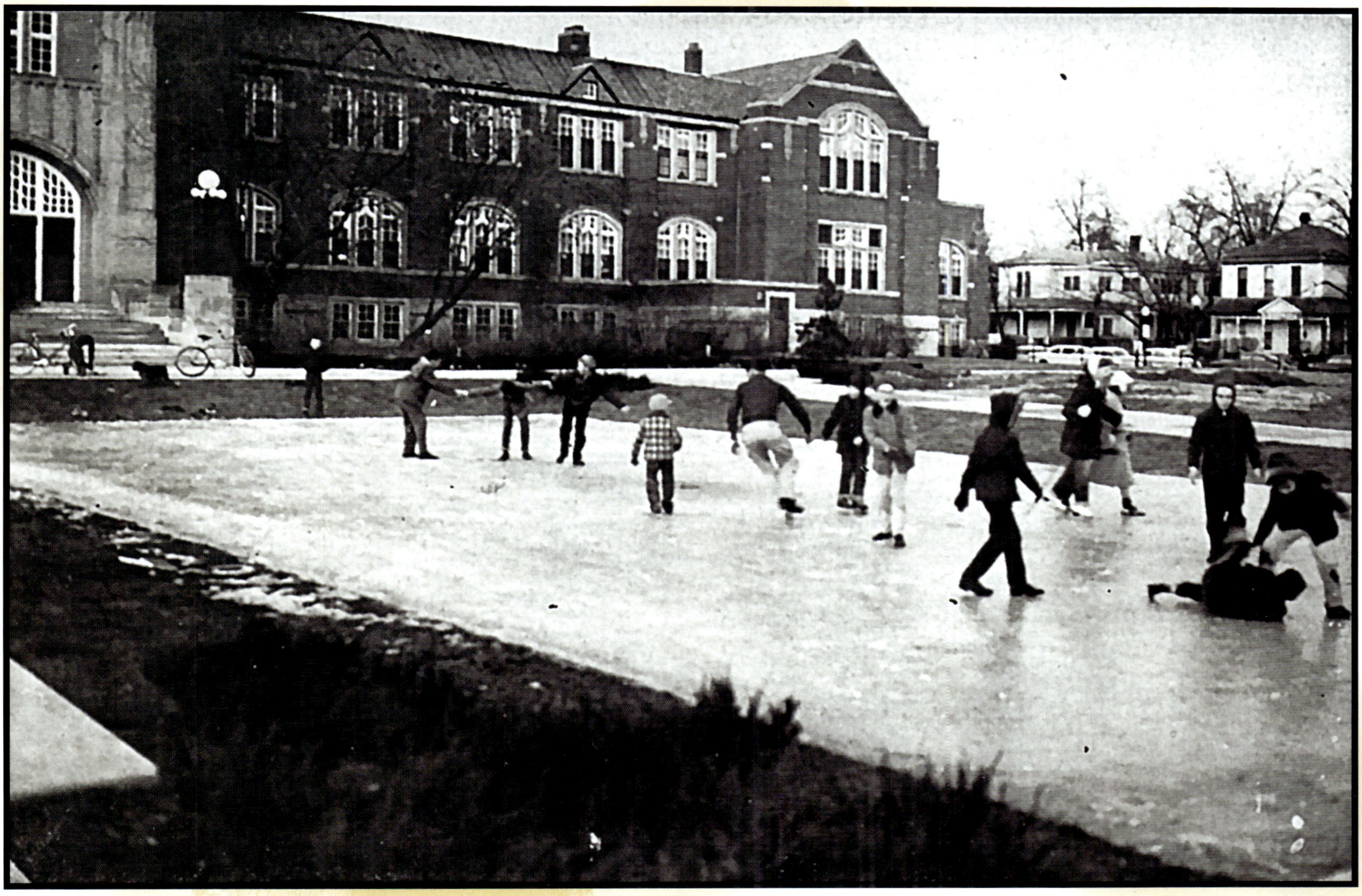

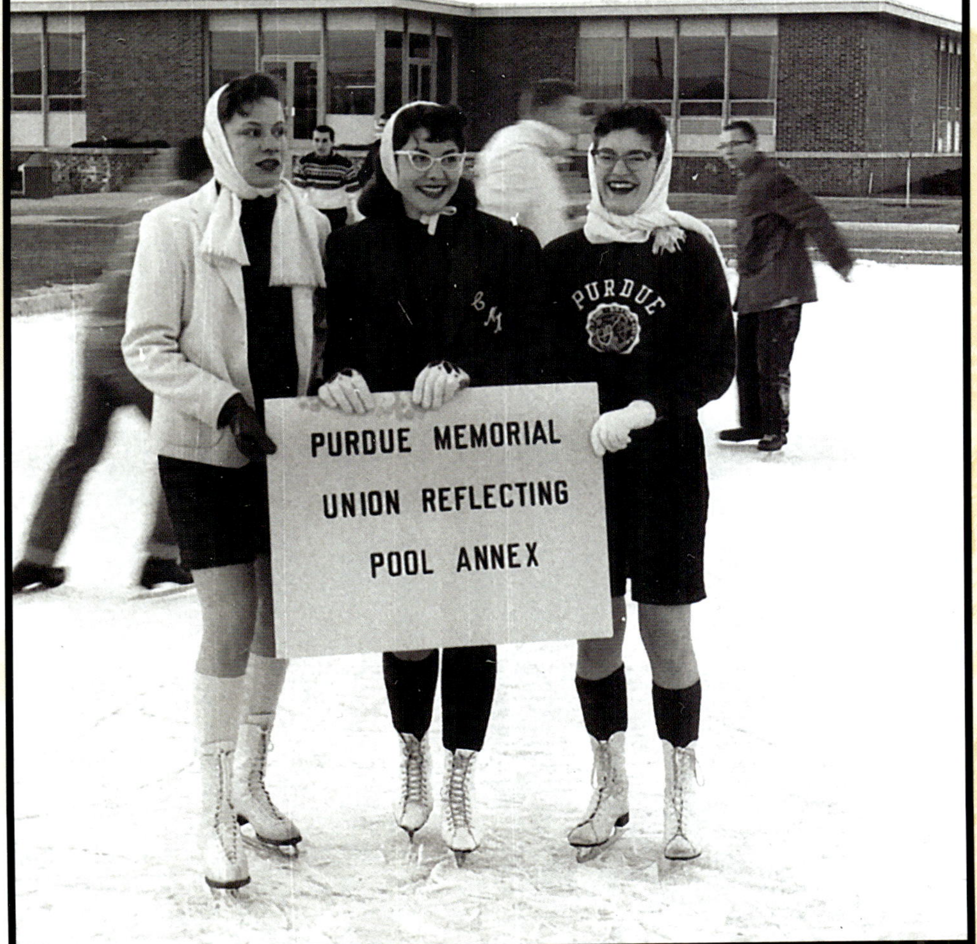

Above: Ice-skating on the reflecting pool outside Purdue Memorial Union, 1957. *(Debris yearbook)*

Left: Students ice-skating on south campus near Terry Courts, 1957. They jokingly call the rink the "Purdue Memorial Union Reflecting Pool Annex" to parody the unusually named Purdue Memorial Union Annex (Stewart Center) under construction at that time. *(J. David Weiss papers)*

Renowned Chinese scientist and nuclear weapons expert Deng Jiaxian earned his PhD in physics from Purdue in 1950. He is recognized today as the father of China's first atomic bomb.

The international student population at Purdue grew steadily throughout its years of existence, but it especially bloomed in the years after World War II. In 1951, the university hired Arthur Tichenor as its first full-time foreign student advisor specifically to assist those students adjusting to a new country and culture in addition to their full course loads. Tichenor remained in the position until his retirement in 1982, overseeing a major period of growth and inclusivity for international students.[6]

Several initiatives of the university administration and the student body brought groundbreaking opportunities to Purdue students. In 1953 the Department of Freshman Engineering was established to prepare new engineering students for their academic careers. In 1958 the Department established the first honors program at Purdue to support academically advanced engineering students.

The Purdue chapter of the Society of Women Engineers formed in 1954, the first student chapter to join the national organization. The group at Purdue originally formed in 1946 as the Gamma chapter of Pi Omicron, a professional society for women in engineering, to support scholarship, fellowship, and professional development. By joining the national organization, Purdue's students gained a network of support expanded across the country, providing new opportunities for women entering a male-dominated field.

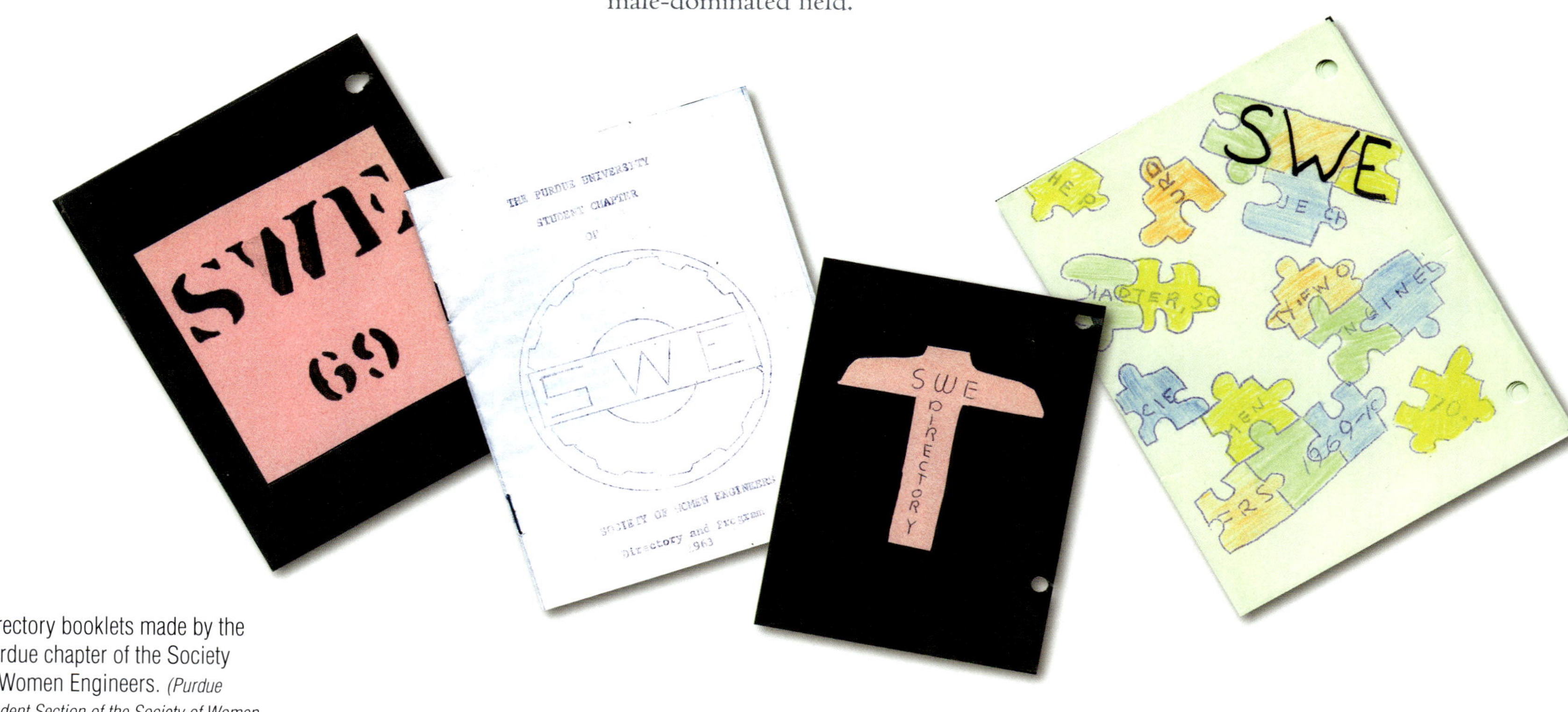

Directory booklets made by the Purdue chapter of the Society of Women Engineers. *(Purdue Student Section of the Society of Women Engineers records)*

Ruth Siems, inventor of Stove Top Stuffing, received her degree in home economics from Purdue in 1953.

Purdue Pete and Golden Girl Valerie Brown, 1960s.
(Purdue University photographs)

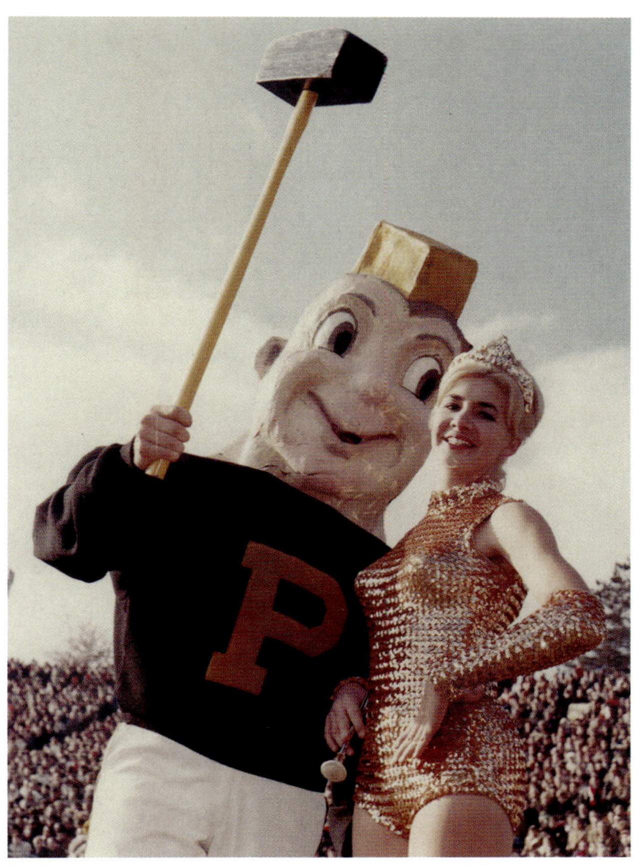

In 1954 Purdue purchased a Datatron 204 computer for $125,000. The Datatron was almost constantly in use by students, faculty, and staff. In 1957 Purdue became the first university to use a computer to assist with course registration.[7] Demand for computing power soon surpassed the Datatron's capacity, and in 1959 a Univac Solid State 80 computer was installed.[8]

The Student Council introduced an "old masters plan" in 1950 that would invite respected industry leaders to stay on campus for a week, living among the students, to provide career advice and professional insights.[9] The first group of ten Old Masters came to Purdue in December 1950 and hosted three days of "bull sessions," engaging with students and helping them prepare for their future professions.[10] The student-led event became an annual tradition, offering students an opportunity to plan and participate in events with successful professionals from a variety of fields.

A new tradition was born in 1954 when Juanita Lee Carpenter became the first "Golden Girl," a featured twirler in gold uniform performing with the Marching Band.[11] After two years, Juanita passed her baton on to Sandie Hutchison and the Golden Girl became a permanent fixture of Marching Band performances.

Purdue's football team drew national attention in 1950 when it ended Notre Dame's twenty-nine-game winning streak with a 28–14 win on October 7. Columnist Al Campbell wrote that "all the newsprint in Canada, all the type in the city of Chicago, and all the words that were written from Bikini Atoll when the test bombs exploded did not and cannot tell the significance and the glory" of the victory.[12] Celebrations filled the streets of West Lafayette for two days. The Boilermakers won only two games that season but made both of them count; in its second victory, the team took down Indiana and brought home the Old Oaken Bucket.

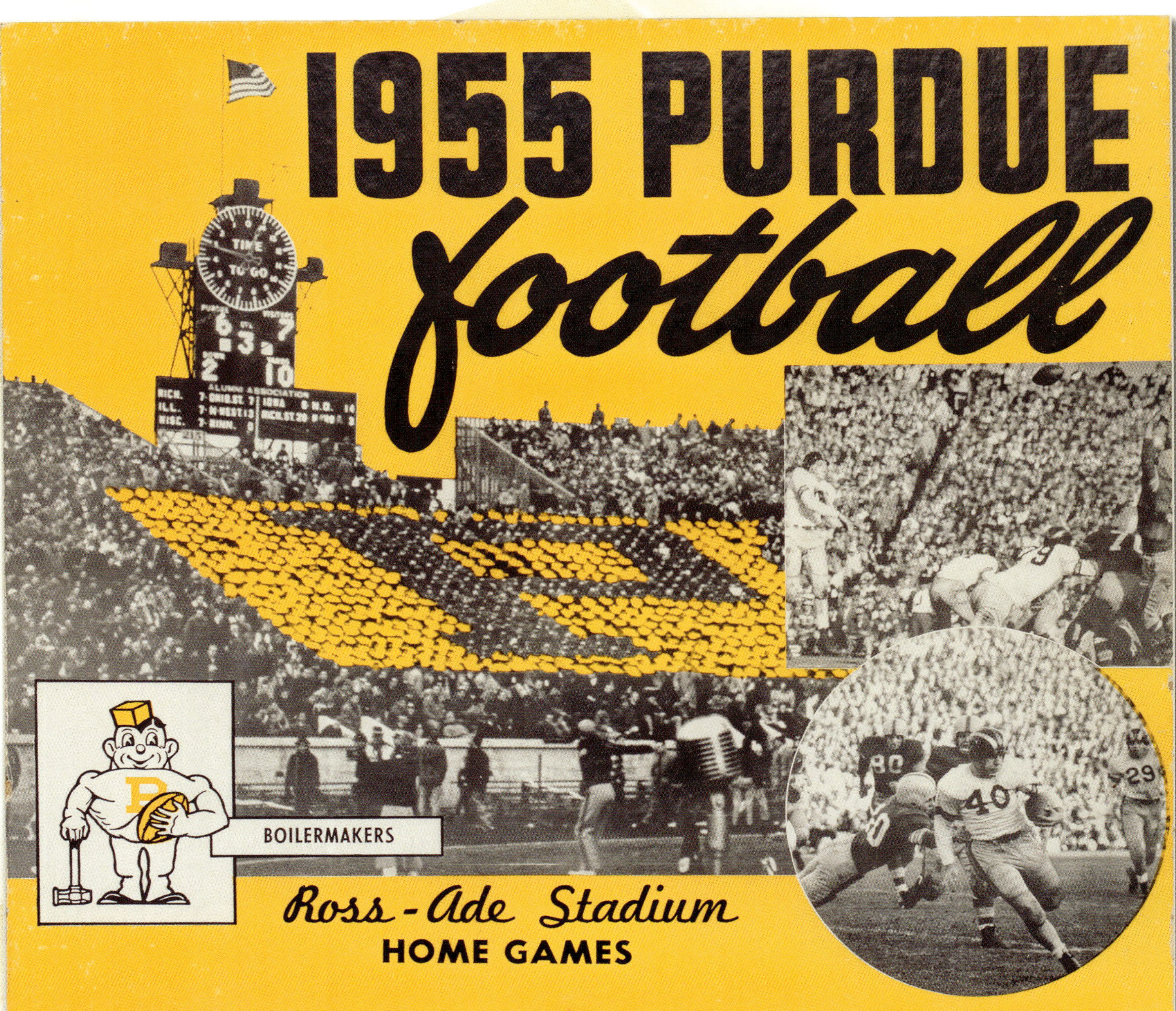

SEPT. 24 – COLLEGE OF THE PACIFIC – $3.60
(High School Band Day)

OCT. 8 – WISCONSIN – $3.60
(Homecoming)

OCT. 22 – NOTRE DAME – $3.60

NOV. 5 – MICHIGAN STATE – $3.60
(Dad's Day)

NOV. 12 – NORTHWESTERN – $3.60
('P' Men's Day)

KICKOFF FOR ALL HOME GAMES 1:30 P.M.

GAMES AWAY

OCT. 1 – MINNESOTA – $3.60

OCT. 15 – IOWA – $3.60

OCT. 29 – ILLINOIS – $3.60

NOV. 19 – INDIANA – $4.00

FOR TICKETS ADDRESS – C. S. DOAN – PURDUE UNIVERSITY – WEST LAFAYETTE

1955 Purdue football poster.
(Fredrick C. Tegeler collection)

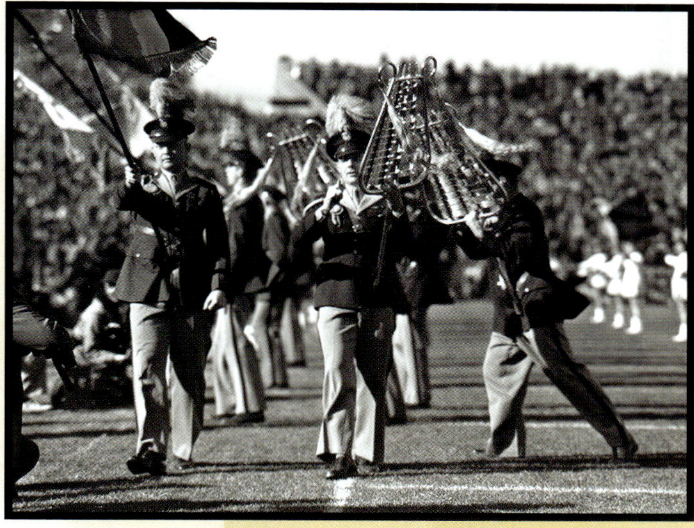

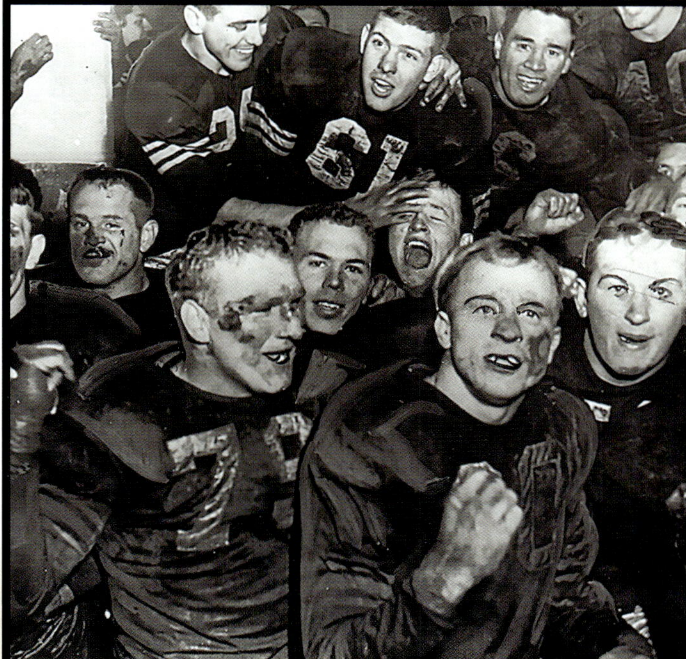

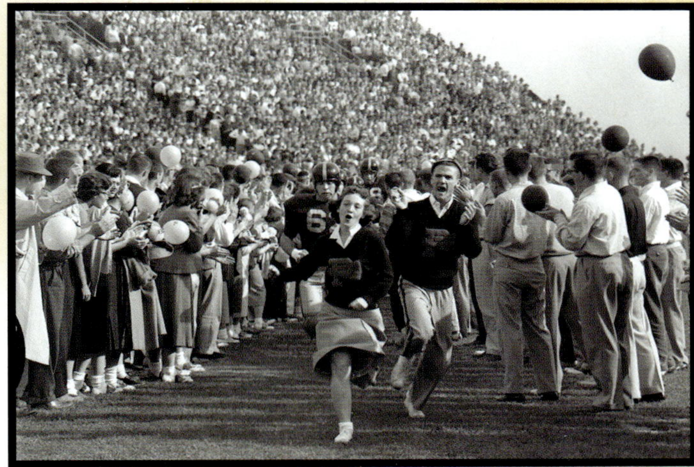

Above from top:

Majorette on the field at a football game. *(Purdue Bands and Orchestras records)*

The football team celebrates a muddy victory. *(Purdue University photographs)*

Cheerleaders leading football players onto the field. *(Purdue University News Service negatives and photographs)*

Below from top:

"Hi Dads!" crowd sign at a Purdue University home football game. *(J. David Weiss papers)*

John Beletic and John Kerestes, football co-captains, with the Old Oaken Bucket, May 17, 1950. *(J. C. Allen and Son Inc. photographs and negatives)*

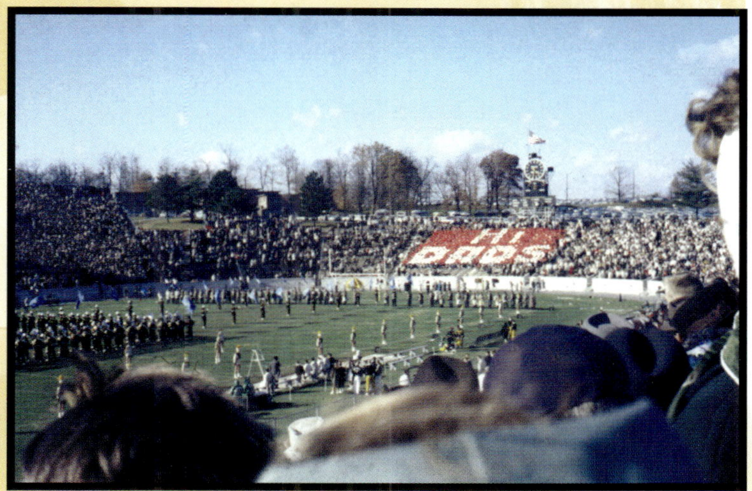

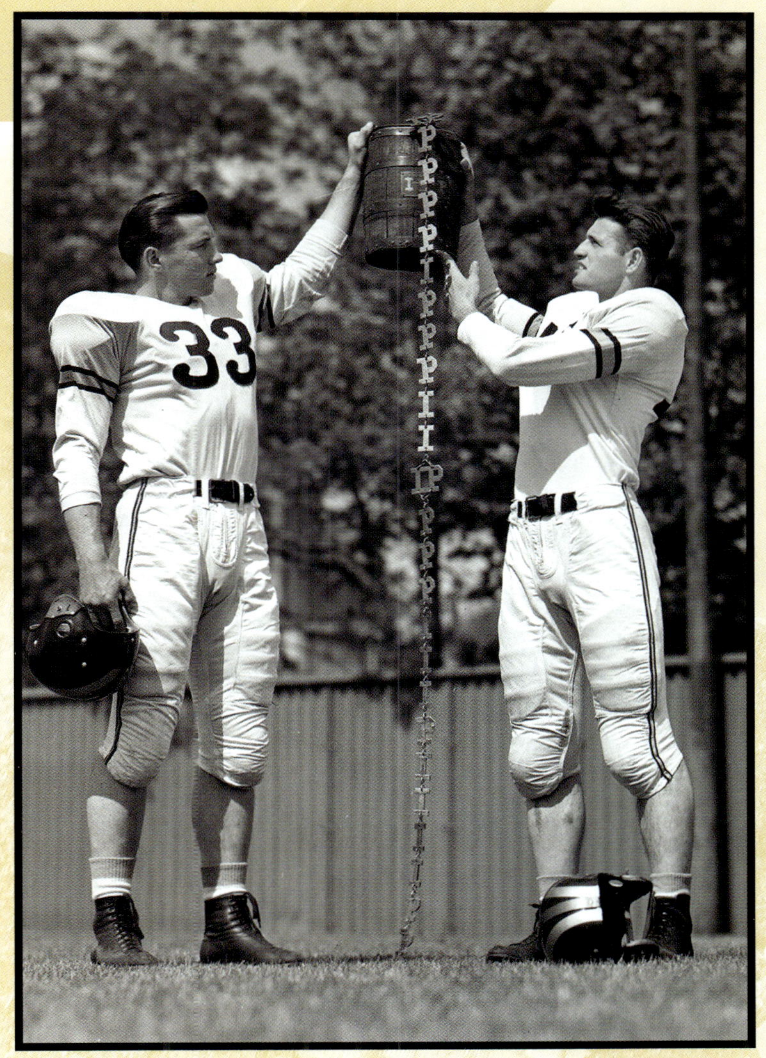

The Grand Prix

On Saturday, May 17, 1958, twenty-one drivers erupted from the starting line in the first Purdue Grand Prix. The next three hours consisted of 144 laps around a sixteenth of a mile track laid out along Intramural Drive in front of Tarkington and Wiley Residence Halls. The event, invented by a group of engineering students in the Delta Upsilon Fraternity, allowed participants representing housing units, clubs, or independent groups to show off their mechanical knowledge and skills. Each cart had its own unique transmission and design, though all had identical one-and-a-half horsepower gasoline engines with a top speed around thirty miles per hour. The team from Gable Courts won that first race, followed by the teams from Kappa Sigma, Cary West, and Dover Co-op.[13]

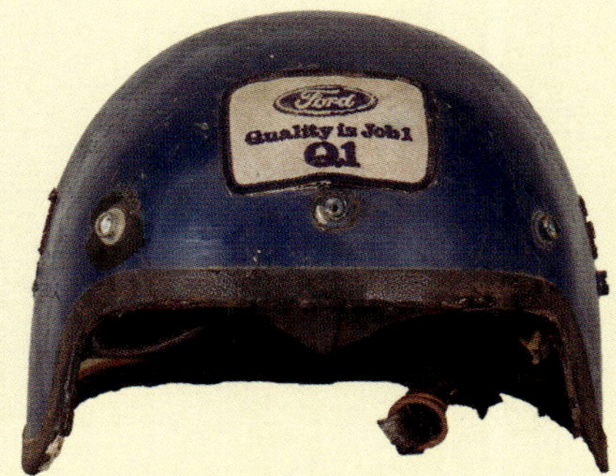

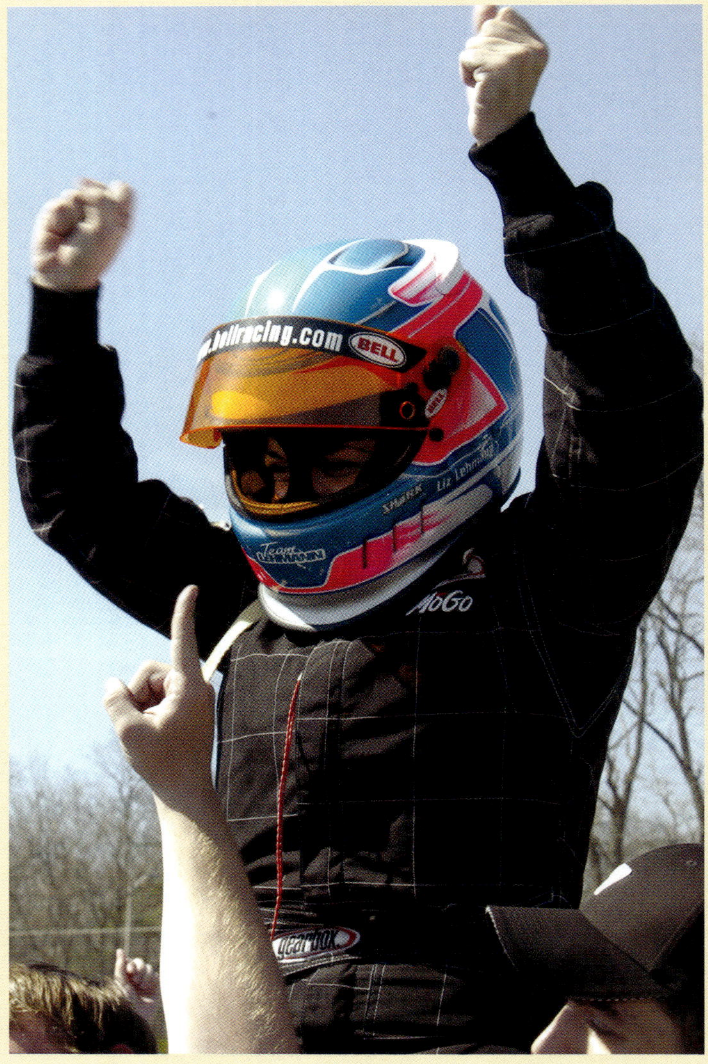

The following year the track moved to the center of campus, with a course passing in front of Hovde Hall and through the Engineering Mall. Fifty-two teams participated, including teams of women and older students. Thirty-two teams made it through two heats to compete in the final race, won by Sigma Chi.

The Grand Prix relocated several times before moving to its permanent home at the corner of McCormick Road and Cherry Lane in 2008. The year 2019 marks the sixty-second running of the Purdue Grand Prix, the "Greatest Spectacle in College Racing."[14]

Above: Liz Lehmann, a junior majoring in management, won the fiftieth Purdue Grand Prix on April 21, 2007. Lehmann was the first female driver to win the fifty-mile race. *(Purdue University photographs)*

Above left: Grand Prix helmet, 1966. *(Purdue University Archives and Special Collections Artifacts collection)*

Below: The Grand Prix courses through campus, 1958. *(Purdue University photographs)*

The Purdue students of the 1950s found multiple unique opportunities to hold lighthearted competitions with their peers. Beginning in 1950, men who lived in the dormitories held an annual tricycle race. Later in the decade, it became a battle between the units of Cary Quad known as the Cary Club Tricycle Race. The racers used standard tricycles in the first 5 laps, then switched to modified trikes for two hours and another 215 to 245 laps. Onlookers threw water at the racers, and after the race the tricycles were donated to charity.

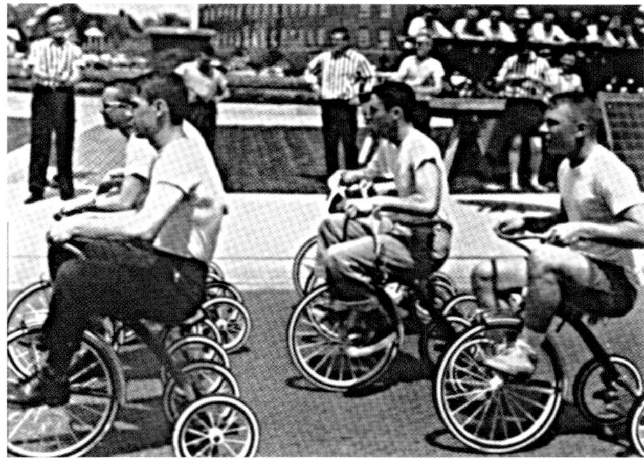

Races were a common sight on Purdue's campus. In addition to the Grand Prix, the pledges of Lambda Chi Alpha and Tau Kappa Epsilon competed in the annual Alley Race each May between 1948 and 1958. Built from an earlier friendly competition between the fraternities, the race saw sororities build an obstacle course through the alley behind the Tau Kappa Epsilon house on Russell Street to be navigated by six pledges, all dressed in pajamas. Obstacles included "chicken wire, cans, tubs, and other items strewn here and there, including ill-timed fire crackers and lots of water, it was also made messy with mud, flour, and garbage thrown by the girls."[15] The tradition ended in 1958 due to safety concerns but was briefly revived in the late 1960s.[16]

Fraternities, sororities, dorms, and co-ops competed annually in the Homecoming Sign Contest. The signs consisted of elaborate decorations on the lawns of the residences that tied in some way to the football game. Judging was based on "originality, slogan, neatness, and day and night effects" with an emphasis on "appropriateness and good taste."[17] The winners were announced during halftime of the Homecoming game and awarded a trophy. The annual competition continued until the 1970s.[18]

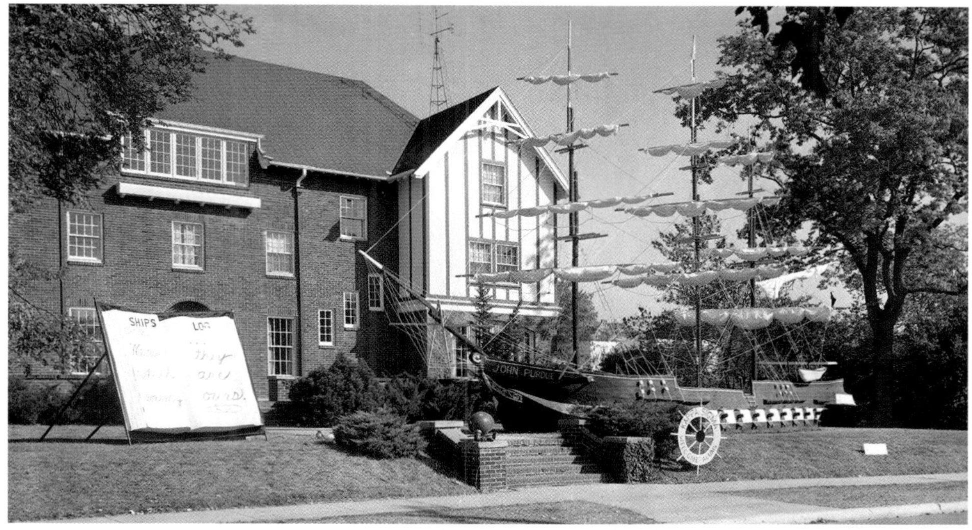

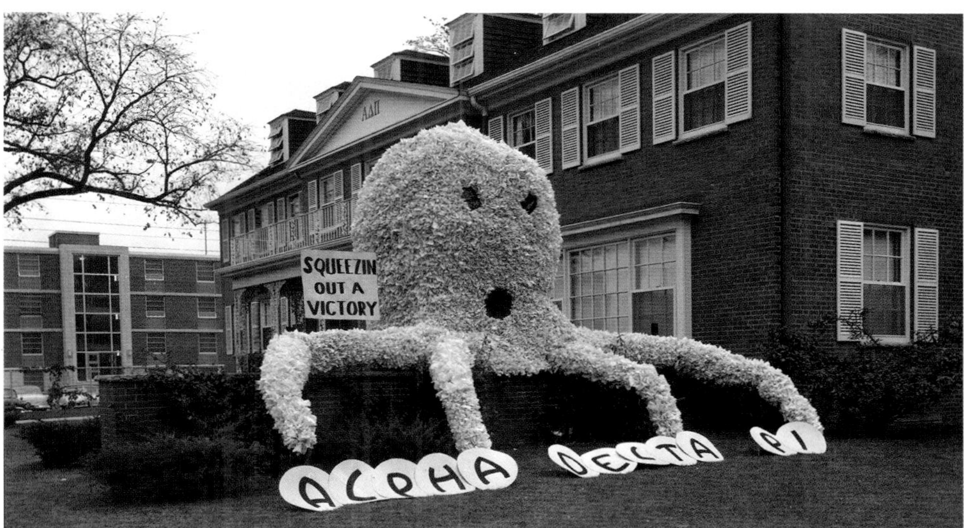

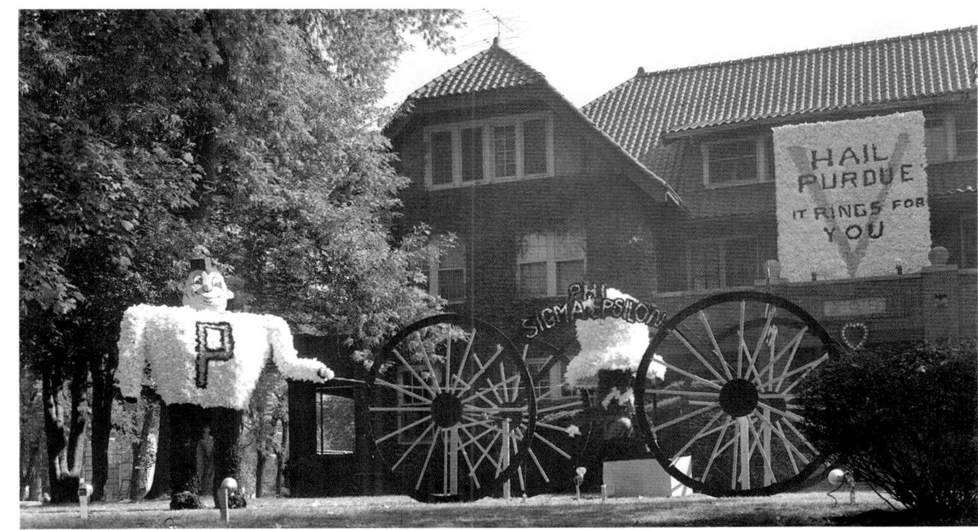

Left: A tricycle race on campus, 1963. *(Debris yearbook)*

Right from top:

The S. S. John Purdue helped Kappa Sigma house win the $60 bracket in the 1957 Homecoming Sign Contest. *(Purdue University News Service negatives and photographs)*

Alpha Delta Pi house's octopus won the women's division of the 1958 Homecoming Sign Contest. *(Purdue University News Service negatives and photographs)*

Victory Bell–themed decorations at the Sigma Phi Epsilon house won the men's $25 bracket in the 1957 Homecoming Sign Contest. *(Purdue University News Service negatives and photographs)*

The 1957 Asian flu epidemic led Purdue to cancel campus activities to curb an outbreak, though two thousand people still fell ill.[19]

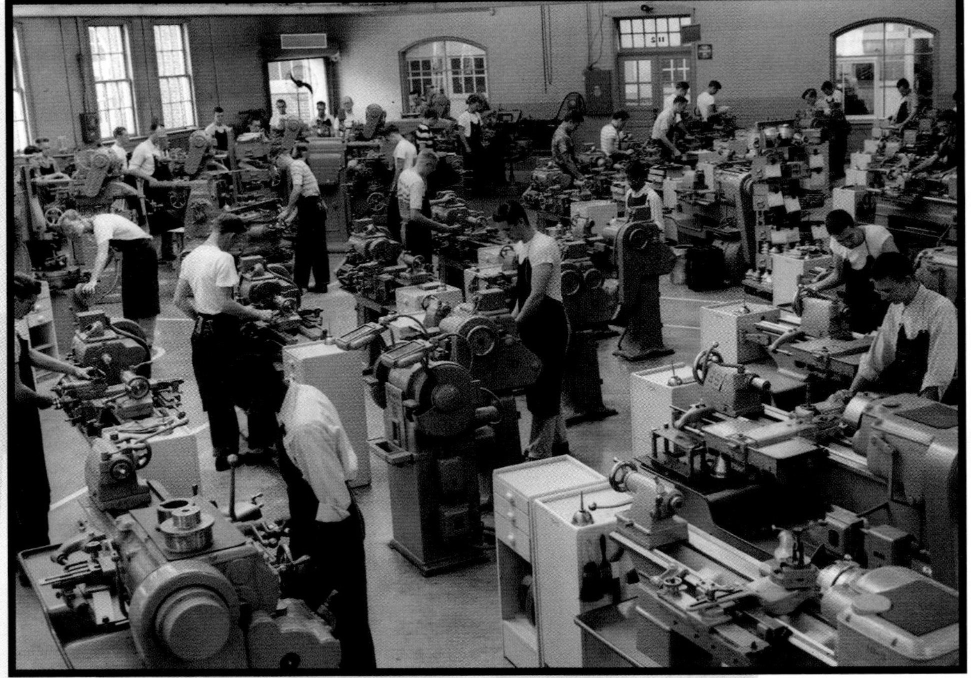

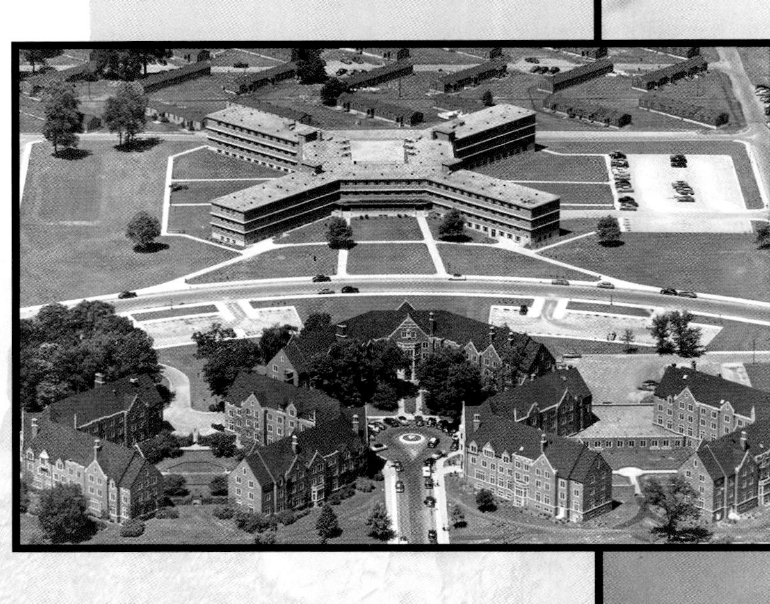

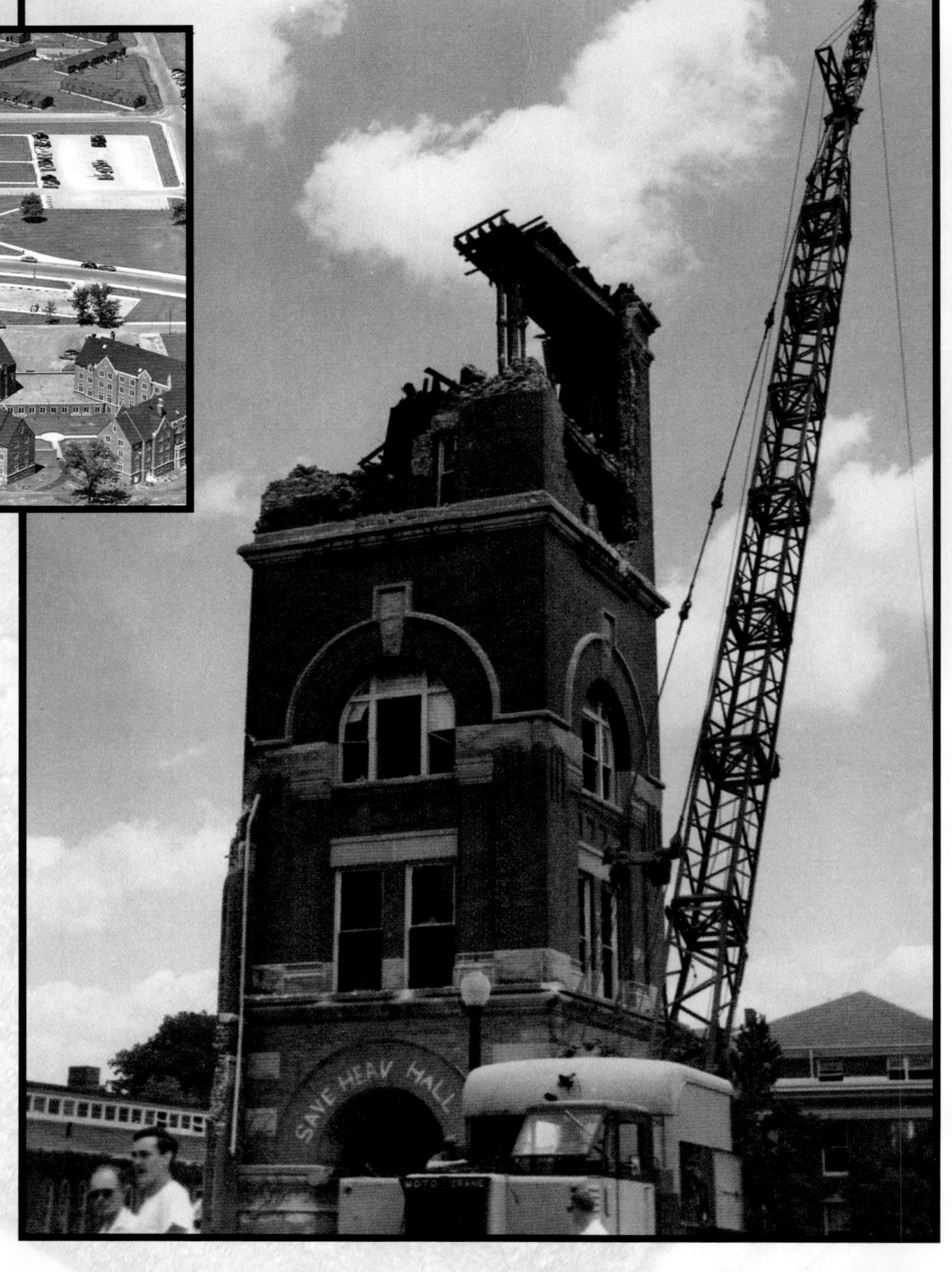

Top: Industrial education students in shop class in Michael Golden Labs, 1955. *(Purdue University photographs)*

Above: Virginia C. Meredith Hall with Windsor Halls in the foreground and temporary wartime housing in background. Meredith Hall was one of several residence halls built during the 1950s to house Purdue's rapidly growing postwar population. *(Purdue University photographs)*

Right: Demolition of the second Heavilon Hall in 1956. "SAVE HEAV HALL" is written on the building. *(Purdue University photographs)*

Top: The Purdue Groove, an annual record of the sounds of campus. *(Purdue University Musical Organizations records)*

Middle: Vinyl records. *(Purdue University Musical Organizations records)*

Bottom: Office of the Grooves, a student group that created the annual Purdue Groove record featuring the sounds of campus, 1958. The records' contents included basketball games, classroom lectures, and ambient sounds on Memorial Mall, allowing Boilermakers to take the sound of Purdue wherever they went. *(Purdue University News Service negatives and photographs)*

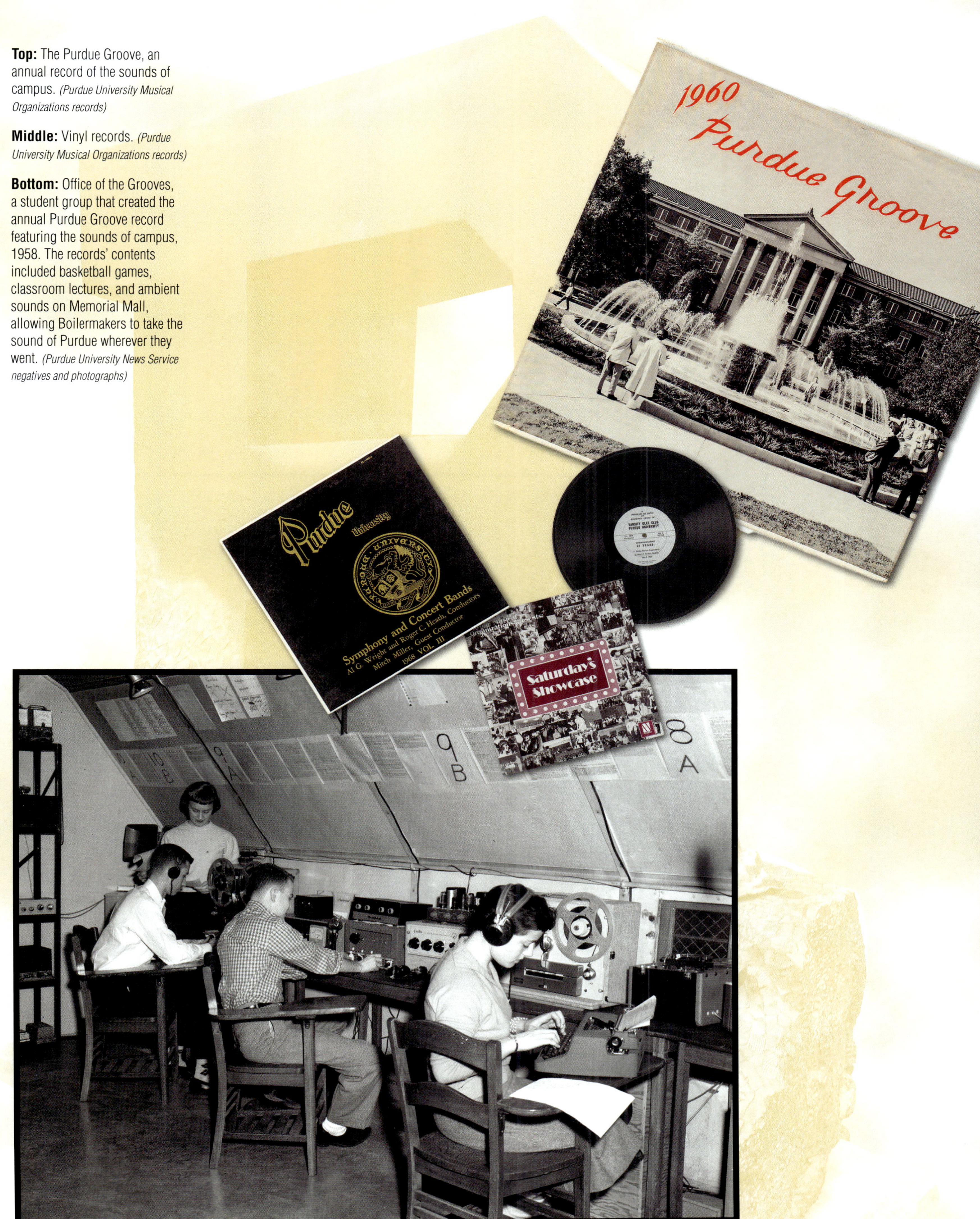

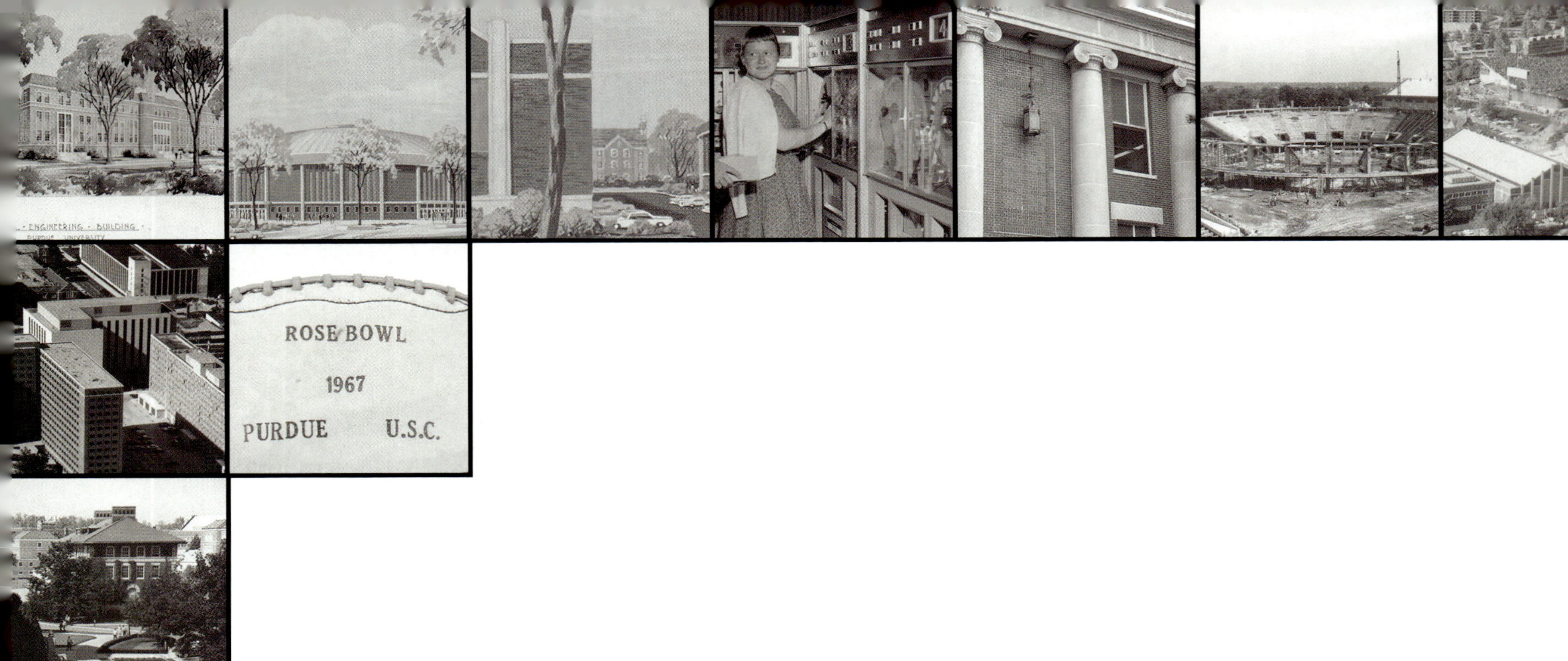

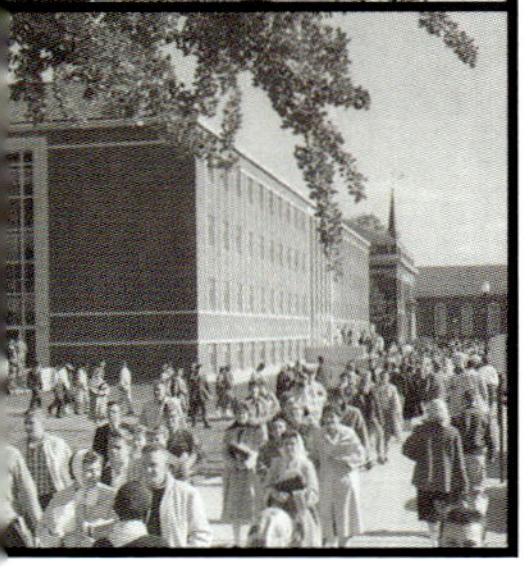

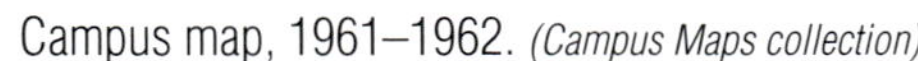

Campus map, 1961–1962. *(Campus Maps collection)*

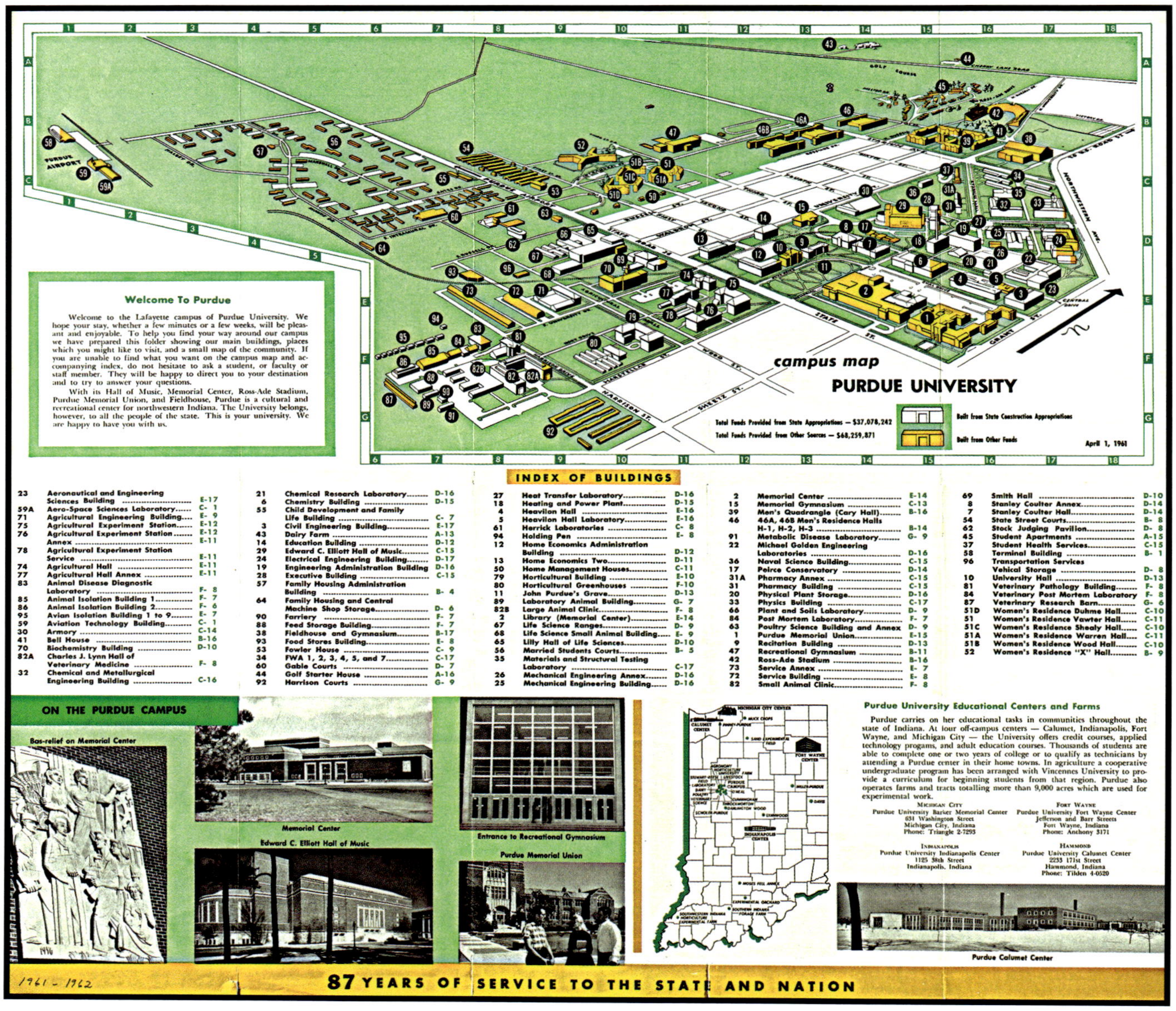

Welcome To Purdue

Welcome to the Lafayette campus of Purdue University. We hope your stay, whether a few minutes or a few weeks, will be pleasant and enjoyable. To help you find your way around our campus we have prepared this folder showing our main buildings, places which you might like to visit, and a small map of the community. If you are unable to find what you want on the campus map and accompanying index, do not hesitate to ask a student, or faculty or staff member. They will be happy to direct you to your destination and to try to answer your questions.

With its Hall of Music, Memorial Center, Ross-Ade Stadium, Purdue Memorial Union, and Fieldhouse, Purdue is a cultural and recreational center for northwestern Indiana. The University belongs, however, to all the people of the state. This is your university. We are happy to have you with us.

campus map

PURDUE UNIVERSITY

Total Funds Provided from State Appropriations — $37,078,242

Total Funds Provided from Other Sources — $68,259,871

Built from State Construction Appropriations

Built from Other Funds

April 1, 1961

INDEX OF BUILDINGS

No.	Building	Location
23	Aeronautical and Engineering Sciences Building	E-17
59A	Aero-Space Sciences Laboratory	C- 1
71	Agricultural Engineering Building	E- 9
75	Agricultural Experiment Station	E-12
76	Agricultural Experiment Station Annex	E-12 / E-11
78	Agricultural Experiment Station Service	E-11
74	Agricultural Hall	E-11
77	Agricultural Hall Annex	E-11
83	Animal Disease Diagnostic Laboratory	F- 8
85	Animal Isolation Building 1	F- 7
86	Animal Isolation Building 2	F- 6
95	Avian Isolation Building 1 to 9	E- 7
59	Aviation Technology Building	C- 1
30	Armory	C-14
41	Bell House	B-16
70	Biochemistry Building	D-10
82A	Charles J. Lynn Hall of Veterinary Medicine	F- 8
32	Chemical and Metallurgical Engineering Building	C-16
21	Chemical Research Laboratory	D-16
6	Chemistry Building	D-15
55	Child Development and Family Life Building	C- 7
3	Civil Engineering Building	E-17
43	Dairy Farm	A-13
14	Education Building	D-12
29	Edward C. Elliott Hall of Music	C-15
24	Electrical Engineering Building	D-17
19	Engineering Administration Building	D-16
28	Executive Building	C-15
57	Family Housing Administration Building	B- 4
64	Family Housing and Central Machine Shop Storage	D- 6
90	Farriery	F- 7
88	Feed Storage Building	F- 7
38	Fieldhouse and Gymnasium	B-17
93	Food Stores Building	E- 8
53	Fowler House	C- 9
34	FWA 1, 2, 3, 4, 5, and 7	C-17
60	Gable Courts	D- 7
44	Golf Starter House	A-16
92	Harrison Courts	G- 9
27	Heat Transfer Laboratory	D-16
18	Heating and Power Plant	D-15
4	Heavilon Hall	E-16
5	Heavilon Hall Laboratory	E-16
61	Herrick Laboratories	C- 8
94	Holding Pen	E- 8
12	Home Economics Administration Building	D-12
13	Home Economics Two	D-11
50	Home Management Houses	C-11
79	Horticultural Building	E-10
80	Horticultural Greenhouses	F-10
11	John Purdue's Grave	D-13
89	Laboratory Animal Building	G- 7
82B	Large Animal Clinic	F- 8
2	Library (Memorial Center)	E-14
67	Life Science Ranges	D- 9
68	Life Science Small Animal Building	E- 9
65	Lilly Hall of Life Sciences	D-10
56	Married Students Courts	B- 5
35	Materials and Structural Testing Laboratory	C-17
26	Mechanical Engineering Annex	D-16
25	Mechanical Engineering Building	D-16
2	Memorial Center	E-14
15	Memorial Gymnasium	C-13
39	Men's Quadrangle (Cary Hall)	B-16
46	46A, 46B Men's Residence Halls H-1, H-2, H-3	B-14
91	Metabolic Disease Laboratory	G- 9
22	Michael Golden Engineering Laboratories	D-16
36	Naval Science Building	C-15
17	Peirce Conservatory	D-14
31A	Pharmacy Annex	C-15
31	Pharmacy Building	C-15
20	Physical Plant Storage	D-16
33	Physics Building	C-17
66	Plant and Soils Laboratory	D- 9
84	Post Mortem Laboratory	F- 7
63	Poultry Science Building and Annex	D- 9
1	Purdue Memorial Union	E-15
9	Recitation Building	D-13
47	Recreational Gymnasium	B-11
42	Ross-Ade Stadium	B-16
73	Service Annex	E- 7
72	Service Building	E- 8
82	Small Animal Clinic	F- 8
69	Smith Hall	D-10
8	Stanley Coulter Annex	D-14
7	Stanley Coulter Hall	D-14
54	State Street Courts	B- 8
62	Stock Judging Pavilion	D- 8
45	Student Apartments	A-15
37	Student Health Services	C-15
58	Terminal Building	B- 1
96	Transportation Services Vehical Storage	D- 8
10	University Hall	D-13
81	Veterinary Pathology Building	F- 8
84	Veterinary Post Mortem Laboratory	F- 8
87	Veterinary Research Barn	G- 6
51D	Women's Residence Duhme Hall	C-10
51	Women's Residence Vawter Hall	C-11
51C	Women's Residence Shealy Hall	C-10
51A	Women's Residence Warren Hall	C-11
51B	Women's Residence Wood Hall	C-10
52	Women's Residence "X" Hall	B- 9

ON THE PURDUE CAMPUS

Bas-relief on Memorial Center

Memorial Center

Edward C. Elliott Hall of Music

Entrance to Recreational Gymnasium

Purdue Memorial Union

Purdue University Educational Centers and Farms

Purdue carries on her educational tasks in communities throughout the state of Indiana. At four off-campus centers — Calumet, Indianapolis, Fort Wayne, and Michigan City — the University offers credit courses, applied technology progams, and adult education courses. Thousands of students are able to complete one or two years of college or to qualify as technicians by attending a Purdue center in their home towns. In agriculture a cooperative undergraduate program has been arranged with Vincennes University to provide a curriculum for beginning students from that region. Purdue also operates farms and tracts totalling more than 9,000 acres which are used for experimental work.

MICHIGAN CITY
Purdue University Barker Memorial Center
631 Washington Street
Michigan City, Indiana
Phone: Triangle 2-7293

FORT WAYNE
Purdue University Fort Wayne Center
Jefferson and Barr Streets
Fort Wayne, Indiana
Phone: Anthony 3171

INDIANAPOLIS
Purdue University Indianapolis Center
1125 38th Street
Indianapolis, Indiana

HAMMOND
Purdue University Calumet Center
2233 171st Street
Hammond, Indiana
Phone: Tilden 4-0520

Purdue Calumet Center

1961 - 1962

87 YEARS OF SERVICE TO THE STATE AND NATION

{Enrollment in 1960: 17,600 students[1]}

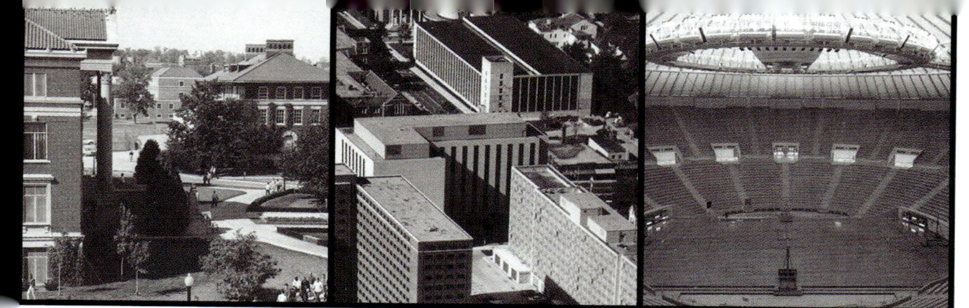

[The 1960s]

PURDUE AT 100

"I visited Purdue when I was . . . a sophomore in high school. I fell in love with the campus, and I said, 'I want to go to school here,' not knowing for sure what I would study, but I felt certain that I wanted to get a degree. So that was my first experience, and it was such a beautiful campus."

—*Mary Lou Siefker, class of 1968*[2]

Overhead view of Purdue University campus and airport, circa 1963. *(Purdue University photographs)*

The Purdue student of 1960 could scarcely imagine the changes in store over the next ten years. Perhaps the first major shift of the decade was the awarding of a new degree in the spring of 1960: the bachelor of arts. Until that time, all Purdue degrees had been variations of scientific degrees, but the bachelor of arts was finally deemed more appropriate for students of liberal arts and humanities. The remainder of the decade would see dramatic changes across the nation and at Purdue.

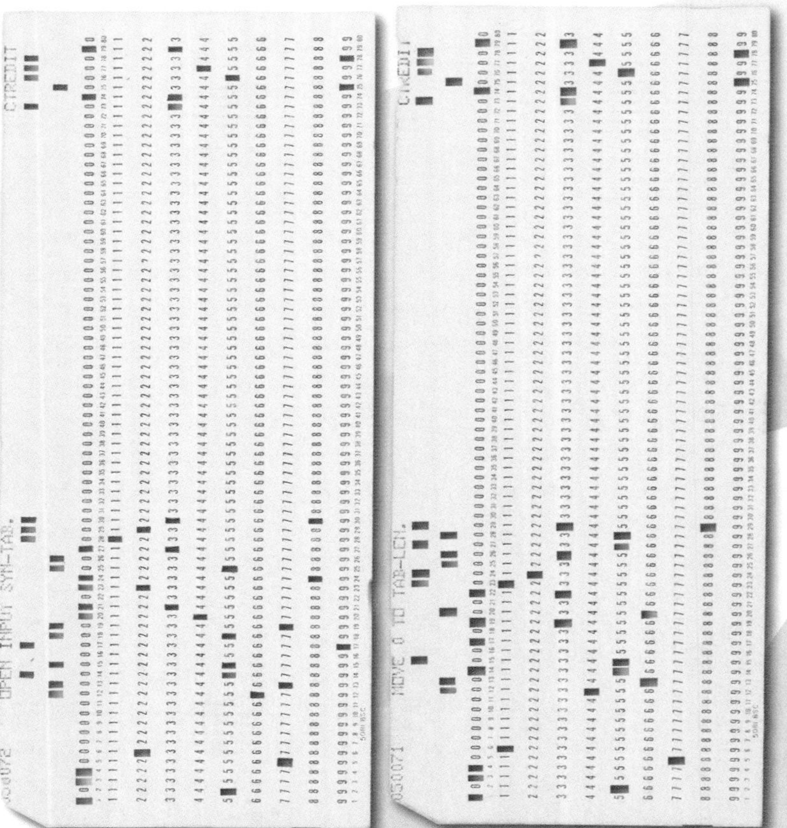

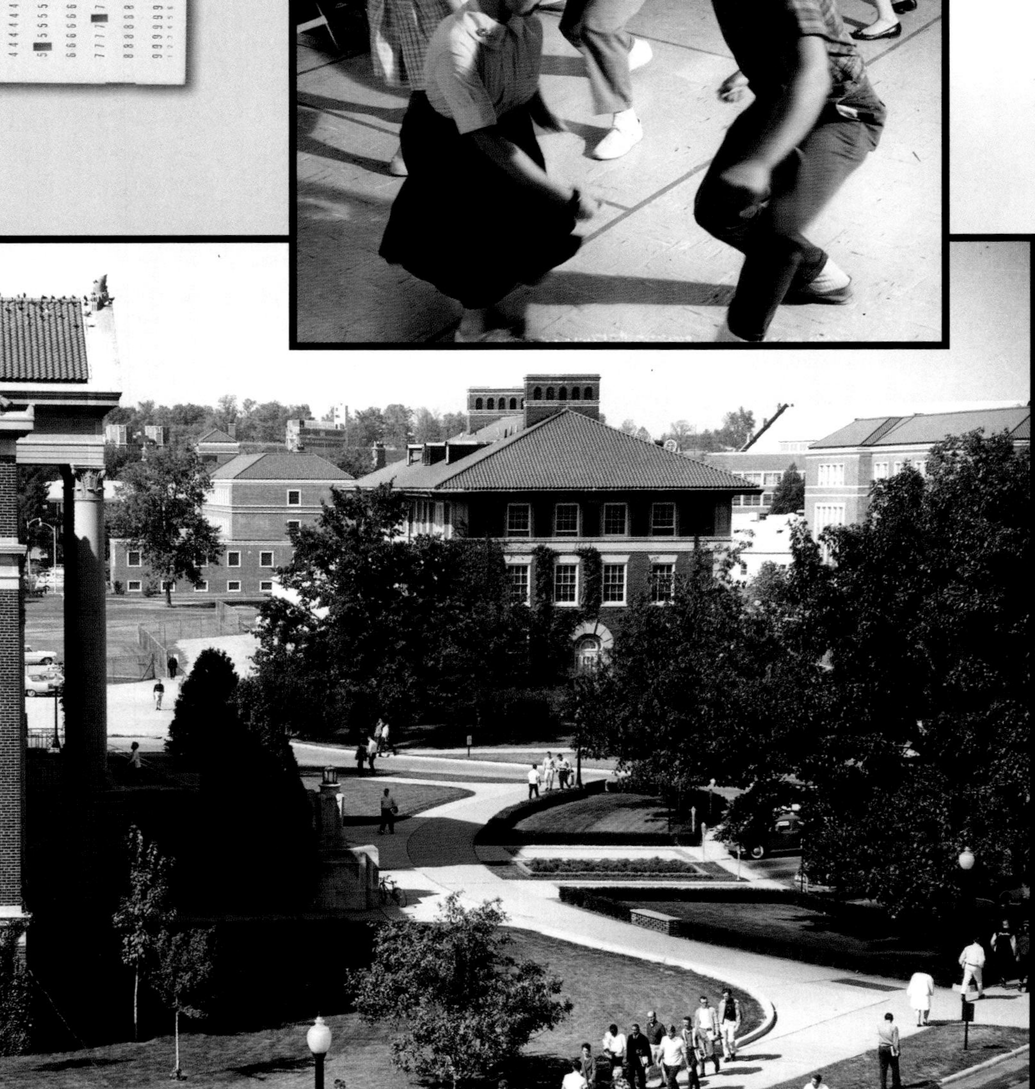

Top left: Computer punch cards used by students to run a COBOL search. *(David A. Studebaker Computer Science papers)*

Top right: Students dance to jukebox music in the Social Room of the CoRec. *(Purdue University photographs)*

Right: View of campus with Hovde Hall at left. *(Purdue University photographs)*

THE WHITE HOUSE

WASHINGTON

TO THE GRADUATING CLASS
PURDUE UNIVERSITY, 1967

It is a pleasure for me to extend my best wishes as you complete your college education.

You are graduating into a society in which you will be warmly welcomed. Our country has never had so great a need for highly educated men and women. Never have young Americans moved from the college campus into a world offering so broad a range of opportunities for individual fulfillment and contribution to the welfare of humanity.

Your generation of students has been distinguished by its fresh and vigorous concern for the quality of American life and its commitment to American democracy. Perhaps the greatest opportunity awaiting you is the challenge to make this a life-long commitment.

Today, Americans from every walk of life are striving together to shape a society that can offer a meaningful and rewarding life to all its members. Never have so many of our countrymen been so deeply dedicated to eradicating the old evils of ignorance, poverty, and bigotry from every corner of the land.

Through your years of study, you have prepared yourselves for positions of leadership in this quest for a better America.

I congratulate you, and urge you to take full advantage of that opportunity.

Sincerely,

Lyndon B. Johnson

Letter written by President Lyndon B. Johnson to the Purdue graduating class of 1967. *(Purdue University Archives and Special Collections vertical files)*

Some of the biggest changes at Purdue happened not in West Lafayette but on campuses throughout Indiana. Indiana University–Purdue University Fort Wayne opened in 1964, merging two independent programs Indiana University and Purdue University had managed in the city. The joint university was established on a new campus alongside the St. Joseph River in Fort Wayne, offering a permanent identity to programs that had grown from a need for wartime training in the 1940s. The two universities partnered again with the 1969 establishment of Indiana University–Purdue University Indianapolis (IUPUI). These two new regional campuses joined the existing Purdue University Calumet and Purdue University North Central, both of which expanded their course offerings from two-year professional degree programs to four-year degree programs in the 1960s.

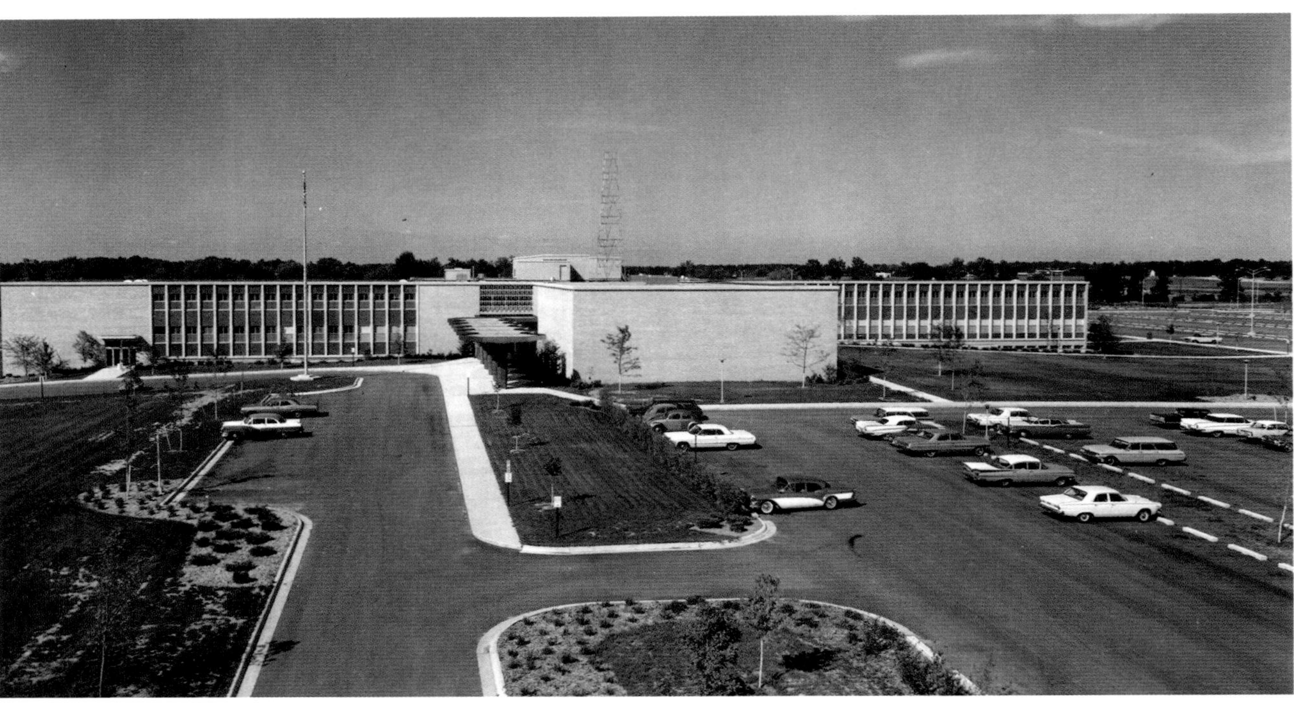

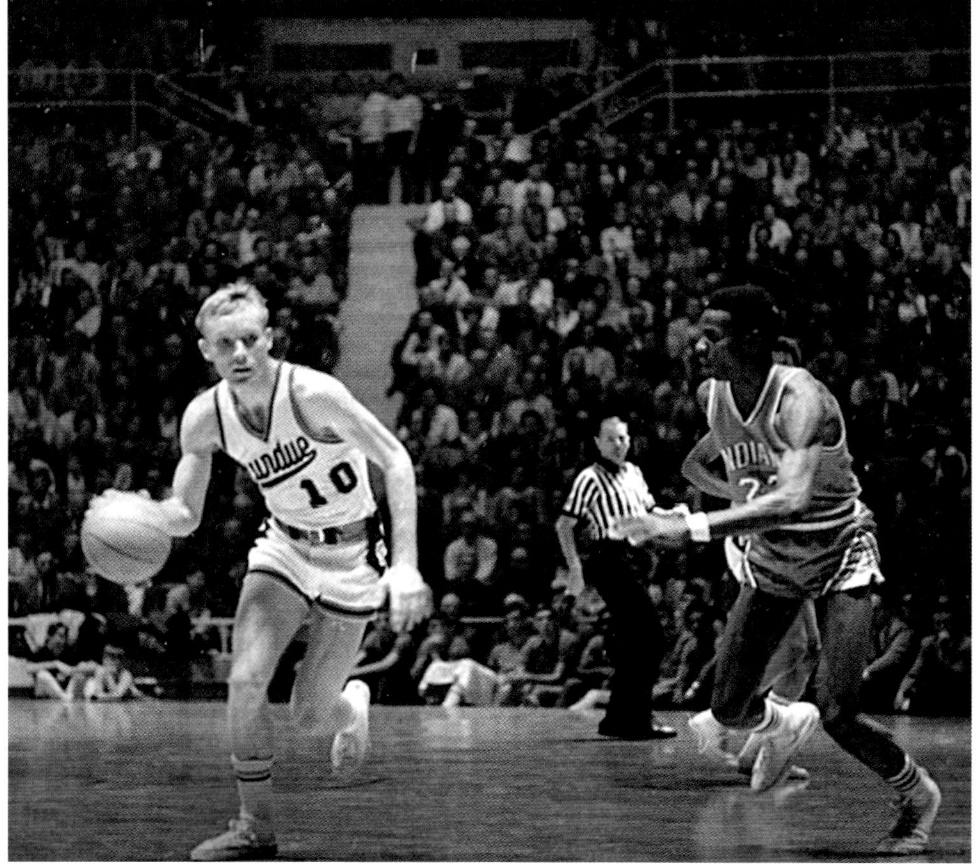

In 1969 the Boilermakers made their first appearance in an NCAA Men's Basketball Championship game. The team defeated Miami University (Ohio), Marquette University, and the University of North Carolina on their way to the final. The Boilermakers, led by star players Rick Mount, Billy Keller, and Herm Gilliam, faced Coach John Wooden and the Bruins in the March 22, 1969, game. Purdue fell 92–72 as the tournament's most outstanding player, Lew Alcindor (later known as Kareem Abdul-Jabbar), scored 37 points and gathered 20 rebounds.

Above: Purdue University, Fort Wayne. *(Purdue University photographs)*

Left: Rick Mount vs. Indiana University, March 8, 1969. Purdue won 120–76. *(Purdue University Marketing and Media collection)*

Purdue's football highlight of the 1960s was undoubtedly the 1967 Rose Bowl. Approximately four thousand students, seven hundred faculty and staff, and thousands of alumni made the trek to California to support the team, including about two thousand students who were part of the university's official "student tour."[3]

The entire football team flew to California a few days before the game. Their time was filled with events and honorary banquets and, when they could find both time and a location, practice. The team was seemingly at a disadvantage compared to their opponents, USC, who could practice on their nearby home field in the days before the game. Years later, Purdue football head coach Bob DeMoss remembered:

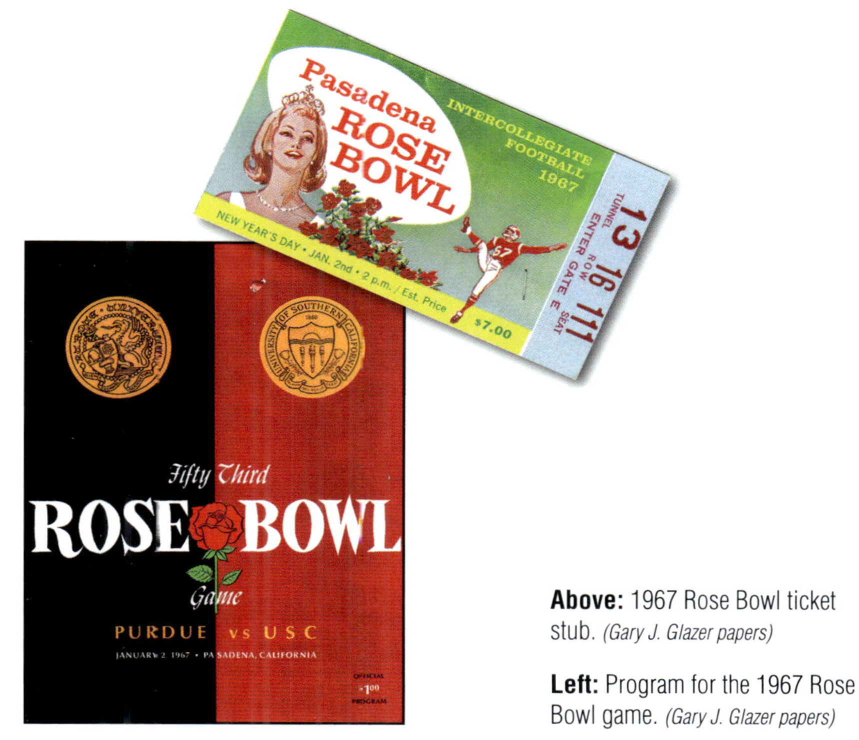

Above: 1967 Rose Bowl ticket stub. *(Gary J. Glazer papers)*

Left: Program for the 1967 Rose Bowl game. *(Gary J. Glazer papers)*

> We practiced here, and we practiced out there. We had to get on a bus and go about 20 miles. . . . Then, we practiced on a baseball field. It wasn't a football field. No, we were in a park. We were in a city park. They found a city park and lined out some—a football field for us, and that was it.[4]

Fans crossed the country by plane, train, or car. The Purdue "All-American" Marching Band traveled across the country by train, including a freight car for the big bass drum. They stopped along the way in Denver, Salt Lake City, and Las Vegas. In Las Vegas the band practiced parading, apparently causing a spectacle: "The headline on the paper said—the only thing that ever has called the gamblers away from the slot machines was the Purdue band marching up and down the street."[5]

When the day of the game arrived, Purdue's team was ready. The Boilermakers and the Trojans faced off through four tense quarters, and in the end, Purdue won a 14–13 victory over USC.

The 1967 Rose Bowl festivities focused not only on football but also on one of Purdue's most illustrious groups of alumni: astronauts. The Tournament of Roses Parade was themed "Travel Tales in Flowers" and Purdue's float represented Purdue as the "Alma Mater of Astronauts." Neil Armstrong, Gene Cernan, Roger Chaffee, and Virgil "Gus" Grissom appeared in the parade and attended the football game.

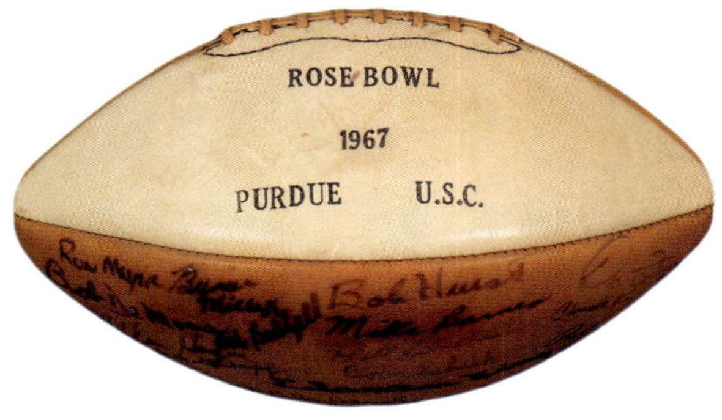

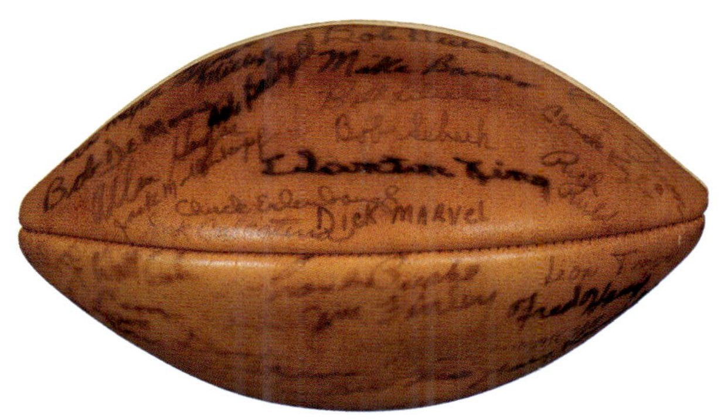

Football signed by the Rose Bowl team and given to Neil Armstrong. Each of the four astronauts received a personalized football. *(Neil A. Armstrong papers)*

Just a few weeks after the Rose Bowl victory, the Purdue community mourned the loss of Grissom and Chaffee in the *Apollo 1* fire. In response to their deaths, the university memorialized both men by renaming the Civil Engineering Building to Virgil I. Grissom Hall and naming a recently opened office building at the Jet Propulsion Center Roger B. Chaffee Hall.[6]

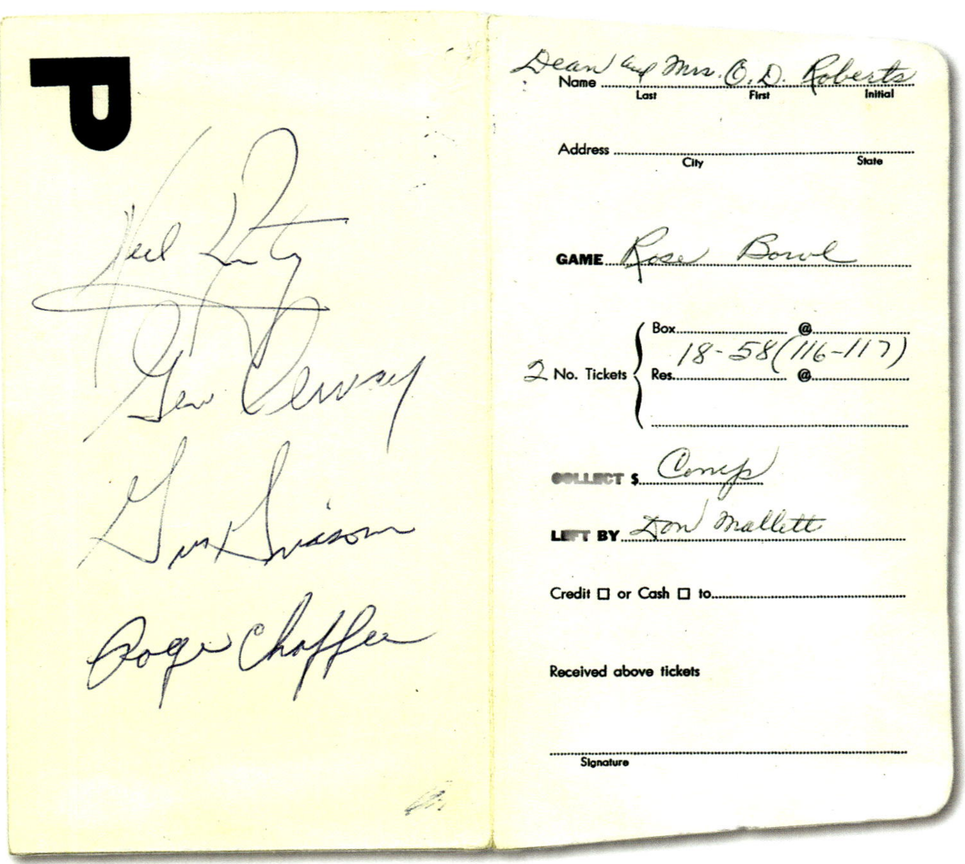

P

Name Last First Initial

Address City State

GAME Rose Bowl

2 No. Tickets Box @ Res. 18-58 (116-117) @

COLLECT $ Comp

LEFT BY Don Mallett

Credit ☐ or Cash ☐ to

Received above tickets

Signature

Above: Ticket envelope signed by the astronauts at the Rose Bowl, 1967. *(Rose Bowl Ticket Envelope Signed by Astronauts)*

APOLLO 11 DAY

MONDAY, JULY 21, 1969

Purdue Libraries + Audio-Visual Center will be closed.

Regular schedule in effect on

SUNDAY, JULY 20 AND TUESDAY, JULY 22

Right: The State of Indiana and Purdue University celebrated Apollo 11 Day on Monday, July 21, 1969, in honor of the first moon landing and alumnus Neil Armstrong's moon walk. *(Purdue University Libraries records)*

Purdue's Astronaut Alumni

In 1959, Purdue graduate Virgil "Gus" Grissom became a member of NASA's first astronaut group, known as the Mercury 7. Loral O'Hara became a member of NASA's twenty-second astronaut candidate group in 2017. Between Grissom and O'Hara were twenty-two Purdue alumni astronauts, including the first human to walk on the Moon, Neil Armstrong, and the last, Eugene Cernan. Though their professional accomplishments mark these men and women as exceptional, and in many minds somewhat superhuman, these astronauts were once students who shared the same experiences as many other Purdue students.

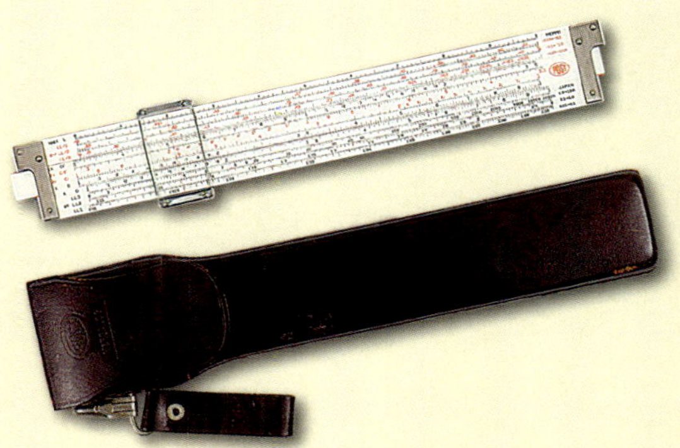

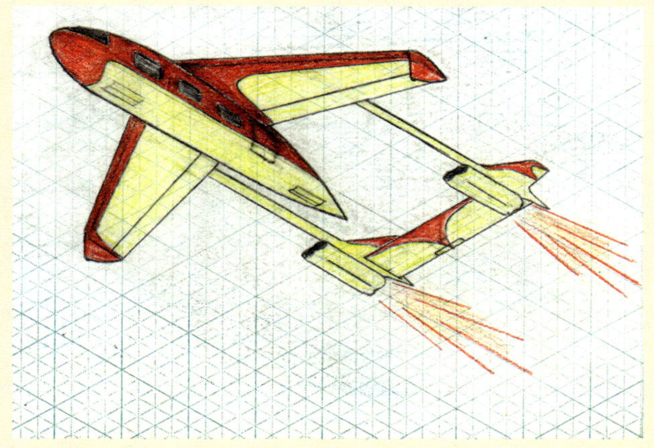

As undergraduates, astronaut alumni shared the experience of rigorous courses and participated in student organizations like so many generations of Purdue students. While a student, Gus Grissom was a member of the American Society of Mechanical Engineers. Neil Armstrong was a member of the marching band, then known as Military Band, and president of the Aero Club. He was also music director for his fraternity, Phi Delta Theta. Eugene Cernan was the editor of the Naval Reserve Officers Training Corps (NROTC) yearbook, president of the Quarterdeck Society, and member of Phi Gamma Delta Fraternity.
Roger Chaffee was a member of the honorary societies Tau Beta Phi, Sigma Gamma Tau, and the Quarterdeck Society, as well as a member of Phi Kappa Sigma Fraternity and an Interfraternity Council member. The Reamer Club found a dedicated member in Donald Williams and the Tomahawk Club in Jerry Ross. Gregory Harbaugh and Mark Polansky were student participants in Old Masters.

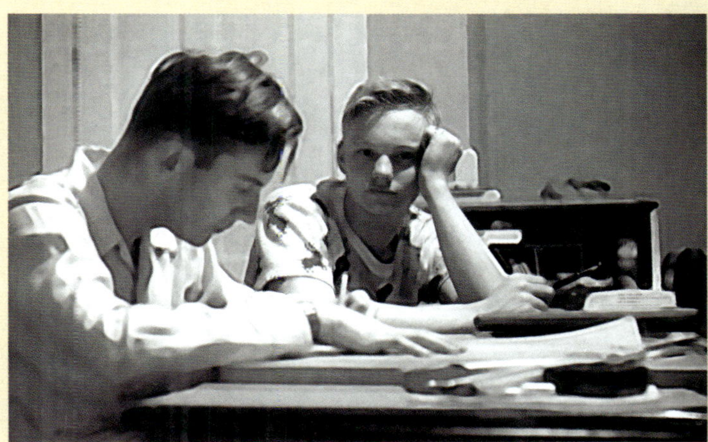

Above: Neil Armstrong's Preliminary Design Analysis for AE 420, January 1955. *(Neil A. Armstrong papers)*

Top: Janice Voss's slide rule. *(Janice Voss papers)*

Above: Neil Armstrong in his dorm room doing homework in his moose pajamas, circa 1948. *(Neil A. Armstrong papers)*

Astronauts found in the *Debris* Yearbook

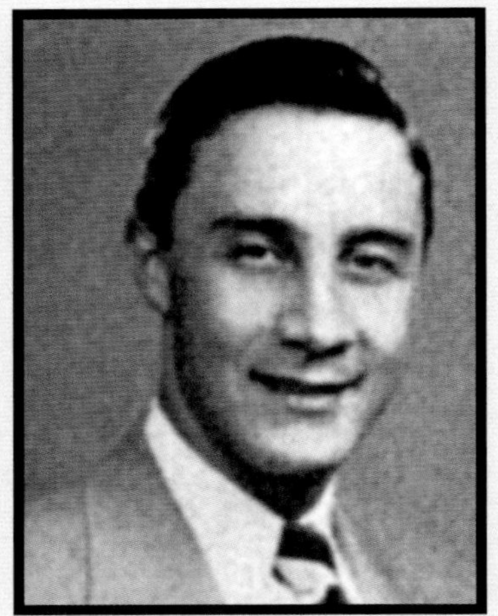

Virgil "Gus" Grissom

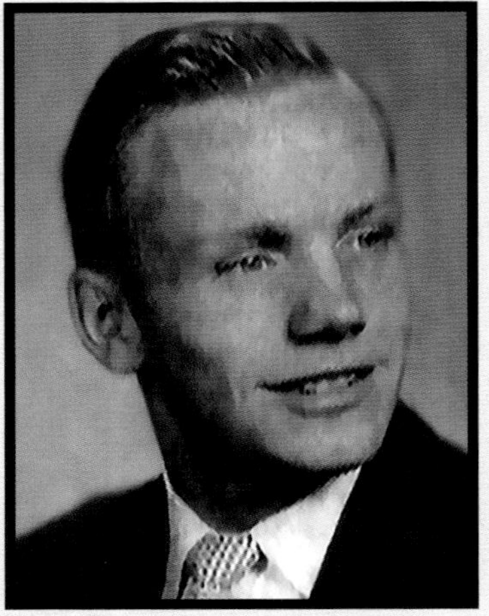

Neil Armstrong

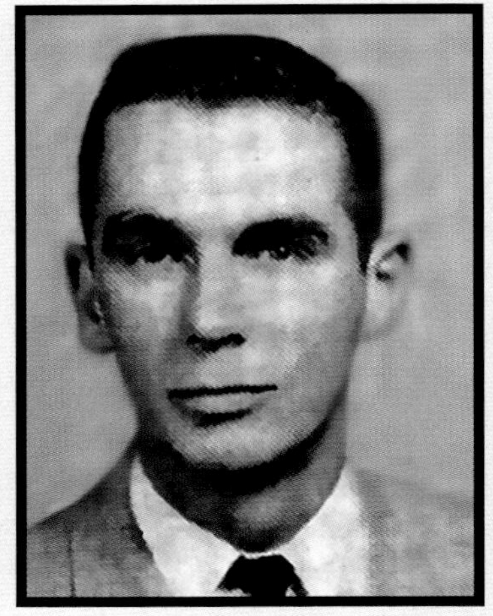

Eugene Cernan

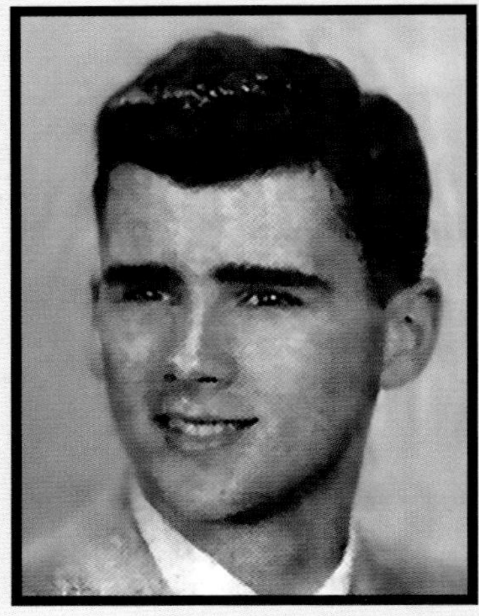

Roger Chaffee

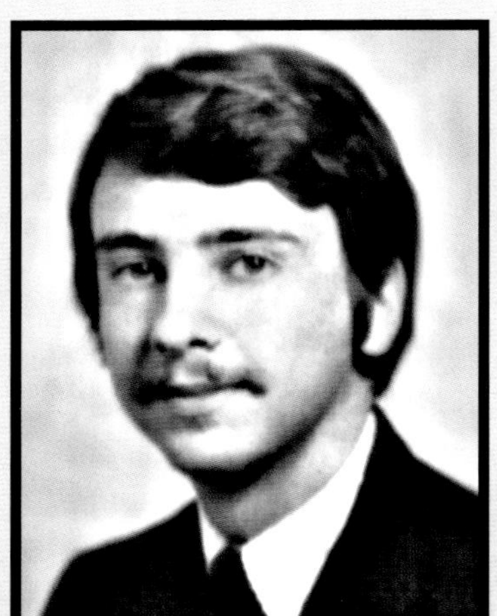

Charles Walker

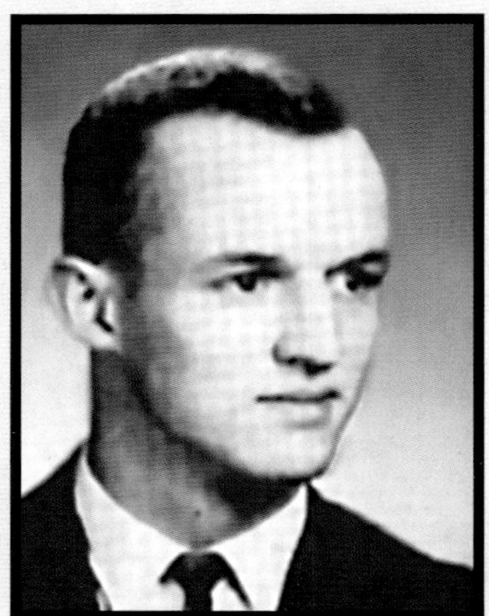

Donald Williams

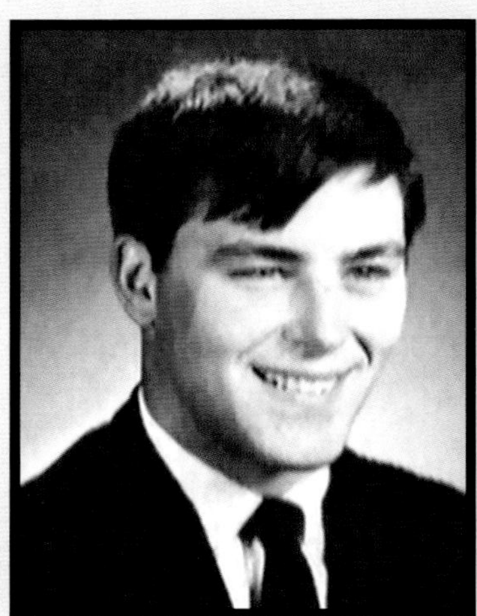

Jerry Ross

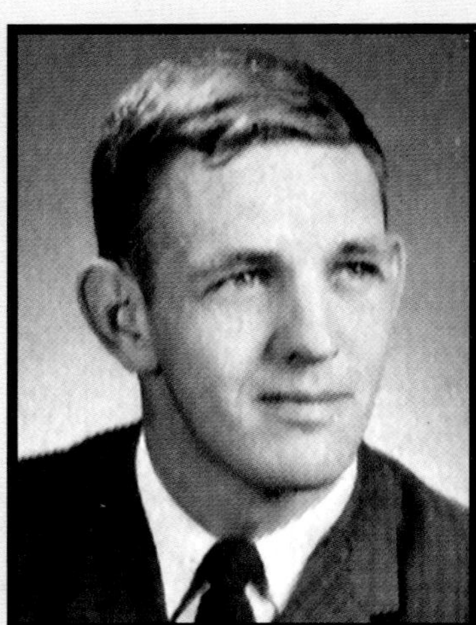

Michael McCulley

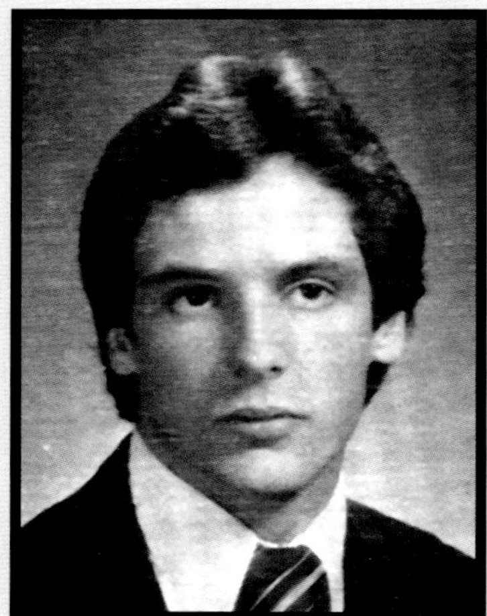

Gregory Harbaugh

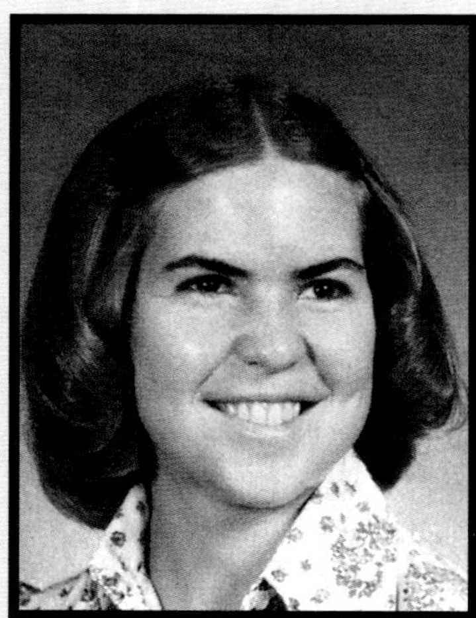

Janice Voss

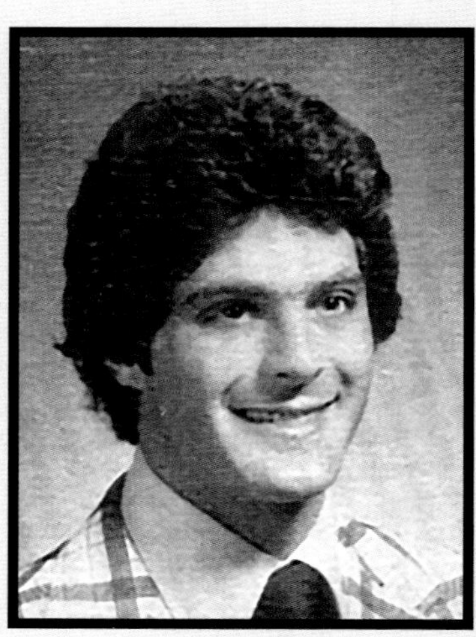

David Wolf

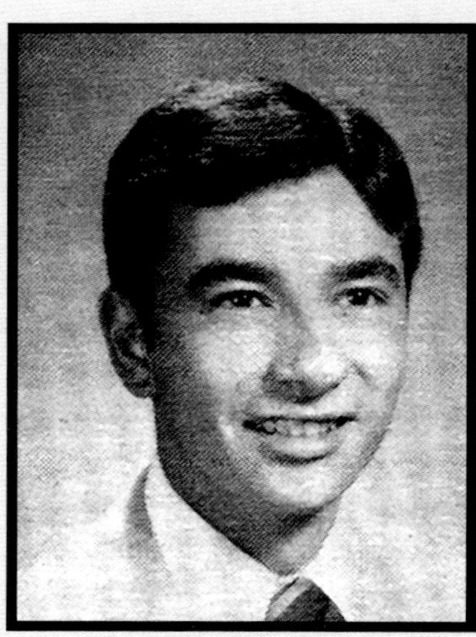

Mark Polansky

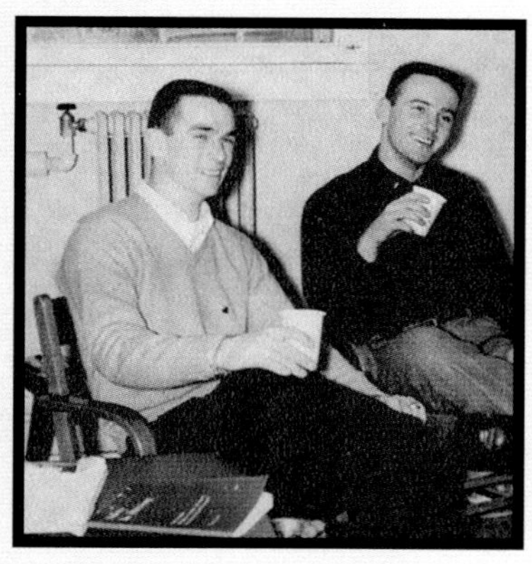

Gregory Harbaugh recalled his experience as an Old Masters student host: "By spending two and a half days with [invited guest] Rusty [Schweickart], I came to see astronauts as real, live human beings, with their strengths and their weaknesses. . . . He made it real for me. He made it a possibility."[7]

Janice Voss was a member of the Angel Flight student group and Mortar Board. David Wolf and Mary Ellen Weber were members of Eta Kappa Nu (an electrical engineering honor society) and Omega Chi Epsilon (the national chemical engineering honor society), respectively. Andrew Feustel worked as a Cary Quadrangle Residence Hall counselor for two years and served as Grand Prix chairman for three years, as well as team kart driver for Sigma Phi Epsilon.[8]

As graduate students, astronaut alumni worked hard and formed connections to their second alma mater. Seven astronaut alumni came to Purdue as selectees for the Purdue University–Air Force Academy cooperative master's degree in astronautics: John Blaha, Roy Bridges Jr., John Casper, Richard Covey, Guy Gardner, Gary Payton, and Loren Shriver. Gardner recalls being on campus in July 1969: "I shared an apartment with three other guys from the Academy. . . . All four of us sat and watched the moonwalk on a little nine-inch black-and-white TV."[9]

Whether these astronaut alumni were at Purdue as undergraduates or graduate students, many returned to the University regularly to share their experiences with current students. Several have worked alongside Purdue students to reach and inspire upward of six hundred elementary school children during the annual student-run Purdue Space Day. Making themselves available to current students and future college students makes the possibilities of space exploration real for just about every student they meet.[10]

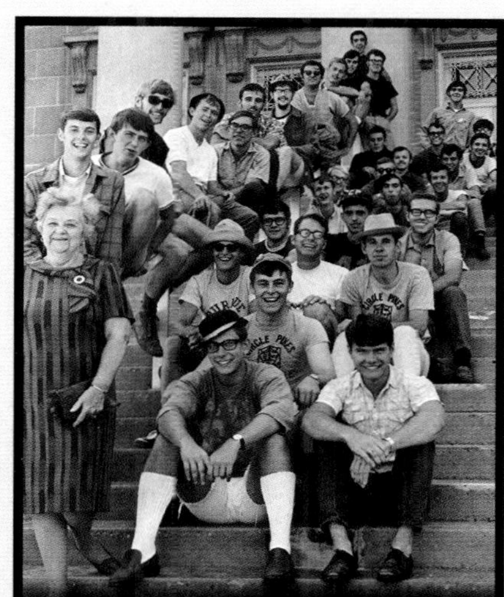

Above left: Eugene Cernan (*left*) as president of the Quarterdeck Society, the honorary society for upperclassmen in NROTC. *(Eugene A. Cernan papers)*

Left: Circle Pines Co-Operative members, including Jerry Ross (*second row*). (Debris *yearbook)*

Purdue University alumni astronauts listed chronologically by NASA Astronaut Group

Group 1, 1959: Virgil "Gus" Grissom

Group 2, 1962: Neil Armstrong

Group 3, 1963: Eugene Cernan, Roger Chaffee

Group 8, 1978: Richard Covey, Loren Shriver, Charles Walker, Donald Williams

Group 9, 1980: John Blaha, Roy Bridges, Guy Gardner, Jerry Ross

USAF Manned Space Flight Program, 1980: Gary Payton

Group 10, 1984: Mark Brown, Michael McCulley, John Casper

Group 12, 1987: Gregory Harbaugh

Group 13, 1990: Janice Voss, David Wolf

Group 14, 1992: Mary Ellen Weber

Group 16, 1996: Mark Polansky

Group 18, 2000: Andrew Feustel

Group 20, 2009: Scott D. Tingle

Group 22, 2017: Loral O'Hara

In honor of its hundredth anniversary, Purdue commissioned a redesign of the university seal. The new design, by visual arts professor Al Gowan, modernized the seal and shifted its focus from a literal illustration of Purdue's areas of expertise to an embodiment of Purdue's values.

PURDUE UNIVERSITY CENTENNIAL

PROCLAMATION

WHEREAS, the Indiana General Assembly did, in the year 1869 A. D. establish a Land-Grant institution in Tippecanoe County, and,

WHEREAS, the said General Assembly did name the institution in honor of its principal benefactor, John Purdue, and

WHEREAS, since that time, Purdue University has flourished for 100 years, serving not only all of the people of the State, nation, and the world, and

WHEREAS, Purdue University has for a century prepared thousands upon thousands of this State's and this nation's young people for useful service to themselves and to the whole fabric of society, and

WHEREAS, this great University has made countless contributions to man's useful knowledge through agriculture, engineering, the sciences, education, the humanities, and to the highest intellectual and cultural pursuits, and

WHEREAS, in this year 1969 A. D. Purdue University celebrates its one hundredth birthday and looks forward to continued Progress Unlimited,

Now, therefore, in behalf of all the citizens of West Lafayette and Lafayette we do hereby problaim 1969, from this date until 12 o'clock at midnight, December 31, 1969, as the Purdue Centennial Year.

In witness whereof we have hereunto affixed our signatures fifteenth day of January, 1969.

James R. Williamson
Mayor, West Lafayette

Mayor, La

Top: Student proclamation commemorating Purdue's centennial year in 1969 signed by the presidents of the Student Body, Student Senate, and Student Union Board. Many activities marked the anniversary, including banquets, lectures, publications, and a fundraising campaign to contribute to the ongoing growth of campus. A special centennial year logo appeared on all university stationery and publications. *(Purdue University Centennial collection)*

Bottom: The new Purdue seal as seen on the cover of the 1969 commencement program. *(Purdue University Commencement programs and invitations collection)*

A student group called the Peace Union formed in 1964, initially to protest the requirement that all underclassmen participate in ROTC training. Once that requirement was removed in 1965 after a change in federal regulations, the Peace Union organized for other causes, including a protest of the University Placement Service due to the corporations included in their career fairs, anti-Vietnam protests, protests against racial injustice on campus, and a protest in April 1969 opposing an increase in student fees.[11]

A sit-in at the Purdue Memorial Union on May 5, 1969, in response to the student fee increase ended in the early hours of the following morning as more than two hundred students who refused to vacate the building were arrested, held, booked, and released without bond. Their cases never went to trial. The next day, the day of Purdue's centennial celebrations, hundreds of students marched to the Administration Building to protest the arrests of the previous night. They surrounded the entrance to the building and, at the peak of the protest, nearly eight hundred students filled the first floor. The protestors dispersed following threat of arrest and the use of mace by state troopers monitoring the situation outside the building.[12]

Even the *Purdue Exponent,* a consistent presence on campus for eighty years, became entangled in the political turmoil on campus. Articles and editorials in the newspaper became increasingly political, drawing ire and praise from students. Competing editorials filled columns of the paper in every issue. The tensions came to a head on October 23, 1968. The recurring column "Notes from a Black Book," written by married students Paul and Deborah Cabbell, took aim at what they called President Hovde's "tyrannical administration" and called for his removal from office using language that many deemed inappropriate for a campus publication.[13] In response, the University removed the paper's editor,

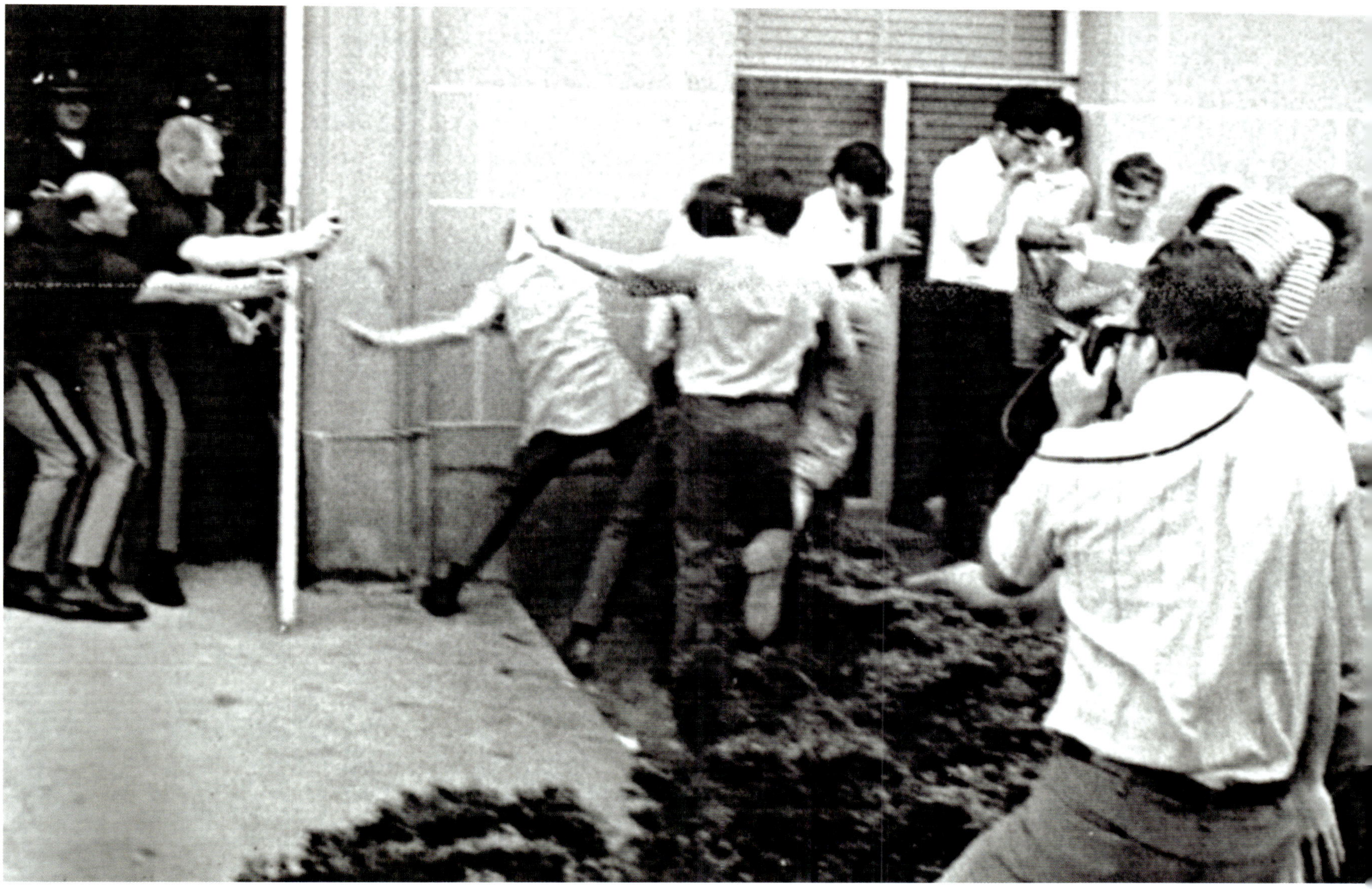

William Smoot, from his position. The *Exponent* ceased print for a brief time as the staff supported their exiled leader. Smoot was reinstated following additional support from students and faculty. As a result of this matter, the complicated administration of the *Exponent* was clarified by removing it from university oversight entirely and establishing The Purdue Student Publishing Association.[14]

On April 22, 1968, approximately one hundred students, staff, and administrators attended the first meeting of the Negro History Club. Discussion focused on the issues facing black students at Purdue and ways to increase awareness of "the past and present accomplishments of the American black people."[15] That same week, the *Purdue Exponent* announced that it would no longer accept classified ads from "landlords who discriminate on the basis of color or nationality."[16]

In 1969 Purdue established the Women in Engineering Program to increase female enrollment in engineering majors. Due to the program's success, similar programs were soon adopted at other institutions across the country. Change continued to come to Purdue through student activism, academics, and organizations into the 1970s.

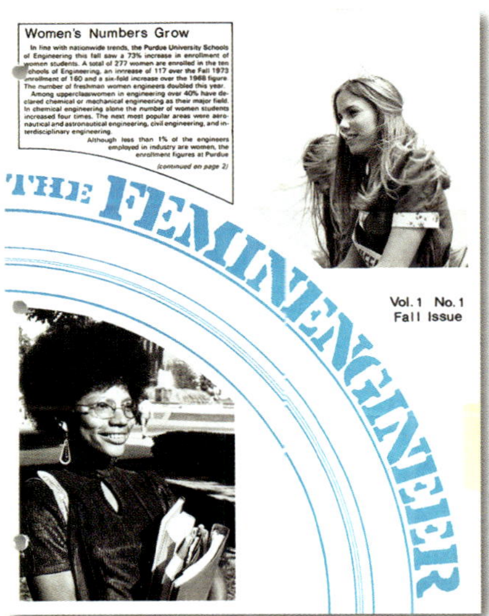

Women's Numbers Grow

In line with nationwide trends, the Purdue University Schools of Engineering this fall saw a 73% increase in enrollment of women students. A total of 277 women are enrolled in the ten Schools of Engineering, an increase of 117 over the Fall 1973 enrollment of 160 and a six-fold increase over the 1968 figure. The number of freshman women engineers doubled this year.

Among upperclasswomen in engineering over 40% have declared chemical or mechanical engineering as their major field. In chemical engineering alone the number of women students increased four times. The next most popular areas were aeronautical and astronautical engineering, civil engineering, and interdisciplinary engineering.

Although less than 1% of the engineers employed in industry are women, the enrollment figures at Purdue

(continued on page 2)

THE FEMINENGINEER

Vol. 1 No. 1
Fall Issue

Above: State Police use mace to keep protestors out of the Administration Building after closing hours. *(Purdue University photographs)*

Left: *The Feminengineer*, Vol. 1, No. 1. *(Women in Engineering Program records)*

Salute to Equal Rights

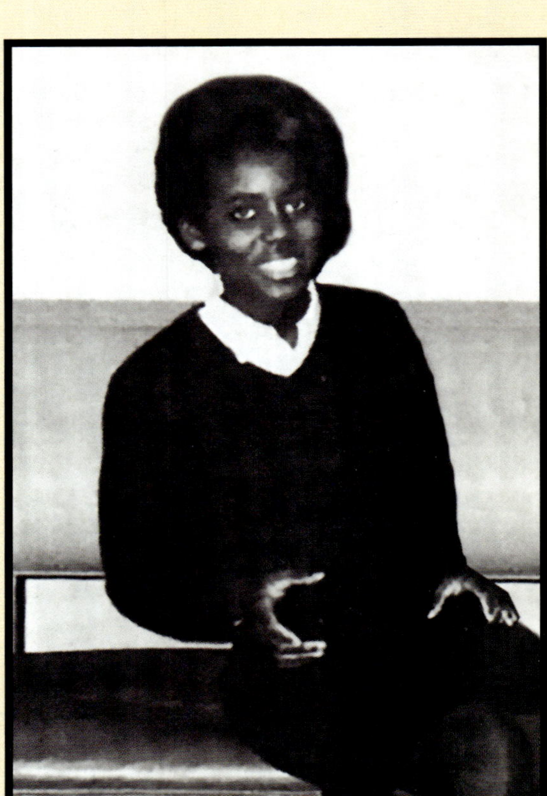

Pamela Tyson King, 1967.
(Debris *yearbook*)

"This is the Black Man's Salute. It is a symbol of pride and dignity for the black man—a symbol of unity. But that does not mean we are automatically at odds with the white man."

—Pamela King

Pamela King was a Purdue student and activist during the 1960s. King participated in the Mortar Board, was one of the first two black Purdue cheerleaders, and also engaged in protests against racial discrimination. During the 1968 football and basketball games, King raised her fist in the Black Salute during the playing of the national anthem.

In December 1968, she and the other cheerleaders were barred from entering the floor at a basketball game against Ohio University. King in turn quit the cheerleading squad and filed a complaint through the Dean of Men's office. In addition to her experiences at Purdue, King was also involved in activism throughout the community.[17]

A Peaceful Demonstration and a Nine-Point Petition

On an overcast morning in May 1968, 129 students from the Black Student Union assembled at the steps of the Administration Building, nonviolently protesting discrimination on campus by symbolically placing bricks on the steps of Hovde Hall. The students delivered a petition to the University listing specific demands for change. It stated:

1. *We demand that the University pressure its departments to recruit qualified black professors for the 1968–1969 school year.*
2. *We demand that the professors of the History Department integrate their segregated, bigoted, and insulting U.S. history courses.*
3. *We demand the immediate integration of student organizations.*
4. *We demand courses dealing with black culture.*
5. *We demand that the black arts be incorporated into the music and art appreciation courses.*
6. *We demand that the University compile a list of discriminatory housing and make this list public.*
7. *We demand more than a token integration of the administration.*
8. *We demand that the University see to it that black professors do not meet discrimination in procuring housing.*
9. *We demand that a course dealing with distortion be instituted as a general core requirement for all students.*[18]

"The day of the march we had already been told that we needed to get a brown paper bag and find a red brick. . . . (Purdue had red brick buildings everywhere). So, we each got our brick, put it in our little paper bag. . . . We assembled in Stewart Center, and we got in a single line, with our bricks in our paper bags, and one by one we marched to Hovde Hall. . . . Single file. Quietly. . . . We took our red bricks out of our brown paper bags and one by one we walked up the steps, and put a brick on the steps."

—Marion Blalock, BS 1969, director of the Minority Engineering Program, 1973–2008[19]

Members of the Black Student Union engaged in a nonviolent protest outside Hovde Hall, 1969. (Debris *yearbook*)

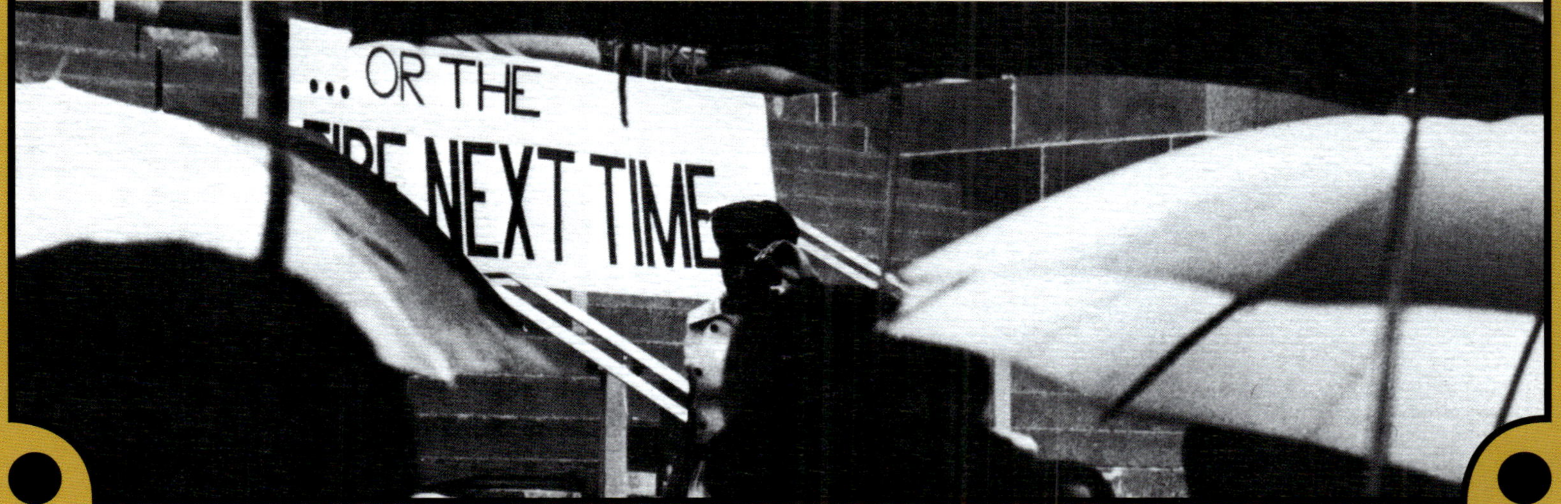

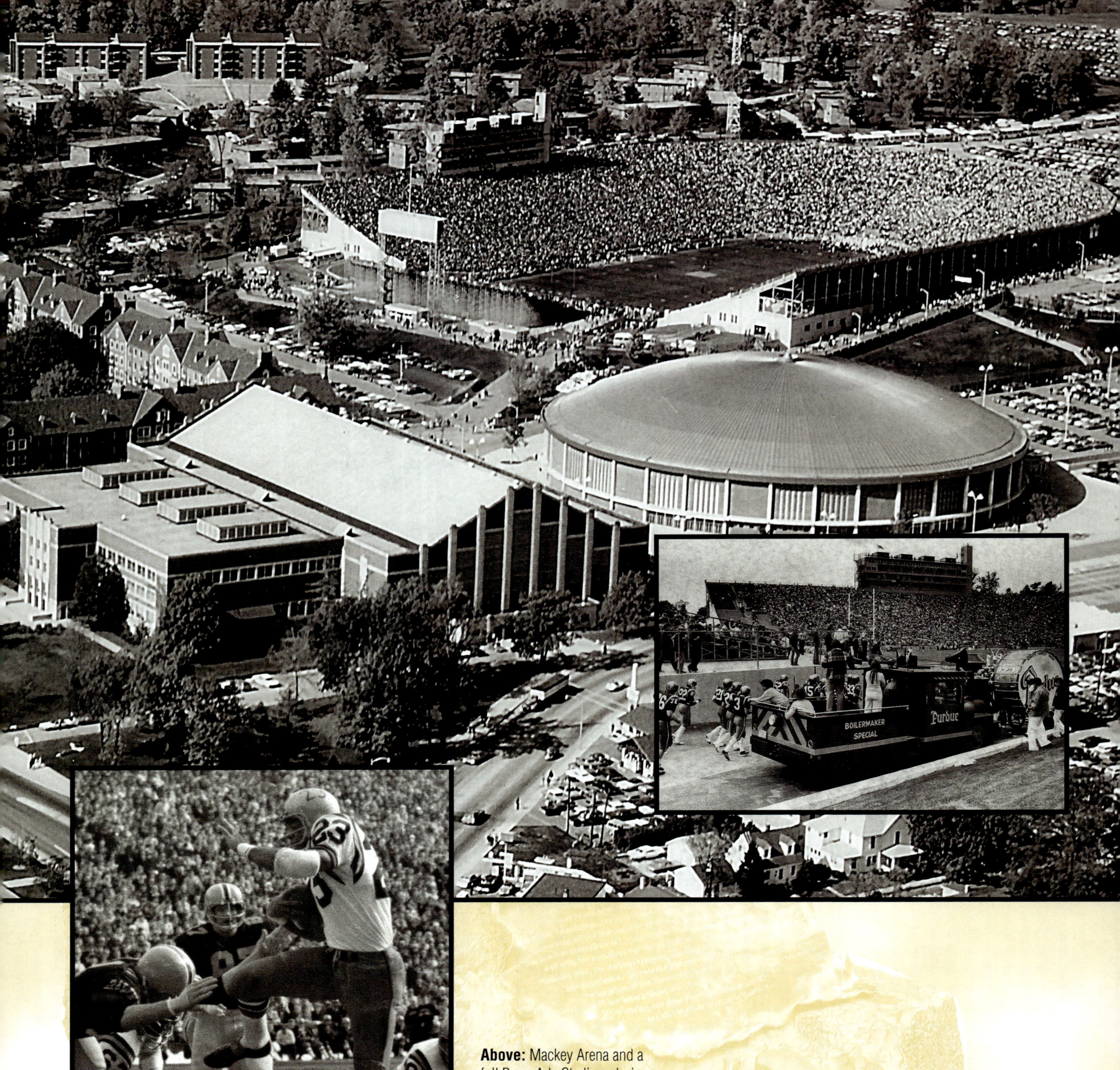

Above: Mackey Arena and a full Ross-Ade Stadium during a football game, circa 1969.
(Purdue University photographs)

Above (inset): The Boilermaker Special and Big Bass Drum greet football players as they run onto the field at Ross-Ade Stadium.
(Purdue University photographs)

Left: Leroy Keyes rushing through the Iowa defense, October 28, 1967. Keyes was selected as a first-team All-American for the 1967 season.
(Purdue University photographs)

Top: Cheerleaders take the floor at a basketball game. *(Purdue University photographs)*

Middle: Students painting senior cords, 1960. *(Purdue University photographs)*

Bottom: Mackey Arena under construction, September 7, 1966. *(Purdue University photographs)*

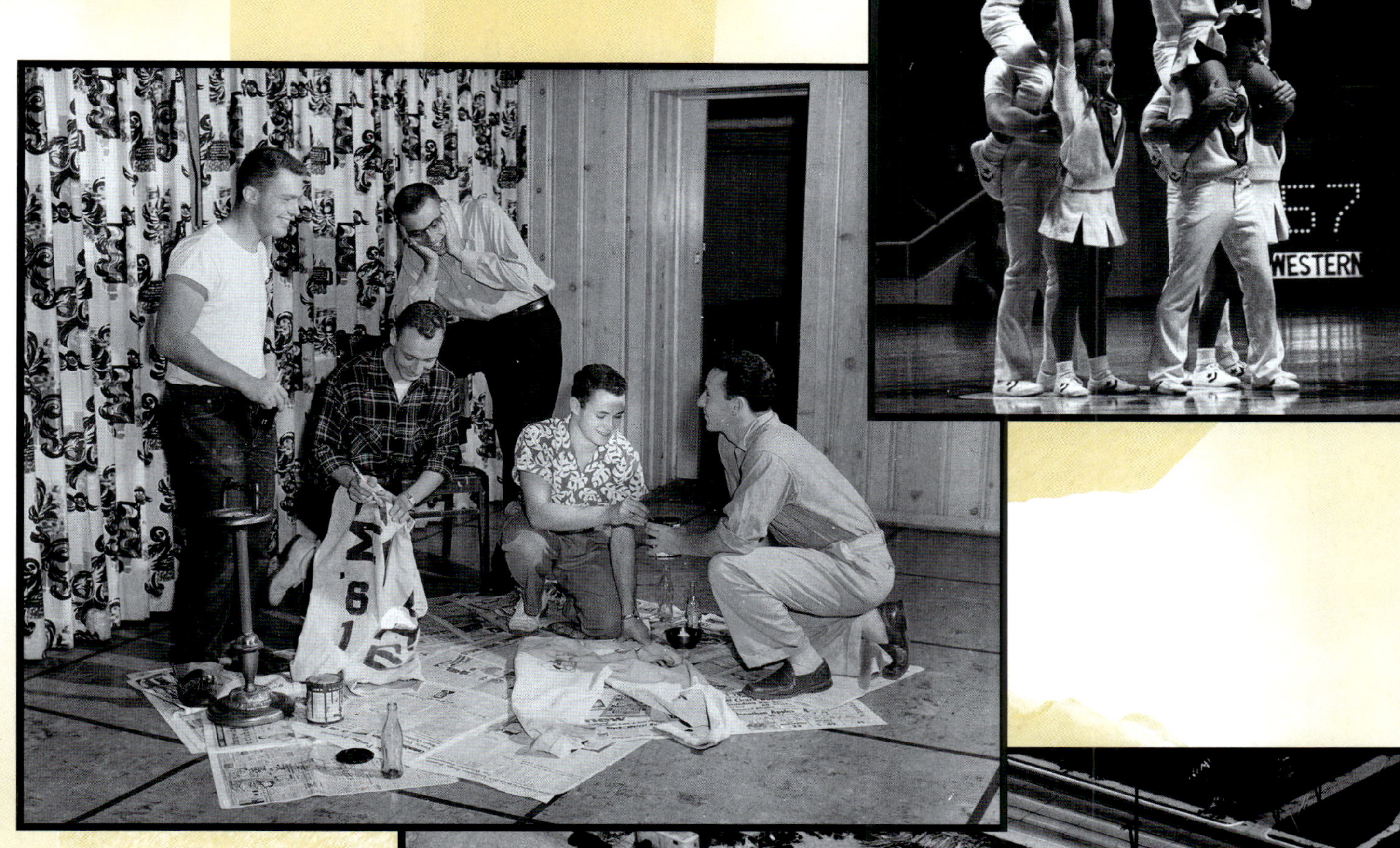

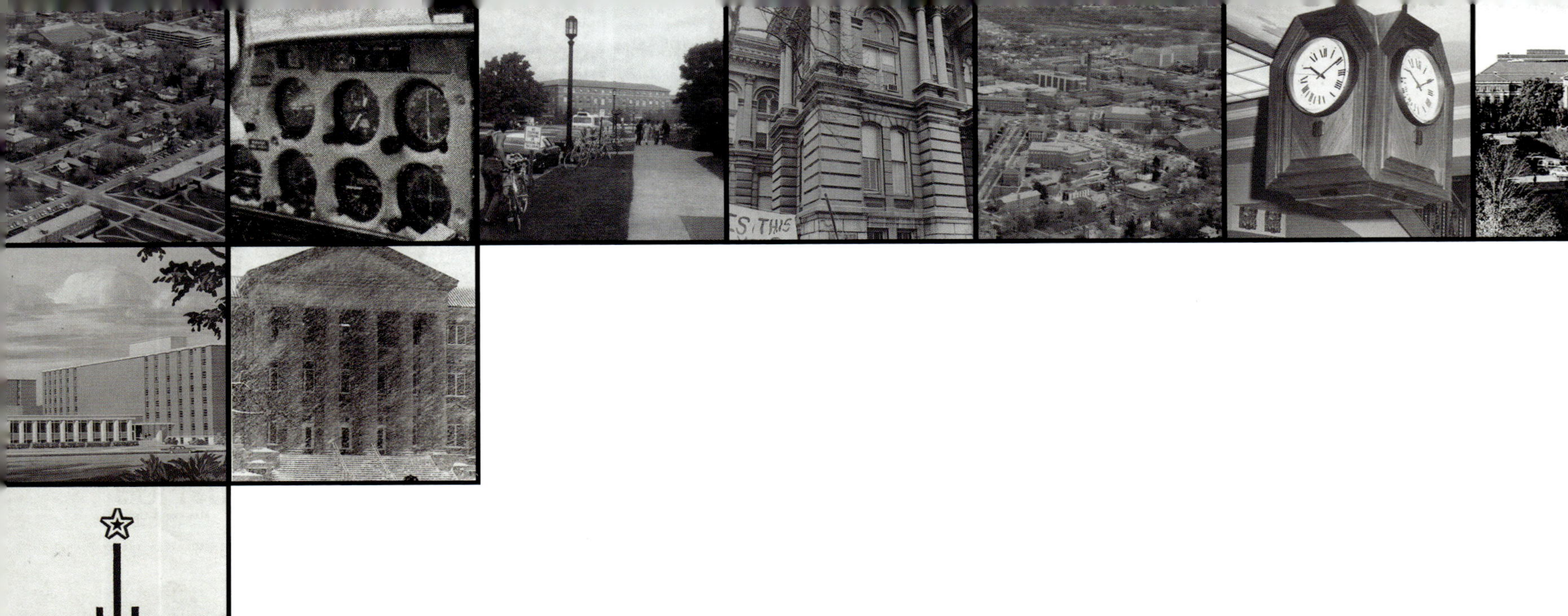

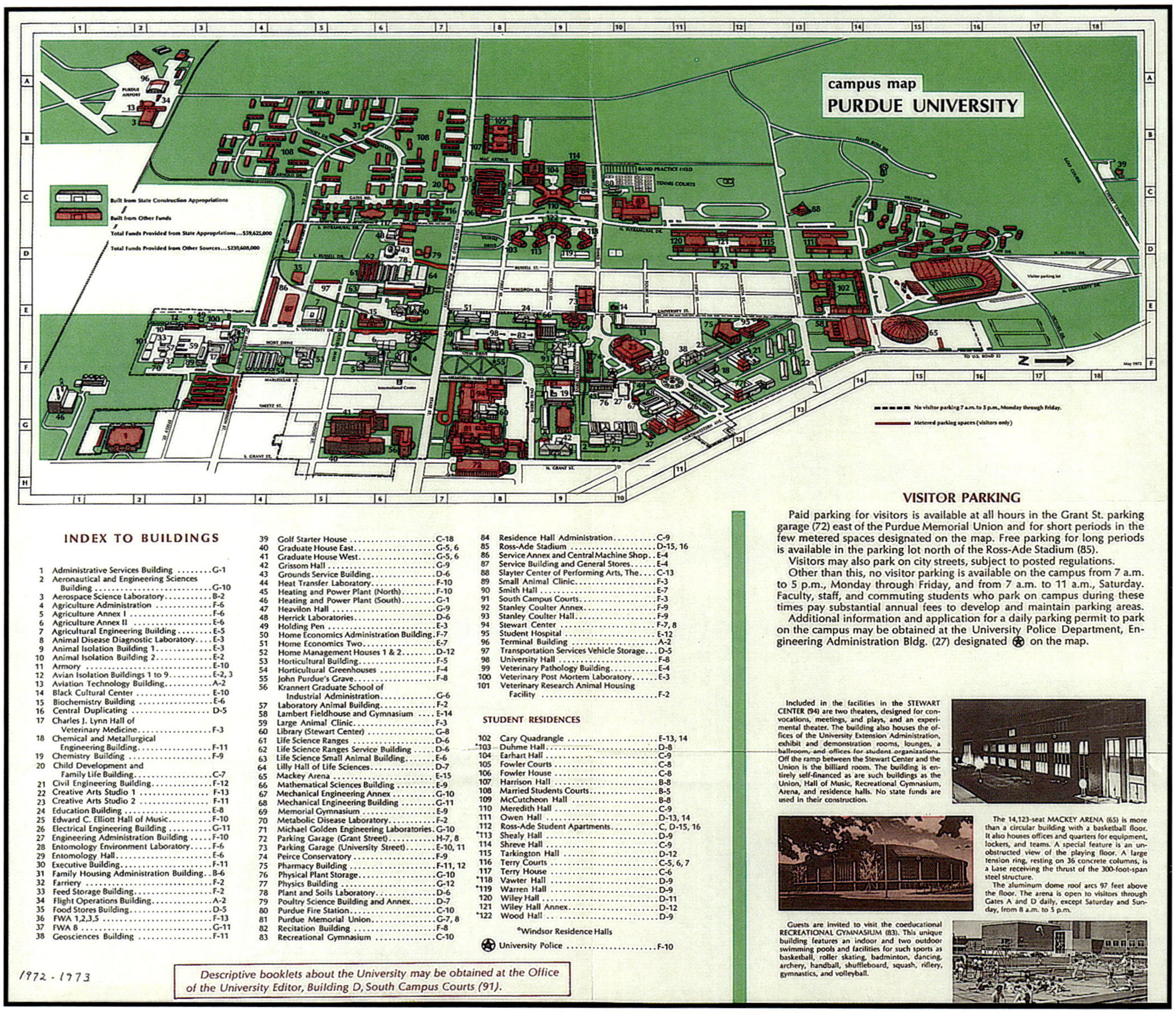

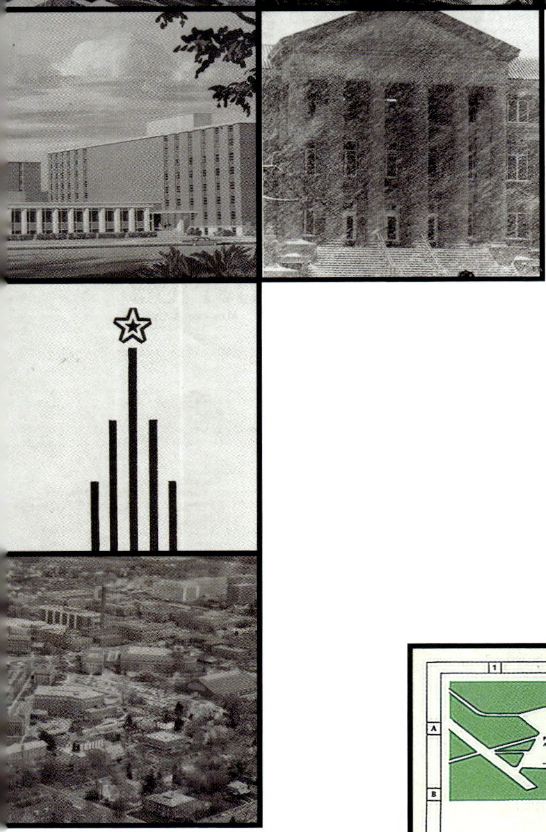

Campus map, 1972–1973. *(Campus Maps collection)*

campus map
PURDUE UNIVERSITY

Built from State Construction Appropriations
Built from Other Funds
Total Funds Provided from State Appropriations...$59,625,000
Total Funds Provided from Other Sources...$230,608,000

No visitor parking 7 a.m. to 5 p.m., Monday through Friday.
Metered parking spaces (visitors only)

INDEX TO BUILDINGS

1 Administrative Services Building G-1
2 Aeronautical and Engineering Sciences Building G-10
3 Aerospace Science Laboratory........B-2
4 Agriculture Administration F-6
5 Agriculture Annex I F-6
6 Agriculture Annex II E-6
7 Agricultural Engineering Building........E-5
8 Animal Disease Diagnostic Laboratory....E-3
9 Animal Isolation Building 1........E-3
10 Animal Isolation Building 2........E-2
11 Armory E-10
12 Avian Isolation Buildings 1 to 9........E-2, 3
13 Aviation Technology Building........A-2
14 Black Cultural Center E-10
15 Biochemistry Building E-6
16 Central Duplicating D-5
17 Charles J. Lynn Hall of Veterinary Medicine........F-3
18 Chemical and Metallurgical Engineering Building........F-11
19 Chemistry Building F-9
20 Child Development and Family Life Building........C-7
21 Civil Engineering Building........F-12
22 Creative Arts Studio 1 ....F-13
23 Creative Arts Studio 2 ....F-11
24 Education Building E-8
25 Edward C. Elliott Hall of Music........F-10
26 Electrical Engineering Building G-11
27 Engineering Administration Building F-10
28 Entomology Environment Laboratory.....F-6
29 Entomology Hall........E-6
30 Executive Building........F-11
31 Family Housing Administration Building..B-6
32 Farriery F-2
33 Feed Storage Building........F-2
34 Flight Operations Building........A-2
35 Food Stores Building........D-5
36 FWA 1,2,3,5 ....F-13
37 FWA 8 ....G-11
38 Geosciences Building F-11
39 Golf Starter House C-18
40 Graduate House East........G-5, 6
41 Graduate House West........G-5, 6
42 Grissom Hall G-9
43 Grounds Service Building........D-6
44 Heat Transfer Laboratory........F-10
45 Heating and Power Plant (North)........F-10
46 Heating and Power Plant (South)........G-1
47 Heavilon Hall G-9
48 Herrick Laboratories........D-6
49 Holding Pen E-3
50 Home Economics Administration Building.F-7
51 Home Economics Two........E-7
52 Home Management Houses 1 & 2........D-12
53 Horticultural Building........F-5
54 Horticultural Greenhouses F-4
55 John Purdue's Grave........F-8
56 Krannert Graduate School of Industrial Administration........G-6
57 Laboratory Animal Building........F-2
58 Lambert Fieldhouse and Gymnasium E-14
59 Large Animal Clinic........F-3
60 Library (Stewart Center) G-8
61 Life Science Ranges D-6
62 Life Science Ranges Service Building D-6
63 Life Science Small Animal Building........E-6
64 Lilly Hall of Life Sciences........D-7
65 Mackey Arena E-15
66 Mathematical Sciences Building E-9
67 Mechanical Engineering Annex G-10
68 Mechanical Engineering Building G-11
69 Memorial Gymnasium E-9
70 Metabolic Disease Laboratory........F-2
71 Michael Golden Engineering Laboratories.G-10
72 Parking Garage (Grant Street)........H-7, 8
73 Parking Garage (University Street)........E-10, 11
74 Peirce Conservatory F-9
75 Pharmacy Building F-11, 12
76 Physical Plant Storage........G-10
77 Physics Building G-12
78 Plant and Soils Laboratory........D-6
79 Poultry Science Building and Annex........D-7
80 Purdue Fire Station........C-10
81 Purdue Memorial Union........G-7, 8
82 Recitation Building F-8
83 Recreational Gymnasium C-10
84 Residence Hall Administration........C-9
85 Ross-Ade Stadium D-15, 16
86 Service Annex and Central Machine Shop..E-4
87 Service Building and General Stores......E-4
88 Slayter Center of Performing Arts, The....C-13
89 Small Animal Clinic........F-3
90 Smith Hall E-7
91 South Campus Courts........F-3
92 Stanley Coulter Annex........F-9
93 Stanley Coulter Hall........F-9
94 Stewart Center F-7, 8
95 Student Hospital E-12
96 Terminal Building A-2
97 Transportation Services Vehicle Storage...D-5
98 University Hall F-8
99 Veterinary Pathology Building........E-4
100 Veterinary Post Mortem Laboratory......E-3
101 Veterinary Research Animal Housing Facility F-2

STUDENT RESIDENCES

102 Cary Quadrangle E-13, 14
*103 Duhme Hall........D-8
104 Earhart Hall C-9
105 Fowler Courts C-8
106 Fowler House C-8
107 Harrison Hall B-8
108 Married Students Courts........B-5
109 McCutcheon Hall B-8
110 Meredith Hall C-9
111 Owen Hall D-13, 14
112 Ross-Ade Student Apartments........C, D-15, 16
*113 Shealy Hall D-9
114 Shreve Hall C-9
115 Tarkington Hall D-12
116 Terry Courts C-5, 6, 7
117 Terry House C-6
*118 Vawter Hall D-9
*119 Warren Hall D-9
120 Wiley Hall D-11
121 Wiley Hall Annex........D-12
*122 Wood Hall D-9

*Windsor Residence Halls

University Police F-10

1972 - 1973

Descriptive booklets about the University may be obtained at the Office of the University Editor, Building D, South Campus Courts (91).

VISITOR PARKING

Paid parking for visitors is available at all hours in the Grant St. parking garage (72) east of the Purdue Memorial Union and for short periods in the few metered spaces designated on the map. Free parking for long periods is available in the parking lot north of the Ross-Ade Stadium (85).

Visitors may also park on city streets, subject to posted regulations.

Other than this, no visitor parking is available on the campus from 7 a.m. to 5 p.m., Monday through Friday, and from 7 a.m. to 11 a.m., Saturday. Faculty, staff, and commuting students who park on campus during these times pay substantial annual fees to develop and maintain parking areas.

Additional information and application for a daily parking permit to park on the campus may be obtained at the University Police Department, Engineering Administration Bldg. (27) designated ⊛ on the map.

Included in the facilities in the STEWART CENTER (94) are two theaters, designed for convocations, meetings, and plays, and an experimental theater. The building also houses the offices of the University Extension Administration, exhibit and demonstration rooms, lounges, a ballroom, and offices for student organizations. Off the ramp between the Stewart Center and the Union is the billiard room. The building is entirely self-financed as are such buildings as the Union, Hall of Music, Recreational Gymnasium, Arena, and residence halls. No state funds are used in their construction.

The 14,123-seat MACKEY ARENA (65) is more than a circular building with a basketball floor. It also houses offices and quarters for equipment, lockers, and teams. A special feature is an unobstructed view of the playing floor. A large tension ring, resting on 36 concrete columns, is a base receiving the thrust of the 300-foot-span steel structure.

The aluminum dome roof arcs 97 feet above the floor. The arena is open to visitors through Gates A and D daily, except Saturday and Sunday, from 8 a.m. to 5 p.m.

Guests are invited to visit the coeducational RECREATIONAL GYMNASIUM (83). This unique building features an indoor and two outdoor swimming pools and facilities for such sports as basketball, roller skating, badminton, dancing, archery, handball, shuffleboard, squash, riflery, gymnastics, and volleyball.

{Enrollment in 1970: 28,356 students[1]}

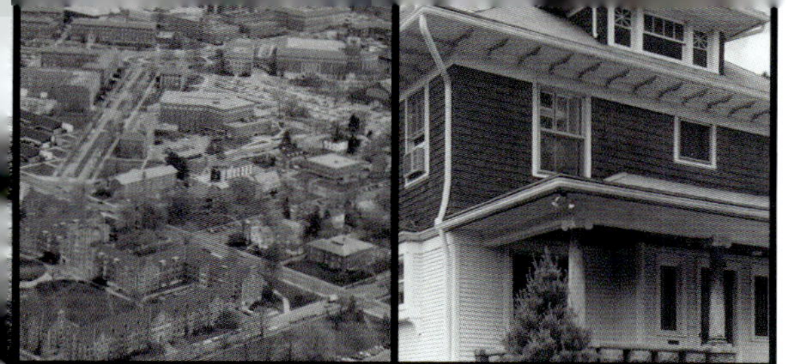

[The 1970s]

PURDUE AT 110

"When I was a student there . . . for the computer programming, we punched cards. We wrote . . . a line of code and punched a card for every line of code, and then we had to take our box of cards to the card reader, and we did this all two sub-basements down under the math-science building. . . . I would usually stay there 'til they closed it at five A.M., writing computer code. I would say those are some of my most heartwarming memories . . . all those many nights spent underground. We used to call ourselves the moles."

—*Jennifer Bradford, class of 1981*[2]

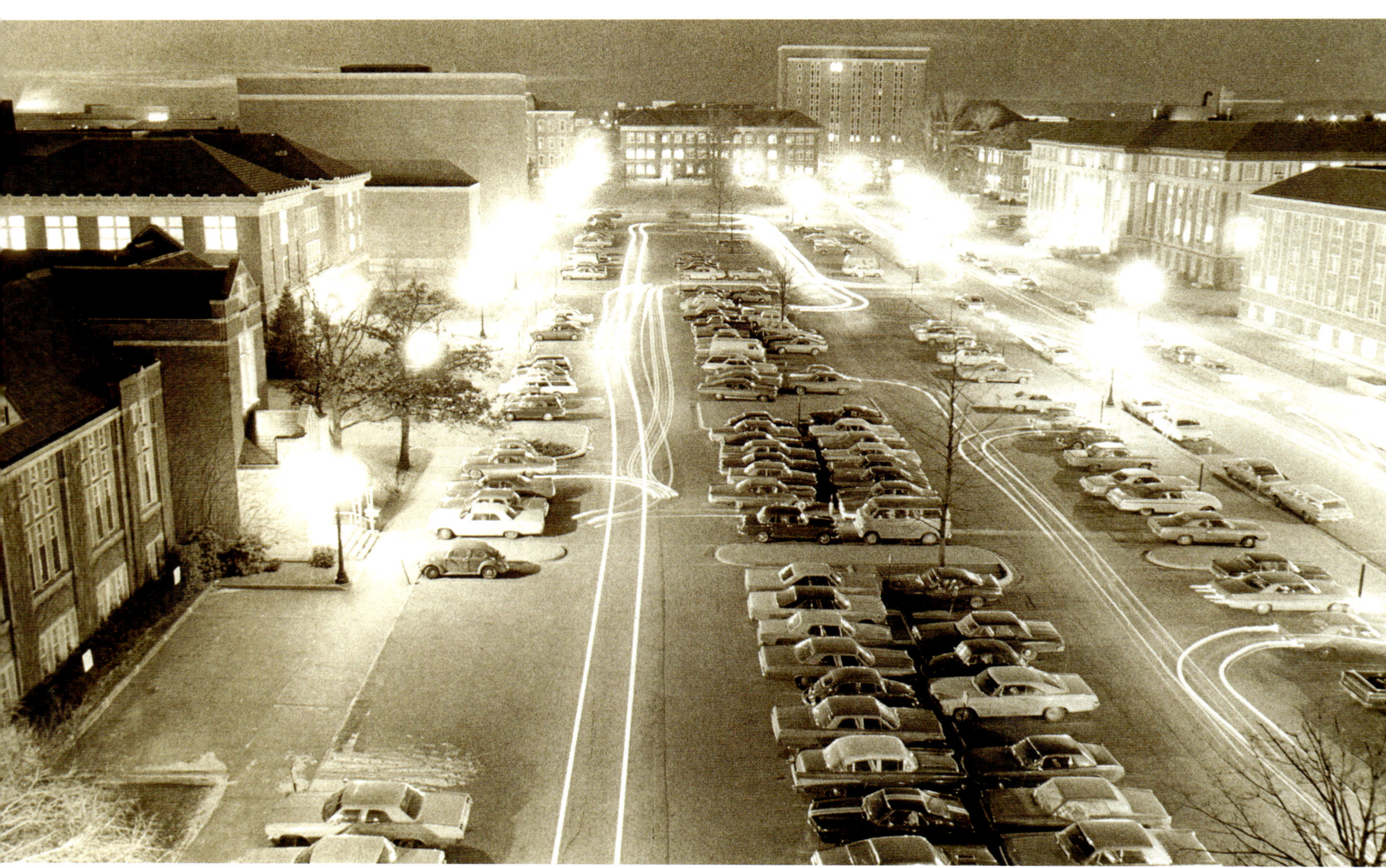

Evening photograph of campus taken in long exposure, 1979. This area transitioned from parking to Academy Park in the 1990s as part of a green spaces movement on campus. *(Purdue University Marketing and Media collection)*

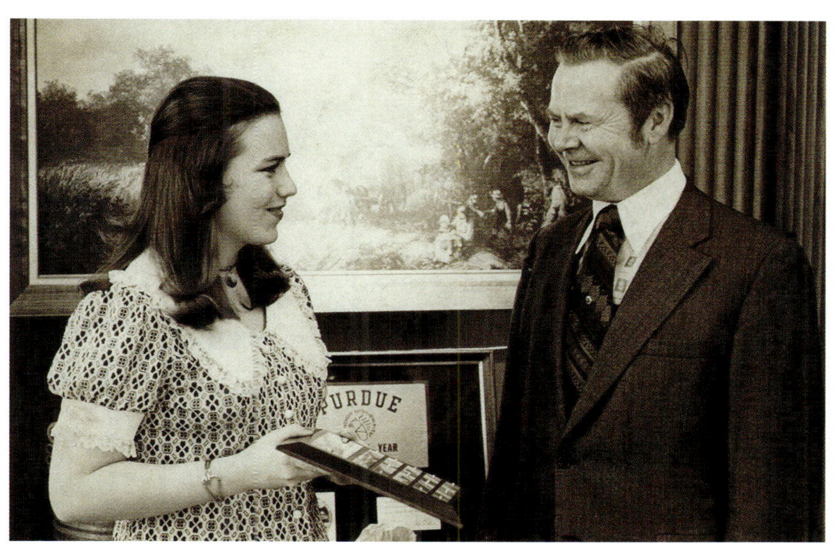

President Arthur Hansen and a student, 1973.
(Purdue University photographs)

In the fall of 1970, Purdue again experienced a record enrollment across its five campuses. In addition to the students enrolled at the West Lafayette campus, 18,684 students were enrolled at the branch campuses.[3] The ensuing decade would be marked by student protests, a new administrative direction for the university, and new beginnings in race relations.

After twenty-five years of service, President Frederick Hovde retired in 1971. Arthur Hansen, a Purdue alumnus who graduated from Purdue the year Hovde started his tenure, was appointed Hovde's successor and the eighth president of the University.

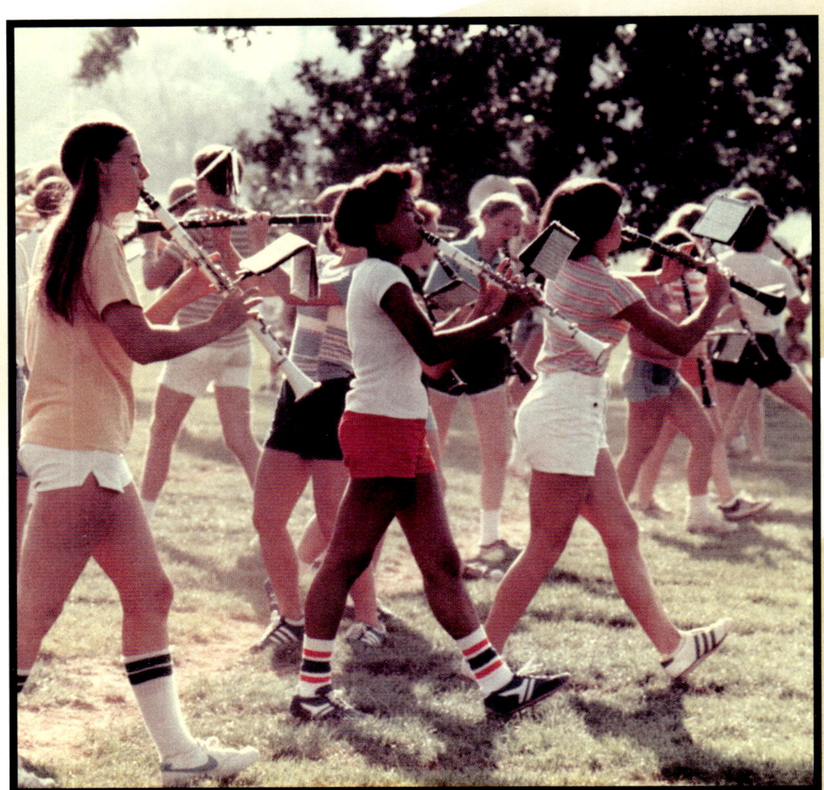

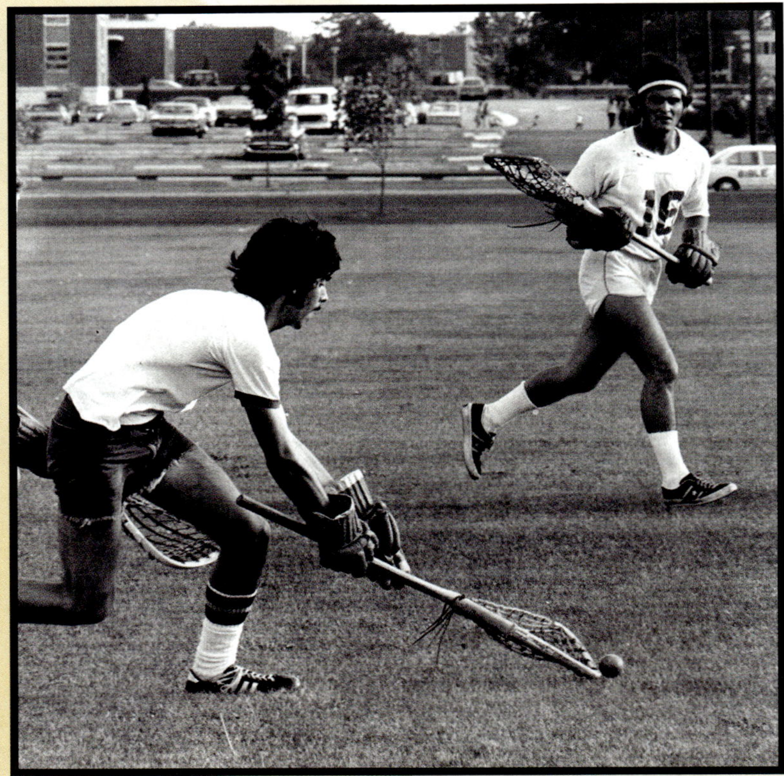

Clockwise from top left:

Clarinet players rehearsing during band camp. *(Purdue Bands and Orchestras records)*

Intramural lacrosse. *(Purdue University Marketing and Media collection)*

The Purdue crew. *(Purdue University Marketing and Media collection)*

Selita Sue Smith, Purdue's eighth Golden Girl. *(Purdue University photographs)*

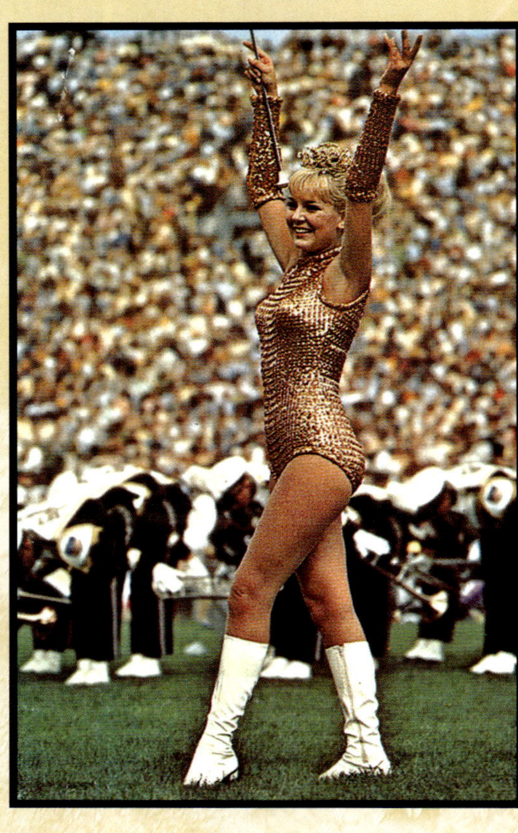

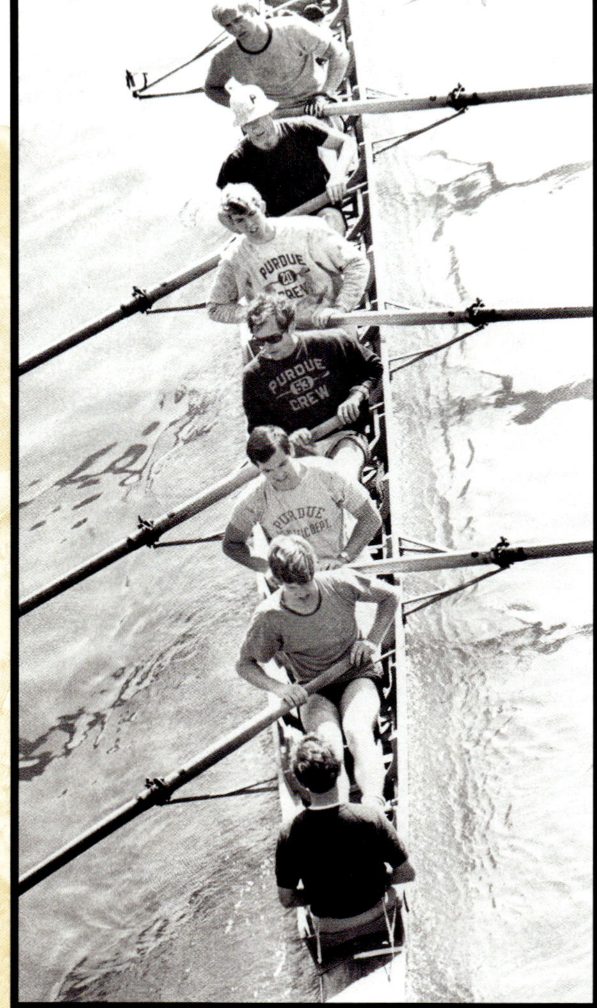

Purdue was defeated by the University of Illinois in the world's first concrete canoe race in 1971.[4]

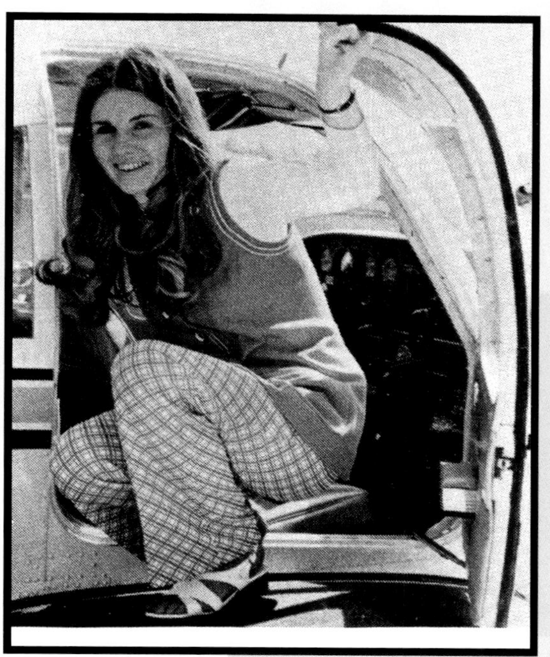

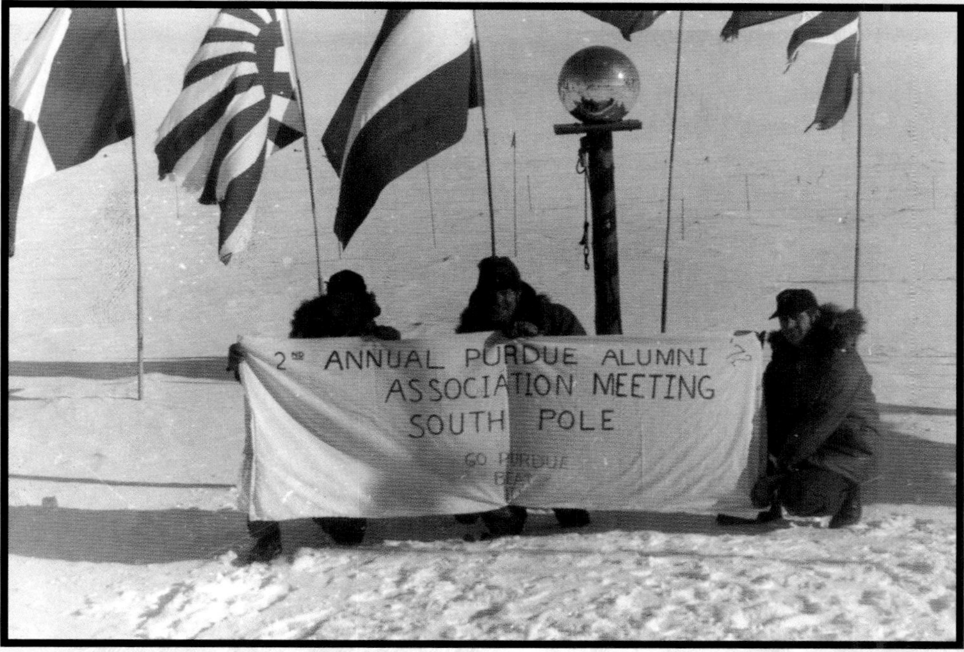

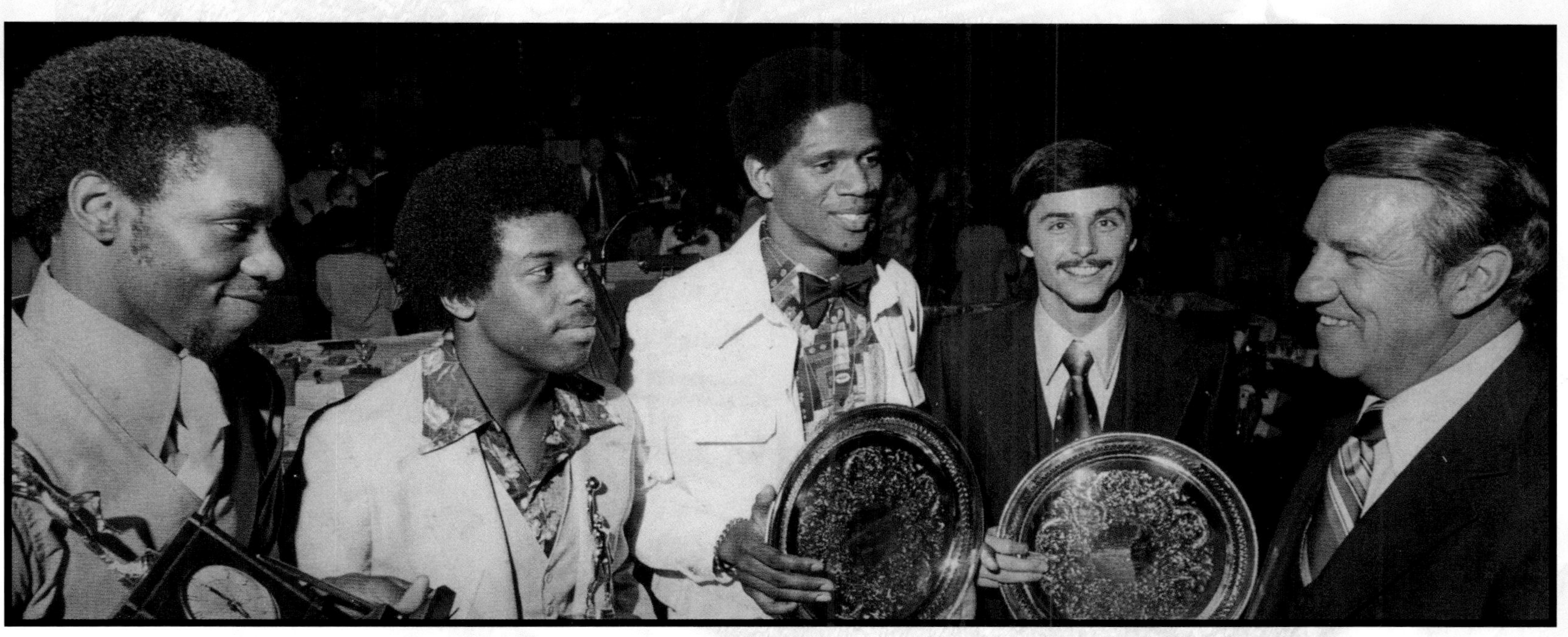

Top: Rosemary Merims, Purdue's first female graduate in aviation technology and the first woman student to achieve a professional pilot rating at Purdue. *(Department of Aviation Technology records)*

Middle: Second annual meeting of the Purdue Alumni Association at the South Pole, 1972. *(Purdue University photographs)*

Bottom: Most valuable player Walter Jordan, defensive player of the year Eugene Parker, team captain Gerald Thomas, Guy J. Mackey postgraduate scholarship nominee Bruce Parkinson, and coach Fred Schaus at the Purdue Basketball Honors Awards on March 30, 1977. *(Purdue University photographs)*

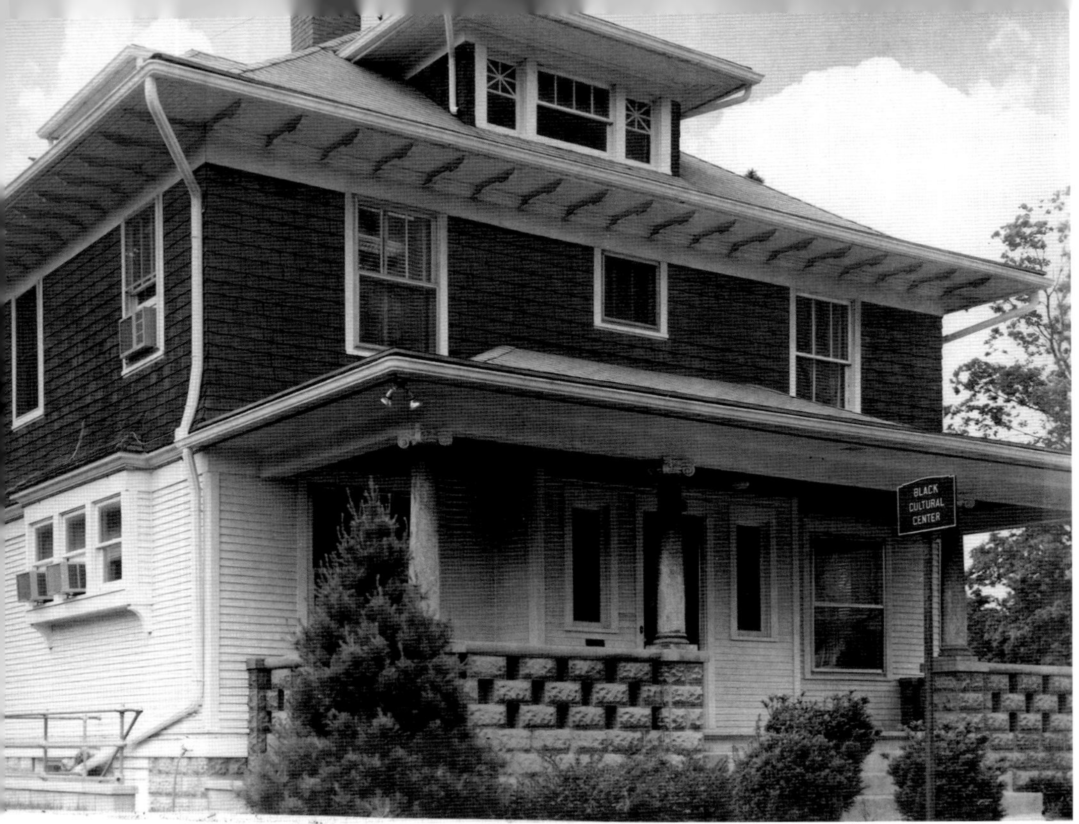

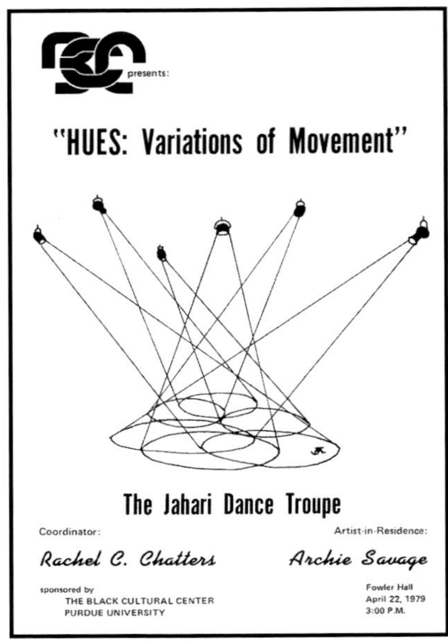
"HUES: Variations of Movement"

The Jahari Dance Troupe

Coordinator: Rachel C. Chatters

Artist-in-Residence: Archie Savage

sponsored by THE BLACK CULTURAL CENTER PURDUE UNIVERSITY

Fowler Hall April 22, 1979 3:00 P.M.

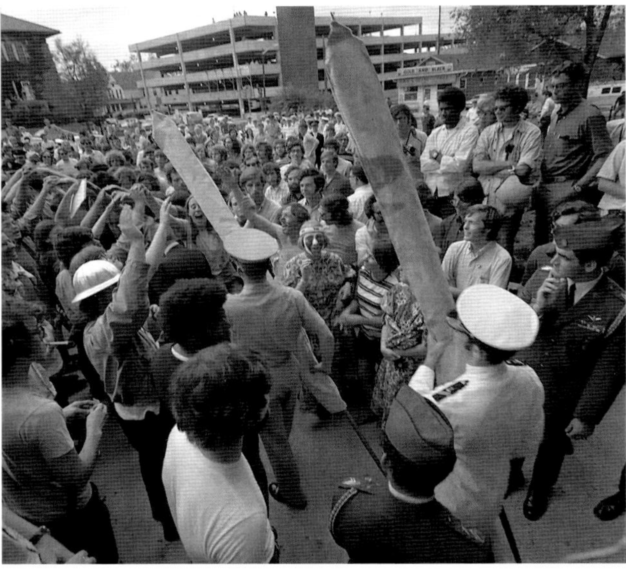

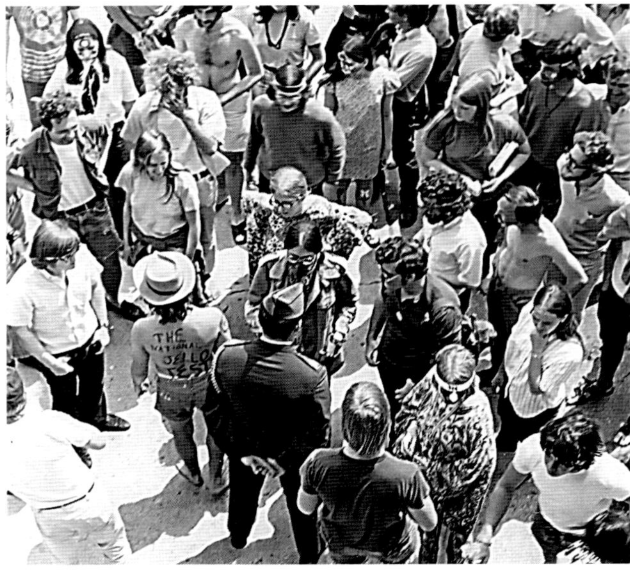

Clockwise from top left:

The first Black Cultural Center, dedicated in 1970. *(Purdue University photographs)*

Leaflet promoting an April 22, 1979, performance of "HUES: Variations of Movement" by the Jahari Dance Troupe, a student dance company sponsored by the Black Cultural Center. The group trained in a range of dances from traditional to contemporary trends of black dance, including African dance, ballet, Caribbean, folk, jazz, modern dance, and music video. *(Black Cultural Center records)*

Student protestors and an ROTC cadet in standoff, 1970. *(Purdue University photographs)*

Student protest on campus, 1970. *(Purdue University News Service negatives and photographs)*

Student protests continued into the 1970s as the Vietnam War persisted. The Board of Trustees passed a resolution supporting automatic suspension of students and dismissal of teachers who disrupted school activities. On May 1, 1970, students protesting an ROTC convocation and the escalation of U.S. involvement in the war staged a sit-in at the Armory. They demanded the abolition of the ROTC and the cessation of classified war research at Purdue. Student activists also sought a statement from University officials calling for an end to the war. Members of the Indiana State Police were called in to remove the students, and about thirty-five students were suspended. Later that same day, a large group of students marched into Lafayette while helicopters from the State Police flew overhead. According to the executive assistant to the president, John Hicks, this was "the last big protest" at Purdue.[5]

After decades of fighting for rights and representation, African American students began gaining new opportunities in academic and cultural programs. The Black Cultural Center (BCC), dedicated in the fall of 1970, offered a location for both learning and community building. Professor Singer Buchanan was hired as Purdue's first coordinator of Black Student Programs in 1970. He articulated a vision for the BCC as an educational and social center, a place for people of different races and backgrounds to discuss issues, exchange feelings, and "emerge hopefully on the other side with a greater understanding of what each thinks, and feels, and believes."[6] Graduate student John Houston became the first director of the BCC in 1972. He was succeeded by Antonio Zamora in 1973.

The Interdisciplinary Afro-American Studies Program at Purdue was approved in 1970. The option for students to major or minor in African American studies became available in the fall of 1971. The College of Engineering's Minority Engineering Program was established in 1974, with alumna Marion Blalock serving as its inaugural director. The BCC brought Muhammad Ali to campus in 1976, sponsoring a lecture he gave on the topic of friendship.[7]

Two undergraduate students, Edward Barnette and Fred Cooper, established the Black Society of Engineers (BSE) in 1971 as a means of improving black engineering student retention and recruitment. Barnette served as the first president of the new student organization. The society's president, Anthony Harris, contacted students at universities across the country and, on April 10–12, 1975, hosted the first meeting of what would become known as the National Society of Black Engineers.[8]

By the 1970s, students were increasingly taking advantage of the press to make their voices heard. The *Black Hurricane* newspaper, a publication of the Black Student Union, published its first issue in 1970. It advocated for total freedom for African American people, with a sphere "like a hurricane" that "knows no boundaries to its destination."[9] Several other independent student newspapers, such as *Red Brick,* made their debuts during the decade.

Top: The Society of Black Engineers, 1975. *(Debris yearbook)*

Bottom left: Flyer for Muhammed Ali's talk at Purdue in 1976. *(Black Cultural Center records)*

Bottom middle: *Black Hurricane*, Vol. 1, No. 1, November 17–30, 1970. *(Collection of Student Newspapers at Purdue University)*

Bottom right: *Red Brick*, Vol. 1, No. 1, circa 1971. *(Collection of Student Newspapers at Purdue University)*

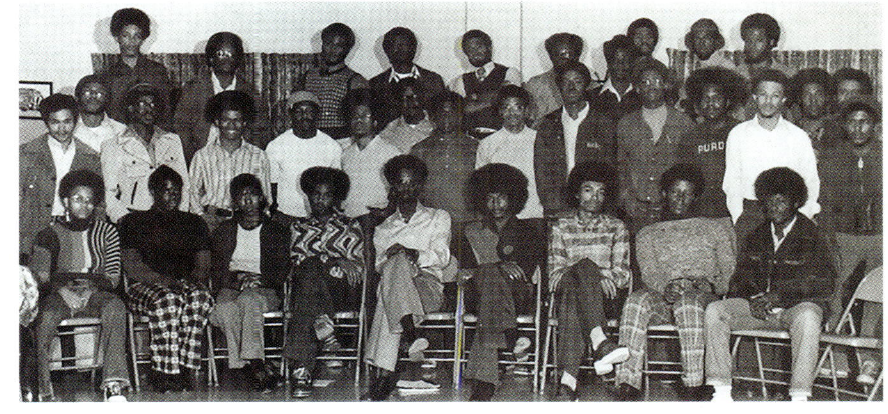

Internationally Famous
WORLD CHAMPION
MUHAMMAD ALI

Guest Speaker
Topic: Friendship
Thursday, November 20, 8:00 p.m.
Reception immediately following in the PMU South Ballroom
free and open to the public

Sponsored by
THE BLACK CULTURAL CENTER
PURDUE UNIVERSITY

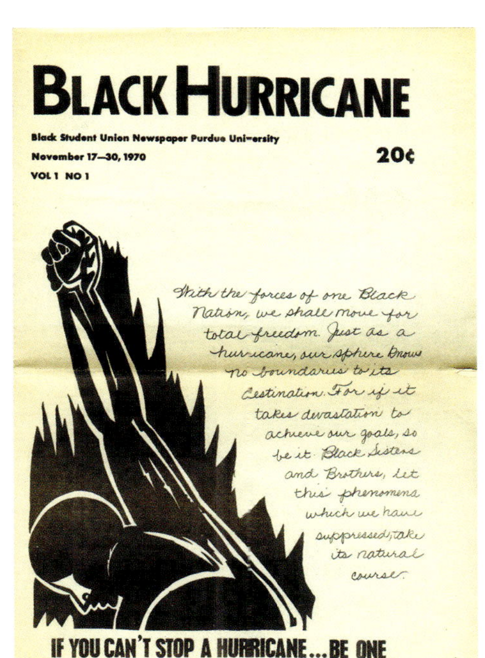

BLACK HURRICANE
Black Student Union Newspaper Purdue Uni-ersity
November 17–30, 1970
VOL 1 NO 1
20¢

With the forces of one Black Nation, we shall move for total freedom. Just as a hurricane, our sphere knows no boundaries to its destination. For if it takes devastation to achieve our goals, so be it. Black Sisters and Brothers, let this phenomena which we have suppressed, take its natural course.

IF YOU CAN'T STOP A HURRICANE...BE ONE

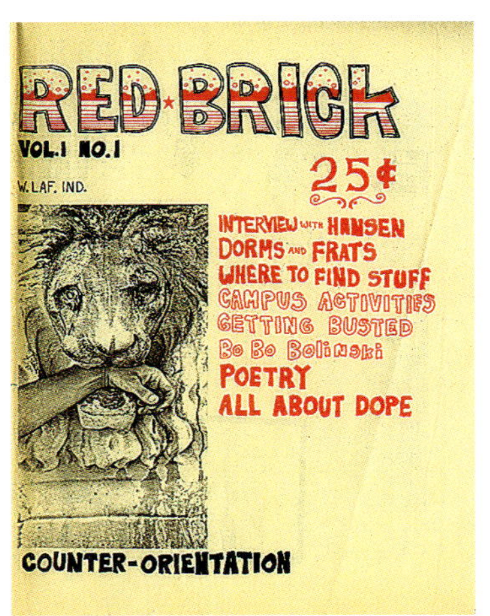

RED★BRICK
VOL. I NO. I
W. LAF. IND.
25¢
INTERVIEW WITH HANSEN
DORMS AND FRATS
WHERE TO FIND STUFF
CAMPUS ACTIVITIES
GETTING BUSTED
Bo Bo Bolinski
POETRY
ALL ABOUT DOPE
COUNTER-ORIENTATION

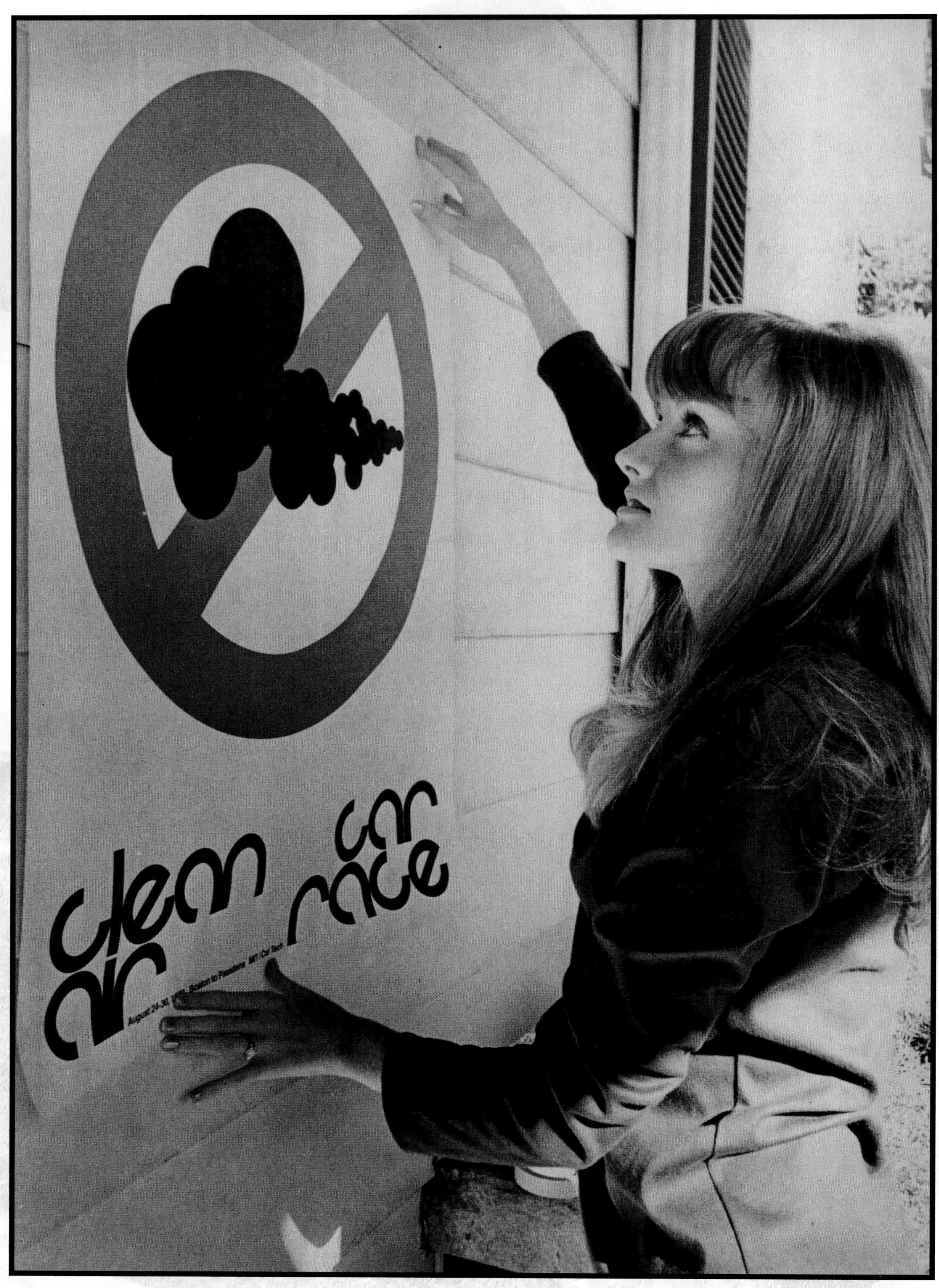

Student putting up poster for clean air car race, circa 1970s.
(Purdue University photographs)

In 1970 the Board of Trustees created a student representative position to participate and provide a voice for student interests. An official student trustee position was created in 1975, following a new state law requiring student membership on the governing boards of each state university. Larry Grieshaber, a pharmacy graduate student, filled the new role. A position for a student representative of the West Lafayette City Council was also approved in 1975 and filled by David Berkey.[10]

Purdue Mortar Board,
1973–1974. *(Debris yearbook)*

As the student body increased, Purdue once again faced a housing shortage. Demand far exceeded supply by 1974, and in 1976 the University broke a new record in number of students living off campus: 14,161.[11] Some students rented rooms in local motels on a semester basis or lived temporarily in Union Club Hotel rooms. The University converted some married student housing for use by single students, and available spaces in dorms, such as workshops and service closets, were converted into rooms for students. Students received the right to have guest hours in 1970, which allowed for dorm room visitation by members of the opposite sex.[12]

Prior to the 1970s, there were separate deans of students for men and women. When the offices of the Dean of Women Students and the Dean of Men Students merged in 1974, Dean of Women Beverley Stone was appointed into the newly combined role. One of the issues Dean Stone championed was equal rights for women, pointing out that although all of the academic programs were available to women students, Purdue could do more to increase the number of women faculty in leadership positions and address issues of equal pay for women employed at the University.[13]

Increasing numbers of women students were entering Purdue. In the 1970–1971 fiscal year, the number of women students exceeded one-third of the total student population for the first time.[14] The ROTC began admitting women students in 1970. Title IX federal regulations, passed in 1972, resulted in enhanced support for women's intercollegiate athletics by the mid-1970s. Purdue soon had one of the best women's college volleyball teams in the nation. Student organizations that were traditionally gender-specific, such as Mortar Board, the Association for Women Students, and Iron Key, were required to admit both men and women.

The Purdue Bells was founded in 1979.

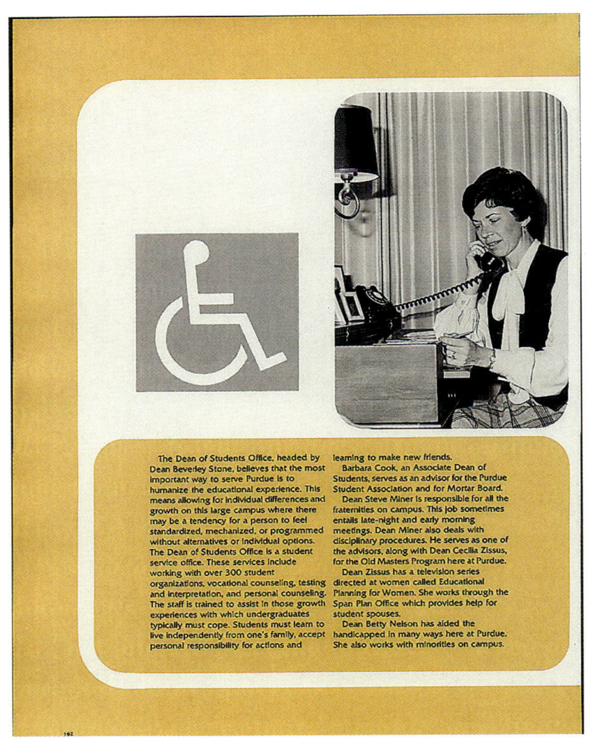

The Dean of Students Office, headed by Dean Beverley Stone, believes that the most important way to serve Purdue is to humanize the educational experience. This means allowing for individual differences and growth on this large campus where there may be a tendency for a person to feel standardized, mechanized, or programmed without alternatives or individual options. The Dean of Students Office is a student service office. These services include working with over 300 student organizations, vocational counseling, testing and interpretation, and personal counseling. The staff is trained to assist in those growth experiences with which undergraduates typically must cope. Students must learn to live independently from one's family, accept personal responsibility for actions and learning to make new friends.

Barbara Cook, an Associate Dean of Students, serves as an advisor for the Purdue Student Association and for Mortar Board.

Dean Steve Miner is responsible for all the fraternities on campus. This job sometimes entails late-night and early morning meetings. Dean Miner also deals with disciplinary procedures. He serves as one of the advisors, along with Dean Cecilia Zissus, for the Old Masters Program here at Purdue.

Dean Zissus has a television series directed at women called Educational Planning for Women. She works through the Span Plan Office which provides help for student spouses.

Dean Betty Nelson has aided the handicapped in many ways here at Purdue. She also works with minorities on campus.

After a much larger turnout of sopranos than tenors answered the callout for the University Choir, the Coed Choral Club was founded in 1972 with forty-four women students, most of whom were freshmen.[15] The size of the University Choir was reduced from approximately three hundred members to fifty. An editorial in the student newspaper criticized Al Stewart for his requirements relating to hair length and dress standards for members of the Purdue Musical Organizations.[16]

The University began to improve conditions for students with disabilities, with advocates such as Betty Nelson working in the Dean of Students Office. The University increased the number of ramps on campus, and the Department of Schedules and Space began a program for students with limited mobility that would "move classes rather than the student."[17]

A new student organization, the Gay Liberation Front, was approved by 1973. President Hansen supported the formation of the group, despite concerns from some members of the University community. He also approved the formation of the Communist Youth Brigade, a short-lived student group that met only once and disbanded. Recalling the unpopularity of these decisions, Hansen stated that if you destroy the right of free speech, you destroy the university.[18]

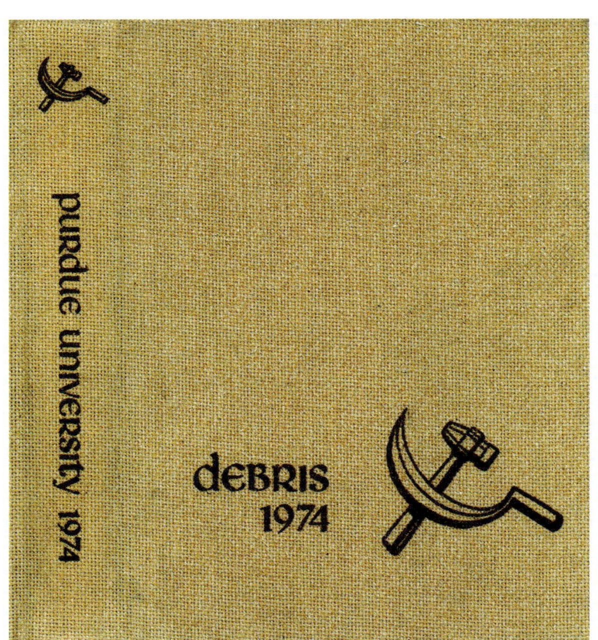

Above: Betty Nelson, 1979. Nelson led renewed efforts to make the campus accessible to all students and visitors. *(*Debris *yearbook)*

Left: Cover of the 1974 *Debris* yearbook featuring a hammer and sickle, which led to an accusation from State Senator John Shawley that the *Debris* staff had been infiltrated by communists. President Hansen defended the students' selection, pointing out that the hammer of mechanical arts and sickle of agriculture were symbolic of Purdue's mission as a land grant university.[19] *(*Debris *yearbook)*

Kassandra Agee Chandler, Purdue's First African American Homecoming Queen

As a sophomore in the fall of 1978, Kassandra Agee Chandler was elected Purdue's Homecoming queen, the first African American Homecoming queen in Purdue's history. A representative of Meredith Residence Halls, she competed against twenty-three other competitors to win her title. When reflecting upon the nomination and campaign experience, she remembered hearing, "They'll never let you win this."[20] But Agee Chandler drew upon the strength of her family, friends, and dorm mates, as well as her own tenacity. She worked tirelessly on her campaign, going door-to-door and hanging posters. She remembered, "I didn't let it get to me. I never let anyone talk me down. . . . In the end, I was able to make my family and sisterhood proud."[21]

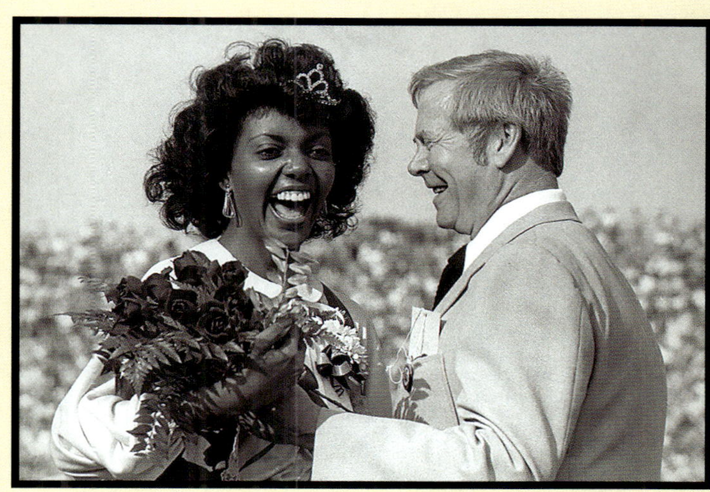

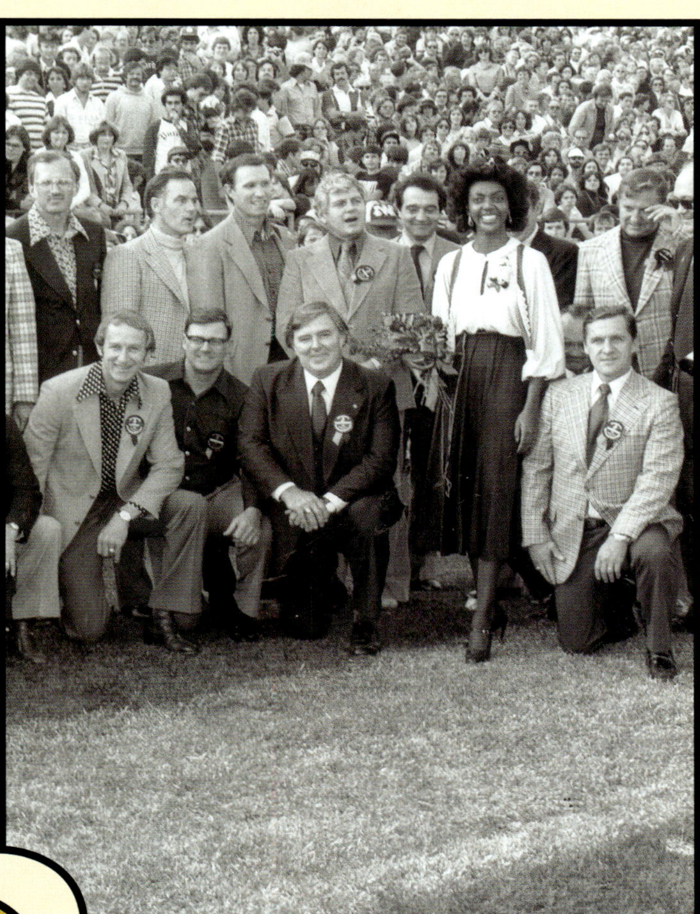

In addition to her roles as Homecoming queen and leader for African American students on campus, Agee Chandler was active in extracurricular activities. She was a member of Alpha Lambda Delta freshman honor society, Purdue Pals, and the Black Voices of Inspiration Choir. Agee Chandler was also a president and founding member of Purdue's Society of Minority Managers. In addition, she served as a social counselor for the Business Opportunity Program in the School of Management and was a member of the Mortar Board senior honor society. Her involvement reflected her role as a leader on campus as well as her excellent academic record.

Top: President Arthur Hansen presenting flowers to 1978 Homecoming queen Kassandra Agee. *(Purdue University Marketing and Media collection)*

Left: Homecoming queen Kassandra Agee. *(Purdue University photographs)*

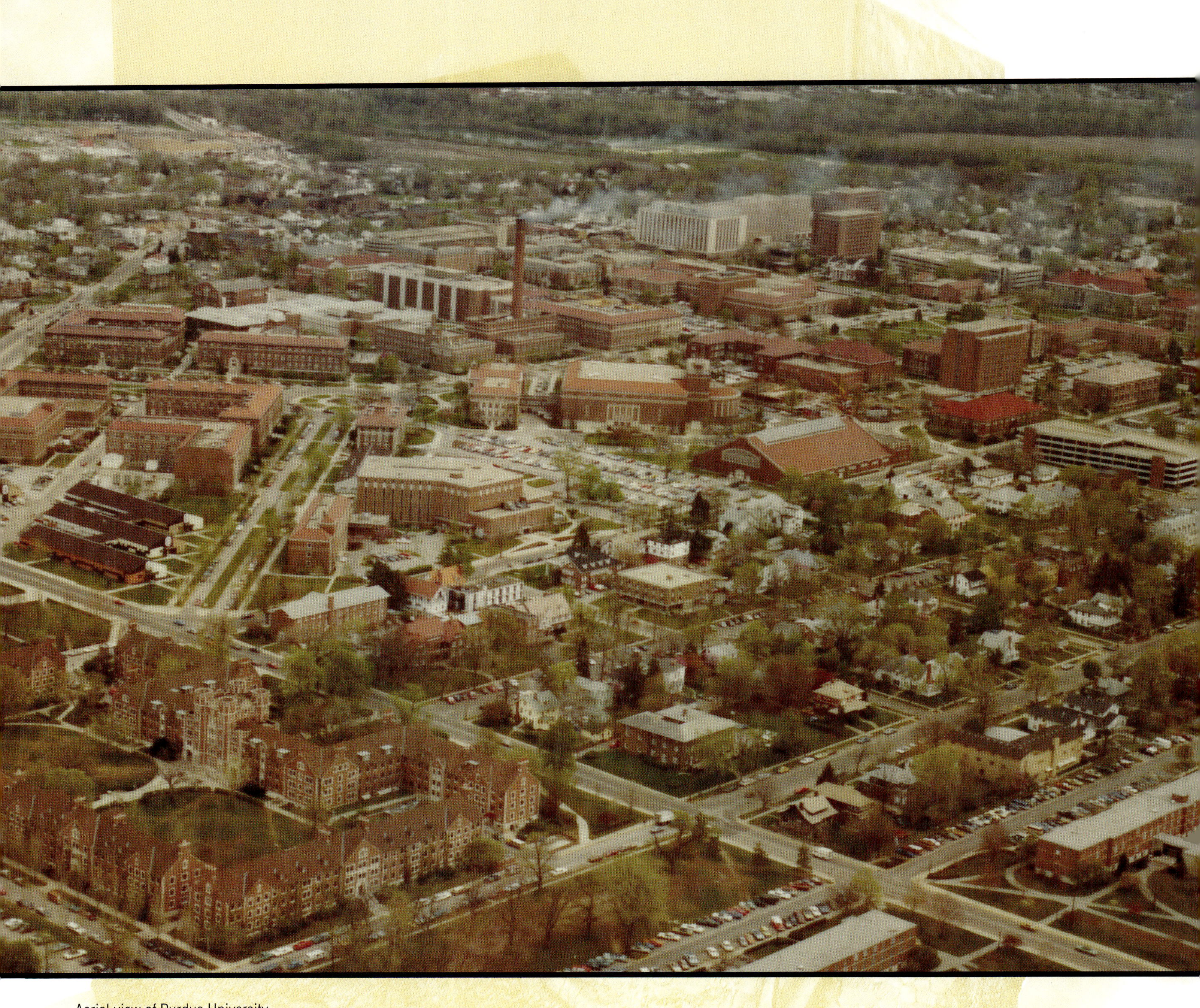

Aerial view of Purdue University campus, looking to the southeast, 1978. *(Purdue University photographs)*

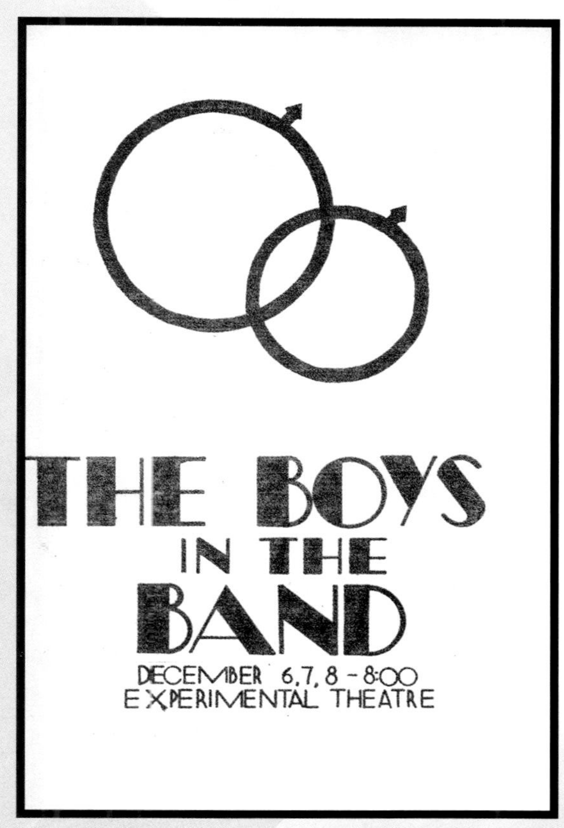

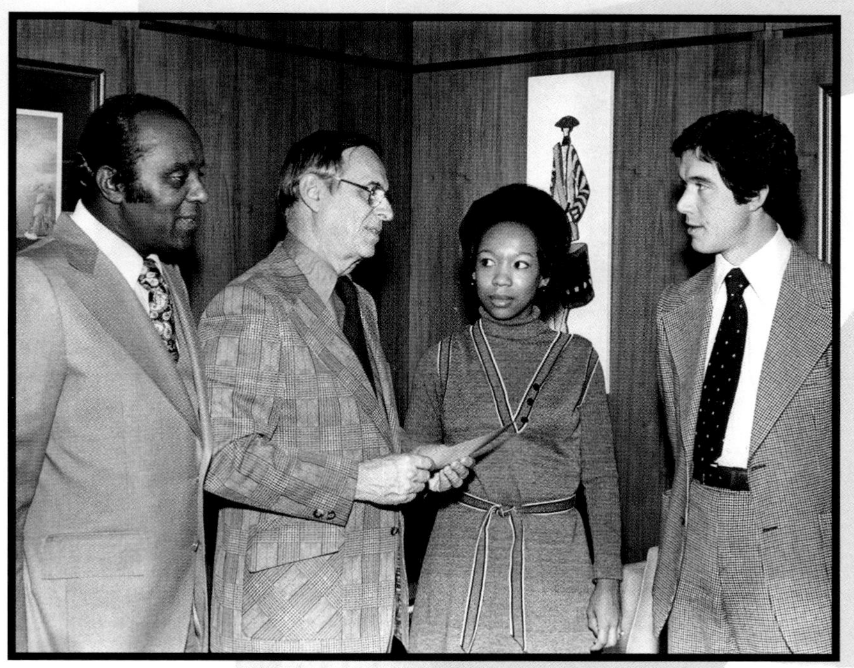

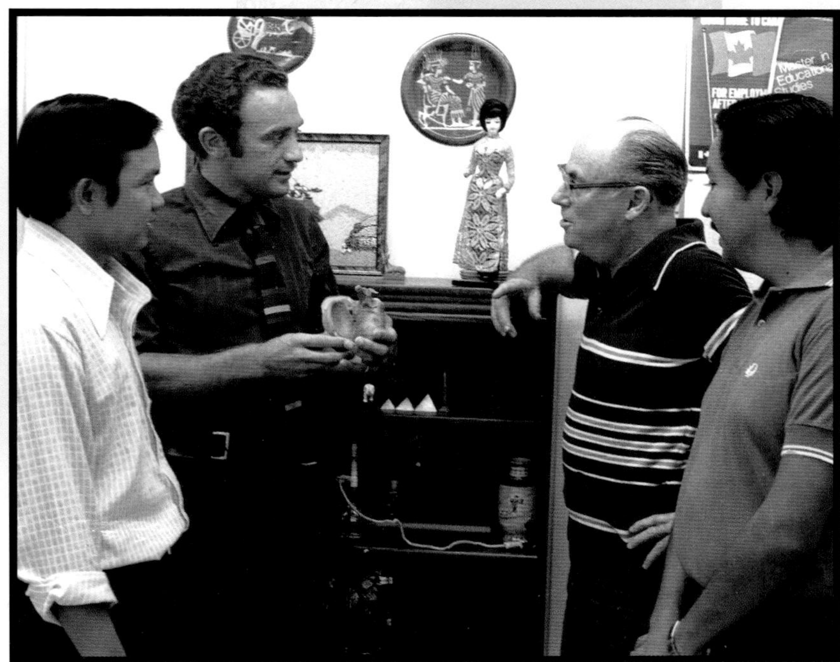

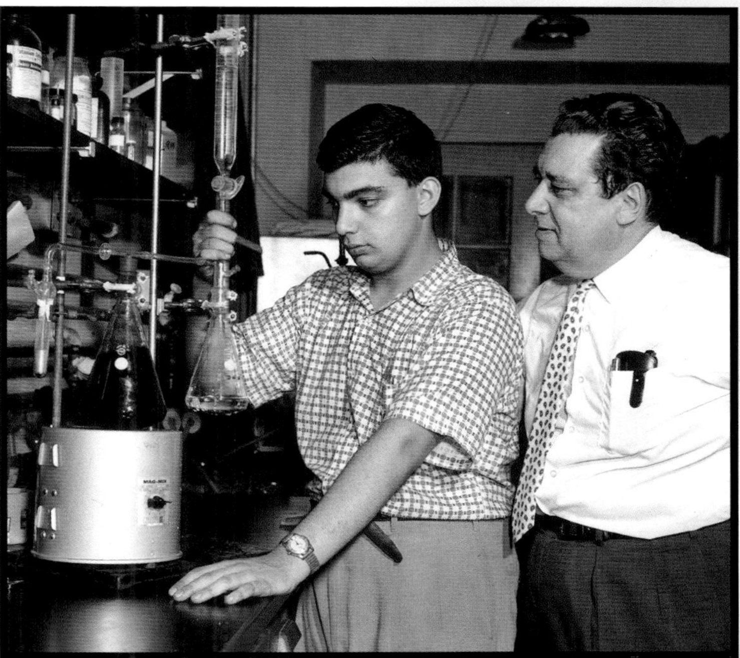

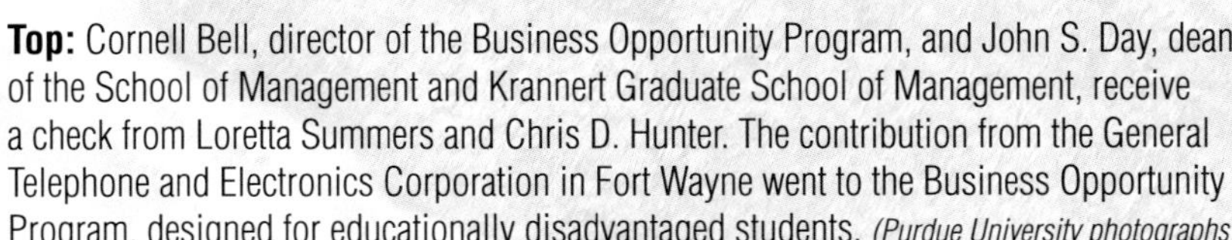

Top: Cornell Bell, director of the Business Opportunity Program, and John S. Day, dean of the School of Management and Krannert Graduate School of Management, receive a check from Loretta Summers and Chris D. Hunter. The contribution from the General Telephone and Electronics Corporation in Fort Wayne went to the Business Opportunity Program, designed for educationally disadvantaged students. *(Purdue University photographs)*

Bottom: Arthur H. Tichenor Jr., advisor to international students, speaks to students in summer 1974. *(Purdue University photographs)*

Top: Program from the 1970 Purdue production of *The Boys in the Band*, a play about young gay men in New York. *(Erling E. Kildahl papers)*

Bottom: Chemistry professor Herbert C. Brown instructing a student. Brown received the 1979 Nobel Prize in Chemistry with Georg Wittig for their development of the use of boron- and phosphorus-containing compounds. *(Purdue University photographs)*

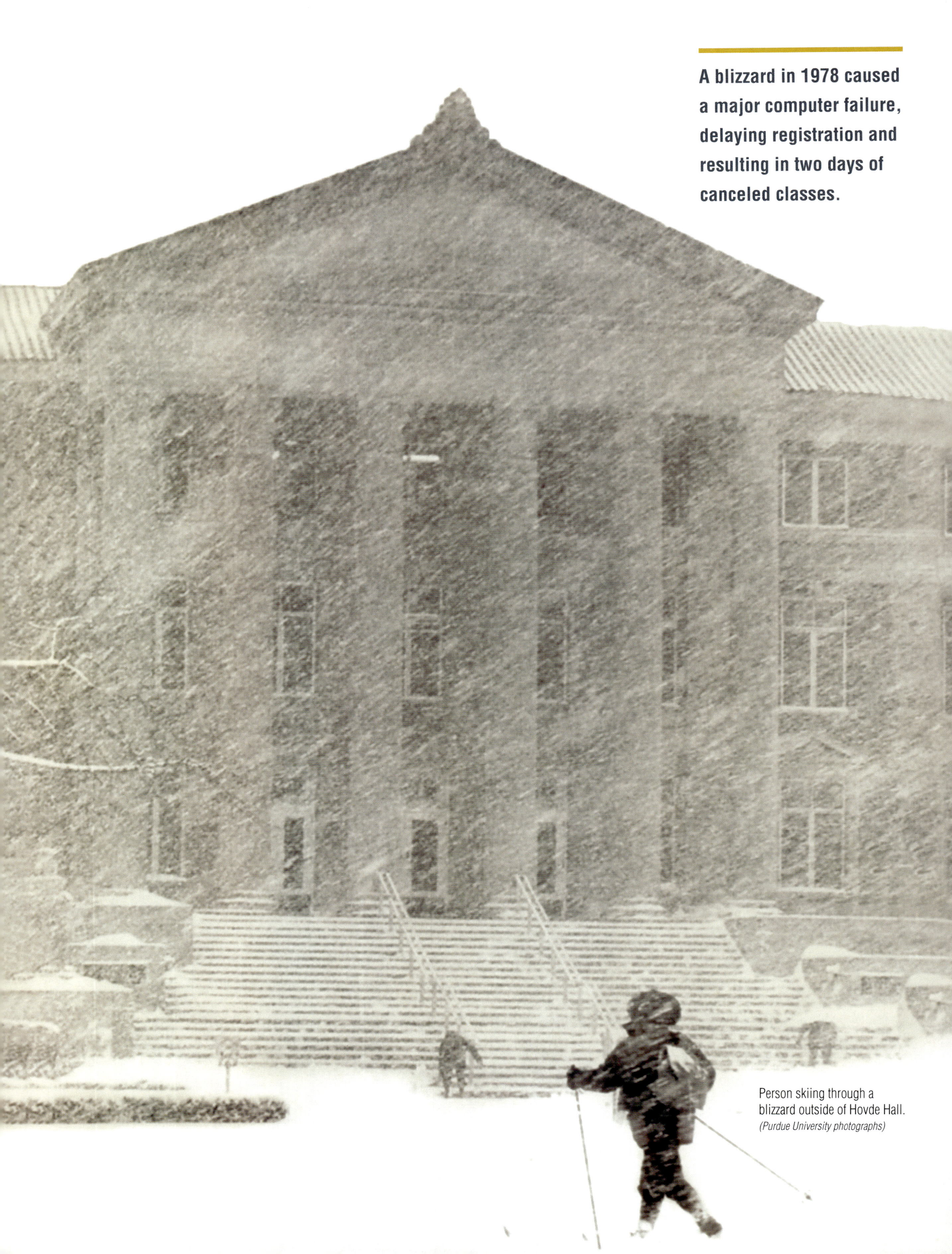

A blizzard in 1978 caused a major computer failure, delaying registration and resulting in two days of canceled classes.

Person skiing through a blizzard outside of Hovde Hall.
(Purdue University photographs)

In the 1970s, calculators were replacing slide rules as the must-have student accessory. One of the most recognized Purdue students to wield a slide rule, Neil Armstrong, followed his 1969 walk on the moon with a campus visit in January 1970. He received an honorary doctorate of engineering from President Hovde at commencement ceremonies, and, in return, Armstrong presented to the University a Purdue centennial flag that he carried with him to the moon. Eugene Cernan, astronaut alumnus, was also honored with an honorary doctorate of engineering in June 1970 in recognition of his leadership in piloting the lunar module for *Apollo 10*.

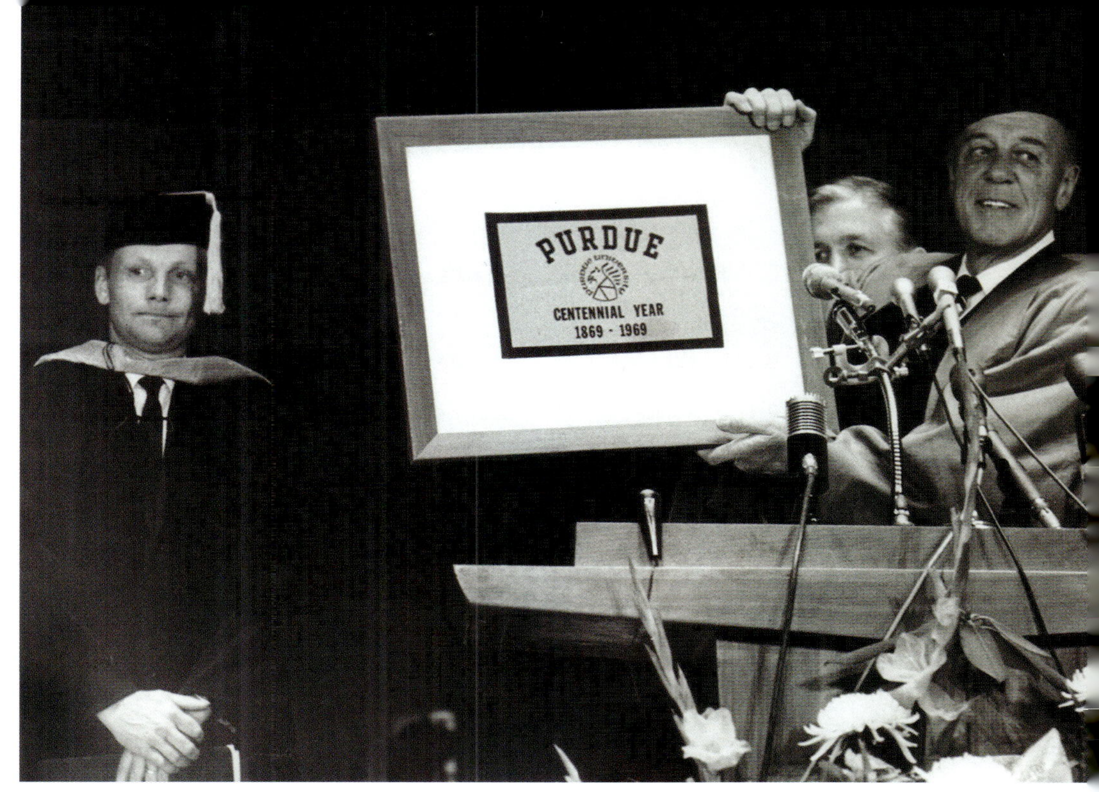

The Boilermakers played against the USSR national basketball team to a sold-out crowd in Mackey Arena in 1977. Part of a twelve-game tour of the United States, the Russian team lost to Purdue, 85–75. Soviet coach Alexander Gomelsky praised the Purdue team and coach Fred Schaus following their win.[22] The basketball team ended the decade with a 27–8 record in 1979, sharing the Big Ten title with Michigan State.

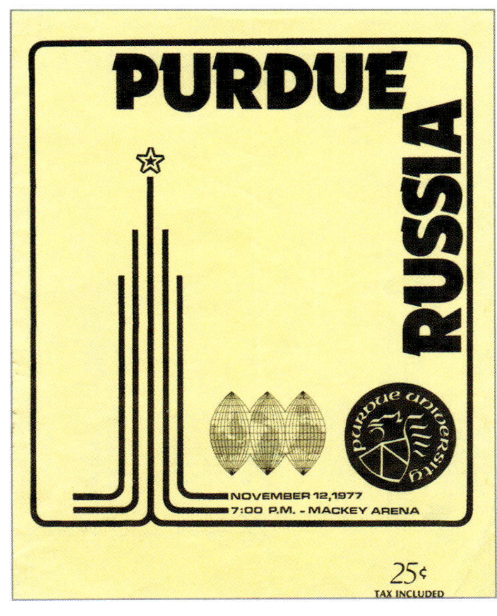

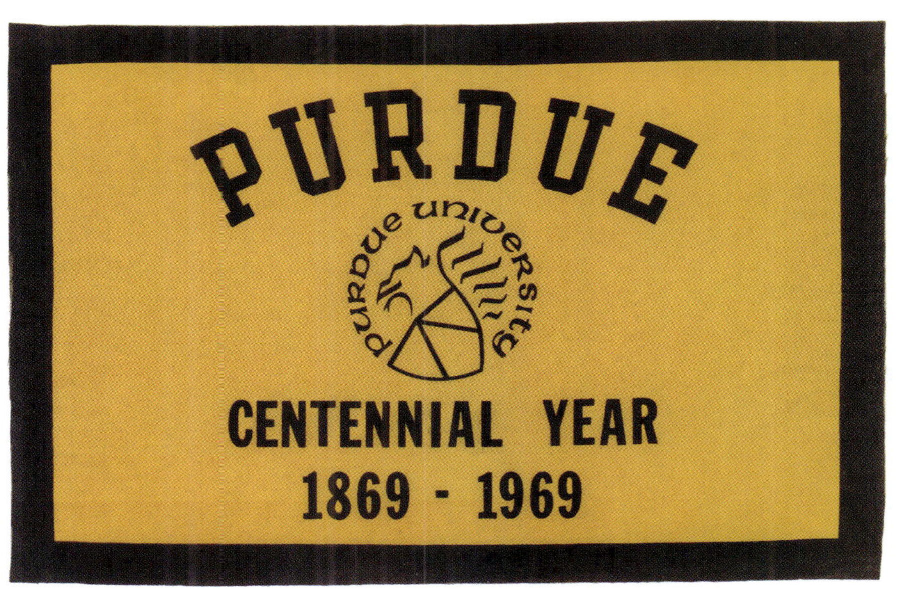

Left: Program from Purdue vs. USSR basketball game, held on November 12, 1977, as part of Indiana's International Basketball Week. *(Purdue Russia program)*

Above: Purdue Centennial flag taken to the moon on *Apollo 11* and presented to the university by Neil Armstrong on January 8, 1970. *(Neil A. Armstrong papers)*

Top: President Hovde accepts the Purdue centennial flag that traveled to the moon with Neil Armstrong. *(Purdue University photographs)*

Purdue's football team had consecutive winning seasons at the end of the decade. The Boilermakers went on to win the Peach Bowl in 1978 and the Bluebonnet Bowl in 1979. In his first season of track, sophomore football player Larry Burton tied the world indoor record for sixty yards and set a new track record for the 100 meters. That same year he won the NCAA finals in 200-meter events and earned a spot at the 1972 Olympics, where he won fourth place in the 200-meter dash.

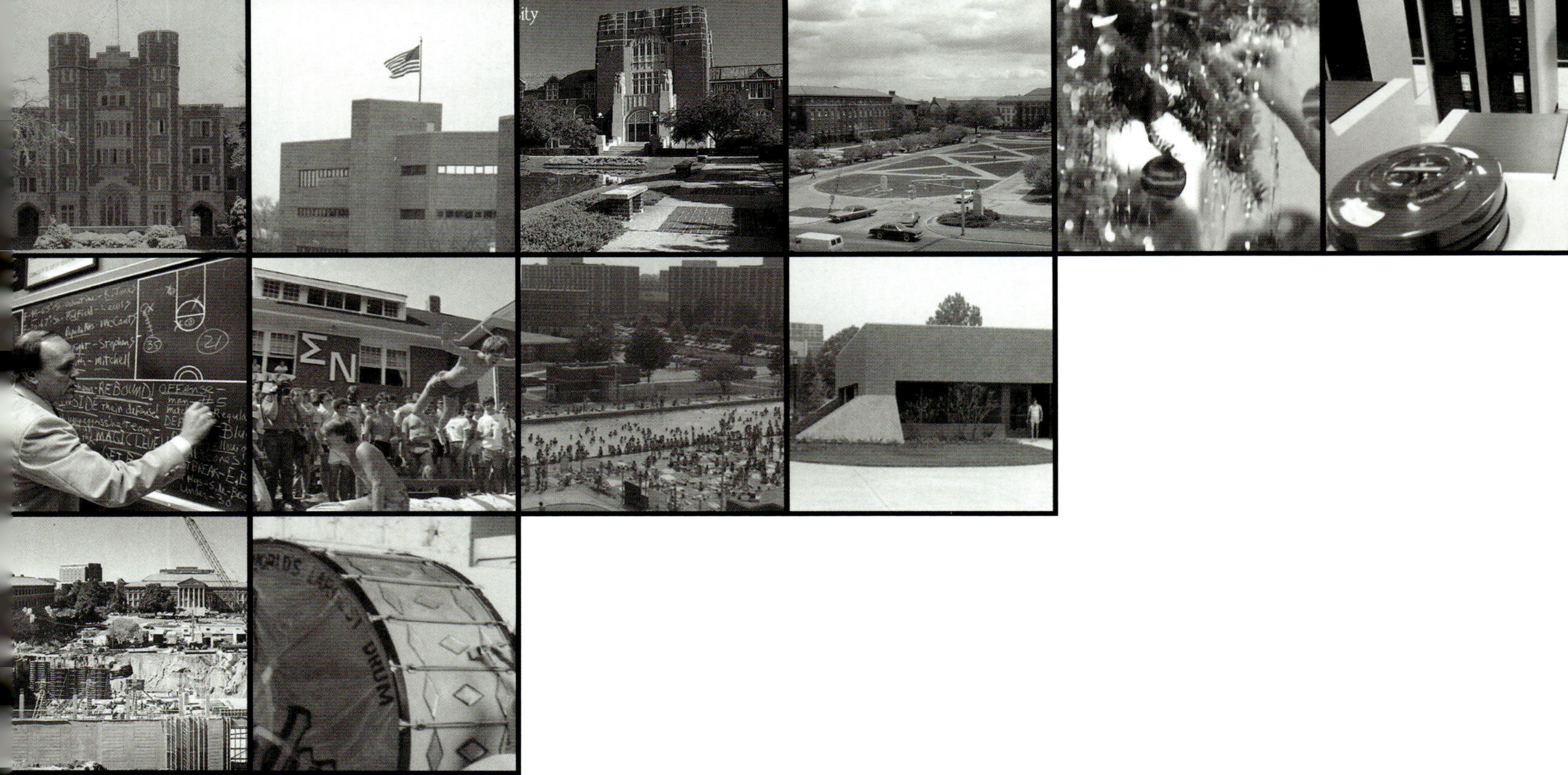

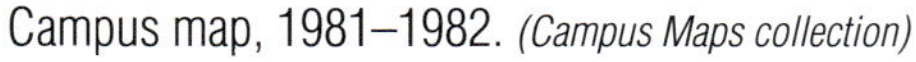
Campus map, 1981–1982. *(Campus Maps collection)*

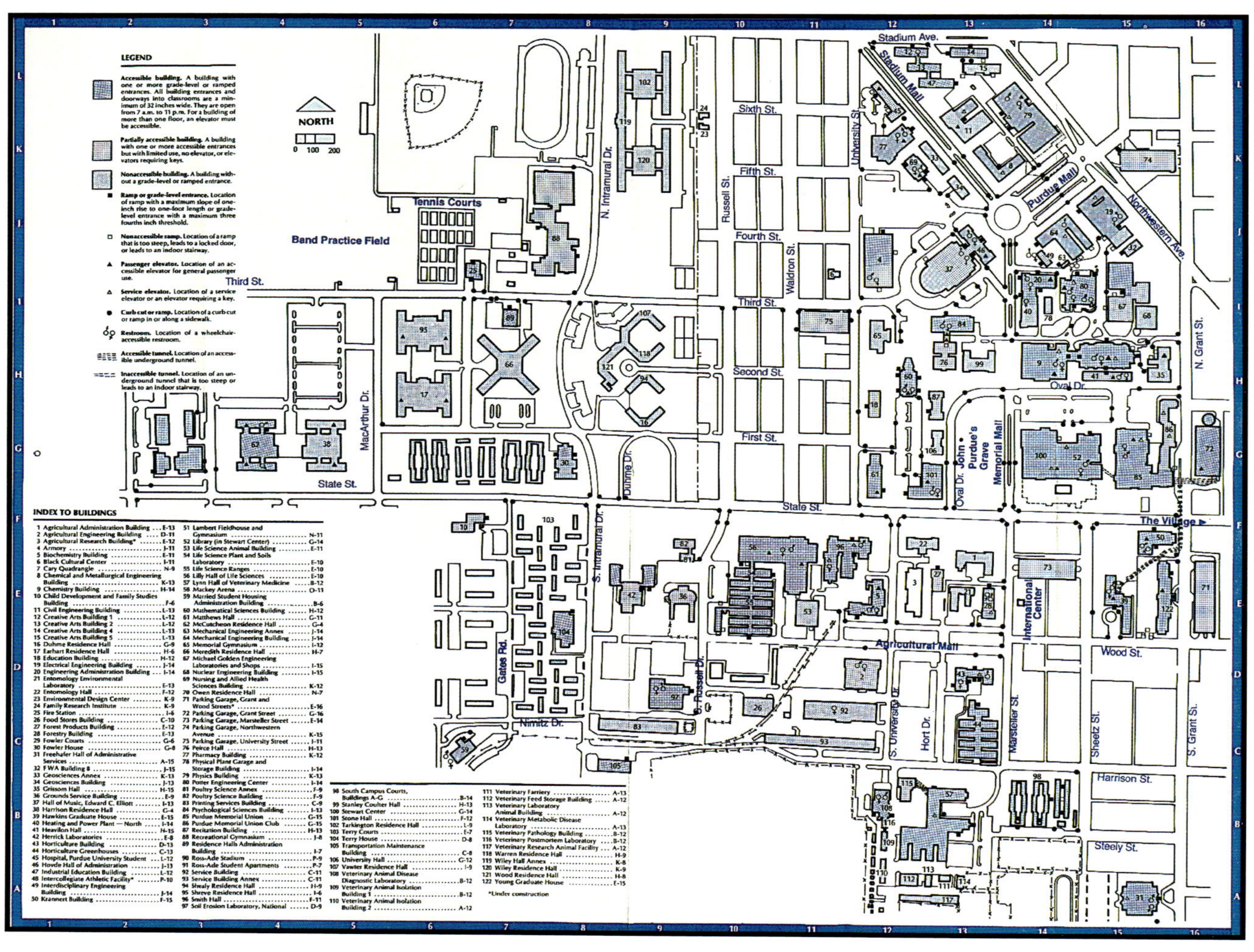

{Enrollment in 1980: 32,366 students[1]}

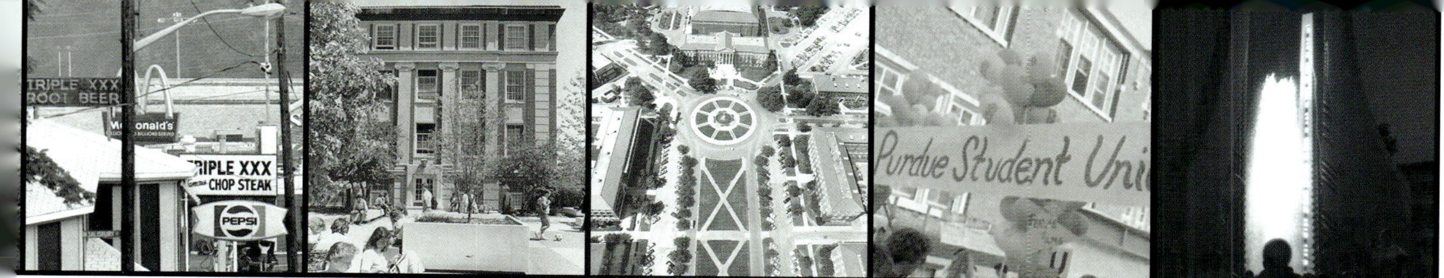

[The 1980s]

PURDUE AT 120

"I'm just very thankful for my years at Purdue, and it's probably the best thing I ever did. I got accepted and just figured it was the best school. . . . It was absolutely the greatest decision I ever made in my life, because it's gotten me everything I've got in my life."

—*Joel Kern, class of 1990*[2]

State Street at River Road, as seen from Chauncey Hill in the late 1980s.
(Purdue University Marketing and Media collection)

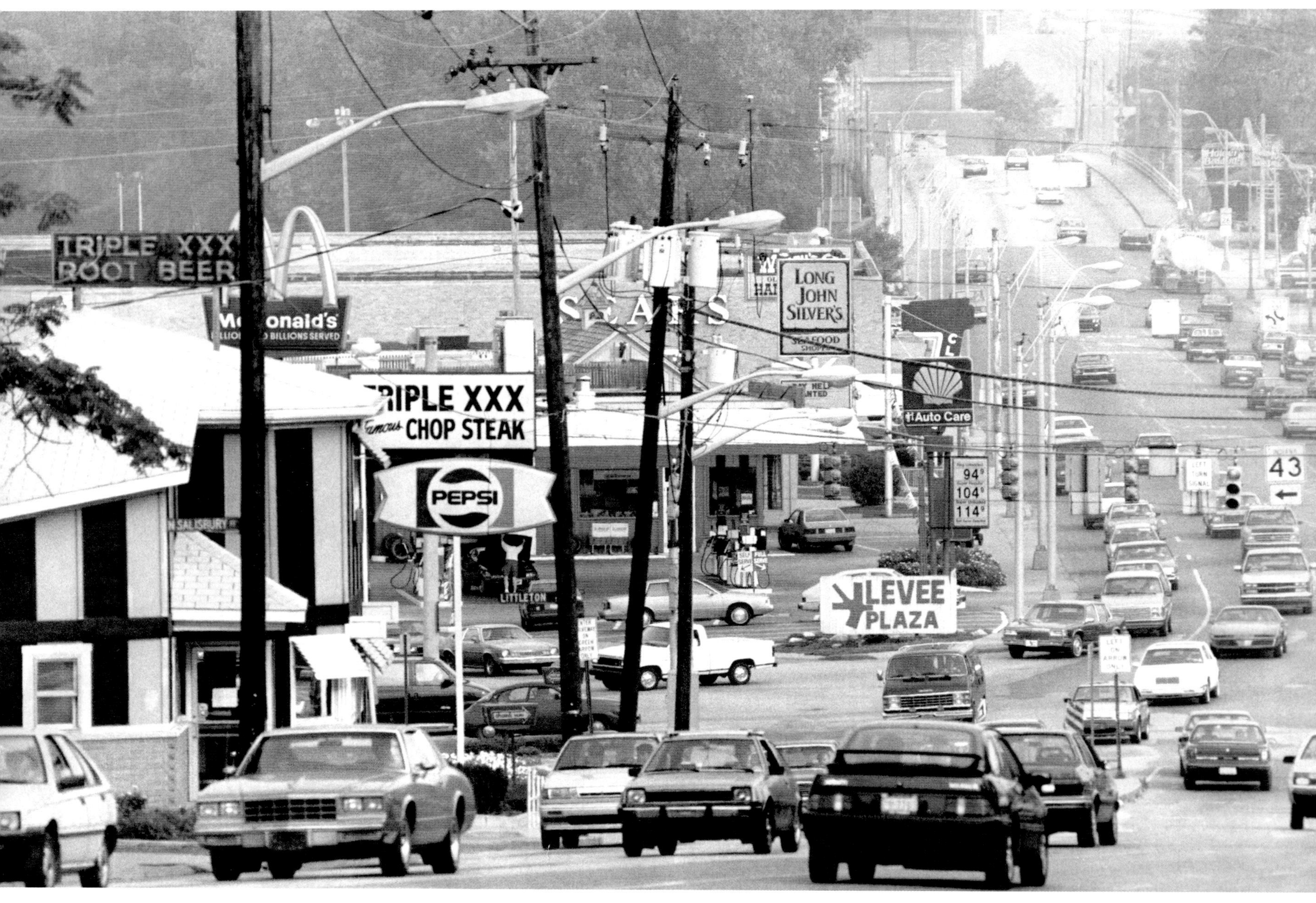

***University*, the first soap opera created and filmed on a college campus, produced one episode per year at Purdue from 1983 to 1985.[3]**

The first *Purdue Exponent* of the 1980s contained news about an ongoing student housing shortage, a story about a fire at McCutcheon Residence Hall, details surrounding a proposed parking garage along University Street, congratulations to the Purdue football team for their appearance in their third-ever bowl game—a 27–22 win over Tennessee in the Bluebonnet Bowl—and a letter to the students from new West Lafayette mayor Sonya L. Margerum. She wrote:

> Together, we are entering the decade of the 80's, which will be a decade full of challenges and opportunities. This administration stands ready to work together with the faculty, staff and students of Purdue University, in order to make West Lafayette a city which is responsive to the needs of all its citizens. There are many problems in the areas of housing, parking and traffic in West Lafayette, and we are actively involved in addressing those problems. Their solution will require cooperation and an active commitment on the part of Purdue, administration, the city of West Lafayette, and the residents and students.[4]

A group of students created a small shanty on Memorial Mall in December 1986 in response to apartheid in South Africa.[5]

Sigma Nu hosts a Jell-O Jump in front of the fraternity house, September 1984. *(Purdue University Marketing and Media collection)*

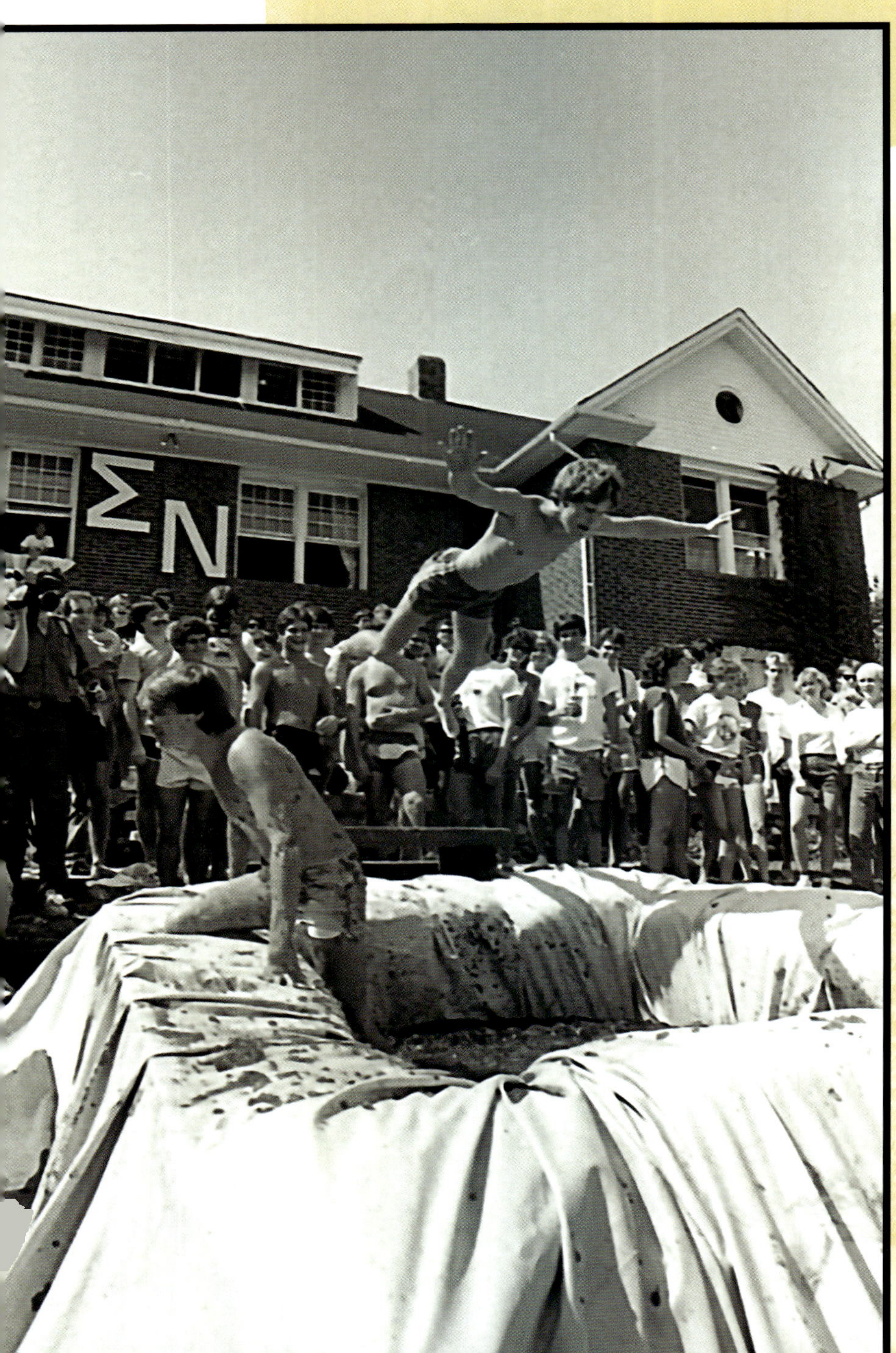

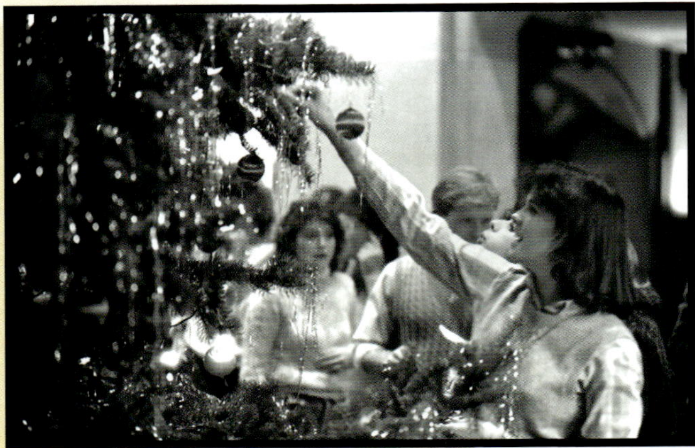

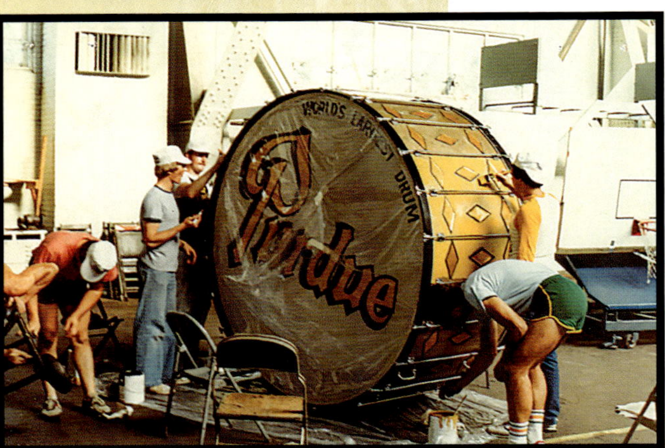

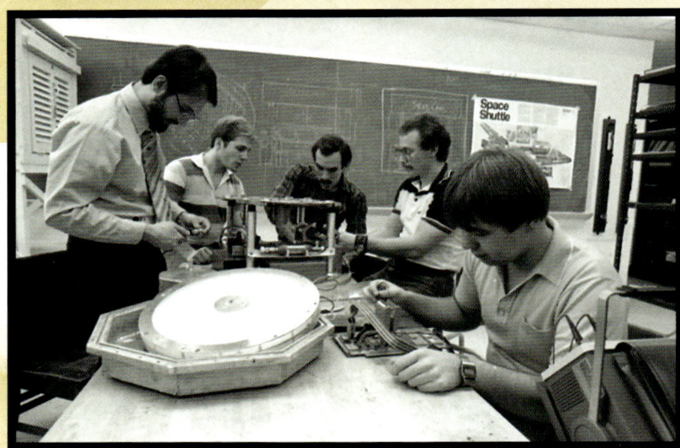

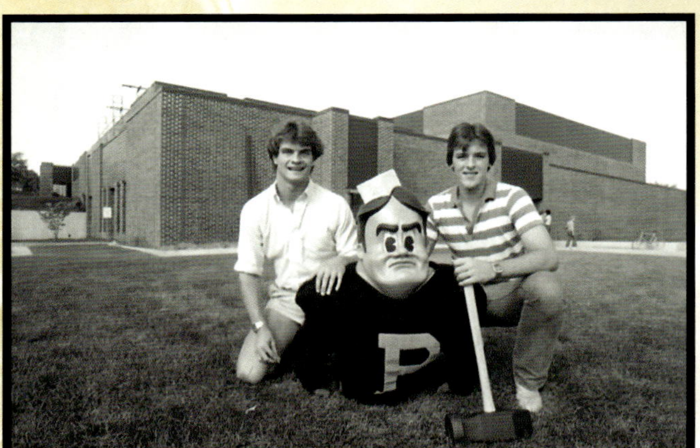

From top:

Students decorating a Christmas tree on campus, November 1984. *(Purdue University Marketing and Media collection)*

Members of the Big Bass Drum crew giving the drum a new paint job. *(Purdue Bands and Orchestras records)*

Students collaborating on research that would travel on the space shuttle *Challenger* the following year, December 1982. *(Purdue University Marketing and Media collection)*

Guy Wilson and Dave McGaughey share the role of Purdue Pete, September 1982. *(Purdue University Marketing and Media collection)*

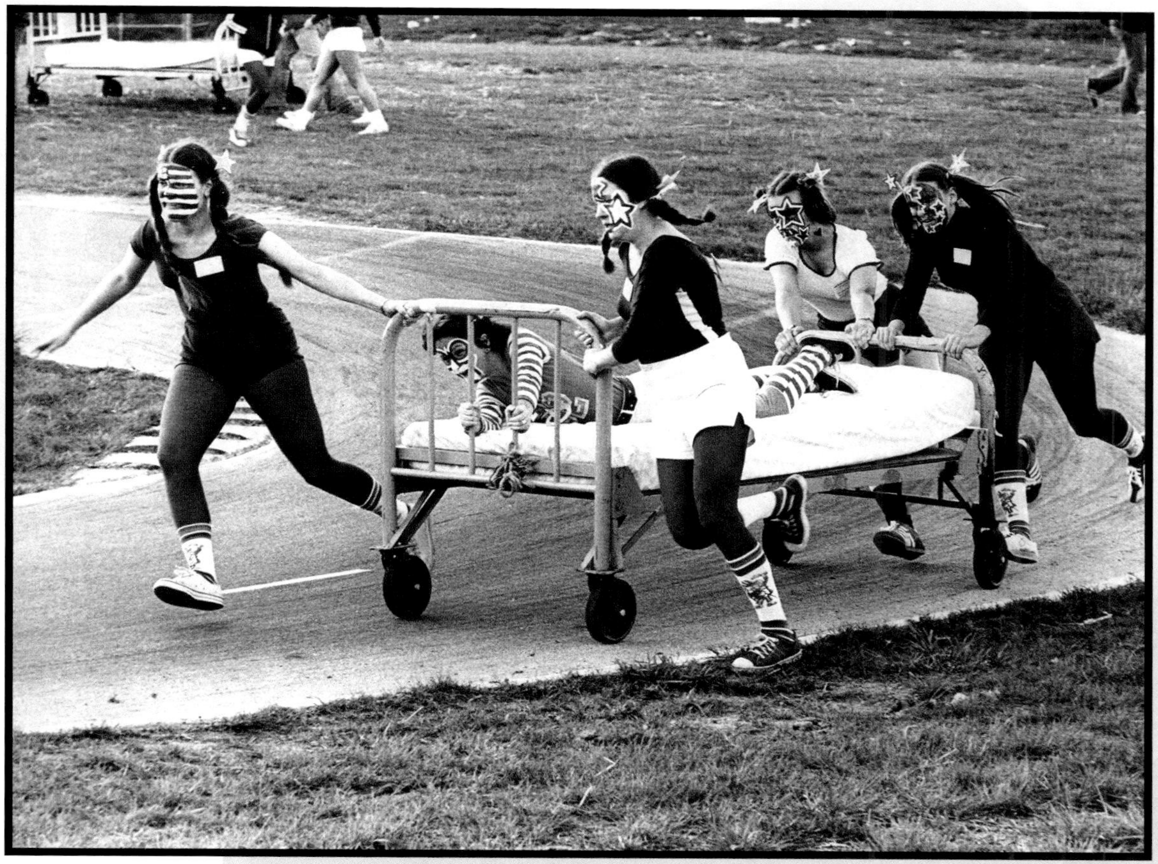

Below: A flyer promoting "An Evening with Maya Angelou," sponsored by the BCC on March 21, 1985, at Loeb Playhouse. *(Black Cultural Center records)*

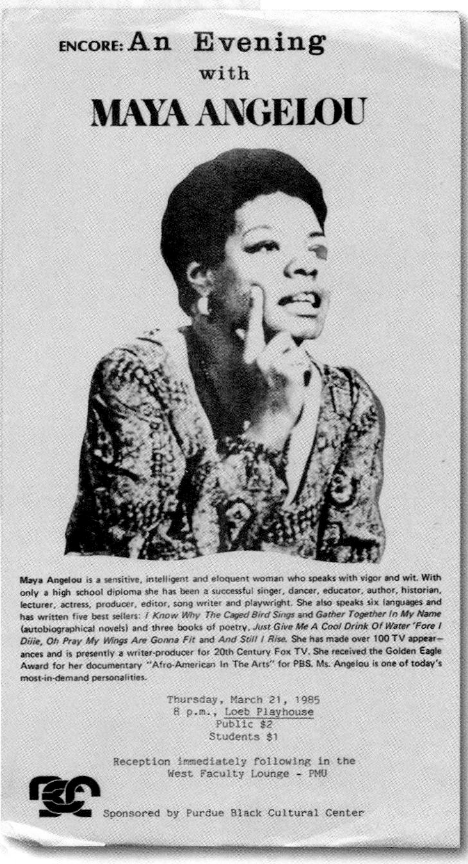

ENCORE: An Evening with

MAYA ANGELOU

Maya Angelou is a sensitive, intelligent and eloquent woman who speaks with vigor and wit. With only a high school diploma she has been a successful singer, dancer, educator, author, historian, lecturer, actress, producer, editor, song writer and playwright. She also speaks six languages and has written five best sellers: *I Know Why The Caged Bird Sings* and *Gather Together In My Name* (autobiographical novels) and three books of poetry, *Just Give Me A Cool Drink Of Water 'Fore I Diiie, Oh Pray My Wings Are Gonna Fit* and *And Still I Rise.* She has made over 100 TV appear–ances and is presently a writer-producer for 20th Century Fox TV. She received the Golden Eagle Award for her documentary "Afro-American In The Arts" for PBS. Ms. Angelou is one of today's most-in-demand personalities.

Thursday, March 21, 1985
8 p.m., Loeb Playhouse
Public $2
Students $1

Reception immediately following in the
West Faculty Lounge - PMU

Sponsored by Purdue Black Cultural Center

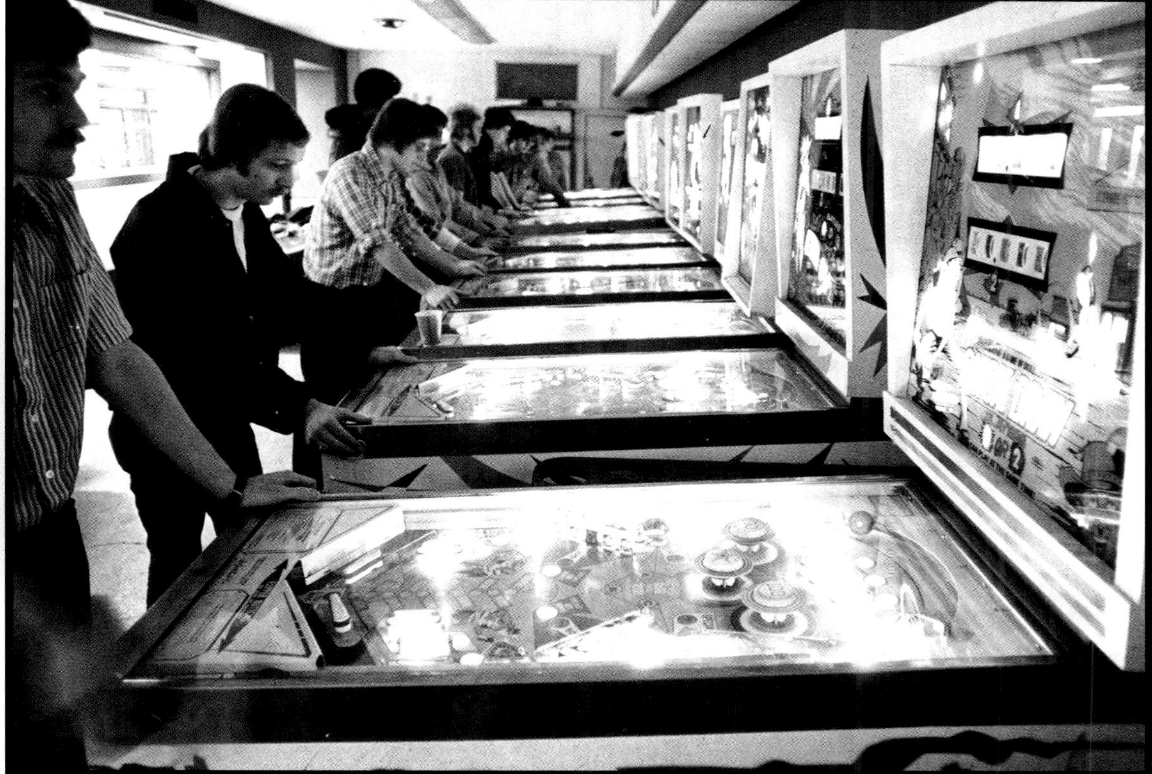

Top: Students participating in bed races before the Grand Prix, circa 1980s. *(Purdue University Marketing and Media collection)*

Bottom: Students play arcade games. *(Purdue University Marketing and Media collection)*

The Purdue Student Association (PSA) changed its name to Purdue Student Government (PSG) on September 14, 1988.[6]

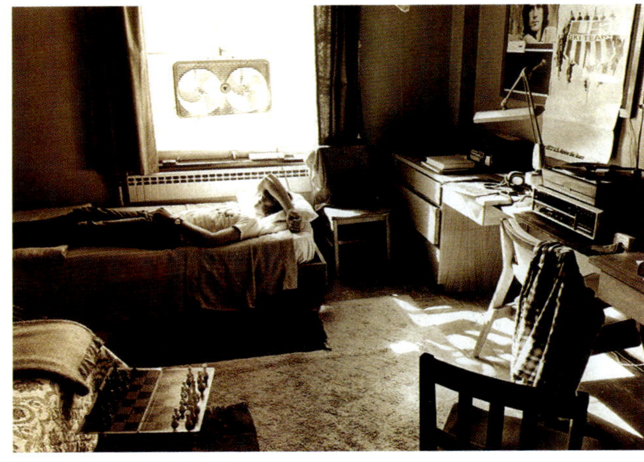

Quiet dorm room scene. *(Purdue University Marketing and Media collection)*

Increases in student population placed great demands on Purdue and West Lafayette. A growing student body found itself short of housing. The shortage continued to cause problems for years, and fees for enrollment and on-campus housing increased. In subsequent years, undergraduates began living in converted dormitory common areas, graduate housing, and Ross-Ade Apartment Units (later known as Hilltop Apartments). Changes would be coming to Purdue in multitudes.

The advent of personal computing dramatically increased student interest and enrollment in computer science. Concurrently, Purdue sought to be a leader in computing. A Cyber 205 super computer was constructed in the Purdue University Computing Center of the Math Building in 1983; Purdue was one of the first two universities in the United States to have one. The Memorial Gymnasium, later renamed Felix Haas Hall, was renovated to house the Department of Computer Science, and enrollment in the program increased following the updates. A team of computer science students finished eighth in a national programming contest in 1988 after winning their regional competition.[7]

Student activities remained a prominent feature of campus life. The Recreational Sports Center (CoRec) began renovations in 1980 in response to student demand. The Slayter Slammer concert, an annual free concert that ran for several years at Slayter Hill, first kicked off the new school year in 1980.

The Rube Goldberg Machine Contest was resurrected by Purdue students in 1983 after a hiatus of nearly three decades. The contest asks participants to complete basic tasks using complex multistep processes. In 1989 the contest went national, with Purdue as host.

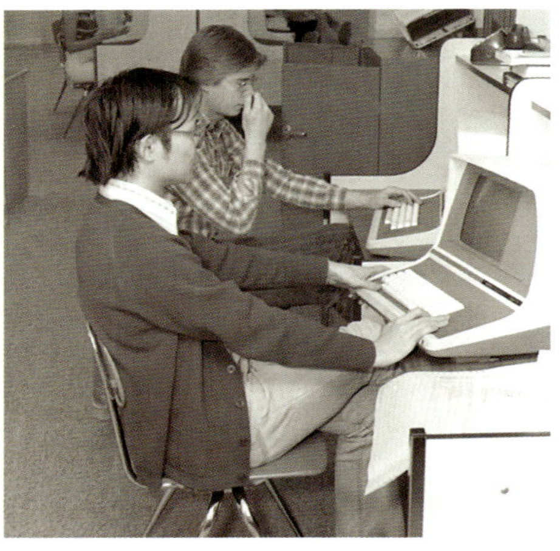

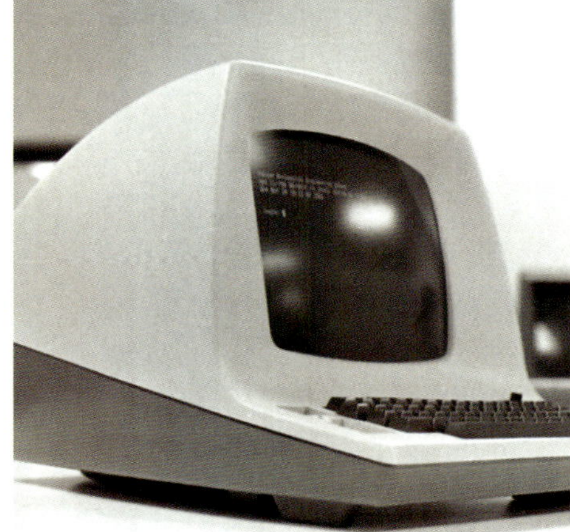

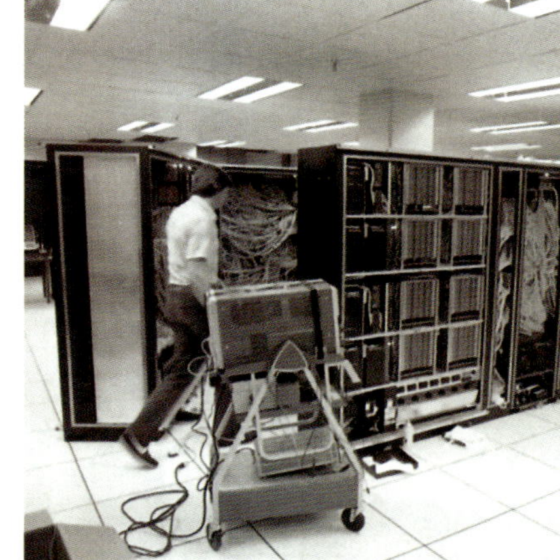

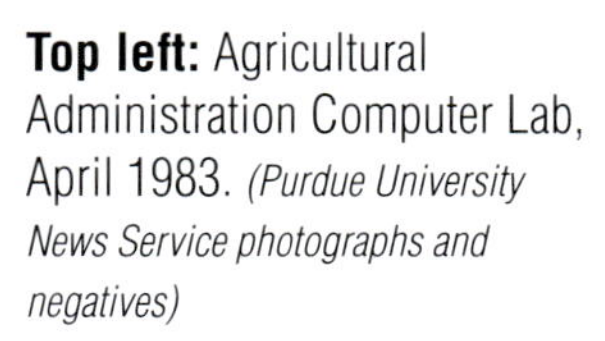

Top left: Agricultural Administration Computer Lab, April 1983. *(Purdue University News Service photographs and negatives)*

Top right: Computer terminal in the School of Mechanical Engineering, March 1982. *(Purdue University Marketing and Media collection)*

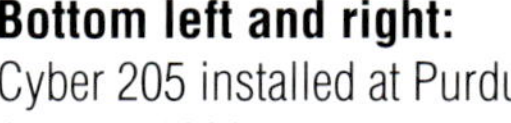

Bottom left and right: Cyber 205 installed at Purdue, January 1983. *(Purdue University Marketing and Media collection)*

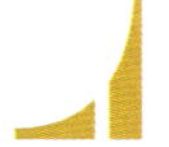

In the early 1980s, Purdue Convocations began using a computerized ticketing system called "concertificates" for events.

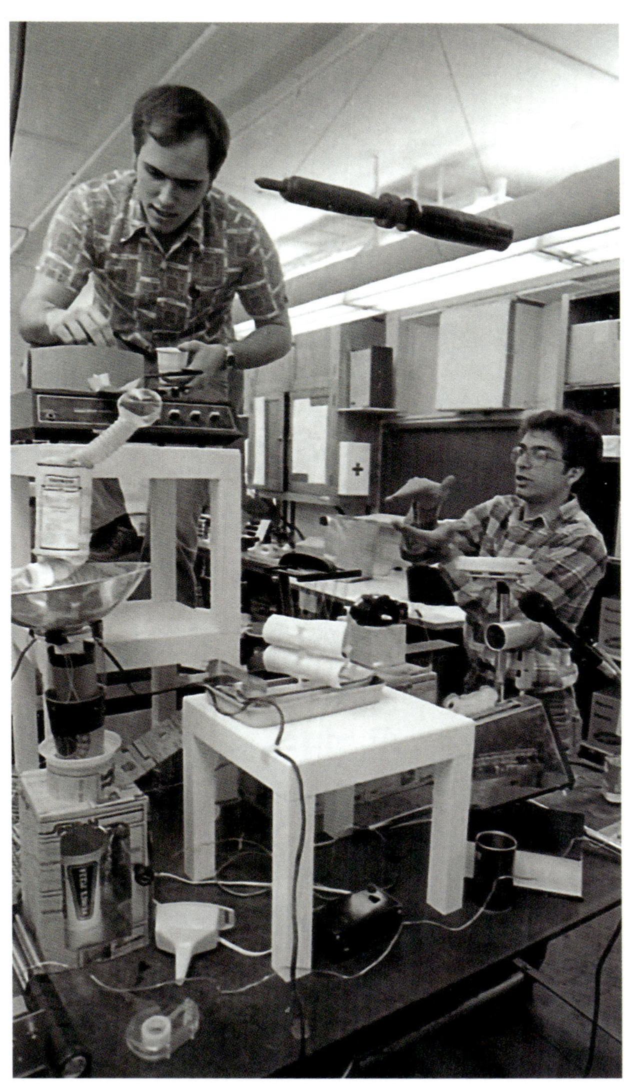

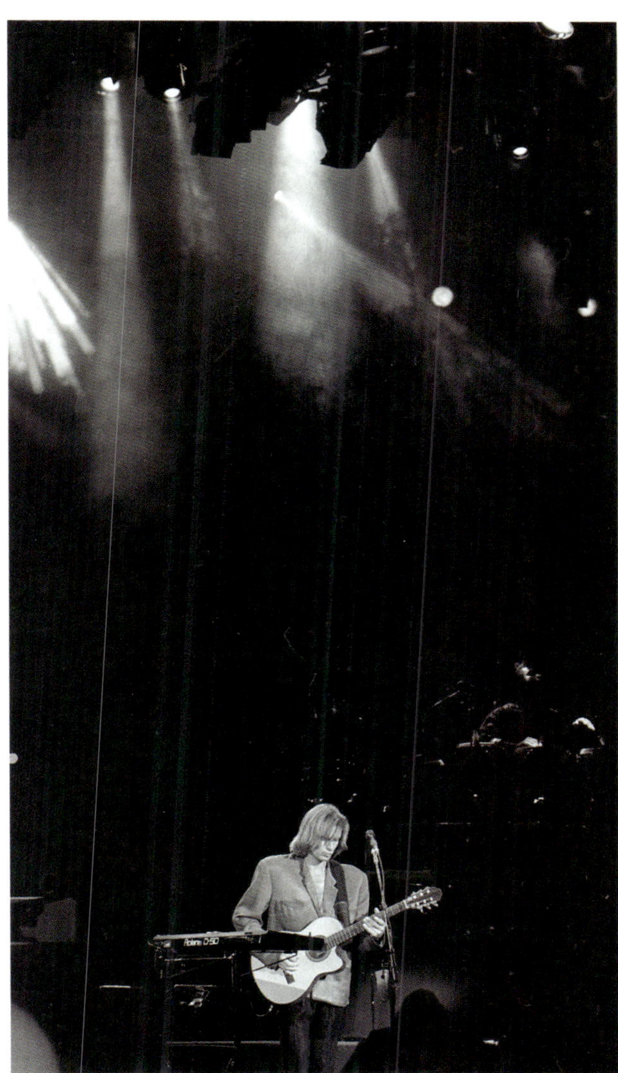

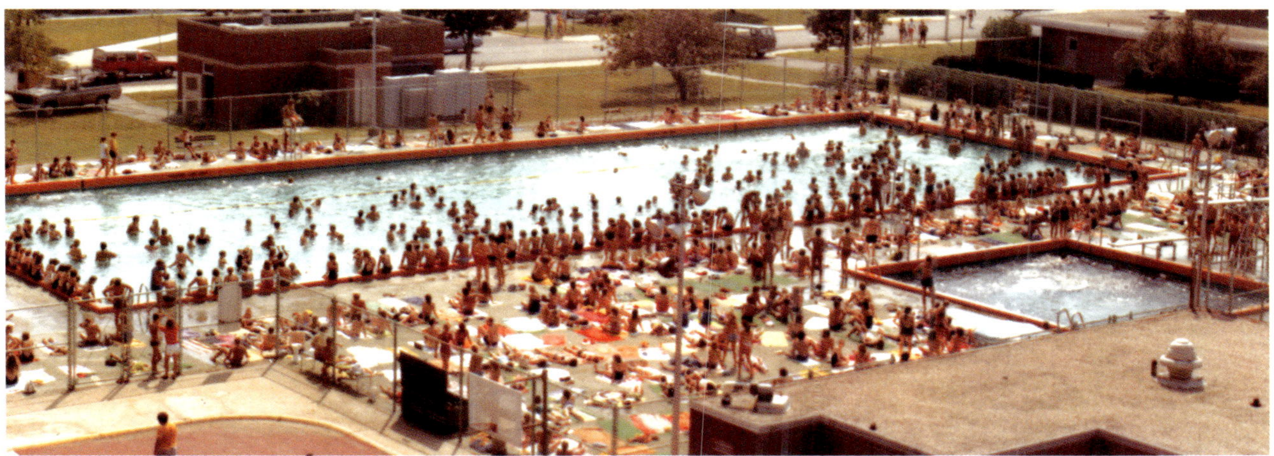

Top left: Two students construct a machine for the Rube Goldberg Machine Contest, March 1983. *(Purdue University Marketing and Media collection)*

Top right: Performance by Sting in the Elliott Hall of Music, February 23, 1988. *(Purdue University Marketing and Media collection)*

Bottom: Students fill the CoRec pool on a hot August day in 1980. *(Purdue University photographs)*

Right: *The Class* of 1939 Water Sculpture, also known as the Engineering Fountain, is installed in Engineering Mall, April 1989. *(Purdue University Marketing and Media collection)*

Below: Hovde Hall and Engineering Mall with the centennial marker visible in the foreground. *(Purdue University photographs)*

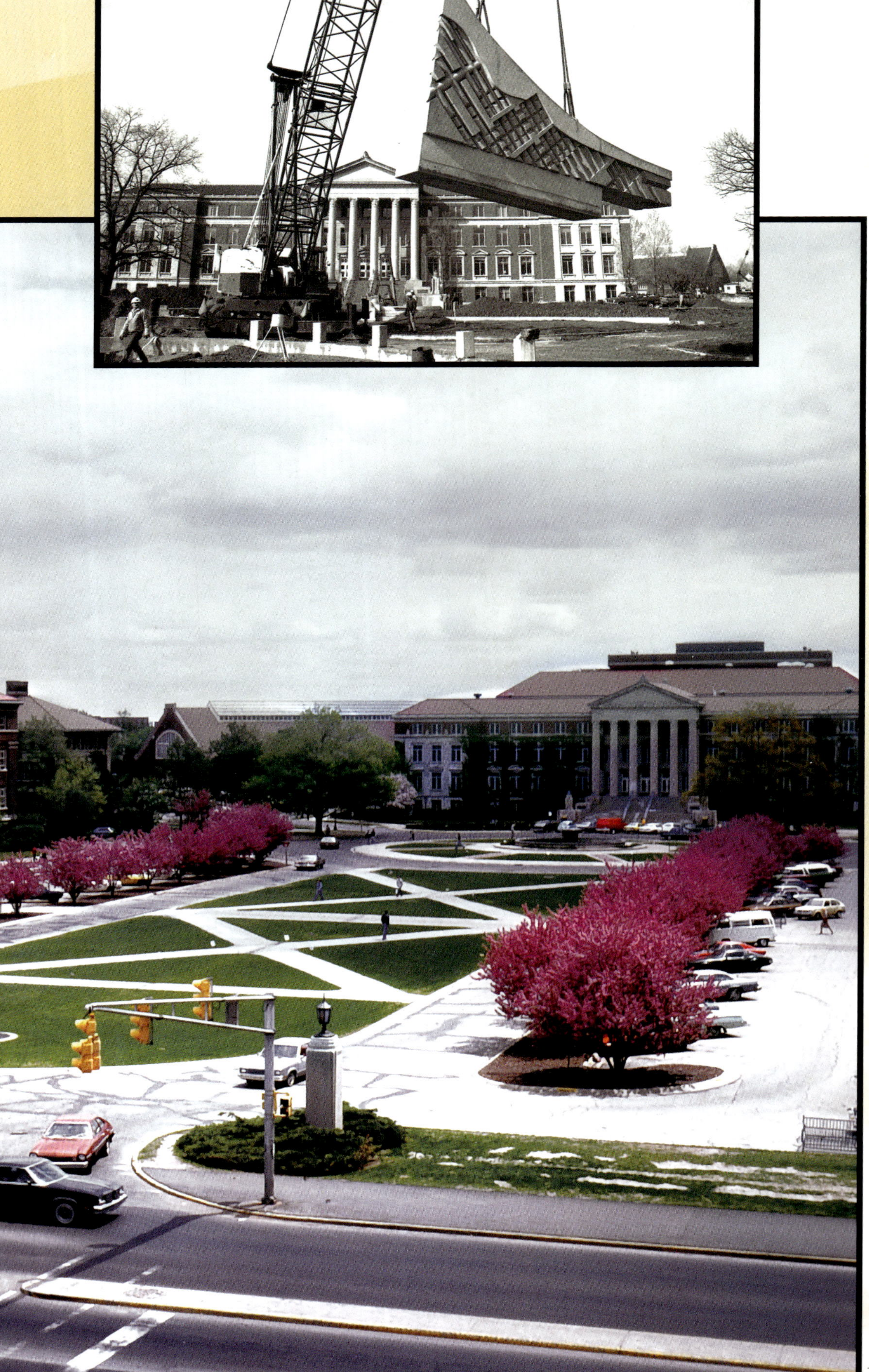

Right: Students relax and study between classes near Wetherill Hall. *(Purdue University Marketing and Media collection)*

Below: President Steven C. Beering speaking with students, July 1983. Beering became Purdue's ninth president that year, replacing Arthur G. Hansen. *(Purdue University News Service photographs and negatives)*

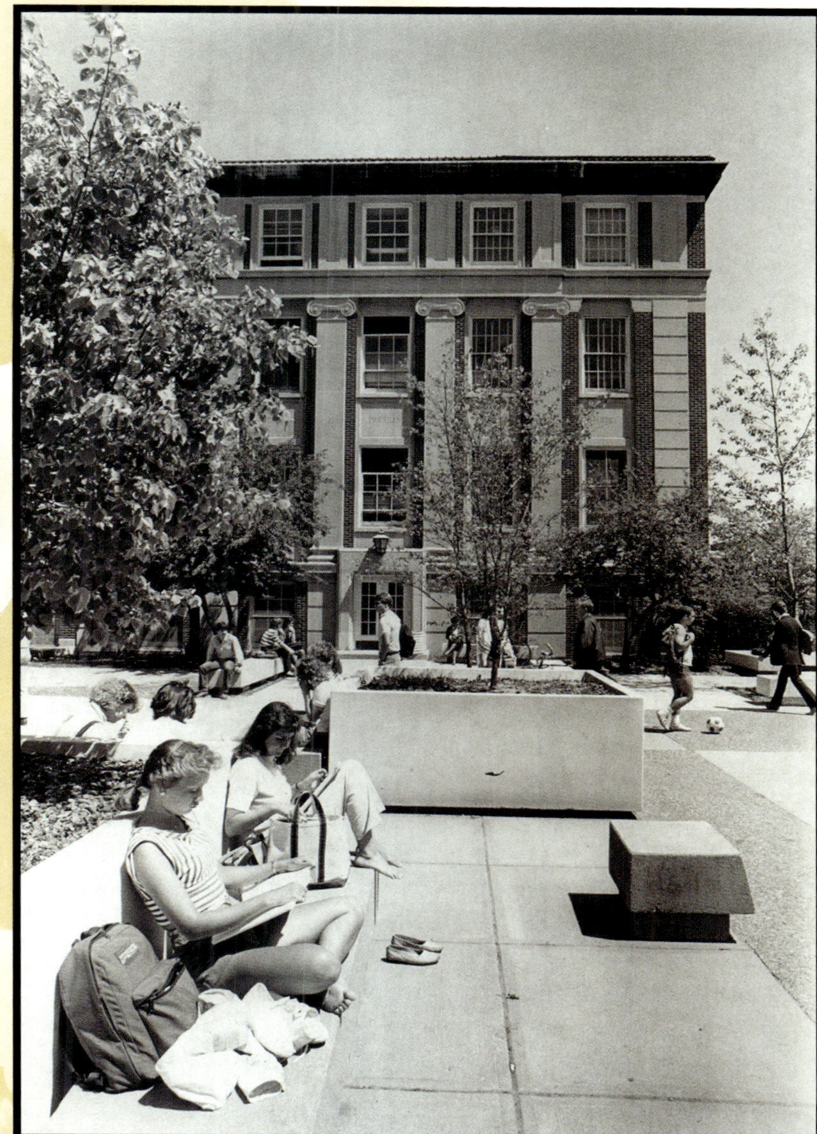

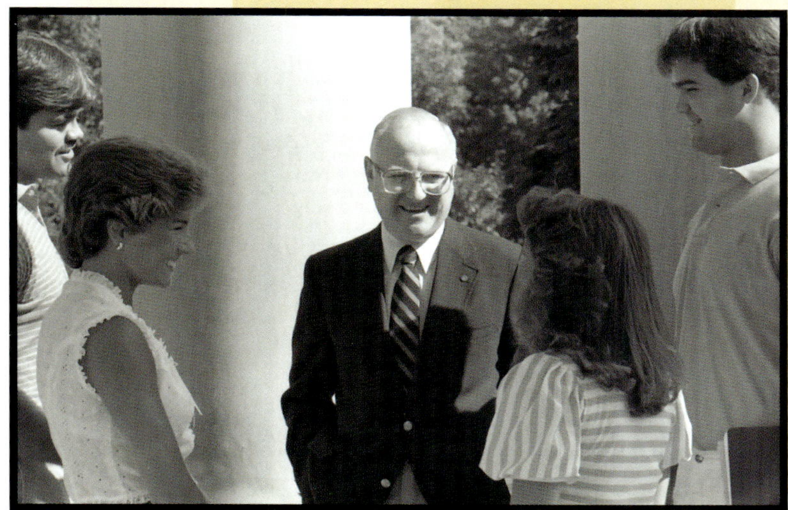

Purdue community members gather as the Engineering Fountain is turned on for the first time, July 1989. *(Purdue University Marketing and Media collection)*

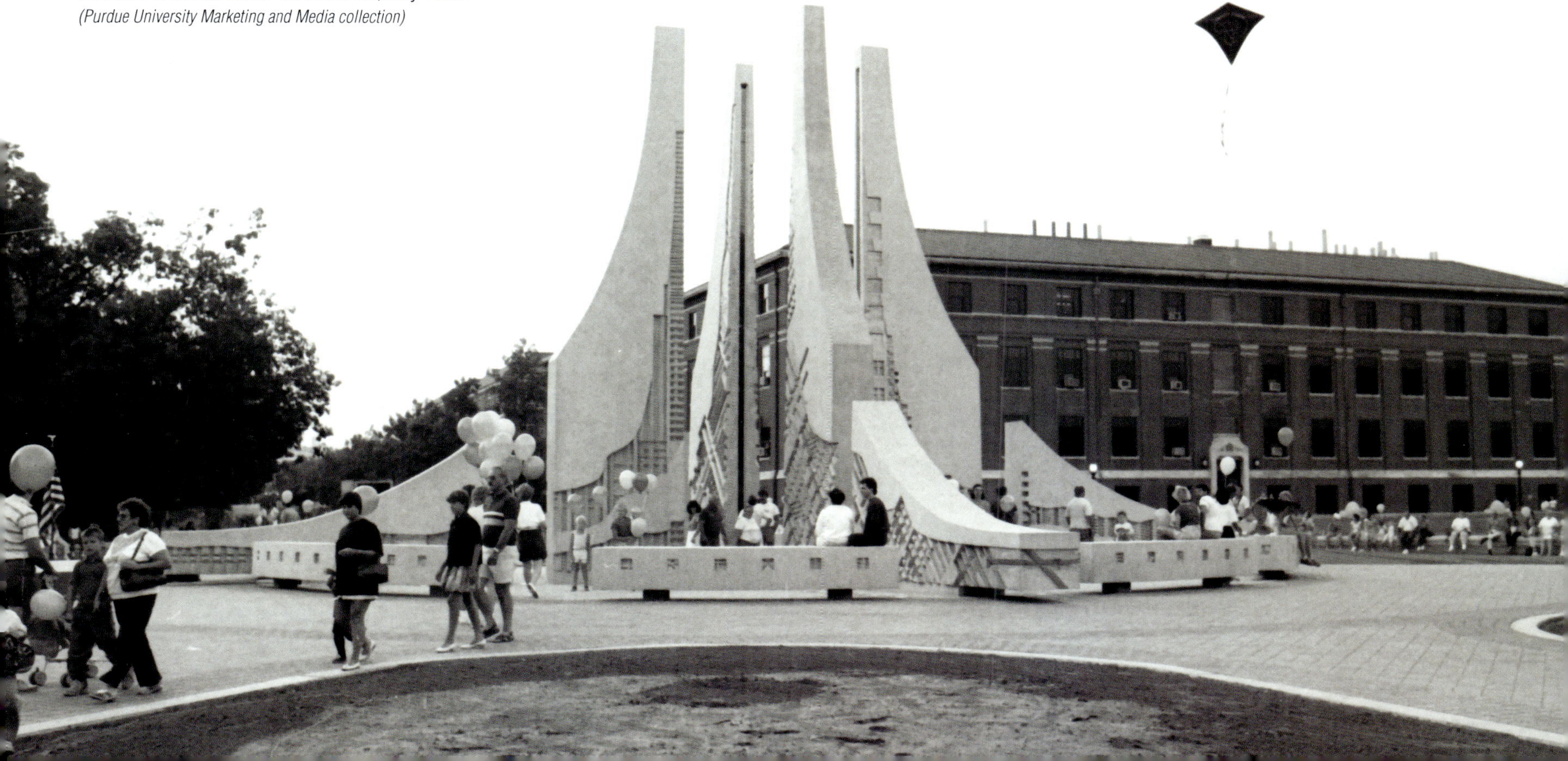

The Nude Olympics

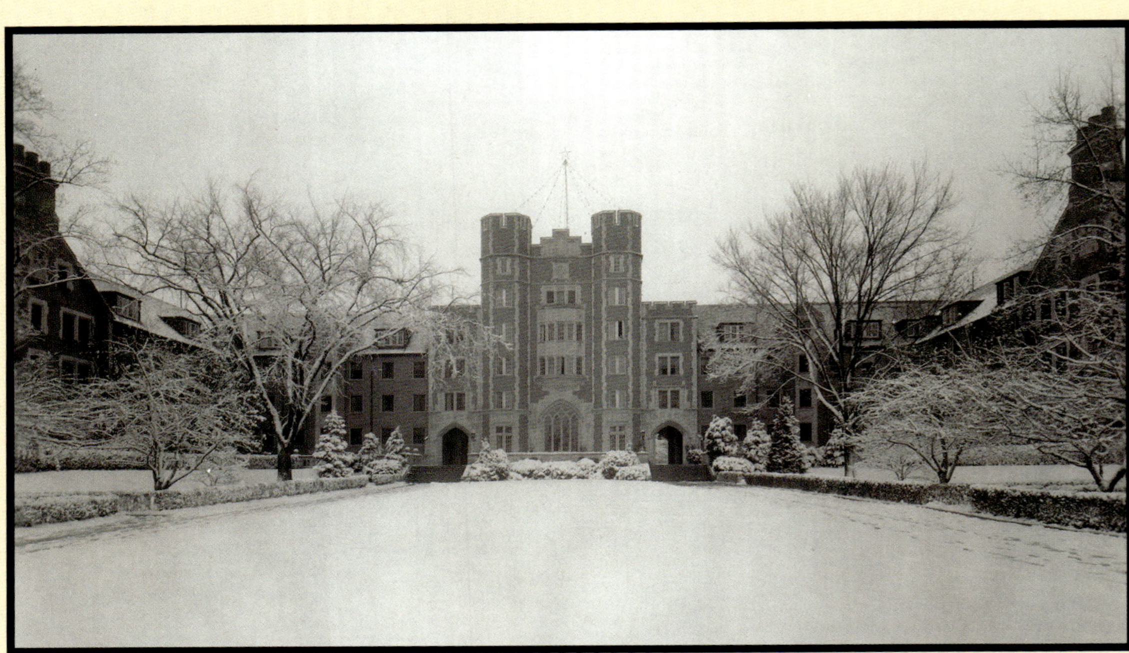

The Nude Olympics was a student-organized winter spectacle on campus. Despite attempts by the university administration to stop this event, it was fiercely defended and much cherished by those who participated.

The Nude Olympics began at some point prior to 1969 after two students creatively settled a bet by running nude across the northern part of campus. In subsequent years, as many as three thousand people observed up to two hundred runners clad only in shoes, hats, ski masks, and scarves run through Spitzer Court in Cary Quad. The run was held on an agreed-upon "coldest night of the year," sometimes more than once during the year, and began around 11:30 p.m. In the first competitions, the last runner remaining was declared the winner. After the event was banned, the declared winner was the runner not caught by the police.[8]

One runner, interviewed in 1982, recalled his first run as a freshman: "My first year, it was only 25 degrees. I was able to run for two hours and 25 minutes."[9] He won the race by running just fast enough to keep warm. He used the same strategy the following year and won again.

For a time, the university administration tolerated the event. Purdue University Police and Cary Quad staff worked together to ensure that the event was as safe as possible. But in 1985, multiple runners dealt with exposure-related injuries, including three who were taken away by ambulance.[10] Subsequently, Purdue banned the Nude Olympics, citing liability issues, health of the students, and Purdue's national reputation.[11] Still, the tradition quietly continued despite threats of disciplinary action, spurred on by a large student fan base. From 1987 to 1995, students were arrested during the now-unsanctioned run. Arrest numbers ranged from six in 1989 to twenty-five in 1992. Many were given probated suspensions, but others had their residence hall contracts terminated for public intoxication, resisting arrest, disorderly conduct, or indecent exposure.

Above: Cary Quadrangle in the snow, March 2013. Photo by Andrew Hancock. *(Purdue University Marketing and Media collection)*

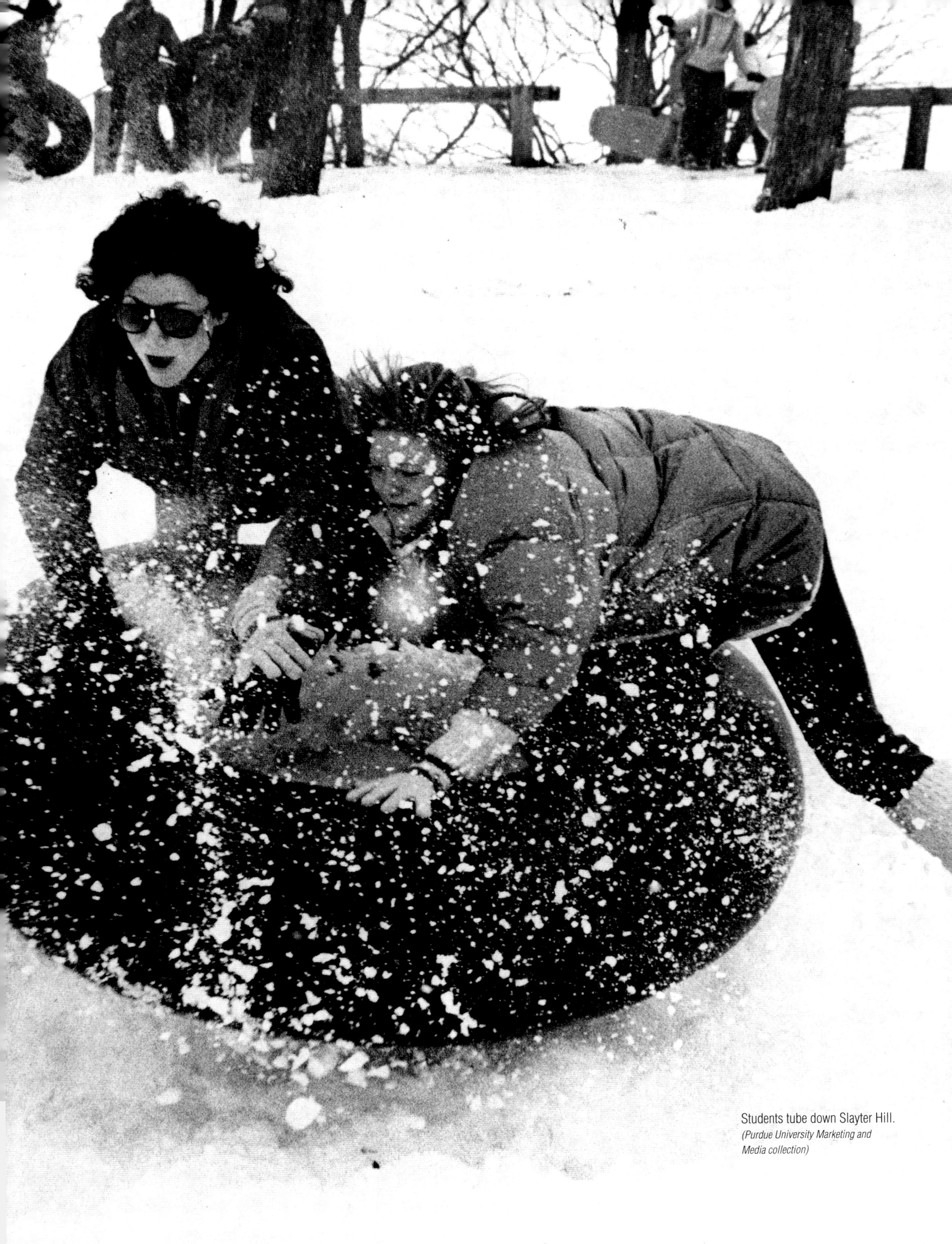

Students tube down Slayter Hill.
(Purdue University Marketing and Media collection)

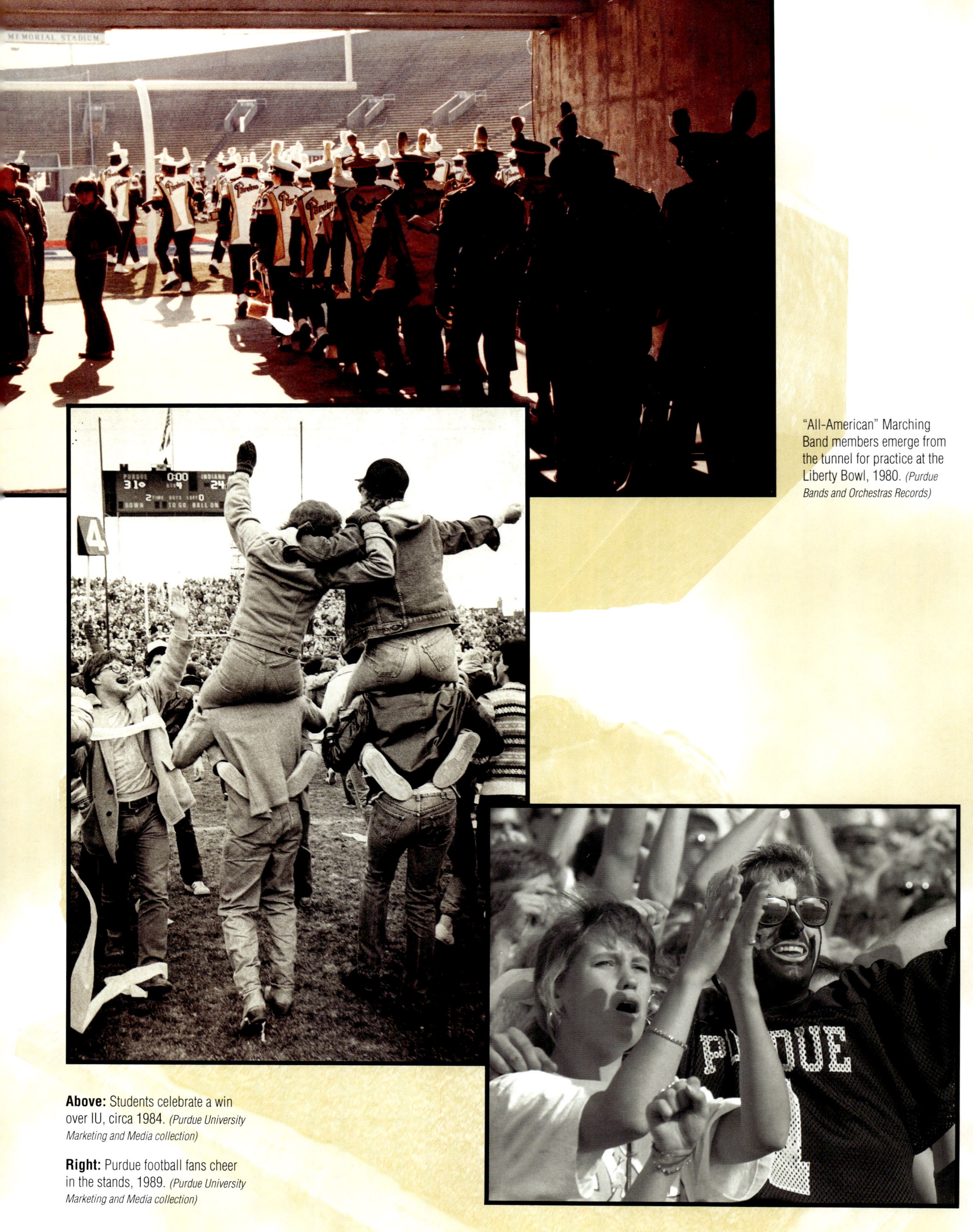

"All-American" Marching Band members emerge from the tunnel for practice at the Liberty Bowl, 1980. *(Purdue Bands and Orchestras Records)*

Above: Students celebrate a win over IU, circa 1984. *(Purdue University Marketing and Media collection)*

Right: Purdue football fans cheer in the stands, 1989. *(Purdue University Marketing and Media collection)*

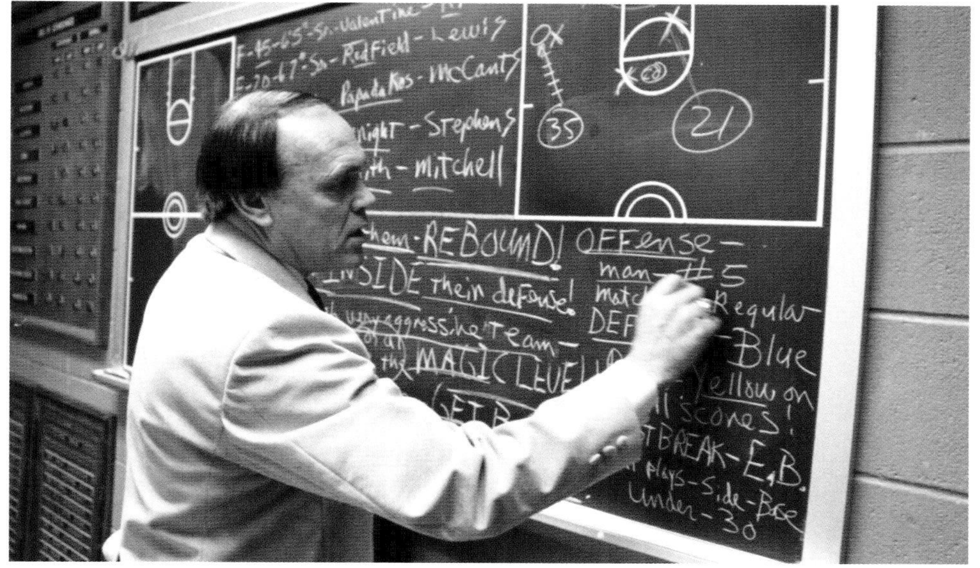

Women's sports during the 1979–1980 year included swimming, volleyball, basketball, track, tennis, crew, and power lifting.

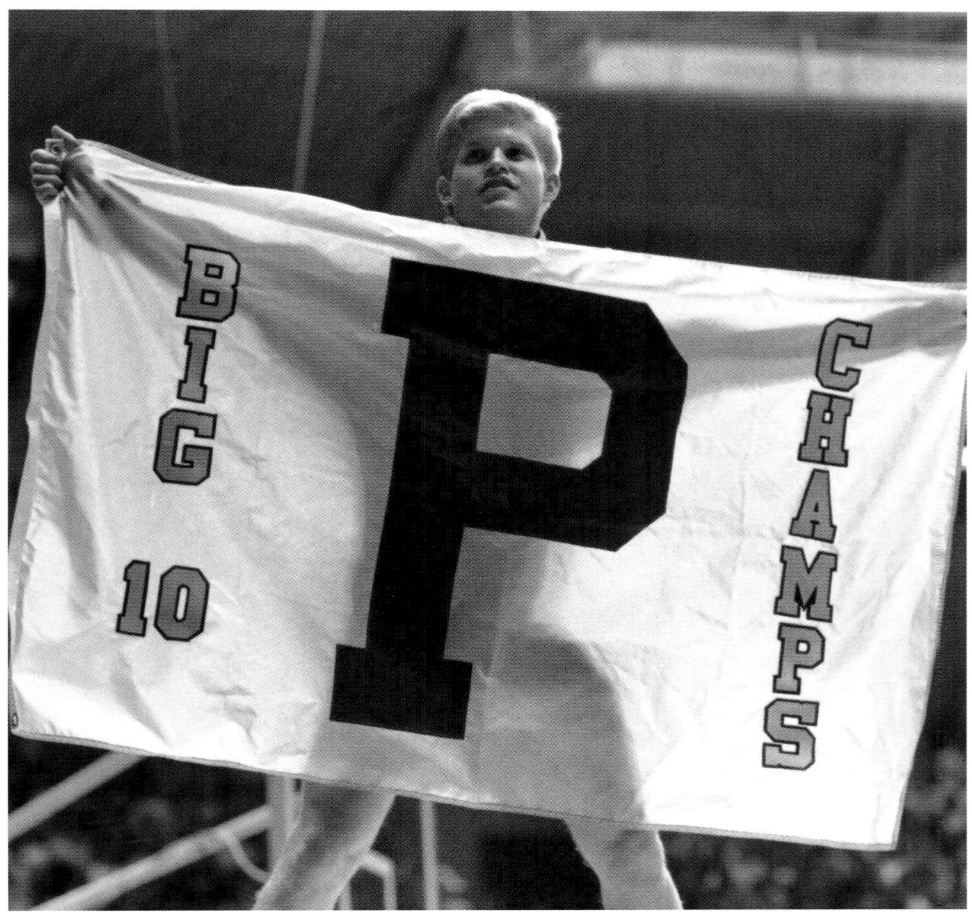

Commencement itself underwent change. In 1981, graduation was split into three separate ceremonies; a year later, four sessions were held. A summer commencement ceremony was held in 1984, marking its return from a thirty-three-year hiatus. In 1987 a winter commencement ceremony was added, and the Purdue tradition of May, August, and December graduation was firmly established.

The football team made its third consecutive bowl game following the 1980 season, winning the Liberty Bowl against Missouri. However, the football program would fall on difficult times for the remainder of the decade; 1984 was the only other winning season for the Boilermakers.

The men's basketball team reached the 1980 NCAA Final Four, where it fell in the national semifinals to UCLA. Purdue defeated Iowa in the consolation (third-place) game. Afterward, coach Lee Rose resigned his position. Star player Joe Barry Carroll was selected as the first overall pick in the 1980 NBA Draft by the Golden State Warriors. Gene Keady was named Purdue men's basketball coach on April 11, 1980. Keady continued the tradition of basketball excellence, as the men's team won three Big Ten titles during the decade and reached the NCAA Tournament Sweet Sixteen in 1988.

Top: Coach Keady diagrams plays for the basketball team, January 1988. *(Purdue University Marketing and Media collection)*

Bottom: A student cheers for the men's basketball team during the NCAA tourrnament, 1988. *(Purdue University Marketing and Media collection)*

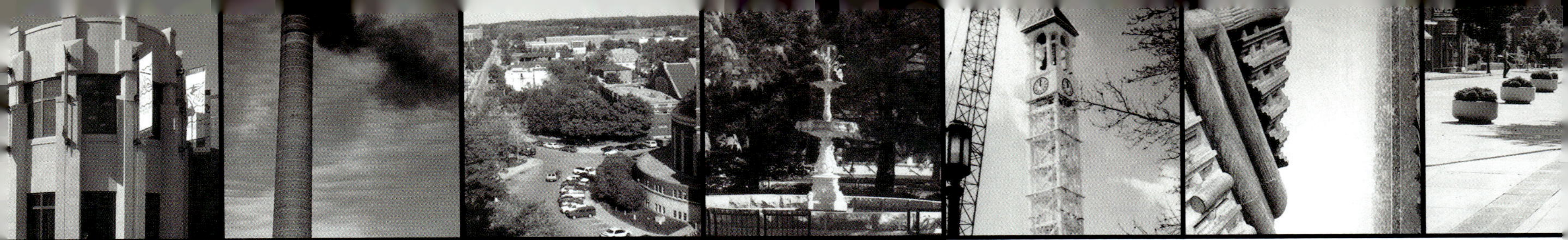

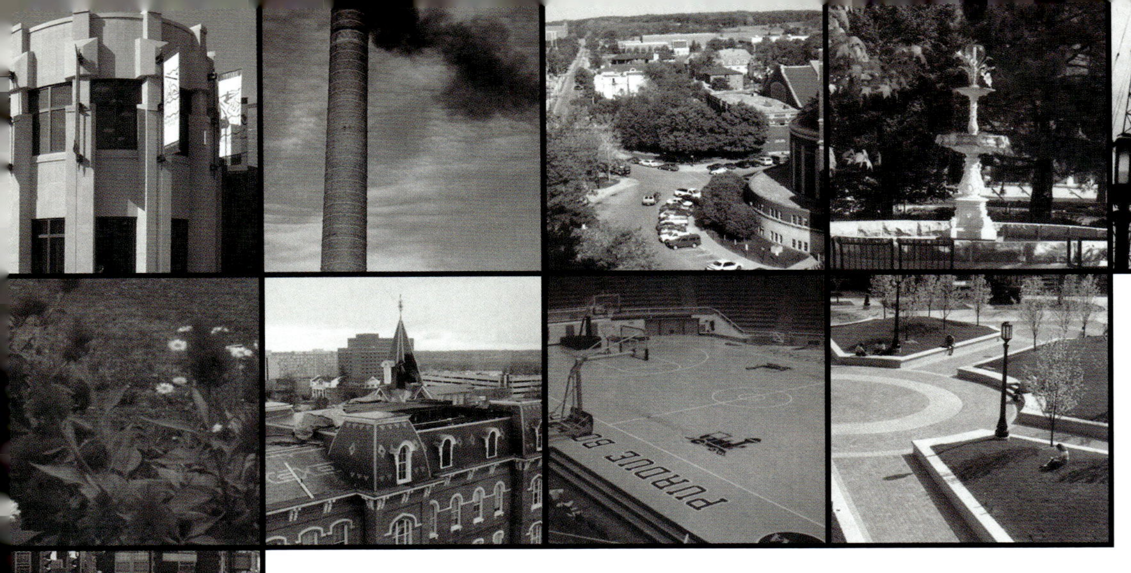

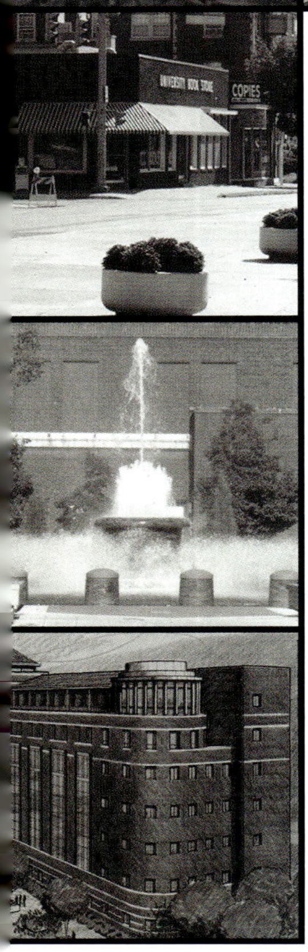

Campus map, 1992–1993. *(Campus Maps collection)*

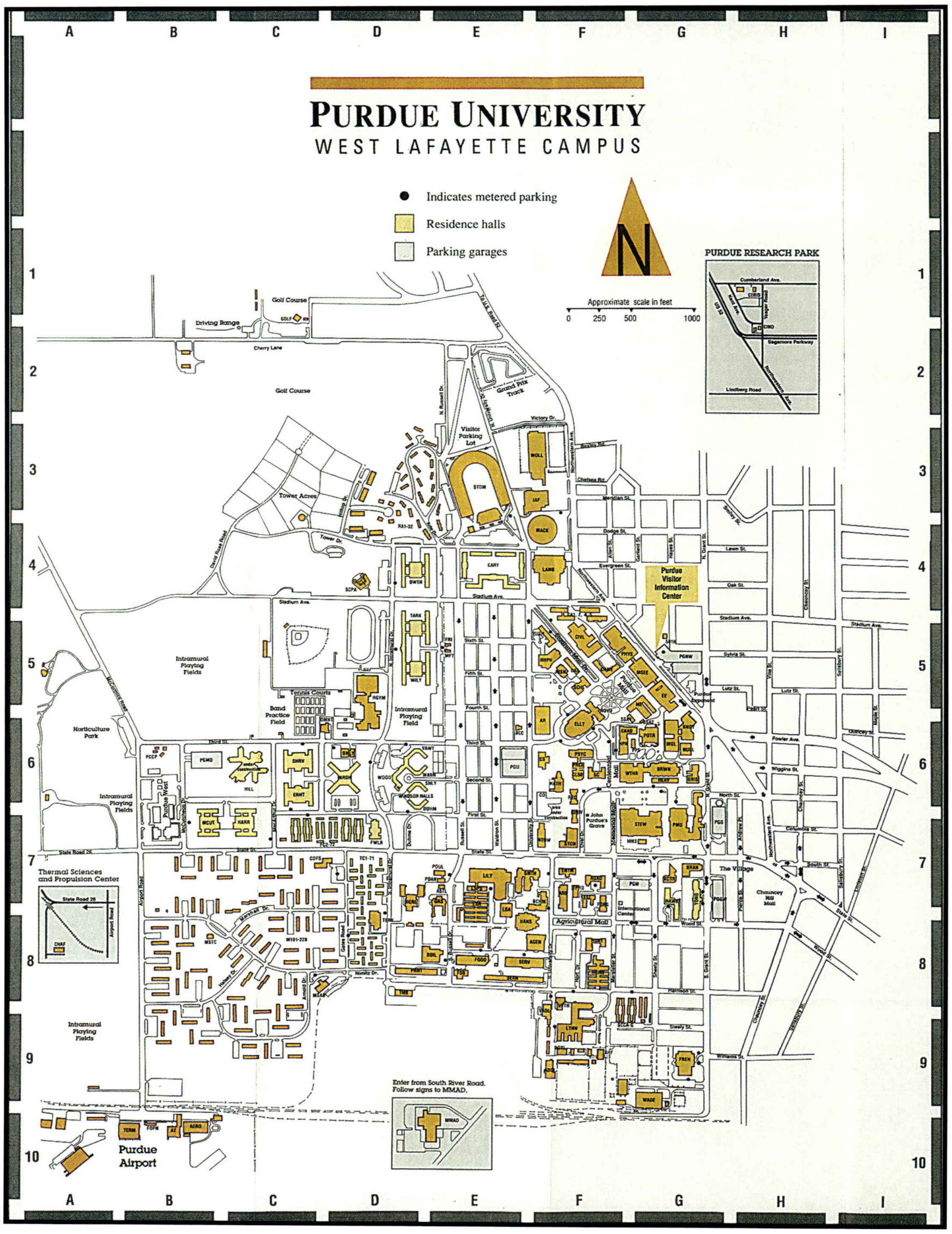

{Enrollment in 1990: 35,647 students[1]}

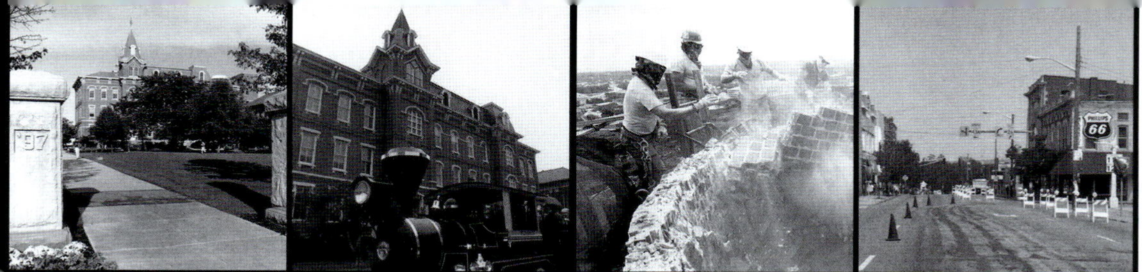

[The 1990s]

PURDUE AT 130

"The twentieth century was a period when college students strived to . . . lead better lives than their parents. While technology advanced to simplify the lives of students, the broad social issues of the year worked to complicate their actions and ideas. Crossing the years from an innocent freshman to a distinguished senior was filled with many hardships, mind-expanding experiences, academic challenges, and most importantly, memories of the greatest years of one's life."

—*Kim Terhune for the 1996* Debris *yearbook*[2]

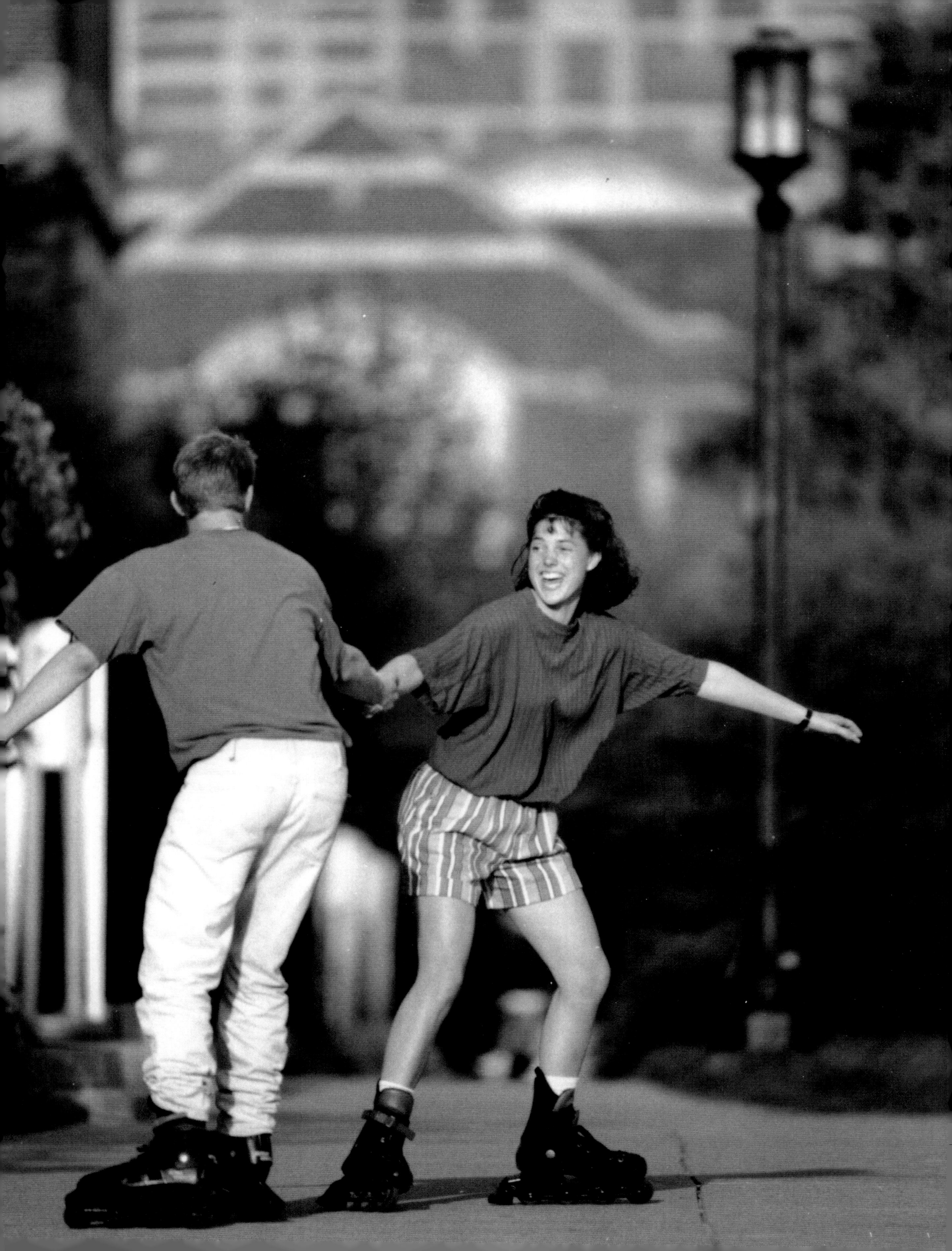

Purdue's grade scale changed from a 6.0 system to a 4.0 system in the summer of 1993.[3]

Two students rollerblade through campus. *(Purdue University Marketing and Media collection)*

The final decade of the twentieth century continued the movement toward a more pedestrian-friendly, green, and accessible campus. The 1990s transformed the physical West Lafayette campus dramatically, perhaps more than any other decade after World War II. Remnants of the smaller campus of decades past were removed from the campus core: parking was largely moved to the periphery and the smokestack was razed. New buildings grew from the prior foundations of century-old structures. Meanwhile, study areas and a newly built, yet reclaimed, bell tower took their places as iconic Purdue landmarks.

The first African American student body president, Tarrus Richardson, was elected to lead Purdue Student Government in the 1990–1991 academic year.[4]

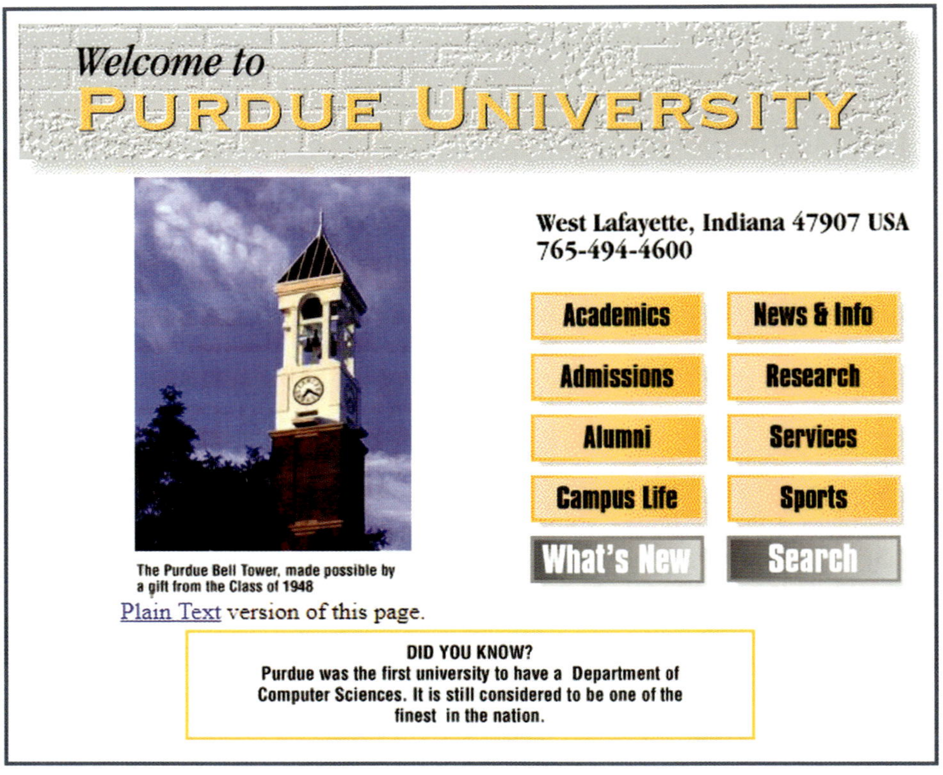

Academy Park opened in 1997 and soon became a favorite stop during campus tours. Trees and other greenery were added in subsequent years. The space included numerous seating areas, trees, and the "clapping circles," geometrically designed spaces that acoustically reverberate. Nearby, a memorial named Golden Taps was created to honor students who had passed away.

Student enrollment rose throughout the decade, and the number of international and minority students continued to increase as well. Purdue had a record number of international students in the fall of 1990, who matriculated to campus from more than one hundred foreign countries. Purdue received recognition for work with minority and women engineers, and African American student enrollment within graduate programs increased. In 1993 the Helen Bass Williams Women's Scholarship, named after Purdue's first female African American faculty member, was created for female African American students. By the end of the decade, Purdue held the distinction of enrolling more international students than any other public research institution in the country.

During the 1990s, Walkmans were replaced with Discmans, and more than a few students could be seen carrying their CD players between classes. Like many academic institutions, Purdue University joined the World Wide Web. Initiatives in online learning, classroom technologies, and telecommuting became a regular aspect of life at the University.

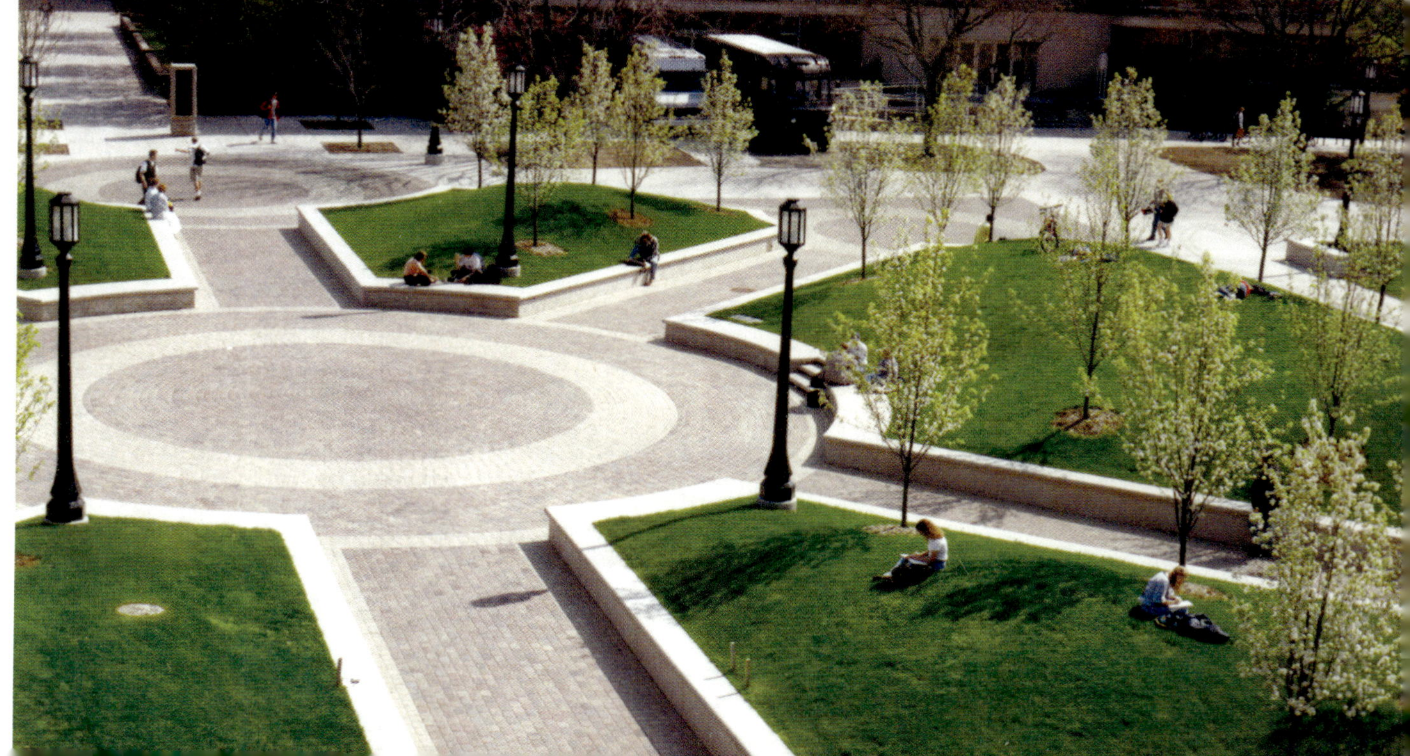

Top: Purdue University website home page, June 5, 1997. *(Purdue University website)*

Right: The clapping circle at the newly opened Academy Park, 1997. *(Purdue University Architect records)*

Down Goes the Smokestack, Up Goes the Bell Tower

For generations, the smokestack in the center of Purdue's campus served as a beacon for Boilermakers. It could be seen for miles and was viewed with affection as a symbol of the University. When the smokestack and its adjoining power plant were deemed unsafe in the mid-1980s, students petitioned for it to stay; nevertheless, the plant completely ceased operations in March of 1992 and the smokestack was torn down a few months later.[5] The Power Plant Building itself, though shuttered, would remain on campus until 2014.

In 1995, the Purdue skyline was again altered as a bell tower rose at the center of campus. The tower was made possible by a gift from the Class of 1948. Placed inside the 160-foot-tall tower were the bells from the second Heavilon Hall, kept in storage since the latter's demolition in 1956. The Bell Tower quickly became part of campus lore: legend states that any student who walks directly under the tower will not graduate in four years.

Right: Power plant smokestack, 1956. *(Purdue University photographs)*

Far right: Construction on the Bell Tower. *(Purdue University Marketing and Media collection)*

Two people enjoy a fountain run.
(Purdue University Marketing and Media collection)

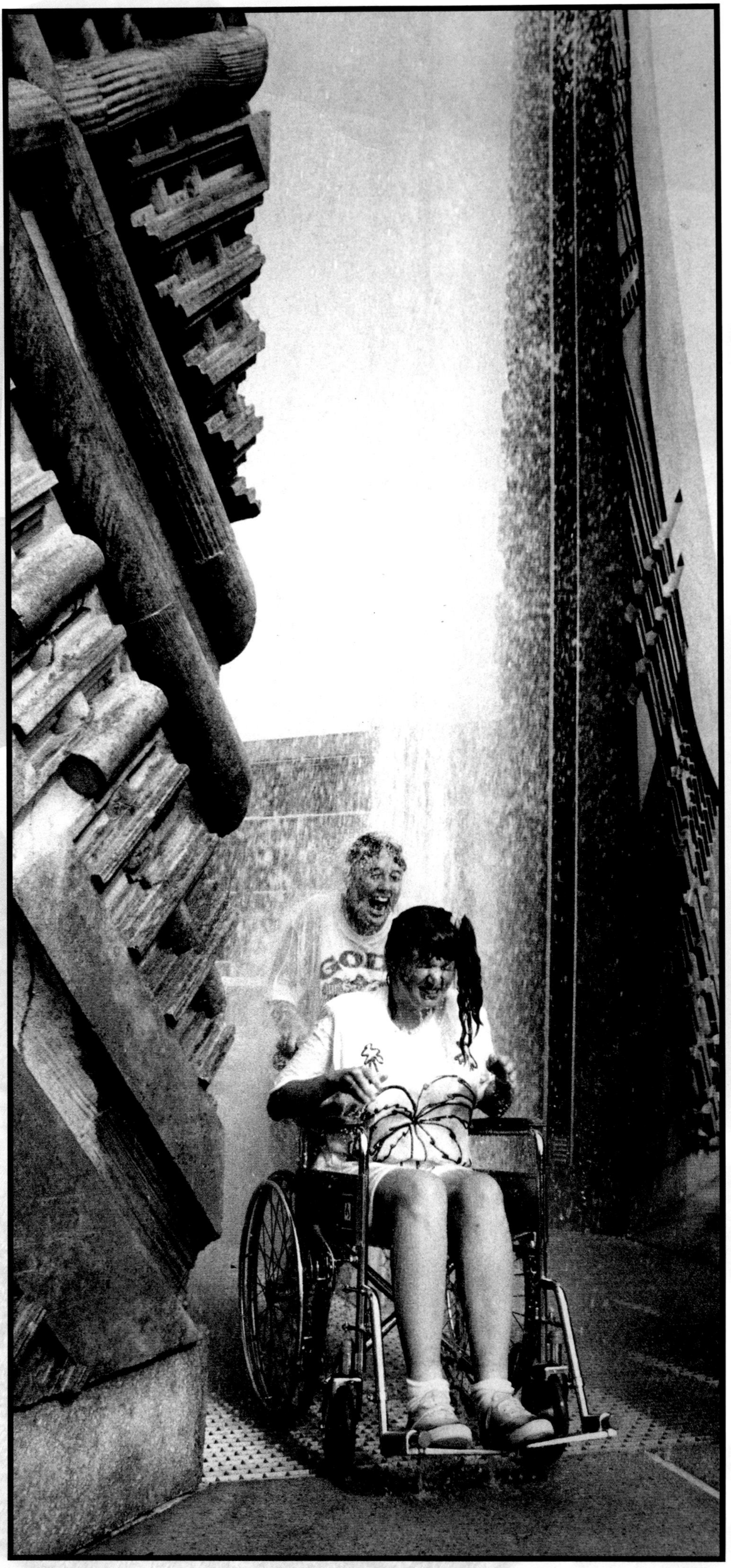

In the 1996–1997 academic year, Purdue Engineering developed Engineering Projects in Community Service (EPICS). This new course aimed to teach students how their engineering contributions would aid the community.

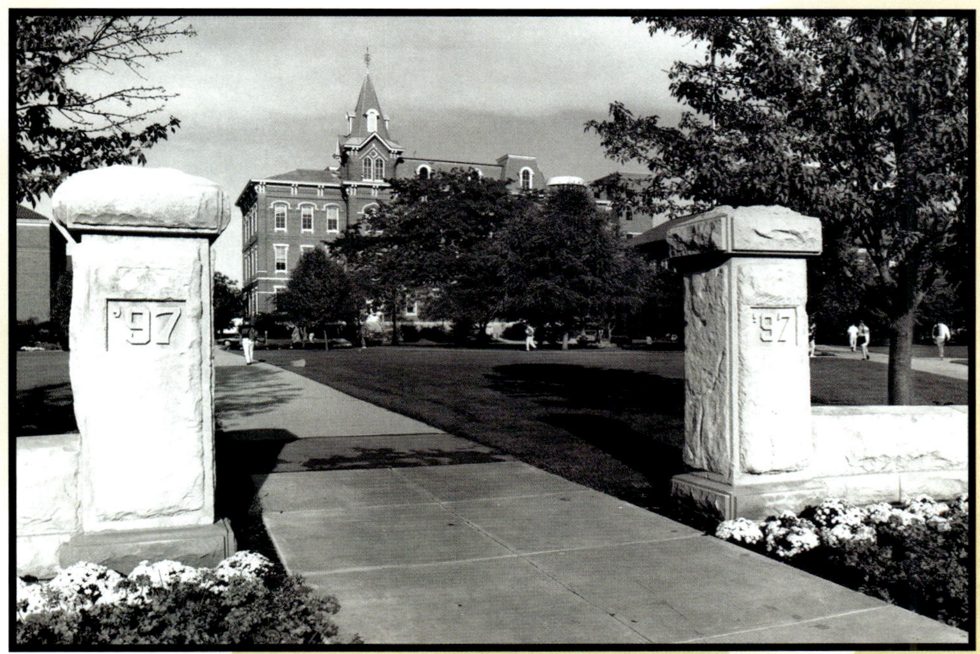

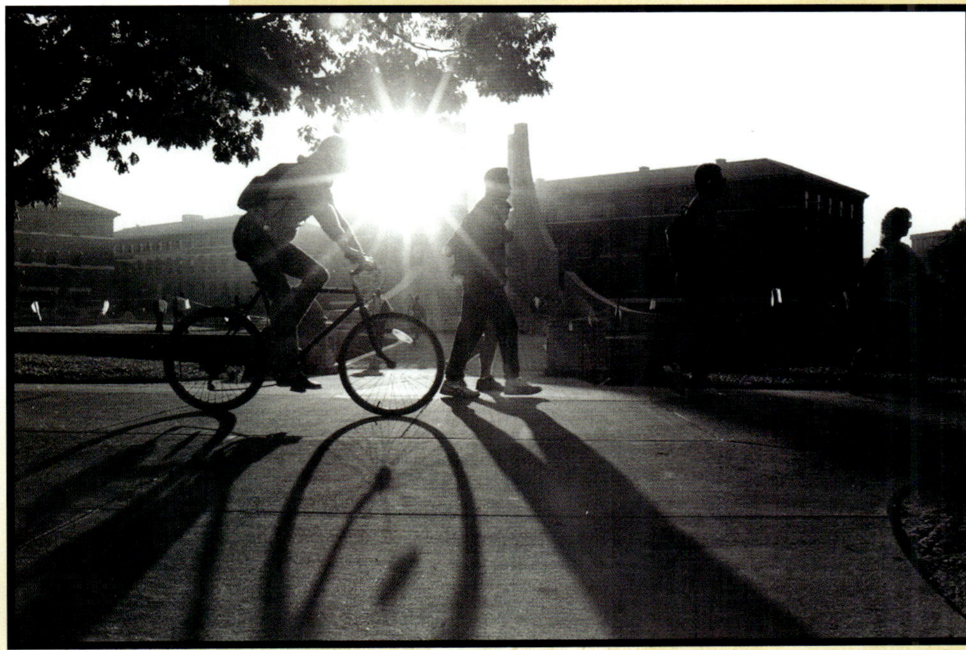

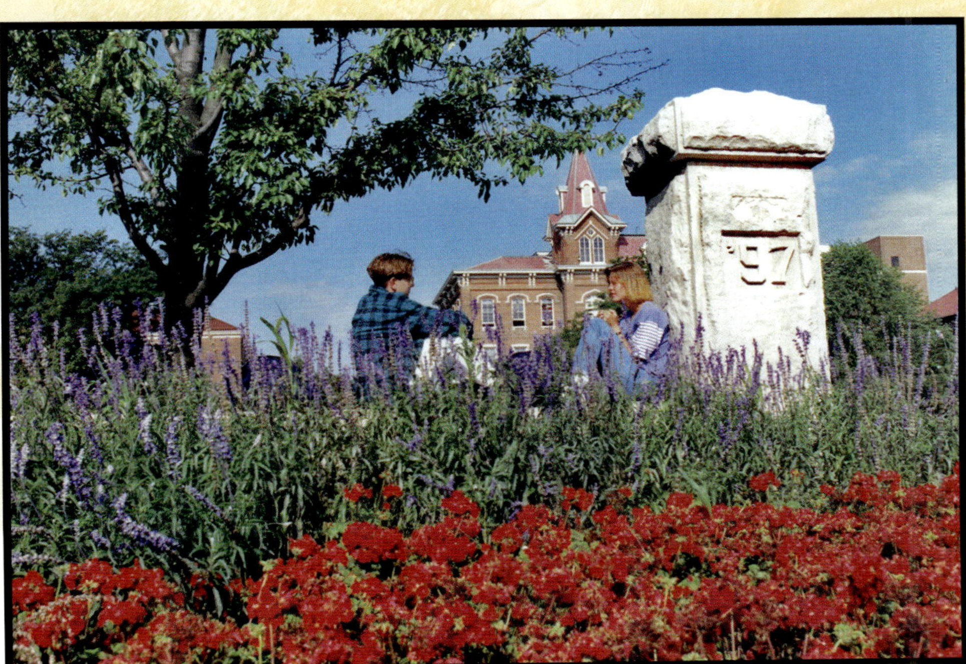

Top: The Class of 1897 gates, initially located at the main entrance to campus on State Street, were reconstructed and installed in Memorial Mall in 1991. The gates and Hello Walk, a path encouraging people to say hello to everyone they pass, harkened to Purdue's past. *(Purdue University Marketing and Media collection)*

Middle: Student traveling through Engineering Mall. *(Purdue University Marketing and Media collection)*

Bottom: Students relax and talk on the Memorial Mall, September 1992. *(Purdue University Marketing and Media collection)*

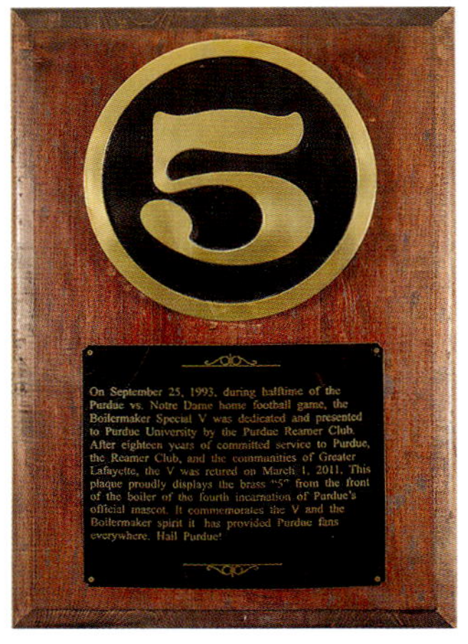

Above: Plaque of the 5 from the front of the Boilermaker Special V. *(Purdue Reamer Club records)*

Below: The Boilermaker Special V. *(Purdue University photograph)*

A new Boilermaker Special arrived on campus in 1993. After twenty-three years of service, the Boilermaker Special III was retired from service. While the Boilermaker Special IV, a smaller version of the Special, continued to participate in campus events, the Special V was the natural successor to the III. On September 25, 1993, the V made its first appearance. This incarnation of the Boilermaker Special remained in service until 2011.

The University founded a new orientation program for incoming freshmen in 1993. The Collegians Orientating Residential Newcomers, or Corn Camp, took place in June with a small number of participants. Two years later the event moved to the week before the start of fall semester and was renamed Boiler Gold Rush (BGR). In the ensuing decades BGR grew to include nearly all incoming freshmen, and in 2011 BGR International was formed to familiarize international students with campus life as well.[6]

Purdue Athletics were a vital part of student life on campus. In January of 1993, Purdue University Softball was established, with Carol Bruggeman hired as the first coach. The softball team played its first game on March 5, 1994, a loss to Canisius College. The team made its first Big Ten Tournament just a few years later in 1997. Women's soccer became an intercollegiate sport at Purdue in 1998, and the men's tennis team reached the NCAA tournament for three consecutive seasons from 1997 to 1999.

The women's basketball program took its place among the nation's best during the 1990s. Coach Lin Dunn and the team won their first Big Ten Conference Championship following the 1990–1991 season. Three years later, the team made its first Final Four. Continued success led the team to multiple conference championships and NCAA Tournament appearances. In 1999, under coach Carolyn Peck, the women's team reached its second Final Four. Following a national semifinal victory against Louisiana Tech, the Boilermakers outclassed Duke 62–45 to win their first national championship. Star players Ukari Figgs, Stephanie White, and Katie Douglas were named to the All-Tournament Team. The team was the first in Purdue Athletics to win a national championship since golf in 1961.

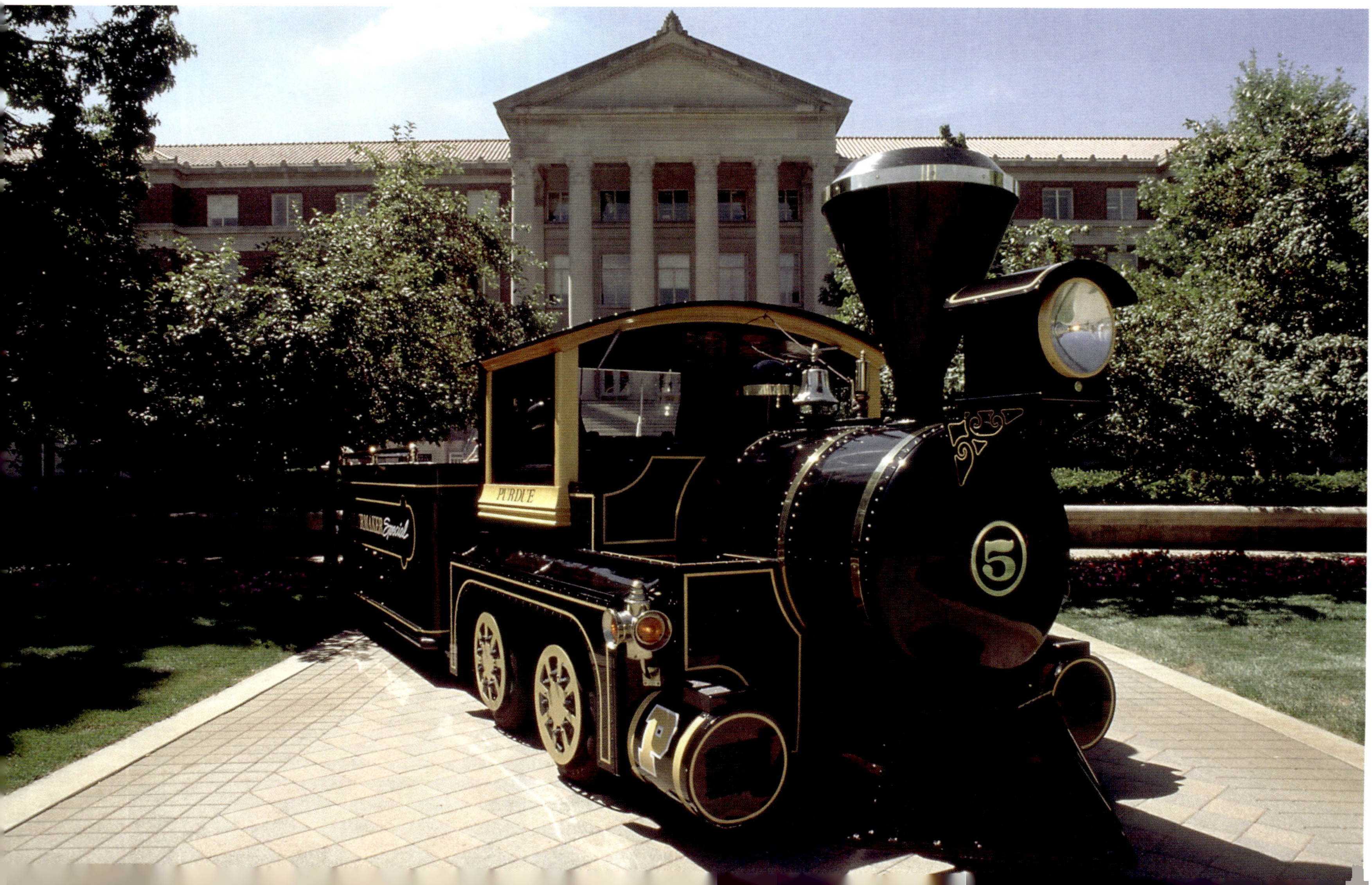

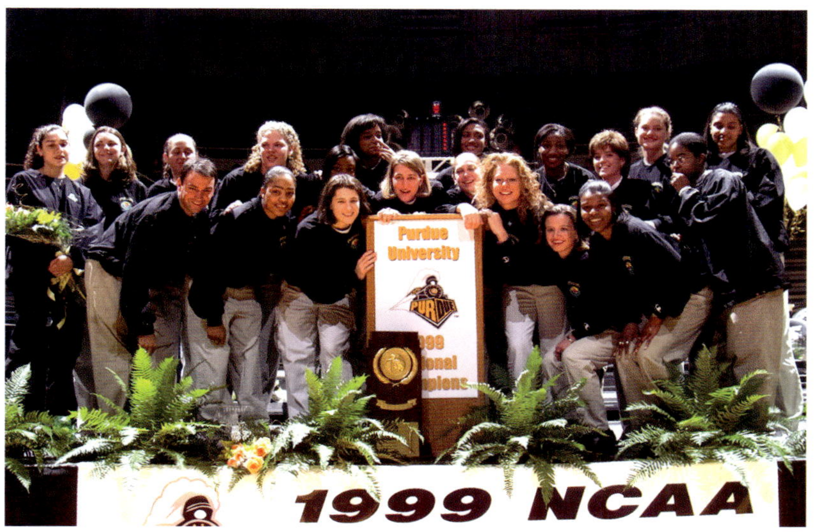

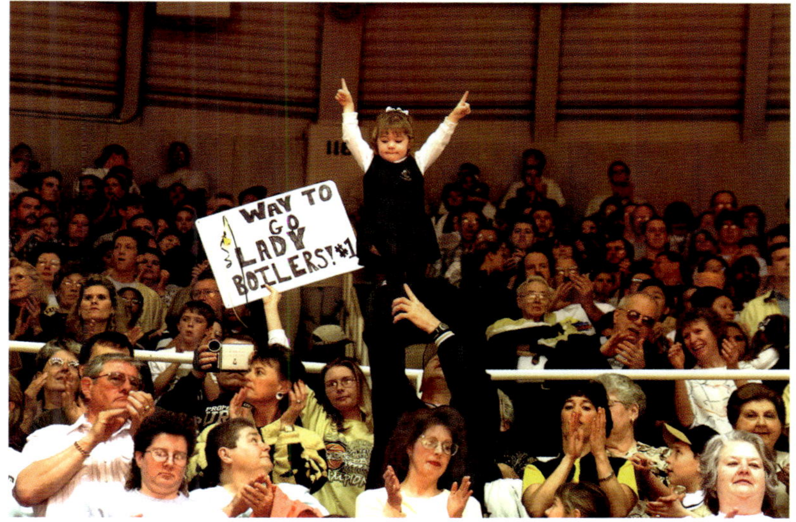

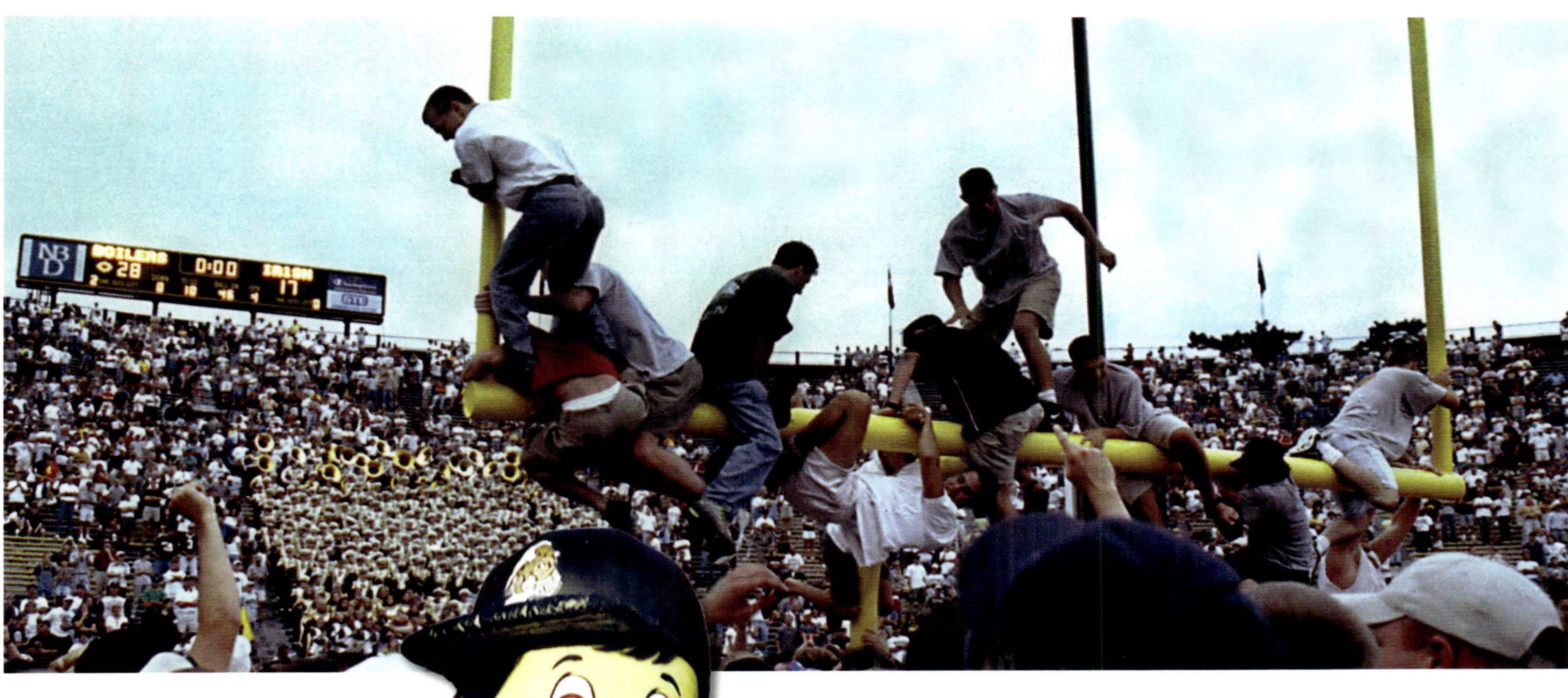

Top left: The Purdue women's basketball team celebrates its national championship, 1999. *(Purdue University Marketing and Media collection)*

Top right: The Purdue community celebrates the women's basketball national championship, 1999. *(Purdue University Marketing and Media collection)*

Above: Purdue students storm the football field after a win against Notre Dame, 1997. *(Purdue University Marketing and Media collection)*

Right: For a few years in the late 1990s and early 2000s, Purdue Pete had a companion: Rowdy, a large, childlike inflatable mascot, who was seen at Purdue home games. *(Purdue University News Service photographs and negatives)*

Men's basketball also achieved great success, winning the Big Ten for three consecutive seasons from 1994 to 1996. The team regularly reached the NCAA Tournament, falling in the Elite Eight in 1994. Following the 1994 season, Big Ten Conference and National Player of the Year award-winner Glenn Robinson was selected first overall in the 1994 NBA Draft by the Milwaukee Bucks.

After more than a decade of difficult seasons, Purdue football hired Joe Tiller as head coach in 1997. Coach Tiller immediately provided a spark to the program. The Boilers went to their first bowl game in thirteen years, winning the Alamo Bowl against Oklahoma State. Under Tiller, the team reached the postseason for the remainder of the decade.

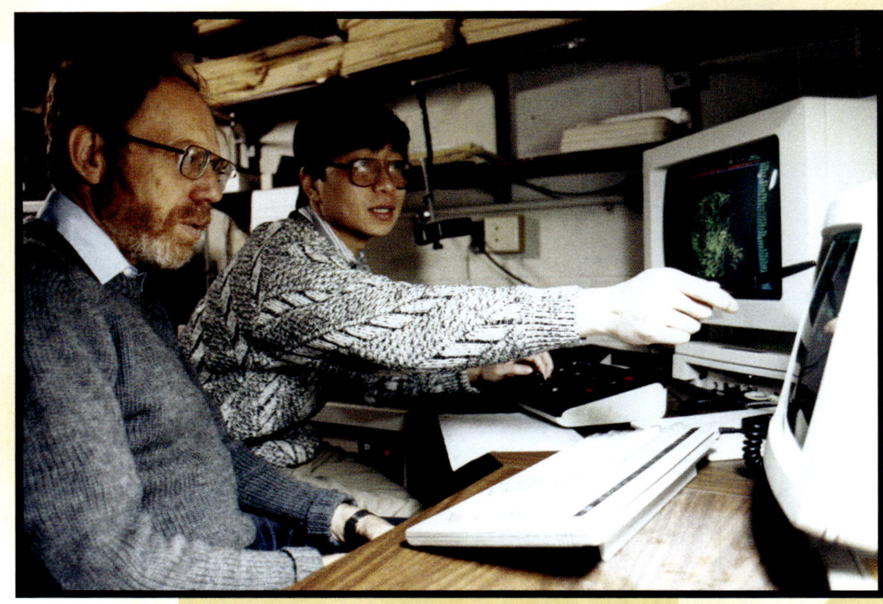

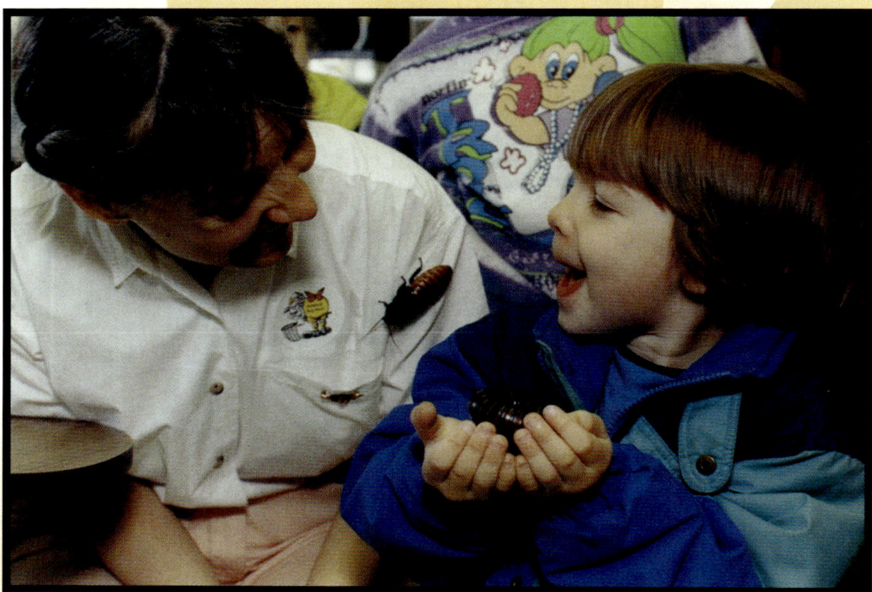

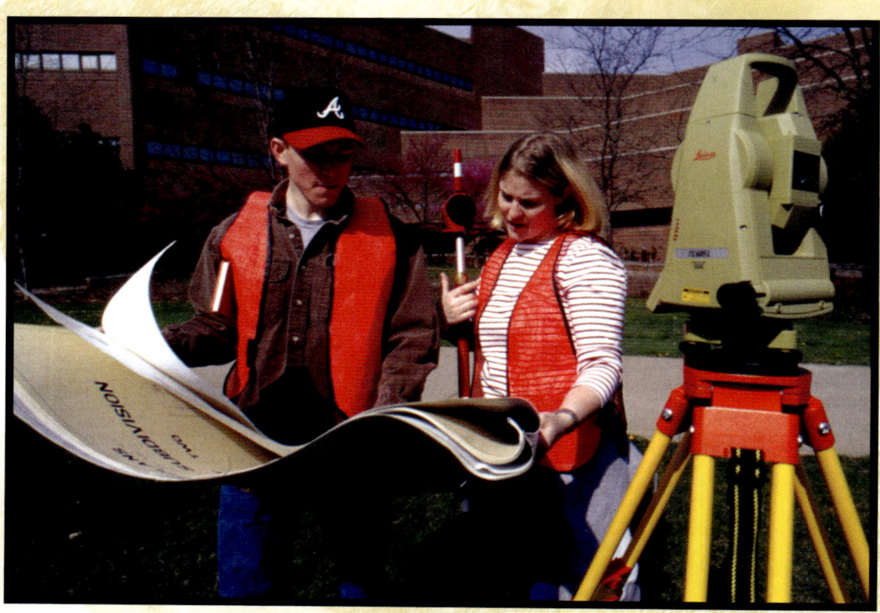

Top: Michael Rossman works with a student to study the common cold structure. *(Purdue University Marketing and Media collection)*

Middle: The Bug Bowl, 1993. Founded in 1990, the Spring Fest activity allows visitors to hold bugs and participate in a bug-spitting contest. *(Purdue University Marketing and Media collection)*

Bottom: Construction management students learn about surveying, 1999. *(Purdue University Marketing and Media collection)*

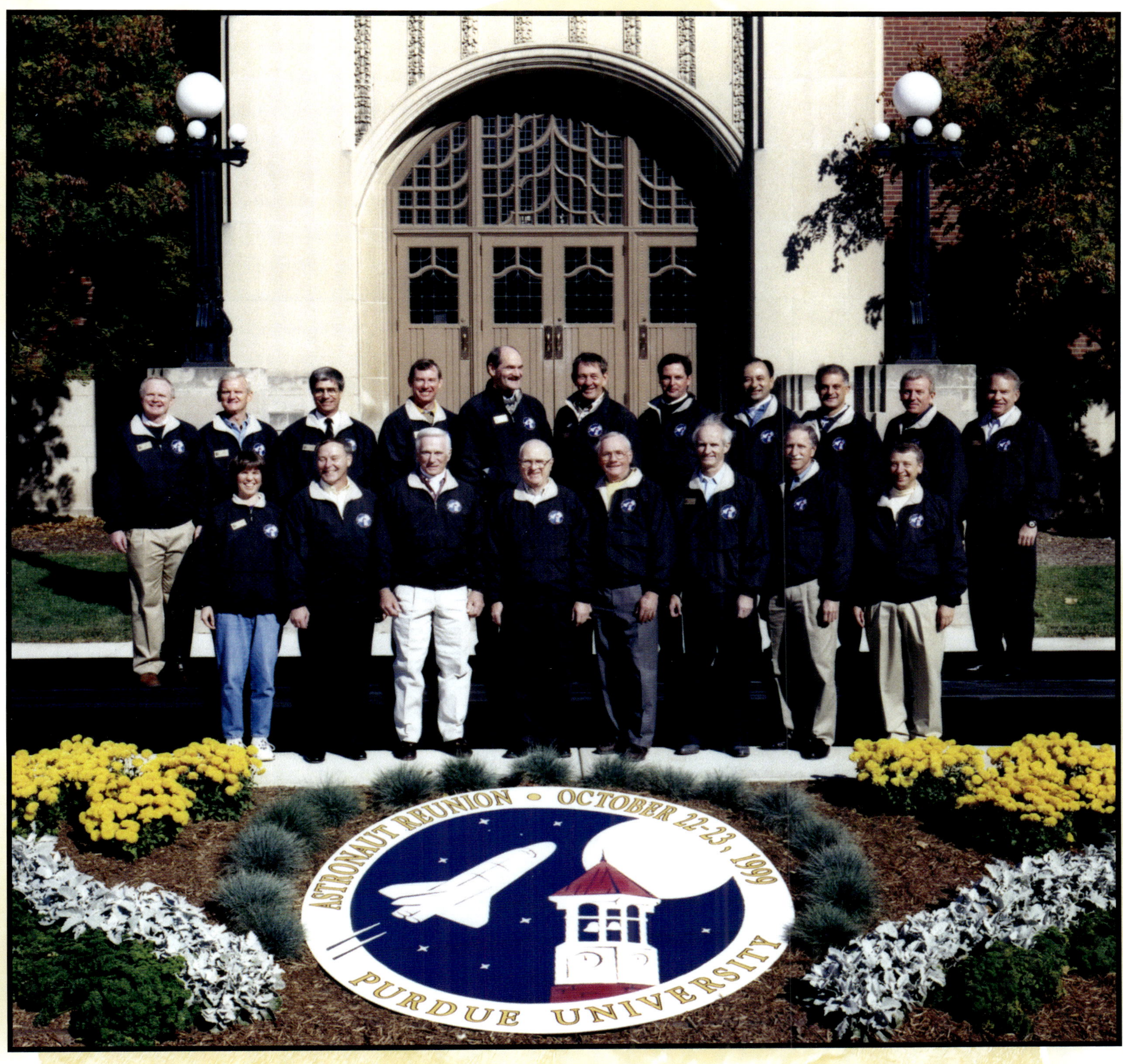

Astronaut alumni attend the astronaut reunion, October 22, 1999.
(Purdue University Marketing and Media collection)

Right: The Purdue Hymn, written in 1941 by Alfred Kirchhoff. The Hymn was adopted as the University's official alma mater in February 1993. *(Purdue University Musical Organization records)*

Background: Graduating students walk across the newly completed Engineering Mall toward their commencement ceremony in Elliott Hall of Music. *(Purdue University Architect records)*

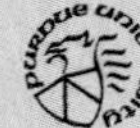

PURDUE HYMN
(Purdue's Alma Mater)

Close by the Wabash in famed Hoosier land
Stands Old Purdue, serene and grand!
Cherished in memory
By all her sons and daughters true,
Fair Alma Mater, All Hail, Purdue,
Fairest in all the land,
Our own Purdue.
Fairest in all the land,
Our own Purdue.

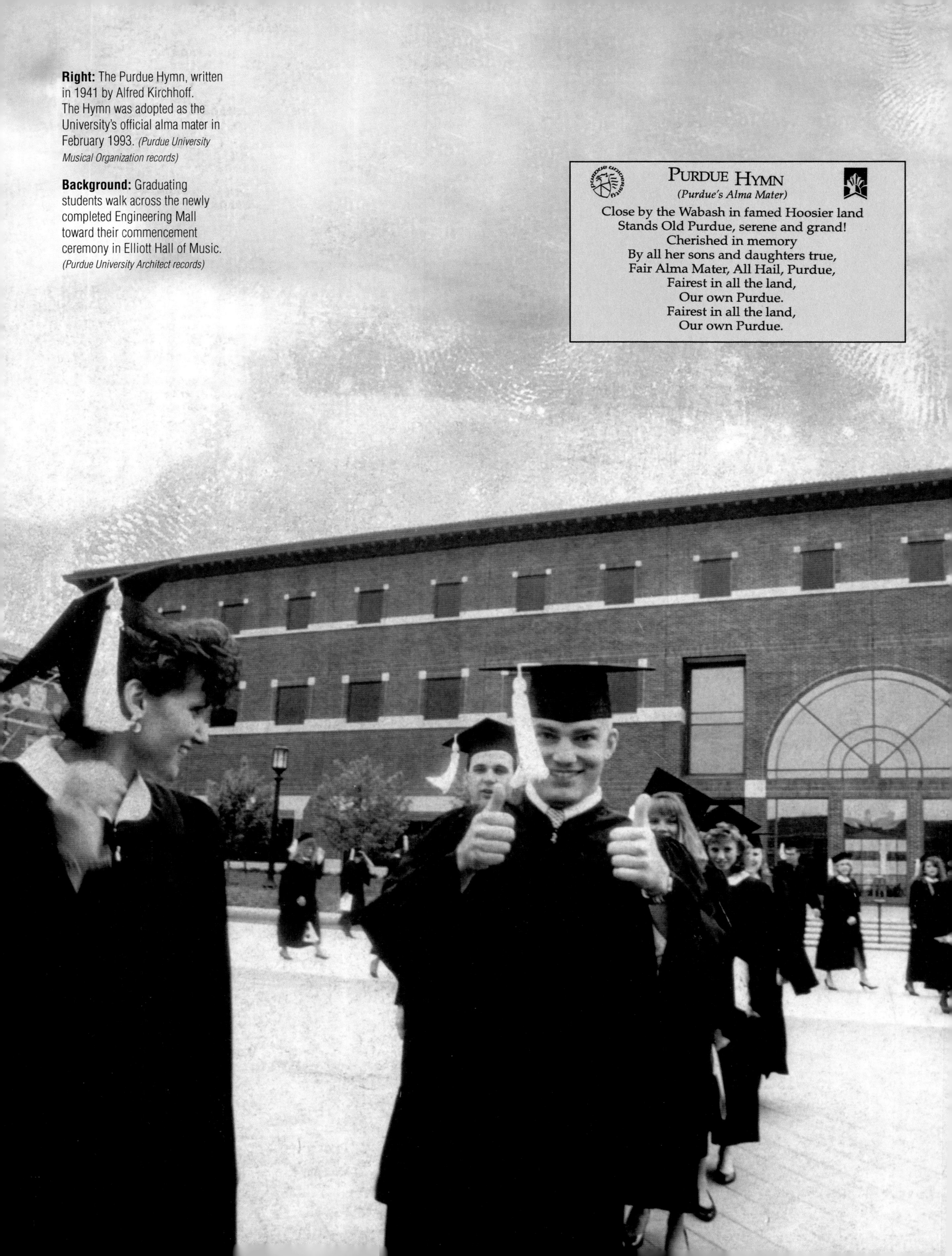

Thirty years after its founding, the Black Cultural Center opened a new facility in 1999. Located at the corner of Russell and Third Streets, the Center continued to provide educational and social programs for the campus community. The new building included a library, event spaces, offices, and study areas for students.

Below left: Jahari dance troupe, 1998. *(Purdue University Black Cultural Center records)*

Below right: Black Voices of Inspiration, 1998. *(Purdue University Black Cultural Center records)*

Bottom: The new Black Cultural Center, opened in 1999. *(Purdue University photographs)*

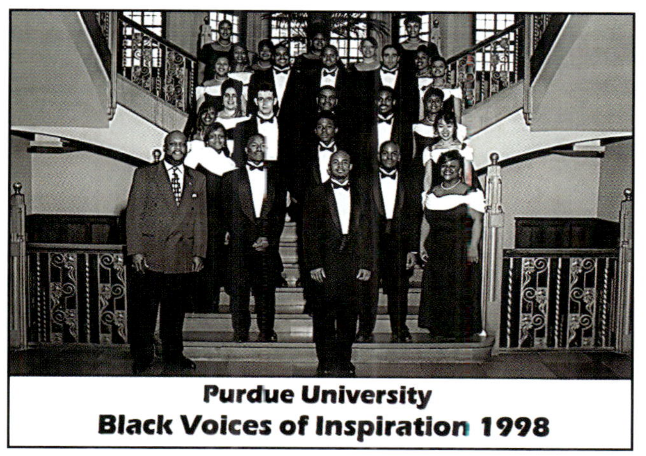

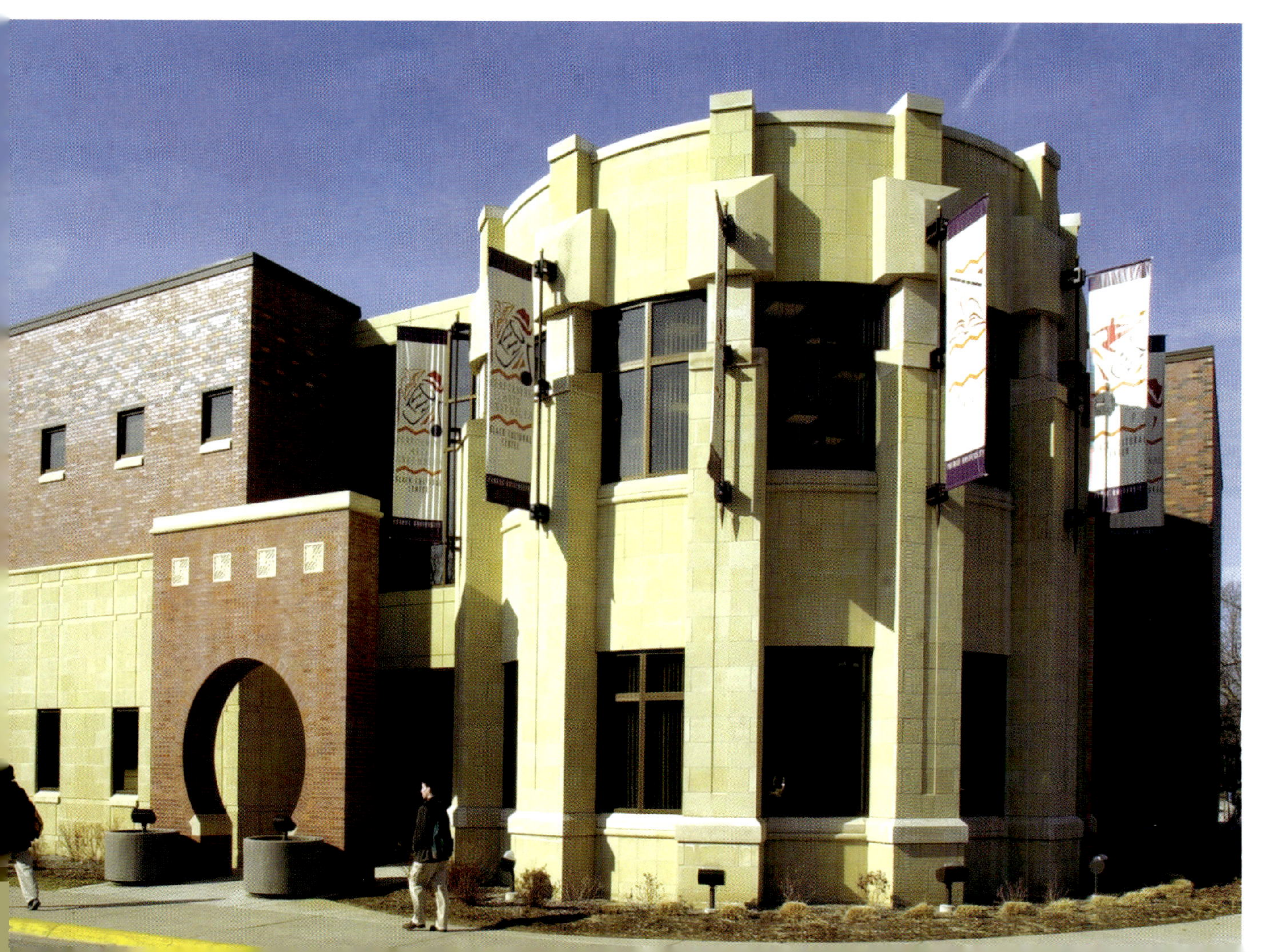

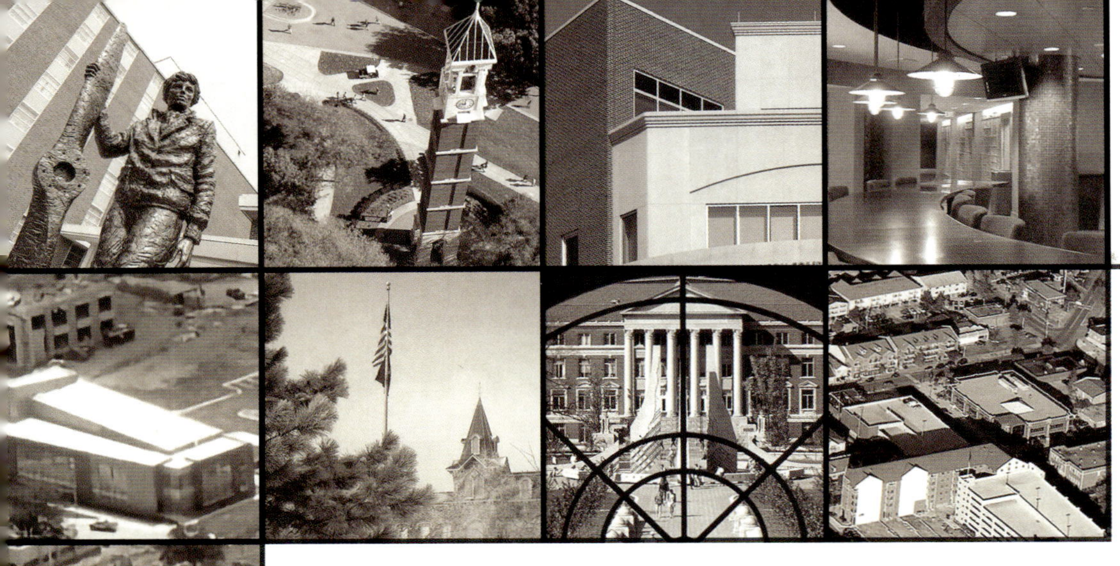

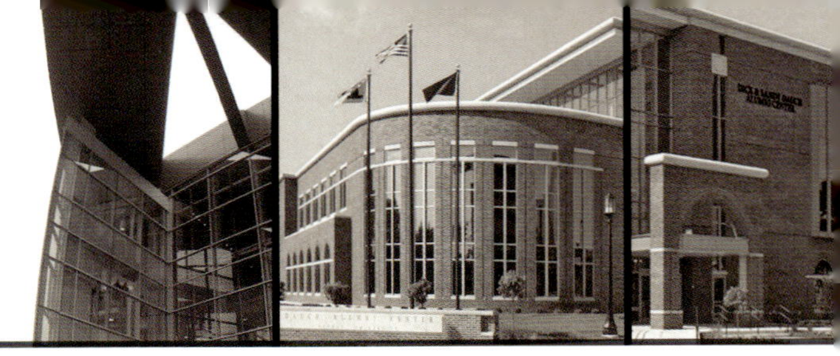

Campus map, 2010. *(Campus Maps collection)*

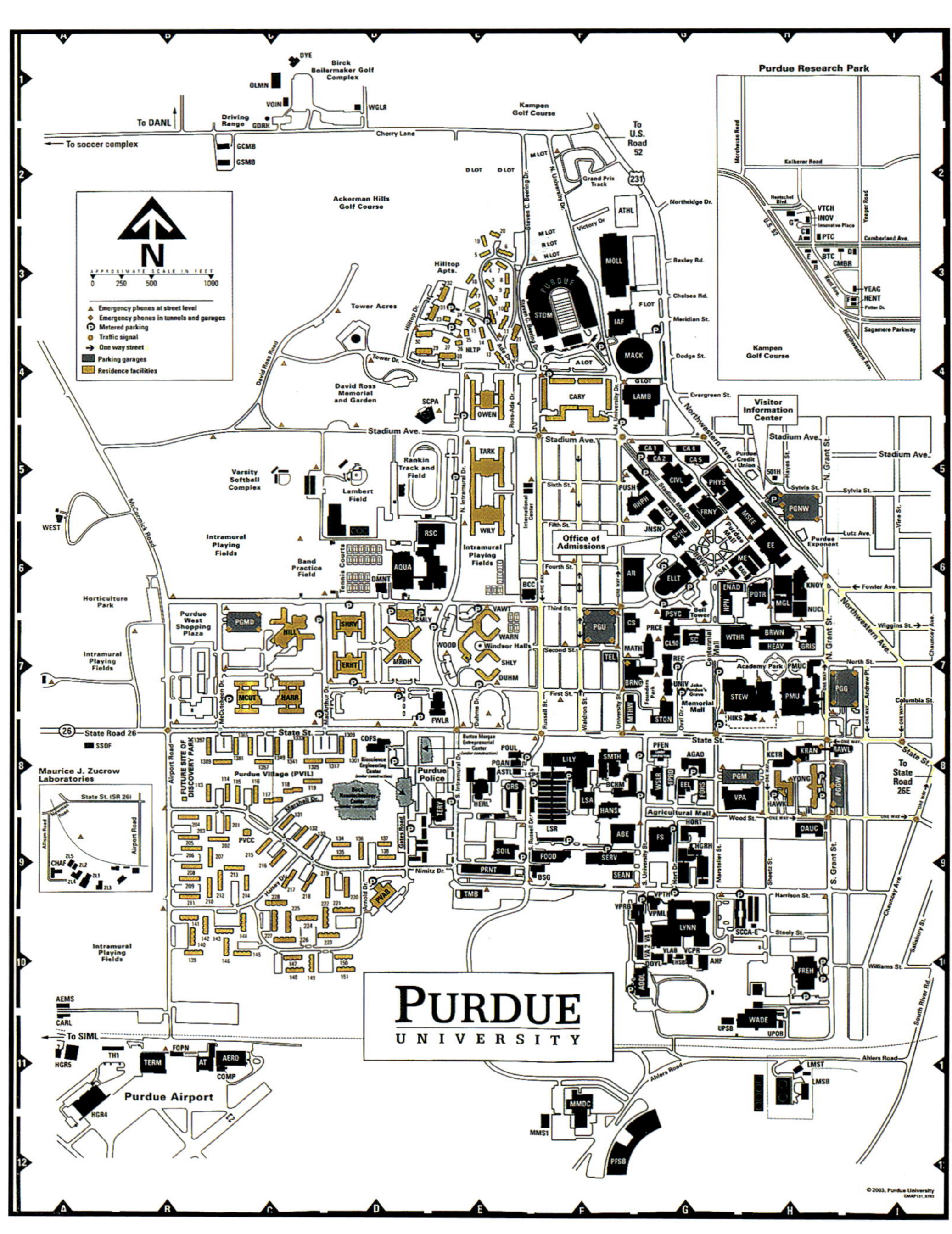

{Enrollment in 2000: 37,871 students[1]}

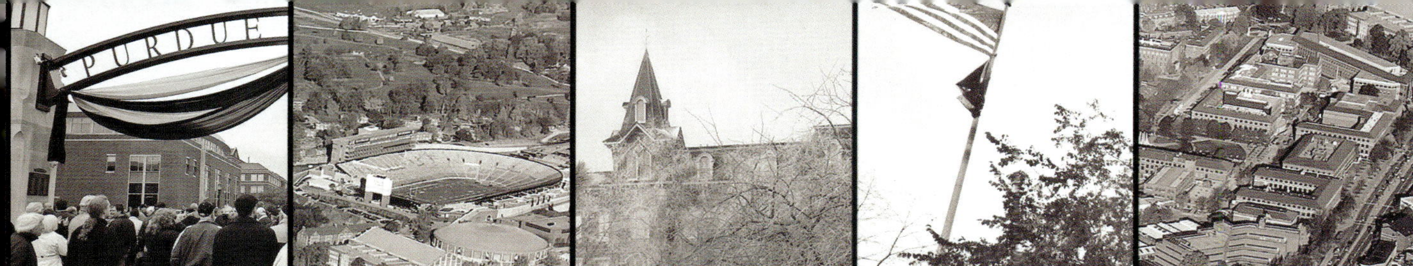

[The 2000s]

PURDUE AT 140

"When August comes around, college students have to prepare for campus life possibly for the first time. This seemingly ordinary month can mean only one thing for millions of teenagers throughout the World pursuing a higher level of education: it is time to leave home. College students everywhere must step out that familiar doorway, shove one last box in the car, run back and forth for forgotten knick-knacks and wave good-bye as they speed away."

—*Kristin Riermaier and Constance Murphy for the 2003* Debris *yearbook*[2]

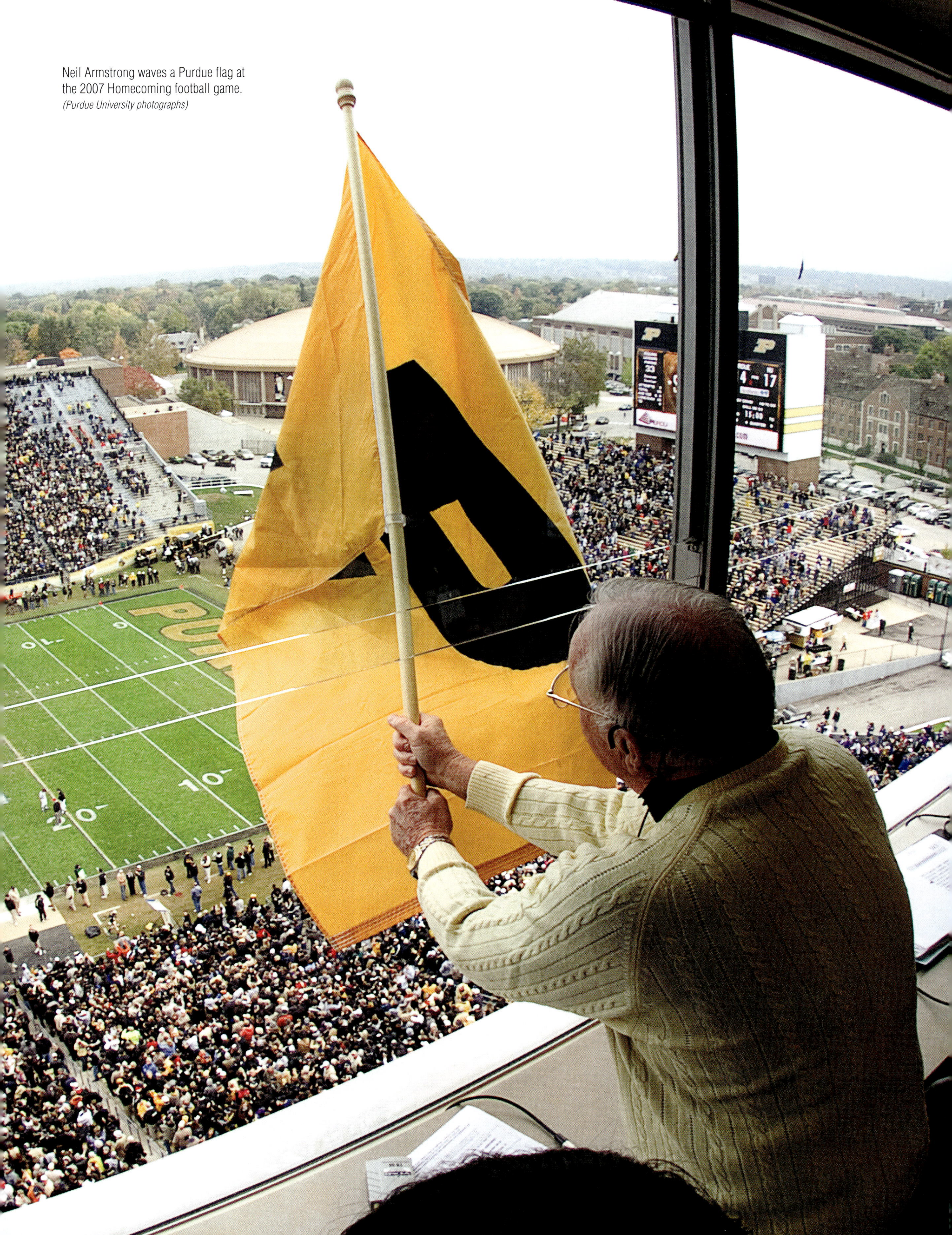

Neil Armstrong waves a Purdue flag at the 2007 Homecoming football game.
(Purdue University photographs)

The first Nearly Naked Mile, harkening back to the Nude Olympics, was run in 2007.[3]

The twenty-first century began with a new university president, a trip to the Rose Bowl, and a national tragedy; by the end of that first decade, the university welcomed another new president, a growing new campus core for discovery, and rapid change in communication technologies. ***"Boiler Up!"*** became a chant heard around the University and beyond.

Purdue embarked upon the new century with renewed vigor in many areas. Following the retirement of President Steven C. Beering, Martin C. Jischke began his tenure as the tenth president of Purdue University on August 14, 2000, just in time for fall semester classes to begin.

Personal and university-based technologies also changed the way in which the University and students carried about regular activities. By the mid-2000s MP3 players replaced CD players. Use of the internet in residence halls proliferated as more students purchased personal computers.

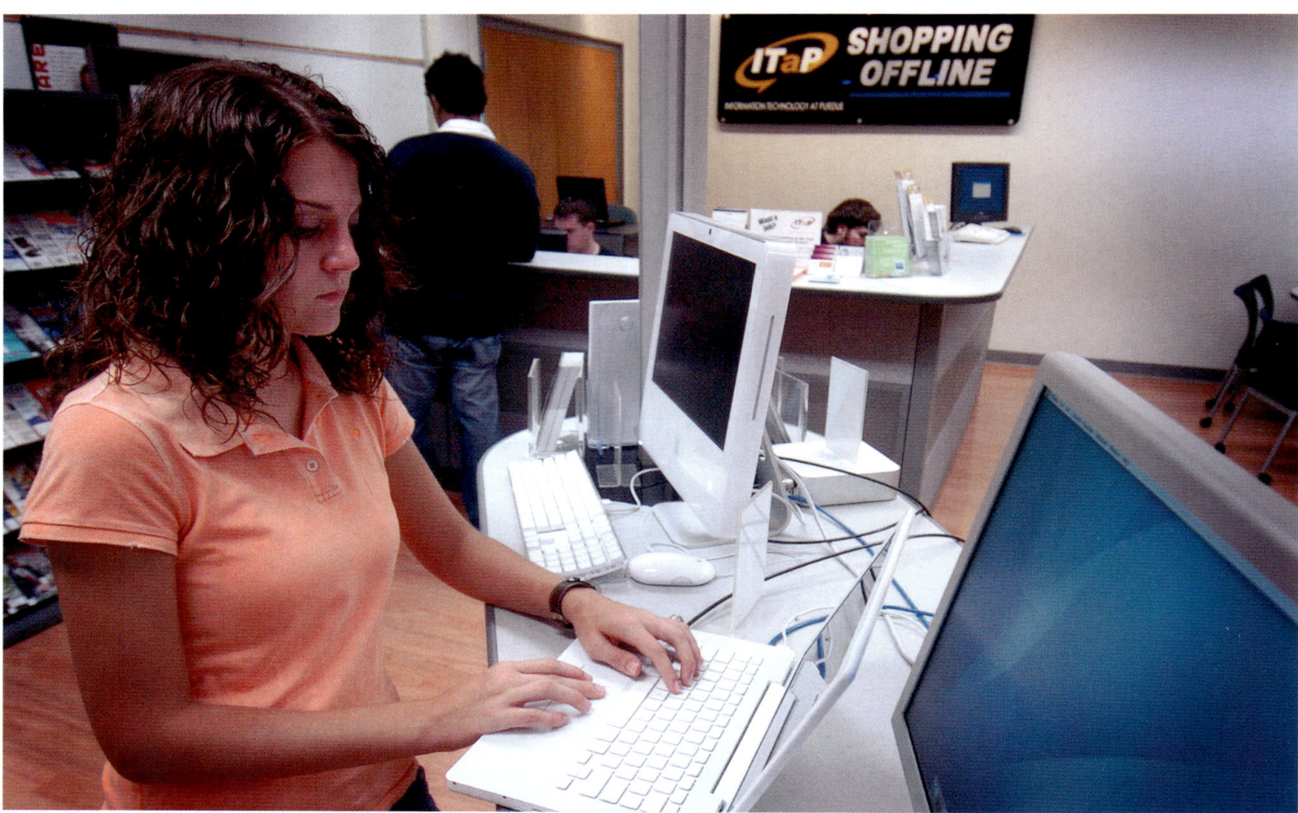

ITaP (Instructional Technology at Purdue) offering students and staff the opportunity to browse and purchase university-recommended computers, 2006.
(Purdue University photographs)

Technology became a tool not merely for coursework but for instant communication. Students used AOL Instant Messenger (AIM), Yahoo! Messenger, or ICQ for instantaneous chats with classmates or keeping up with family and friends. Conceptually, long-distance phone calls became more outdated. Music downloads and other peer-to-peer file sharing platforms became more prevalent. Facebook expanded to all college campuses, including Purdue. By decade's end, many students had exchanged desktop computers for laptops and flip phones for smartphones. WBAA, Purdue's radio station, maintained its long-standing position at the forefront of communications by webcasting its programs to a worldwide audience.

Purdue University students received online access to grades and class schedules in the year 2000 as the university launched SSINFO (Student Services Information).[4] Students of this era anxiously awaited 8:00 a.m. on the Wednesday following final exams for their grades to populate on the site. Class assignments, quizzes, and general information were available on WebCT/WebCTVista, a web-based course suite used by instructors. Prior to the start of the fall 2008 semester, Purdue moved to a new system for managing student course registration, schedules, financial information, and transcripts. The myPurdue portal was a significant change from SSINFO, which was based in the COBOL programming language.[5] For the first time in Purdue's history, students possessed the ability to review course catalogs and to register for classes online.[6]

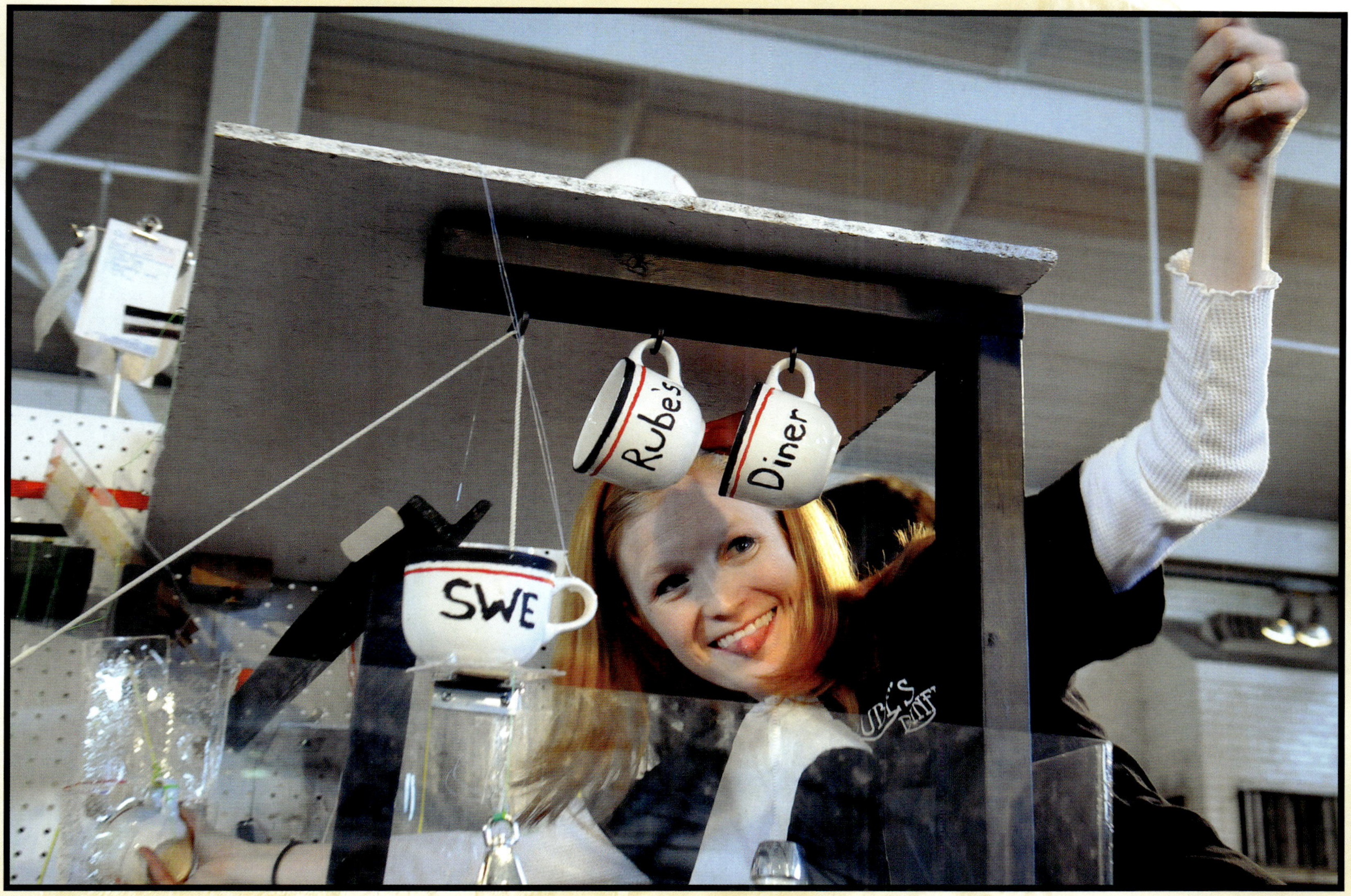

Above: Holly Mundt, a senior in industrial engineering from Fort Wayne, Indiana, helps set up her team's machine, Rube's Diner, during the 2008 Rube Goldberg Machine Contest. Her team, the Society of Women Engineers, placed third in the competition, which challenged teams to assemble hamburgers complete with four toppings and a bun. *(Purdue University photographs)*

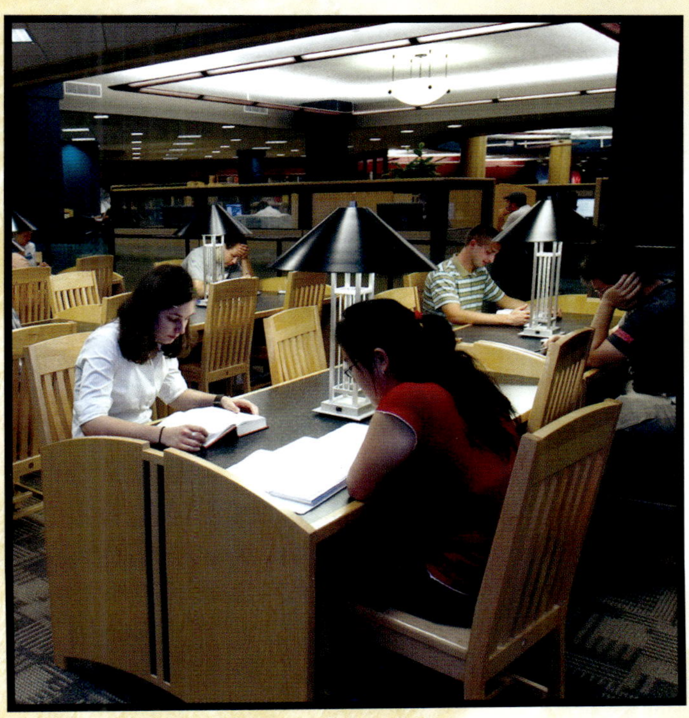

Right: Students at the Humanities, Social Science, and Education Library, 2005. *(Purdue University Libraries records)*

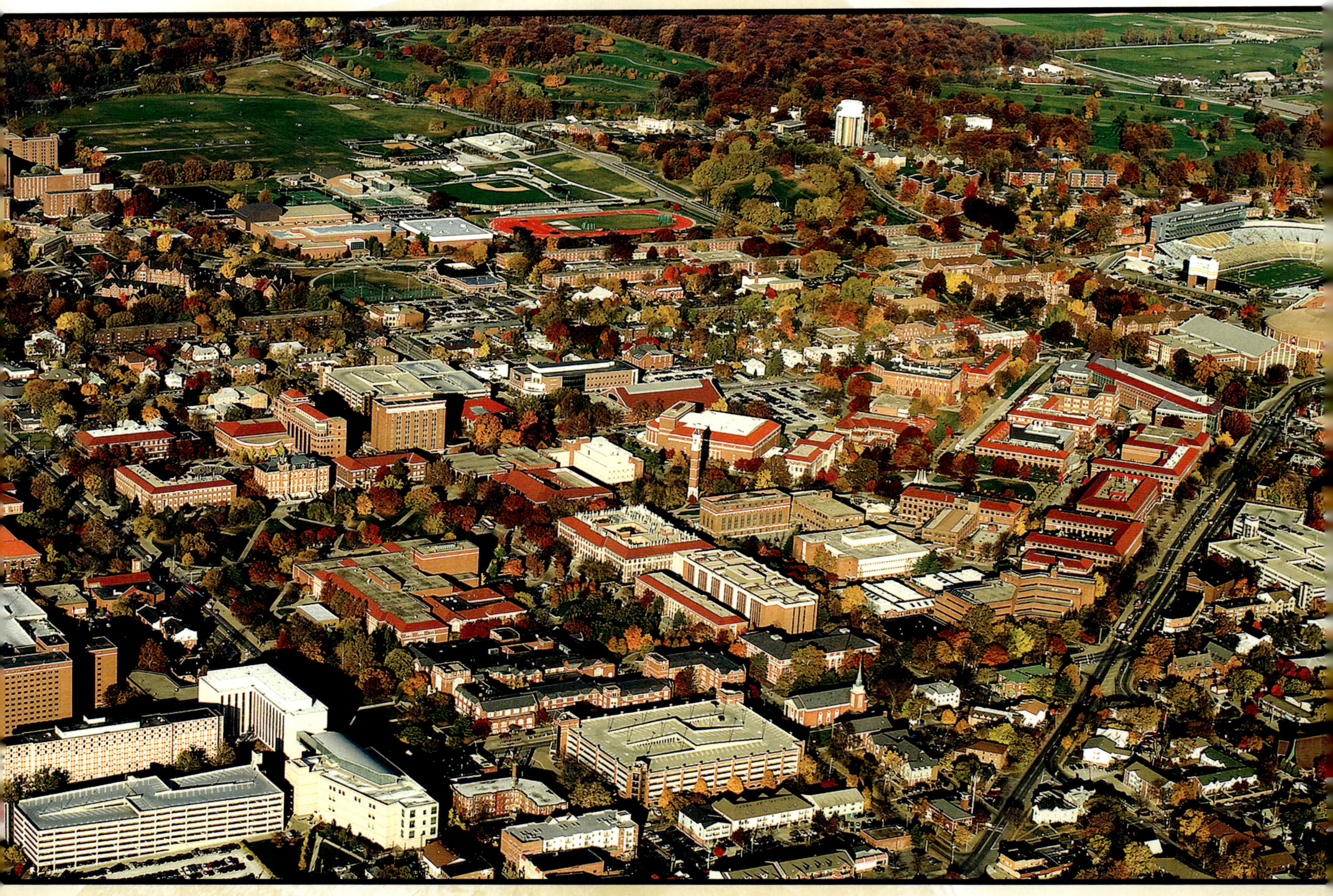

Above: Aerial view of the West Lafayette campus, November 2008. *(Purdue University Marketing and Media collection)*

Right: A statue of former faculty member and aviator Amelia Earhart outside of Earhart Hall, dedicated on April 16, 2009. Photo by Rebecca Wilcox. *(Purdue University Marketing and Media collection)*

Far right: Snow-covered lantern and gate at Windsor Halls, January 2005. *(Purdue University photographs)*

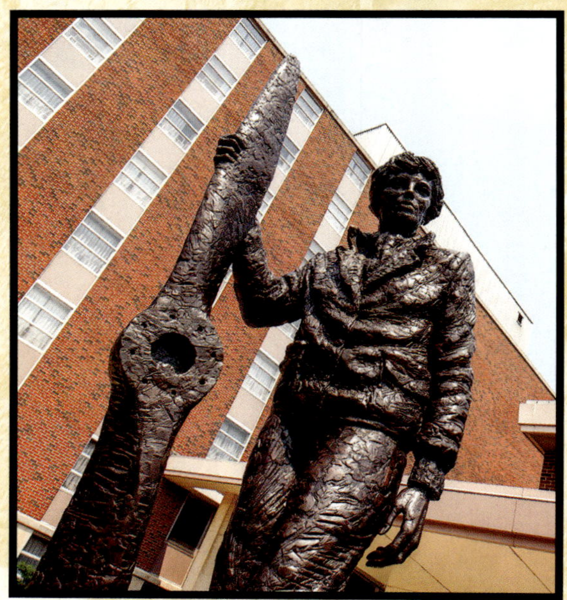

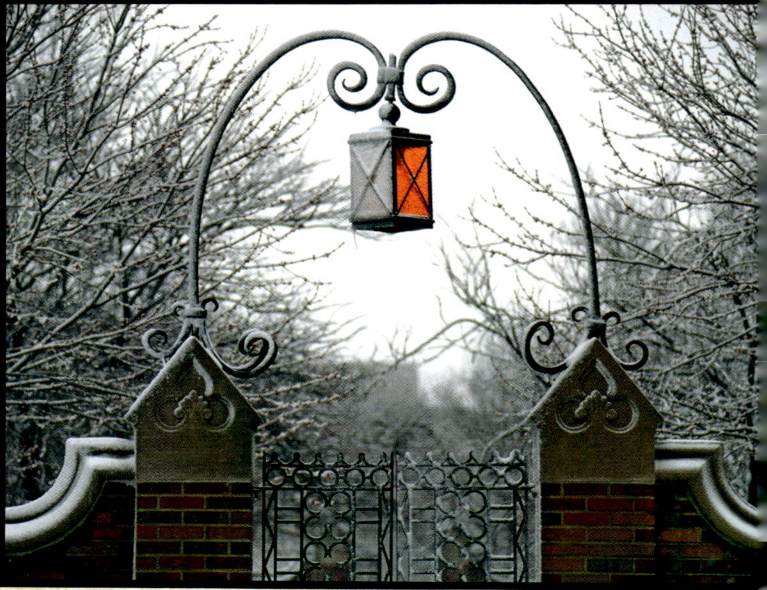

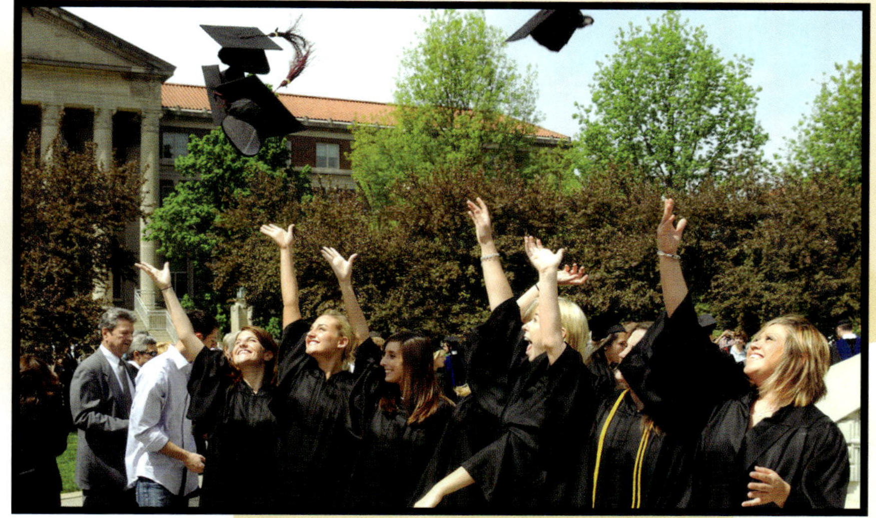

Left: Sisters from the Delta Zeta sorority at Purdue University toss their mortarboards in celebration of earning their degrees, 2008.
(Purdue University photographs)

Below left: "The Compliment Guys," students Brett Westcott and Cameron Brown gave out free compliments to passersby, 2009.
(Purdue University photographs)

Below right: Student on a Purdue campus lawn, April 2009.
(Purdue University Marketing and Media collection)

Bottom: Purdue Contemporary Dance Company Dance Works production of *Her Own Skin*, choreographed by student Michal Nevitt, spring 2007.
(Purdue University Division of Dance records)

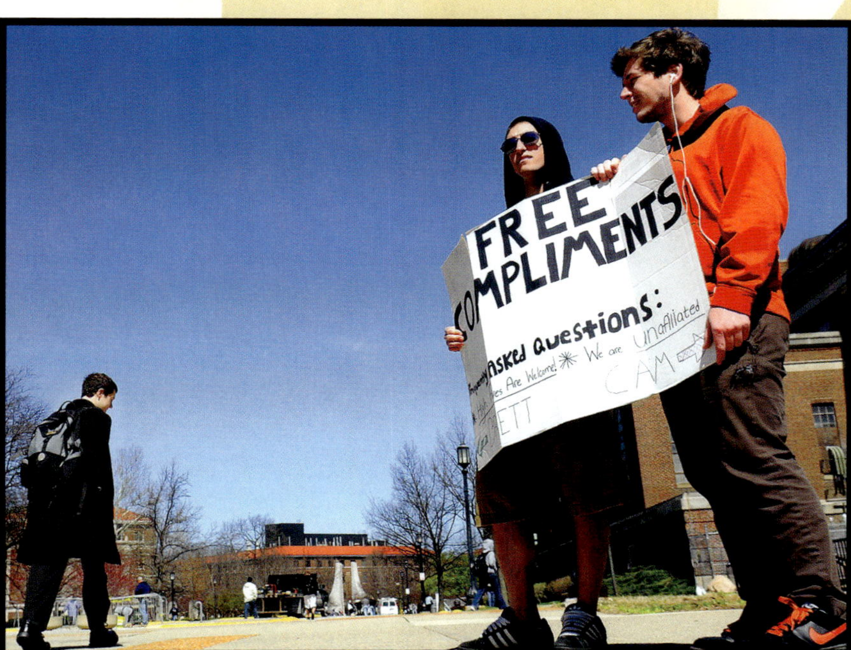

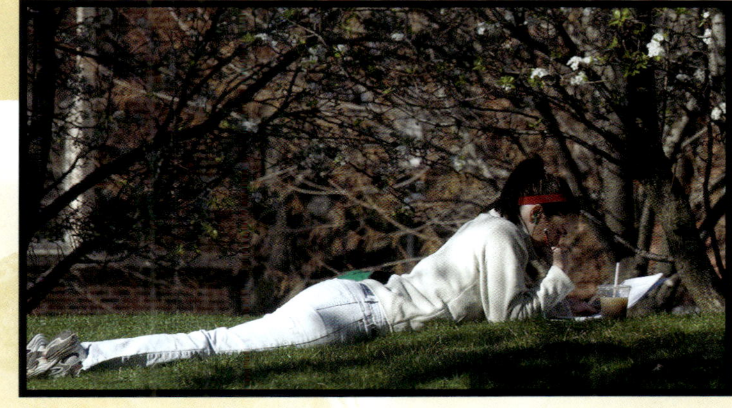

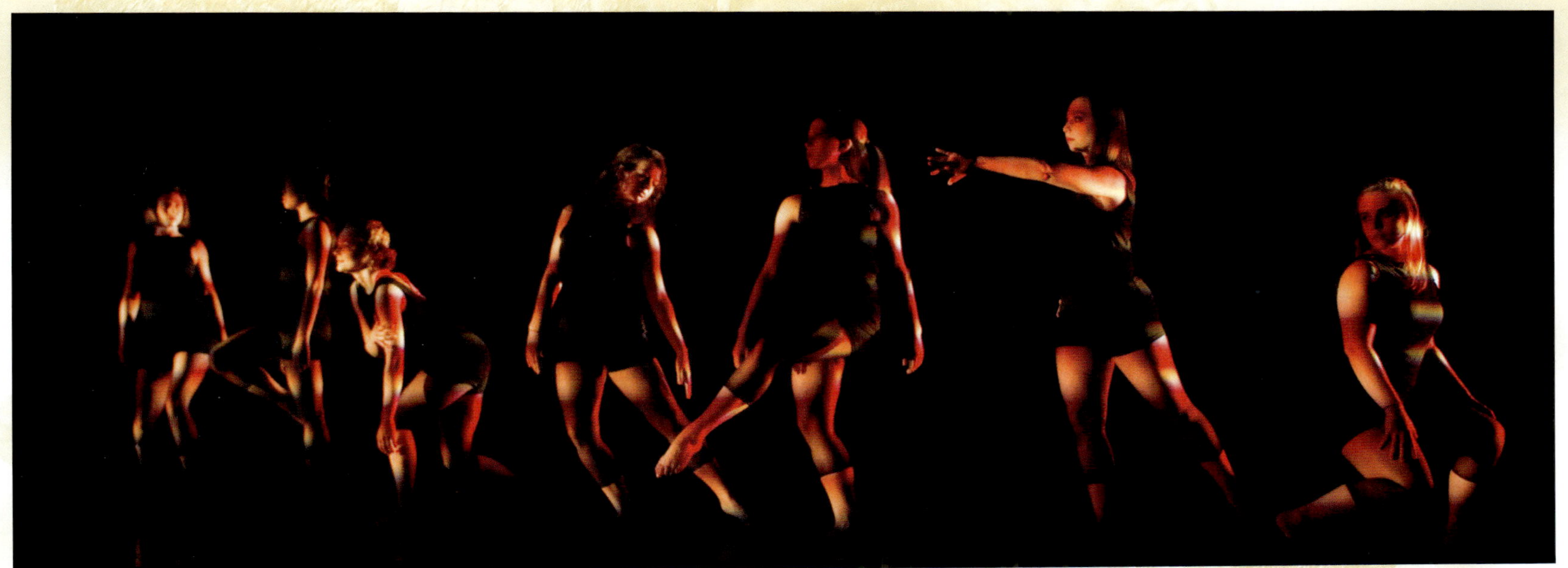

The 2000 Purdue football team won the Big Ten co-championship and a trip to the Rose Bowl. Led by star quarterback Drew Brees, Purdue's season included victories over Wisconsin, Michigan, and Ohio State. The trip to the Rose Bowl was the team's second overall visit and first in thirty-four years; the team faced the Pac-10 Conference champions, the Washington Huskies, in the marquee New Year's Day bowl game. The game was very competitive, yet the Huskies were the victors, 34–24.

Top: Coach Joe Tiller and quarterback Drew Brees celebrate invitation to the Rose Bowl after the Old Oaken Bucket game in Ross-Ade Stadium, November 1999. Photo by Tom Campbell. *(Purdue University Athletics collection)*

Below right: Team captain Akin Ayodele tackles a University of Washington running back during the Rose Bowl game, 2001. *(Purdue University Marketing and Media collection)*

Below left: 2001 Rose Bowl teddy bear by AT&T. *(Purdue University Archives and Special Collections Artifacts collection)*

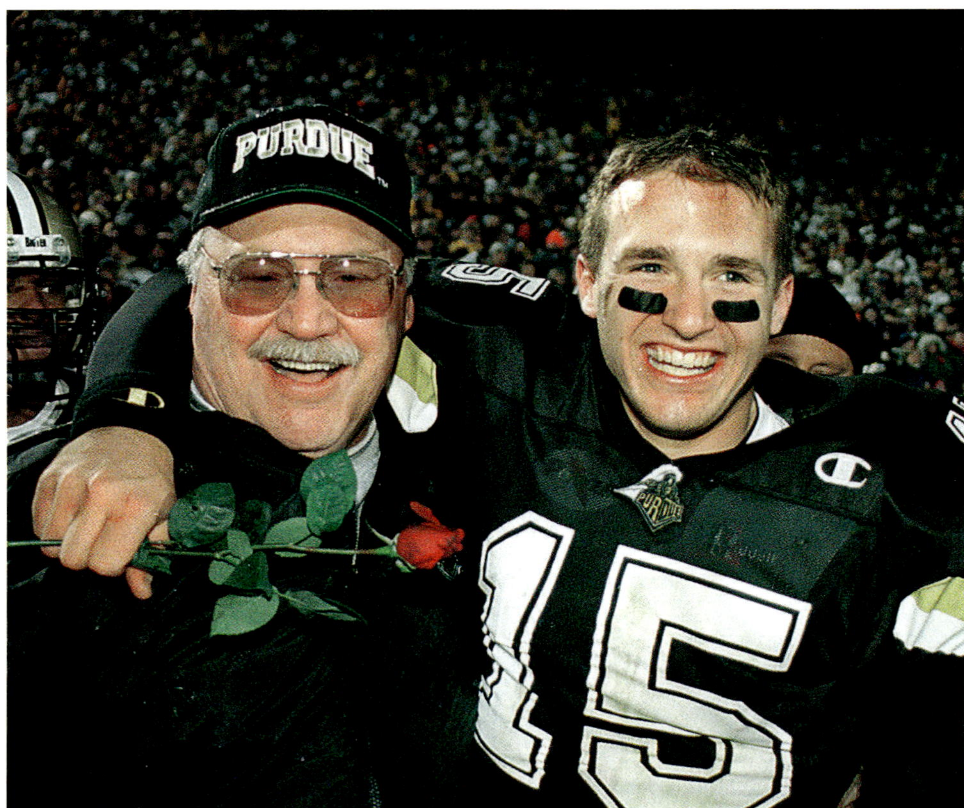

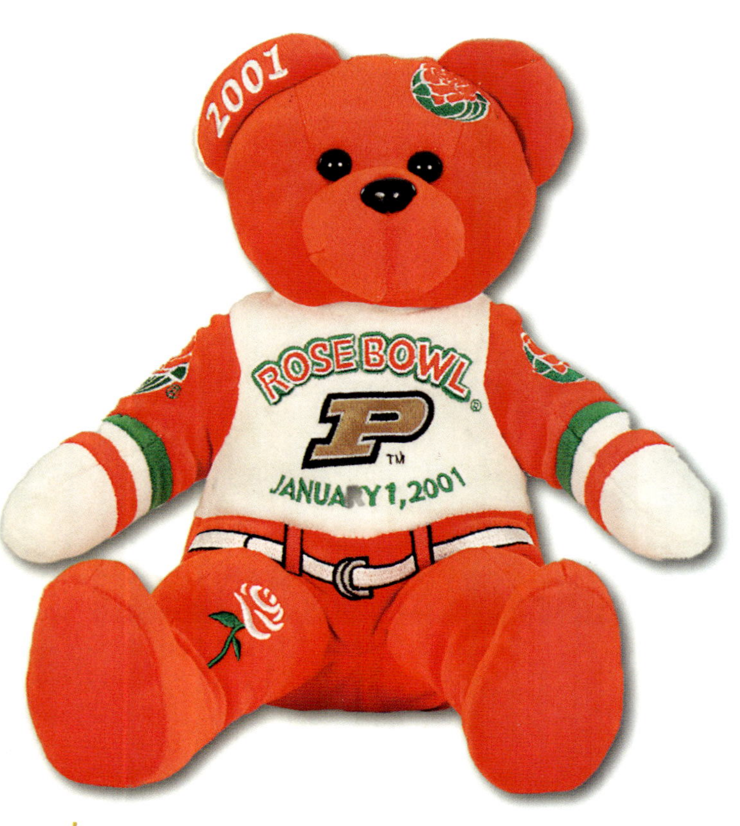

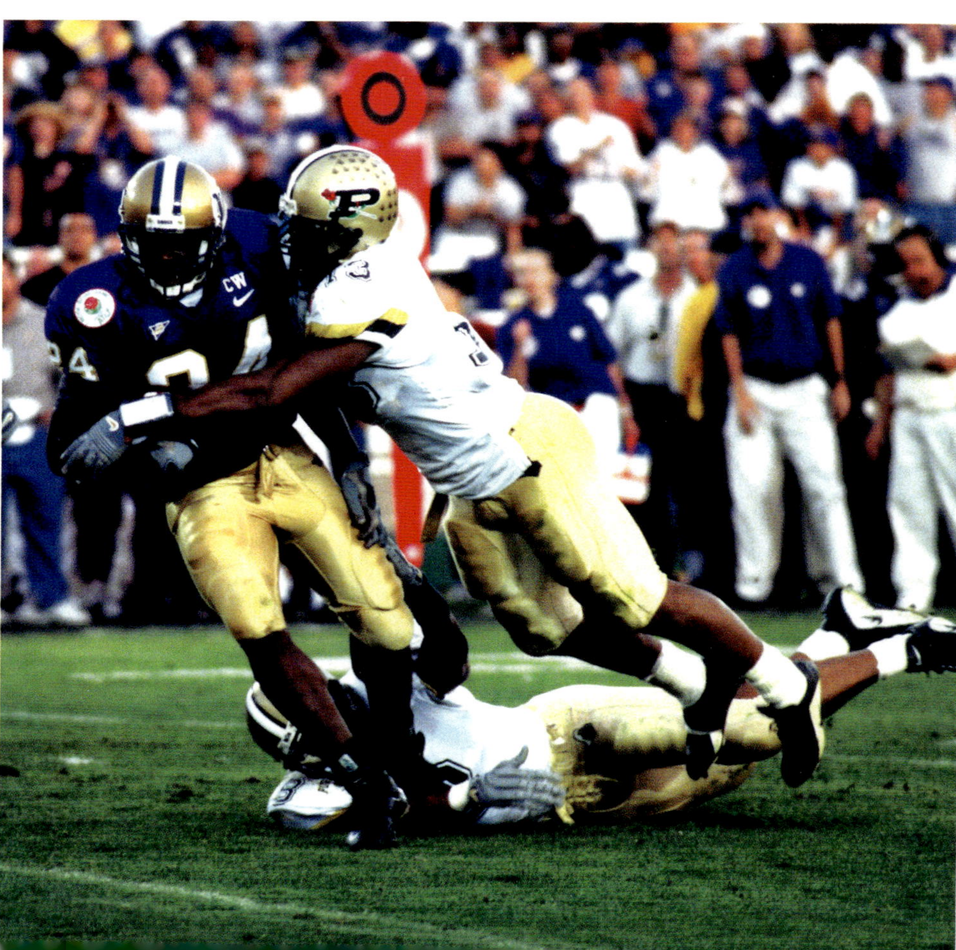

Left: Coach Tiller celebrates a victorious final game as Purdue head coach, November 22, 2008. *(Purdue University Marketing and Media collection)*

Right: Purdue vs. Wisconsin Homecoming 2004 poster. *(Purdue Broadsides collection)*

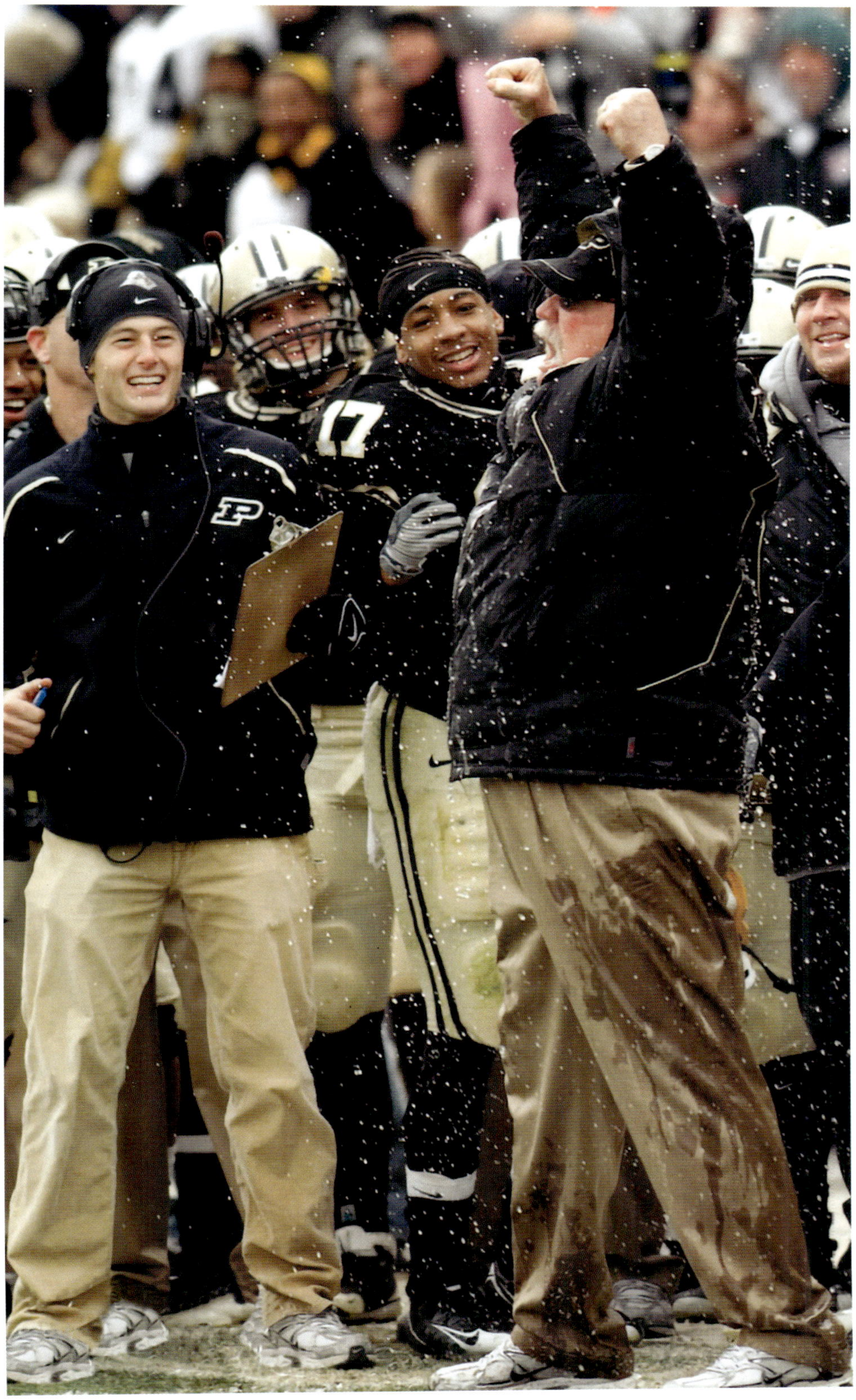

In October 2004, ESPN's College GameDay came to Purdue for the first time as the undefeated fifth-ranked Boilermakers hosted the twelfth-ranked Wisconsin Badgers for Homecoming. The Badgers won the hard-fought game following a late turnover by the Boilermakers.[7]

Despite the loss, the team continued to thrive under coach Joe Tiller and played in several bowl games throughout the remainder of the decade. Tiller retired in 2008 as the winningest football coach in Purdue history.[8]

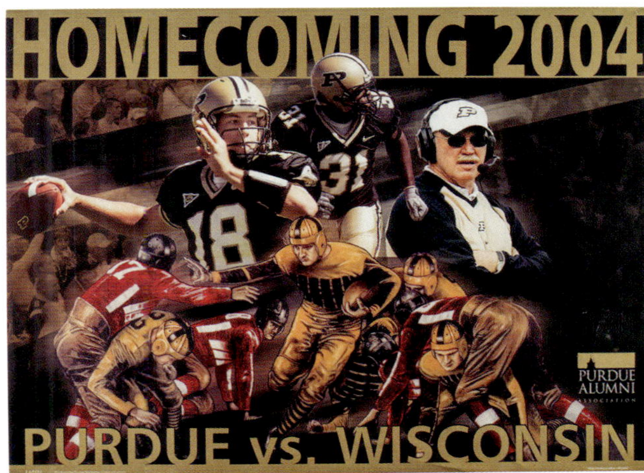

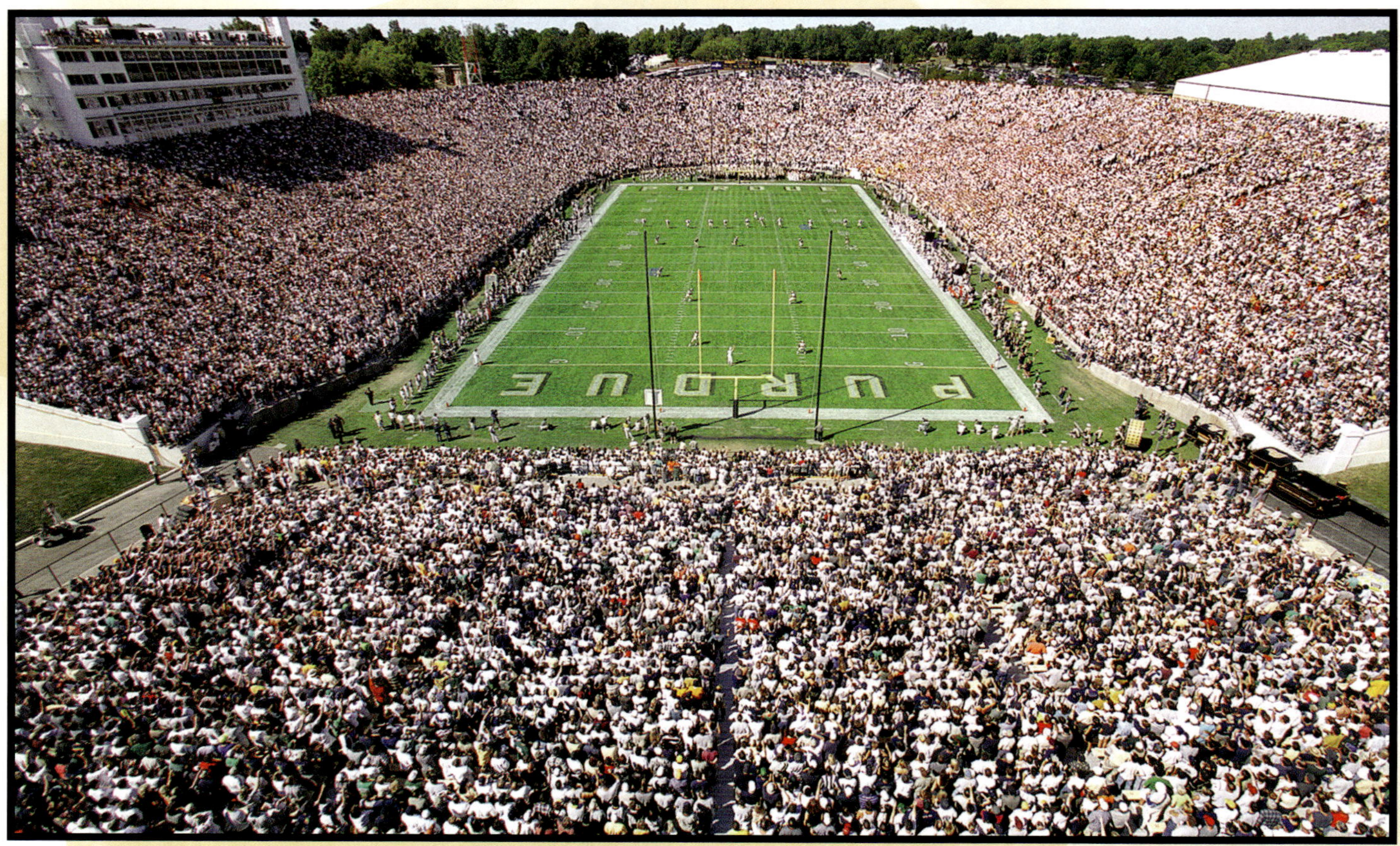

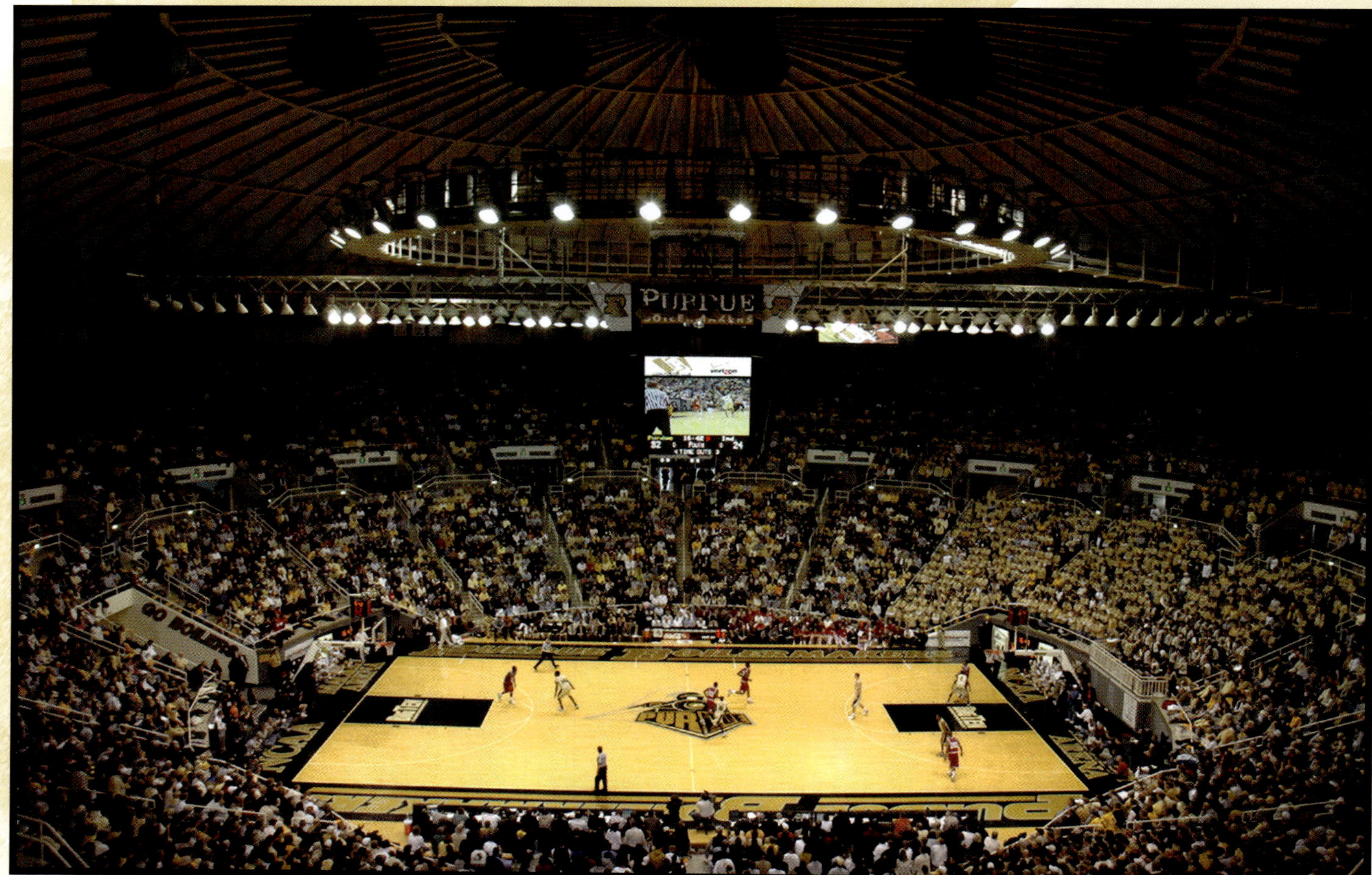

Top: Ross-Ade Stadium, 2005. *(Purdue University photographs)*

Bottom: Purdue men's basketball home game vs. Indiana University, January 15, 2005. *(Purdue University Marketing and Media collection)*

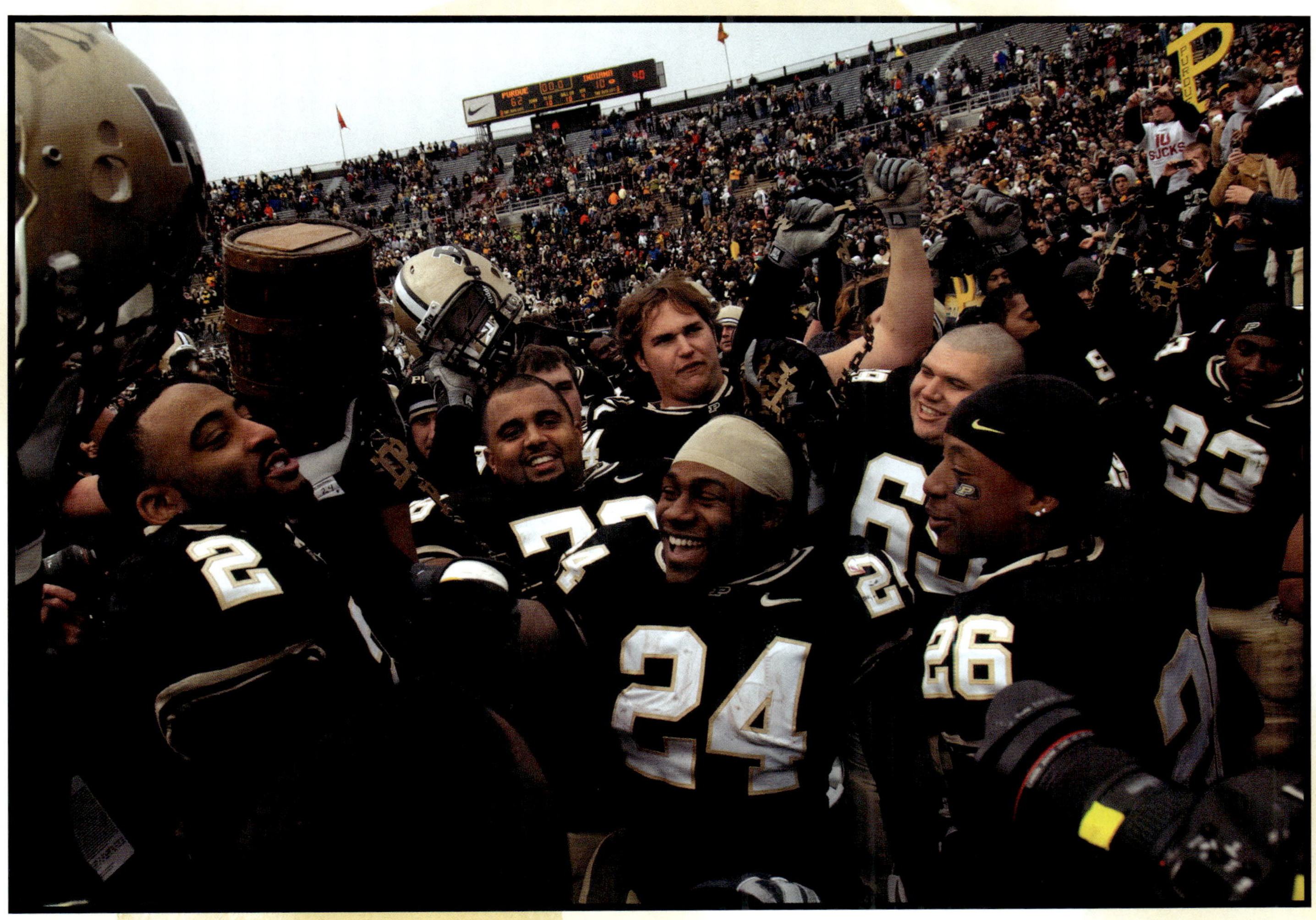

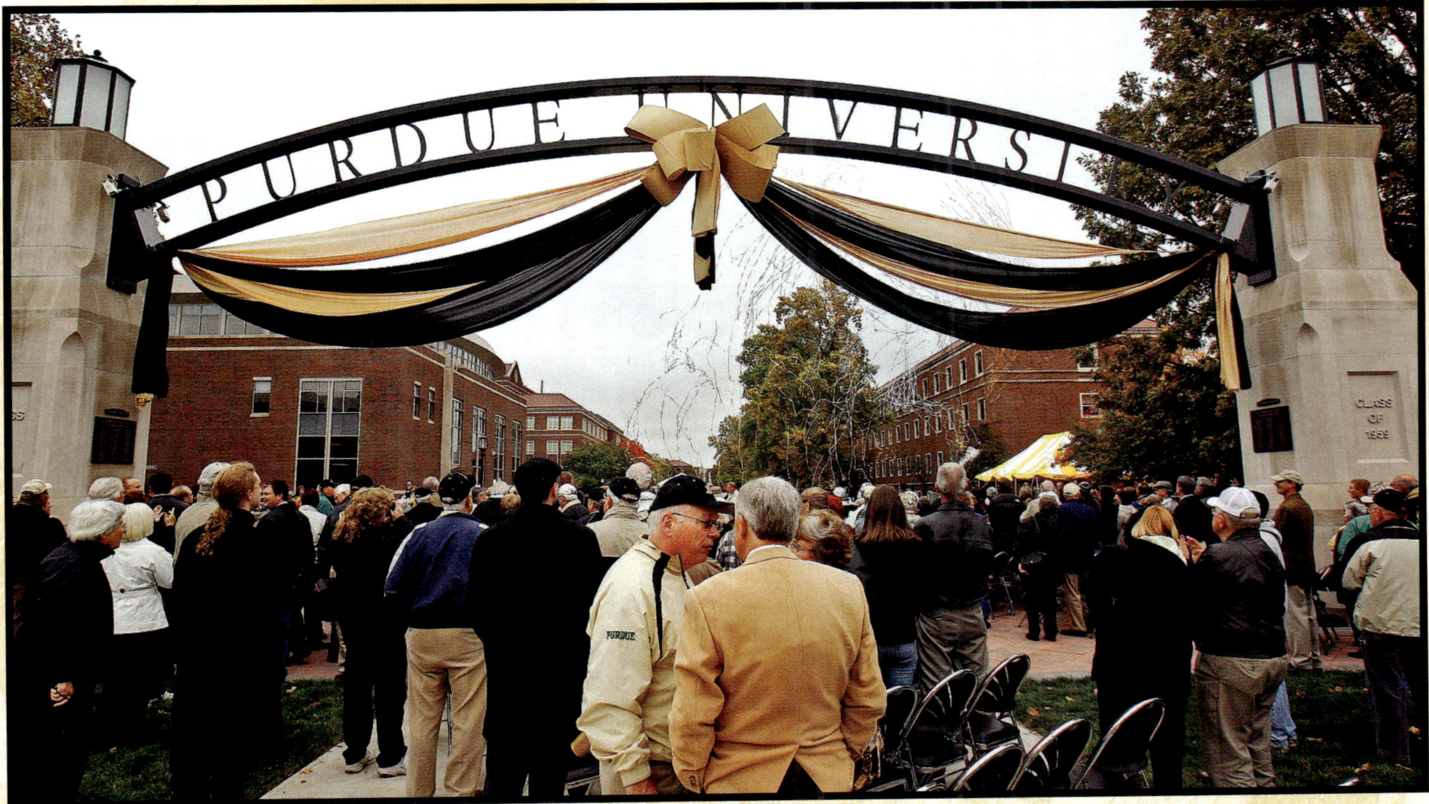

Top: Purdue football team celebrates winning the Old Oaken Bucket from IU, November 22, 2008. *(Purdue University Marketing and Media production samples)*

Bottom: Confetti flies through the air and guests cheer as the Gateway to the Future arch, a gift from the Classes of 1958 and 1959, is dedicated during Homecoming 2008. *(Purdue University photographs)*

Opposite page: Purdue basketball player E'Twaun Moore shoots during the game against Duke, December 12, 2008. *(Purdue University Marketing and Media collection)*

Below: Fans celebrate the women's basketball team for reaching the Final Four, 2001. *(Purdue University Marketing and Media collection)*

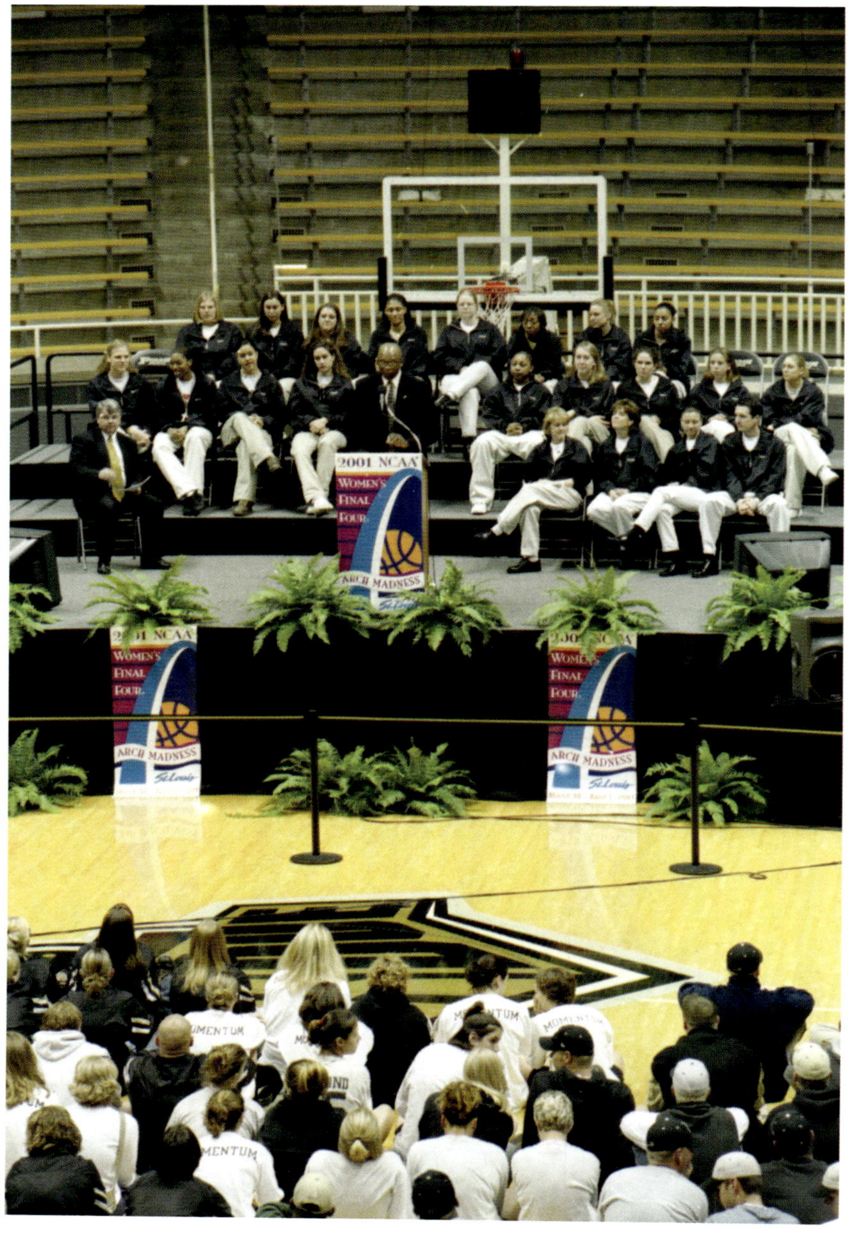

Other sports also flourished. Purdue tennis moved into a new facility, the Dennis J. and Mary Lou Schwartz Tennis Center, in December 2006. Women's golf celebrated a Big 10 title during its twenty-fifth anniversary year in 2000; in 2009 Maria Hernandez won the NCAA Individual Women's Golf Championship. The Purdue Crew became one of the top college rowing clubs in the country and, by decade's end, a new boathouse was under construction along the Wabash River.

Two years after winning the national championship, the Purdue women's basketball team again reached the Final Four and title game in 2001. Playing in-state rivals Notre Dame, star Katie Douglas and the Boilermakers eventually fell 68–66 in a disappointing end to a tremendous season. The team—coached until 2006 by Kristy Curry and 2006 onward by former Purdue player Sharon Versyp—continued its success throughout the decade, earning NCAA Tournament appearances and winning multiple Big Ten titles.

The men's basketball team continued its decades-long success, reaching the Elite Eight in 2000. Long-time coach Gene Keady retired in 2004 after reaching the NCAA Tournament eighteen times during his twenty-five years as head coach. The court in Mackey Arena was named Keady Court in honor of Coach Keady. Former Purdue player and assistant coach Matt Painter succeeded Keady as head coach. The men's team remained nationally ranked, as the trio of Robbie Hummel, E'Twaun Moore, and JaJuan Johnson led the Boilers to the Big Ten Tournament championship and NCAA Tournament Sweet Sixteen in 2009.

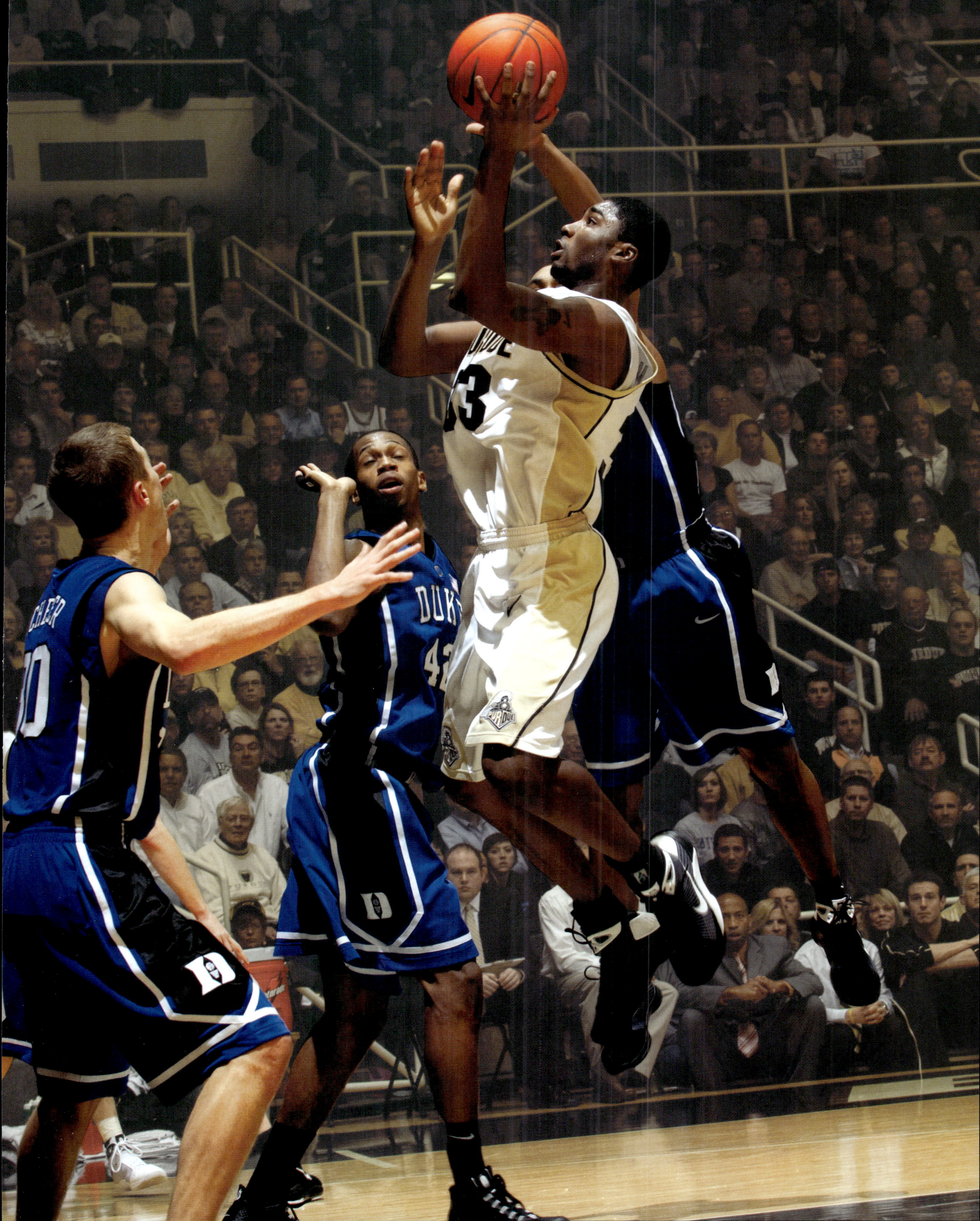

September 11

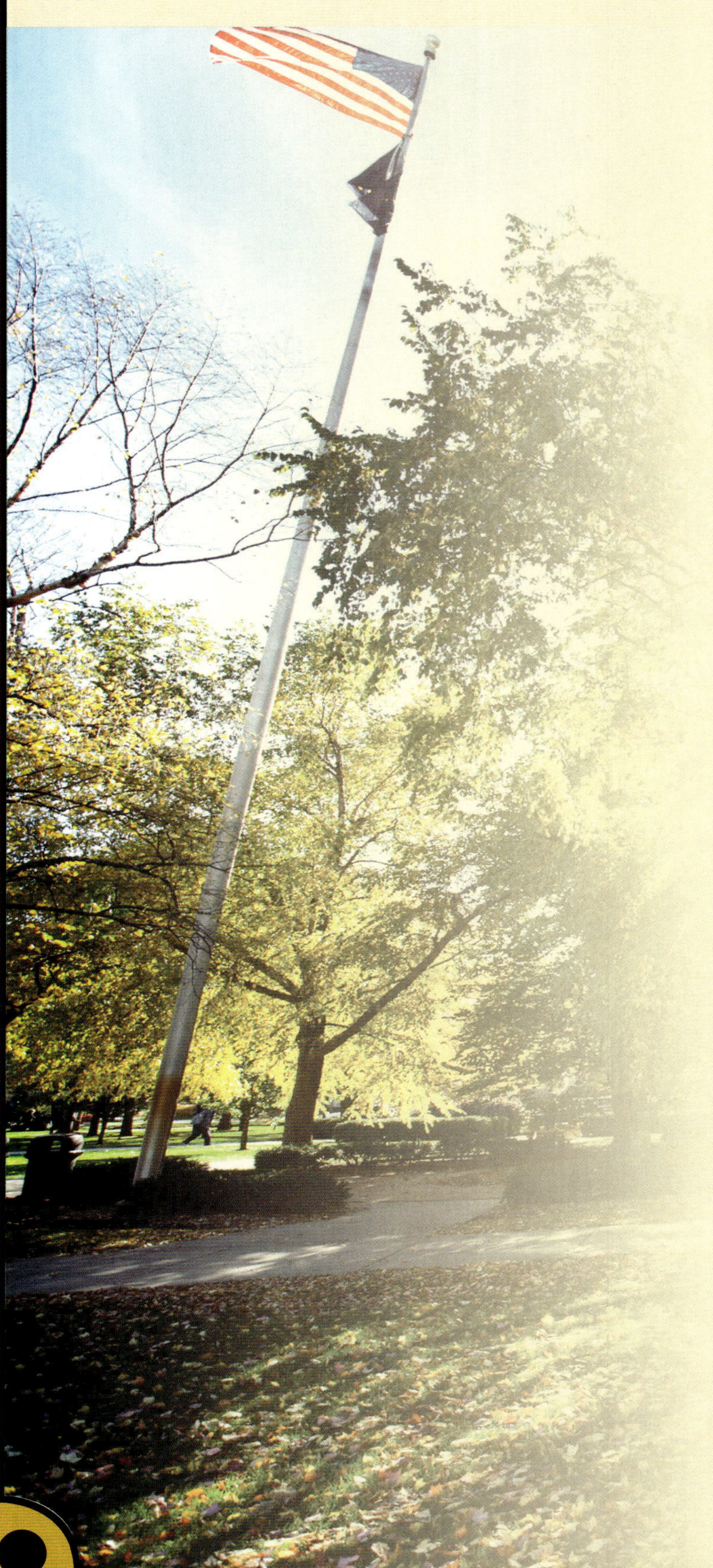

The terrorist attacks on September 11, 2001, left an indelible mark upon all Americans; Purdue University was no different. As the news spread across campus, first by word of mouth and then through news reports, students continued to attend classes. Few students possessed cell phones in 2001, and frantic landline long-distance calls were made to loved ones. In the Memorial Union, a large crowd stood in rapt attention around the large television in the basement dining area. Outside, students stopped between classes to give blood at an American Red Cross Bloodmobile parked near Schleman Hall of Student Services. In the days that followed, memorial services were held in honor of the victims of the attacks, and students announced a plan to raise $60,000 for the American Red Cross.

The American flag flies on the Purdue campus. Photo by Matthew Thomas. *(Purdue University Marketing and Media collection)*

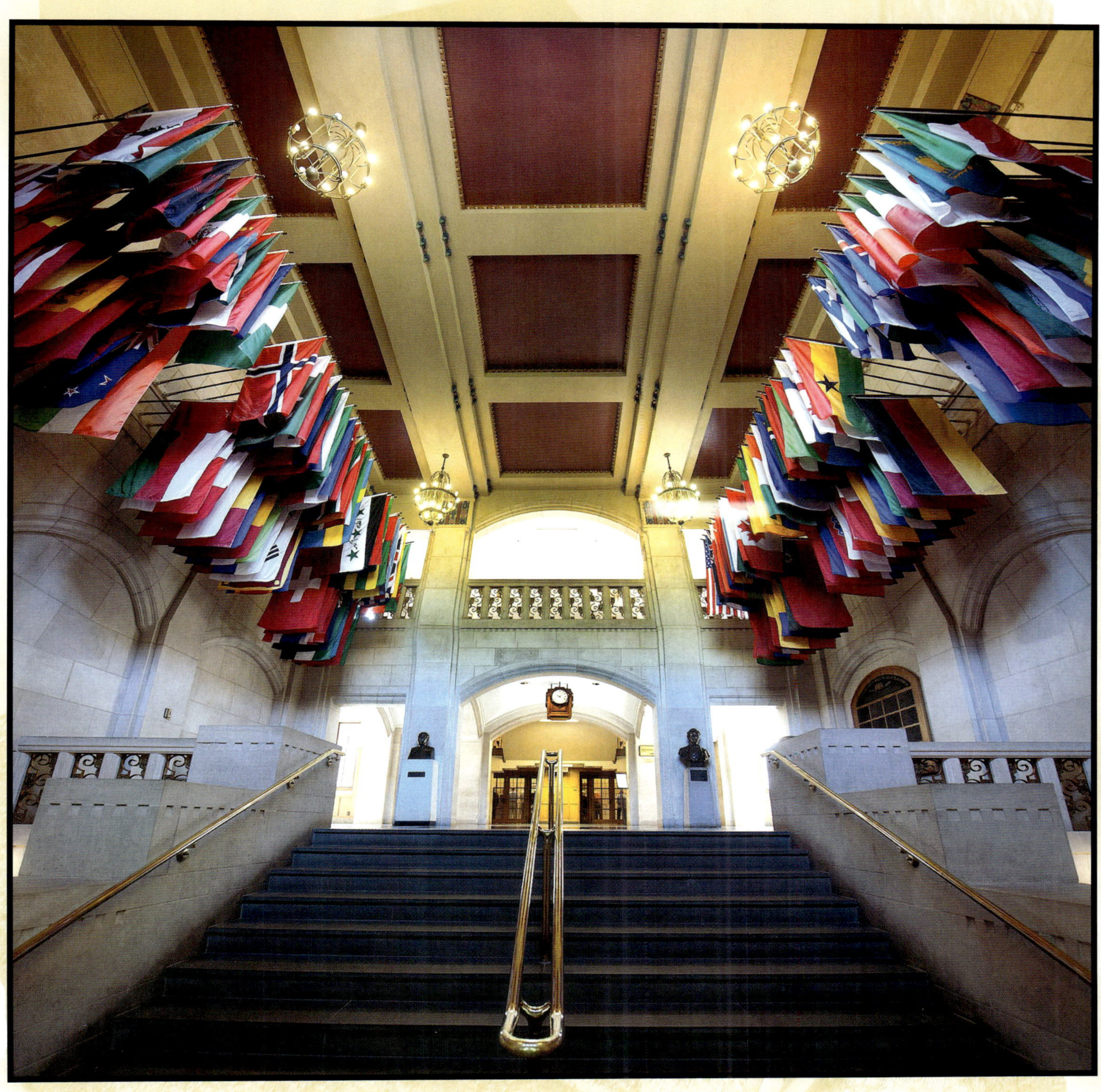

The International Flag Display in the Purdue Memorial Union, established by the Iron Key student honorary in 2006 to represent the home countries of all students at Purdue. Photo by Mark Simons. *(Purdue University Marketing and Media collection)*

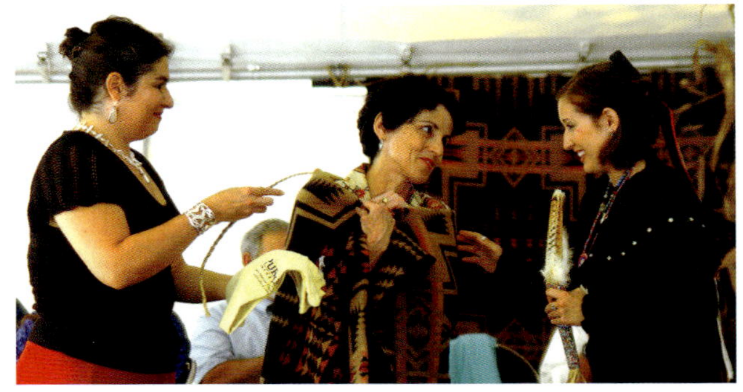

as the Engineering Fountain. Due to safety concerns regarding the high-pressure waterworks, the fountain was turned off in 2001 while a campus committee discussed options. In September 2001, a large cylindrical tube was placed at the center of the fountain to prevent direct contact with the water as it jetted upward.[11] The fountain run tradition continued—albeit with a change or two.

President Jischke retired in 2007 and France A. Córdova was named as the first female president of the university on July 16, 2007. Soon after President Córdova joined Purdue, she welcomed the creation of the Native American Educational and Cultural Center to campus.[9] The Center joined the Latino Cultural Center, created in 2003, as newly established resources available in the community.

For decades, a rite of passage for incoming students had been the fountain run—a gallop through cool jets of water on hot August days. Older alumni may recall racing through the Loeb Fountain outside of Hovde Hall before it moved to Founders Park; younger alumni will remember the Engineering Fountain in the days before a large tube stood in its center. Yet for a time in the early 2000s, fountain runs were imperiled. In Founders Park, Loeb Fountain access was restricted and the fountain turned off for more than a year from 2001 to 2002. Eventually a renovation of the fountain took place to ease safety worries, and fountain runs continued unabated.[10] Meanwhile, debate raged on campus regarding the fate of the Class of 1939 Water Sculpture, better known

New partnerships and endeavors in diversity and inclusiveness took place. For the first time, the Jahari Dance Troupe joined the "All-American" Marching Band during a halftime show in 2001. That year, the Black Cultural Center and the Office of Human Relations sponsored a lecture about race and acceptance from National Association for the Advancement of Colored People (NAACP) president Kweisi Mfume.

Social clubs and student traditions old and new made their mark on the 2000s. The number of student organizations continued to grow. Boiler Gold Rush, founded in the 1990s, grew significantly in importance to incoming freshmen. In 2006 the university created a new tradition as part of Boiler Gold Rush: crossing the tracks. Replica railroad tracks were installed between Stanley Coulter Hall and Wetherill Hall near the site where railroads once traveled a century prior. Students then "crossed the tracks" to signify their entrance into the university. Meanwhile, activities such as Big Man on Campus and the Purdue University Dance Marathon raised money for charity.

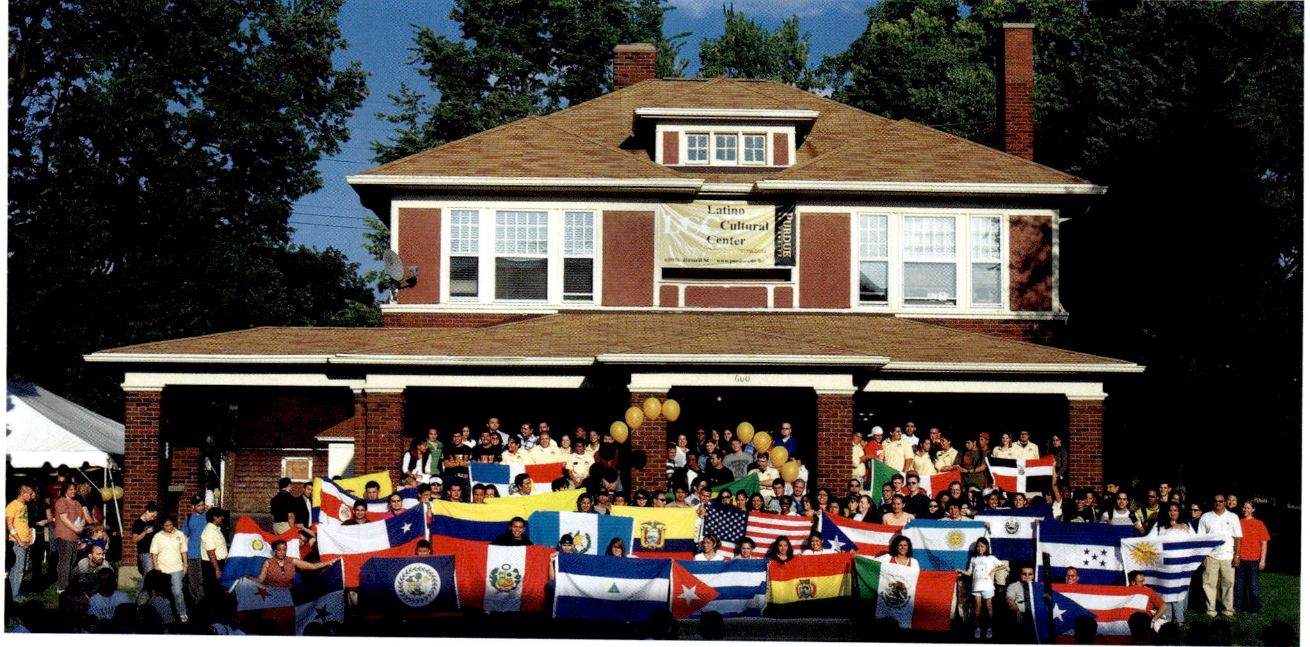

Top: Verónica Hirsch and graduate student Candice Guy present a Pendleton blanket as a gift to Purdue president France A. Córdova during the October 6, 2007, dedication ceremony of the University's Native American Educational and Cultural Center. Photo by Dave Umberger. *(Purdue University News Service photographs)*

Right: Opening of the Latino Cultural Center, 2006. *(Purdue University photographs)*

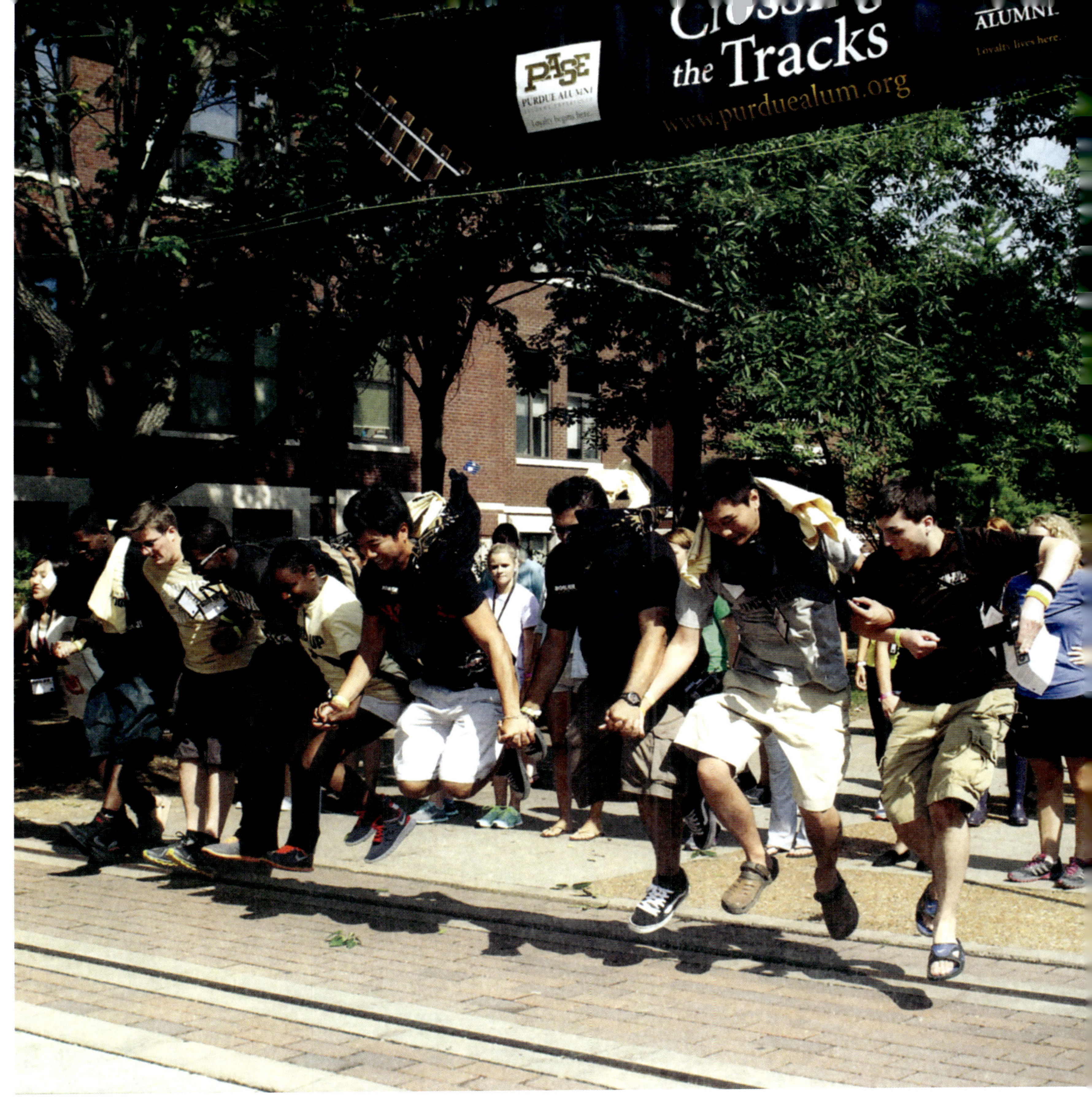

Freshmen "cross the tracks" during the 2014 Boiler Gold Rush. *(Purdue University Marketing and Media production samples)*

Less philanthropic was the Breakfast Club, held the mornings of home football games and the Grand Prix race. Breakfast Club began in the late 1980s, as students awoke early on football game days and traveled to local bars for drinks.[12] By the 2000s, Purdue students had added dressing in costumes to this uniquely Purdue tradition. When speaking about Breakfast Club, the 2001 *Debris* yearbook designated barhopping as "Purdue's Pastime."[13]

Sadly, a Purdue tradition ceased in 2008 as the *Debris* discontinued following its release that year. The yearbook was published continuously from 1889 to 2008, producing an annual (two issues were produced in 1893, 1943, and 1972) compendium of student life and student activities. The rise of social media, declining student interest, and production costs were cited as reasons to end the yearbook.[14]

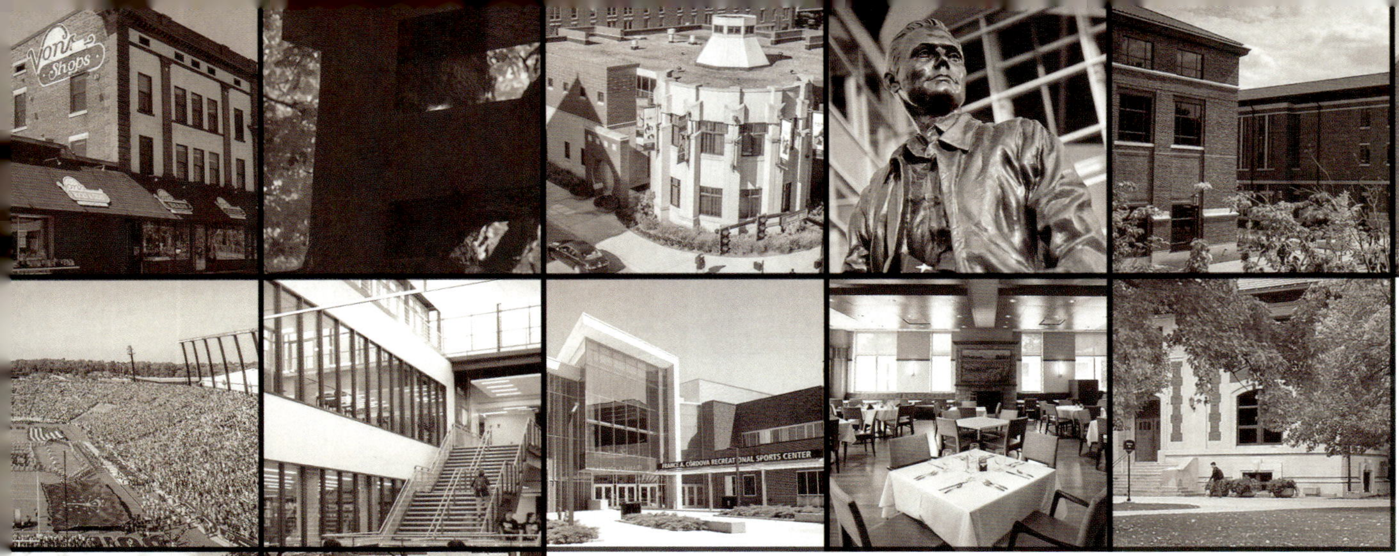

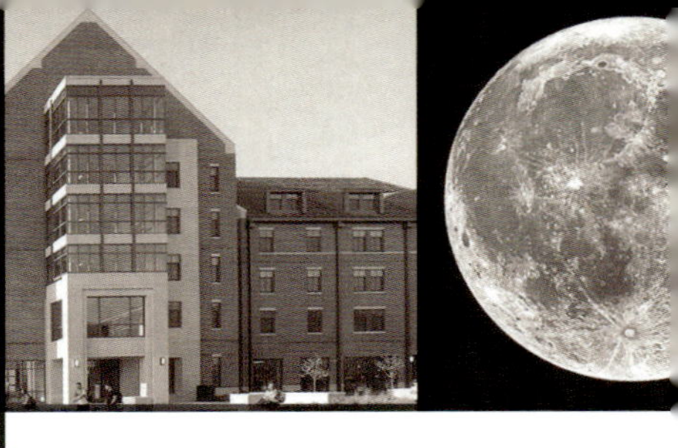

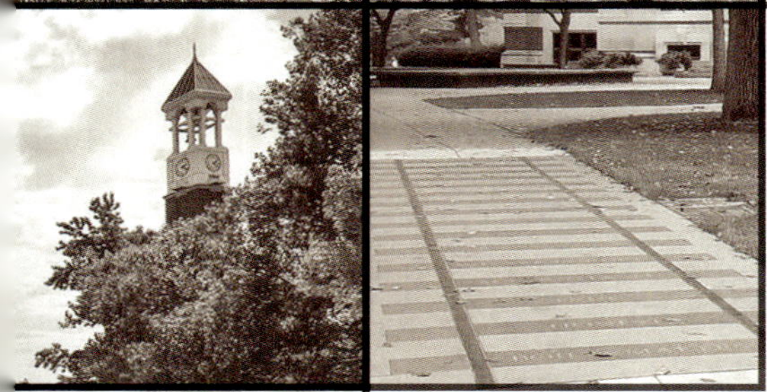

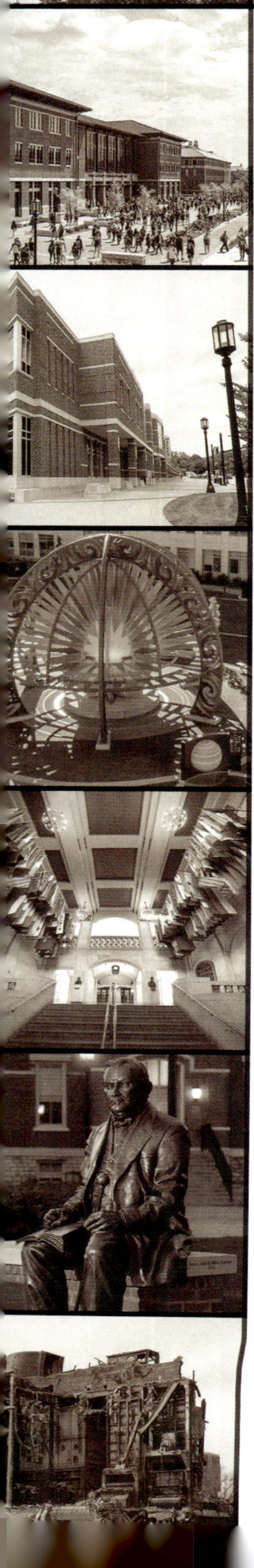

Purdue University West Lafayette campus map, 2017. *(Campus Maps collection)*

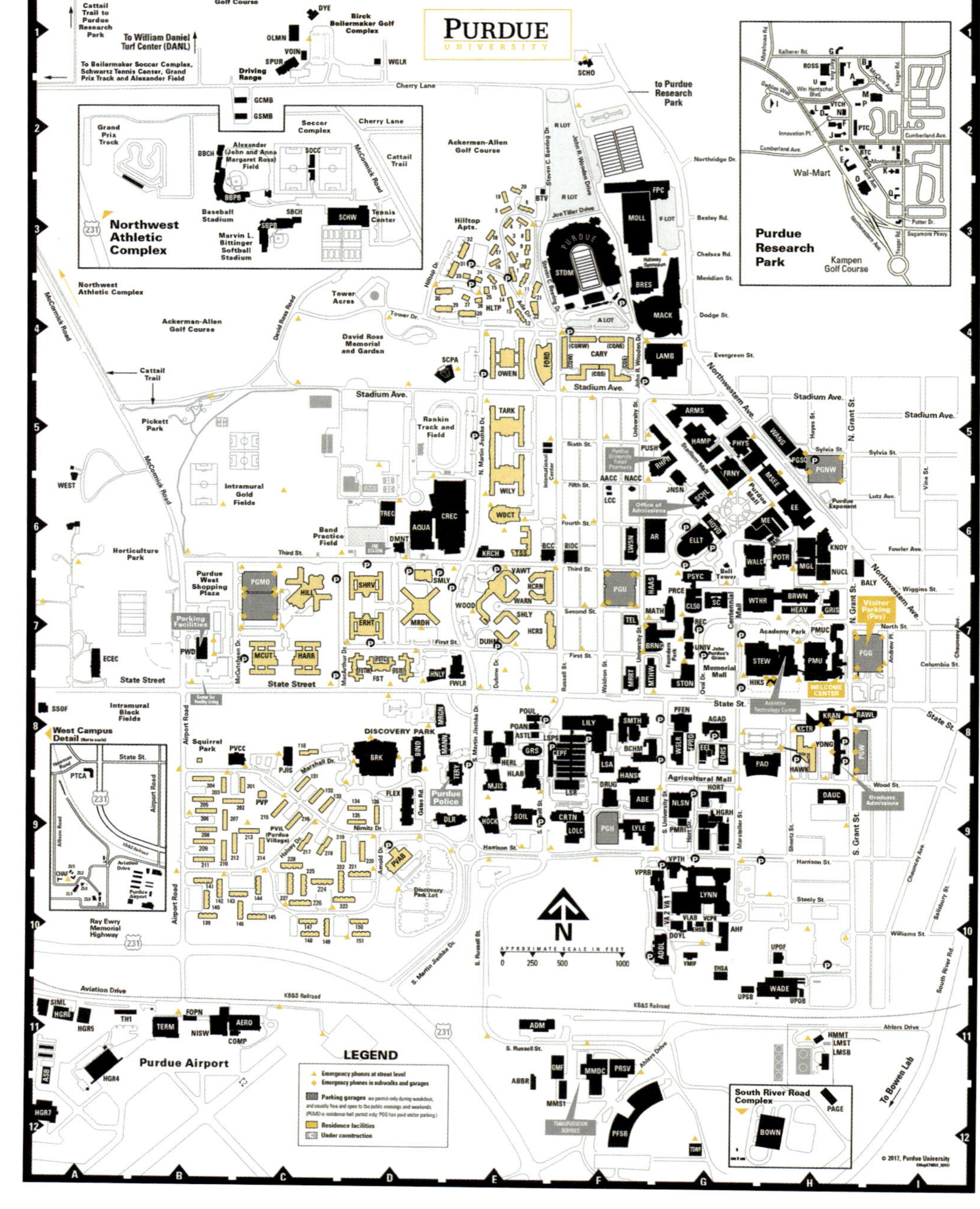

{Enrollment in 2010: 39,726[1]}

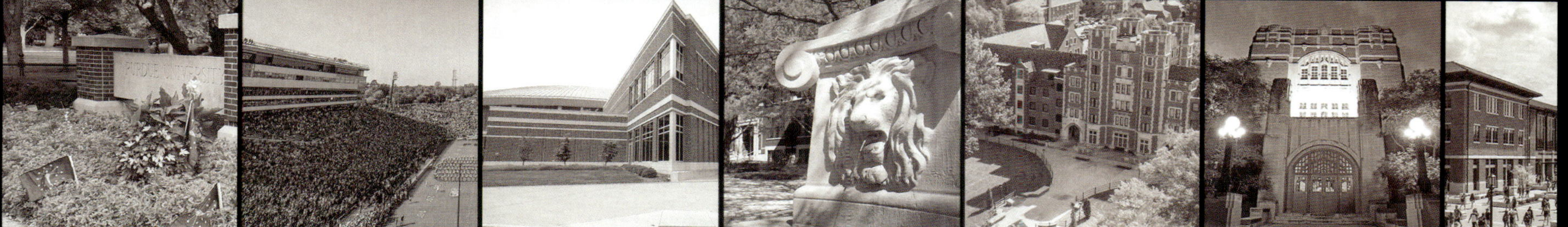

[The 2010s]

PURDUE AT 150

"When I think Purdue, I think of this massive campus but it's also very small. You . . . see the same faces, and the same things, and it feels like home when you're there. I love Purdue."

—*Becca Lax, class of 2020*[2]

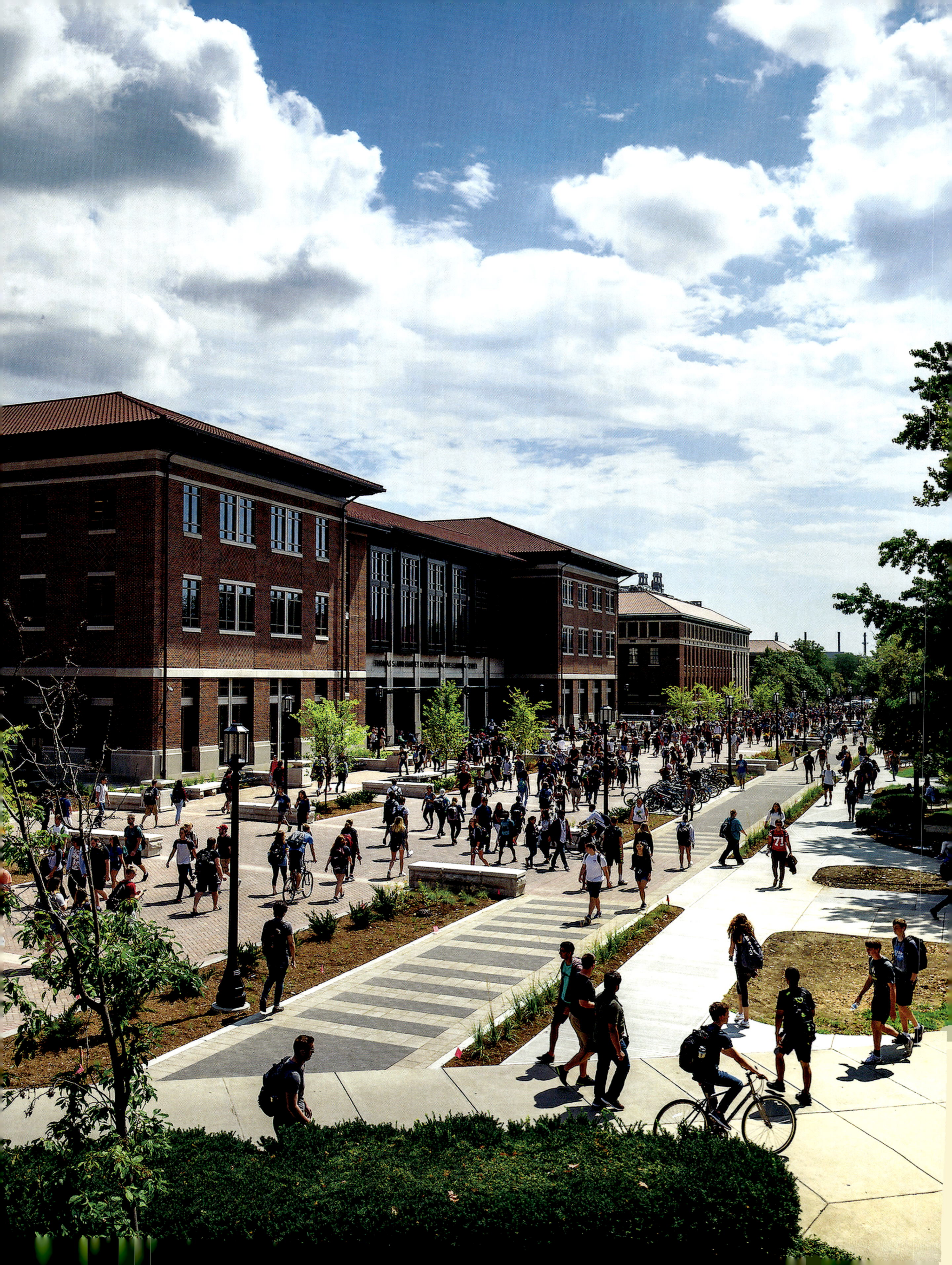

Opposite page: Brick walkway outside the Wilmeth Active Learning Center, 2017.
Photo by Alex Kumar. *(Purdue University Marketing and Media collection)*

Left: Students researching in the Wilmeth Active Learning Center Mullins Reading Room.
Photo by Teresa M. Brown. *(Purdue University Libraries records)*

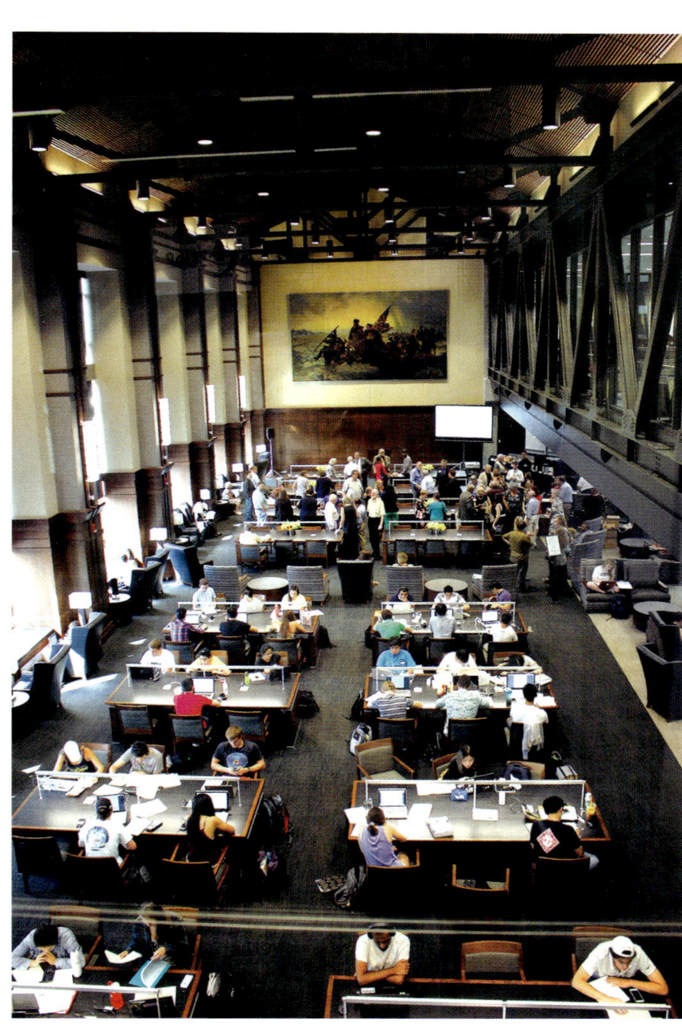

The second decade of the twenty-first century at Purdue University continued the growth of the West Lafayette campus, in both student population as well as the campus itself. Most notably, the Thomas S. and Harvey D. Wilmeth Active Learning Center altered the core of Purdue's campus, creating a multifaceted teaching and student learning space.

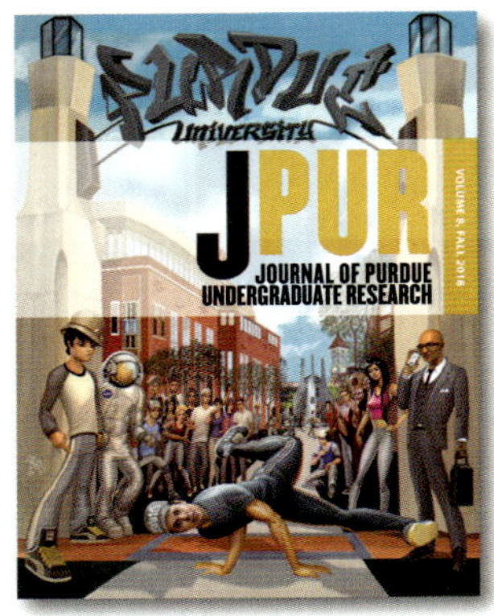

Journal of Purdue Undergraduate Research, Vol. 8. *(Journal of Purdue Undergraduate Research)*

During the 2010s, technology fully integrated itself into everyday activities, both socially and academically. More so than at any other time in human history, Purdue students were connected to the world around them. iPods were quickly replaced with smartphones. Social networking platforms Twitter, Instagram, and Snapchat became avenues for student social customs, interactions, and movements. Meanwhile, streaming services such as Netflix, YouTube, and Spotify brought entertainment immediately to students' devices. Faculty also took advantage of new technologies, increasingly providing lecture recordings and instruction information online.

The Purdue University Honors College was established in 2011.[3] The Honors College replaced the University Honors Program and other existing honors programs at the university; its first courses were offered in the 2013 fall semester.[4] Honors students had to meet and maintain stringent academic, leadership, and engagement requirements. The four main tenets set forth within the Honors College in its formative years were undergraduate research, interdisciplinary academics, leadership development, and community and global experiences. Honors College students were also expected to complete a capstone project prior to graduation.[5]

Undergraduate research, always a mainstay of Purdue, received additional prominence with the creation of the *Journal of Purdue Undergraduate Research* (*JPUR*) and creation of the Office of Undergraduate Research (OUR). *JPUR*, an annual journal, began in 2011. Each issue includes original research conducted by undergraduate students. The OUR was created to connect undergraduate students to research and learning experiences. Conferences and poster symposiums managed by the OUR provide Purdue students the opportunity to present their research to faculty and staff across campus.

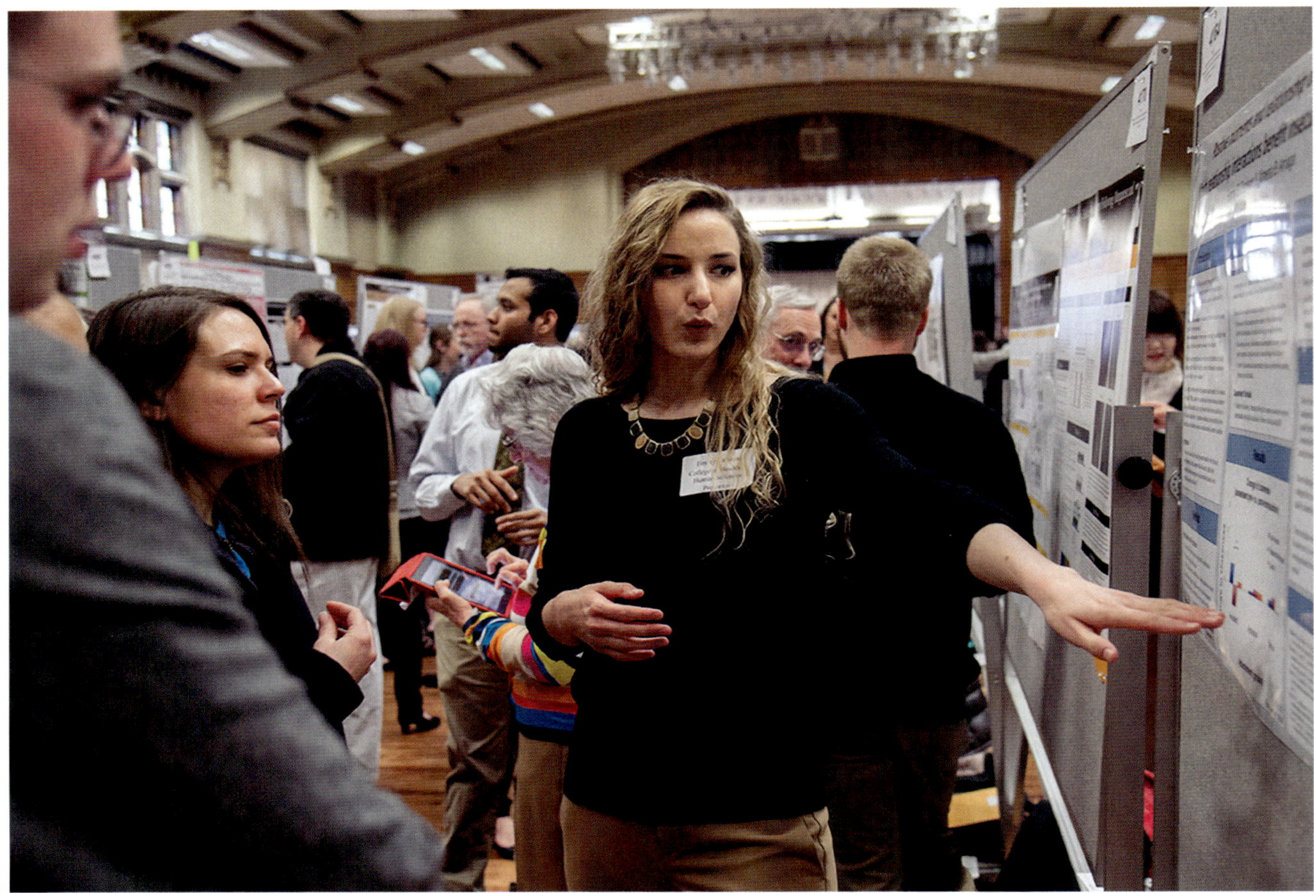

Emmy Denison presenting her research poster "Positive Moments and Relationship Outcomes: Which Relationship Interactions Benefit Insecure Individuals?" during the 2018 Office of Purdue Undergraduate Research Symposium. Photo by Mark Simons. *(Purdue University Marketing and Media collection)*

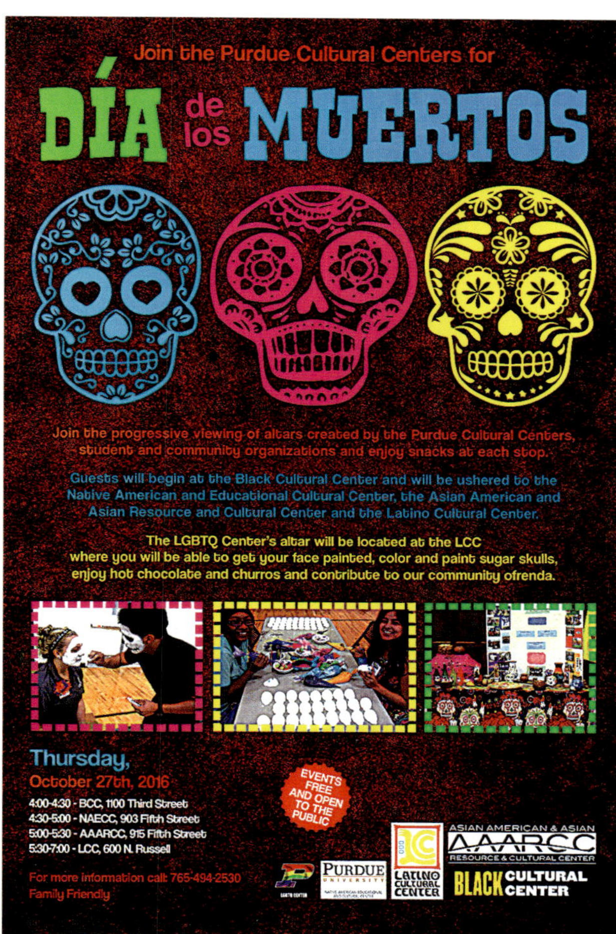

Left: Poster for the Purdue Cultural Centers Dia de los Muertos activities, October 27, 2016. *(Purdue University LGBTQ Resource Center records)*

Below: LGBTQ Study Abroad at the Stonewall Inn and National Monument in New York City, 2016. *(Purdue University LGBTQ Resource Center records)*

The decade was also a time of substantial change for Purdue regional campuses. Purdue's two northern regional campuses, Purdue Calumet and Purdue North Central, merged to form Purdue Northwest in 2016 after two years of planning. In 2016, Indiana University and Purdue University announced that Indiana University–Purdue University Fort Wayne would undergo realignment and much of the campus would come under the management of Purdue University. In 2017, the university was renamed Purdue University Fort Wayne, and the campus realignment took formal effect on July 1, 2018.[6]

Cultural centers continued to be an integral component of the Purdue experience for many students, staff, and faculty. These centers provided safe spaces, programs, education, and community events centered on important social, health, economic, and academic issues. New cultural centers formed within the decade, joining the Latino Cultural Center and Black Cultural Center. The LGBTQ (Lesbian, Gay, Bisexual, Transgender, and Queer) Center opened its doors in 2012, and the Asian American and Asian Resource and Cultural Center (AAARCC) formed in 2015. The Veterans Success Center, a Purdue-based resource for veterans and military students, opened in 2014. In 2019, the Black Cultural Center celebrated its fiftieth anniversary and twentieth anniversary of its facility. Social justice movements also marked the decade, as Purdue students voiced their expectations for increased university action regarding diversity, inclusion, and equality.

In the fall of 2018 Purdue Northwest enrollment was 10,473 students. Total enrollment at Purdue Fort Wayne was 10,139. West Lafayette campus enrollment reached its highest mark in history, with 43,411 students.[7]

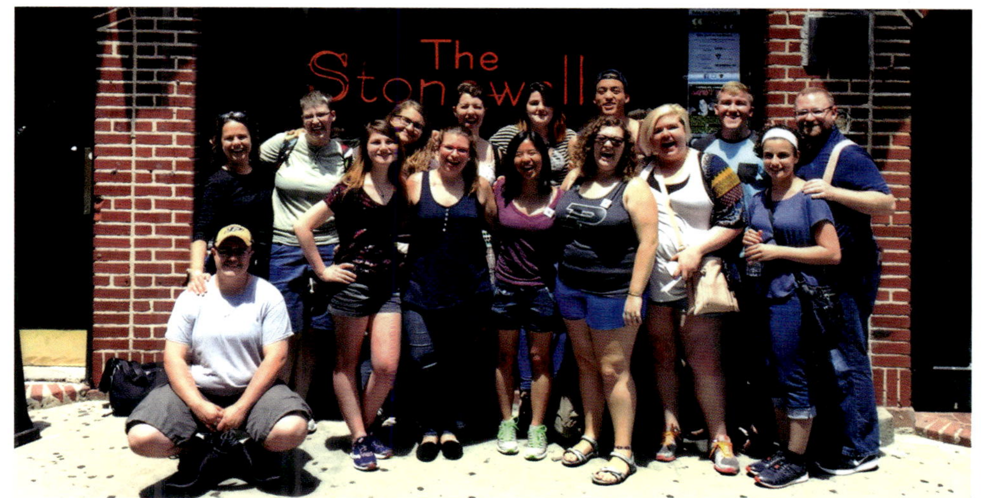

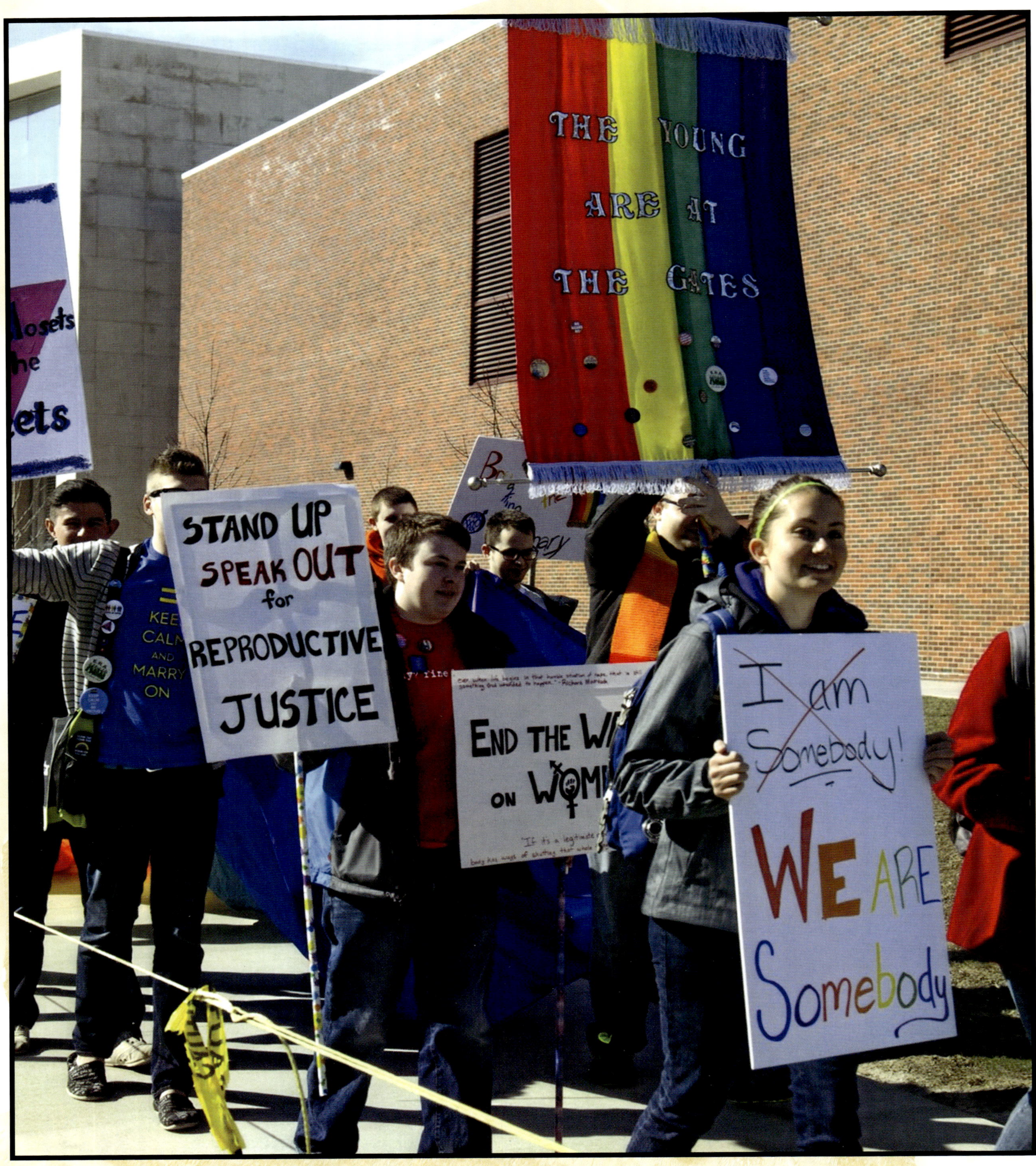

The March at Purdue, celebrating the hundredth anniversary of the women's march on Washington and progressive movements, March 22, 2013. *(Purdue University LGBTQ Resource Center records)*

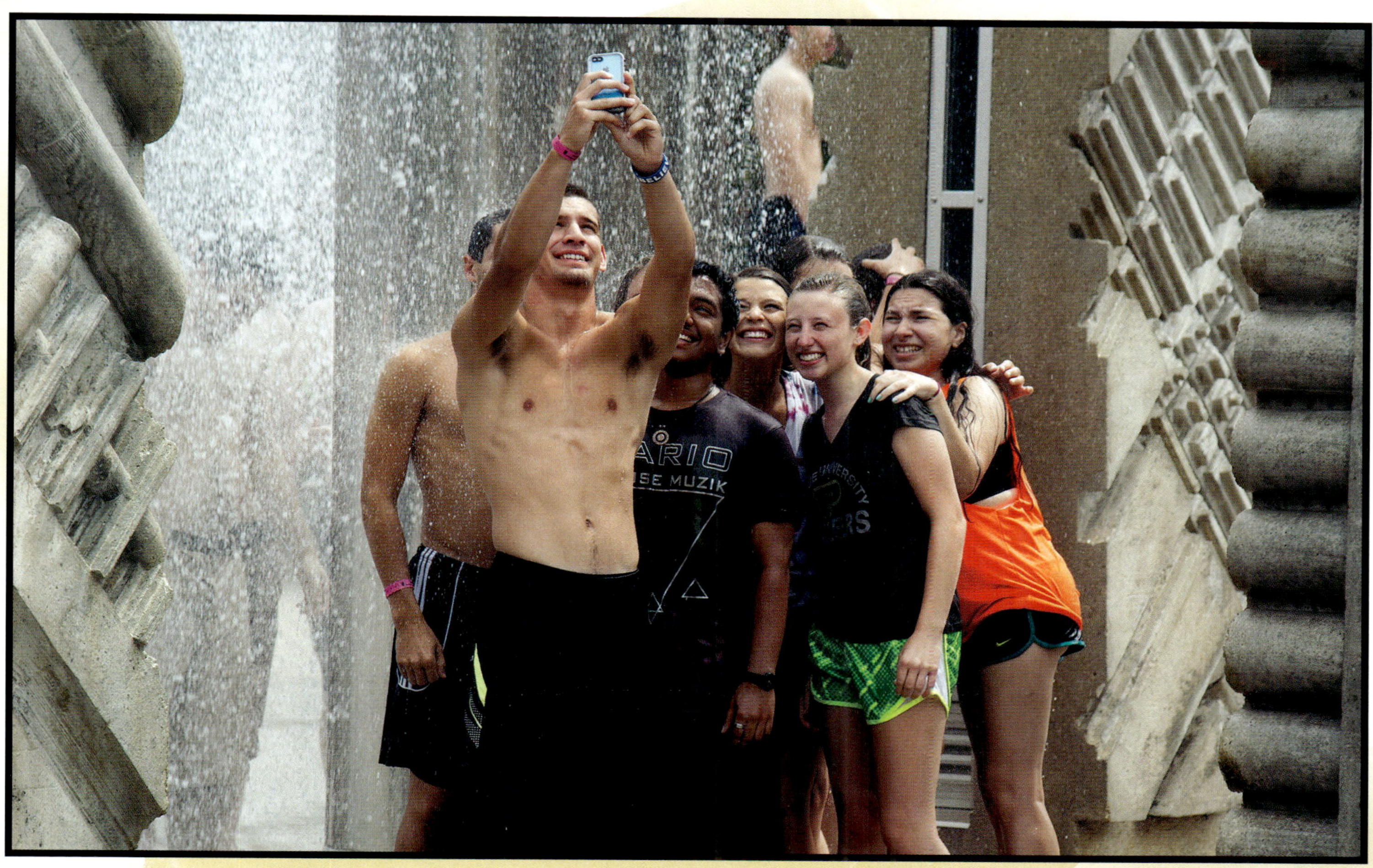

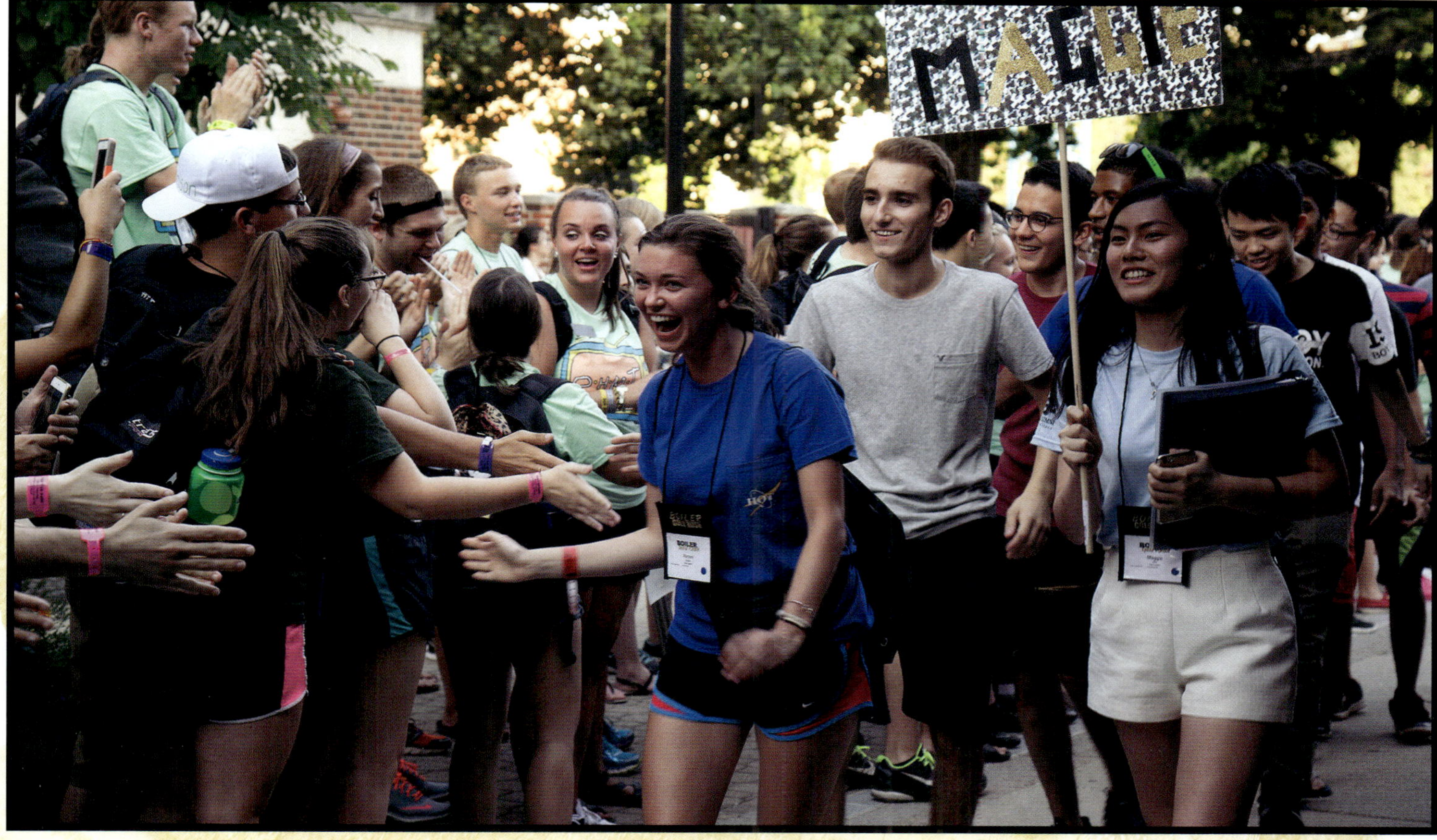

Top: Students pause for a photo during a Boiler Gold Rush fountain run in 2014. Photo by Mark Simons. *(Purdue University Marketing and Media collection)*

Bottom: Boiler Gold Rush 2015. *(Purdue University Marketing and Media collection)*

Purdue Celebrates the Indiana Bicentennial

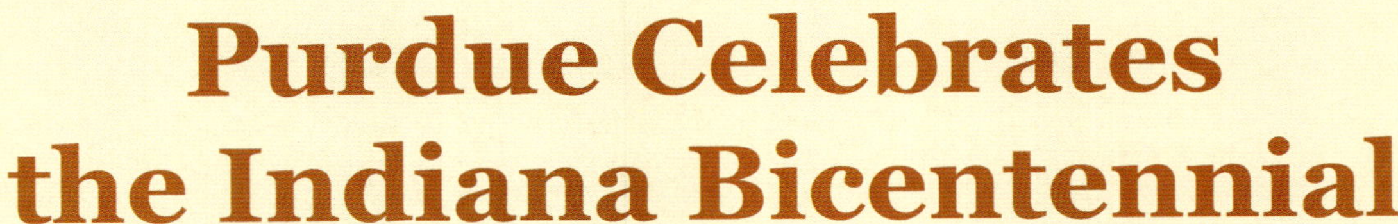

In 2016 the state of Indiana celebrated its two-hundredth birthday with a yearlong series of special activities to commemorate the occasion. A ceremonial torch relay, in the same vein as the Olympic torch relay that precedes each Olympic Games, was one such activity. A bicentennial torch was designed and manufactured at Purdue by students from Agriculture and Biological Engineering and the College of Engineering.[8]

The torch relay wound its way through the state, stopping in all ninety-two counties along the way. On Wednesday, October 12, the torch traveled through Tippecanoe County and the Purdue West Lafayette campus. Hundreds of spectators lined the streets along the torch relay route. Torchbearers included Dean of Students Emerita Betty Nelson, Student Body president Geri Denger, Purdue president Mitch Daniels, Purdue astronaut alumnus David Wolf, Purdue alumnus and former football star Leroy Keyes, and many other members of the community selected by the State Bicentennial Commission.

Indiana Bicentennial flag with the Torch Relay and Purdue Engineering emblems. *(Collection of Indiana Bicentennial materials)*

Left: Betty Nelson, Mitch Daniels, and David Wolf carrying the Bicentennial Torch through Purdue's campus. *(Collection of Indiana Bicentennial materials)*

Background: Indiana Bicentennial flags line the corner of State and Grant Streets. *(Collection of Indiana Bicentennial materials)*

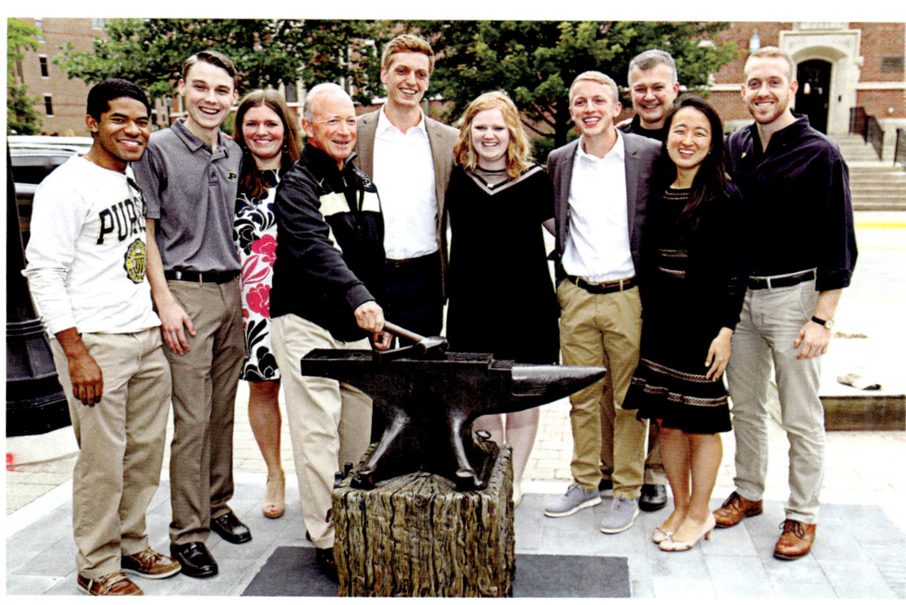

Left: President Mitch Daniels and Provost Jay Akridge joined faculty and students at the dedication of *The Forge* statue outside Krach Leadership Center, September 22, 2018. Photo by Michael Zoltowski.

Bottom: Flyover before a 2017 Purdue home football game. Photo by Alex Kumar. *(Purdue University Marketing and Media collection)*

In 2012, France Córdova stepped down as university president; Mitch Daniels, former governor of Indiana, was named Purdue's twelfth president. Daniels began his presidency in January 2013. Several initiatives, known collectively as Purdue Moves, were begun under Daniels, including a tuition freeze and increases in science, technology, engineering, and math (STEM) faculty.

Several Purdue Athletics teams and individuals distinguished themselves during the 2010s. In 2010, the women's golf team won the NCAA title; the team went on to compete in the NCAA championships several more times during the decade. David Boudia won a gold medal in diving at the 2012 Olympic Games in London; he and Purdue undergraduate Steele Johnson won a silver medal in synchronized diving at the 2016 Olympic Games in Rio de Janeiro. Alumna Amanda Elmore won a gold medal in rowing for the U.S. women's eight-person team in the Rio 2016 Games, becoming the first female Purdue Olympian to win a gold and the fifth Boilermaker to win an Olympic gold medal.[9]

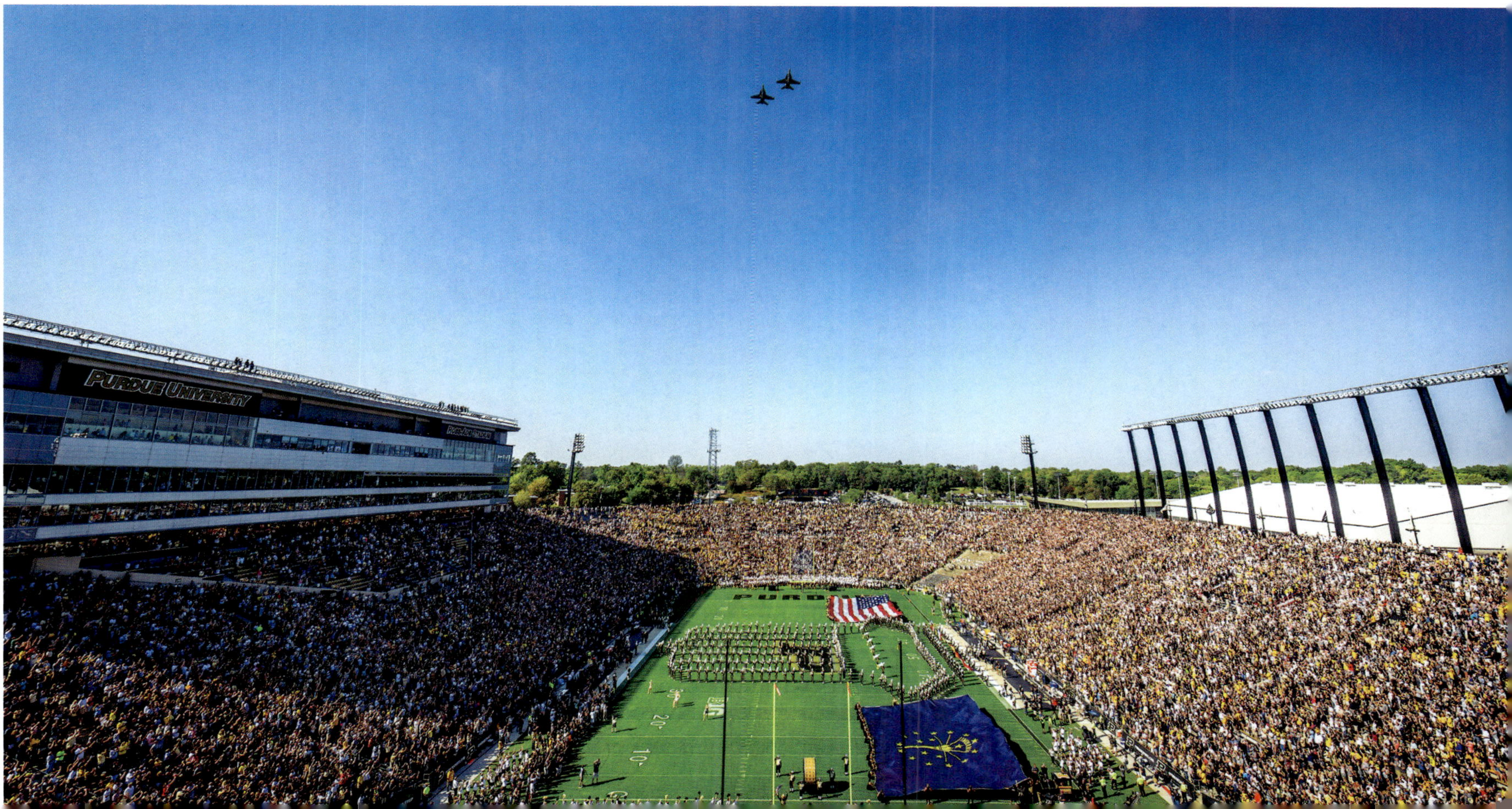

Top: Autographed Neil DeGrasse Tyson lecture flyer, 2013. *(Purdue Broadsides collection)*

Middle: The VOSS (Visiting Our Solar System) permanent installation opened in 2015 in Discovery Park. Named in honor of Purdue astronaut alumna Janice Voss, the scale model provides a walking tour of the solar system. Photo by Smith Donovan. *(Purdue University Marketing and Media collection)*

Bottom left: Aerial view of campus looking southeast in early 2018. Cary Quadrangle is in the foreground. Photo by Smith Donovan. *(Purdue University Marketing and Media collection)*

Bottom right: A statue of John Purdue was dedicated in April 2013. The sculpture sits on Memorial Mall near both University Hall and the grave of Purdue. Photo by Mark Simons. *(Purdue University Marketing and Media collection)*

NEIL DEGRASSE TYSON

BIG IDEAS LECTURES AT PURDUE

This Just In: Latest Discoveries in the Universe

FREE ADMISSION

SEPT 19 / 7PM
DOORS OPEN AT 6PM
THURS / ELLIOTT HALL

Presented By
DISCOVERY LECTURE SERIES
PURDUE UNIVERSITY
and
PURDUE UNIVERSITY
LIBRARIES

WITH SUPPORT FROM
College of Engineering,
Purdue Convocations,
and the College of Science

AND ADDITIONAL SUPPORT FROM
Indiana Space Grant Consortium,
the Black Cultural Center,
the Global Policy Research Institute,
and the Vice Provost for Diversity & Inclusion

CONVOCATIONS.ORG

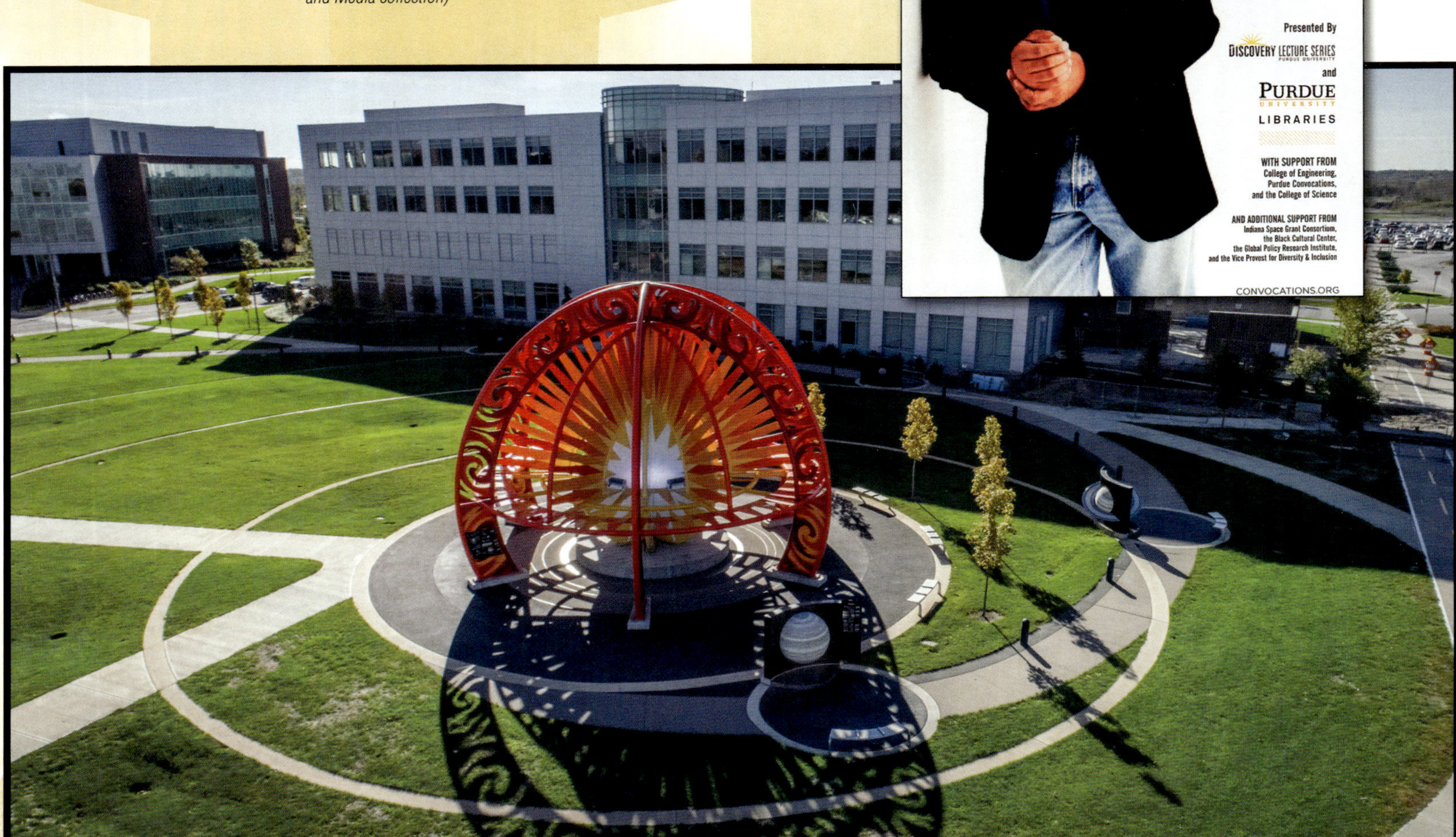

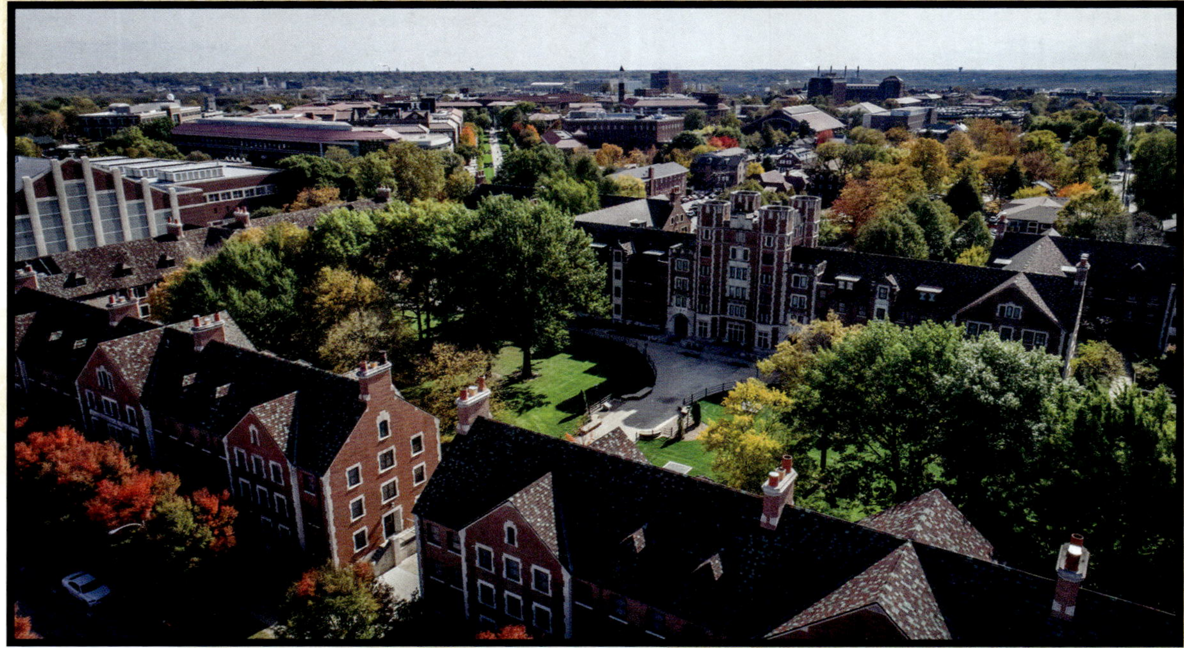

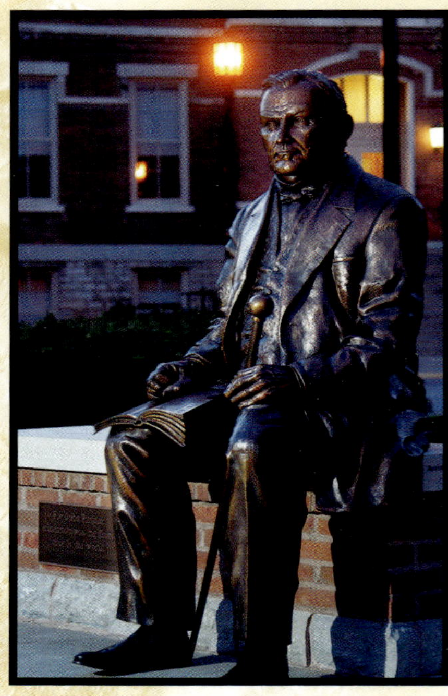

Lily Bishop and Grant Wood became the first Homecoming royalty in 2018. Purdue replaced the traditional Homecoming king and queen to select the top two candidates regardless of gender.

The women's volleyball team rose in national prominence, advancing to the NCAA Tournament Elite Eight in 2010 and 2013. In 2012, the baseball team won its first Big Ten title since 1909. The women's basketball team continued its excellence, earning repeated invitations to the NCAA Tournament; meanwhile, the men's basketball team reached the Sweet Sixteen of the NCAA Tournament in 2010, 2017, and 2018.

Left: Purdue volleyball fans congratulate the team after defeating Louisville to reach the Elite Eight, December 3, 2010. *(Purdue University Marketing and Media collection)*

Right: The baseball team celebrates after scoring against Michigan, April 9, 2011. *(Purdue University Marketing and Media collection)*

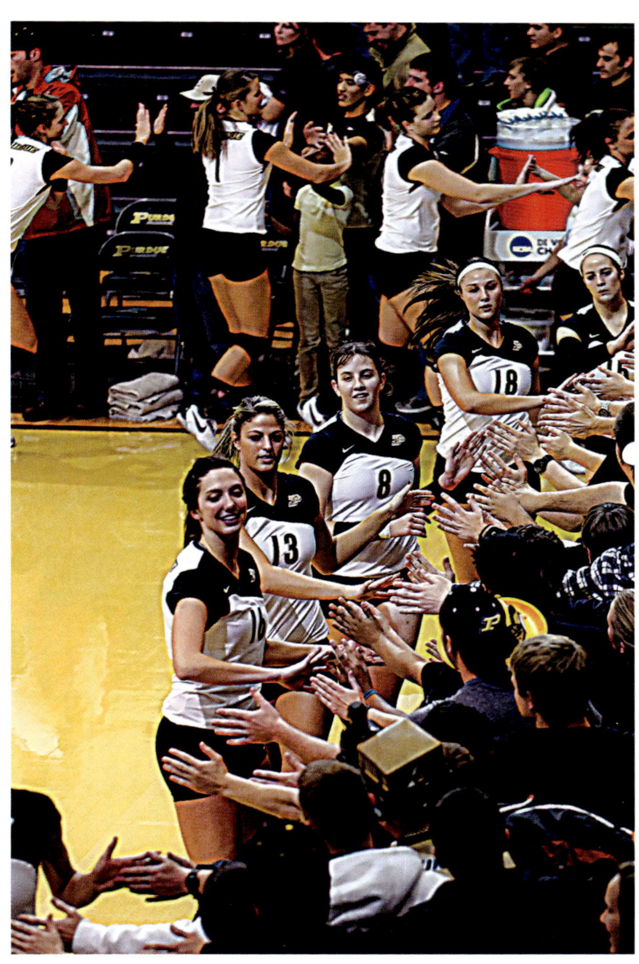

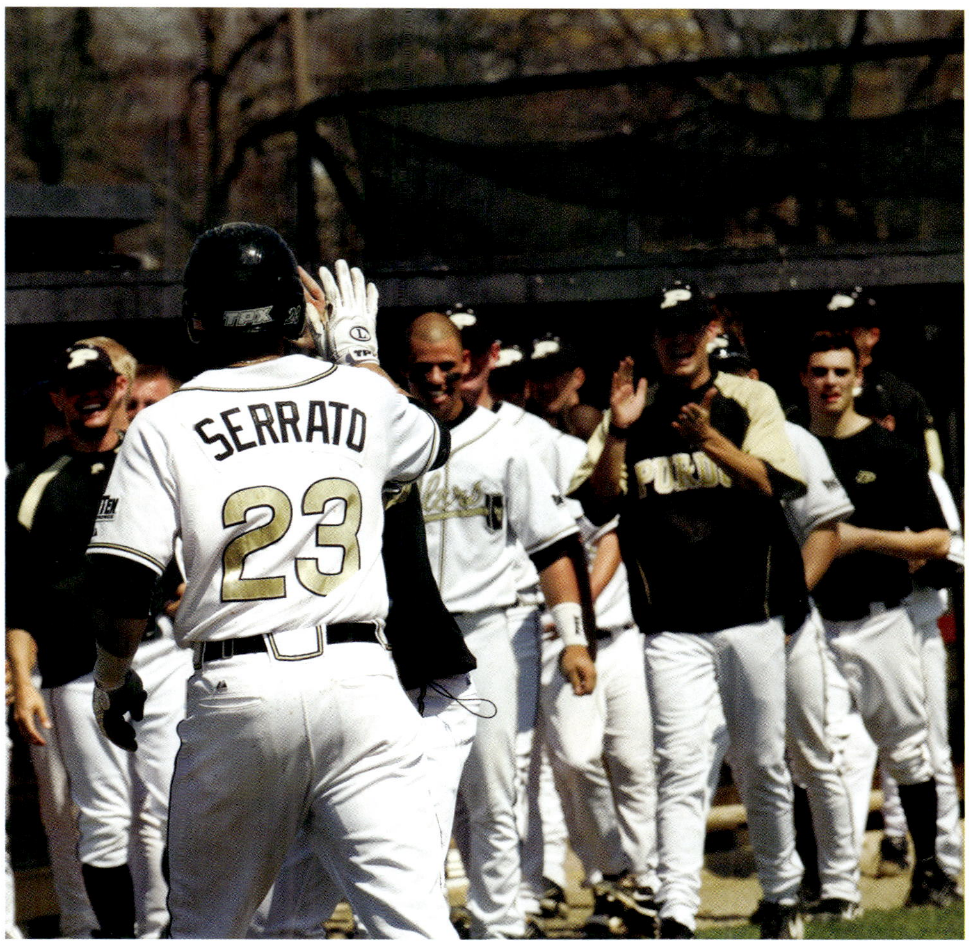

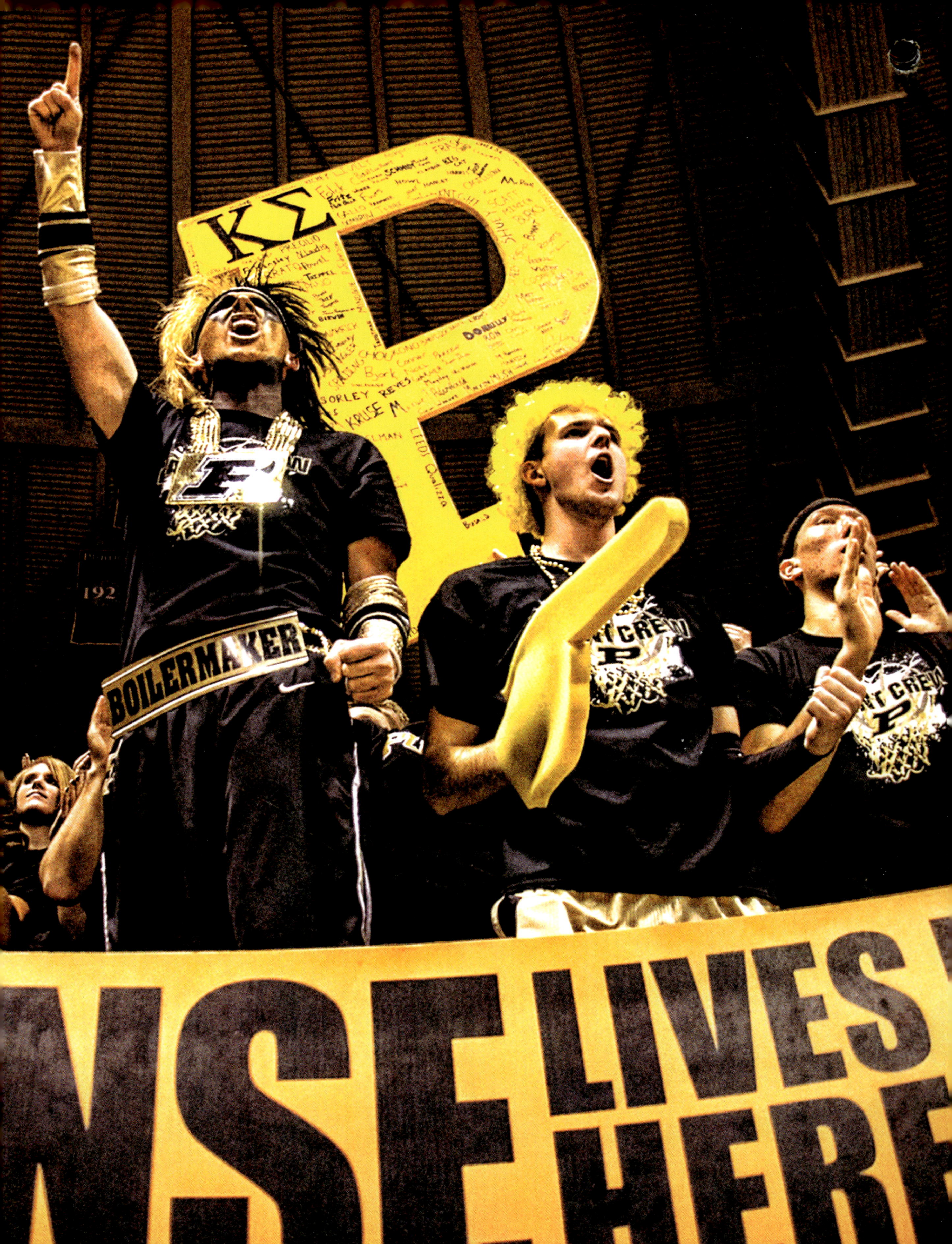
KΣ
BOILERMAKER
LIVES

Top: The Purdue football team unveils the Old Oaken Bucket at a Purdue men's basketball game, November 28, 2017. Photo by Alex Kumar. *(Purdue University Marketing and Media collection)*

Middle: Past and present iterations of Purdue Pete celebrate a birthday in 2016. *(Purdue University Newsreels and Year in Review collection)*

Bottom: Purdue softball team huddles during a game against Ball State, October 10, 2010. *(Purdue University Marketing and Media collection)*

Opposite page: The student section at a Mackey Arena basketball game. *(Purdue University Marketing and Media production samples)*

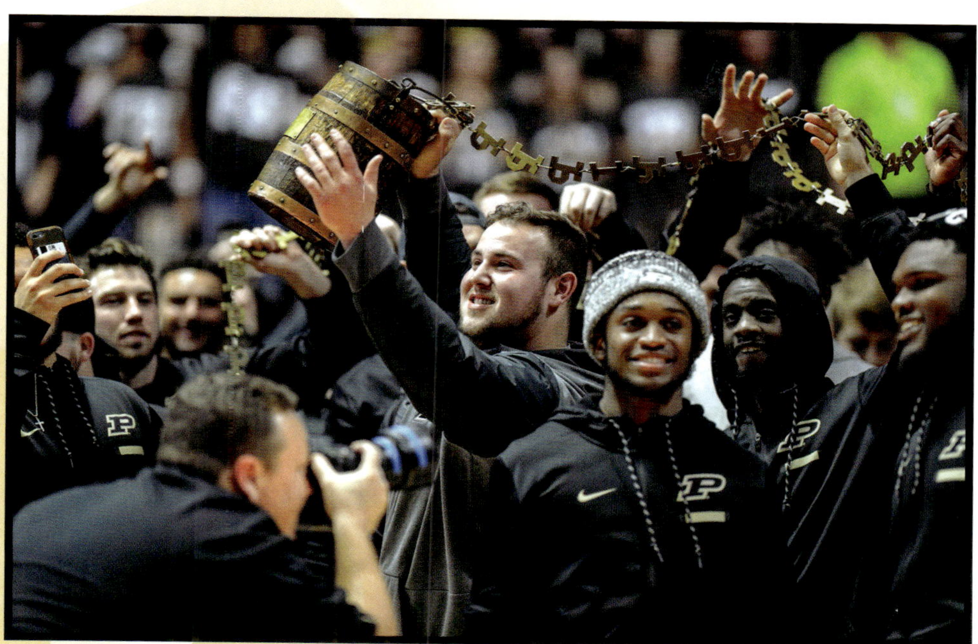

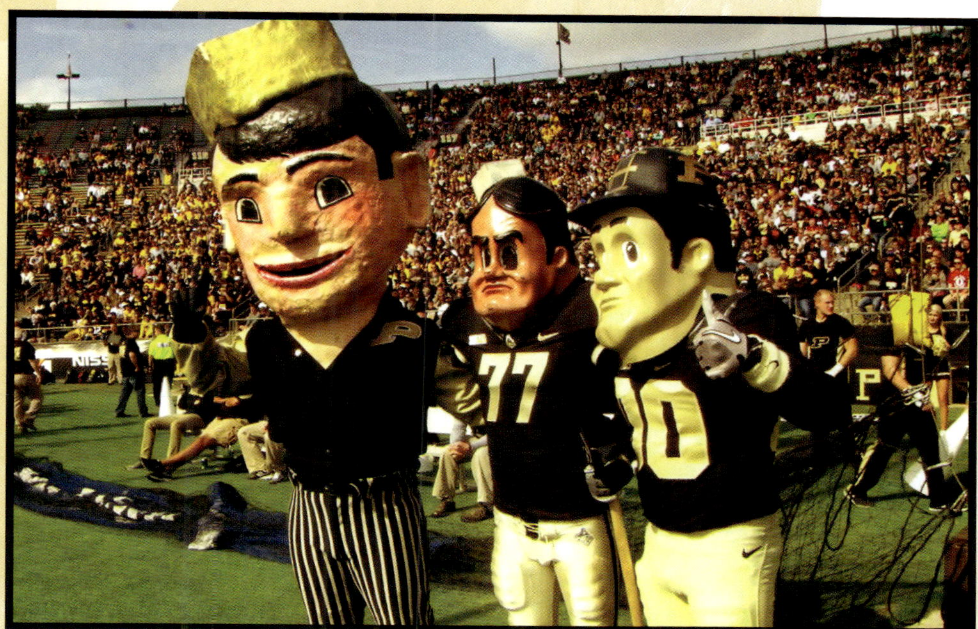

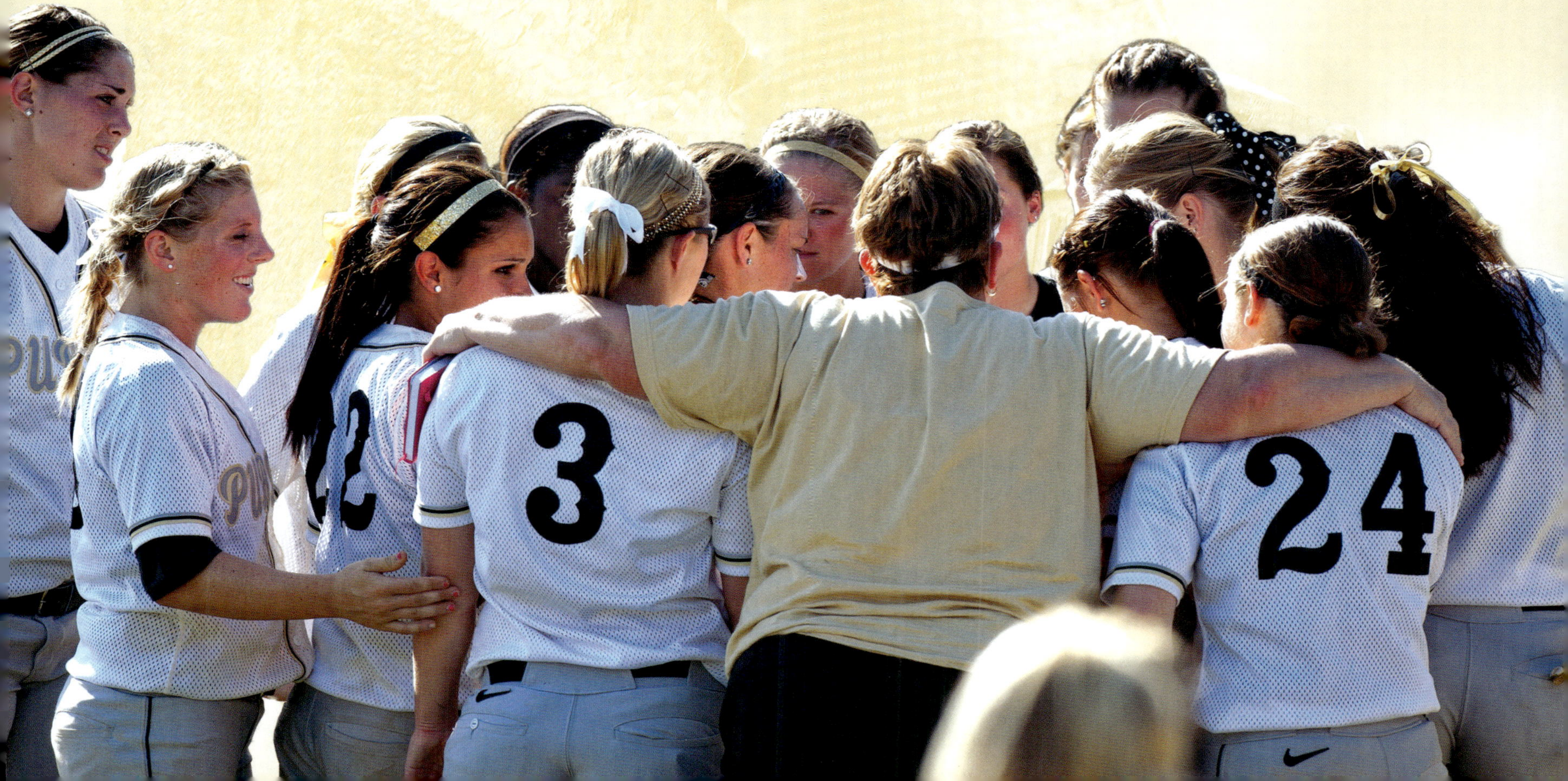

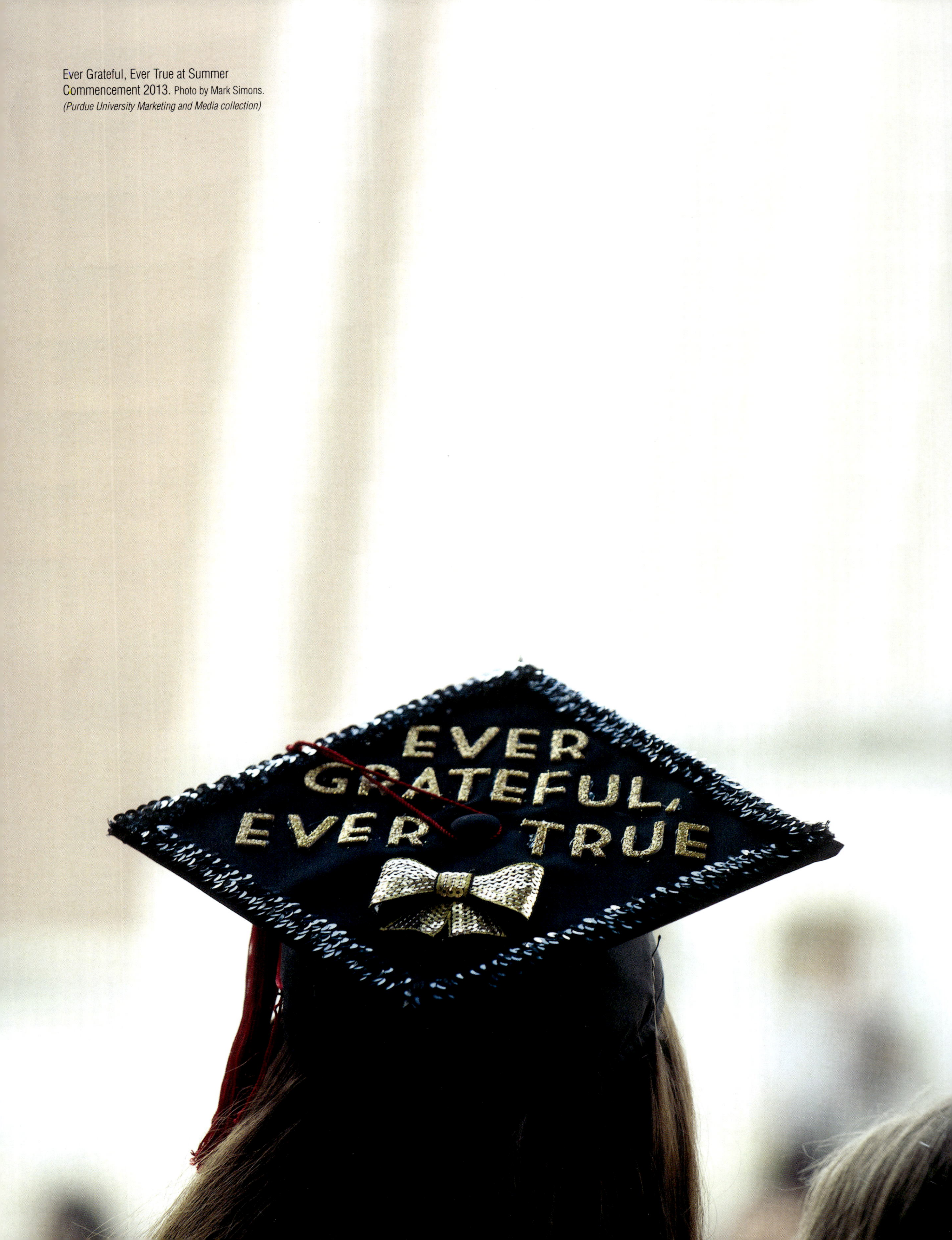

Ever Grateful, Ever True at Summer Commencement 2013. Photo by Mark Simons. *(Purdue University Marketing and Media collection)*

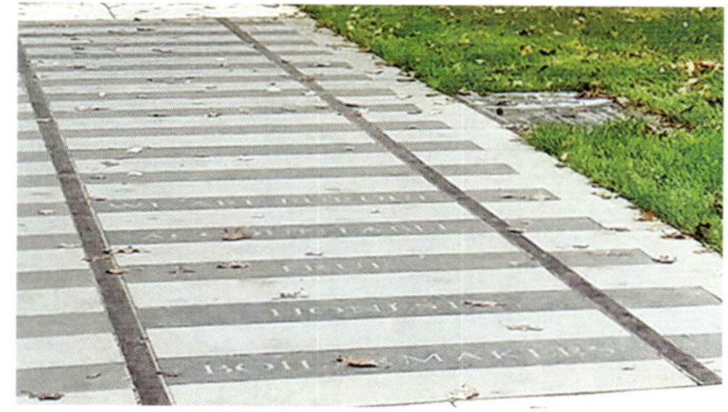

Student Honor Pledge outside of Felix Haas Hall. *(Purdue University photographs)*

As new academic approaches took root, commitment to honorable and ethical actions by all students was reaffirmed with a new permanent marker on campus. A student honor pledge was adopted and a monument placed in the walkways between Felix Haas Hall and the Psychological Sciences Building. The pledge stated: "As a Boilermaker pursuing academic excellence, I pledge to be honest and true in all that I do. Accountable together—We are Purdue."

Another major change came to the University as Purdue launched new initiatives into public university online education with the acquisition of Kaplan University. In 2017, President Mitch Daniels and the Board of Trustees announced the purchase of Kaplan, which was renamed Purdue University Global in 2018. As President Daniels announced Purdue Global, he invoked the reasons Purdue was founded:

Nearly 150 years ago, Purdue proudly accepted the land-grant mission to expand higher education beyond the wealthy and the elites of society. We cannot honor our land-grant mission in the 21st century without reaching out to the 36 million working adults, 750,000 of them in our state, who started but did not complete a college degree, and to the 56 million Americans with no college credit at all. None of us knows how fast or in what direction online higher education will evolve, but we know its role will grow, and we intend that Purdue be positioned to be a leader as that happens.[10]

The first class of Purdue Global, numbering over nine thousand students, graduated in May 2018.[11] Later in 2018, the West Lafayette campus welcomed its largest freshman class in history, as eighty-three hundred incoming students arrived for the academic year.[12]

In 2019 Purdue celebrated its sesquicentennial, marking 150 years since the founding of the university. The anniversary, "150 Years of Giant Leaps," was commemorated in a series of events, activities, and tributes as Purdue looked fondly to its past and expectantly toward its future.

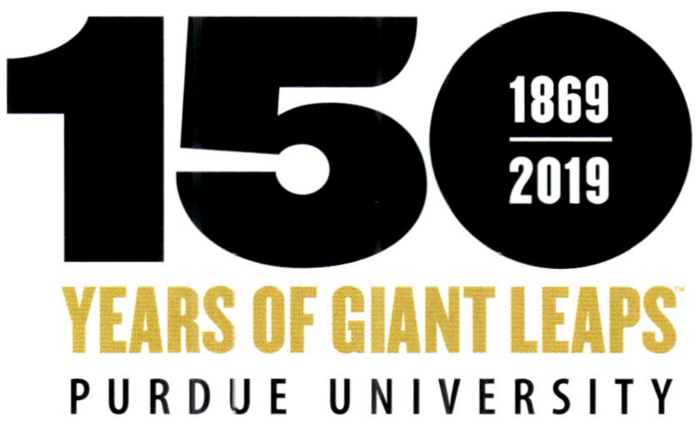

[Epilogue]

Purdue University Archives and Special Collections, a division of Purdue Libraries, is pleased to share historical photographs, documents, and artifacts from the collections in honor of Purdue's sesquicentennial. With 150 years of University history, it was at times challenging to determine what content would be included within our page limits and what would be omitted. We used two guiding principles in our coverage: to focus, whenever possible, on the experiences of Purdue students and to use only collections contained in the Archives and Special Collections.

The Archives and Special Collections exists to support the discovery, learning, and engagement goals of Purdue University by identifying, collecting, preserving, and making available unique collections of enduring value. These collections of photographs, scrapbooks, diaries, letters, and student memorabilia bring Purdue history to life while preserving the legacies of the many individuals who are part of that history. Our team takes pride in our mission to preserve Purdue's heritage and to provide access to it. Because the items in our collections are one of a kind and irreplaceable, they are used in the secure Archives reading room. Yet it is important to our team that we make them available easily to people who are unable to visit the Archives by increasingly digitizing the collections for online access and sharing them in publications like this one. Our collections are accessible to both the University community and the public, and the Archives is eager to assist researchers both near and far.

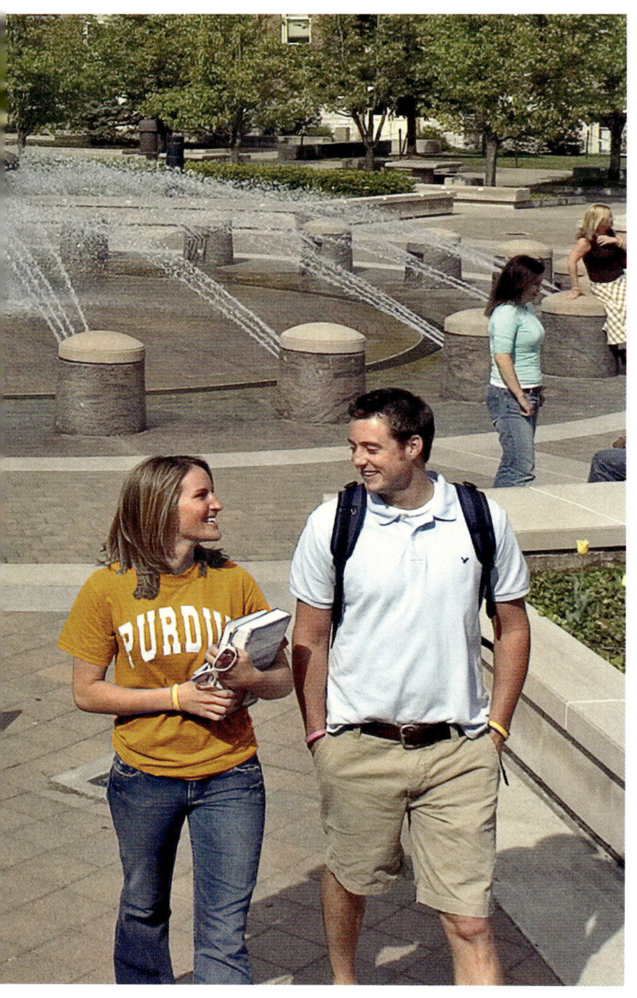

Students at Loeb Fountain, 2005.
(Purdue University photographs)

We assume full responsibility for omissions in the text and regret not being able to include many significant people, events, and developments in Purdue's history as part of this volume. Rather, we reviewed what collections the Archives contained and shaped our narrative around the existing documentary record. Where there are gaps in the history, this reflects the lack of archival collections available on those topics. Many official Purdue publications also offer conflicting dates for major events, so when in doubt we made an educated choice and cited our sources.

We are dedicated to growing our collections on Purdue history and filling in gaps or silences in the record. A major goal of the Archives and Special Collections is to represent as full, accurate, and diverse of a University history as possible. We rely on the donations of collections from loyal Boilermakers and Purdue friends like you to help us in our mission to preserve and share Purdue's history. Thank you for engaging with us and being a part of our rich heritage.

Hail Purdue!

Sammie L. Morris, Professor
University Archivist and Head, Archives and Special Collections Division
Director of the Virginia Kelly Karnes Archives and Special Collections Research Center

[Afterword]

When I started working in the Purdue University Archives during August of 2017, I had no idea that the Archives was releasing a book for the university's 150th anniversary, let alone that I would be involved in the process of bringing it to life. Working in the Archives is an opportunity that not a lot of people have; I consider myself fortunate to have "seen backstage" into not only Purdue's history, but also how that history is maintained and recorded in the present. From hundred-year-old film negatives to mid-century underground student newspapers to alumni interviews recorded within the last decade, all carefully stored and preserved, the pieces of history I have had the opportunity to work with have allowed me to understand and appreciate Purdue for what it is, despite its shortcomings and even more for its merits. Contributing to *Purdue at 150* by selecting images to use in its pages was a small way for me to wholeheartedly give back to the school that had provided me with so much.

My work on *Purdue at 150* began during my last semester as a Purdue student when I was handed several photographs and asked to scan them for "the book project." Scanning pre-chosen images gradually turned into poring over scrapbooks and pinpointing specific collections, trying to decide which pictures best captured Purdue's rich past. Through this work, I was able to see what Purdue started out as: a small college specializing in agriculture, fifty students large. It changed with the times throughout the decades, adding majors and allowing minorities to enroll and live on campus. From pictures taken during the World War II years, I learned that Purdue was a center of aviation technology that people visited from all over the world. After that, campus became a place where students programmed computers with punch cards and held protests on Memorial Mall. As I gained more knowledge of Purdue's history I was also aware that, as a senior, my time at Purdue was nearing an end. Looking back on Purdue's past gave me a deep appreciation for the university as it is today, as well as hope for Purdue's future.

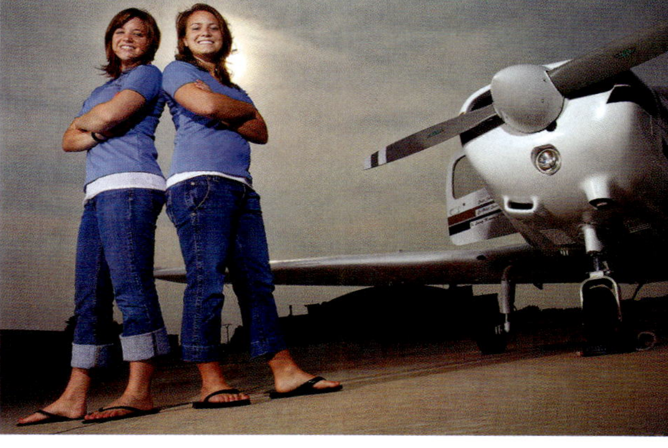
Juliana Lindner and Lauren Steele with their plane at the Purdue University Airport. Lindner and her co-pilot, Lauren Steele, competed in the June 2009 all-women's, cross-country air race, finishing fourth among collegiate teams. *(Purdue University photographs)*

There is always one part of Purdue that is changing. I am sure the next time I visit there will be a new building or road to remind me of how long it's been since the last time I was on campus. The construction may be a nuisance at times, but it's a reminder that Purdue is constantly growing. From a small handful of buildings scattered around Memorial Mall to today's multitude of academic and athletic facilities, residence halls and study areas, and recreational and cultural spaces, Purdue's growth has been steady and marked. I can only imagine how different it will be in another 150 years, by which time this book will be an archival object itself for others to marvel over and use to understand Purdue and its past. I am grateful to have played a part in documenting its first 150 years and for everything I have gained in the process.

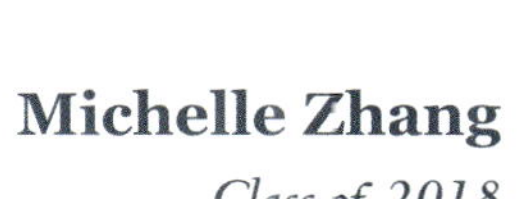
Michelle Zhang
Class of 2018

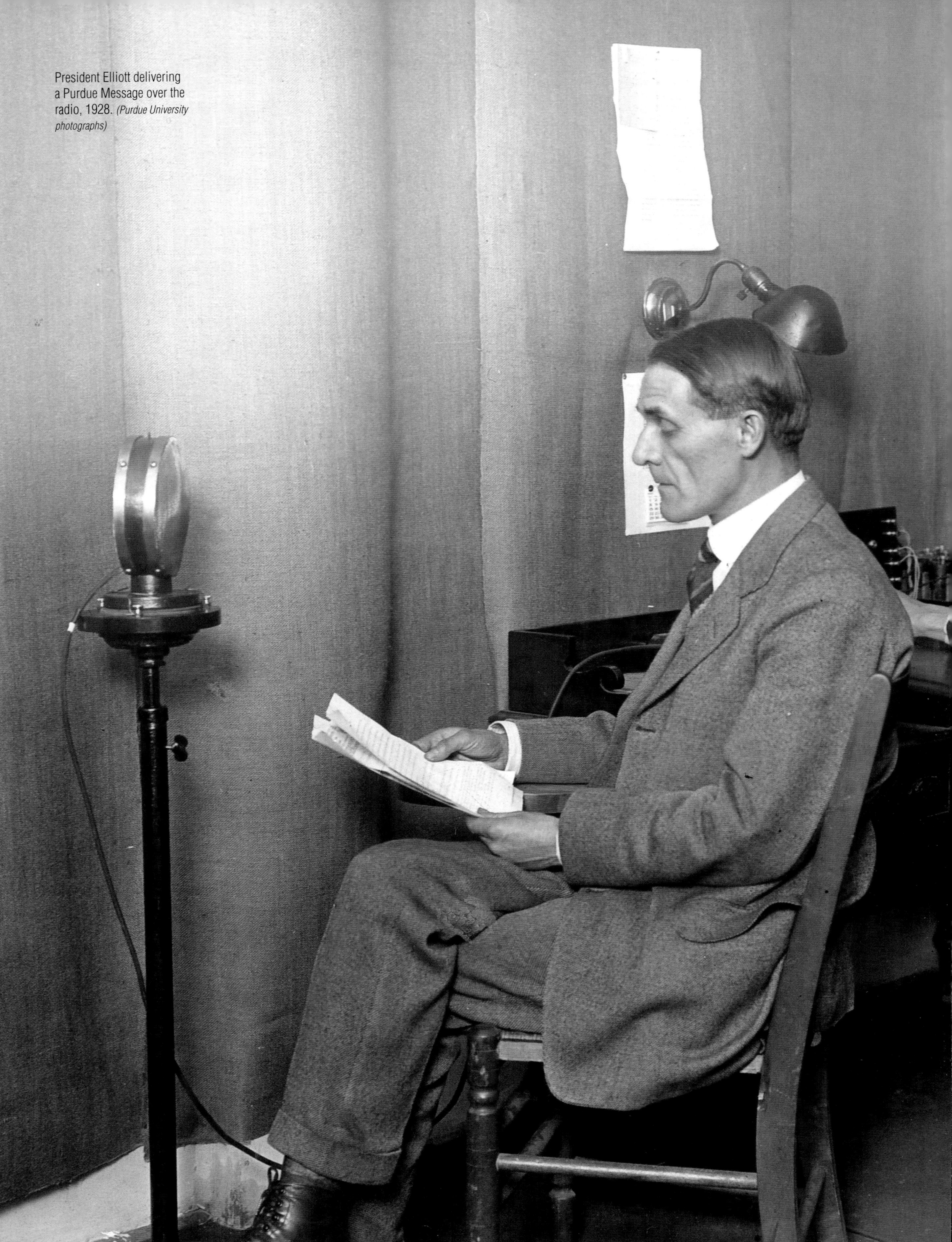

President Elliott delivering a Purdue Message over the radio, 1928. *(Purdue University photographs)*

[Notes]

Preface

1. William Murray Hepburn and Louis Martin Sears, *Purdue University: Fifty Years of Progress* (Indianapolis: Hollenbeck Press, 1925), 168.

Introduction

1. Title 7 U.S. Code § 301—Land Grant Aid of Colleges. July 2, 1862, ch. 13, § 1, 12 Stat. 503.
2. William Murray Hepburn and Louis Martin Sears, *Purdue University: Fifty Years of Progress* (Indianapolis: Hollenbeck Press, 1925), 31–33.
3. Fassett A. Cotton, *Education in Indiana* (Bluffton, Ind.: Progress Publishing, 1934).

The 1870s

1. William Murray Hepburn and Louis Martin Sears, *Purdue University: Fifty Years of Progress* (Indianapolis: Hollenbeck Press, 1925), 171–72.
2. Worth Reed, "Notes from Away Back," *Purdue Alumnus*, October 1919, 14.
3. *Annual Report of the Board of Trustees of Purdue University for the Year Ending October 31, 1874* (Indianapolis: Sentinel Company Printers, 1875), 9.
4. Faculty meeting minutes, October 6, 1874, p. 18, box 1, folder 1, Purdue University Faculty and Senate records, UA 8.
5. "Purdue's First Co-ed Tells of Trials and Tribulations," Scrapbook, box 5, Purdue University Semi-Centennial collection, MSP 120; Eulora Miller, "When Co-eds Were Scarce," *Purdue Alumnus*, March 1920, 7.
6. Hepburn and Sears, *Purdue University*, 173–74.
7. "Alumni Notes," *Purdue Engineer*, March 1929, 162.
8. Reed, "Notes from Away Back," 14.
9. George Munro, *John Purdue and Purdue University: A Study of the Relations between Them from Its Organization to His Death* (unpublished, 1946), 140.
10. *Annual Circular of Purdue University, Lafayette, Ind., for 1876-77* (Indianapolis: Sentinel Company Printers, 1876), 18.
11. Harvey W. Wiley, *An Autobiography* (Indianapolis: Bobbs-Merrill, 1930), 127–28; Hepburn and Sears, 177.
12. "Local," *The Purdue*, June 1875.
13. Wiley, *An Autobiography*, 128.
14. Hepburn and Sears, *Purdue University*, 6[illegible].
15. "Purdue's First Co-ed Tells of Trials and Tribulations."
16. Miller, "When Co-eds Were Scarce," 7; George M. Eberhart, "Things You Didn't Know about ALA History, 1876–1900," *American Libraries Magazine*, February 11, 2016, https://americanlibrariesmagazine.org/blogs/the-scoop/things-you-didnt-know-about-ala-history-1876-1900/.

The 1880s

1. *Seventh Annual Report of Purdue University for the Year Ending June 30, 1881* (Indianapolis: William B. Burford, 1881), 14.
2. Journal, 1881–1882, box 1, folder 1, E. C. White papers, MSA 355.
3. *Seventh Annual Report*, 54.
4. "Bugle Notes," *The Purdue* 1, no. 1 (November 1882): 10.
5. William Murray Hepburn and Louis Martin Sears, *Purdue University: Fifty Years of Progress* (Indianapolis: Hollenbeck Press, 1925), 70–71.
6. "Purdue's First Football Team," *Purdue Exponent*, October 16, 1909.
7. George Munro, "RE: The Purdue Extra," in *The New Purdue: Sketches of Hitching Back Days* (unpublished, 1945).
8. *Purdue Exponent*, December 15, 1889.
9. Purdue University Semi-Centennial collection, MSP 120, Box 5: Scrapbook, p. 11.

The 1890s

1. *Seventeenth Annual Report of Purdue University for the Year Ending June 30, 1891* (Indianapolis: William B. Burford, 1891), 8.
2. DeWitt Buchanan interview, July 21, 1972, Purdue Office of Publications Oral History Program collection, MSO 2.
3. Bob Kriebel, "One Brick Higher: The Story of Heavilon Shops," *Lafayette Journal & Courier*, January 23, 1994.
4. "President Smart as a Friend," *Purdue Exponent*, March 1, 1900.
5. "Slaughter of the Innocents," *Daily Argus News*, October 26, 1891; "Purdue vs. Wabash," *Purdue Exponent*, October 28, 1891, p. 36.

6. "The Purdue of Yesterday," box 1, folder 4, L. Murray Grant and Bernice Nelson Grant Papers, MSA 330.
7. William T. Berkshire interview, May 1, 1971, Purdue University Office of Publications Oral History Program collection, MSO 2.
8. *Debris* yearbook, 1905, 310.

The 1900s

1. *Thirty-Seventh Annual Report of Purdue University for the Year Ending June 30, 1911* (Indianapolis: William B. Burford, 1912), 25.
2. William T. Berkshire interview, May 1, 1971, Purdue University Office of Publications Oral History Program collection, MSO 2.
3. "'Hello!' Cried Captain Osborne, When He Fell," box 12, Winthrop E. Stone papers, UA 49.
4. "Young Girls Work Amid Death and Suffering," box 12, Winthrop E. Stone papers, UA 49.
5. Frank Kovalcik, "Blanche Annis Miller," *Purdue Alumnus,* June–July 1948, 6.
6. Announcement concerning a memorial gymnasium at Purdue University, folder 2, Memorial Gymnasium Records, UA 133.
7. "Editor's Corner," *Purdue Exponent,* May 19, 1904.
8. Helen Walters, "The Purdue Scrapbook for Friday, December 7, 1934"; "Customs and Traditions—Victory Bell," Purdue University Archives and Special Collections vertical files, MSK 1.
9. *Debris* yearbook, 1908, 138 and 258.
10. "Dr. E. C. Elliott Entertains Foreign Students at Tea," *Purdue Exponent,* March 16, 1944.
11. *Debris* yearbook, 1946, 181.
12. "Joshes, Customs, Cutups," 1914 *Debris* yearbook, 1914, 344; *Debris* yearbook, 1904, 102 and 117.
13. "The Dubois Club," *Purdue Exponent,* October 29, 1909.
14. "Provident Hospital Graduate Secures a Good Position," *Chicago Defender,* April 17, 1915.

The 1910s

1. *Thirty-Seventh Annual Report of Purdue University for the Year Ending June 30, 1911* (Indianapolis: William B. Burford, 1912), 25.
2. Purdue Class of 1915 40th anniversary booklet, 9, Class of 1915 collection, MSA 369.
3. "'S.H.' painted on the tank," *Purdue Exponent,* January 23, 1912.
4. "The Burning of Mechanics," *Purdue Exponent,* February 4, 1903.
5. "The Burning of the Mechanics," *Purdue Exponent,* February 4, 1904.
6. "Mechanic's Burning: Class of 1911," folder 1, John Heiss collection, MSF 172.
7. "Circus a Great Success," *Purdue Exponent,* May 2, 1913.
8. 1915 Purdue Circus program, box 3, folder 5, Purdue University Customs and Traditions collection, MSP 151.
9. "University Sing to Create Springtime Atmosphere," *Purdue Exponent,* May 1, 1958.
10. "May Day Queen to Reign at Sing," *Purdue Exponent,* April 4, 1946.
11. "May Day Festivities Hatched U-Sing Idea," *Purdue Exponent,* April 11, 1977.
12. Letter to parents from France, November 3, 1917, folder 1, Julius L. Born correspondence, MSA 58.
13. "Historic Armory Constructed in 1873 Consumed by Fire," *Purdue Exponent,* February 25, 1916.
14. "Your Paper," *Purdue Exponent,* January 6, 1919; *Debris* yearbook, 1919, 55.
15. Fred L. Willis, "Watchtower of Health: A Half-Century with the Student Health Center, Purdue University, 1912–1966," 1966, typescript, Watchtower of Health manuscript, 20180212.2.
16. T. F. Moran, "A New Start," *Purdue Exponent,* January 6, 1919.

The 1920s

1. *Annual Reports of the President and Other Officers of Purdue University for the Year Ending September 30, 1921* (Lafayette: Purdue University, December 1921), 14.
2. "Seniors," *Debris* yearbook, 1925, 242.
3. "The Chinese Students at Purdue," Box 1, folder 3, Purdue University Chinese Students collection, MSP 155.
4. "Home Management Experience Provided by Practice House," *Purdue Exponent,* May 1, 1920.
5. Jeff Sterrett, Becky Gick, and Bob Mindrum, *75th Anniversary: Purdue Memorial Union* (West Lafayette: Purdue University, 1999).
6. "Home-Coming Odds and Ends," *Purdue Alumnus,* December 1924, 16.
7. "Will Lay Dorm Cornerstone Today," *Purdue Exponent,* November 5, 1927.
8. Robert W. Topping, *A Century and Beyond: The History of Purdue University* (West Lafayette: Purdue University Press, 1988), 288.
9. "Destructive Fire Brings Modernization to WBAA," *Purdue Exponent,* November 16, 1929.
10. Excerpt from *Purdue University Hand-Book, 1920-1921* (West Lafayette: Young Men's and Young Women's Christian Associations of Purdue University, 1920), 22–23.

The 1930s

1. *Reports of the President and Other Officers of Purdue University for the Year Ending September 30, 1931* (Lafayette: Purdue University, November 1931), 6.
2. Edward M. Purcell interview, November 20, 1970, Purdue University Office of Publications Oral History Program collection, MSO 2.
3. "Personal Letters from Purdue University to Students of the World," 1934, p. 3, International students, Purdue University Archives and Special Collections vertical files, MSK 1.
4. *Debris* yearbook, 1931, 78.
5. Edward M. Purcell interview, November 20, 1970, Purdue University Office of Publications Oral History Program collection, MSO 2.
6. H. B. Knoll, *The Story of Purdue Engineering* (West Lafayette: Purdue University Studies, 1963), 349.
7. John Estes, Bob Pence, and Jim Vruggink, *Purdue Athletics: A Century of Excellence* (West Lafayette: published jointly by John Purdue Club Office and Athletic Public Relations Office, 1987), 25.

8. Doug Griffiths, Alan Karpick, and Tom Schott, *Tales from Boilermaker Country: A Collection of the Greatest Stories Ever Told* (Champaign, IL: Sports Publishing, 2003), 10.
9. Estes et al., *Purdue Athletics*, 4.
10. Griffiths et al., *Tales from Boilermaker Country*, 19.
11. Griffiths et al., *Tales from Boilermaker Country*, 16.
12. Estes et al., *Purdue Athletics*, 4.
13. "'Miss Indiana' Burns as 4,000 Loyal Fans Watch Blazing Pyre," *Purdue Exponent*, November 18, 1938.
14. John Norberg, *Hail Purdue* (Owatonna, Minn.: "All-American" Band Club, 1987), 40.
15. Norberg, *Hail Purdue*, 40–41.
16. Joseph L. Bennett, *Boilermaker Music Makers: Al Stewart and the Purdue Musical Organizations* (West Lafayette, Purdue University, 1986), 50.
17. Bennett, *Boilermaker Music Makers*, 75.
18. Knoll, *The Story of Purdue Engineering*, 88–89.

The 1940s

1. *Reports of the President and Other Officers of Purdue University for the Session 1940-1941* (Lafayette: Purdue University, 1941), 7.
2. *Debris* yearbook, August 1943, 10.
3. H. B. Knoll, *A Record of the University in the War Years, 1941-1945* (Lafayette: Purdue University, 1947), 6.
4. Knoll, *War Years*, 7; H. B. Knoll, *The Story of Purdue Engineering* (West Lafayette: Purdue University Studies, 1963), 107–8.
5. Knoll, *War Years*, 6.
6. Byron Anderson interview, June 27, 2007, Purdue University Archives and Special Collections Oral History Program collection, MSO 1.
7. A. F. Grandt Jr., W. A. Gustafson, and L. T. Cargnino, *One Small Step: The History of Aerospace Engineering at Purdue University* (West Lafayette: Purdue Research Foundation, 1995), 32–39.
8. Knoll, *The Story of Purdue Engineering*, 107.
9. *Debris* yearbook, 1944, 114.
10. *Purdue Engineer*, September 1943, 239.
11. Recollections, folder 1, Esther Conelley Boonstra collection, MSA 57.
12. Knoll, *The Story of Purdue Engineering*, 107.
13. *Debris* yearbook, 1944, 217–21.
14. *Debris* yearbook, 1944, 227.
15. Board of Trustees minutes, 2 May 1942, p. 25, box 9, Purdue University Board of Trustees meeting minutes, UA 58.
16. Myrna Oliver, "Frederick C. Branch, 82; First Black Officer in U.S. Marine Corps," *Los Angeles Times*, April 12, 2005, http://articles.latimes.com/2005/apr/12/local/me-branch12.
17. *Debris* yearbook, 1944, end pages.
18. Purdue Reamer Club, *A University of Tradition: The Spirit of Purdue*, second ed. (West Lafayette: Purdue University Press, 2013), 174.
19. Joseph L. Bennett, *Boilermaker Music Makers: Al Stewart and the Purdue Musical Organizations* (West Lafayette, Purdue University, 1986), 7.
20. *Debris* yearbook, 1944, 197–99.
21. Robert W. Topping, *A Century and Beyond: The History of Purdue University* (West Lafayette: Purdue University Press, 1988), 255.
22. *Debris* yearbook, 1947, 20.
23. Board of Trustees minutes, 10 May 1945, p. 1, box 9, Purdue University Board of Trustees meeting minutes, UA 58.
24. Topping, *A Century and Beyond*, 383.
25. Board of Trustees minutes, January 21–22, 1948, 783.
26. Purdue "Facts at Your Fingertips," 1969–1970, 29.
27. Bleacher collapse report, addition 1, box 3, Board of Trustees Office records, 20110426.
28. Testimony of R. C. Forney, March 4, 1947, pp. 1–2, addition 1, box 3, Board of Trustees Office records, 20110426.
29. "Bleachers Crash," *Debris* yearbook, 1947, 298.
30. *Debris* yearbook, 1949, 140.
31. Knoll, *War Years*, 192.
32. Knoll, *The Story of Purdue Engineering*, 106.

The 1950s

1. *Annual Report of the President 1951* (West Lafayette: Purdue University, 1952), 62.
2. Richard E. Grace interview, May 29, 2008, Purdue University Archives and Special Collections Oral History Program collection, MSO 1.
3. *Annual Report of the President 1950* (West Lafayette: Purdue University, 1951), 8; A. F. Grandt Jr., W. A. Gustafson, and L. T. Cargnino, *One Small Step: The History of Aerospace Engineering at Purdue University* (West Lafayette: Purdue Research Foundation, 1995), 259.
4. Mary Lou Siefker interview, September 23, 2017, Purdue University Archives and Special Collections Oral History Program collection, MSO 1.
5. Julia Jackson, "Purduvians Nominate Kennedy," *Purdue Exponent*, March 29, 1960.
6. Board of Trustees minutes, 14 May 1982, p. 14, box 17, Purdue University Board of Trustees meeting minutes, UA 58.
7. Robert W. Topping, *The Hovde Years: A Biography of Frederick L. Hovde* (West Lafayette: Purdue University, 1980), 253.
8. Robert W. Topping, *A Century and Beyond: The History of Purdue University* (West Lafayette: Purdue University Press, 1988), 300; H. B. Knoll, *The Story of Purdue Engineering* (West Lafayette: Purdue University Studies, 1963), 151.
9. Jim Mayer, "SCEB Drops Idea of Auditing Fee Slash," *Purdue Exponent*, January 26, 1950.
10. Jim Mayer, "Assembly to Start Poll on Graduation Question," *Purdue Exponent*, October 18, 1950.
11. "Juanita Carpenter Gives Band 'New Look' This Year," *Purdue Exponent*, November 17, 1954.
12. Al Campbell, "Time Out . . . Purdue" *Purdue Exponent*, October 10, 1950.
13. "Purdue Grand Prix Uses 'La Mans' Start," *Purdue Exponent*, May 16, 1958; "History," Purdue Grand Prix Foundation. http://www.purduegrandprix.org/foundation/history; Larry Miller with Tom Pearson, *Purdue Grand Prix: 1958-2007; A Rich History and Tradition* (West Lafayette: Larry Miller and Tom Pearson, 2006).
14. Purdue Grand Prix Foundation. http://www.purduegrandprix.org/foundation/history.
15. "Lambda Chi's Win Annual Alley Race," *Purdue Exponent*, May 25, 1951.
16. Margaret Cannon, "Fraternities Battle in Traditional Race," *Purdue Exponent*, May 2, 1968.
17. "Student Council Sets Rules for Sign Contest," *Purdue Exponent*, October 13, 1953.

18. "Judges Pick Four Winners of Homecoming Signs," *Purdue Exponent*, October 31, 1950; "Homecoming Spectacle for Alums," *Purdue Exponent*, October 6, 1971.
19. "State Board of Health Confirms Fact That Asian Flu Hit Campus," *Purdue Exponent*, January 9, 1958.

The 1960s

1. *Annual Report of the President 1961* (Lafayette: Purdue University, November 1962), 34.
2. Mary Lou Siefker interview, September 23, 2017, Purdue University Archives and Special Collections Oral History Program collection, MSO 1.
3. Carol Thompson, "California Holds Memories of Sight-Seeing, People, Fun," *Purdue Exponent*, January 6, 1967.
4. Robert DeMoss interview, November 14, 2007, Purdue University Archives and Special Collections Oral History Program collection, MSO 1.
5. Al G. Wright interview, April 30, 2007, Purdue University Archives and Special Collections Oral History Program collection, MSO 1.
6. Sandi Cannon, "Purdue Honors Astronaut Alumni," *Purdue Exponent*, February 2, 1967.
7. John Norberg, *Wings of Their Dreams: Purdue in Flight* (West Lafayette: Purdue University, 2003), 304.
8. "Andrew J. Feustel," National Aeronautics and Space Administration, accessed January 14, 2018, https://www.jsc.nasa.gov/Bios/htmlbios/feustel-aj.pdf.
9. Norberg, *Wings of Their Dreams*, 169.
10. John Norberg, interviews with Purdue astronaut alumni, 20141104.1; Purdue Space Day Student Organization records, 20130128.
11. Robert W. Topping, *A Century and Beyond: The History of Purdue University* (West Lafayette, Purdue University Press, 1988), 331.
12. Ron Thornburg, "Students React to Union Arrests, *Purdue Exponent*, May 7, 1969.
13. Paul and Deborah Cabbell, "Notes from a Black Book," *Purdue Exponent*, October 23, 1968.
14. *Debris* yearbook, 1970, 446.
15. Puff Crary, "History Study Group Stresses Negro Cultural Achievements," *Purdue Exponent*, April 24, 1968.
16. Karen Rasmussen, "Exponent Announces Anti-discrimination Policy," *Purdue Exponent*, April 24, 1968.
17. "Support Schuhmann Resolution," *Purdue Exponent*, February 17, 1969; ". . . Or the Fire Next Time," http://collections.lib.purdue.edu/timelines/orthefire#event-or-the-fire-next-time/.
18. Petition circulated by black students to the University Administration in 1968, Frederick L. Hovde papers; ". . . Or the Fire Next Time" ; "Black Purdue," http://www.purdue.edu/blackpurdue/.
19. "Black Purdue."

The 1970s

1. *Annual Report of the President 1970* (West Lafayette: Purdue University, 1971), 11.
2. Jennifer Bradford interview, August 4, 2017, Purdue University Archives and Special Collections Oral History Program collection, MSO 1.
3. *Annual Report of the President 1970*, 11.
4. "1971," *Purdue Exponent*, January 14, 1980.
5. Mike Backus, "Purdue No Kent State, but Had Protests, Sit-Ins," *Purdue Exponent*, January 14, 1980.
6. Singer Buchanan interview, 1970 Newsreel, Purdue Alumni Association, 1971.
7. Muhammad Ali poster, Black Cultural Center records, UA 176.
8. "NSBE History," National Society of Black Engineers. https://www.nsbe.org/About-Us/NSBE-History.aspx#.WrFFEOj482w.
9. *Black Hurricane*, vol. 1, no. 1, box 3, folder 1, Collection of Student Newspapers at Purdue University, MSP 99.
10. Jan Wewe, "First District Councilman Works for Student Goals," *Purdue Exponent*, January 14, 1980.
11. Silvia Ascarelli, "Housing Shortage Began with '74 Enrollment Rise," *Purdue Exponent*, January 14, 1980.
12. Francis McCorkel, "Guest Hours Added as Decade Advances," *Purdue Exponent*, January 14, 1980.
13. Rani Tewari, "Stone: 'Students More Mature,'" *Purdue Exponent*, January 14, 1980.
14. *Annual Report of the President 1971* (West Lafayette: Purdue University, 1972), 11.
15. "New Group Joins PMO," *Purdue Exponent*, September 7, 1972.
16. "Hair Length and Singing: Value Conflict," *Purdue Exponent*, September 7, 1972.
17. Tewari, "Stone: 'Students More Mature.'"
18. Robert W. Topping, *A Century and Beyond: The History of Purdue University* (West Lafayette, Purdue University Press, 1988), 367.
19. "Hammer, Sickle: Yearbook Cover Riles Lawmaker," *Daily Report* (Ontario-Upland, CA), April 22, 1974, 7
20. Kassandra Agee Chandler, "My Pieces of History: A Queen's Journey to Archival Peace (and Release)," February 6, 2018, Krannert Auditorium, West Lafayette, Indiana.
21. Chandler, "My Pieces of History."
22. Phil Britt, "Boilers Beat USSR," *Purdue Exponent*, November 14, 1977.

The 1980s

1. Francis McCorkel, "Togetherness: Enrollment Hits Record 32,366," *Purdue Exponent*, September 8, 1980.
2. Joel Kern interview, November 4, 2017, Purdue University Archives and Special Collections Oral History Program collection, MSO 1.
3. "Behind the Scenes: Community Talent Used in Campus Soap Production," *Debris* yearbook, 1984, 45.
4. Sonya L. Margerum, "Welcome," *Purdue Exponent*, January 14, 1980.
5. Susan Oberlander, "Students Shiver in Shanty," *Lafayette Journal and Courier*, December 4, 1986, Purdue University Archives and Special Collections vertical files, MSK 1.
6. Lana Bandy, "It's Official: PSA Changes Name in 23–3 Vote," *Purdue Exponent*, September 15, 1988.
7. "Purdue Programs a Winning Team," Purdue University Special Report, January 20, 1988; Lana Bandy, "Computer Team Gets 8th Place in Competition," *Purdue Exponent*, March 3, 1988.
8. Becky Boyd, "Snowball Fights, Sledding, and Nude Olympics Signal Winter on Campus," *Debris* yearbook, 1993, 52.
9. John Norberg, "Nude Olympian Shows Cold Endurance," *Lafayette Journal and Courier*, February 5, 1981.

10. Dan Lance, "Olympics Runners Race in 'Unbareable' Cold," *Purdue Exponent*, January 23, 1985.
11. "Controversy." *Debris* yearbook, 1986, 562–63.

The 1990s

1. Audrey Hungerford, "Census Shows West Lafayette Population Growth," *Purdue Exponent*, February 1, 1991.
2. *Debris* yearbook, 1996, 6.
3. Ellen Chang, "Grade Scale to Change Soon," *Purdue Exponent*, April 8, 1993.
4. Heather Seigel, "Tarrus & Tina Win Election by Landslide: Voting Turnout Increases Tremendously," *Purdue Exponent*, February 8, 1990.
5. Paul Delnero, "Smokestack Begins Coming Down Today," *Purdue Exponent*, May 11, 1992.
6. "Upcoming Events Will Celebrate 25th Anniversary of BGR," last updated September 4, 2018, https://www.purdue.edu/orientation/bgr/celebration.html.

The 2000s

1. Purdue University Office of the Registrar, "Purdue University West Lafayette, Enrollment Summary, Fall Semester 2000–2001."
2. *Debris* yearbook, 2003, 46.
3. "Donating Clothes to Those in Need the Goal of Nearly Naked Mile," *Purdue News*, March 13, 2013, https://www.purdue.edu/newsroom/releases/2013/Q1/donating-clothes-to-those-in-need-the-goal-of-nearly-naked-mile.html; "Nearly Naked Mile a Fully Lame Substitute for Naked Olympics," *Purdue Exponent*, March 28, 2014, https://www.purdueexponent.org/opinion/article_69a27d13-d5f2-528a-8687-bab634536d6d.html.
4. Brad Ramsay, "SSINFO Allows Records Access," June 12, 2000, https://www.purdueexponent.org/campus/article_eaf167ea-3993-50c7-adcc-536b31ccfb2c.html.
5. Laura Hoffman, "SSINFO Switches to Banner," June 15, 2008, https://www.purdueexponent.org/features/article_dfc5bc9f-20a0-5f20-95c2-7976a7c4eafc.html.
6. "myPurdue Portal Redesign Coming in October," October 5, 2009, https://web.archive.org/web/20110527165808/https://www.purdue.edu/onepurdue/mypurduenews/Purdue_portal_redesign_coming_in_October.html.
7. John Jeanguenat, "'College GameDay' Prepares for Long Day at Purdue," *Purdue Exponent*, October 15, 2004, https://www.purdueexponent.org/sports/article_38e158f0-8e35-5b73-85ef-3438a409ab80.html.
8. "Joe Tiller: 1942–2007," https://purduesports.com/sports/2018/5/21/joe-tiller-1942-2017.aspx.
9. "Native American Educational and Cultural Center Dedication to Highlight Heritage," *Purdue News*, October 1, 2007, https://news.uns.purdue.edu/x/2007b/071001NativeDedicate.html.
10. "Loeb Fountain Runs Return after Renovation," *Purdue Exponent*, April 17, 2002, 9.
11. "Fountain's New Additional Earns Ridicule, Criticism by Students," *Purdue Exponent*, September 14, 2001, 4.
12. *Debris* yearbook, 1988, 151.
13. *Debris* yearbook, 2001, 40.
14. Brittany Collins, "Last Year for *Debris*: Yearbook Out with the Old and In with the New," *Purdue Exponent*, May 12, 2008.

The 2010s

1. Purdue University, "Data Digest," https://www.purdue.edu/datadigest.
2. Becca Lax interview, August 4, 2017, Purdue University Archives and Special Collections Oral History Program collection, MSO 1.
3. "Purdue to Establish New Honors College," *Purdue News*, July 12, 2011, http://wayback.archive-it.org/6053/20120626195555/http://www.purdue.edu/newsroom/academics/2011/110712BOTHonors.html.
4. Jake Schmidt, "Rhonda Phillips to Become the First Dean of Purdue's Honors College," *Purdue Exponent*, June 14, 2013, https://www.purdueexponent.org/campus/article_b2a3b706-c11b-5636-afb2-af369a6b92d8.html.
5. Purdue University Honors College, "Our Mission," accessed July 20, 2018, https://honors.purdue.edu/about-us/mission/index.php.
6. Purdue University Fort Wayne Office of Academic Affairs, "Realignment," accessed September 10, 2018, https://www.pfw.edu/offices/oaa/realignment/university-realignment.html.
7. "Purdue Celebrates More Students Than Ever Seeking High-Quality, Affordable Education," *Purdue News*, September 11, 2018, https://www.purdue.edu/newsroom/releases/2018/Q3/purdue-celebrates-more-students-than-ever-seeking-high-quality,-affordable-education.html.
8. "Purdue University Fact Sheet: Bicentennial Torch," *Purdue News*, September 9, 2016, https://www.purdue.edu/newsroom/releases/2016/Q3/purdue-university-fact-sheet-bicentennial-torch.html.
9. Amy Patterson Neubert and Brian Huchel, "Purdue Olympians Earn Four Medals, Including First Female Boilermaker to Win Gold," *Purdue Today*, August 22, 2016, https://www.purdue.edu/newsroom/purduetoday/releases/2016/Q3/purdue-olympians-earn-four-medals,-including-first-female-boilermaker-to-win-gold.html.
10. "Purdue to Acquire Kaplan University, Increase Access for Millions," *Purdue News*, April 27, 2017, http://www.purdue.edu/newsroom/releases/2017/Q2/purdue-to-acquire-kaplan-university,-increase-access-for-millions.html.
11. "Purdue University Global Holds First Commencement: Over 9,000 Graduates Make Up Historic Cohort," *Purdue Today*, June 14, 2018, https://www.purdue.edu/newsroom/purduetoday/releases/2018/Q2/purdue-university-global-holds-first-commencement-over-9,000-graduates-make-up-historic-cohort.html.
12. "Purdue's Pleasant Surprise: Largest, Most Well-Prepared Class in History Expected," *Purdue News*, May 4, 2018, https://www.purdue.edu/newsroom/releases/2018/Q2/purdues-pleasant-surprise-largest,-most-well-prepared-class-in-history-expected.html.

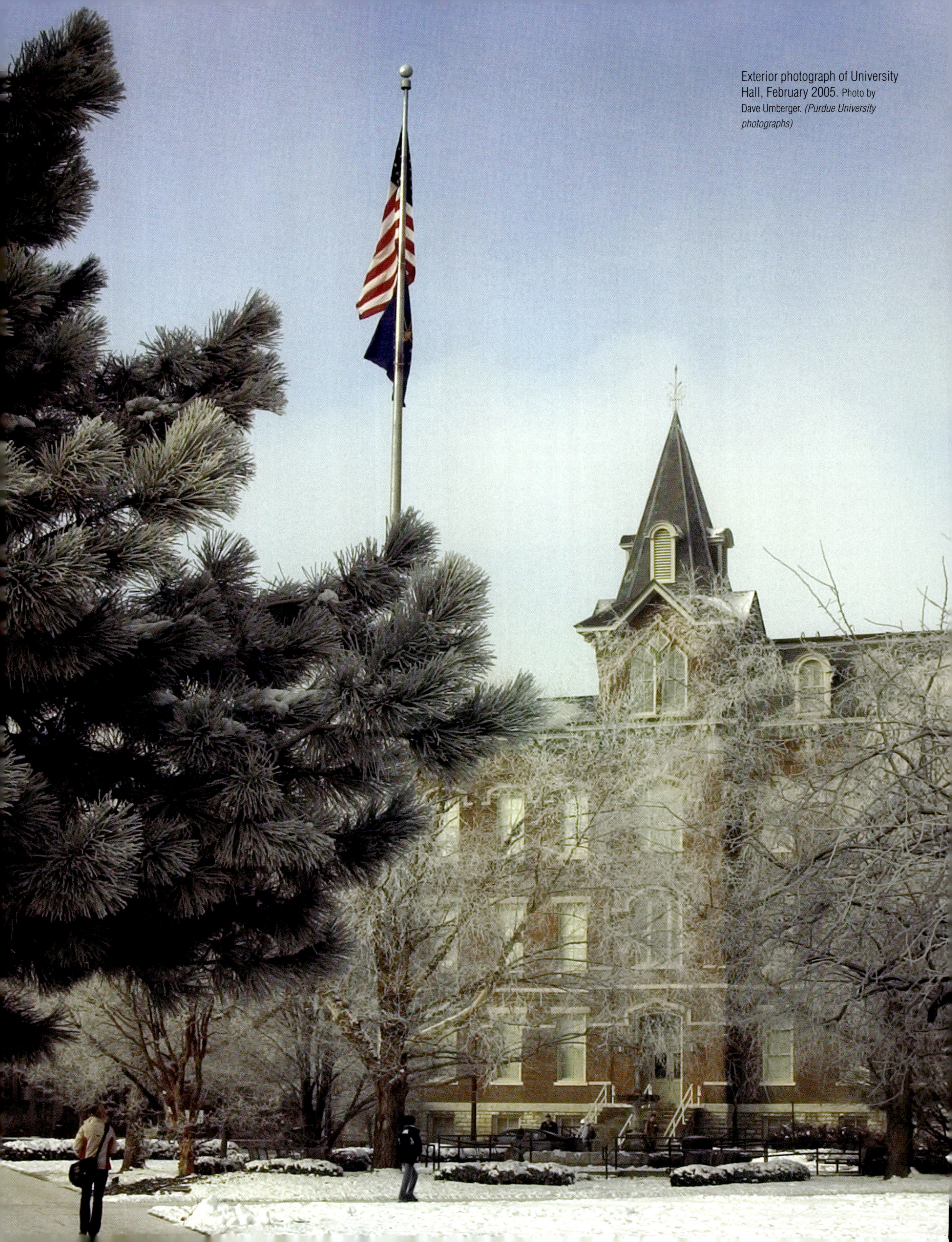

Exterior photograph of University Hall, February 2005. Photo by Dave Umberger. *(Purdue University photographs)*

[Bibliography]

Sources

American Libraries Magazine (Chicago, IL), https://americanlibrariesmagazine.org/

Annual Register of Purdue University (Indianapolis, IN)

Annual Report of Purdue University (Indianapolis, IN)

Bennett, Joseph L. *Boilermaker Music Makers: Al Stewart and the Purdue Musical Organizations.* West Lafayette: Purdue University, 1986.

Catalogue of Purdue University, The (West Lafayette, IN)

Chandler, Kassandra Agee. "My Pieces of History: A Queen's Journey to Archival Peace (and Release)" speech. Purdue University, West Lafayette, IN, February 6, 2018.

Chicago Defender (Chicago, IL)

Chinese Students Year Book. West Lafayette: Purdue University, 1927.

Cotton, Fassett A. *Education in Indiana.* Bluffton, IN: Progress Publishing, 1934.

Daily Argus News (Crawfordsville, IN)

Debris yearbook (West Lafayette, IN)

Estes, John, Bob Pence, and Jim Vruggink. *Purdue Athletics: A Century of Excellence.* West Lafayette: John Purdue Club Office and Athletic Public Relations Office, 1987.

Grandt, A. F., Jr., W. A. Gustafson, and L. T. Cargnino. *One Small Step: The History of Aerospace Engineering at Purdue University.* West Lafayette: Purdue Research Foundation, 1995.

Griffiths, Doug, Alan Karpick, and Tom Schott. *Tales from Boilermaker Country: A Collection of the Greatest Stories Ever Told.* Champaign, IL: Sports Publishing, 2003.

Hepburn, William Murray, and Louis Martin Sears. *Purdue University: Fifty Years of Progress.* Indianapolis: Hollenbeck Press, 1925.

Journal of Purdue Undergraduate Research (West Lafayette, IN)

Knoll, H. B. *A Record of a University in the War Years.* West Lafayette: Purdue Alumnus, 1948.

Knoll, H. B. *The Story of Purdue Engineering.* West Lafayette: Purdue University Studies, 1963.

Lafayette Journal & Courier (Lafayette, IN)

Los Angeles Times (Los Angeles, CA)

Miller, Larry, and Tom Pearson. *Purdue Grand Prix: 1958–2007; A Rich History and Tradition.* West Lafayette: Purdue University, 2006.

National Aeronautics and Space Administration website, https://www.nasa.gov/

National Society of Black Engineers website, https://www.nsbe.org/

Norberg, John. *Hail Purdue.* Owatonna, MN: "All-American" Band Club, 1987.

Norberg, John. *Wings of Their Dreams: Purdue in Flight.* West Lafayette: Purdue University, 2003.

Purdue Alumnus, The (West Lafayette, IN)

Purdue Data Digest, Purdue University, https://www.purdue.edu/datadigest

Purdue Engineer, The (West Lafayette, IN)

Purdue Exponent (West Lafayette, IN)

Purdue Grand Prix Foundation website, Purdue University, http://www.purduegrandprix.org/

Purdue News, Purdue University, https://www.purdue.edu/newsroom/

Purdue Reamer Club. *A University of Tradition: The Spirit of Purdue.* 2nd ed. West Lafayette: Purdue University Press, 2013.

Purdue Russia: November 12, 1977, 7:00 P.M., Mackey Arena. West Lafayette: Purdue University, 1977.

Purdue, The (West Lafayette, IN)

Purdue University Fort Wayne website, https://www.pfw.edu/

Purdue University Sports website, http://www.purduesports.com/

Purdue University Student Handbook (West Lafayette, IN)

Purdue University Web Archive, https://www.archive-it.org/collections/6053

Purdue University website, https://www.purdue.edu

Sterrett, Jeff, Becky Gick, and Bob Mindrum. *75th Anniversary: Purdue Memorial Union.* West Lafayette: Purdue University, 1999.

Topping, Robert. *A Century and Beyond: The History of Purdue University.* West Lafayette: Purdue University Press, 1988.

Topping, Robert. *The Hovde Years: A Biography of Frederick L. Hovde.* West Lafayette: Purdue University, 1980.

Wiley, Harvey W. *An Autobiography.* Indianapolis: Bobbs-Merrill, 1930.

Archival Collections

1903 Train Wreck materials, MSP 117

George Ade papers, MSA 4

Purdue University African American Students, Alumni, and Faculty collection, MSF 154

J. C. Allen and Son Inc. photographs and negatives, MSP 25

Josiah H. Andrews scrapbook, MSA 266

Purdue University Architect records, UA 154

Neil A. Armstrong papers, MSA 5

Purdue University Archives and Special Collections artifacts collection, MSR 4

Asian American and Asian Resource and Cultural Center records, UA 164
Purdue University Athletic collection, MSP 160
Henry C. Balcom collection, MSA 325
Purdue University Bands records, UA 160
Arthur and Roberta Bitzer papers, MSA 259
Black Cultural Center records, UA 176
Board of Trustees Office records, 20110426
Purdue University Board of Trustees meeting minutes, UA 58
Charles J. Bohrer thesis, MSA 279
Esther Conelley Boonstra collection, MSA 57
Julius L. Born correspondence, MSA 58
Purdue University Campus and Lafayette photo albums, MSP 255
Purdue University Campus Maps collection, MSR 6
Purdue University Centennial collection, MSP 121
Eugene A. Cernan papers, MSA 288
Kassandra Agee Chandler papers, MSA 363
Purdue University Chinese Students collection, MSP 155
Class of 1915 photo album, MSP 260
Collection of early Purdue University publicity materials, MSP 233
Collection of Indiana Bicentennial materials, MSP 296
Collection of Purdue University Photographs, MSP 43
Collection of Sigma Chi Fraternity Court Case materials, MSP 37
Collection of Student Newspapers at Purdue University, MSP 99
College of Agriculture, Administration of the College of Agriculture records, UA 44
Purdue University Commencement programs and invitations collection, MSP 158
Purdue University Customs and Traditions collection, MSP 151
Department of Aviation Technology records, UA 12
H. C. Dimmich papers, MSA 153
Purdue University Division of Dance records, UA 10
Amelia Earhart at Purdue, MSF 450
James R. Eaton photo album, MSA 284
Edward C. Elliott papers, UA 50
Purdue University Faculty and Senate records, UA 8
Arthur H. Fisher papers, MSA 29
John C. Franks papers, MSP 171
Robert Gagen engineering tools, MSA 38
Gary J. Glazer papers, MSA 31
Helen Gould collection of Purdue dance cards and theater programs, MSA 294
L. Murray Grant and Bernice Nelson Grant papers, MSA 330
Otis E. Griner papers, MSA 129
William Chester Halstead photographs, MSA 262
Purdue University Harlequin Club collection, MSP 173
Eleanor Harrison collection, MSA 339
Robert T. Hatt scrapbook, MSP 35
Heavilon Hall records, UA 123
John Heiss collection, MSF 172
Thomas Hendrix letters to Margaret Kennedy, MSA 287
Judy Herd cord skirt, 20160922
Frederick L. Hovde papers, UA 51
Purdue University International Students collection, MSP 152
Irving Literary Society records, MSP 34
James Johnson papers, MSA 13
Erling E. Kildahl scrapbooks and papers, MSF 480
LGBTQ Resource Center records, UA 162
Purdue University Libraries records, UA 30
Purdue University Marketing and Media collection, UA 62
Marketing and Media Production Samples, 20160616
J. Holmes Martin Battery B papers, MSA 269
Robert L. Matthews collection, MSA 167
Richard Mayoras senior cords and gimlet hat, 20160901.2
Memorial Gymnasium records, UA 133
Eulora Miller papers, MSA 380
Glennard Miller photo album, MSA 348
Paul Million papers, MSF 512
Purdue University Musical Organizations records, UA 40
Purdue University News Service negatives and photographs, MSP 19
Purdue University Newsreels and Year in Review, UA 65
Purdue Office of Publications Oral History Program collection, MSO 2
Purdue University Archives and Special Collections Oral History Program collection, MSO 1
Horace W. Payne collection, MSA 186
Philalethean Literary Society records, MSP 101
Purdue University Postcard collection, MSP 39
Purdue Broadsides collection, MSR 5
Purdue Club of Chicago, MSP 216
Purdue Memorial Union records, UA 111
J. E. Raffensperger collection, MSA 196
Reamer Club records, 20111004
Orville Redenbacher papers, MSA 37
Betty J. Lynch Roberts papers, MSA 307
Martha Bemis Rogers dance cards, MSA 256
Charles M. Romanowitz papers, MSA 345
Rose Bowl Ticket Envelope Signed by Astronauts, MSP 249
Jerry L. Ross papers, MSA 283
School of Medicine collection, MSP 174
School of Pharmacy and Pharmacal Sciences records, UA 53
Purdue University Semi-Centennial collection, MSP 120
Guy R. Smith scrapbook, MSA 324
Purdue Society of Women Engineers records, MSP 182
Purdue Space Day Student Organization records, 20130128
Opal D. Stech scrapbook, MSA 36
Stewart Center records, UA 110
Winthrop E. Stone papers, UA 49
David A. Studebaker Computer Science papers, MSA 296
Fredrick C. Tegeler collection, MSA 141
Charles E. Thompson collection, MSA 227
Miller J. Tonkel papers, MSA 15
University Hall records, UA 151
University Photographic Services photos, MSP 78
Leslie and Ruth Vaught papers, MSA 362
Purdue University Archives and Special Collections Vertical Files collection, MSK 1
Janice Voss papers, MSA 9
Loretta Mae Wallace scrapbook, MSA 327
Warranty deed signed by John Purdue, MSP 244
Watchtower of Health manuscript, 20180212.2
WBAA records, MSP 211
J. David Weiss papers, 20120302
E. C. White papers, MSA 355
Carlton A. Wilmore papers, MSA 293
Totsye Harper Winslow papers on the Curtiss Wright Cadettes, MSA 195
Purdue Women in Engineering Program records, UA 7
Purdue World War I Announcements and Publications, MSP 251
Purdue World War II Announcements and Publications, MSP 252
John S. Wright papers, MSA 27

[Illustrations]

Foreword, Preface, and Acknowledgments

Introduction

The 1870s

The 1880s

The 1890s

The 1900s

The 1910s

The 1920s

The 1930s

The 1940s

The 1950s

The 1960s

The 1970s

The 1980s

The 1990s

The 2000s

The 2010s

Epilogue and Afterword

Notes and Bibliography

[Index]

Page numbers in italics refer to images and spotlights.

B

C

D

E

H

I

J

K

O

P

Q

R

S

T

U

V

W

Y

Z